The Pillar New Testament Commentary

General Editor

D. A. CARSON

The Second Letter to the CORINTHIANS

Mark A. Seifrid

William B. Eerdmans Publishing Company
Grand Rapids, Michigan / Cambridge, U.K.

APOLLOS
NOTTINGHAM, ENGLAND

Published 2014
in the United States of America by
Wm. B. Eerdmans Publishing Co.
2140 Oak Industrial Drive N.E., Grand Rapids, Michigan 49505 /
P.O. Box 163, Cambridge CB3 9PU U.K.
www.eerdmans.com

and in the United Kingdom by
APOLLOS
Norton Street, Nottingham,
England NG7 3HR

Printed in the United States of America

28 27 26 25 24 9 8 7 6 5 4

Library of Congress Cataloging-in-Publication Data

Seifrid, Mark A.
The second letter to the Corinthians / Mark Seifrid.
pages cm. — (The Pillar New Testament commentary)
Includes bibliographical references.
ISBN 978-0-8028-3739-4 (cloth: alk. paper)
1. Bible. Corinthians, 2nd — Commentaries.
I. Title.

BS2675.53.S45 2014
227'.307 — dc23

2014012059

British Library Cataloguing in Publication Data

A catalogue record for this book is available from the British Library
ISBN 978-1-78359-161-9

Scriptures taken from the English Standard Version

Contents

INDEXES

Editor's Preface

Commentaries have specific aims, and this series is no exception. Designed for serious pastors and teachers of the Bible, the Pillar commentaries seek above all to make clear the text of Scripture as we have it. The scholars writing these volumes interact with the most important informed contemporary debate, but avoid getting mired in undue technical detail. Their ideal is a blend of rigorous exegesis and exposition, with an eye alert both to biblical theology and to the contemporary relevance of the Bible, without confusing the commentary and the sermon.

The rationale for this approach is that the vision of "objective scholarship" (a vain chimera) may actually be profane. God stands over against us; we do not stand in judgment of him. When God speaks to us through his Word, those who profess to know him must respond in an appropriate way, and that is certainly different from a stance in which the scholar projects an image of autonomous distance. Yet this is no surreptitious appeal for uncontrolled subjectivity. The writers of this series aim for an even-handed openness to the text that is the best kind of "objectivity" of all.

If the text is God's Word, it is appropriate that we respond with reverence, a certain fear, a holy joy, a questing obedience. These values should be reflected in the way Christians write. With these values in place, the Pillar commentaries will be warmly welcomed not only by pastors, teachers, and students, but by general readers as well.

* * *

In the world of New Testament scholarship, Mark Seifrid is best known for his careful and fulsome treatments of Paul's doctrine of justification, on which he has made himself a remarkably competent expert. Here he turns to what is arguably Paul's most emotionally wrenching epistle, a letter that soars to a kind of pastoral ecstasy and plunges to pastoral despair, a letter with some of the most difficult Greek in the New Testament and some of the most memorable passages. In the past two hundred years or so, Second Corinthians has also been beset by scholars who have put forward a variety of creative reconstructions that sometimes make the text as we have it almost unrecognizable. Through all of these Dr. Seifrid proves to be a patient and sure-footed guide. The result is a commentary that makes 2 Corinthians come alive again as a letter that provides its own unique contribution to the Pauline corpus, to the New Testament, and to the entire Bible — and thus to the church of God in the twenty-first century.

D. A. Carson

Author's Preface

I owe thanks to the trustees and administration of the Southern Baptist Theological Seminary, who granted me a sabbatical in the fall of 2011, during which a substantial portion of this commentary was written. Thanks are due, as well, to two doctoral seminars that I had the privilege of leading, one of them at the Southern Baptist Theological Seminary in the spring of 2012, the other at Concordia Theological Seminary, St. Louis, in January 2013. The participants in those seminars, through both their questions and their observations, contributed more than I can fully acknowledge. Last, but not least, I owe thanks to my wife, Janice, who has patiently borne with the writing of this commentary.

MARK A. SEIFRID
Louisville, Kentucky, February 2013
Verbum crucis, virtus Dei.

Abbreviations

AB	Anchor Bible
ABD	*Anchor Bible Dictionary,* 6 vols.
ACCS	Ancient Christian Commentary on Scripture
ANRW	H. Temporini and W. Haase, eds., *Aufstieg und Niedergang der römischen Welt,* 37 vols.
BDAG	F. W. Danker, W. Bauer, W. F. Arndt, and F. W. Gingrich, eds., *A Greek-English Lexicon of the New Testament and Other Early Christian Literature*
BDF	F. Blass, A. Debrunner, and R. W. Funk, *A Greek Grammar of the New Testament and Other Early Christian Literature*
BDR	F. Blass and A. Debrunner, ed. F. Rehkopf, *Grammatik des neutestamentlichen Griechisch*
BHT	Beiträge zur historischen Theologie
BJRL	*Bulletin of the John Rylands University Library of Manchester*
BWANT	Beiträge zur Wissenschaft vom Alten und Neuen Testament
BZNW	Beihefte zur Zeitschrift für die neutestamentliche Wissenschaft
EDNT	H. Balz and G. Schneider, eds., *Exegetical Dictionary of the New Testament,* 3 vols.
EKK	Evangelisch-katholischer Kommentar (zum Neuen Testament)
FB	Forschung zur Bibel
FRLANT	Forschungen zur Religion und Literatur des Alten und Neuen Testaments
HCSB	Holman Christian Standard Bible
HTKNT	Herders theologischer Kommentar zum Neuen Testament
ICC	International Critical Commentary
JAC	*Jahrbuch für Antike und Christentum*
JSNT	*Journal for the Study of the New Testament*
JSNTSupp	Journal for the Study of the New Testament: Supplement Series
KEK	Kritisch-exegetischer Kommentar über das Neue Testament
LAB	*Liber Antiquitatum Biblicarum*

LCL	Loeb Classical Library
LQ	*Lutheran Quarterly*
LSJM	H. G. Liddell and R. Scott, rev. H. S. Jones and R. Mackenzie, *A Greek-English Lexicon*
LW	J. Pelikan and H. Lehman, eds., *Luther's Works,* 55 vols.
LXX	Septuagint
MT	Masoretic Text
NA	E. Nestle and K. Aland, eds., *Novum Testamentum Graece*
NAC	New American Commentary
NIGTC	New International Greek Testament Commentary
NovT	*Novum Testamentum*
NTAbh	Neutestamentliche Abhandlungen
NTOA	Novum Testamentum et Orbis Antiquus
NTS	*New Testament Studies*
NTTS	New Testament Tools and Studies
RAC	*Reallexikon für Antike und Christentum,* 24 vols.
RGG3	K. Galling, ed., *Die Religion in Geschichte und Gegenwart,* 7 vols., 3rd ed.
RGG4	H. D. Betz, D. S. Browning, B. Janowski, and E. Jüngel, eds., *Die Religion in Geschichte und Gegenwart,* 8 vols., 4th ed.
SBLDS	Society of Biblical Literature Dissertation Series
Smyth	H. W. Smyth, *Greek Grammar*
SNTSMS	Society for New Testament Studies Monograph Series
Str-B	H. Strack and P. Billerbeck, *Kommentar zum Neuen Testament aus Talmud und Midrasch,* 6 vols.
TDNT	G. Kittel and G. Friedrich, eds., trans. G. Bromiley, *Theological Dictionary of the New Testament,* 10 vols.
TRE	G. Müller, ed., *Theologische Realenzyklopädie,* 36 vols.
TynB	*Tyndale Bulletin*
UBS	United Bible Societies, *The Greek New Testament*
WA	Martin Luther, *D. Martin Luthers Werke,* 120 vols., Weimar Ausgabe
WBC	Word Biblical Commentary
WdF	Wege der Forschung
WMANT	Wissenschaftliche Monographien zum Alten und Neuen Testament
WUNT	Wissenschaftliche Untersuchungen zum Neuen Testament
ZNW	*Zeitschrift für die neutestamentliche Wissenschaft und die Kunde der älteren Kirche*

Bibliography

Althaus, P. "Kenosis," *RGG3* 3 (1957): 1243-46.

Austin, J. L. *How to Do Things with Words* (William James Lectures; Cambridge, Mass.: Harvard University Press, 1962).

Avemarie, F. "Bund als Gabe und Recht," in *Bund und Tora: Zur theologischen Begriffsgeschichte in alttestamentlicher, frühjüdischer und urchristlicher Tradition* (WUNT 92; ed. F. Avemarie and H. Lichtenberger; Tübingen: Mohr Siebeck, 1996), 163-216.

Back, F. *Verwandlung durch Offenbarung bei Paulus: Eine religionsgeschichtlich-exegetische Untersuchung zu 2 Kor 2,14–4,6* (WUNT 2/153; Tübingen: Mohr Siebeck, 2002).

Barth, K. "Evangelium und Gesetz," in *Gesetz und Evangelium: Beiträge zur gegenwärtigen theologischen Diskussion* (WdF 142; ed. Ernst Kinder and Klaus Haendler; Darmstadt: Wissenschaftliche Buchgesellschaft, 1968), 1-29.

———. *The Resurrection of the Dead* (trans. H. J. Stenning; New York: Fleming H. Revell, 1933).

Bauckham, R. *Jesus and the God of Israel: God Crucified and Other Studies on the New Testament's Christology of Divine Identity* (Grand Rapids: Eerdmans, 2009).

Bayer, O. *Autorität und Kritik: Zu Hermeneutik und Wissenschaftstheorie* (Tübingen: Mohr Siebeck, 1991).

———. *Contemporary in Dissent: Johann Georg Hamann as Radical Enlightener* (trans. R. A. Harrisville and M. C. Mattes; Grand Rapids: Eerdmans, 2012).

———. "The Ethics of Gift," *LQ* 24 (2010): 447-68.

———. *Freedom in Response: Lutheran Ethics; Sources and Controversies* (Oxford Studies in Theological Ethics; Oxford: Oxford University Press, 2007).

———. *Freiheit als Antwort: Zur theologischen Ethik* (Tübingen: Mohr Siebeck, 1995).

———. *Gott als Autor: Zu einer poietologischen Theologie* (Tübingen: Mohr Siebeck, 1999).

———. *Martin Luther's Theology: A Contemporary Interpretation* (trans. Thomas H. Trapp; Grand Rapids: Eerdmans, 2008).

———. "Rupture of Times: Luther's Relevance for Today," *LQ* 13 (1999): 35-50.

———. "Scheidekunst und Ehekunst: Glaube und Geschichte bei Kant und Hamann," in *Heil und Geschichte: Die Geschichtsbezogenheit des Heils und das Problem der Heilsgeschichte in der biblischen Tradition und in der theologischen Deutung* (WUNT

248; ed. J. Frey, S. Krauter, and H. Lichtenberger; Tübingen: Mohr Siebeck, 2009), 611-32.

———. *Schöpfung als Anrede: Zu einer Hermeneutik der Schöpfung* (Tübingen: Mohr Siebeck, 1990).

———. *Theology the Lutheran Way* (Lutheran Quarterly Books; ed. and trans. J. G. Silcock and M. C. Mattes; Grand Rapids: Eerdmans, 2007).

———. *Vernunft ist Sprache: Hamanns Metakritik Kants* (Spekulation und Erfahrung 2; Stuttgart–Bad Cannstatt: Frommann-Holzboog, 2002).

Beard, M. *The Roman Triumph* (Cambridge, Mass.: Harvard University Press, Belknap Press, 2007).

Belleville, L. L. *Reflections of Glory: Paul's Polemical Use of the Moses-Doxa Tradition in 2 Corinthians 3.1-18* (JSNTSupp 52; Sheffield: JSOT Press, 1991).

Betz, H. D. *Der Apostel Paulus und die sokratische Tradition: Eine exegetische Untersuchung zu seiner Apologie 2 Korinther 10–13* (BHT 45; Tübingen: Mohr Siebeck, 1972).

Bjerkelund, C. J. *Parakalō: Form, Funktion und Sinn der parakalō-Sätze in den paulinischen Briefen* (Bibliotheca Theologica Norvegica 1; Oslo: Universitets forlaget, 1967).

Bonhoeffer, D. *The Cost of Discipleship* (New York: Simon & Schuster, 1995 [1939]).

———. *Letters and Papers from Prison* (ed. E. Bethge; New York: Macmillan, 1972).

———. *Life Together* (trans. J. W. Doberstein; New York: Harper & Brothers, 1954).

———. *Widerstand und Ergebung: Briefe und Aufzeichnungen aus der Haft* (16 ed.; ed. E. Bethge; Munich: C. Kaiser, 1997 [1951]).

Bray, G. L., ed. *1-2 Corinthians* (ACCS 7; Downers Grove, Ill.: InterVarsity Press, 1999).

Breytenbach, C. *Versöhnung: Eine Studie zur paulinischen Soteriologie* (WMANT 60; Neukirchen: Neukirchener Verlag, 1989).

Bultmann, R. *Der Zweite Brief an die Korinther* (KEK 6; Göttingen: Vandenhoeck & Ruprecht, 1976).

Busch, E. *Glaubensheiterkeit: Karl Barth, Erfahrungen und Begegnungen* (Neukirchen: Neukirchener Verlag, 1987).

Cameron, M. *Christ Meets Me Everywhere: Augustine's Early Figurative Exegesis* (New York: Oxford University Press, 2012).

Collange, J.-F. *Énigmes de la Deuxième Épître de Paul aux Corinthiens: Étude exégétique de 2 Cor. 2:14–7:4* (SNTSMS 18; Cambridge: Cambridge University Press, 1972).

Collins, J. N. *Diakonia: Re-interpreting the Ancient Resources* (New York: Oxford University Press, 1990).

Derrida, J. *The Gift of Death* (Religion and Postmodernism; Chicago: University of Chicago Press, 1995).

———. *Given Time*, vol. 1: *Counterfeit Money* (Chicago: University of Chicago Press, 1992).

Ebeling, G. "Geist und Buchstabe," *RGG3* 2 (1957): 1290-96.

Ebner, M. *Leidenslisten und Apostelbrief: Untersuchungen zu Form, Motivik und Funktion der Peristasenkataloge bei Paulus* (FB 66; Würzburg: Echter, 1991).

Eckert, J. "Christ als 'Bild Gottes' und die Gottebenbildlichkeit des Menschen," in *Vom Urchristentum zu Jesus: Für Joachim Gnilka* (ed. H. Frankenmölle and K. Kertelge; Basel: Herder, 1989), 337-57.

Eckstein, H.-J. *Der Begriff Syneidesis bei Paulus* (WUNT 2/10; Tübingen: Mohr Siebeck, 1983).

Ehrman, B. D. *God's Problem: How the Bible Fails to Answer Our Most Important Question — Why We Suffer* (New York: HarperOne, 2008).

Figal, G. "Metapher III: Religionsphilosophisch," *RGG4* 5 (2002): 1166-67.

Fitzgerald, J. T. *Cracks in an Earthen Vessel: An Examination of the Catalogues of Hardships in the Corinthian Correspondence* (SBLDS 99; Atlanta: Scholars Press, 1988).

Forde, G. O. *Justification by Faith: A Matter of Death and Life* (Philadelphia: Fortress Press, 1982).

———. *On Being a Theologian of the Cross: Reflections on Luther's Heidelberg Disputation, 1518* (Grand Rapids: Eerdmans, 1997).

Fuller, D. P. *Gospel and Law: Contrast or Continuum? The Hermeneutics of Dispensationalism and Covenant Theology* (Grand Rapids: Eerdmans, 1980).

———. *The Unity of the Bible: Unfolding God's Plan for Humanity* (Grand Rapids: Zondervan, 1992).

Funk, R. W. "The Apostolic *Parousia:* Form and Significance," in *Christian History and Interpretation: Studies Presented to John Knox* (ed. W. R. Farmer, C. F. D. Moule, and R. R. Niebuhr; Cambridge: Cambridge University Press, 1967), 249-68.

Furnish, V. P. *II Corinthians* (AB; New York: Doubleday, 1984).

Garland, D. E. *2 Corinthians* (NAC 29; Nashville, Tenn.: Broadman & Holman, 1999).

Georgi, D. *The Opponents of Paul in Second Corinthians* (Philadelphia: Fortress Press, 1986).

Gestrich, C. "Luther mit Leib und Seele: Impulse für die christliche Eschatologie," in *Denkraum Katechismus: Festgabe für Oswald Bayer zum 70. Geburtstag* (ed. J. von Lüpke and E. Thaidigsmann; Tübingen: Mohr Siebeck, 2009), 289-314.

———. *The Return of Splendor in the World: The Christian Doctrine of Sin and Forgiveness* (Grand Rapids: Eerdmans, 1997).

Gnilka, J. *Der Kolosserbrief* (HTKNT; Freiburg: Herder, 1980).

Grindheim, S. J. "The Law Kills, but the Gospel Gives Life: The Letter-Spirit Dualism in 2 Corinthians 3:5-18," *JSNT* 84 (2001): 97-115.

Gunton, C. *The Actuality of the Atonement: A Study of Metaphor, Rationality, and the Christian Tradition* (Edinburgh: T&T Clark, 1988).

Hafemann, S. J. *Paul, Moses, and the History of Israel: The Letter/Spirit Contrast and the Argument from Scripture in 2 Corinthians 3* (WUNT 81; Tübingen: Mohr Siebeck, 1995).

———. *2 Corinthians* (NIV application commentary; Grand Rapids: Zondervan, 2000).

———. *Suffering and Ministry in the Spirit* (Grand Rapids: Eerdmans, 1990).

Hahn, S. *Kinship by Covenant: A Canonical Approach to the Fulfillment of God's Saving Promises* (New Haven: Yale University Press, 2009).

Harris, M. J. *The Second Epistle to the Corinthians: A Commentary on the Greek Text* (NIGTC; Grand Rapids: Eerdmans, 2005).

Hays, R. B. *The Conversion of the Imagination: Paul as Interpreter of Israel's Scripture* (Grand Rapids: Eerdmans, 2005).

———. *Echoes of Scripture in the Letters of Paul* (New Haven: Yale University Press, 1989).

Heckel, T. K. *Der innere Mensch: Die paulinische Verarbeitung eines platonischen Motivs* (WUNT 2/53; Tübingen: Mohr Siebeck, 1993).

Heckel, U. "Der Dorn im Fleisch: Die Krankheit des Paulus in 2Kor 12,7 und Gal 4,13f," *ZNW* 84 (1993): 65-92.

———. *Kraft in Schwachheit: Untersuchungen zu 2. Kor 10–13* (WUNT 2/56; Tübingen: Mohr Siebeck, 1993).

Hengel, M. *The Cross of the Son of God* (London: SCM Press, 1986).

Hengel, M., and A. M. Schwemer. *Paul between Damascus and Antioch: The Unknown Years* (Louisville, Ky.: Westminster John Knox Press, 1997).

Himmelfarb, M. *Ascent to Heaven in Jewish and Christian Apocalypses* (New York: Oxford University Press, 1993).

Hobbes, T. *Leviathan* (ed. E. Curley; Indianapolis, Ind.: Hackett, 1994).

Hofius, O. "Gesetz und Evangelium nach 2. Korinther 3," in *Paulusstudien* (WUNT 51; Tübingen: Mohr Siebeck, 1989), 75-120.

———. " 'Gott hat unter uns aufgerichtet das Wort von der Versöhnung' (2 Kor 5:19)," in *Paulusstudien* (WUNT 51; Tübingen: Mohr Siebeck, 1989), 15-32.

Hofmann, K.-M. *Philema hagion* (Beiträge zur Förderung christlicher Theologie 2/38; Gütersloh: C. Bertelsmann, 1938).

Horn, F. W. *Das Angeld des Geistes: Studien zur paulinischen Pneumatologie* (FRLANT 154; Göttingen: Vandenhoeck & Ruprecht, 1992).

Janowski, B. *Sühne als Heilsgeschehen: Studien zur Sühnetheologie der Priesterschrift und zur Wurzel KPR im Alten Orient und im Alten Testament* (WMANT 55; Neukirchen: Neukirchener Verlag, 1982).

Jervell, J. *Imago Dei: Gen. 1,26f. im Spätjudentum, in der Gnosis und in den paulinischen Briefen* (FRLANT 58; Göttingen: Vandenhoeck & Ruprecht, 1960).

Jewett, R. *A Chronology of Paul's Life* (Philadelphia: Fortress Press; London: SCM Press, 1979).

Joest, W. *Ontologie der Person bei Luther* (Göttingen: Vandenhoeck & Ruprecht, 1967).

Johnson, M. "Philosophy's Debt to Metaphor," in *The Cambridge Handbook of Metaphor and Thought* (ed. R. W. Gibbs Jr.; Cambridge: Cambridge University Press, 2008), 39-52.

Käsemann, E. *Commentary on Romans* (trans. G. W. Bromiley; Grand Rapids: Eerdmans, 1980).

———. "Justification and Salvation History," in *Perspectives on Paul* (trans. M. Kohl; Philadelphia: Fortress Press, 1971), 60-78.

———. *Die Legitimität des Apostels: Eine Untersuchung zu II Korinther 10–13* (Reihe Libelli 33; Darmstadt: Wissenschaftliche Buchgesellschaft, 1964).

Kelly, H. A. "Teufel V: Kirchengeschichtlich," *TRE* 33 (2001): 124-34.

Kierkegaard, S. "Of the Difference between a Genius and an Apostle," in *The Present Age* (trans. A. Dru; London: Oxford University Press, 1940), 138-63.

———. *Purity of Heart Is to Will One Thing* (trans. D. V. Steere; New York: Harper & Row, 1948).

Klassen, W. "The Sacred Kiss in the New Testament: A Example of Social Boundary Lines," *NTS* 39 (1993): 122-35.

Klauck, H.-J. *Herrenmahl und hellenistischer Kult: Eine religionsgeschichtliche Untersuchung zum ersten Korintherbrief* (NTAbh 15; Münster: Aschendorff, 1982).

Kleinknecht, K. T. *Der leidende Gerechtfertigte: Die alttestamentlich-jüdische Tradition vom "leidenden Gerechten" und ihre Rezeption bei Paulus* (WUNT 13; Tübingen: Mohr Siebeck, 1984).

Knauf, E. A. "Zum Ethnarchen des Aretas 2 Kor 11:32," *ZNW* 74 (1983): 145-47.

Krischer, T. "Νόος, νοεῖν, νόημα," *Glotta* 62 (1984): 141-49.

Lessing, G. E. "Über den Beweis des Geistes und der Kraft," *Gotthold Ephraim Lessing Werke 1774-1778* (ed. A. Schilson; Deutscher Klassiker Verlag, 1989), 8:437-45.

Levenson, J. D. *The Death and Resurrection of the Beloved Son* (New Haven: Yale University Press, 1993).

Lincoln, A. T. *Paradise Now and Not Yet: Studies in the Role of the Heavenly Dimension in Paul's Thought with Special Reference to His Eschatology* (SNTSMS 43; Cambridge: Cambridge University Press, 1981).

Lüpke, J. von. "Geist und Buchstabe," *RGG4* 3 (2002): 578-82.

Marshall, P. *Enmity in Corinth: Social Conventions in Paul's Relations with the Corinthians* (WUNT 2/23; Tübingen: Mohr Siebeck, 1987).

———. "A Metaphor of Social Shame: ΘΡΙΑΜΒΕΥΕΙΝ in 2 Cor. 2:14," *NovT* 25 (1983): 302-17.

Martin, R. P. *2 Corinthians* (WBC 40; Waco, Tex.: Word Books, 1985).

Metzger, B. M. *A Textual Commentary on the Greek New Testament* (2nd ed.; New York: United Bible Societies, 1994).

Mitchell, M. M. *Paul, the Corinthians, and the Birth of Christian Hermeneutics* (Cambridge: Cambridge University Press, 2010).

Moltmann, J. *The Crucified God: The Cross of Christ as the Foundation and Criticism of Christian Theology* (trans. R. A. Wilson and J. Bowden; New York: Harper & Row, 1974).

Niebuhr, H. R. *The Kingdom of God in America* (New York: Harper & Row, 1959).

Nüssel, F. *Allein aus Glauben: Zur Entwicklung der Rechtfertigungslehre in der konkordistischen und frühen nachkonkordistischen Theologie* (Forschungen zur systematischen und ökumenischen Theologie 95; Göttingen: Vandenhoeck & Ruprecht, 2000).

Obama, B. *The Audacity of Hope: Thoughts on Reclaiming the American Dream* (New York: Crown Publishers, 2006).

Otto, R. *The Idea of the Holy: An Inquiry into the Non-rational Factor in the Idea of the Divine and Its Relation to the Rational* (trans. J. W. Harvey; London: Oxford University Press, 1958).

Pickett, R. *The Cross in Corinth: The Social Significance of the Death of Jesus* (JSNTSupp 143; Sheffield: Sheffield Academic Press, 1997).

Porter, S. E. *Καταλλάσσω in Ancient Greek Literature, with Reference to the Pauline Writings* (Estudios de filología neotestamentaria 5; Córdoba: El Almendro, 1994).

———. "Reconciliation and 2 Corinthians 5,18-21," in *Studies on 2 Corinthians* (ed. R. Bieringer and J. Lambrecht; Leuven: Leuven University Press, 1996), 693-705.

Rensberger, D. "2 Corinthians 6:14–7:1 — a Fresh Examination," *Studia Biblica et Theologica* 8 (1978): 25-49.

Savage, T. B. *Power through Weakness: Paul's Understanding of the Christian Ministry in 2 Corinthians* (SNTSMS 86; New York: Cambridge University Press, 1996).

Schlatter, A. *Paulus, der Bote Jesu: Eine Deutung seiner Briefe an die Korinther* (3rd ed.; Stuttgart: Calwer, 1962 [1934]).

Schmeller, T. *Der zweite Brief an die Korinther* (EKK 8/1; Neukirchen: Neukirchener Verlag, 2010).

Schmitz, O. *Neutestamentliche Forschungen*, 4th ser., *Evangeliumsprobleme*, 2 vols. (Gütersloh: C. Bertelsmann, 1933).

Schnider, F., and W. Stenger. *Studien zum Neutestamentlichen Briefformular* (NTTS 11; Leiden: Brill, 1987).

Schweitzer, A. *The Quest of the Historical Jesus: A Critical Study of Its Progress from Reimarus to Wrede* (ed. J. M. Robinson; trans. W. B. D. Montgomery; New York: Macmillan, 1968).

Segal, A. "Heavenly Ascents in Hellenistic Judaism, Early Christianity, and Their Environments," *ANRW* 2.23.2 (1980), 1333-94.

Seifrid, M. A. "Romans 7: The Voice of the Law, the Cry of Lament, and the Shout of Thanksgiving," in *Perspectives on Our Struggle with Sin* (ed. T. L. Wilder; Nashville, Tenn.: B&H Publishing Group, 2011), 111-65.

Seitz, C. R. *Figured Out: Typology and Providence in Christian Scripture* (Louisville, Ky.: Westminster John Knox Press, 2001).

Shi, W. *Paul's Message of the Cross as Body Language* (WUNT 2/254; Tübingen: Mohr Siebeck, 2008).

Sjöberg, E. *Gott und die Sünder im Palästinischen Judentum nach dem Zeugnis der Tannaiten und der apokryphisch-pseudepigraphischen Literatur* (BWANT 79; Stuttgart: W. Kohlhammer, 1938).

Starling, D. I. *Not My People: Gentiles as Exiles in Pauline Hermeneutics* (BZNW 184; Berlin: Walter de Gruyter, 2011).

Steinmetz, D. C. *Luther in Context* (Grand Rapids: Baker, 1995).

Stockhausen, C. K. *Moses' Veil and the Glory of the New Covenant: The Exegetical Substructure of II Cor. 3,1–4,6* (Analecta biblica 116; Rome: Editrice Pontifico Istituto Biblico, 1989).

Strecker, G. "Entrückung," *RAC* 5 (1962):461-76.

Strecker, G., and U. Schnelle. *Neuer Wettstein: Texte zum Neuen Testament aus Griechentum und Hellenismus* (Berlin: Walter de Gruyter, 1996).

Stuhlmacher, P. *Biblische Theologie des Neuen Testaments*, vol. 1: *Grundlegung: Von Jesus zu Paulus* (Göttingen: Vandenhoeck & Ruprecht, 1992).

Sumney, J. L. *Identifying Paul's Opponents: The Question of Method in 2 Corinthians* (JSNTSupp 40; Sheffield: JSOT Press, 1990).

———. *'Servants of Satan,' 'False Brothers,' and Other Opponents of Paul* (JSNTSupp 188; Sheffield: Sheffield Academic Press, 1999).

Taatz, I. *Frühjüdische Briefe: Die paulinischen Briefe im Rahmen der offiziellen religiösen Briefe des Frühjudentums* (NTOA 16; Freiburg: Universitätsverlag; Göttingen: Vandenhoeck & Ruprecht, 1991).

Tabor, J. D. *Things Unutterable: Paul's Ascent to Paradise in Its Greco-Roman, Judaic, and Early Christian Contexts* (Studies in Judaism; Lanham, Md.: University Press of America, 1986).

Taylor, J. "The Ethnarch of King Aretas at Damascus: A Note on 2 Cor 11,32-33," *Revue Biblique* 99 (1992): 719-28.

Thiselton, A. "Realized Eschatology at Corinth," *NTS* 24 (1978): 510-26.

Thraede, K. "Ursprünge und Formen des 'Heiligen Kusses' im frühen Christentum," *JAC* (1968/1969): 124-80.

Thrall, M. E. *A Critical and Exegetical Commentary on the Second Epistle to the Corinthians* (ICC 47; Edinburgh: T&T Clark, 1994).

Vegge, I. *2 Corinthians — a Letter about Reconciliation: A Psychagogical, Epistolographical, and Rhetorical Analysis* (WUNT 2/239; Tübingen: Mohr Siebeck, 2008).

Versnel, H. S. *Triumphus: An Inquiry into the Origin, Development, and Meaning of the Roman Triumph* (Leiden: Brill, 1970).

Vorholt, R. *Der Dienst der Versöhnung: Studien zur Apostolatstheologie bei Paulus* (WMANT 118; Neukirchen: Neukirchener Verlag, 2008).

Wannenwetsch, B. "Lob der Äußerlichkeit," in *Denkraum Katechismus: Festgabe für Oswald Bayer zum 70. Geburtstag* (ed. J. von Lüpke and E. Thaidigsmann; Tübingen: Mohr Siebeck, 2009), 387-413.

———. *Political Worship: Ethics for Christian Citizens* (Oxford Studies in Theological Ethics; Oxford: Oxford University Press, 2004).

Webb, W. J. *Returning Home: New Covenant and Second Exodus as the Context for 2 Corinthians 6.14–7.1* (JSNTSupp 85; Sheffield: JSOT Press, 1993).

Weima, J. A. D. *Neglected Endings: The Significance of the Pauline Letter Closings* (JSNTSupp 101; Sheffield: Sheffield Academic Press, 1994).

Weissenrieder, A. "Der Blick in den Spiegel: II Kor 3,18 vor dem Hintergrund antiker Spiegeltheorien und ikonographischer Abbildungen," in *Picturing the New Testament: Studies in Ancient Visual Images* (WUNT 2/193; ed. A. Weissenrieder, F. Wendt, and P. von Gemünden; Tübingen: Mohr Siebeck, 2005), 313-43.

Wright, N. T. *The Climax of the Covenant: Christ and the Law in Pauline Theology* (Minneapolis: Fortress Press, 1992).

———. *Jesus and the Victory of God* (Christian Origins and the Question of God 2; Minneapolis: Fortress Press, 1996).

———. *The New Testament and the People of God* (Christian Origins and the Question of God 1; Minneapolis: Fortress Press, 1992).

———. "On Becoming the Righteousness of God," in *Pauline Theology,* vol. 2: *1 & 2 Corinthians* (ed. D. M. Hay; Minneapolis: Fortress Press, 1993), 200-208.

———. *Paul in Fresh Perspective* (Minneapolis: Fortress Press, 2005).

———. *Surprised by Hope: Rethinking Heaven, the Resurrection, and the Mission of the Church* (New York: HarperOne, 2008).

———. *What Saint Paul Really Said: Was Paul of Tarsus the Real Founder of Christianity?* (Grand Rapids: Eerdmans, 1997).

Young, F. M., and D. Ford. *Meaning and Truth in 2 Corinthians* (Grand Rapids: Eerdmans, 1988).

Zahn, T. *Der Brief des Paulus an die Römer* (Kommentar zum Neuen Testament 6/3; 3rd ed.; Leipzig: A. Deichertsche Verlagsbuchhandlung, 1925), 265-69.

Introduction

I. BEFORE AND AFTER SECOND CORINTHIANS

Paul's first visit to Corinth may be dated fairly precisely to A.D. 50-51. The Lukan report that Paul was brought before Gallio, the Roman proconsul, locates him in Corinth within this time frame (Acts 18:12-17).[1] A rescript from Claudius to the citizens of Delphi upon his twenty-sixth acclamation as emperor in which he mentions Gallio, who served as proconsul for only a brief period, provides the most reliable point at which the chronology of Acts (and the Pauline letters) may be correlated with external history. It was during this first visit that the church in Corinth came into existence.

We do not possess Paul's first letter to the church in Corinth. It most likely was written from Ephesus and included within its instruction a warning to the Corinthians against "mixing together" with immoral people (1 Cor 5:9-13). In Paul's understanding, association in common worship or common meals implies and effects a form of union of persons.[2] It is possible, and in fact it is likely, that Paul recalls or even cites a section of this first letter in 2 Cor 6:14–7:1, where he calls the Corinthians to separate themselves from unbelievers.[3] In this latter instance, he has in view the apostolic claimants who have made their way to Corinth. Insofar as he echoes his earlier instruction, it adds weight to his injunction.

As becomes clear in First Corinthians, the Corinthians misunderstood Paul's first letter to be enjoining a withdrawal from contact with unbelievers, a mistake that may very well lie behind the question as to whether a believer should remain with an unbelieving spouse (1 Cor 7:10-15). But Paul is concerned with immoral persons within the church, not without it.[4]

1. See the brief discussion at 12:14, pp. 460-61.

2. See 2 Thess 3:14; LXX Hos 7:8; cf. LXX Ezek 20:18.

3. See the discussion at pp. 287-92.

4. In his response, in First Corinthians, Paul insists that the Corinthians remove from

We do not know who carried this first letter to Corinth. Perhaps it was Timothy, who would have been known to the church already. It was followed by at least two visits by members of the Corinthian church to Paul while he was in Ephesus (cf. Acts 19:1-41).

In the first place, a group of prominent members of the church, which included Stephanas, one of the first converts in Corinth, brought a financial gift to Paul (1 Cor 16:15-18). Paul apparently did not regard his reception of this gift as a violation of his sworn commitment not to accept compensation from the Corinthian church (9:15-18).[5] Indeed, Paul praises the gift as a compensation for that which is lacking from the church (16:17). Yet it was given to Paul in support of his labors in Ephesus, not in Corinth. It therefore did not threaten to place Paul in a benefactor-beneficiary relation with the Corinthian church, a relationship that Paul is determined to avoid. His acceptance of the gift corresponds to his acceptance of gifts from the churches in Macedonia that supported his labor in Corinth (2 Cor 11:8-9).

Second, a group of slaves belonging to a certain Chloe informed Paul that factions had developed within the church, each centering on a favorite apostolic figure (1 Cor 1:10-17).[6] They also made Paul aware of other serious problems within the church: the tolerance of the man who had taken his fa-

---

the church a man who has his father's wife (1 Cor 5:1-8). This case of immorality may be the most flagrant instance in Corinth, but it is far from being the only instance: "a little leaven leavens the entire loaf" (1 Cor 5:6; see 6:1-20). When Paul later writes Second Corinthians, he remains concerned about "the many" who "previously" sinned and have not repented (2 Cor 12:19-21). The Corinthian toleration of immorality within the life of the church is one manifestation of their vacillation concerning Paul's apostolic authority. The problems Paul dealt with in his initial letter to Corinth have not gotten better by the time he came to write Second Corinthians. Indeed, they have gotten worse.

5. Paul emphatically restates this commitment in 2 Cor 11:7-11.

6. Admittedly, Apollos appears in this list alongside Paul and Cephas. But he may well have been accorded apostolic status, even if he had not directly encountered the risen Jesus. The apostolic claimants who later made their way to Corinth boasted in having experienced apparitions of the risen Lord (2 Cor 12:1-10). Such an experience could have been ascribed to Apollos. His rhetorical skill would have made him a favorite in Corinth, where he apparently arrived not too long after Paul departed (Acts 18:24-28). That Paul names him alongside himself as an "assistant laborer" of Christ and a steward of "the mysteries of God" likewise implies that Paul accepts the Corinthian estimation of Apollos as an apostle (1 Cor 4:1-13). It may well be that Apollos's refusal to travel to Corinth at Paul's urging may have been due to fears of making the situation in Corinth worse by his presence (1 Cor 16:12). Even at this early stage, the problems in Corinth center on the legitimation of Paul as apostle. Furthermore, it is possible that Apollos is the "brother whose fame in the Gospel is throughout all the churches," whom Paul has sent to Corinth. Paul does not name him precisely because he has been accorded apostolic status: "the Gospel" in this early period is not a written document, but apostolic proclamation (2 Cor 8:18-19). Naming Apollos would only have complicated the delicate situation in Corinth at that moment.

ther's wife (5:1-13), the lawsuits by members of the church against one another (6:1-11), and the open practice of immorality (6:12-20). It is unclear whether "those of Chloe" had been sent to Corinth in order to report on these matters or whether they carried the letter of the Corinthians to Paul and used the occasion to communicate with Paul. It is possible, too, although less likely, that they had been sent to Ephesus on other business and communicated with Paul while there. Their task, most likely, was the delivery of the Corinthian letter with its questions for the apostle (7:1).

In any case, both the report of Chloe's slaves and the letter with its questions from the Corinthians prompted Paul to write the letter that we now know as First Corinthians. Several features of this letter stand out as bearing particular significance for the interpretation of Second Corinthians. In the first place, Paul's lengthy and substantial response to the report concerning the factions in Corinth takes a primary place in the letter (1 Cor 1:10–4:21). The significance of this opening argument is underscored by the "apostolic parousia" that appears at its conclusion (4:16-21).[7] Normally, Paul refers to an upcoming visit, or a visit by one of his representatives, in the conclusion of a letter. Paul's reference to his impending visit appears remarkably early in First Corinthians. In speaking already of his travel to Corinth, Paul signals that he already has dealt with his fundamental concern at this point in the letter. The instruction that follows is significant but will have no effect if the Corinthians, or some of the factions among them, should reject Paul's authority as apostle.

Correspondingly it is significant that Paul repeatedly and in various ways appeals to his authority as apostle in First Corinthians.[8] Particularly in 1 Cor 9:1-27, in the midst of his discussion of eating meat that had been sacrificed to idols, Paul refers directly to his calling as apostle and to the questioning of that authority within the Corinthian church (9:1-7). The interjection of this issue into the discussion of idol meats should come as no surprise. As the Corinthians themselves recognize, the life and existence of an apostle is merely Christian existence written large. In his life and practice, Paul is the test case for the form of knowledge within the life of faith (8:1-3), and likewise for the form of Christian freedom within the world (9:1, 19). It is no accident that, in the discussion of idol meats, Paul repeats and again corrects the Corinthian slogan, "All things are permitted for me!" (10:23).[9] Nor is it accidental that he closes his instruction on idol meats with the appeal to the Corinthians to "become imitators of me, as I am of Christ" (11:1). His opening discussion of apostolic service concludes in the very same manner (4:16-21). Already in First Corinthians the form of apostolic life is the fundamental issue. It becomes the

7. See the discussion on pp. 314-16.

8. See 1 Cor 7:12, 25, 40; 9:1-27; 11:2-16, 17-34; 14:37; 15:1-11.

9. Cf. 1 Cor 6:12.

focal issue in Second Corinthians. The Corinthians implicitly recognize that the apostle who is thrust into weakness and suffering represents the form and nature of Christian existence. They prefer other apostolic claimants, who offer something that appears far more glorious than that which they find in Paul.

As is the case in Second Corinthians, Paul by no means seeks to bind the Corinthians to his own person. The Corinthian recognition of his apostolic authority will mean that the church will be more closely bound to all the other churches.[10] The collection "for the saints" serves this end. Already by the time he writes First Corinthians, Paul has enlisted the Corinthians in this cause. The instruction that he provides in the conclusion of the letter as to administration of the gift serves as a practical reinforcement of his authority (1 Cor 16:1-4). Difficulties in his relations with the Corinthians will delay the completion of the collection, so that Paul must take up the question of the collection again in Second Corinthians. Here, too, his instruction, which now appears at greater length, serves to further the Corinthian recognition of his apostolic authority and, concomitantly, to bind them to the other churches (2 Cor 8:1–9:15).

Both in the early "apostolic parousia" (1 Cor 4:16-21, esp. 18-21) and in the closing one that appears in connection with the instructions concerning the collection (16:5-12, esp. 5-8), Paul announces his intention to visit Corinth for a lengthy period on his way to Macedonia, "if the Lord permits" (16:7).[11]

That plan changed dramatically. Rather than making an extended visit in Corinth as he brought the collection to a conclusion, Paul found it necessary to make an emergency visit to Corinth from Ephesus (1 Cor 16:8).[12] It is impossible to discern precisely what brought Paul to make the journey, but the visit did not end well. As Paul sums up the matter in 2 Cor 2:1, he notes that he "came to them in grief." A leading figure within the church stood up to Paul, resisting his authority (2 Cor 2:1-4). The church, by doing nothing, tacitly gave its support to this person. Whoever this person might have been, it is not likely that he was the "immoral man" of 1 Cor 5:1-13. If that were the case, Paul most likely would have referred to his instructions to the church concerning this person

10. See 1 Cor 11:2-16, 17-34, esp. v. 16.

11. See also Acts 19:21. The plan to visit the Corinthians twice — once on his way to Macedonia and once on his way from Macedonia to Jerusalem — that Paul recounts in 2 Cor 1:15-16 does not appear explicitly in 1 Cor 16:5-9. It may well have been apparent to the Corinthians, who would have been aware of his plan to accompany the "collection for the saints" to Jerusalem.

12. When writing First Corinthians, Paul indicates that he is sending Timothy to the church. It is unlikely that Timothy carried the letter, since Paul reckons with the possibility that Timothy may have decided to cancel or postpone that visit, as Apollos also did (1 Cor 4:17; 16:10). Paul's co-workers obviously exercised a considerable degree of freedom in their responses to his requests. It is possible that it was Timothy who, after his visit, reported the situation in Corinth that prompted Paul's unexpected, emergency travel to Corinth.

when he takes up the matter again in 2 Cor 2:1-11. Furthermore, the "immoral man," as he appears in Paul's instructions in 1 Cor 5:1-13, does not seem to have borne any particular authority within the church, even if it is likely that he was a prominent member. There must have been, of course, some presenting issue that prompted Paul's unplanned visit from Ephesus. But we cannot discern precisely what it was. It could well have involved immorality, although strife and contention, or any of the other questions that Paul handles in First Corinthians, may have precipitated Paul's action. Perhaps it was all of them together.

It is significant that Paul does not mention any particular issue. He only recalls the affront that he had suffered in Corinth and reframes the matter so as to deflect attention from his own person. He directs the Corinthians to the restoration of the offender, as well as to the recognition that the offense had done damage to all of them: it was not Paul who had been "grieved" but (whether they knew it or not) the Corinthians (2 Cor 2:5). The authority of the apostle is at stake. Everything else recedes into the background. In the end, it is this issue that must have prompted Paul's visit.

Following his emergency visit to Corinth and the unhappy confrontation that had taken place there, Paul sent yet another letter (presumably from Ephesus) that we do not possess. It was written, Paul tells the Corinthians, "out of much affliction and anguish of heart, through many tears" (2 Cor 2:4). The relationship between apostle and church is the fundamental issue. Later, in Second Corinthians, Paul wants to communicate to the Corinthians the love and wrenching concern he had for them, even in the face of their rejection of him. The relationship with the church had not been severed, even if it had been damaged, at least from the perspective of the apostle.

It was Titus who carried Paul's "tearful letter" to Corinth and who also conveyed Paul's message personally to the church (2 Cor 2:13; 7:5-16). Upon his return to Paul, he likewise communicated to him the change of heart that had taken place in the Corinthian church. They, too, had come to tears over their broken relationship with the apostle. They now have a fervent love for him. They now have zeal for him, an excessive one, manifest in their (mis-) treatment of the offender (7:6-7, 11; cf. 2:5-11). Paul structures the entire body of Second Corinthians around his broken relationship with the Corinthians and his paralyzing concern for them. He concludes with his reception of the happy news of their reconciliation to him brought to him by Titus. The deepest affliction of the apostle is the affliction of his love for this wayward church (2:11-12; 7:5-16).

The unhappy encounter in Corinth caused Paul to change his plans. He did not visit the Corinthians on his way to Macedonia as he had promised but instead, as we have noted, sent Titus, his co-worker. Paul's broken promise further complicated his broken relationship with the church. He finds it necessary to take up the matter again in Second Corinthians (2 Cor 1:12–2:17).

As he informs the Corinthians, he judged it best not to come to them again "in grief" (2:1). He decided to avoid another confrontation. The relationship between the apostle and his church is to be one of mutual love and encouragement. His commission as an apostle of Christ is not the destruction of the church but its edification (10:8; 13:10). In sending Titus rather than appearing in Corinth himself, Paul keeps his own person (and in this case, any further wounding of his person) out of the contention with the Corinthians. It is not Paul and his gifts, or his lack of them, but the apostolic mission itself that is at stake in Corinth. Just as Apollos may well have decided not to visit Corinth because a faction of the church was attracted to his person (1 Cor 16:12), Paul appears to have decided not to visit Corinth because of the strife that was attached to his person.

The letter we know as Second Corinthians was written in response to the Corinthians' positive reception of Titus. It was sent at a moment in which there had been healing in the fragile relationship between the apostle and the church. Paul seeks to build on the reconciliation that has taken place between him and the Corinthians, as it had been effected by the "tearful letter" and by Titus's visit. As we have noted, it is not Paul's person that had been at stake. It is the legitimation of an apostle. At least that is Paul's understanding. Not merely in the opening and body of the letter (2 Cor 1:1–2:17; 3:1–7:16) but also in the collection chapters (8:1–9:15) and in Paul's closing defense of his apostolic ministry in Corinth (10:1–13:13 [ET 13:14]), this is the theme of the letter. Paul's adversaries, who have now made their way to Corinth, receive only indirect mention until the closing defense.[13] Even there it is clear that they are mere intruders, not merely in Corinth, but into the relationship between the apostle and the church.[14] Paul seeks afresh to win the hearts and minds of the Corinthians for the Gospel, which he bears in his body and life. The legitimation of the apostle is not carried out in the abstract. The question is whether Paul, who lives in weakness, bears the power and authority of Christ as the apostle to the Corinthians. Does the risen Lord speak in Paul, the weakling (13:3)?

Paul writes Second Corinthians from Macedonia, where he has met Titus, his emissary to the church (2 Cor 7:5-6). He is underway to visit Corinth yet again. It is his third visit, as he himself reminds them (13:1-2). Before he arrives, Titus will have completed a return trip to Corinth, carrying this letter (8:16-17; 12:17-18). He is accompanied by two others, who, together with Titus, are to assist in bringing to completion the Corinthian "mission for the saints" (in Jerusalem; 8:18-19, 22; 12:17-18). By the time Paul makes his third visit to Corinth, his letter and the mission of his representatives will have made their impact on the church.

13. 2 Cor 2:17; 3:1; 5:12; 6:14–7:1.

14. 2 Cor 10:7-11, 12; 11:1-4, 5, 12-15, 18-21, 22-23; 12:11.

The letter must have performed its work among the Corinthians: its preservation attests its positive reception in Corinth. The mission of Paul's representatives, the letter, and Paul's final visit to Corinth appear to have brought about the recognition of Paul as apostle in Corinth and an enduring change in the relationship between the apostle and the church. When Paul, near the end of his third visit to Corinth, writes to the Christians in Rome, he regards his work in the eastern Mediterranean as complete and stable. For that reason, once he has delivered the collection to Jerusalem, he is prepared to visit Rome and then to expand his mission into Spain (Rom 15:15-29).

Long afterward, at the end of the first century, strife and contention seem to have broken out again in the Corinthian church. But even Clement of Rome, who admonishes the church, regards the church as "most surely confirmed" *(bebaiotatos)* and "early" (or "old," *archaios*).[15] Its recent problems are an aberration from its happier past. The letter of the apostle performed its work.

II. PAUL'S OPPONENTS IN CORINTH AND THE PURPOSE OF SECOND CORINTHIANS

The identity of Paul's opponents has been a vexing conundrum for the interpreters of Second Corinthians. The same is true, correspondingly, of a description of the purpose of the letter.[16] The best reading of the letter surely is to be based on a minimal "mirror-reading" of the opponents, keeping itself as closely bound to Paul's statements as possible.

Although it has sidetracked interpreters, Paul's lengthy presentation of apostolic mission in contrast with that of Moses in 2 Cor 3 must be taken into account in any reading of the letter. Quite understandably, it often has been taken to indicate that Paul is battling against familiar opponents, the advocates of Judaizing who had made their way to Galatia and who presented problems for other churches as well.[17] But Paul's usual argument for faith apart from "works of the Law" is lacking here, as is any reference to circumcision and uncircumcision. It is not "Jews" who appear in 2 Cor 3 but the "sons of Israel" (2 Cor 3:13): Paul employs the honorific title. Only in passing does he urge Gentiles not to be circumcised in First Corinthians, and that after having urged Jews not to undergo epispasm (1 Cor 7:18). Unlike Galatia, the first Corinthian believers came from the synagogue and already have gone through an unhappy

15. *1 Clem.* 47:1-7. The adjective βεβαιότατος recalls Paul's descriptions of God's work among the Corinthians (1 Cor 1:6, 8; 2 Cor 1:7, 21).

16. See the excursus on this topic below, pp. 100-110.

17. Phil 3:1-11.

and violent divorce from it (Acts 18:1-17). It is unlikely that they are tempted to return to Judaism. Nowhere does Paul charge his opponents with tempting the Corinthians to Judaize. Paul has another purpose in appealing to the story of Moses: he finds fundamental truths about God's ways with human beings revealed in it.

While the opponents who have now appeared in Corinth present Jewish credentials (2 Cor 11:22), there is no indication that they appeal to Moses or the Law as a means to spiritual power. On the contrary, they too preach "Jesus," at least *some* Jesus or another (11:4). We know nothing of what they offer the Corinthians. Indeed, it is unlikely that they offer a single message: they are battling not only Paul but also one another for recognition in Corinth (10:12-18).

The intruders who have gained recognition as apostles in Corinth apparently bring a new situation.[18] Or rather, they make a bad situation worse. It is possible that they have exploited the recent breach in the relationship between Paul and Corinth. In any case, they present a new problem. The prior, unhappy confrontation in Corinth involved a member of the church. This much is clear from Paul's exhortation to the church to comfort the offender (2 Cor 2:7). An outsider more likely would have simply departed, moving on to greener pastures.

Paul's explicit statements concerning his opponents reveal nothing of a developed theology on their part. Of course, they bring "another Jesus, another Spirit, and another Gospel" (2 Cor 11:4). But Paul attacks a practical theology, one that legitimates apostolic mission (and thus Christian living) on the basis of the open display of rhetorical skill, deeds of power, and ecstatic visions. Whatever their message might have been, Paul regards the real danger that they present as lying in the implicit theology that measures God's saving work in Christ by outward marks of success. Already, before the arrival of the intruders, the Corinthians have embraced this theology. As we have noted, Paul battles for the hearts and minds of the Corinthians before all else. It is the Corinthian misunderstanding of the apostle and the Gospel that is finally at the center of the argument.

III. THE INTEGRITY OF SECOND CORINTHIANS

Perhaps more than any other letter of Paul, Second Corinthians has been thought to represent a compilation of letter fragments. The self-contained

18. It is no surprise that apostolic claimants have arrived in Corinth. It was a center of commerce and travel. The Corinthians were familiar not only with Paul but also with Apollos and Cephas, and perhaps others as well.

rhetoric and unusual language of early Jewish polemic of 6:14–7:1 has led many to regard it as an insertion.[19] The collection chapters appear abruptly after the denouement of Paul's happy meeting with Titus.[20] Furthermore, they seem to present two discrete arguments, at least at first reading. Perhaps two independent Pauline fragments have been inserted into Second Corinthians at this point. Finally, the strident tone with which Paul defends himself in 2 Cor 10–13 seems to be at odds with the resolution of the conflict with the Corinthians that Paul reports in 7:5-16.[21] Nor does it appear to match the argument in 2 Cor 1–7, in which Paul explicitly refuses to commend himself to the Corinthians (3:1; 5:12). One might find as many as five letter fragments that have been pieced together in the letter that we now possess.

The unusual features of the text deserve consideration. The theory that our Second Corinthians is a composite letter is not to be rejected out of hand. It is possible that, out of reverence for Paul, portions of his letters were preserved and that honor was offered to the late apostle by the supplementation of a shorter original letter with sections drawn from others.

Yet this scenario is not likely, especially not in Paul's relationship with the Corinthians. No matter how one slices the matter — or the letters — the issue in contention is Paul's apostolic authority in Corinth. It is a wonder that Second Corinthians has been preserved at all, given the state of the relationship between Paul and the Corinthians. The notion that a letter that was instrumental in cementing the bond between the church and the apostles would be subject to a scissors-and-paste operation, even at a later time, is difficult to imagine. The burden of proof surely lies upon any theory of a composite letter.

Furthermore, the incoherence or inconcinnity of argument that one might find in the letter is more apparent than real. We must not judge Paul's letters by the standard of Romans. At the end of the day, a coherent rhetoric may be discerned rather easily throughout Second Corinthians. The apparent disruptions make sense in context. The discrete argument of 6:14–7:1, presented in the form and language of early Jewish polemics, anticipates the heated rhetoric of 2 Cor 10–13. It more likely comes from the hand of a Jewish apostle rather than being inserted later by a Gentile. Jewish thought was basically foreign to the second generation of Christians.

As we have suggested already, the collection chapters are by no means alien to Paul's aim of securing the recognition of his apostolic authority in Corinth. As the apostle of Christ, he wants to bind the Corinthians to the larger circle of churches. The collection has this aim in any case. It is perfectly natural for Paul to seek to reinforce Titus's successful visit to Corinth by urg-

19. See the discussion at pp. 287-92.

20. See the discussion at pp. 305-8.

21. See the discussion at pp. 305-13.

ing the Corinthians to complete their promised contribution. Titus, the very emissary through whom the reconciliation was achieved, returns to Corinth to further this cause among the Corinthians (2 Cor 8:16-17; 12:18). The unusual, inverted form of Paul's argument in 2 Cor 8–9, in which the theology of giving follows the exhortation to give, surely reflects the situation as it stands. Paul already has instructed the Corinthians on the collection. They already have been eager to participate. As he indicates to them at the beginning of 2 Cor 9, it is superfluous for him to write to them about this mission. Nevertheless, his fresh instruction on the nature of giving, even as it appears delayed in the argument, is quite understandable, given the Corinthians' delay in completing the project.

Finally, the contrast between 2 Cor 10–13 and 2 Cor 1–7 is more apparent than real. The moment of reconciliation that has been effected through Titus is a mere calm within the stormy relations between Paul and the church in Corinth. It should not be given more weight than is due. There are repeated signals within the body of the letter that not all is well in Corinth, despite the recent success (3:1; 5:12; 6:1-2, 11-13, 6:14–7:1). Paul's assertion of apostolic authority is ironic in 2 Cor 10–13, from his very opening words in 10:1-2 (which are regularly mistranslated) through the "fool's speech" that effectively concludes his defense (11:22–12:10). The irony is effective only because of Paul's lengthy description of the apostolic mission that appears in 2 Cor 1–7. An argument for apostolic authority based on weakness would not normally have been persuasive, especially in a church enamored with power. Likewise the paradoxical nature of God's work in Christ and Christ's apostle, in which life is given in death, light in darkness, comfort in affliction that Paul presents in 2 Cor 1–7, receives its necessary theological articulation only in 2 Cor 10–13: power is made perfect in weakness (12:9-10). This word of Christ to Paul constitutes his defense of the apostolic mission — not merely that mission in general, but the mission in Corinth. The defense of that mission constitutes the thematic unity of the letter.

IV. THE THEOLOGY OF SECOND CORINTHIANS

As even a cursory reading of the letter shows, Second Corinthians is an intensely personal letter. That is so, even though Paul makes every effort to deflect attention from himself and his gifts. The fundamental issue at stake in First Corinthians has become the focal issue in Second Corinthians: what are the marks of a true apostle? As both Paul and the Corinthians agree, to ask this question is to ask in what form Christ's power appears in the world: "You are seeking proof of the Christ who speaks in me" (2 Cor 13:3). The form of

Christian life is therewith decided. The life of the apostle is nothing other than the life of a Christian in large-screen display: "Our hope for you is confirmed, knowing that as you are partakers of sufferings, so also you are partakers of salvation" (1:7). As we have noted, the Corinthians implicitly recognize this truth, and for that reason prefer other apostolic claimants who have made their way to Corinth, and who confirm their calling with outward displays of speech and power.

The battle for the hearts and minds of the Corinthians therefore cannot be separated from Paul's person, even if it does not finally have to do with his person. Paul is the battleground between the Gospel and the world. Nowhere other than in Galatians do we find such dramatic expressions of emotion and affections on Paul's part, as we find them here. Paul opens his heart wide to the Corinthians, appealing to them to open their hearts wide to him as well (2 Cor 6:11-13). He speaks to them without reserve of his struggles and weaknesses, his joys and his sorrows. At this point in Paul's mission, these sorrows have to do primarily with the Corinthians. He seeks not merely for them to recognize him as an apostle, he seeks for them to recognize him as *their* apostle. His words in First Corinthians apply here: "even if I am not an apostle to others, I am indeed an apostle to *you*" (1 Cor 9:2). His very salvation is bound to their salvation, just as their salvation is bound to his (2 Cor 1:12-14). He is prepared "to die with them and live with them" (2 Cor 7:3).

The problem with Paul in Corinth is the jarring contrast between his powerful letters and his pitiful presence.[22] The apostle "bears the deadness of Jesus" in his body, in order that the resurrected life of Jesus might be manifest in him (2 Cor 4:10-11). He is thrust again and again into distress, including his distress over the Corinthians, in order that God's power, and not his own, might be manifest in him. The life of an apostle, and thus the life of a Christian, is fundamentally passive. It is not a "purpose-driven life" but a "God-driven life." This passivity by no means excludes the activity of the apostle. It creates the space in which faith operates. To attempt to measure the work of God by the outward and visible standards of human activity is to completely misunderstand that work (10:12-18). The issue between Paul and the Corinthians, then, is the difference between faith and appearance, the difference between what the eyes can see and what the ears can hear in the apostolic proclamation of the cross. The apostle bears "the word of the cross" (1 Cor 1:18), not merely in his proclamation, but in his body and life. God's saving work takes place *sub contrario* in the crucified Jesus, contrary to all human thought and expectations. The delivery of that work in the apostolic word takes the same form.

This is the fundamental theological issue of the Corinthian correspon-

22. His practices, too, have alienated the Corinthians: not only his refusal to accept compensation from them (11:7-11) but also his failure to visit them as he had promised (1:15–2:4).

dence as a whole, one that bears hermeneutical implications. Indeed, Paul's contention with the Corinthians finally has to do with the profound hermeneutical question as to whether the human being has the capacity of recognizing, understanding, and judging the work of God within the world, or whether it is the work of God that recognizes and judges the human being. This question is present within the Corinthian assumption that they are capable of judging and approving apostles. To judge an apostle is to judge Christ. The apostle is a bearer of Christ, and as such a bearer not only of Jesus' life but also of "the deadness of Jesus" (2 Cor 4:10). Will the Corinthians finally embrace another Jesus, different from the one they have found through Paul (11:4)? The controversy in Corinth therefore runs through the very heart and understanding of the Corinthians. The battle — and Paul is not ashamed to call it a battle (10:3-5) — has to do not merely with false judgments but with false judgment, namely, the self-seeking reasoning that is inherent to every human being. We cannot get outside of our own skin. We cannot gain the perspective of an all-seeing "eye" or become an all-seeing "I." Our heart, with its affections, beats faster than our head can think. Second Corinthians may be regarded as an extended commentary on "the word of the cross" (1 Cor 1:18). God's saving work is necessarily hidden under its opposite, not only in Christ, but also in Christ's apostle — as well as in all Christians. In this way alone humans are removed from themselves and made new. Salvation comes through judgment, and in no other way. Paul's message in Second Corinthians, therefore, is that salvation never becomes a possession of the human being but remains a communication between the God who saves and the human being who is lost in blindness. Saving communication between God and the fallen human being is found in Christ alone, in whom life is hidden within death, wealth within poverty, wisdom within foolishness.

The hermeneutic that Paul presents in Second Corinthians is thus *material,* bound to God's work in Christ. It cannot properly be universalized. It cannot be reduced to a set of rules. Nor can it be reduced to transcendental judgments about the nature of human understanding. It is a work that is communicated in the "word of God" that the apostle bears (2 Cor 2:17; 4:2; cf. 1:18). As we have observed, it is the disjunction between the overwhelming word of the apostle and the "underwhelming" presence of the apostle that has scandalized the Corinthians. As Paul makes clear, the whole of the Scriptures are thereby at stake. His appeal to the story of Moses in 2 Cor 3 bears an unmistakably hermeneutical message: the veil that rests on the hearts and minds of the "sons of Israel," which prevents them from seeing the face of Moses, prevents them also from seeing God in his saving work. This veil is removed only "in Christ" and thus through the free and open speech of Christ's apostle. What happened to the "sons of Israel" is a figure in which the truth about all of humanity is revealed: the god of this world has blinded the minds of unbelievers (4:4). Our blindness may be overcome only by a fresh act of the Creator, who causes light to arise in darkness, just as he has done in the heart of the apostle (4:6). For Paul, therefore, there is no going behind God's saving work through "the letter" and by the Spirit (3:6). Life and righteousness are given only through death and condemnation. That is true not only of Christ but also of the apostle, who has delivered the word of reconciliation to Corinth and delivers it now afresh. It is also true of the Corinthians, who share in comfort and salvation only as they also share in the sufferings of Christ as they are distributed to them. The question at stake is whether we have the power and ability to interpret the message of Scripture, or whether the Scripture of itself, without any help from us, has the power to interpret us and impart itself to us through the apostolic message — a message that has now been proclaimed through the mouths of weak and suffering human beings through the centuries. It is the question as to whether we are to master Scripture, or whether Scripture is to master us. Paul's hermeneutic does not at all exclude the reading and study of Scripture. In a rare moment, he boasts of his own knowledge, which can only be understood as knowledge of Scripture (11:6). As interpreters long have recognized, he expects the Corinthians, Gentiles though they are, to possess a remarkable knowledge of the biblical text. But to know the text, the words of the text, and the divine demands is not the same thing as knowing the message of Scripture. That knowledge must come from the work of the Scriptures themselves as they are interpreted and proclaimed in the "word of the cross" (1 Cor 1:18). Current fascination with metanarratives that we might construct from the text or with the virtue of the interpreter as a means of "theological interpretation" receives here a fundamental correction from the apostle.

Commentary

I. THE OPENING OF THE LETTER: THE CALL TO FELLOWSHIP WITH THE APOSTLE IN CHRIST (1:1–2:17)

The openings of Paul's letters take a consistent form, in which Paul announces his calling by Christ as apostle and with it expresses the message of the Gospel. Nevertheless, no two openings of Paul's letters are alike. In each instance, the apostle communicates his pastoral concern for the concrete needs of his addressees. His variations on the theme of the Gospel speak to their needs at that moment in their life. His word is always a word targeted to his churches.[1] As he tells the Corinthians, it is a "word to you" (1:18).

The letter openings, then, generally take the following pattern: (1) a prescript and address (or "superscript"), in which Paul identifies himself and those to whom he writes; (2) a "grace pronouncement," in which the apostle blesses the church by the power and authority of the Gospel; (3) a prayer of thanksgiving, in which Paul communicates the presence of his addressees in his heart and prayer; and (4) a self-disclosure, in which Paul reports concerning himself and his activities to his readers. The shift from Paul's report concerning his person to his message to his addressees marks the transition from the opening to the body of the letter.[2]

Letters are a substitute for personal presence. This is dramatically so in this letter, in which Paul must explain to the Corinthians why he did not visit them as he had promised.[3] His absence raised suspicions and may well have provided opportunity to his opponents. Did he fail to come to Corinth because he was not reliable and did not really care about them? Or perhaps he was

1. I have borrowed this language from J. Christiaan Beker, who used it on many occasions in reference to Paul and his letters.

2. On the form of the Pauline letter openings, see esp. F. Schnider and W. Stenger, *Studien zum Neutestamentlichen Briefformular* (NTTS 11; Leiden: Brill, 1987), 1-68.

3. 1:15-22; 2:3-4.

ashamed of his inadequacies and was embarrassed to appear there? The Corinthians — likely under the influence of Paul's opponents — perceived an obvious difference between Paul's letters and his personal presence: "His letters, they say, are weighty and strong. But his bodily presence is weak and his speech is contemptible" (10:10). This suspicion, however, is a misjudgment of the apostle, in whom Christ's death and life, the saving work of God, is present. Paul's own person was at the center of his contention with the church in Corinth.[4] There was no room in this church, which lived for power, for an apostle who lived in weakness. Outward, visible presence and performance — measured, as it must be, by mere human tastes — had become the standard by which the Corinthians judged the presence of Christ, the ministry of the Gospel, and the legitimacy of the apostle.[5] Indeed, they regarded *their* letters of commendation as necessary for Paul's accreditation.[6] In the height of irony, Paul now must defend his apostolic authority to a church that was the fruit of his apostolic labor. As he tells them more than once, they themselves are the proof of his apostleship — so long as they hold to the true apostle through whom they received the Gospel.[7] Paul writes "boldly" to the Corinthians so that he might spare them from the severity that he would otherwise be forced to exercise in a personal visit (13:10), a severity that he already had avoided in his decision to cancel his promised visit (1:23–2:4). Such apostolic severity would also have meant sorrow, tears, and self-humiliation on Paul's part — an expression of weakness that the Corinthians thus far have failed to comprehend.[8]

As Paul makes clear, this contention over apostolic authority does not have to do with him but with the Gospel, and therefore with the very salvation of the Corinthians.[9] In his understanding, the authority of an apostle rests not in office or in personal charisma or in the genius of rhetoric. It is an authority that rests solely in the call of Christ and in the Gospel, of which Paul is neither master nor interpreter.[10] It is the Gospel that masters and

4. See 1 Cor 2:1-5.

5. Käsemann's argument that 2 Cor 10–13 is Paul's defense and definition of apostolic ministry remains convincing and fruitful, even if his assumption that Paul's adversaries claimed the support of Jerusalem must be revised. See E. Käsemann, *Die Legitimität des Apostels: Eine Untersuchung zu II Korinther 10–13* (Reihe Libelli 33; Darmstadt: Wissenschaftliche Buchgesellschaft, 1964). This reading of 2 Cor 10–13 may be expanded to the entire letter: Paul is not dealing with a series of problems, as interpreters generally assume, but with only one — the wayward heart of the Corinthians. See the excursus on Paul's opponents (pp. 100-110), as well as the introduction to 2 Cor 10–13 (pp. 368-73).

6. 3:1-3.

7. See, e.g., 1:12-14; 3:1-3.

8. 10:10-11; 12:19-21.

9. 1:12-14; 12:19-21.

10. On this theme, see S. Kierkegaard, "Of the Difference between a Genius and an Apostle," in *The Present Age* (trans. A. Dru; London: Oxford University Press, 1940), 138-63.

interprets the apostle in word and life — and with him the Corinthians as well. It must run its course with him through this conflict with the Corinthians, and through all others whom it provokes in this world. The apostle bears the message of the Gospel, not merely in his word and speech, but also in his body and life.[11] The story of Jesus Christ, in which all God's people share — past, present, and future — must repeat itself in the apostle for the comfort and strengthening of those to whom he has been sent. While Paul's authority as an apostle does not rest in his person, it cannot be separated from his person.

A. Prescript (1:1-2)

> [1]*Paul, an apostle of Christ Jesus by the will of God, and Timothy our brother. To the church of God that is at Corinth, with all the saints who are in the whole of Achaia:* [2] *Grace to you and peace from God our Father and the Lord Jesus Christ.*

1. *Superscript (1:1a)*

1a The superscript, address, and pronouncement of grace follow the usual pattern of Paul's letters in a rather restrained manner (vv. 1-2). Unlike other occasions (as, for example, First Corinthians), Paul's particular theological concerns here hardly come to expression. Or perhaps they do in Paul's silence. In the absence of elaboration, the fundamental matters receive full attention. The Gospel itself is at stake. To those familiar with Paul's letters, as the Corinthians were by this time (having received four of them), the simplicity of his opening words very likely communicated this very point.

Paul here names himself "apostle by the will of God" as he does in First Corinthians and elsewhere.[12] No additional designation (such as "slave") appears.[13] Nor does Paul elaborate his calling, as he does in Galatians and Romans.[14] Here it is necessary for him merely to make his fundamental claim: by the will of God he is apostle. That is to say, he is not apostle by virtue of his own abilities, powers, or self-assertion. The Corinthians were

11. See A. Schlatter, *Paulus, der Bote Jesu: Eine Deutung seiner Briefe an die Korinther* (3rd ed.; Stuttgart: Calwer, 1962 [1934]), 533: "As the herald of Jesus, he recounted the history of Jesus' passion, but he not only recounted it, he experienced it as well."

12. The designation "apostle by the will of God" also appears in 1 Cor 1:1; Eph 1:1; Col 1:1; 2 Tim 1:1; cf. 1 Tim 1:1.

13. See Rom 1:1; Phil 1:1.

14. Gal 1:1; Rom 1:1-5.

looking for a genius. God sent them an apostle, who was theirs in weakness and suffering.[15]

"Apostles" were those eyewitnesses of the crucified and risen Lord who had been called by Jesus himself to proclamation and witness. The immediate background to this apostleship most likely lay in the practice of the Jewish authorities in Jerusalem, who authorized delegates with authority to act in their name.[16] This early Jewish practice had roots, or at least its precedent and legitimation, in the divine sending of the prophets as messengers.[17] Similar Hellenistic practices also existed in this period. Paul elsewhere characterizes his apostolic calling in the language of Jeremiah's call as a prophet, and he strikingly appeals to the words of the prophets as an anticipation of apostolic witness, suggesting that the biblical background of the suffering prophets also shaped his understanding of the apostolic calling.[18] It was of course Jesus — standing outside the sphere of scribal or high-priestly authority — who first had made an implicit claim to authority in appointing apostles, especially in his original naming of twelve apostles. The circle was expanded after the resurrection (1 Cor 15:5-11). The requirement that an apostle be a direct witness of Jesus, appointed by him, was well known to the Corinthian church (1 Cor 9:1-18). Undoubtedly, it was also known to the adversaries with whom Paul has to deal in this letter, who themselves claimed to be apostles of Christ.[19] Paul does not attack them on this ground. How could he? The claim would be difficult if not impossible to challenge. It would have been beside the point, in any case. For Paul, apostolic calling expresses itself in fidelity to the Gospel. Proclamation or conduct that did not conform to the Gospel of Christ was not apostolic, no matter from whom it came.[20] At this point in their relations, Paul's conflict with the church at Corinth had finally focused on the question of the legitimation of an apostle. This question had been present from the start, playing a role within all the other issues that had troubled Paul's relationship with the church. It was already present in the factions within the Corinthian church, a situation that Paul addresses in First Corinthians: "Each of you says, I am of Paul, I am of Apollos, I am of Cephas, I am of Christ."[21] Now others

15. Again, see Kierkegaard, "Of the Difference between a Genius and an Apostle."

16. K. H. Rengstorf, "ἀπόστολος," *TDNT* 1:414-20.

17. E.g., Jer 7:25; 25:4; 26:5; 29:19; 35:15; 44:4.

18. Gal 1:15-16; Rom 9:25–11:9.

19. Perhaps 2 Cor 5:16 and possibly 10:7; 11:23.

20. Cf. Gal 1:6-9; 2:11-21.

21. 1 Cor 1:12. The claim to be "of Christ," which falls at the end of Paul's listing of the factions, bears a twofold significance. On the one hand, it designates a distinct faction within the church who most likely claimed that they had experienced an apparition of the risen Lord (cf. 2 Cor 12:1-10). On the other hand, Paul's immediate response (whether an exclamation or a rhetorical question) that Christ had been divided (1 Cor 1:13) indicates that all of the factions

had presented full "apostolic credentials," including Jewish identity, offering themselves as an alternative to Paul. At this point, the entire debate came to be centered on the question as to what constituted the marks of an apostle. Who could rightly claim the title?

Paul is an "apostle of Christ Jesus" (v. 1). In the Pauline prescripts, "Christ" is often placed before "Jesus," which suggests that something of its titular force is retained. Paul thus describes himself as apostle of "Messiah Jesus," the Anointed One of Jewish hope. Behind the question of the legitimating marks of the apostle stood the question of the identity of the Christ. As we have noted, already at the beginning of the troubles, when divisions arose in the church, there was a group who refused to identify themselves with any earthly leader and named themselves as those "of Christ."[22] But what sort of "Christ," what sort of "Anointed One" did they imagine that they followed? One who imparted heavenly speech perhaps? One who endued them with outward and visible power? Paul, for his part, refused to abandon "the word of the cross" for "the wisdom of word."[23] He refused to surrender God's wisdom "hidden in a mystery"[24] for the overt wisdom of rhetorical skill and a pleasing presentation. Paul preached Christ *crucified*, namely, the Crucified One, who now lives by the power of God alone.[25] In him all human wisdom and power is brought to an end, so that the wisdom and power of God may have its place.[26] It was not merely other apostles to whom the Corinthians were attracted, but to another, false "Jesus" in whom there was a corruption of "the simplicity and purity" that belongs to the *crucified* and risen Christ.[27] The question of apostolic authority is nothing other than the question as

---

supposed that they possessed Christ, either in their favored leader (2 Cor 10:7; 13:4) or in an immediate apparition of Christ. The presence of a faction that claimed to be immediately "of Christ" shows that, already at this stage, a direct challenge to Paul's apostolic authority existed within the Corinthian church. That challenge manifests itself in the confrontation that took place in Corinth on Paul's second, "tearful" visit (2 Cor 2:5-11), as well as in the questions about Paul's authority that appear already in 1 Cor 9:1-27. The arrival of Jewish apostolic claimants added a new dimension to the problem and brought it to a point of crisis (2 Cor 11:4). Although their claim to authority is based in part on their Jewish identity (v. 22), they apparently made no appeal to Jerusalem authorities. They hardly could do so, if an opposing group already claimed to follow Cephas! The Corinthian church supposed itself to be capable of judging who was an apostle and who was not (3:1-3; 13:3). The criterion clearly was the authority of the risen Christ, who was understood to be present in an apostle (10:7; 13:3; cf. 11:13, 23). See the discussion of the opponents and the purpose of the letter, pp. 100-110.

22. 1 Cor 1:12.

23. 1 Cor 1:17-18.

24. 1 Cor 2:7.

25. 13:4.

26. 1 Cor 1:23-24.

27. 11:3-4.

to who is "of Christ."[28] The Corinthians, who seek proof of the presence of Christ in Paul, here receive a definitive answer from him.[29] It was an answer that they hardly expected.

Paul names Timothy alone as co-sender of and witness to the letter, which was probably sent from Macedonia.[30] Timothy had been present as one of Paul's co-workers at the first proclamation of the Gospel and the founding of the church in Corinth (v. 19).[31] In the course of Paul's troubles with the Corinthians, Timothy also had served as Paul's messenger and representative in difficult circumstances.[32] He would have been familiar to the Corinthians. They would have been familiar to him as well. His earlier visit, like that of Paul's, had failed to resolve the problems in the church.

Paul's simple description of Timothy as "brother" is by no means an indication of secondary status (v. 1). Rather, it is an acknowledgment of him as a genuine fellow Christian, an equal to Paul in Christ.[33] They differ only in their callings.

2. *Address (1:1b)*

1b Paul addresses the letter first to the "church of God that is at Corinth." The expression "church of *God*" recalls the scriptural description of the gathering *(qahal)* of Israel as the people of the Lord.[34] By virtue of its root (*kaleō,* "to call"), the term *ekklēsia* connotes the calling and work of God by the Gospel — a calling that is therefore effective. The "church" is no mere gathering of the pious, but rather "the church of God,"[35] the gathering of those whom God has called as his people.[36] The term *ekklēsia* signifies "assembly" or "gathering";

28. 10:7.

29. 13:3.

30. Titus, who had brought Paul the dramatic and comforting news of the repentance of the Corinthians, most likely carried the letter to Corinth, again serving as Paul's representative to the Corinthian church and preparing for the third visit of the apostle himself (7:6; 8:16-17; 12:18).

31. See also Acts 18:1-11.

32. 1 Cor 4:17; 16:10; see also Rom 16:21.

33. The same form appears in Col 1:1; Phlm 1; cf. 1 Cor 1:1. Paul names himself and Timothy "slaves of Christ Jesus" in Phil 1:1. They appear together without designations in 1 Thess 1:1; 2 Thess 1:1.

34. E.g., Num 16:3; 20:4; Deut 10:4; 23:2-8.

35. 1 Cor 10:32; 11:22; 15:9.

36. It is therefore *one* church, extended throughout the entire world, as Paul indicates in the prescript of 1 Corinthians (1:2). Of course, Paul also names the individual gatherings of believers in their scattered locations "churches" (e.g., Rom 16:4, 16, 23; 1 Cor 7:17; 11:16; 16:19; 2 Cor 8:1), including the individual house churches, which were part of a larger body (Rom

in secular usage it often refers to the assembly of the citizens of a city.[37] As Bernd Wannenwetsch observes, it is striking that the earliest Christians chose a distinctively political (and yet, as we have noted, simultaneously biblical) term for their collective existence, speaking of themselves as an *ekklēsia,* a public assembly, rather than as a "religious gathering" ("synagogue").[38] They thereby confessed that the church is a political entity. They did not insist that it *become* political in its espousal of one cause or another. They confessed that it is *essentially* political because it already shares in the new creation, which inevitably challenges the present world and *all* its judgments (and not merely those of the right or the left).[39] No matter that the church remains within the present, fallen world and continues to be marked by sin and death; it knows the crucified and risen Christ, in whom it is forgiven and by whom it is possessed.

In his address, Paul recognizes the Corinthian church as having influence throughout the Roman province. In other contexts, he speaks of churches in a region as a plurality.[40] Later in this letter, in speaking to the Corinthians, he refers simply to "Achaia," the entire Roman province.[41] Conversely, in Romans he refers to the *church* in Cenchreae[42] and gives the same designation to the group that met in the home of Gaius, his later host in Corinth.[43] His address to "the saints who are in the whole of Achaia" implies the influence of the church in Corinth on the surrounding region, and most likely its extension into this larger area in the form of numerous house churches.

Together with those throughout Achaia, Paul addresses the church at Corinth as "saints," or, better, "holy ones" *(hagioi).* This is Paul's most frequent designation of Christians (43x), the term by which he most often greets them in the prescript of his letters.[44] Consciously or unconsciously, he chooses this word over others: "the elect," "the called," "brothers and sisters," "the righteous," "believers." The expression "holy ones" recalls a series of biblical texts that locate the holiness of God's people in the redemptive action of God, who, in saving them, takes possession of them.[45] Therefore, while "holiness" in-

---

16:5, 23). As is clear from the last verse here, the phenomenon was more widely spread than Rome. The connotation of a physical and local gathering of persons clearly emerges in some contexts, esp. where Paul speaks of being "in church" (e.g., 1 Cor 11:18; 12:28; 14:19, 28, 34, 35).

37. E.g., Acts 19:32, 39, 41.

38. B. Wannenwetsch, *Political Worship: Ethics for Christian Citizens* (Oxford Studies in Theological Ethics; Oxford: Oxford University Press, 2004), 137-38.

39. Wannenwetsch, *Political Worship,* 21-40.

40. E.g., Gal 1:2; 2 Cor 8:1.

41. 9:2.

42. Rom 16:1.

43. Rom 16:23.

44. Rom 1:7; 1 Cor 1:2; 2 Cor 1:1; Eph 1:1; Phil 1:1; Col 1:2.

45. E.g., Exod 19:4-6; Lev 11:44; 19:1-2; 20:7, 26; 21:6; Num 15:40. In the Prophets and the

cludes moral purity, it signifies something larger and greater: the wonder of being made God's own in the whole of our body and life.

Paul thus names the Corinthians "holy ones," not on the basis of their morality, conduct, or progress, but solely on the basis of God's redemptive act in Christ. The claim that the Lord laid upon Israel in bringing it out of Egypt is fulfilled and transcended in his redemptive work in Jesus. This understanding of sanctification as the effective work of God in Christ could not be any clearer or more significant than in Paul's dealings with the Corinthians. Despite their worldliness, weakness, and many failures, they have been "sanctified [made holy] in Christ Jesus, called [by God] as saints."[46] If Paul had taken their life and conduct into account, it would have been impossible for him to describe them in this way. Christ alone is their righteousness, holiness, and redemption.[47] They *are* the holy temple of God, both corporately and individually.[48] In faith and baptism they had been "washed, *sanctified,* and justified" by Jesus' name and by the Spirit of God.[49] In Jesus Christ, to whom they belong, holiness is not a goal yet to be attained but a reality that has arrived, unconditioned by their works. The holiness that Paul hopes will come to perfection in the Corinthians is the very holiness that has been given to them already in Christ.[50] Paul's reminders to them of God's work are intended to bring them back to Christ, in whom not merely their attitudes and habits but their entire being and person have been re-created: "such were some of you" (1 Cor 6:11). "Being-made-holy" is not some second stage in an *ordo salutis* of the Christian life. Nor is sanctification a steady, upward process of growth and development. It is decidedly not a matter of self-improvement. Indeed, it does not rest in the actions, plans, or self-discipline of the Corinthians. Thank God, our growth is not given into our hands! As Paul makes clear to the Corinthians, sanctification is *God's work* that believers do not themselves perform but "suffer," as God — in his own times and ways, not theirs — drives them outside themselves to Christ, who alone remains their sanctification (1 Cor 1:30).[51] Growth is nothing other than growth in the faith that grasps Christ

---

Psalms, not only those who fear and trust God are described as God's "holy ones" (קְדֹשִׁים; e.g., MT Pss 16:3; 34:10[9]; LXX Ps 150:1; Isa 4:3; 62:10-12), but also the heavenly beings (MT Ps 89:6[5], 8[7]; see also Sir 42:17; 45:2; so also in the eschatological vision of Daniel, which bridges this difference between angels and human beings: Dan 7:17-18; see also Wis 5:5; 18:9).

46. 1 Cor 1:2.

47. 1 Cor 1:30.

48. 1 Cor 3:17.

49. 1 Cor 6:11.

50. 7:1; 10:15; cf. 1 Cor 3:5-17.

51. Thus Luther: "Our 'activity' is to permit God to do His work in us," *LW* 26:401. On this topic see W. Joest, *Ontologie der Person bei Luther* (Göttingen: Vandenhoeck & Ruprecht, 1967), 292-94. See further the useful reflections on current interest in "spirituality" in B. Wan-

and his saving work again and again in the ever-changing circumstances of life — that is, in trouble and deliverance, affliction and comfort.

3. *Grace-Pronouncement (1:2)*

2 In place of the usual greeting, which in Hellenistic letters was occasionally supplemented with a wish for the health of the recipient(s), Paul pronounces what we might call an apostolic blessing intended to impart the Gospel to his addressees, and thus to call them afresh to faith.[52] The formula "grace and peace" is a creation of the apostle that bore liturgical significance: his letters were intended for public reading in the worship of the congregations. As we have noted, the twofold form of the greeting is shared by Hellenistic letters. It is also approximated by early Jewish letters, which sometimes open with the wish, "mercy and peace be with you."[53] Paul replaces the term "mercy" with "grace,"[54] and at the same time he plays upon the usual Hellenistic *chairein* ("greeting") with the term *charis* ("grace"). He thus signals from the start that the letter is purely about the Gospel, as it speaks to his addressees at that moment. There is probably a further semantic motivation for Paul's choice of the term "grace" over "mercy." To speak of "mercy," as Paul does almost immediately in this letter (v. 3), is to presuppose a situation of trouble or suffering. "Grace," in contrast, usually signifies the favor and loving attention of God, particularly as it is undeserved in the face of sin and guilt.[55] While the term "grace" certainly does not exclude the idea of deliverance from distress, it speaks first of God's favor. Consciously or unconsciously, Paul approximates the Aaronic benediction in the form and content of his apostolic pronouncement: "The Lord bless you and keep you, the Lord cause his face to shine unto you, and *be gracious* unto you, the Lord lift up his countenance upon you, and grant you *peace*" (Num 6:24-26). In both instances, the "vertical" reality of grace takes on a "horizontal" dimension and yet is not exhausted within it. The Gospel announces not only our deliverance from the misery of sin and death but also the unfathomable love of God by which God gives himself to us in Christ. As we shall see, this is the theme of the letter. The Corinthians imagine that salvation is empowerment. Paul makes it clear that salvation brings an abiding confession of our

---

nenwetsch, "Lob der Äußerlichkeit," in *Denkraum Katechismus: Festgabe für Oswald Bayer zum 70. Geburtstag* (ed. J. von Lüpke and E. Thaidigsmann; Tübingen: Mohr Siebeck, 2009), 394-96.

52. Cf. Acts 15:24; Jas 2:1.

53. E.g., 2 *Bar.* 78:2; cf. 2 Macc 1:1; see I. Taatz, *Frühjüdische Briefe: Die paulinischen Briefe im Rahmen der offiziellen religiösen Briefe des Frühjudentums* (NTOA 16; Freiburg: Universitätsverlag; Göttingen: Vandenhoeck & Ruprecht, 1991), 106.

54. See 1 Pet 1:2; 2 Pet 1:2; Rev 1:4; cf. 1 Tim 1:2; 2 Tim 1:2.

55. See 2 Cor 1:12; 4:15; 6:1; 12:9.

weakness. It establishes a relationship of communication: in the crucified and risen Christ, God's power comes to be present in our weakness.[56]

The apostle's pronouncement of grace presupposes that, although God's undeserved and unmerited favor has been granted fully and finally in Christ, it nevertheless must be granted ever again to believers. We, likewise, are to grasp and receive this grace again and again, in the midst of our tasks, trials, and temptations. That is to say, Paul speaks of "grace" as it is concretely experienced in the varying circumstances of life.[57] This usage appears again significantly in Paul's encouragement and instruction concerning the collection for Jerusalem.[58] Just as he is able to speak of grace as a gift, so he also speaks of gifts as (acts of) grace.[59] In both instances, he underscores the presence and activity of the one who gives within the gifts given.[60]

The second member of the blessing, "peace," communicates the salvation *(shalōm)* God has promised in the Scriptures.[61] It is therefore not to be understood primarily in psychological terms. Nevertheless, in speaking of peace, Paul does not merely refer to external well-being but also signifies an inward reality, just as he does elsewhere.[62] "Peace" is the objective reality of eschatological blessing, which is already present in the heart by the Gospel, yet presently hidden in hope.

It should not be overlooked that most of Paul's letters, including Second Corinthians, close with a reversal of the order of the elements in the opening apostolic blessing.[63] A concluding pronouncement of "peace" precedes a final pronouncement of "grace."[64] This chiasm, or x-pattern, again signals the single, unswerving purpose of the apostle of proclaiming the Gospel to his churches in their particular needs. Each of his letters, including Second Corinthians, is a fresh announcement and defense of the Gospel in the face of the threats that have arisen against it.

According to the apostolic pronouncement, "grace and peace" proceed from "God, our Father, *and* from the Lord, Jesus Christ." Christ is thus not merely the means of salvation but the source of it. In speaking of Jesus Christ in this way, Paul effectively identifies Christ with God.[65] This identification is

56. The primacy of Christology and the cross in the letter is expressed finally in Paul's closing benediction, in which he names "the grace of Christ" prior to "the love of God" (13:14).

57. E.g., 1:15; 4:15; 6:1; 8:1, 4, 6, 7, 9; 12:9.

58. 8:1–9:15.

59. See 8:6, 19.

60. See the discussion below, p. 319.

61. E.g., Isa 9:7; 52:7; 55:12; 57:19.

62. E.g., Rom 14:17; 15:13; Gal 5:22; Phil 4:7.

63. Schnider and Stenger, *Studien,* 88-91.

64. See 13:11, 13.

65. On "divine identity," see R. Bauckham, *Jesus and the God of Israel: God Crucified and*

essential to his Gospel: Christ's love and saving work cannot be separated from that of God himself.[66] For Paul, in Jesus Christ we see and find nothing other than God's heart of fatherly love.[67]

Consequently, Gentile believers in Corinth have become God's own people, the objects of his love and care as "father." Just as God became Israel's father in the exodus from Egypt, through Jesus Christ, God is now the father of those who believe.[68] As our father, who loves us and has made us his own, he calls us to live as his children: to know, obey, and experience him as the self-giving father who loves us and gives himself to us without measure.[69] No one should hesitate to name God "father." Human fatherhood — which is always imperfect, and sometimes is tragically so — is measured by God's love and care, and not the reverse.

B. The Apostolic Benediction of God (1:3-7)

> [3]*Blessed be the God and Father of our Lord Jesus Christ, the Father of mercies and God of all comfort,* [4]*who comforts us in all our affliction, so that we may be able to comfort those who are in any affliction, with the comfort with which we ourselves are comforted by God.* [5]*For as we share abundantly in Christ's sufferings, so through Christ we share abundantly in comfort too.* [6]*If we are afflicted, it is for your comfort and salvation; and if we are comforted, it is for your comfort, which you experience when you patiently endure the same sufferings that we suffer.* [7]*Our hope for you is unshaken, for we know that as you share in our sufferings, you will also share in our comfort.*

This second element of the letter opening already signals trouble between the apostle and the church in Corinth. As we have noted, at this point in the letter Paul usually gives thanks for God's work through the Gospel in the church he addresses. Even in First Corinthians he does so, despite the considerable problems that were present in the church.[70] Here, however, the prayer of thanksgiving is missing, as it also is in his letter to the Galatian churches. In this case,

---

Other Studies on the New Testament's Christology of Divine Identity (Grand Rapids: Eerdmans, 2009), 60-106.

66. Paul's thought here remarkably parallels that of the Johannine writings, esp. John's Gospel, e.g., John 14:1-11.

67. As Luther rightly urges, *LW* 24:141.

68. E.g., Exod 4:22; Jer 31:9; Hos 11:1.

69. Paul takes up this theme in 6:18, in a "democratized" expansion of 2 Sam 7:14: "And I shall be a father to you, and you shall be to me sons and daughters, says the Lord Almighty."

70. 1 Cor 1:4-9. See also Rom 1:8-10; Phil 1:3-11; 1 Thess 1:2-10; 2 Thess 1:3-12; Phlm 4-7.

it is replaced by a benediction of God. Paul blesses God for the comfort that he receives in his afflictions (vv. 3-4) and explains the significance of God's work in him for the Corinthians (vv. 5-7). At this moment, the Corinthians are a large part of those afflictions. As quickly becomes clear, the fundamental issue at stake is the relationship between the church and the apostle. Paul's usual thanksgiving expresses his affection for the church and the bond that exists between them. This very relationship is now in jeopardy. For all the wrong reasons, the Corinthians have been attracted to others who claim to be apostles,[71] and they have become suspicious of Paul's qualifications. Here in the benediction, as well as throughout the letter, Paul answers their suspicions. He does so, not by defending himself, but by defending the apostolic ministry with which he has been entrusted. He instructs the Corinthians in the nature of apostolic ministry — and therewith in the meaning of salvation itself. His benediction of God is an invitation to the Corinthians to embrace him afresh as their apostle, and thereby to grasp the Gospel that they are in danger of abandoning.[72]

We again must not overlook the liturgical significance of Paul's words. Apostolic letters were written to be read in the worship of the church. Paul's substitution of a blessing of God for his thanksgiving for the church likely made a point with the first hearers, whose reading of our First Corinthians (and likely also Paul's other two letters to them) would have prepared them for the usual thanksgiving. Paul here shifts attention away from the gifts given to the church (which constituted the usual topic of his thanksgiving) to God the Giver himself. At the same time, he speaks to the Corinthians of the gift of "comfort and salvation" (v. 6), which is delivered only through those in suffering and need. He thus counters the Corinthian tendency to measure all things, including the apostles and the Gospel itself, by outward displays of power and charisma.

As becomes apparent in vv. 6-7, the first-person language in vv. 3-7 does not include the Corinthians. The "we" refers to the apostle alone. Paul's use of the plural merely shifts attention away from his own person, to the life and experience of all those called as apostles.

As we have noted, in his letter openings the apostle instructs his churches in the Gospel in the face of the challenges, questions, and problems among them. This is clearly the case in Paul's benediction. We find here the theology of the entire letter in a nutshell: God's fatherly comfort is given ever only to those in weakness and affliction, a comfort that is salvation itself. Such is the nature of apostolic ministry and Christian life, which the Corinthians have refused

71. See, e.g., 1:15-22; 6:11–7:16; 10:7-11; 11:1-15.

72. The blessing of God in Ephesians introduces the apostle and his Gospel afresh to addressees largely unfamiliar with him and describes what God has done in Christ for us.

to accept. Paul thus reminds the Corinthians that the final gift of comfort is not given apart from the reality of suffering. The apostle first must trouble the comfortable in order to later comfort the troubled.

The blessing of God by which Paul begins this letter must have been unexpected and, indeed, alien and jarring to the Corinthians. In their own mind, they had little need of comfort. In First Corinthians, Paul ironically describes the self-understanding that the Corinthians have adopted, which continues to mark them: "Already you have become filled, already you have become rich, without us you have begun to reign!"[73] Only the comfortable and the self-assured (such as our contemporaries) can dispense with the hope of the resurrection.[74] The Corinthians were attempting to comfort themselves with earthly goods. They had substituted the creature for the Creator and, without knowing it, had fallen into idolatry. Of course the comfort for which they had opted was no real comfort but a temporary anesthetic with a mere dulling effect. Paul's benediction of "the Father of mercies and God of comfort" is intended to shake them out of their narcotic slumbers, to bring them back to the harsh realities from which they, in their imagination, had taken flight. To confess that the present world is a "vale of tears," as Paul effectively does, is not to say that there is nothing in it but suffering and sorrow. It is, however, to open one's eyes to the sorrow and suffering that are present in the world. It is to see beyond the temporary security of the earthly goods to the suffering that in one measure or another must come to each who belongs to Christ. Indeed, according to the apostle, comfort and salvation come only through trial and suffering. True happiness comes only to those who know sorrow. Paul seeks to bring the Corinthians back to this realism.

As becomes clear in the benediction itself, the comfort that God gives in suffering is bound to Christ, and thus to the message of the apostle. It is not a general truth but is specific to the crucified and risen Christ. The communication of light within darkness, life within death, and wealth within poverty takes place in him.[75] These opposites of divine omnipotence and human weakness coincide in Christ in such a way that not only human suffering but also human rebellion is overcome: God's triumph and righteousness are thereby established. As Paul will shortly affirm to the Corinthians, God's Yes is found in Christ (1:20). As Paul earlier has reminded the Corinthians, they have been called into a "*koinōnia* of Christ," in which communication and exchange with Christ takes place (1 Cor 1:9). Here and elsewhere, Paul reminds the Corinthians that God's saving work in the fallen human being follows the pattern of his saving work in Christ and the "word of the cross," by which God distributes

73. 1 Cor 4:8.

74. 1 Cor 15:12-58.

75. See, e.g., 4:6, 10; 6:10; 8:9.

salvation.[76] That which God has effected for us in Christ, God effects in those who belong to Christ. We thus are stripped of our idols so that we may be given the true God.

It is sufficient for Paul here to announce the Gospel to the Corinthians. He does not delve into the mystery of the origin and end of suffering, sin, and death — the question of the hidden God. His attention is focused on the comfort given in the crucified and risen Christ. The Gospel in which God's love and power are displayed can be grasped only as the effective and final comfort of all human need, suffering, and sorrow. Paul's message thus stands in stark contrast to the old, unanswered human question of the origin of evil: *unde malum?*[77] In contrast to the *question* of suffering that seeks an *answer* that we might then carry around in our heads to our own satisfaction, Paul speaks of the *comfort* that God has given in Christ. He understands that we need something more, something larger and greater than an intellectual answer to the question of suffering, just as we need something more than mere outward aid or assistance. He announces a *comfort* in which the warmth of God's love and understanding is present, *along with* the hope of deliverance from evil. In Christ, God promises to wipe away, not only the questions in every mind, but also the tears from every eye. This comfort — which can come from God alone — cannot be found in an "answer" but only in a relationship of communication with God, in which there is a place for petition and lament, and also thanksgiving and praise. This communication, according to Paul, has taken place in the crucified and risen Christ, in whom is found God's decisive Yes to all God's seemingly broken promises. This Yes, which contains the hope of the rectification of all things, is no mere apocalyptic date for which we wait. It is the deliverance that has entered into the world in Jesus Christ and is *effective* in the face of evil and the seeming meaninglessness of life that suffering brings. This is very good news, which surpasses all our expectations — and questions.

The apostle's blessing of God *identifies* God with the Gospel and does so *in relation to Paul in his apostolic life and ministry in such a way that it also identifies* those to whom the apostle ministers and who receive the Gospel. In thus reminding the Corinthians of the way the Gospel has come to them and the course it must run with them, Paul reminds the Corinthians of their true identity. They are not what they imagine themselves to be. They are not defined by their abilities, powers, or performance, but by the works that God performs in them. They are to suffer these works of God, and to be driven by misery and suffering to find comfort in the crucified Christ

76. 1 Cor 1:18.

77. See B. D. Ehrman, *God's Problem: How the Bible Fails to Answer Our Most Important Question — Why We Suffer* (New York: HarperOne, 2008).

who is risen.[78] As Paul makes clear, this suffering of God's work in us, and not our acting, is fundamental to the life of faith.

Before all else, then, Paul wants his readers to be recipients of comfort through him. He does not comfort them out of his own resources. Just as the Corinthians could not bring themselves comfort, Paul cannot finally comfort them either. Nor does he put himself forward as a mere example of one who has received comfort. As the bearer of the Gospel, the apostle is the battleground between the old, fallen world and the new creation that has arrived in Jesus Christ. The apostle is the *vehicle* of divine comfort to the Corinthians; God comforts them *through* him. Just as he has received and handed on the Gospel,[79] so through Christ, he receives and hands on comfort. This comfort, which extends into the present hour, has been received and handed on in a long chain of tradition stretching back to the apostle, and beyond him to Christ: the God whom Paul blesses is none other than "the God and Father of our Lord, Jesus Christ." The psalmists' experience of trouble, deliverance, their proclamation, and their giving forth of comfort culminates in Christ, who was thrust into the ultimate affliction and granted decisive and final comfort.[80] Even here and now, we are the recipients of that comfort, given by Christ, through the apostle. The mere instrumental role of the apostle notwithstanding, it makes all the difference in the world that the words spoken and written here came *through him*. Paul is able to speak true comfort because he, like the psalmists, is one who received true comfort in the midst of all his hardships: "My soul boasts in the Lord. The poor hear it and rejoice" (Ps 34:2). Like all biblical pronouncements of blessing on God, the apostle's benediction of God here is neither remote nor abstract. It is a response to the goodness of God, which Paul experiences concretely as God's work of comfort and salvation in Christ.

Paul speaks here as apostle. His blessing of *God* and his own experience of comfort are inseparable from his hope for the comfort and salvation of the *Corinthians*. Conversely, God speaks comfort to the Corinthians *only through the bodily life and words of the apostle*. Their first "task" — and ours as well — is to be recipients of that comfort. Their life and salvation is bound to that of the apostle and his to theirs, as he makes clear again and again in the letter. His ministry is no mere matter of words that might be peddled. It is the sharing of life, the life that is present in the risen Christ. Paul's life is bound to theirs

78. On this topic, see O. Bayer, *Martin Luther's Theology: A Contemporary Interpretation* (trans. Thomas H. Trapp; Grand Rapids: Eerdmans, 2008), 19.

79. 1 Cor 11:23; 15:1. The apostle is not excluded from receiving the Gospel, despite his direct encounter with the risen Lord (Gal 1:16; 1 Cor 9:1). Despite the dramatic vision, the *verbal* communication through another remains necessary.

80. See, e.g., Pss 34; 69:29-32.

through Jesus Christ, to whom he has betrothed them. This is true in a unique and unqualified sense for the life of the apostle, to whom we remain bound even today through his written witness. In a derivative way, however, it applies to all the relationships of giving and receiving of comfort within the life of the Church. Here Bonhoeffer's words concerning Christian community are fitting:

> I have community with others and I shall continue to have it only through Jesus Christ. The more genuine and deeper our community becomes, the more will everything else between us recede, the more clearly and purely will Jesus Christ and his work become the one and only thing that is vital between us. We have one another only through Christ, but through Christ we do have one another, wholly, and for all eternity.[81]

3 Paul's benediction of God follows a scriptural pattern and likewise bears similarities to the forms of early Jewish benedictions. As in most instances (esp. in use of the *baruk*-form),[82] the expression of blessing (Gk. *eulogētos,* Heb. *baruk*) is fronted. The naming of God follows.[83] Often in Scripture the *nomen proprium* of God appears, followed by a further description of his saving deeds: "Blessed be the Lord, who. . . ."[84] In accord with the twofold usage of the Hebrew verb *brk,* which, according to context, may describe either divine blessing of human beings or the human response of thanksgiving,[85] benedictions of God are expressions of thanksgiving for blessings — either those already received or those for which one hopes.[86] Like the "comfort" that Paul is about to describe, "blessing," whether it is the bestowal of good or the benediction returned in response, is a *verbal* event that takes place in the context of exchange. Benedictions differ from thanksgivings in their focus upon the Giver rather than upon the gifts received. Yet, while we can distinguish between benediction and thanksgiving, and between gift and Giver, it is impossible to separate the two. We receive God's benefits as *gifts* only insofar as we recognize and thank the *Giver.* We bless God rightly only as we recognize

81. D. Bonhoeffer, *Life Together* (trans. J. W. Doberstein; New York: Harper & Brothers, 1954), 25-26.

82. Otherwise the *pi'el* form of the verb ברך appears and often is fronted as well (e.g., MT Pss 16:7; 34:2[1]; 103:2).

83. Alternatively, the blessing in the בָּרוּךְ form may be addressed directly to God, in which case the Septuagintal translation generally supplies the second-person verb, while the Hebrew simply uses the second-person pronoun, e.g., "Blessed are you, Lord, the God of Israel, our Father . . ." (1 Chr 29:10).

84. E.g., LXX Exod 18:10; Ruth 4:14; 1 Kgdms 25:32, 39; 2 Kgdms 6:21; 3 Kgdms 8:15; 2 Chr 2:12; 6:4; Ps 27:6 (28:6); 2 Esd 7:27.

85. Of course, the "blessing" of God also is used ironically in the opposite sense of "curse" (e.g., Ps 10:3; Job 1:9: 2:9).

86. E.g., Pss 18:46; 34:1; 41:13; 66:8-9; 68:19; 72:18-20; 103:1-5; 106:48.

God as the Giver of all good gifts, including our very life and existence. Faith is a relationship of communication. It is therefore entirely fitting to the situation Paul addresses that he substitutes the blessing of God for his usual thanksgiving for God's gifts among his addressees. It had long been a temptation of the Corinthian church — which had been remarkably blessed by God — to worship the gifts of God in the place of God the Giver, and thus to pervert and idolize those gifts. They had succumbed to that temptation in their embrace of apostolic claimants, who apparently had displayed remarkable gifts of rhetoric and other powers. In so doing, the Corinthians not only rejected Paul but had failed to give thanks to God, and thus failed to *receive* what had been given to them as gifts of God.[87] The returning of thanks to God is not finally an act of *giving* but an act of *receiving,* namely, the reception and acknowledgment of God as *Giver.* Only in this reception of the Giver do God's many benefits become *God's gifts* to us: otherwise they are imagined to be good fortune or the recompense for good works. In blessing God, the apostle offers the thanks that the Corinthians have failed to yield, thus inviting them to thanksgiving. In so doing, he introduces another of the fundamental themes of the letter.[88]

Frequently in early Jewish benedictions, but also occasionally in Scripture, God is identified as the God in whom Israel or the patriarchs trust, and whom they worship and serve, for example, "Blessed be the Lord, the God of Israel!" (LXX Ps 71[72]:18).[89] Paul identifies God in the same way, yet with his own apostolic distinctive. He replaces the usual naming of God as the "God of Israel" or "God of Abraham" or "God of the fathers" with another name: it is "the God and Father of our Lord, Jesus Christ," whom Paul blesses.[90] He draws this blessing from his preceding pronouncement of grace on the church in v. 2, taking up his reference to "God, our Father" and to "our Lord, Jesus Christ" and strikingly rearranging it. In so doing, he again makes clear that his blessing of God springs from and is entirely bound up with the Gospel.

In speaking of God as "the God and Father of Jesus Christ," Paul also dramatically shifts the language of his grace-pronouncement. There he identifies Jesus Christ with God. Here he speaks of Jesus Christ as a human being who knew suffering and comfort (v. 5). Indeed, Jesus is *the* human being whose experience of suffering and comfort was anticipated by the people of God in the past, and in whom their own experience reached its promised fulfillment:

87. Cf. 1 Cor 4:7.

88. See 1:11, 14; 2:14; 5:12; 9:15, and the discussion of "gift" below in connection with the collection for Jerusalem, p. 319.

89. See also Gen 9:26; 24:27; 1 Sam 25:32; 1 Kgs 8:15; 1 Chr 29:10; 2 Chr 2:12; 6:4; 2 Esd 7:27; Dan 3:28; Tob 8:5; Luke 1:68.

90. Only rarely does Paul speak of "the God of Jesus." Beyond Paul's use of this characterization later in this letter (2 Cor 11:31), it appears only in the opening of Ephesians (Eph 1:3, 17). See also 1 Pet 1:3, where the characterization of God likewise appears in a benediction.

in *Jesus* God has revealed himself as "the Father of mercies and God of all comfort." As Paul makes clear shortly, all the promises of God find their Yes in him (v. 20). The Christ is Jesus, the Suffering Servant of God (6:2; cf. Isa 49:8). He is the one in whom the hope of the patriarchs is fulfilled. His name therefore replaces theirs and that of Israel in the apostolic benediction. We know God rightly and give him thanks only as the God of Jesus Christ. Already here in the letter Paul again warns the Corinthians against imagining that they may know God in any other way than in the crucified Christ who lives.[91] They are not to accept "another Jesus" (11:4).

Paul fills out his benediction of God theologically, identifying the *God* and *Father* of our Lord, Jesus Christ, as the "*Father* of mercies" and "*God* of all comfort."[92] In his use of this x-pattern, or chiasm, the apostle signals that the two elements of his benediction interpret one another. The God and Father in whom Jesus hoped is for us what he was and is for Jesus. The "mercies" and "comfort" of God are found solely in the resurrection of the crucified Jesus, in whom is the Yes to all of God's promises (v. 20).

As in biblical usage elsewhere, in his genitive constructions "father of mercies" and "God of all comfort" Paul *names* God. As with Paul's characterizations of God elsewhere, his naming of God stands apart from prior biblical usage in its *open* universality of hope and its eschatological finality.[93] The psalmists, who likewise name and characterize God, speak of him in immediate relation to their need or that of Israel.[94] Their appeals to God are paradigmatic, of course, so that they bear an implicit universal dimension. Yet Paul's universalism is explicit. Likewise, the psalmists' naming of God bears

91. Cf. 1 Cor 1:18–2:16.

92. Broadly speaking, in Hellenistic Greek the term παράκλησις bears the sense of "request" or "appeal" in a polite or persuasive sense. Within the NT it might generally be rendered "encouragement," which may signify either "exhortation" or "comfort," according to context. This latter meaning, "comfort," is uniquely biblical, deriving from Septuagintal usage, in which the noun and the corresponding verb, παρακαλέω, render the Hebrew verb נחם and related terms. See J. Thomas, "παρακαλέω," *EDNT* 3:23-24. As vv. 5-6 show, the idea of "comfort" is clearly in view here, in the concrete sense of *saving help* (on which, see below).

93. The most frequent characterization of God in Paul's letters is the decisively eschatological and universal name "the God of peace" (Rom 15:33; 16:20; 1 Cor 14:33; Phil 4:9; 1 Thess 5:23), which appears in 2 Corinthians in expanded form, "the God of love and peace" (13:11). The characterizations of God that appear in the ending of Romans are closely related to Paul's language here: "the God of perseverance and comfort" (Rom 15:5), "the God of hope" (Rom 15:13).

94. E.g., Ps 4:1, "God of my righteousness"; Ps 18:46, "God of my salvation"; Ps 85:4, "God of our salvation." Even the appeal to the "God of vengeance" (Ps 94:1) bears this particular and temporal orientation. Likewise the naming "the Lord, the God of hosts" (e.g., Ps 80:4, 7, 14, 19) speaks of God's power, yet without the obvious eschatological dimension that appears in Paul's naming of God as "the God of peace," as is esp. apparent in Rom 16:20.

eschatological implications: what they confess of God in their particular need shall also be manifest finally and decisively in the world. But this dimension, too, remains implicit with them. In contrast, while Paul's naming of God retains particular and immediate dimensions, it is bound up with God's dealings with the apostle (and the Corinthians) through the crucified and risen Jesus. In him we find God's final and decisive revelation of himself.

In his naming of God, then, the apostle tells the Corinthians *who God is.* He discloses God's identity and teaches them to know him *as nothing other than as a merciful and comforting father.* In Jesus Christ, sin, suffering, and death have been overcome. There is nothing more of God, no evil or judgment, that we must fear or dread. Yet within the fallen world, God's self-giving self-revelation is localized: the "mercies" and "comfort" of which Paul speaks, as well as the God who freely gives them, are found nowhere but in Jesus. Only in him — and therefore only in faith and in hope — do we find God as our merciful Father.

This does not at all mean, of course, that God's mercy was unknown prior to Jesus. The Lord who revealed himself to Moses is the God who is "merciful and gracious, abounding in active love for thousands" (Exod 34:6-7). Israel in its distress, and the psalmists in their trials, appeal to the Lord to show his mercies to them.[95] Especially in and after Israel's exile, Israel's prophets recall the Lord's mercy and set their hope upon it.[96] What is new is Paul's *unqualified* naming of God as the Father of mercies and the source of all comfort. The tension between mercy and judgment, which is apparent already in the Lord's announcement to Moses (Exod 34:6-7), and which shaped Israel's history,[97] has now come to its resolution in Jesus Christ, in whom condemnation and death have been overcome, and in whom the gift of the Spirit and life is now given (3:3-11).[98] "Justice" and "mercy" have met one another in Christ. In Jesus Christ we meet God in absolute and unconditioned mercy. This is so,

95. E.g., Pss 25:6; 40:11; 51:1; 69:16; 79:8; 86:15; 103:8-11; 119:77.

96. E.g., Neh 9:6-37; Lam 3:22; Hos 2:19; Zech 1:16.

97. E.g., Jer 16:5; Lam 2:2; Hab 3:2.

98. Parallels to Paul's language appear in 1QM XIV, 6 ("God of mercies") and *b. Ketub.* 8b ("Lord of comfort"). See further 11QMelch II, 19-20; 1QH XVII, 13 ("comfort"). Within early Jewish writings, along with affirmations of or appeals to God's mercy (e.g., Tob 6:17; 7:13; 8:4, 7; Jdt 7:30; 13:14; 16:15; Wis 6:6; 12:22; Bar 3:2; 4:22; Pr Azar 12-19, 67; *b. 'Abod. Zar.* 4b; *b. Ber.* 16a, 17a; and esp. 1QS X, 4; XI, 12-13; 1QH V, 5; XXIII, 14), there also appear attempts to resolve the biblical tension between God's mercy and judgment by measuring and balancing them (e.g., Sir 5:6; *m. 'Abot* 3.16; *b. Ber.* 7a; *b. Yebam.* 64a), further Str-B 3:494. On this topic, see esp. E. Sjöberg, *Gott und die Sünder im Palästinischen Judentum nach dem Zeugnis der Tannaiten und der apokryphisch-pseudepigraphischen Literatur* (BWANT 79; Stuttgart: W. Kohlhammer, 1938), 62-71, 201-10. Christians remain subject to the same temptation of rationalization and the taming of God that it entails.

not because judgment has been set aside, but because it has been overcome. It is "the God and Father of our Lord, Jesus Christ," whom we know and confess as the "Father of mercies and God of all comfort."

In naming God "the Father of mercies and God of all comfort," Paul identifies God as the Creator and source of all human experience of mercy and comfort, who is present and active in the world. Mercy and comfort have their single and final source in God, the Giver of all good. Paul's language is a warning against the Corinthian idolatry that seeks comfort in creaturely things that in themselves can bring no comfort — even if human words and earthly gifts (such as the deliverance in Asia and the report of Titus)[99] themselves serve as the vehicles and messengers of divine comfort. Paul's language thus may be regarded as an appropriation of the *Shema* (Deut 6:4). The apostolic description of God is therefore not diffuse or undefined. It is only in God's identity as the Father of Jesus Christ, in whom he has fulfilled all the promises of Scripture, that we know his mercy and comfort. Otherwise, God's mercy is not experienced and known as such but is misinterpreted as happenstance or luck, attributed to skill, cleverness, works, or piety, or perhaps regarded as the benefit of another god, whose kindness must be coaxed or otherwise obtained by human efforts.

Paul's identification of God is not naive. He does not imagine that the eschaton has arrived in the world apart from the risen Christ, or that God's mercy and comfort appear automatically at all times and all places. Nor does he suppose that they do away with present sufferings. Despite the comfort he has received, one trouble is soon replaced with another. His deliverance in Asia was overshadowed by his trouble with the Corinthians. Everything has its time. The apostle still awaits the final deliverance and comfort, of which present deliverance remains a mere promise. His benediction of God is contrary to all outward appearance and any reasonable human assessment of his own experience. It is a confession of Christ and God's saving work in him. The Corinthian defection from the Gospel is nothing other than their expectation of visible and complete comfort in the present time. They have embraced a Gospel that requires no faith or hope. They would rather ignore the misery of the world and imagine that nothing terrible will befall or disturb them. They have placed their trust in the creature rather than the Creator. Paul's aim is to trouble the comfortable Corinthians, to awaken them to the reality of suffering of the world, which they themselves must endure in some measure if they belong to Christ. In Paul's description of what it means to be an apostle, the Corinthians are to learn what it means to be Christians. Paul's apostolic identification of God is no romantic vision of the present order of things. It is an expression of biblical hope, a confession of faith in Christ that pierces the darkness of misery and sin.

The second description, "God of all comfort," enlarges and deepens the

99. 1:8-11; 7:5-7.

first, emphasizing the sufficiency of divine comfort for every human need. No loss is too deep, no sorrow or pain too great, for the overwhelming and transcendent comfort that God freely gives in Christ. Paul's language comes close to that of 1 Pet 5:10, which in a similar way speaks of "the God of all grace," who meets Christians in their trials. While Jdt 9:14 and 13:4 speak of "the God of all power," Paul speaks of "the God of all comfort," and thus of God's love and God's power *to help and heal.*[100] This help and healing include the overcoming of our sin.

Paraklēsis here (and, in similar contexts, the verb *parakaleō*) expresses the idea of "help" that arrives and is experienced as "comfort," i.e., as personal encouragement, relief, and support in time of need in the form of a word of address.[101] "Comfort" is help that *speaks.* It brings not merely outward relief but the knowledge that there is One who loves and cares, a God who sees distress and answers lament. Those who are in the midst of distress need something more than the external assistance that a mere technician might deliver. They need the warmth of compassion and concern, and they need it from the One who has power over all things, the ability to bring true help and deliverance. According to the apostle, deliverance is "comfort" and not merely external help. It is certainly not a matter of luck or of human skill and effort. It is God's loving and caring response to human misery, which speaks and promises help in all trouble — no matter that we have brought that trouble upon ourselves by our sins, failures, and foolishness:

> "Comfort, comfort my people," says your God, "speak to the heart of Jerusalem, and call out to her that her warfare has been fulfilled, that her guilt has been satisfied, that she has received from the Lord a twofold [recompense] for her sins." (Isa 40:1-2)[102]

Paul likewise speaks of "the God of all comfort" and the "comfort" that God gives in an all-encompassing manner. As a "comfort" that may be communicated, the comfort that Paul receives in his afflictions is a *"word"* that he hands on to others in their affliction.[103] As Paul shortly makes clear, it is the word of God's promise that has been fulfilled in the resurrection of the crucified Christ, which is effective through and in him (v. 20). Paul's language in v. 3 parallels

100. See also Jer 32:27, "God of all flesh"; Sir 36:1; 50:22, "God of all."

101. See p. 18, n. 92.

102. See also LXX Pss 70(71):21; 85(86):17; 89(90):13; 93(94):19; 118(119):50, 52, 76, 82; 134:14; Isa 49:10, 13; 51:3, 12; 61:2; 66:11-13; Luke 2:25; 6:24; cf. O. Schmitz, "παρακαλέω," *TDNT* 5:793-99; J. Thomas, "παρακαλέω," *EDNT* 3:23-24 and n. 92.

103. This word simultaneously brings help and relief. In vv. 8-11 Paul describes the affliction and comfort that he has experienced in concrete example of the deliverance granted to him in Asia. See, likewise, 7:4-13, where he describes his meeting with Titus and the good news of the Corinthians' repentance as God's comforting him in his troubles.

that in Rom 15:4-5, where he speaks of hope arising through "perseverance and the comfort of the Scriptures," and similarly names God as "the God of perseverance and comfort." In both contexts "comfort" is bound up with hope. One might, in fact, describe this comfort as the promises of God directed to human misery and fulfilled in Jesus Christ. Comfort, in other words, is nothing other than the Gospel at work, as God speaks to human need through it. As Paul's larger argument in the letter shows, he understands God's mercies and comfort to be given in the face of physical distress, failure of health, disability, illness, and weakness.[104] They cover all human sins and failures, including those of the Corinthian church, that Paul must endure.[105] They extend to the condemnation and death that the Law brings on all human beings, including the apostle.[106] The mercies and comfort of God give life to the dead.

As we have noted, Paul does not tie up all loose ends in his confession of God as the God of all comfort. He leaves the question of the ultimate cause of suffering unexplored and unexplained. Indeed, he later gives this question radical dimensions when he speaks of "the god of this age" (4:4). It is sufficient for him that God has triumphed over sin and death in Jesus Christ. The resolution of the problem of evil remains until the final translation to glory, even for one who has been caught up to heaven itself (12:1-10).

4 Paul expands his identification of God in v. 3. Just as he is the "God of *all* comfort," so he is the One who comforts Paul in *all* his affliction. The wonder of overwhelming comfort meets all of Paul's lack and need. This further identification of God by the use of a participle ("the one who comforts us") is not unlike the benedictions of the Scriptures and of early Judaism, which often express thanksgiving in a following relative clause,[107] or also occasionally with a participle.[108] As we have noted, benediction and thanksgiving are bound up with one another in biblical thought. One cannot praise God without speaking of his benefits, nor can one speak of God's benefits without praising God. Paul's use of the participle here fixes attention more fully on God's identity than a relative clause that speaks of God's saving action. The apostle is driving home to the Corinthians precisely who God is.

Paul's expansion also elaborates his preceding benediction: the "Father of mercies and God of all comfort" is the one who comforts the apostle in every affliction. The elaboration continues in vv. 5-7. As we have noted, Paul explains the meaning of his benediction for his Corinthian readers, making explicit what is implicitly the case in the biblical psalms. The benedictions of

104. 2 Cor 1:8-11; 2:14-17; 4:7-15; 6:3-10.

105. 2 Cor 2:14-17; 7:5-16.

106. 2 Cor 3:4-18.

107. E.g., Gen 24:27; Ruth 4:14; 1 Sam 25:32, 39; 2 Sam 6:21; 1 Kgs 8:15, 56, 2 Chr 2:12.

108. See Ps 72:18; Jdt 13:17; Tob 13:2.

God that appear there are also invitations to the readers and hearers to believe and confess the God whom the psalmists praise, and thus to enter into the same experience as the psalmists. Paul here is merely making clear to the Corinthians the meaning of his benediction. Indeed, this entire letter to the Corinthians might be described as a biblical psalm, expanded and explained. Paul has been given the same Spirit of faith about which the psalmists have written, and thus out of his hardships follows the pattern of their response to trial: "I believed, therefore I spoke" (4:13; Ps 116:10 [LXX 115:1]).

The term *thlipsis,* which usually bears the sense "pressure, constraint, or burden," is used frequently in the LXX and the NT in metaphor, in the sense of "oppression, distress, affliction," as are the corresponding Hebrew terms (esp. *tsarah*). This metaphorical sense is not unknown in extrabiblical Greek, but its frequency in Scripture is an expression of the experience of the people of God and the theology of lament that arises from that experience. To render the word "trouble" (NIV) is not entirely wrong, but it is weak and unfortunately omits the inward experience of trial that *thlipsis* communicates. "Distress" or "affliction" more accurately conveys the meaning of the term. Paul will shortly take up the metaphor in the image of his "being burdened" (2:5; 5:4).

The following distinction that Paul draws between himself and the Corinthians makes clear that he speaks here not of Christian suffering in general but of his own sufferings as an apostle. A subtle shift in the referent of "we" and "our" takes place between v. 2 and v. 3, a pattern that is repeated throughout the letter. In v. 2 Paul obviously refers to himself together with the Corinthians when he speaks of "God our Father" and "our Lord." But as Paul's words about the Corinthians in v. 7 make clear, the "we" in vv. 4-6 refers to Paul in distinction from the Corinthians. The subtlety of the transition, which already takes place in v. 3, allows Paul to invite the Corinthians to life together in the Gospel under the sufferings and comfort of Christ. As we have noted, that invitation is a fundamental theme of the letter. The first-person plural form that Paul continues to use frequently in reference to himself in the letter makes clear that it is not Paul's person that is finally at stake in the conflict with the church but Paul's calling as apostle, a calling that has been given to others as well. The use of the first-person plural form as an expression of authority in witness to the Gospel, especially apostolic authority, is not unique to Paul. It appears elsewhere in the letters of the New Testament.[109] This usage frequently serves as a means of inviting the readers to share in truths that the author communicates, or as an affirmation that the author and readers already participate in the realities brought into the world by the Gospel.[110] Similarly,

109. E.g., Heb 6:9, 13:18-23; 2 Pet 1:16-18; 1 John 1:1-5.

110. These transitions in reference from the author to audience and author are frequent. See, e.g., 2 Peter 1:19; 1 John 1:6-10; Heb 13:10-15.

Paul uses first-person plural forms to include his co-workers (e.g., 1:19; 1 Thess 1:1-10), or even others who independently minister the Gospel (e.g., 1 Cor 3:9; 4:6-13). It is best, therefore, to interpret Paul's use of the first-person plural in self-reference as communicating the twofold understanding that (1) apostolic authority rests not in the person of the apostle but in the Gospel, and that (2) the Gospel creates a community of faith, and thereby a common experience of suffering and labor.

Paul speaks of his trials collectively in the singular ("all our affliction"), indicating that they are multiple and varied, and yet come to him in his experience as a whole.[111] They are the sufferings of Christ (v. 5). It is God who comforts the apostle in these afflictions. Paul's reference to the crucified and risen Christ and the following description of his "affliction" in Asia, as well as his further reports of trials and deliverance, indicate that, in speaking of "comfort" here, he has in view concrete acts of help and deliverance.[112] It is God who comforts Paul, yet God does so through concrete and creaturely means, including the Corinthians themselves. Behind and in the events that bring him relief, Paul sees the saving hand and hears the comforting voice of God.[113]

The very purpose of Paul's sufferings and weakness as an apostle is to *enable* him to comfort those in affliction with the comfort with which he himself is comforted by God. Indeed, his very strength lies in his weakness, according to his own report of the words of the risen Christ to him (12:9). This, again, is Paul's apostolic ministry in a nutshell, the ministry of the Gospel, the new covenant established in Christ. Paul's sufficiency is not from himself but from the God who performs his work in the apostle (3:5-6). The God who sends affliction does so in order to deliver and save the apostle, and not only the apostle, but all who hear him (4:11-12; 6:4-13; 12:1-10).

The objects of his ministry are "those who are in all affliction." They are the ones to whom the Gospel comes. English translations (ESV, NIV, NRSV) interpret the expression *tous en pasē thlipsei* distributively and indefinitely ("in any affliction"). But the parallelism with Paul's description of his own experience ("all our affliction"),[114] the recollection of Scripture,[115] and the

111. The predicate position of πᾶς might also be distributive ("every affliction"), but the biblical precedents that Paul recalls are decidedly collective (1 Kgdms 26:24; 2 Kgdms 4:9; 3 Kgdms 1:29; LXX Ps 53:9 [54:7]; Isa 63:9), as is Paul's usage in 2 Cor 7:4. The preceding reference to "the God of all comfort" likewise prepares for a collective expression here.

112. See 2 Cor 1:8-11; 4:7-15; and esp. 7:5-7.

113. According to Paul, even the final deliverance from death itself shall come through the incarnate Son; cf. 1 Cor 15:20-28.

114. The absence of the article is no clear indication that Paul uses πᾶς indefinitely. See, e.g., Rom 1:18, 29; 3:20; 7:8; 11:26; 15:13; 2 Cor 7:1; 8:7; 9:8 (2x); 9:11; 10:6; 12:12, all of which are collective. Of course, even if a reference is not collective, it may well be definite "every."

115. See esp. 1 Sam 26:24; 2 Sam 4:9; 1 Kgs 1:29; 2 Chr 15:16; LXX Ps 53:9 (54:7); Isa 63:9.

apostle's indication that the Corinthians share in the same sufferings as he suffers (vv. 6-7) suggest that the reference is instead collective, and therefore intensive. The apostle is empowered to comfort those "in all affliction," those who find themselves in the depths, so that all they are able to see around them is affliction in the midst of overwhelming affliction. Their comfort and help come from God alone. This characterization of the recipients of comfort has an edge, as Paul's following statements make clear: the Corinthians share in comfort only as they share in sufferings and affliction (vv. 6-7).

The "comfort" that Paul gives to others is nothing other than the "comfort" that he has been given by God. As we have observed, in speaking of the comfort he receives, Paul has in view God's concrete acts of deliverance on his behalf. The same is true of the comfort that he gives to others. The comfort that he describes is not that of mere words or of mere sympathy. It is saving help and deliverance from distress that arrives here and now in limited, temporal, and yet wonderful ways, and shall yet arrive ultimately in the resurrection from the dead.[116] Paul himself seeks to relieve the need of the saints in Jerusalem temporally through the collection. Nevertheless, the comfort of which Paul speaks consists *also* in word, the effective word of the Gospel, by which he distributes the comfort that he receives. Never entirely free from affliction and assault, *faith* causes the apostle to speak, to proclaim that which he himself has received (4:13-15).

The apostolic experience of affliction and deliverance is essential to this distribution of comfort. The Corinthians cannot grasp the Gospel without grasping it as it is concretely given through the suffering apostle, the messenger of the crucified and risen Christ. As we have noted, together with countless other Christians through the centuries, we are the recipients and beneficiaries of this apostolic ministry and comfort. Precisely because the apostle speaks out of affliction, he speaks comfort to all human affliction, even to *our* affliction in whatever form it might take. What power would have been present in Paul's preaching if he had lived in ease, as the false apostles wished to do? Paul wants nothing else for the Corinthians than that they learn to see themselves as the recipients of the Gospel as it is given through him. Through them, he invites us to see ourselves in the same way.

5 The afflictions that come to Paul are nothing other than the "sufferings of Christ" (v. 5), which in turn are all the sins and suffering of the world that Christ took on himself in a "wonderful exchange."[117]

While the initial usage of the article with *Christos* in this verse *("ta pathēmata tou Christou")* might be attributed to Apollonius's Canon,[118] Paul

116. See 2 Cor 1:8-11; 4:7-15; 5:1-10.

117. See 5:21; 8:9; 1 Cor 5:7; 11:23-26.

118. See also 2 Cor 2:12; 4:4; 5:14; 9:13; 10:1, 5, 14; 11:3; 12:9.

only infrequently uses the article after the preposition as he does in the second instance *(dia tou Christou)*. It is not unlikely, then, that the use of the article with *Christos* in this verse bears a titular force, as it probably does in several other instances in Second Corinthians,[119] as it clearly does in other contexts.[120] Paul here speaks of "the sufferings of *the* Christ." Over against the Hellenistic "theology of glory," which the Corinthians had embraced, Paul thus reasserts the biblical understanding of the Lord's anointed as one who is delivered over to suffering and yet is granted the Lord's help and deliverance.[121] The motif is closely related to that of "the beloved son," who is subject to rejection, suffering, and death, a motif that he takes up in v. 19. At the same time, Paul inverts the tradition that later appears in the rabbinic expectation of the "travails of the Messiah" *(heblē shel meshiaḥ)*. These were the times of suffering that were expected to precede the coming of the Messiah, and from which one hoped to be spared.[122] Paul speaks instead of Christ's sufferings, in which he shares as an apostle, and which belong to all Christians.

Christ has borne the suffering and death of all human beings (5:14).[123] Nevertheless, those who share in Christ share in his sufferings. Paul's thought disrupts all salvation-historical schemes: Christ's suffering and death are complete and lie in the past; yet Christ's suffering and death continue into the present, even though they have been overcome in his resurrection. The risen Lord whom Paul proclaims is the crucified Christ (1 Cor 1:18–2:5). The apostle carries about "the deadness of Jesus" with him in his bodily life (4:10). Those who belong to Christ share in his sufferings (1:7). Their Lord remains the Crucified One who lives. Christ, who was crucified in weakness, lives solely by the power of God (13:4).

According to Paul, salvation is thus a participation in Christ, one that *necessarily* includes sharing in suffering: "*just as* the sufferings of Christ abound to us, *so* through Christ our comfort *also* abounds."[124] Paul emphatically returns to this point in relation to the Corinthians in v. 7. Paul's shift in language from "affliction" to "sufferings" places even greater emphasis on the *human experience* of pain and sorrow. It also recalls the experience of Christ and thus expresses a starkly realistic conception of union with Christ.[125] The pattern of Christ is repeated first in the apostle, and then — in varying mea-

119. 2 Cor 2:14; 11:2; 13:3.

120. E.g., Rom 9:3, 5; 15:3; 1 Cor 10:4, 9.

121. See Pss 2; 18; 20; 28; 89.

122. See *b. Šabb.* 118a; *b. Pesaḥ.* 118a; *b. Sanh.* 98b.

123. See also 1 Cor 1:13; 15:3; Rom 5:8; 14:15.

124. This understanding of our participation in Christ is fundamental to Paul's Gospel, as is clear from Rom 8:12-39, esp. v. 17.

125. See esp. Phil 3:10 and Col 1:24; also 2 Cor 1:7; 2:14-15; 4:10-11; 5:14-17, 18; 6:15; 11:2; 13:3, 5; Rom 8:17-18; Phil 1:29-30; further Heb 2:9-10; 1 Pet 1:11; 4:13; 5:1, 9.

sures — in all those who belong to Christ. In him, and in him alone, God becomes our God to whom we look for all help in distress, and who finally shall deliver us from all affliction. Strangely, yet wonderfully, this suffering in Christ works eternal glory (4:16-18). Perhaps for this reason Paul can speak elsewhere of suffering on behalf of Christ as being *given* to the Philippians.[126] The gift of salvation cannot be separated from the Giver of salvation. The absolutizing of the gifts of which the Corinthians were guilty, and from which the apostle seeks to deliver them, is nothing other than idolatry. They had been entrapped in the worship of power, wealth and pleasure, rather than seeking the God who grants all good gifts according to his time and wisdom.[127]

As Paul's following description of the effect of his experience in v. 6 makes clear, his suffering works the salvation of the Corinthians, yet not as his suffering, but as the sufferings of Christ. Paul's suffering is not properly his own. He is the *recipient* of Christ and his suffering, and thereby likewise of the comfort that he *hands on* to the Corinthians. The apostle is not the source or basis of their salvation. In that sense, the rhetorical questions of 1 Cor 1:13 must be heard alongside this text: "Paul was not crucified for you, was he? Or were you baptized into the name of Paul?" Nevertheless, in his participation in Christ's sufferings, the apostle is placed in the role of Christ in relationship to the Corinthians. Salvation comes to them through the apostle, even if Paul in no way displaces Christ. Paul is merely Christ's apostle, yet he is *Christ's* apostle, in whom Christ is present.

6 The apostle's affliction takes place for the sake of the "comfort and salvation" of the Corinthians. The pairing is clearly a hendiadys: the "comfort" that comes to the Corinthians is nothing other than their salvation. As Paul indicates later in the letter, death is at work in him, so that "life" might be at work in them (4:12). Everything that God works in the apostle is for the saving benefit of the Corinthians (4:15). The eschatological orientation of Paul's thought becomes clear here. The "comfort and salvation" that have entered the world in Jesus Christ constitute nothing other than the entrance of the eschaton into the present time. Paul sees in Christ the intersection of the fallen world with the age to come. This intersection is marked by battle. "The sufferings of the present time" and the groaning of the children of God are nothing other than the "sufferings of Christ" in which the apostle and the Corinthians share.[128] In these afflictions, God performs his strange, backward work, destroying the Corinthians' false trust in themselves and their creaturely powers. He does so in order that they might trust in him alone, as Paul expressly indicates in v. 9.

126. Phil 1:29; see also 3:10.

127. On this theme, see O. Schmitz, *Neutestamentliche Forschungen,* 4. Reihe, *Evangeliumsprobleme,* vols. 1-2 (Gütersloh: C. Bertelsmann, 1933), 104-5.

128. Rom 8:18-27.

In v. 6 one might have expected a simple chiasm, a balanced x-pattern: if we are afflicted, it is for your "comfort" and salvation; if we are "comforted," it is for your (help in) *affliction*. Instead, as we have noted, Paul speaks twice of the "comfort" that comes to the Corinthians. His asymmetrical statement underscores the unconditioned benefits that come to the Corinthians through him: "If we are comforted, it is on behalf of your comfort." As he later tells them, "All things are for your sake."[129]

Yet Paul does not abandon the chiastic form entirely but merely modifies it so that the references to "comfort" retain their priority. The references to "comfort" are followed by explanations. In the first case, as we have noted, Paul speaks of comfort as "salvation." In the second case in v. 6b, Paul refers to the sufferings that the Corinthians must endure. The comfort that the Corinthians are given through the apostle meets them in their sufferings, which are, as Paul tells them, "the same sufferings that we ourselves suffer." The Gospel brings the whole Christ, *crucified* and *risen* to the human being. On the one hand, the Corinthians also have their sufferings to endure. On the other hand, as Paul instructs them, these sufferings are the same sufferings that "we" (namely, Paul and all apostles) endure. They are the sufferings of Christ. Furthermore, the "comfort" that Paul receives is for the "comfort" of the Corinthians. This comfort is no mere experience (as the ESV and NRSV have it) but bears its own power and performs its work in effecting the Corinthians' endurance of these sufferings: "If we are comforted, it is for the sake of your comfort, which works effectively in the endurance of the same sufferings that we ourselves suffer."[130] As we have noted, "comfort" is nothing other than the Gospel at work.

Paul continues to use the term *pathēmata* ("sufferings") and not *thlipseis* ("afflictions"), emphasizing human experience and recalling "the sufferings of Christ" that come to him as an apostle (v. 5). The sufferings that belong to the Corinthians are the sufferings of Christ. The Corinthians would rather pretend that they were immune to this reality. For that reason, they have long been skeptical of Paul's authority and have been attracted to other apostles who offer them a more appealing model of the Christian life.

7 The last word of Paul's blessing *of God* includes a surprisingly positive and confident statement about the Corinthians. Something of Paul's usual

129. Cf. 1 Cor 3:21-23.

130. Here the ESV and NRSV misread the subject of the participle ἐνεργουμένης. It is not "you" but "comfort." They also misinterpret the meaning of the participle: it does not mean "to experience" but "to work" or "to effect," just as it does in Rom 7:5; 2 Cor 4:12; 1 Thess 2:13, and also, debate notwithstanding, Gal 5:6. The same is true of the usage in the active voice. In these instances Paul may employ the middle form in order to underscore the self-operative nature of the powers he names as subjects of the verb. In this instance, it is "comfort" that acts as a power. Rightly, the NIV: "If we are comforted, it is for your comfort, which produces in you patient endurance of the same sufferings we suffer."

prayer of thanksgiving appears here. His benediction of God includes the Corinthians, just as they are included in his apostolic calling and salvation. Yet Paul places emphasis on the God who saves, and not on the unstable Corinthians. In fact, Paul's concluding pronouncement very nearly becomes the missing apostolic blessing. The Corinthians, viewed in terms of their conduct, could hardly inspire the confidence he expresses ("our hope for you is firmly established"). Paul's apostolic pronouncement is a statement of *faith,* a confidence in the work of God through the Gospel among the Corinthians. For this reason, his *hope* for them is "confirmed" *(bebaia)* and certain,[131] knowing that, as they share in sufferings, they share in comfort.[132] Hidden though it is, the eschaton makes its mark within the world and thus confirms its triumph over the present, fallen age.[133] In First Corinthians, Paul names the Spirit's gifts as marking that confirmation (1 Cor 1:6, 8). Here, on account of their misunderstanding and abuse of those gifts, Paul's emphasis necessarily shifts. The mark of the age to come — and thus also the true sign of an apostle — is the presence of comfort in affliction (12:12).

The note that Paul sounds here is not only that of confidence, but also that of invitation. He calls the Corinthians to share in the sufferings of Christ. They must yet learn that their salvation is inseparable from that of the apostle (1:12-14): God's "confirming" him *(bebaioō)* takes place only together with them. Their confirmation in faith is Paul's confirmation as apostle (1:21).[134] By locating their "confirmation" and stability in Christ, Paul implicitly indicates that the Corinthians are unstable in themselves. Paul hopes for their salvation against all appearances. His blessing of God serves as an exhortation to the Corinthians to recognize their calling to Christ,[135] and to accept the sufferings that necessarily come with that calling.

The main English versions are somewhat misleading at this juncture. Paul does not speak of his sufferings or comfort (ESV "our sufferings . . . "our comfort"), but merely of "sufferings" and "comfort." As the larger context makes clear, they are the "sufferings" and "comfort" of Christ, and not prop-

131. The call to *wait* for the coming of the Lord, which plays such a large role in 1 Corinthians, also has its place in this letter. God's "confirmation" of the Corinthians is the certainty of their salvation.

132. This is a noticeable shift over against 1 Cor 1:4-9, where Paul speaks of the witness of Christ confirmed among the Corinthians as included in the gifts that God had given them through Christ. The situation has become more serious.

133. See Phil 1:7.

134. With this statement, Paul introduces a note of irony into his argument. His failure to visit them as promised has made him appear "unstable."

135. V. P. Furnish, *II Corinthians* (AB; New York: Doubleday, 1984), 121, "Such expressions of confidence, however, including those which occur in the opening thanksgivings, are often implicitly hortatory."

erly those of Paul. While these sufferings come to the apostle in special measure, and while some of these sufferings come to the apostle alone,[136] Christ's sufferings belong to *all* Christians. Indeed, as Paul here makes clear, if the Corinthians are to share in comfort — and therefore salvation itself — they must also share in sufferings, the same sufferings as those of the apostle himself (vv. 6-7). As Paul's description of his apostolic experience indicates, the sufferings that have come to him include the whole range of affliction: not only outward hardships (11:23-27), physical suffering and illness (12:7-8), and death itself (4:7-15), but also inward weakness and struggle (2:12-13; 11:28-29). The apostle has experienced "fightings without and fears within" (7:5). The apostle, together with all Christians who hold to the apostolic message, shares in the sufferings of the creation under the power of sin and death.[137] In this sense, the sufferings that come to Christians are simply *human* sufferings and do not differ from those of other human beings. They are specifically *Christian* sufferings — indeed, the sufferings of Christ — in that the Corinthians *accept* these sufferings as the confession of Christ. At this moment in its life, the criterion of the Gospel in the Corinthian church is its acceptance of Paul as a suffering apostle. Before all else, they are to embrace the suffering apostle, enter into petition for him, and give thanks for God's acts of deliverance on his behalf. In so doing, they embrace the God who has shown us mercy and has given us eternal comfort in the crucified and risen Christ.

C. The Apostolic Report: The Deliverance from Trouble and the Trouble with the Corinthians (1:8–2:17)

Paul regularly reports his activities and circumstances to his addressees in his letters before he delivers his message to their situation.[138] As is especially evident in Second Corinthians, this element of the letter is not accidental. The life of the apostle cannot be separated from the Gospel that he preaches. He bears the message in his own person. In the usual prayer of thanksgiving — absent in this letter — he communicates to his audience that they are present with him in his heart and in his prayer. In his report concerning himself he makes himself present with them.

The length of the apostolic report varies widely in Paul's letters, depending on the relationship between Paul and his addressees. In Second Corinthians we find, not only one of Paul's lengthier apostolic reports (1:8–2:17), but an extended report that Paul later resumes (7:5-16), forming a bracket around

136. 4:7-15; cf. 1 Cor 4:9-12.

137. See Rom 8:12-17, 18-39.

138. Schnider and Stenger, *Studien*, 50-68.

the entire body of the letter. The letter revolves around the bond between Paul and the Corinthians, which they now threaten to dissolve. Paul renders only a brief account of how in Asia God delivered him from death itself (1:8-11), and devotes his apostolic report almost entirely to a recounting of his strained relationship with the Corinthians (1:12–2:17). What must have been a truly dramatic event in Asia yields its significance in comparison with Paul's concern for the Corinthians. As he describes how his anxiety concerning the Corinthians rendered him unable to make use of the opportunity for mission in Troas, he suddenly breaks off his account of his activities (2:12-13, 14-17) and turns to a defense of his apostolic calling, a calling that had been misunderstood and despised by the Corinthians (3:1–7:4). At the conclusion of this argument, he abruptly returns to his account of his distress over the Corinthians and of his joy over Titus's report of their repentance (7:5-16). He thus poignantly envelops his description of apostolic ministry within the fear and joy that has characterized his experience with the Corinthians. His defense of his apostolic ministry is not abstract and distant but living and personal. He wants to show the Corinthians not only that he is an apostle but that he is *their* apostle and that his experience with them is part of his life as an apostle of *Christ.* Through Christ he loves them deeply, and just as deeply he hopes that they will return his love. This deeply personal relationship is not secondary or accidental to the Gospel but integral and essential to it. Paul's opening account of his trial in Asia is of fundamental significance to this relationship. His weakness, trials, and suffering represent an offense to the Corinthians, who mark the presence of the Spirit by outward success and visible power. They must now accept the suffering apostle of Christ, or they will not accept the crucified Christ whom the apostle proclaims.

As is the case in other letters, Paul's self-report is both an account of his recent experiences and instruction in the Gospel for his readers. His narratives about himself are never merely self-narratives. They are narratives of the Gospel as it runs its course with him.[139] Paul's life follows the pattern of the Gospel, the word of God, which always meets with trouble in the world. The "word of the cross" is present within the chronology of the apostolic account (1 Cor 1:18). The deliverance in Asia and the enduring threat that emerged from it bind the Corinthians to Paul — or at least ought to do so (1:8-11, 12-14). The defection of the Corinthians from the apostle, and thus from faith, forced him to distance himself from them and cancel his visit (1:15–2:4). The subsequent judgment of the church on the person who had resisted the apostle now opens the way for him to forgive the offender and to urge the church to do so as well (2:5-11). When Paul reached Troas, however, he was not aware of the repentance of the Corinthian church. He breaks off his narrative at this

139. On the *cursus evangelii,* see O. Bayer, *Luther's Theology,* 8.

point and recounts to the Corinthians the troubles of his heart concerning them (2:12-13). Before all else, he seeks to win their hearts for the Gospel that he bears in his body and life. By the grace of God, they must come to see the suffering apostle *through the eyes of faith* (2:14-17).

1. *Trouble and Deliverance in Asia (1:8-11)*

> [8]*For we do not want you to be unaware, brothers, of the affliction we experienced in Asia. For we were so utterly burdened beyond our strength that we despaired of life itself.* [9]*Indeed, we felt that we had received the sentence of death. But that was to make us rely not on ourselves but on God who raises the dead.* [10]*He delivered us from such a deadly peril, and he will deliver us. On him we have set our hope that he will deliver us again.* [11]*You also must help us by prayer, so that many will give thanks on our behalf for the blessing granted us through the prayers of many.*

Paul apparently had sent Titus to the Corinthians while he was still in Ephesus, quite likely as the bearer of the "tearful letter."[140] The Corinthians therefore were unaware of Paul's trial in Asia.[141] Their first knowledge of it comes to them in the brief report here (1:8-11). Paul's narrative of that experience concludes with an invitation to the Corinthians to work with God for him in prayer (v. 11). He reinforces and interprets that invitation with his following boast in "simplicity and purity" in all his dealings with the Corinthians (vv. 12-14). Consequently, the opening narrative and its explanation provide the basis for the whole of the continuing account that Paul provides, and indeed for the body of the letter that follows. Already here Paul commends himself to the Corinthians — or, more properly, he does not commend himself but the new covenant with which he has been entrusted (3:1-8; 6:3-10). Paul likewise an-

140. Cf. Act 19:21-22. It is Titus who met Paul in Macedonia with news of the repentance of the Corinthians (2 Cor 2:12-13; 7:5-16). This sorrow and repentance appear to be bound up with the reception of the "tearful letter" (2 Cor 7:8-16). It is possible that the letter preceded Titus to Corinth: Paul speaks of their receiving him "with fear and trembling" (2 Cor 7:15). But given the tension and misunderstanding that existed between Paul and the Corinthians, it is likely that he sent his trusted co-worker, Titus, to them with the letter. If someone other than Titus had delivered the "tearful letter," it is likely that Paul would refer to that representative and the reception (or lack thereof) that he had experienced from the Corinthians. The "brother" whom Paul also sent appears only in association with Titus (2 Cor 12:17-18). It is only the conduct of the latter that Paul asks the Corinthians to judge. Given his positive reception by the Corinthians, Titus quite possibly at the same time initiated the arrangements for the transfer of the Corinthian gift for Jerusalem to appointed representatives (2 Cor 8:6; cf. 1 Cor 16:1-4).

141. See Acts 19:23-40.

swers the questions about himself that were present in the church, but he does not answer them in terms that the Corinthians expected. He answers in terms of the Gospel, under which the apostle and his church are bound together.

8 Having spoken of all his "afflictions" in vv. 3-7, Paul now describes the trial that he endured in Asia. As we shall see shortly, there are good reasons to suppose that the situation was critical, and that it most likely brought with it a continuing threat for the apostle. At the same time, we must be careful not to exaggerate the effect of the experience on Paul. His report not only begins with a narration of affliction, it ends with one as well, an affliction that affects Paul even more deeply than the trial in Asia (2:12-13). It is not that trial in Asia but Paul's paralyzing concern over the state of the Corinthian church that shapes his discourse in the letter all the way up to 7:5-16, where he announces its resolution.

Viewed outwardly, of course, the trial in Asia, far surpasses Paul's trouble with the Corinthians. The life-threatening danger emerging from that trial remains for the apostle. Paul uses it as an opportunity to invite the Corinthians to work with God for him in prayer. In that way, they too shall render thanks to God for him. The God who delivered him once in Asia shall do so again through their prayer. This opening section of Paul's report (1:8-11), unlike the ending (2:14-17), concludes with an invitation to thanksgiving. This thanksgiving is to come from the Corinthians themselves. The usual roles in the opening of the letter are thus reversed: it is not the apostle who gives thanks for God's work among the Corinthians, but the Corinthians who are to give thanks for God's work with Paul.

In v. 8 Paul introduces his narrative as an explanation (*gar;* "for") of the sufferings that belong not only to him but also to the Corinthians themselves under the Gospel. He thus calls the Corinthians to the realism of the Gospel, in which the weakness and failure of the fallen human being serve as the vehicle for the display of the love and power of God in Christ. At the same time, however, he exposes himself again to the false standards by which his opponents in Corinth, and indeed many of the Corinthians themselves, judge the apostolic mission. Paul battles for the hearts of the Corinthians and, indeed, for their salvation (13:5).

The brief formula "I do not want you to be unaware, brothers [and sisters]" alerts Paul's readers to the new information he wishes to impart to them.[142] He follows it with somewhat unusual usage: "*on behalf* [*hyper*] of our affliction in Asia" (not, "concerning our affliction").[143] Paul's language serves

142. See Rom 1:13; 11:25; 1 Cor 10:1; 12:1; 1 Thess 4:13.

143. Usually a genitive-governing ὑπέρ refers to a person, signifying "on behalf of," "in the interest of," or even "on account of" someone (cf. ἕνεκα + gen., διά + acc.). A genitive governing περί may refer either to a person or to a thing ("concerning" someone or something). The potential of semantic overlap arises when a verb governing ὑπέρ + gen. appears to call

his theological point. It is not the matters concerning his own person that he wants them know; it is rather "on behalf of" the sufferings of Christ given to him as apostle that he wants them to be aware of what happened in Asia. He wants to communicate the course of the Gospel with him as apostle. As we have noted, this report is the first the Corinthians have heard of the events in Asia. Other than indicating the life-and-death seriousness of the situation, Paul offers no indication of the nature of the trial that came upon him, leaving his interpreters considerable room for speculation. As Paul's invitation to prayer itself suggests (v. 11), the bearer of the letter (most likely Titus) would have filled in the details for the Corinthian church. We shall consider the two main possibilities that interpreters have suggested for the nature of Paul's trial in connection with v. 9.

It is of first importance, however, not to overlook Paul's general and decidedly theological description of his affliction. Perhaps without their being aware of it, for the Corinthians the gifts of God had taken the place of God the Giver. They had come to regard "spiritual things" — they did not see them as *gifts* — as the inherent possessions of apostles and other Christian leaders.[144] The display of power, especially the exercise of oratory and rhetoric, was the mark of spiritual authority. For this reason, the apostle himself is now under suspicion and even attack in the Corinthian church. His gifts do not match up to those of others — or at least they do not seem to do so (10:7-11). As we have seen, Paul takes up this theme in his opening benediction of God, where he characterizes the apostolic mission as the communication of comfort received in affliction (vv. 3-7). One cannot rightly read this paradox as a general truth, a description of human life and the normal course of events in the world, as if it were a trick that one might learn in order to live successfully. God's overturning of the world remains a matter of faith and hope in the God whose promises find their Yes in Christ. The specifically christological anchoring of this theme becomes quite clear in Paul's theological description of his experience, where he spells out what it means to be granted comfort in the midst of affliction.

Paul's continuing use of the term *thlipsis* ("affliction" or "burden"; see

---

for a sense of "relation" rather than one of "benefit" (e.g., Rom 9:27) or, more often, when a genitive-governing ὑπέρ refers to a thing. This usage is infrequent and, within the NT generally, is confined to Paul (BDF §231). It mostly concerns benefits (e.g., "your comfort and salvation," 2 Cor 1:6), futurities (e.g., the [both present and coming] kingdom, 2 Thess 1:5), or metonyms involving persons (e.g., the "name" of Christ, Rom 1:5). In these instances ὑπέρ often (always?) retains the sense "in the interest of" or "on behalf of" (rightly, BDAG, "ὑπέρ," 1031). It is likely, then, that ὑπὲρ τῆς θλίψεως ἡμῶν is to be understood as "on behalf of our affliction." Paul already has used ὑπέρ + gen. in the sense of "on behalf of" three times in vv. 6-7. As the variant reading περὶ τῆς θλίψεως ἡμῶν v. 8 shows, scribes discerned a semantic difference between the two prepositions and found the usage of ὑπὲρ τῆς θλίψεως ἡμῶν suspect.

144. See 1 Cor 12:1; 14:1.

vv. 4-8) lends biblical overtones to the report, since, as we have noted, it is in biblical usage that the Greek term most often bears the metaphorical sense "burden" that appears here: Paul's following description of the experience as "being exceedingly burdened, beyond [human] power" corresponds to this metaphor of trial as a pressure or burden.[145] Paul may also recall biblical idiom here, especially Psalm 38:4, where the psalmist laments that his sins have become too great a burden for him to bear.[146] The form of Paul's statement follows the biblical pattern of the psalms of thanksgiving. The report of distress is followed by the report of deliverance, in which the speaker announces and confesses God's saving help, offering God thanksgiving in the presence of the gathered community. Paul thus invites the Corinthians to enter into this thanksgiving and thereby to share in his experience of distress and deliverance. In this quite practical and concrete way they enter into the fellowship, the *koinōnia,* of suffering and comfort, the end of which is the thanksgiving that confesses God as Creator (see vv. 7, 11). According to Paul, the saving knowledge of God is found nowhere other than in such thanksgiving.

It is instructive to compare the language of this opening statement with related descriptions of the apostolic experience later in the letter. On first hearing, it is the opening language that informs the interpretation of the later statements. But since Paul undoubtedly meant the letter to be used repeatedly in worship, and certainly not discarded after its first reading, the later statements may be regarded as shedding light on his language here. Paul speaks more dramatically in the opening than he does in his subsequent descriptions of the apostolic experience. Later he understates his affliction, in a play upon words as "being at a loss, yet not absolutely at a loss" (4:8; *aporoumenoi all' ouk exaporoumenoi*). Here, in contrast, he depicts his experience in Asia in the very terms that he later excludes: we despaired of life itself, we were at an utter loss *(exaporēthēnai).* In a similar way, he later speaks of affliction as a temporary, light matter (4:17; *elaphron*), in contrast with the hope of the "eternal weight [*baros*] of glory." Here, however, he speaks of being burdened *(ebarēthēmen)* beyond measure. In these latter instances, Paul drives home his message concerning present deliverance and future hope through juxtaposition and contrast. The slight understatement in 4:8 allows room for the measured contrast between his distress and the earthly and temporary deliverance granted him. The meiosis in 4:17 similarly has its significance solely in relation to the coming glory. Paul paints with a different brush in the letter opening, giving full expression to the seriousness of the situation

145. Although the term "oppression" remains opaque for most speakers of English, its Latin antecedent likewise pictures trial as a pressure or a burden *(oppressio, opprimo).*

146. Likewise, the deliverance from Egypt, as well as deliverance from oppression by other nations, is pictured as release from a burden. See, e.g., Ps 81:6; Isa 9:4; 10:27; 14:25.

and presenting the deliverance that God worked for him as equivalent to a resurrection from the dead (1:10).

There is no need to suppose that Paul misrepresents his circumstances. In the later contexts of the letter, too, he depicts his experiences of distress and deliverance as those of death and resurrection.[147] These "exaggerations" represent biblical idiom, which reckons with the *effect* of severe trials on the human being: more than once, in terms of all *human reckoning,* and thus in his own mind and heart, Paul was dead. The radical language parallels similar usage in the Psalms[148] and corresponds to the tradition of the sacrifice of Isaac.[149] Far more effectively than any detached report, Paul's vivid language communicates the event in all its impact on the apostle's life. He opens his heart to the Corinthians (6:11). This perspective is reflected in the poem Bonhoeffer composed in prison for the family of his fiancée, Maria Wedemeyer, for Christmas 1944 and the new year 1945. The fourth verse, a prayer to God, reads as follows:

> Yet if you still will to grant us / joy in this world and the glory of its sun, / we shall recall all that has come to pass, / and our life with yours shall be wholly one.[150]

In context, Paul further indicates that his affliction bore a legal and forensic dimension: he was under a decree of death, a judgment. It becomes quite clear, then, how he is able to speak of his "death" and "resurrection." In a very real way he carries the "deadness of Jesus" in his body. Jesus, too, was condemned and put to death by "the rulers of this age" (1 Cor 2:8).

Paul wants the Corinthians to know that the affliction that came to him in Asia burdened him "exceedingly, beyond all power." His unqualified statement presents an implicit paradox, not unlike the later contrasts he employs in 4:7-18. Paul was in such desperate straits that no power could deliver him. Nevertheless, God, who has power beyond all human thought and imagination, did so.

9 The apostle has been thrust into a life-and-death struggle. His situation is desperate: "We have [*eschēkamen*] the decree of death [*to apokrima tou thanatou*] in ourselves."[151] Interpreters often have understood the form *eschēkamen* as an "aoristic perfect" that simply refers to a past event. It is

147. See 2 Cor 4:11; 6:9; 13:4; also 1 Cor 4:9; 15:31.

148. E.g., Ps 18:4-6 (2 Sam 22:5-7); 116:3-4.

149. See, e.g., Heb 11:17; Jas 2:21; *b. Sanh.* 89b.

150. D. Bonhoeffer, *Widerstand und Ergebung: Briefe und Aufzeichnungen aus der Haft* (16th ed.; ed. E. Bethge; Munich: C. Kaiser, 1997 [1951]), 219 (here and throughout, author's free translation).

151. In the NT and LXX the perfect of ἔχω appears only here and in 2 Cor 2:13; 7:5; Rom 5:2; Mark 5:15; 2 Macc 14:30; 3 Macc 5:20; 17:16, 24; Sir 13:6.

likely, however, that the perfect expresses a past event with a present effect, as it usually does.[152] There are good reasons for understanding Paul to speak here in present time.[153] He describes a *continuing* situation: "we *have* the decree of death in ourselves."[154] This burden has come upon him so that he might not trust in himself but in the God who raises the dead. Such trust is not merely temporary. It continues indefinitely. The event corresponds to the theology of the letter, especially as it appears in the hardship catalogs.[155] The apostle bears in his body the deadness of Jesus in order that the life of Jesus might be manifest in his body (4:10). In the present context, he goes on to speak not only of God having delivered him but also of the hope that God will *yet* deliver him (v. 10). This expression of trust points ultimately to the resurrection of the dead. It is not at all clear, however, that Paul here refers first and foremost to that event. It is more likely that, in the first instance, he expresses the hope of fresh deliverance from the threat that continues to hang over him. For this reason he invites the Corinthians to work together with God for him in prayer, and he expects that they will have opportunity to give thanks on his behalf (v. 11).

To read the perfect form of *eschēkamen* in present time corresponds to a literal reading of his report that he bore within himself "the decree of death" (v. 9). This literal interpretation of the description of his plight as the formal verdict of a death sentence is by far the most likely reading.[156] The term

152. That is to say, it presupposes an event, for which it expresses a continuing effect. Thus, for example, when we say, "Christ is risen," the perfect form expresses the present resurrected life of Christ, while presupposing the event of the resurrection. See Paul's usage of ἐσχήκαμεν in Rom 5:2. For ἔχω, the aorist form was available, but the pluperfect was missing.

153. Interpreters frequently appeal to 2 Cor 2:13 as a corroborating example of Paul's usage of the perfect of ἔχω as an "aoristic perfect." But again, that sense is not likely. The verb most likely expresses stative aspect in any case. The lexical option of the aorist was available and would have located Paul's distressed state in the past. But that is not the apostle's point! He vividly presents his state upon his arrival in Troas. See the discussion *in loc.*

154. The ESV, together with the NRSV and NIV, thus misreads Paul's statement. Paul does not say that he "felt" that he had received the sentence of death. It is neither a mere feeling, nor is it an experience that now lies in the past. Paul currently has the decree (or sentence) of death in himself.

155. See 2 Cor 4:7-15; 6:3-10; 11:23-33; 12:1-10.

156. None of the objections that Harris brings against this conclusion bears any weight: (1) it is not clear that ἀπόκριμα (which appears infrequently in any case) must here signify merely an official decision and not a juridical one, nor is there reason to suppose that God must be the one who pronounced the death verdict; (2) that Paul should describe his "sentence of death" as taking place in Asia, and not specifically in Ephesus, is no real obstacle to seeing it as related to a legal judgment related to events there, which likely would have come through provincial authorities; (3) it is simply wrong to think that this experience was without parallel

apokrima that appears here is a *hapax* within the biblical writings. It occurs otherwise very rarely in Greek literature, and only somewhat more often in inscriptions and papyri. The infrequency of the term makes it unlikely that Paul uses it as a literary metaphor: one normally employs common images in such metaphors. In Paul's time, the term was used in reference to decrees that decided formal petitions, and thus bore a judicial sense.[157] This is the meaning that it bears as it appears in Josephus and the inscriptions.[158] Paul's use of the expression appears to be rather specialized, implying a petition to Roman authorities and thus, perhaps, a protracted legal battle.[159] Admittedly, in contrast to the otherwise positive usage of the term within this period, the "decree of death" is negative. It is not too surprising, however, that evidence for a negative usage of the term is lacking. The rejection of petitions would not be a matter of civic commemoration, especially not in inscriptions, where much of the usage is to be found. One did not celebrate the rejection of a petition. Negative *apokrimata* might well have been frequent, but they would rarely have been recorded by their recipients. There is evidence — admittedly later — that *apokrima* could mean "condemnation."[160] Without question, the term also appears with the neutral sense of "judgment" or "estimation."[161] Even so, the evidence supports a literal interpretation of the term here as referring to a condemning verdict, judgment, or decree. Paul anticipates the image that he will employ in 3:2-3: while the Corinthians are "a letter of Christ," the apostle bears within himself the *apokrima*, the rescript of death. He bears the deadness of Jesus, and death is at work in him, while life is at work in the Corinthians (4:10-12). The metaphors of being led to death in a provincial theater (1 Cor 4:9) and of being led to death in a Roman triumph (2:14-17) are not far removed from the actual experience of the apostle.

---

in Paul's life thus far (cf. 1 Cor 15:31; 2 Cor 4:10-11; 6:9; 11:23-29); (4) the apostle clearly reckons with the possibility of execution in Philippians (Phil 2:12-13), which would correspond quite well with an Ephesian imprisonment, as well as the situation he describes here. M. J. Harris, *The Second Epistle to the Corinthians: A Commentary on the Greek Text* (NIGTC; Grand Rapids: Eerdmans, 2005), 155-57, 166-70.

157. C. J. Hemer indicates that the term is verdictive but denies that it bore a juridical sense. Either there is confusion here or Hemer has understood judicial action far too narrowly. See Hemer, "A Note on 2 Corinthians 1:9," *TynB* 23 (1972): 103-7; also F. Büchsel, "ἀπόκριμα," *TDNT* 3:945-46; Furnish, *II Corinthians,* 113-14.

158. Whether ἀπόκριμα was merely a technical term for the response to official petitions as Hemer and Harris claim is an open question. There is evidence of a broader usage, on which see below.

159. Luke indicates (Acts 19:31) that some provincial authorities (Ἀσιάρχαι) befriended Paul, which might fit this scenario.

160. The evidence from the fifth-century lexicographer Hesychius, who glosses ἀπόκριμα with κατάκριμα ("condemnation"), is not to be set aside lightly.

161. See Aristophanes Grammaticus, *Epitome* 2.63.4 (second-third century A.D.).

In contrast, it is highly unlikely that Paul uses *apokrima* to indicate that the trouble that came upon him in Asia was a severe illness. He indicates elsewhere, even in this letter, that he already had serious ailments, long before his trouble in Asia. The "thorn in the flesh," with which he still lives, came upon him fourteen years prior to his writing this letter, well before his trial in Asia (2 Cor 12:1-10). The "weakness of the flesh" that brought Paul to the Galatian churches likewise came upon him much earlier in his ministry (Gal 4:12-15). If in the present context he refers to a fresh illness, it is unusual that he does not describe it here with some reference to weakness or suffering "in the flesh." It would be even more unusual for him to describe it figuratively with a relatively infrequent term *(apokrima)*. Furthermore, if he has borne a new illness, why does he not in some way relate it to the "thorn in the flesh" that he later mentions? Does he have two thorns in his flesh? If the "verdict of death" represents God's rejection of Paul's petition for healing, why does Paul ask the Corinthians to intercede for him with the expectation that their petition will be granted? Those who want to read Paul as referring to a deadly illness generally argue that there is no evidence that Paul faced legal trouble or imprisonment during his Ephesian ministry. The claim is overstated. The opposite holds: we have no indication elsewhere that Paul became seriously ill during his mission in Asia.

The book of Acts describes a near riot in Ephesus that evidently brought Paul into serious danger. Admittedly, the connection between this event and Paul's trial in Asia is not entirely clear. The hints in the text are nevertheless suggestive. Already in First Corinthians Paul speaks of having "fought wild beasts" in Ephesus (1 Cor 15:32). His language, which (unlike that of Ignatius) is almost certainly figurative, may well refer to the tumult that Luke reports at length (Acts 19:23-40).[162] As Paul writes First Corinthians, he is still in Ephesus, where he plans to remain until Pentecost (1 Cor 16:5-8).[163] He continues to have opportunity for ministry ("a large door is open for me"), although "there are many opponents" (1 Cor 16:9). One might have expected from the Lukan report that Paul made a swift exit from Ephesus after the uproar, but the circumstances that Paul describes in First Corinthians are not incompatible with Luke's account that "after the tumult ceased" Paul departed for Macedonia (Acts 20:1).[164] One need only suppose some delay.[165] There is no report in Acts

162. It makes little difference that Luke indicates that some of the provincial officials (Asiarchs) persuaded Paul not to enter into the theater in Ephesus, where an agitated crowd had gathered. Nor is it likely that there is a real discrepancy here. Paul's language is metaphorical in any case.

163. He here indicates the plan that he later abandoned of visiting Corinth on his way to Macedonia (1 Cor 16:5-6).

164. Furnish, *II Corinthians*, 123.

165. In conjunction with the writing of 1 Corinthians, Paul sent Timothy to Corinth

concerning a judicial proceeding against Paul following the Ephesian disturbance. But the Lukan report is obviously selective. Other significant details of Paul's ministry are lacking in Acts, not least the collection for Jerusalem. There is, in fact, a hint within Acts that trouble might have continued for Paul after the uproar. According to Luke, the town-clerk *(grammateus)* suggests to the gathered crowd that Demetrius and the other craftsmen should take any claim they have against anyone to the courts and the proconsuls (Acts 19:38).[166] One would expect that they did so. It is not at all inconceivable that Paul came into serious difficulties as the result of such a legal proceeding.[167] Luke, for his own understandable reasons, simply does not report the event.

There is no need to suppose that Paul's affliction in Asia was unparalleled in his experience up to that point. Already in First Corinthians he describes apostles as "those condemned to death" (*epithanatioi,* 1 Cor 4:9) and protests to his all-too-comfortable readers that "I die daily" (1 Cor 15:30-31). If he *always* carries about in his body the deadness of Jesus, then the affliction in Asia could not be *entirely* new or unexpected (4:10-12). He had been in such straits before (6:9). Indeed, he had been as good as dead many times (11:23). Even more unlikely is the suggestion that Paul was forced to abandon the hope of surviving until the *parousia* by his experience in Asia.[168] It is doubtful that he ever held such a conviction. In any case, the interpretation entails a fundamental misreading of the passage. It is not the trouble in Asia that stands in the back-

---

(1 Cor 4:16-21; 16:10-11). By the time he writes this letter, he has also made an unhappy — and perhaps all too brief — visit there himself (2 Cor 1:23–2:4; 13:1-2). The visit implies some passage of time and a delay between the Ephesian riot and Paul's subsequent trouble, but not an extended period.

166. Any connection between the later reference of 2 Tim 4:14 ("Alexander the coppersmith did me great harm") and the Lukan report that the Jews attempted to put forward a certain Alexander during the Ephesian disturbance (Acts 19:33) can only be speculative.

167. It is quite possible that Paul wrote the letter to the Philippians during an Ephesian imprisonment. The imminent threat of execution is the most prominent link between Paul's report in 2 Corinthians and the letter to the Philippians (Phil 1:19-30; 2:17-18). But other circumstances reflected in this letter also correspond to what we know of Paul's ministry at this juncture. Timothy is present with Paul in both 2 Corinthians and Philippians (2 Cor 1:1, 19; Phil 1:1; 2:19), and Paul intends to travel to Philippi if he is spared, which is precisely what he has done, according to 2 Corinthians (Phil 2:24; 2 Cor 2:12-13; 7:5). See further Furnish, *II Corinthians,* 123.

168. Against Harris, *The Second Epistle to the Corinthians,* 182. The proposal is based in part upon an overinterpretation of 1 Thess 4:17. Paul there speaks in the first-person plural in a way that encompasses all believers. As the context shows, however, it is quite clear to him that some believers have died and yet shall die before the Lord comes (1 Thess 4:13-18). The uncertainty as to when "the day of the Lord" will come means that Paul too must reckon with death (1 Thess 5:10). The thought runs along the same lines as 1 Cor 15:50-58, where Paul obviously allows that he and others might die before "the last trumpet."

ground to Paul's message in Second Corinthians, but rather the trouble with the Corinthians, which was of such consequence to him that it paralyzed his service to Christ at a critical moment in Troas.[169] As grave as the consequences of the judgment in Asia might have been, they are not beyond the power of the God who raises the dead. As we have noted, Paul informs the Corinthians about his burden — about which he might have well remained silent — in order to invite them to participate in his sufferings. They are to labor for him with God in prayer. The outcome will be thanksgiving to God voiced through many. Precisely through his trouble, Paul invites the Corinthians to embrace him as their apostle, and in doing so to believe the Gospel that he proclaims. Admittedly, Paul's language finally leaves the question open as to whether God will deliver him within the present life or at the resurrection of the dead. But his very leaving the question open in his invitation to the Corinthians to intercede for him means that he was *not* certain that God had determined that he should now die. Indeed, the positive note with which Paul concludes his report in v. 11 closely parallels his tone in Philippians 1:19-26, which may well relate to the same incident.

The apostle bears the decree of death *in himself* so that he might not trust *upon himself,* but rather upon God. The parallelism of the pronouns ("we"), together with that of the prepositions ("upon"), is fundamental to Paul's point. The circumstances that have come upon him cast him upon God entirely and without reserve. He bears the word of condemnation in his person, *in order that* he might place his trust outside himself in God and thus come to know true deliverance. His confession here is based on the *unconditioned* assurance that "the God who raises the dead" stands with him to keep, carry, and deliver him, just as God does with all who believe. This theme of boasting and confidence in God and in Christ provides the foundation for Paul's defense of apostolic ministry in the letter.[170] Through trial and suffering the apostle himself must experience what it means to know "the God who raises the dead." He is not, "like many, peddling the word of God" but speaks "from purity," i.e., out of his heart and person (2:17). His work of proclamation does not come from him but from "the Spirit of faith" given through the Gospel. By this Spirit — and not by his own strength — in the very midst of trial, he speaks.[171] As he makes clear in his subsequent citation of LXX Ps 115:1 (116:10), he stands in the company of the many witnesses in Scripture, who in trial and temptation were cast upon the Lord alone as their deliverer.[172] Paul thus speaks of the fundamental and determinative question concerning the human being

169. 2 Cor 2:12-13; 7:5-16.

170. See 2 Cor 1:12, 15; 3:4-5; 4:1, 6-7; 5:6; 10:1-2; 12:9-10; 13:4-6.

171. Cf. 2 Cor 3:4-6; 4:13-15.

172. 2 Cor 4:13.

according to the Scriptures — namely, whether one lives in trust in the divine word or in unbelief and idolatry.[173] As strange and wonderful as it is, through death the apostle receives life. Through the word and work of God, Paul is removed from himself. As he makes clear in this letter, his entire ministry is an exercise of boasting and confidence in God, not in himself. He speaks to the Corinthians in order that they too might believe and might share in the comfort and life given and found in the Gospel. Not only his sufferings, but also his comfort "abounds." His trials as apostle effect life for the Corinthians and for all who listen to the message he bears: they too receive life in death, joy in suffering, peace in trial, healing in sickness.[174] At the same time, the apostle is the point of judgment and division. As the bearer of the Gospel, he works not only life but death for those who disbelieve and reject the word of God that he bears (2:14-17). It is in this danger that the Corinthian church itself stands. In recounting his experience in Asia and soliciting their prayers, he invites them to life.

The apostle bears the sentence of death so that he might trust in "the God who raises the dead."[175] As in v. 3, Paul again *identifies* God.[176] We are to know and understand God in no other way than as this God revealed and made known in this work: the Creator who has promised to give us life, even within death. The language here nearly parallels that of Rom 4:17, where Paul speaks of "the God who gives life to the dead and calls [for his purposes] that which is not, as if it exists." In the present context he speaks distinctly of God as "*raising* the dead" (and not merely "making alive"), most likely because he still faces the prospect of execution. Both descriptions of God tell, not merely what God shall do on the last day, but what God does already here and now, in the present time. Paul, of course, does not suppose that God performs acts of resurrection in all places and in all circumstances — else the kingdom would have come in its fullness. Nevertheless, his words imply that God through Christ is constantly bringing forth life from death. As Paul's appeal to Abraham in Rom 4 makes clear, his identification of God is bound up not only with the resurrection of Christ but also with the Scriptures in which

173. See, e.g., Gen 3:1-7; Num 13:1–14:45; Isa 7:1-9; Jer 17:1-8; 2 Sam 24:1-25 (1 Chr 21:1-30); Dan 4:4-37. The contrast between trusting or boasting in oneself and boasting in God runs through the Psalms: Pss 20:7; 44:6; 49:6; 75:4; 82:7; 94:1-7; 115:8; 118:8; 135:18; 146:3.

174. See esp. 1:3-7; 4:12-15; 5:18-21.

175. Paul continues to employ first-person plural language, so that attention is directed away from his person, although he speaks of a trial that came to him. Even in his individuality he remains nothing more than a paradigm of the experience of all apostles and, by implication, of all Christians.

176. Such characterizations of God often appear at pivotal points in Paul's letters, or in the openings and closings where he is summarizing his message. In 2 Corinthians, see 1:18; 2:14; 4:6; 11:31; 13:11.

Christ's resurrection is promised and prefigured. One thinks, for example, of the stories of Joseph, Elijah, and Elisha, of the experience of Jeremiah, of the promise given to Ezekiel, as well as the psalms of lament and praise.[177] These acts of "resurrection" are concrete and definite, bound up with the promises of God that have been fulfilled in Christ and *his resurrection*. This was obviously so with Abraham in the birth of Isaac (Rom 4:16-25). It is also the case for the apostle, who does not speak of a general human experience, but specifically and concretely of the death and resurrection of Christ, in which he shares (4:10-12; 13:4). All those who believe — but only those who believe — share in this Christ and are given over to death and raised to life by the power and promise of God in him (see v. 7). In the present time, this experience comes to us in varying ways and measures. All of God's acts of resurrection within this world are anticipatory, mere figures of the final resurrection, when death shall be conquered. They are nonetheless real. In the form of promise, they make God known.

10 Here we should ignore the division between verses. Paul's characterization of God in v. 9 continues into v. 10. The God who raises the dead acted on behalf of the apostle, who here responds in confession and thanksgiving to this One "who delivered us from so great a death."[178] Paul's striking use of the quantitative adjective ("so great a") underscores the inevitability of his death in this situation and its overwhelming power. He was beyond rescue by any human power, yet God rescued him.

God "shall yet deliver" him. The future tense, which, despite variant readings, most likely is original, presupposes that the decree of death remains for Paul and thus supports the reading of the perfect *eschēkamen* in v. 9 as signifying a past event with enduring effect.[179] Although God has delivered him, the sentence of death remains on the apostle.

Paul rounds out his thought in the latter part of v. 10 by again speaking of his trust in God: "in whom we have hoped that he shall deliver [us]." Trust in

177. Gen 37:1–50:26; 1 Kgs 17:17-24; 2 Kgs 4:8-37; Jer 38:1-28; Ezek 37:1-14; Deut 32:39; 1 Sam 2:6; Pss 30:3; 40:2; 71:19-20. Against N. T. Wright, Israel's return from exile was not merely an event that awaited fulfillment in Christ. It was an event that had taken place already within human history *and thereby* serves as a figure of what was (and is) yet to come, in Christ, as the elevated promises attached to it make clear (e.g., Isa 65:17-25). Cf. N. T. Wright, *Paul in Fresh Perspective* (Minneapolis: Fortress, 2005), 138-40.

178. The textual variant "ἐκ τηλικούτων θανάτων," attested by 𝔭[46] along with Western witnesses, most likely represents an attempt to smooth out an apparent difficulty. According to this reading, God has delivered Paul out of many such "deaths" in the past and shall do so yet. The alteration tames an unusual use of the quantitative adjective.

179. The absence of καὶ ῥύσεται in part of the Western tradition and the use of the present tense in the Western and Byzantine traditions probably again represent attempts to smooth out the text.

God necessarily includes a hope that encompasses our future. Strikingly, Paul does not use the present tense, which would emphasize his present stance. He instead employs the perfect tense: "in whom we have hoped."[180] The apostle thus introduces a certain ambiguity into the statement. On the one hand, he may refer to the moment in which he placed hope in God for deliverance from his trial. On the other hand, he may also refer to the initial moment of faith in his life. Yet the two thoughts meet. For Paul, the whole of Christian living, after all, is nothing but the hope that God will deliver us — and all creation — from death. This intentional ambiguity leaves the present outcome of Paul's trouble open. Even if God should not deliver him from death *now,* God shall do so *finally,* without question. Whatever may come, his deliverance is certain and assured. Yet Paul's "ambiguity of faith" does not constitute a resignation to his circumstances or to his apparent fate. The very recognition that deliverance lies with God, and that the "when" and the "how" of that deliverance must lie with God as well, creates the place for continued resistance rather than immediate surrender. For this very reason he invites the Corinthians to enter into petition for him.

11 Paul thus accentuates his hope for a present deliverance. The sentence that began in v. 9 continues into v. 11. The apostle now locates the Corinthians themselves within the divine act of deliverance for which he hopes. They are "to work together in petition" on his behalf. As the verbs of action in this context make clear, the Corinthians are to co-operate with God. The verb should *not* be read as an imperative (ESV) but as an indicative, which again invites the Corinthians to participation in the Gospel: "as you work together [with God] in petition on our behalf."

Prayer is thus neither surrender to the inevitability of God's will nor the attempt to manipulate God to do our will. Prayer is the entrance — at God's marvelous invitation — into the effecting of deliverance and salvation in the world. This real participation in God's will cannot be grasped by human reason.

The participation in God's work on behalf of the apostle, to which Paul invites the Corinthians, has its own purpose. They are to enter into petition for him "in order that thanksgiving might be made for us by many persons for the *gift* given to us through [those] many."[181] The deliverance for which Paul hopes is an anticipation of his final salvation at the coming of the Lord. Or perhaps, since he leaves the matter slightly ambiguous, he presents his hope in the resurrection itself. In that case, the thanksgiving of the Corinthians will

180. Cf. ESV, "on him we have set our hope."

181. Against the ESV and NRSV, Paul speaks not of "blessing" (εὐλογία, or perhaps μακαρισμός) but of "gift" (χάρισμα). The emphasis lies on that which is given rather than the word of giving or the happiness of the recipient.

come from the redeemed Corinthians. Whether they know it or not, they are bound to the apostle and the Gospel he proclaims (v. 14). They are thus to enter into God's work for the apostle in order that they may voice thanksgiving to God for the deliverance that comes to him. God's saving work — the work of the Creator in raising Paul from the dead — is to effect the thanksgiving of *many* persons, working in them the right and true relation between Creator and creature that we have abandoned in rebellion and sin.[182] Just as Paul's present deliverance is a prolepsis of the resurrection of the dead, the Corinthians' petition and thanksgiving anticipates "the day of the Lord Jesus," when they are the apostle's boast, and he is theirs (1:14; cf. 7:5-16). The psalmist's lament "Will you work wonders on the dead?" finds its Yes in God's work in Jesus Christ, which is effective in the apostle — and in the Corinthians as well.[183]

Paul's language is more graphic than English translations express. The Greek term rendered here (in the plural) as "persons" is *prosōpon* (depending on context, also translated "appearance" or "face"), which may well bear the connotation of the personality and emotion expressed in the face. Paul's usage recalls the language of the psalmists who speak of their "faces not being ashamed" when their hope of deliverance is fulfilled.[184] The Corinthians shall be radiant with thanksgiving at the Lord's deliverance of his suffering apostle — if only they embrace him and enter into petition on his behalf.

God remains the absolute and unqualified Giver, beyond both Paul and the Corinthians. The deliverance of the apostle shall be nothing other than the free gift of God's grace to him *(to eis hēmas charisma)*. This gift shall come, Paul hopes, *through the many,* even as it comes from God. The work of the Corinthians in petition is to end not in self-boasting but in thanksgiving *alone.* Our labors and prayers are nothing more than a participation in God's work in the world, which remains God's work and not our own.

2. *The Trouble with the Corinthians: The Broken Promise of the Apostle (1:12–2:17)*

As we have noted, Paul in his apostolic report gives nearly all his attention to the stormy course of his relationship with the Corinthians. That is not to say that his trial in Asia is irrelevant to this drama. If the Corinthians are to accept the apostle, they must accept him in his weakness. This weakness includes his unbounded concern for them, a concern that constrains, and indeed paralyzes, him at crucial moments of his life. It was out of apostolic concern for them that

182. Cf. Rom 1:18-21.

183. See Pss 6:5; 30:9; 88:10-12; 115:7-8; Isa 38:18-20.

184. Pss 34:5; 42:11; 43:5; and cf. Pss 44:15; 69:7; 83:16.

he determined not to visit them, despite having promised to do so. Paul's life thus takes the form that God himself takes in his dealings with the Corinthians. Just as God hides himself and his saving work in weakness, failure, and suffering, so the apostle has dealt with the Corinthians. Beneath and behind his apparent inconstancy, in which he appears uncaring and unreliable, lie an unswerving love and concern for the Corinthians.

Correspondingly, Paul's response to his broken promise is not a self-defense but a defense of the Gospel that he bears as apostle. As we have seen, his Gospel and the crucified Lord that he announces cannot be separated from his life. Interpreters often "mirror-read" much more than is warranted from Paul's claim to integrity in this section, imagining that he is responding directly to the claims of his adversaries in Corinth. There is no doubt that Paul is answering Corinthian suspicions and wounded feelings in the face of his canceled visit, as becomes clear in 1:23–2:4. It is likewise possible that the opponents of Paul have taken advantage of his failure to come to Corinth as promised, in order to sow doubts about his integrity in the minds of the Corinthians. Some in Corinth seem to regard him as covering up his weaknesses or ulterior motives by failing to appear.[185] Paul's claim to integrity, which he repeats at significant points in the letter, correspondingly serves to undermine his opponents.[186] Nevertheless, it is not finally Paul, but the Gospel that is at stake. Indeed, the Corinthians themselves are being tested (cf. 13:5). The question is whether they will accept the weak and suffering apostle, who out of love suffers on their behalf. Already at the beginning of this section, Paul appeals to the bond between him and the Corinthians, a bond that is essential to their salvation (1:14). At the conclusion of this section, where he likewise insists on his integrity, he underscores God's work through him in the world, the reception or rejection of which is a matter of life and death (2:14-17). Between the two he unfolds the theological significance of his dealings with the Corinthians, especially in 1:18-22 and 2:5-11.

The section begins with Paul's boast in his "simplicity and sincerity," which, as we have noted, serves as a declaration of God's work in the apostle (1:12-14). The Corinthians, who also share in Christ, are likewise to share in such simplicity.[187] Paul then addresses the question of his failure to visit the Corinthians, first rooting his response in the Gospel (1:15-22) and then speaking directly of his motive for canceling his visit (1:23–2:4). This explanation of his decision is the pivotal point of the passage. After providing it, Paul moves on to recount the earlier conflict between him and the Corinthians that shaped his decision not to visit them (2:5-11). He concludes his report with a

185. 10:2, 7-11; 12:16-18.

186. 2:16-17; 4:1-3; 5:11-12; 6:11-13; 12:16-18.

187. 9:11, 13; 11:2; cf. 8:2.

description of his alternate travel to Macedonia, his paralyzing distress over the Corinthians (2:12-13), and a thanksgiving to God, who accomplishes his purposes through him (2:14-17). The final section thus forms an inclusio that rounds off the entire report, recalling the trial in Asia, the course of Paul's dealings with the Corinthians, and his claim to integrity.

a. Paul's Boast in Simplicity and Purity (1:12-14)

> [12]*For our boast is this, the testimony of our conscience, that we behaved in the world with simplicity and godly sincerity, not by earthly wisdom but by the grace of God, and supremely so toward you.* [13]*For we are not writing to you anything other than what you read and understand and I hope you will fully understand —* [14]*just as you did partially understand us — that on the day of our Lord Jesus you will boast of us as we will boast of you.*

Just as Paul links the call to fellowship to intercession for him in his experience of suffering in Asia (vv. 7-8), so he links his invitation to intercession for him to his following boast in a good conscience (vv. 11-12). In both cases, he is providing grounds (*gar,* vv. 8, 12) for his preceding summary statements. The whole of this first section of his report (vv. 8-14), and indeed, the whole of 1:8–2:17 and of the body of the letter that follows (3:1–7:16), is an announcement of the essential bond between the apostle and the Corinthians, their *koinōnia* in Jesus Christ.

Paul here grounds the petition of the Corinthians and their thanksgiving for his deliverance in the transparency of his conduct, his "simplicity and sincerity" (v. 12). This transparency, which itself is a gift of God, allows the work of God to be seen in the apostle. The Corinthians and the apostle are thus to boast in one another, as they are bound together by the work of God in them. Just as trial and testing is necessary to the work of God, so too is the simplicity and purity of the apostle, through whom the Gospel is not only proclaimed but also manifest in his body and life. This is Paul's theme in vv. 12-14. At this moment in his relationship with the Corinthians, his integrity remains in question on account of his failure to visit them as he had promised. He will take up that matter shortly. Yet his concern is broader and deeper. The whole course of his apostolic relationship with them, including their understanding of that relation, is at stake. This larger dimension of Paul's concern is especially evident in his return to his claim to sincerity in 2:17, by which he contrasts his apostolic service with "the many," implicitly calling into question the practices of his adversaries. The theme of "sincerity" thus forms an inclusio around the whole of 1:12–2:17.

As we have seen, Paul's "boasting" in vv. 12-14 serves as a defense, not of himself, but of the Gospel, in which the apostle and the Corinthians are bound together. This bond between the apostle and his church, their *koinōnia* in Christ — the topic of the entire section — is presently exposed to testing and trial. Paul's averments of integrity point away from his qualities and powers to the Gospel, which performs its work in him. The Corinthians must learn the true marks of the Gospel and of the presence of Christ as they are manifest in the apostle and thus not give heed to those who boast in "appearance and not in heart" (5:12). Naturally, Paul's "boasting" serves to undermine the apostolic claims of the intruders. But his argument is not a defense of his own person, nor is it in the first instance directed against adversaries. As he does throughout this letter, Paul above all else seeks to edify the Corinthians, to confirm them in Christ and draw them away from temptation (12:19).

12 Paul grounds *(gar)* his preceding implicit call to the Corinthians to petition on his behalf in his "boasting," that he has been simple and sincere in all his involvement in the world, and especially in relationship to them. His report of the deliverance God granted him in Asia, in which his frailty and vulnerability are apparent, is already an instance of that transparency. He has not hidden his weakness from them, despite their disdain of it.[188] As Paul later makes clear, such simplicity and sincerity are necessary to the display of God's work in him.[189] The Corinthians are to do the same. He wants them likewise to open themselves to him and embrace him as apostle. This is his purpose throughout the letter, as he later states explicitly (6:3-13).

True "boasting" for the apostle is paradoxical. It is contrary to outward appearance and human standards of judgment. This is especially apparent in this context. In the first place, Paul boasts about matters that do not concern the Corinthians, or at least, do not concern them primarily. Their present distrust of the apostle notwithstanding, they are much more interested in a display of skill and power than in purity of heart. Second — and this aspect of boasting underlies the first — true and proper "boasting" is always "eccentric."[190] Those who boast necessarily speak about themselves, else there is no boast. Yet, according to the Scriptures, those who boast rightly do not speak *of themselves,* their achievements or qualities, but rather *of God* and what God has done for them.[191]

188. 11:21-33; cf. 1 Cor 4:6-13.

189. 4:1-2; 5:11a; 6:3.

190. See R. Bultmann, "καυχάομαι," *TDNT* 3:648-52; J. Zmijewski, "καυχάομαι, καύχημα, καύχησις," *EDNT* 2:276-79; and esp., U. Heckel, *Kraft in Schwachheit: Untersuchungen zu 2. Kor 10–13* (WUNT 2/56; Tübingen: Mohr Siebeck, 1993), 144-214, who notes the stark difference between the Hellenistic rejection of boasting, which recognized the possibility of it becoming an affront against the gods, and the biblical tradition, which saw boasting as a robbery of the honor that belongs to God. In Paul's context, all proper boasting is necessarily extrinsic to the human being.

191. Paul takes up the Jeremianic call to set aside human boasting and to boast "in the Lord" at critical points in both our canonical letters to the Corinthians (1 Cor 1:31; 2 Cor 10:17; cf. Jer 9:24).

God's power is displayed ever only in our weakness (12:9). Paul stands within this biblical tradition. All of us necessarily believe and trust in something, either in the Lord or in the idols. We speak and boast about that in which our trust lies: our "mouth overflows with that with which the heart is full" (cf. Luke 6:45).[192]

As its appearance in the opening report of the letter signals, the topic of boasting is fundamental to Paul's argument. He is responding to the Corinthian attraction to those who based their claim to apostolic status on the visible display of their powers, and thus boasted in themselves. In the body of the letter (3:1–7:16), Paul sets forth his proper boast. He himself will engage in improper boasting in its closing (11:16–12:10). The vocabulary varies in the development of the argument in the body, but the theme is consistent. Despite all outward circumstances and his own human weakness, Paul boasts, acts in boldness and remains confident, because — and only because — he is the object of divine grace and mercy, which makes him new and carries him along with the Corinthians to the end of the good purposes of the Creator.[193] As he indicates to the Corinthians, he is giving them reason for boasting about him — or again, more properly, about God's work in him — in the face of boasting "in appearance" (5:12). Only after he has laid this foundation does he counter the boasting of his opponents with a form of boasting in himself, and that only with reserve and irony.[194]

Paul boasts here in "the witness of his conscience," that he has acted in "simplicity and purity." His boast stands in striking contrast to his own statement to the Corinthians that, even though he knows of nothing against himself, he is not thereby justified (1 Cor 4:4). This judgment belongs solely to the Lord, who at the last day will "make manifest the purposes of human hearts" (1 Cor 4:5). For Paul, the conscience can be only an imperfect anticipation of being manifest before Christ (5:10). It performs only a limited function in the life of the human being.[195] It can be "weak" and prohibit conduct that is legitimate, or conversely condone behavior that is wrong. As we have just noted, according to Paul, the conscience does not possess exhaustive self-knowledge. To have a good conscience does not necessarily mean that one is free from guilt. Our own hearts and motives remain finally hidden from us.[196] Paul's claim here to the "witness of his conscience" is limited to his dealings in

192. See 1 Cor 3:21; 2 Cor 5:12; 11:18.

193. See 2 Cor 1:15; 3:1, 4-6, 12; 4:1-2, 16; 5:6.

194. See 2 Cor 10:8, 12-18; 11:5-15, 16-30; 12:5, 9.

195. On this topic, see esp. H.-J. Eckstein, *Der Begriff Syneidesis bei Paulus* (WUNT 2/10; Tübingen: Mohr Siebeck, 1983).

196. Nevertheless we must not violate either our conscience or that of another, even in its limited capacity. In practice and conduct we are to adapt to the weak consciences of other Christians; in teaching and instruction we are to seek to strengthen their conscience. See 1 Cor 8:7-13; Rom 14:1-23.

the world *coram hominis.* It is *not* an assertion of absolute purity *coram Deo* — and therefore not a claim to absolute authority. Paul appeals to the witness of his conscience with respect to the Corinthians. Limited though its function may be, a good conscience is essential to Paul's mission as apostle: by his good conscience, and therefore *the transparency of his life,* he commends himself to the conscience of the Corinthians, and, in fact, that of every human being (4:2; 5:11).[197] Paul's boast in the witness of his conscience is bound up with his call to boast "in the heart," where God has performed his saving work, rather than in appearance (5:12).

As we have noted, Paul speaks of his conduct, not as his own work, but as the work of God and an outworking of the Gospel. His simplicity and purity are "of God." The grace of God operative in the apostle takes the same form as it does in all of God's work in the world: the singleness of God is reflected in the simplicity and purity of the apostle. Although it is hidden under contrary appearance, God's unqualified Yes to his good promises is found in Jesus, the Son of God (1:19-20). Paul has not acted "in fleshly wisdom, but in the grace of God." It is a gift of God's grace to Paul that he has so conducted himself.[198] Otherwise, he too would have followed the pattern of "fleshly wisdom," as, in fact, he once did. This single reference to "wisdom" in Second Corinthians displays the link between its theme and Paul's opening attack on human wisdom in 1 Cor 1–2, a wisdom that has been revealed as foolishness by "the word of the cross" (1 Cor 1:18). God's saving wisdom is found where human beings would never seek it and least expect it: in the suffering and death of Christ. Human wisdom operates on that which is visible, perceptible, and comprehensible. "Fleshly wisdom" is invariably bent toward personal advantage, no matter how good and devout it might appear outwardly. We thus hide our true motives, even from ourselves, and use other persons for own gain under the mask of godly goals. Paul later charges the opponents in Corinth with precisely such self-seeking.[199] Indeed, from the very beginning, his fundamental contention with the Corinthians has been that they are thinking and acting "as mere human beings" (1 Cor 3:1-3), judging the world according to outward appearance (10:7; cf. 5:12).[200]

Although he begins his response to the Corinthians with a reference to his own person and conscience, Paul immediately shifts his focus to the work

197. Likewise, according to Paul, we are not to violate our conscience or provide an offense to that of our neighbor. See, e.g., Rom 13:5; 1 Cor 8:7-12; 10:25-29.

198. See 1 Cor 15:10.

199. See 5:12; 11:16-21.

200. Conversely, although the language is undoubtedly Paul's own, some in Corinth suppose that Paul himself "walks according to the flesh" (10:2). They suppose that Paul's letters and his failure to visit the Corinthians (see 1:15-22) are a means of hiding his weakness and lack of gifts.

of God in Christ that is the basis of his boasting. He concludes his opening remarks by underscoring that work (v. 14) and then speaks of the "confidence" or "persuasion" *(pepoithēsis)* in which he acts (1:15; 3:4). As the term *pepoithēsis* suggests and the context shows, this "persuasion" is defined by God's work. The confidence of the apostle is determined by its object. It is passively received, yet it works Paul's action. Because of this "confidence" and "hope" (3:12), Paul speaks boldly (3:12), does not fail (4:1, 16), and has courage (5:6, 8). At the conclusion of his argument in the body of the letter, Paul uses the same language in reference to the Corinthians, in whom also the Gospel is at work. He speaks boldly and boasts about them (7:4). Indeed, their reception of Titus, his messenger, has proved his boasting true (7:14). In all respects, he is confident *(tharreō)* in them. The vocabulary by which he describes his apostolic calling reappears in relation to the objects of his apostolic ministry. As he reminds them here, he and they are bound together in Christ.

Paul's boast, and the witness of his conscience, is that he has acted in "simplicity and purity." He continues to insist in similar terms that he has dealt with the Corinthians in this way,[201] and he later charges those who have presented themselves to the Corinthians as apostles with precisely the opposite conduct (2:17; 11:12-15, 16-21). In contrast to their boast in superior gifts, he will boast in the pure motives and openness with which he has dealt with the Corinthians.

The first term that Paul employs, *haplotēs* ("simplicity"), might also be rendered "sincerity."[202] The Latin term that underlies the English bears much the same sense as the Greek: the prefix *sin-* (or *sim-*) conveys the idea of simplicity, wholeness, or purity. The apostle claims to have acted with singleness of heart, without duplicity in his dealings. He has acted with the Corinthians in a purity of heart and mind that seeks their good. As Paul indicates later in the letter, he, as apostle, likewise seeks to guard the "simplicity" of the Corinthians that is directed to Christ (11:3). As is the case in other Jewish writings

201. In 4:2 Paul presents his claim as the rejection of the negative: "the hidden things of shame," "walking in guile," and "corrupting the word of God." Rather, he "manifests the truth." The apostle is thus bound to the Gospel. In 5:11-12, correspondingly, it is the apostle who has been manifest before God: the "truth" is found in God's work in him. See further 1:17; 6:11-13; 7:2-4.

202. Despite the impressive witnesses to the reading ἁγιότητι (including $\mathfrak{p}^{46}$, ℵ*, A, B), ἁπλότητι is to be preferred. Although ἁγιότητι at first glance seems to be the *lectio difficilior,* the term found increasing usage in the second through fourth centuries and could have easily displaced an original ἁπλότητι because of the similarity in spelling. It would be a *hapax* with Paul, and nearly so in the New Testament (cf. Heb 12:10). In contrast, Paul employs the term ἁπλότης four times in Second Corinthians, aside from this instance. See B. M. Metzger, *A Textual Commentary on the Greek New Testament* (2nd ed.; New York: United Bible Societies, 1994), 507.

of this period, "simple-mindedness" appears as a positive quality, a dimension of devotion to God.[203] Paul will go on to urge the Corinthians to "simplicity" in sharing with others.[204]

The second term, *eilikrineia,* usually signifies "purity" and correspondingly carries associations of "transparency," especially in this context. In 2:17 Paul follows his use of this term with the brief elaboration, "we speak in Christ in the sight of God." The roots of the term, which would have been obvious to Greek speakers, likewise seem to be reflected in Paul's usage: *eili-krineia* connotes the judgment of the sunlight, which is "the best disinfectant" (Louis Brandeis). In contrast with those who "peddle the word of God" and thus have hidden and impure motives, Paul speaks in purity and transparency. As is clear from Paul's earlier word to the Corinthians, "purity [*eilikrineia*] and truth" constitute the fundamental effect of the Gospel on Christian life and worship.[205] Likewise, the fleshly conduct, which Paul later indicates that he has renounced, is the negative form of the claim he makes here (4:2). As he indicates in this later context, it is through the manifestation of the truth — namely, the truth of the Gospel manifest in his bodily life — that he commends himself to every conscience. Within the limited sphere in which his conscience can judge his actions, he knows that he has dealt honestly and openly with the Corinthians under the power of the Gospel. He speaks from his good conscience to their consciences.

13 Paul's avowal, "we do not write anything other to you but that which you read and comprehend," is occasioned, in part, by his failure to visit them, as he had promised them in an earlier letter that we do not possess. But Paul's apparent unreliability is only one manifestation of his failure to live up to the Corinthians' standards. Suspicions about him have arisen, not only because of his failure to come to Corinth, but also because of the poor impression he made with the Corinthians when he was there (10:10-11). The Corinthians find a discrepancy between the message and the messenger, between Paul's *parrēsia* and his *parousia* and *praxis.*[206] They cannot yet see that Christ's strength is made perfect in the apostle's weakness.

In response, Paul avers that there are no hidden motives, no hidden meanings to be deciphered from his letters. As he tells them later, if his Gospel

203. See one of Jesus' parables with the related term ἁπλοῦς ("single, simple"; Matt 6:22; Luke 11:34). The two terms appear fairly frequently in Philo, and esp. in the *Testaments of the Twelve Patriarchs.* In a broader Hellenistic context, the term could signify simple-mindedness. See LSJM, "ἁπλόος," 190-91.

204. The term reappears in this sense in 2 Cor 8:2; 9:11, 13.

205. 1 Cor 5:8.

206. Nicely put by M. M. Mitchell, *Paul, the Corinthians, and the Birth of Christian Hermeneutics* (Cambridge: Cambridge University Press, 2010), 81, and modified here with the addition of *praxis.*

is hidden, it is hidden to those whose minds have been blinded by the "god of this world" (4:3-4). Especially in this letter he has opened his mouth and heart wide to them (6:11). There is nothing in Paul's letters beyond what they read and recognize. The hermeneutic of Scripture as a whole comes to expression in this word to the Corinthians: Paul hides nothing behind the words he writes, yet — despite his expression of hope — the meaning of his words remains hidden to the Corinthians.[207] He thus recalls the theme of the "wisdom of God, hidden in a mystery" (1 Cor 2:1-16) and anticipates the theme of the work of the Spirit (2 Cor 3:1-18).

The term "recognize" (*epiginōskō;* ESV "understand") bears special significance. It often signifies an approving knowledge or a recollection of something already known. Paul elsewhere uses the term with the former sense,[208] and sometimes also with the latter.[209] In some instances, both ideas are present, as they appear to be in the present context. Insofar as the Corinthians are believers and possess the Gospel, they recognize and approve that which Paul openly writes as apostle. In this respect, the apostle has no authority over them: in their faith they stand (v. 24). In his final statement in v. 13, Paul expresses his hope that the Corinthians *recognize* (and thus *approve*) what he has written to them all the way to the end, namely, to the end of this age and the coming of the Lord, the consummation of all things. Therein lies their salvation.

14 Just as he has invited the Corinthians to share in his trials, Paul now invites them to share in his boasting. In a certain measure they have understood (*epegnōte;* ESV "acknowledged") the apostle, that he is their boast, just as they are his (1 Cor 13:12). Here again *epiginōskō* connotes "recognition" and, very likely, prior knowledge as well. The Corinthians are to recognize Paul as their apostle. The boast of the Corinthians is to be located beyond themselves and their powers, in their apostle, who passes through suffering and deliverance, and through whom they have received and continue to receive the Gospel. It is again clear that the apostle and the Gospel cannot be separated. The Gospel takes a specific form in the bodily life of Christ and Christ's apostle, from which it cannot be removed without being distorted. Conversely, the Corinthians are the apostle's boast. As he makes clear shortly, they are the proof and demonstration that he is a true and faithful apostle. As we have noted, Paul will yet report his boasting in them (7:4, 14). The lives of the apostle and the church are now indissolubly bound together, to "die together and to live together" (7:3). This mutual boasting will be fulfilled

207. It is thus the whole of the apostle's life, not merely his letters, that the Corinthians fail to comprehend. We shall return to this topic in a brief critique of Mitchell, *The Birth of Christian Hermeneutics.* See pp. 142-50.

208. 1 Cor 13:12; 14:37; 16:18.

209. Rom 1:32; 2 Cor 6:9.

openly only "in the day of our Lord, Jesus."[210] In the present time, the basis of the Corinthian boasting in the apostle is hidden beneath his trials and suffering, just as the cause for the apostle's boasting in the Corinthians is hidden behind their present disobedience. Paul's unusual reference to "the day of our Lord, Jesus" underscores this radical contrast between appearance and hope. In speaking of "Jesus" (as opposed to "Christ"), he points to Jesus' earthly ministry, suffering, and death, in which God's glory is hidden and simultaneously revealed.

b. The Word of the Apostle as the Yes of God (1:15-22)

15*Because I was sure of this, I wanted to come to you first, so that you*
might have a second experience of grace. 16*I wanted to visit you on my*
way to Macedonia, and to come back to you from Macedonia and have
you send me on my way to Judea. 17*Was I vacillating when I wanted to*
do this? Do I make my plans according to the flesh, ready to say "Yes, yes"
and "No, no" at the same time? 18*As surely as God is faithful, our word to*
you has not been Yes and No. 19*For the Son of God, Jesus Christ, whom*
we proclaimed among you, Silvanus and Timothy and I, was not Yes and
No, but in him it is always Yes. 20*For all the promises of God find their Yes*
in him. That is why it is through him that we utter our Amen to God for
his glory. 21*And it is God who establishes us with you in Christ, and has*
anointed us, 22*and who has also put his seal on us and given us his Spirit*
in our hearts as a guarantee.

Originally Paul had announced to the Corinthians that he would visit them directly and at length upon his departure from Ephesus.[211] Here he explains his failure to complete that promised visit. As we have noted, it is not at all clear that Paul's explanation of the matter is a response to charges against him. The Corinthians obviously are unhappy that he failed to visit and were grieved by the letter that he sent in place of that visit (7:8-13). They nevertheless have been reconciled to Paul by that letter and by Titus, its carrier — at least for the time being (7:5-16). Wounded feelings remained, as well as suspicions (7:11-12). Paul's denial that he has been untrustworthy is part of his larger aim of securing their faith in the Gospel, which is expressed in their love and loyalty to the apostle, who has brought and still brings that Gospel to them.

210. The reading "our Lord Jesus" is to be preferred to the variant omission of the pronoun. As the UBS committee notes, this expression is unexpected and therefore more likely to have come from Paul than to have been introduced by copyists. The external evidence is rather evenly balanced. See Metzger, *Textual Commentary,* 507-8.

211. See 1 Cor 16:5-9.

Paul immediately dismisses the possibility that carelessness or self-interest in planning led to his failure to complete his promise. He first does so, moreover, not by providing a defense of his actions — that comes only in 1:23–2:4 — but on the basis of the Gospel, or more precisely, on the basis of the Christ proclaimed in the Gospel. In the certainty of God's Yes in Christ, the Corinthians are secured for salvation together with the apostle. Paul avers that, just as God is faithful, so, through Christ, he, as apostle, is faithful as well. His argument is an extension of his preceding description of the bond forged by the Gospel between him and the Corinthians. It is remarkably similar to his declarations of integrity and love for his addressees in 1 Thessalonians, which likewise were written at a time when he unexpectedly had been separated from the church for an extended period.[212] Just as there no reason to think that he is responding to concrete charges from the Thessalonian church, there is no need to do so here either. In both instances, Paul seeks to ward off potential suspicions that might have driven a wedge between him and his churches. And there were, to be sure, negative judgments about Paul's qualifications as an apostle with the church in Corinth. He is on trial, under suspicion as a fraud (12:16, 19). Nevertheless, it is by no means apparent that Paul is responding to open complaints. Not even his invocation of God as his witness is a conclusive indication that he is here defending himself against explicit charges (1:23). Paul's oaths appear regularly in contexts in which he communicates his sincerity and integrity as an apostle, apart from any particular distrust on the part of his addressees.[213] The relation of love with his churches was essential to his ministry. His following appeal to God as his witness (1:23) corresponds to his opening boast in his good conscience concerning *all* his dealings with them (1:12).

The apostle bears the form of Christ in relation to the church. This is so, not only in his outward afflictions, but also in his suffering with their failures. These failures are what have kept him from visiting Corinth. As a result of their unfaithfulness, he has appeared to be unfaithful. Like God's own promises in the face of human suffering, and especially in the cross of Christ, his promise seems to be unreliable. But as with God's work in Christ, Paul's No turns out to be a Yes, since all that he has done serves the salvation of the Corinthians, including his bearing grief on their account and his freely forgiving the one who had offended him (2:1-4, 5-11). Paul has wounded the Corinthians only in order that they might be healed, following the pattern of God's saving work. This healing entails the restoration of their relationship to the apostle, a healing that Paul seeks to further here.

At the time of his writing First Corinthians, Paul planned to visit Corinth

212. See 1 Thess 2:3-6, 10 (2 Cor 1:12); 2:19-20 (2 Cor 1:13-14); 3:6-7, 10 (2 Cor 7:5-16).

213. See Rom 1:9; 9:1; Phil 1:8; 1 Thess 2:5, 10.

upon leaving Ephesus, after passing through Macedonia.[214] Timothy's unsuccessful visit prompted Paul to make an unanticipated journey from Ephesus to Corinth (13:1-2), at which time he decided to alter his original plans and travel via Corinth to Macedonia and return there on the way to Judea. Because of continuing problems in the congregation, Paul decided not to visit ("not to come to you again in grief," 2:1), but to send a letter instead (the tearful letter, 2:3, 4). Paul attempts in this section to explain his actions as motivated by concern for their good.

15 "And in this confidence, I planned to come to you first." As we have noted, "confidence" *(pepoithēsis)* is a fundamentally passive term: a glance at its usage quickly shows that the *object* of trust, and not merely the act of trusting, is in view where the term appears.[215] The "confidence" with which Paul planned to come to the Corinthians is not simply subjective, but it is his objective confidence in the Gospel, which works an abiding relationship between him and the Corinthians, including his sincerity and their recognition of him (vv. 12-14).

On account of this confidence, he speaks of his planned visit to the Corinthians as their receiving "a second gift" (or "grace": *charis*).[216] As in his apostolic greeting (1:2) and elsewhere, he speaks of "grace" in the concrete, in the moment of its being given and received, so that the sense of the term approaches that of "gift."[217] The grace of God that has been given to him and that determines his conduct (v. 12) is what he wants to impart to them, quite concretely in his two visits.

16 Paul not only expects to bring a gift to the Corinthians, he also hopes to receive a blessing from them. He had planned for them to help him travel to Judea. This would have meant a contribution for his travel to Judea, as he accompanied the collection for "the holy ones."[218] Even with the Corinthians, with whom he avoids a benefactor-beneficiary relation, the apostle lives in a relationship of giving and receiving.[219]

214. 1 Cor 16.5-9; but see 1 Cor 4:19, "I shall come to you quickly, *if the Lord wills.*"

215. See LXX 4 Kgdms 18:19; Phil 3:4; Josephus, *Ant.* 1.73; 3.45; 5.74; 10.16; 11.299; 19.317; Philo, *Virt.* 226.5.

216. His following description in v. 16 of his plan to visit them *first* (πρότερον) on his way to Macedonia, and then on his way from Macedonia to Jerusalem, makes it clear that the "second [δευτέραν] grace" is the second visit, for which he had made provision in his travel plans.

217. See the discussion at 8:1, p. 319 below.

218. He is not thereby violating his determination not to receive support from the Corinthians; the help in traveling to Jerusalem is not the same as wages for his apostolic service to them. See 1 Cor 9:15; 2 Cor 11:7-11.

219. See Rom 1:11-12; Phil 4:14-20, and the discussion of this theme in connection with the collection in 8:1–9:15 in the present letter.

17 Although Titus's visit already has brought a reconciliation between the Corinthians and the apostle (7:5-16), Paul himself raises questions that most likely had led to suspicions about him in the Corinthian church. He rhetorically casts them in a form of a denial: "Did I then make this plan carelessly? Or do I plan what I plan according to the flesh?" He does not follow this denial with a personal defense. He speaks instead of the work of God through the Gospel, which is at work in him in his apostolic relation with the Corinthians. The word and message of the apostle to the Corinthians (v. 18) is not limited to merely his preaching. His entire life is an expression of the Gospel and of God's work in Christ.

Of course, there had been a brief, intervening painful visit (2:1-5). Moreover, Paul originally had indicated expressly to the Corinthians that his lengthier visit was contingent upon "the will of the Lord" (1 Cor 4:19; 16:7), just as he likewise indicates to the Roman Christians his hope that a way might be made free for him to come to them (Rom 1:10).[220] Paul had made no absolute promises to the Corinthians. He made it clear that his planning was contingent upon the purposes of God. Of course, this sort of language may easily be used to hide personal motives. Paul understandably makes no reference to it here.

Paul denies that he plans "according to the flesh." To think, act, or speak "according to the flesh" is to do so on the basis of the powers, abilities, and inclinations of the fallen human being. As becomes apparent in this letter, to so think and act is to operate on the basis of that which is outward and perceptible. Living "according to the flesh" inevitably comes to entail duplicity and hypocrisy: appearances are used to hide our self-seeking lives.

Paul already has denied that he has conducted himself in "fleshly wisdom" in relation to the Corinthians (1:12), and later in the letter he will similarly deny that he "walks according to the flesh" (10:2). As we have observed, the Corinthian church suspects that Paul is attempting to hide his weaknesses, and thus his lack of qualification as an apostle. The standards by which an apostle is to be legitimated are at stake. Consequently, the Gospel is at stake as well. The Corinthians have been entranced by outward displays of power. Paul seeks to bring them back to the Gospel, in which God's saving power is hidden in weakness.

The wording at the close of this verse is somewhat difficult. According to Paul, if he planned according to the flesh, there would be with him "the 'Yes, yes' and 'No, no.'" The language bears obvious similarities to the saying of Jesus found in Matthew 5:37 and the similar warning in James 5:12. In these contexts, the doubling of the Yes and No expresses one's fidelity and commitment, in contrast to swearing an oath based on some "thing" of honor,

220. Implicitly pointing to the persecution present in Thessalonica, he reports to the Thessalonian church that Satan has hindered him from coming to them (1 Thess 2:18).

value, or holiness.[221] Paul's statement likely reflects this background. His use of this doubling serves as an emphatic and ironic expression of unreliability: he denies that there is with him a *simultaneous* "yes, yes" *and* "no, no."[222] This combination of asseveration and ambiguity is the height of fickleness and inconstancy. But this is precisely how Paul appears to the Corinthians in his failure to complete his promised visit. Thus, too, apart from the word of the Gospel, God appears in the crucified Christ.

18 The certainty of the apostle's message to the Corinthians does not lie in himself, but in God: *God* is faithful that our "word" *(logos)* to you is not Yes and No.[223] As we have noted, the whole of the apostle's dealings are encompassed within the work of the Gospel. Not merely his preaching to the Corinthians but his entire life with them is an outworking of God's work in Christ. This includes his failure to visit them, as he is about to make clear. God does not deal with the Corinthians in ambivalence, nor does his apostle.

Twice in First Corinthians Paul affirms that God is faithful: faithful in his calling of the Corinthians to confirm them (in salvation) until the end, so that they shall be "blameless at the day of Jesus Christ" (1 Cor 1:8-9), and faithful not to allow them to be tempted beyond what they can bear, providing a way of escape (1 Cor 10:13). In both instances Paul speaks contrary to outward appearances. He does so here as well, now with respect to his own actions. As he will shortly make clear, God leads him in Christ as captive in a Roman triumph, so that the outward circumstances of the apostle *contradict* the hope of the Gospel he bears. God's word is not Yes and No. Yet God hides his Yes in a No, drawing the Corinthians away from themselves and their own wisdom to his wisdom in Christ.

19 Paul's assurance concerning the certainty of the "word" he bears to the Corinthians has its basis *(gar)* solely in Jesus Christ. Indeed, *Jesus Christ,* who was proclaimed through Paul among the Corinthians, has been communicated to them by that proclamation. It is present and at work in it: God's Yes has come about *in him.*

Here, for the only time in this letter, Paul names Jesus "God's Son"; indeed, he emphatically fronts the title and emphasizes that Jesus is *God's* Son.

221. The doubling of an affirmation or denial could also be regarded as an oath, even if the form is different. See esp. *b. Šebu.* 36a and further *b. Meg.* 32a; cf. Str-B 1:337 and the double "Amen" in Johannine usage.

222. His following reference to God's unqualified "yes" to his promises in Christ (v. 20) and his own oath in v. 23 ("I invoke God as witness on my life") support this reading.

223. The δέ that marks v. 18 as a continuation of Paul's statement in v. 17 might be omitted from the translation, as we have done here, or it could be rendered with "and." Against the ESV and NRSV, which seem to follow the variant reading ὁ λόγος ἡμῶν ὁ πρὸς ὑμᾶς οὐκ *ἐγένετο* Ναὶ καὶ Οὔ ("our word to you *has* not *been* Yes and No"), the ἔστιν is to be preferred, expressing the present time: "our word to you *is* not 'Yes and No.'"

Although the title "Son of God" appears only infrequently in Paul's letters, it communicates a fundamental and essential element of his Gospel, as is clear from the contexts in which it appears.[224] It is closely related to Paul's earlier reference to "the Christ" and his sufferings in v. 5. As becomes apparent from its resonance with the Old Testament, the title communicates a *story,* one of salvation. Although it is also applied to Israel in Scripture, and to the godly in early Judaism, Paul's use of the title especially recalls the king of Israel, the offspring of David. God's conferral of the title on the king is associated with God's defeat of the king's enemies and instatement of him as ruler of the nations: it thus expresses the fulfillment of God's promise to David, namely, that he would be a father to David's seed.[225] This decisive moment of deliverance presupposes a time of trial and suffering in which the Lord's promise is tested in the one who bears it.[226] The experience of the king thus fits into the pattern of suffering — and even death — to which "the beloved son" is subject in Scripture. This is the experience of Abel, Isaac, Jacob, Joseph, and Israel itself.[227] In delivering Christ from all trouble and instating him as king, God as "Father" identifies himself with the "Son." The distinction between them remains, of course, in petition and answer, receiving and giving.[228] As becomes apparent in many of the psalms, the suffering and delivered king is God's vehicle of deliverance and salvation for the world, in which suffering and oppression rule.[229]

Several elements of Paul's wider usage of the title "Son" in reference to Jesus are worth noting here as well:

1. Paul elsewhere names Jesus as the *preexistent* Son. Jesus' experience thus provides the pattern that all the other figures in Scripture anticipate; his coming is the eschatological event that fulfills the saving purpose of God.[230]
2. Paul's identification of Jesus the *preexistent* Son with God the Father is of a different order than the identification of an earthly, Davidic king as God's son.
3. This identification expresses itself in Paul's descriptions of Jesus' actions.

224. See Rom 1:4, 9; 5:10; 8:3, 29; 1 Cor 1:9; Gal 1:16; 2:20; 4:4, 6; 1 Thess 1:10; Col 1:13; Eph 4:13. On the earliest development of Christology and Paul's use of the title, see esp. M. Hengel, *The Cross of the Son of God* (London: SCM, 1986), 1-81.

225. Pss 2; 89; 2 Sam 7:12-14.

226. See esp. Ps 89:38-52.

227. On this motif, see J. D. Levenson, *The Death and Resurrection of the Beloved Son* (New Haven: Yale University Press, 1993).

228. See again Pss 2; 89.

229. See, e.g., Pss 3; 18; 20; 72.

230. Gal 4:4; Rom 1:3-4; 8:3.

Not only does the Father give up his Son (Rom 8:3, 29), the Son gives himself up, and in so doing implicitly acts as God (Gal 2:20; cf. 1:4).[231]

4. God's deliverance of Jesus, his Son, works the deliverance of those who belong to Jesus, just as the deliverance of the king brought salvation to Israel.[232]
5. Those who believe in Jesus share in him and thus become "sons" (and "daughters") of God themselves, sharing in both suffering and final deliverance.[233]

It is of considerable significance that Paul *explicitly* indicates that his Gospel is nothing other than the proclamation of "the Son of God."[234] It is *this* story of the suffering and deliverance of Jesus, the Son of God, that provides the basis of Paul's theology and the new covenant, of which he is an emissary (3:1-18). The very "newness" of this covenant implies the radical break of death and resurrection that is taken up in the story of God's Son.

Already in First Corinthians, Paul has reminded the Corinthian church that they have been "called into the fellowship [*koinōnia*] of [God's] Son, Jesus Christ, our Lord" (1 Cor 1:9). He brings this reminder there as a confession of God's faithfulness, just as he here affirms God's faithfulness in his Son. The brief reference to Jesus as God's Son in 1 Cor 1:9 already implies the story of suffering and deliverance that "makes foolish the wisdom of the world" (1 Cor 1:20). Paul there reminds the Corinthians that their call to faith and salvation contradicts all human standards (1 Cor 1:19-31). Their wisdom, strength, and worth, Paul reminds them, are found in the crucified and risen Lord. The Corinthians, in their lust for power, have forgotten that the work of God takes place in suffering and weakness. It is not too much to say, then, that the entire message of the Corinthian correspondence is contained with Paul's brief naming of Jesus as "God's Son." Just as God accepts those who are unacceptable in his Son, the Corinthians are called to accept what appears to them to be

231. Paul's understanding of Jesus as Son thus approaches Paul's identification of him as the "image of God." See esp. 2 Cor 4:4; cf. 3:18.

232. This deliverance takes place in a twofold way. On the one hand, the death and resurrection of Jesus the Son *includes* fallen human beings, delivers them from sin, and reconciles them to God (Rom 5:10-11), just as God's deliverance of the Davidic kings brought deliverance to Israel as well. On the other hand, just as the one who had experienced deliverance announced it to others, so that they would (1) know "God's name," (2) likewise trust in him, and (3) know deliverance (e.g., Ps 22:22-26), so now the risen Christ savingly makes known God's name to the nations, thereby creating faith (Rom 15:10; Ps 18:49-50).

233. See Rom 8:29. Paul's description of his coming to faith as God's revelation of his Son "in him" (Gal 1:16) is to be understood in this story of deliverance as well. The "in me" is not an interior experience but signifies the course of his life (cf. Gal 2:20; 4:6).

234. Rom 1:9; Gal 1:16.

unacceptable, namely, the crucified Jesus, who is present in the apostle. As we have noted, in v. 19 Paul fronts the reference to God and thus speaks emphatically of the proclamation of Jesus as "God's Son." He thus underscores that God's faithfulness and identity are bound up with the crucified and risen Jesus. The Jesus whom he proclaims as God's Son is the crucified Christ (1 Cor 1:23). God savingly reveals himself *sub contrario.* The "word of the cross" (1 Cor 1:18) remains foolishness to the world — and to the Corinthians.

"The Son of God, Jesus Christ, . . . *was proclaimed among you through us,* namely, through me and Silvanus and Timothy."[235] Corresponding to his emphatic reference to God, Paul describes his proclamation of the Gospel in Corinth in the passive voice. It was not that he and Silvanus and Timothy made proclamation, but that Jesus Christ, God's Son, *was proclaimed* through them. He and his co-workers were the mere vehicle of God's work in Jesus. It was "*God's* Son, Jesus Christ" who was proclaimed. All attention is deflected away from the proclaimers to the One whom they proclaimed, whose message they bear in body and in life.

Paul's use of the verb *ginomai* in v. 19b is to be understood as describing an event that has taken place, not merely a state of affairs. He affirms that the Son of God, Jesus Christ, "did not *come to be* 'Yes and No,' but 'Yes' *has come about* in him."[236] Paul here has in view the effect of his proclamation among the Corinthians, to which he refers in his description of Christ ("who was proclaimed among you"). The faith of the Corinthians is nothing other than a manifestation of God's Yes in Christ. Indeed, their faith marks the presence of the crucified and risen Christ among them. In implicit form, Paul's first affirmation is that Jesus Christ, the Son of God, himself came to be Yes. He clearly has in view the resurrection. His second, explicit affirmation is that Yes has come about "in" Christ. The proclamation of Christ establishes a defined "place" within the world in which God's Yes is present. This "place" is "in"

235. Against the ESV and NRSV, the passive voice of the verb is not to be changed to the active ("we proclaimed"). Against the NIV, the διά does not express agency but, as usual, instrumentality ("Jesus Christ . . . was proclaimed through us"; Ἰησοῦς Χριστὸς ὁ ἐν ὑμῖν δι' ἡμῶν κηρυχθείς).

236. The English versions handle this verse rather badly. The ESV, NIV, and NRSV render γίνομαι (2x) as expressing a state of affairs ("the Son of God . . . was not Yes and No" [ESV]), and then attempt to account for the perfect tense of the second use of the verb (γέγονεν) by adding the adverb "always" ("in him it is always Yes" [ESV]). By reading the usage of the verb in this way, the translations miss Paul's focus upon the resurrection of Christ and the effecting of the faith of the Corinthians by the apostolic proclamation. They also fail to recognize that the subject of the verb in the final clause is "yes" and must therefore introduce an impersonal subject in order to maintain their reading of the verb as a predication ("in him *it* is always Yes" [ESV]). The concrete and specific event of the resurrection and its counterpart in the coming-to-faith of the Corinthians thereby becomes an undefined and vague experience. That is esp. the case with the NIV: "in him it has always been 'Yes.'"

Christ. The saving work of God cannot be abstracted or separated from the person of Christ. Where God is savingly at work, Christ is present, and vice versa.

The faithfulness of God is found in his Yes, which has come to pass in his apparent No in the Crucified. This Yes is manifest in the faith of the Corinthians, which was effected by the apostolic proclamation of Christ among them. It likewise shall be manifest in the apostle who presently appears unfaithful to them.

20 "For as many as may be the promises of God, in him is the Yes." A second explanation of Paul's confidence follows the first that appears in v. 19. The crucified and risen Christ, in whom God's Yes has come to reality among the Corinthians, is the one "place" on earth in which all God's promises have come to fulfillment. Unlike Galatians and Romans, Paul here does not identify God's promises as having been given to Abraham. He instead speaks of their fulfillment in Christ. Furthermore, while he can view the whole of salvation as being comprehended within the single promise given to Abraham in Gen 15:1-6,[237] he now stresses the particularity and multiplicity of God's promises.[238] The uncounted number of the promises of God implies the countless dimensions of God's love and care: "as many as may be the promises of God."[239] At the same time, Paul's reference to the multiplicity of God's promises may also signal the hopes and dreams of the Corinthians. In any case, Paul draws a sharp contrast with the multiplicity of the promises and their fulfillment: all God's promises have their Yes in God's Son, Jesus Christ. There is no promise that finds its fulfillment outside of Jesus. Apart from and outside of him, the promises of Scripture remain fragmentary and unanswered. Paul here presents a profoundly material hermeneutic that pervades his entire argument in the letter, and that appears again prominently in his distinction between the "letter" and the Spirit that appears in 2 Cor 3. Christ, crucified and risen, is himself the metanarrative and key to all of Scripture.[240] In him the eschaton has intersected the present time — which nevertheless, for a time, continues.

237. Rom 4:13-20; Gal 3:14, 17, 22; cf., however, Gal 3:16, 21.

238. See Rom 9:4; 15:8; 2 Cor 7:1. In this way, Paul's thought corresponds to that found in later rabbinic literature, which likewise, in contrast with the Scripture, speaks of (and, indeed, delights in) a plurality of covenants. Cf. Str-B 3:262. Against this background, the primacy that Paul assigns the promise to Abraham of "seed" in Galatians 3 and Romans 4 stands out all the more sharply. For Paul, this promise implicitly encompasses all others. The fulfillment of this promise in Christ, which he announces in differing ways in both contexts (Gal 3:16; Rom 4:24-25), signals that his thought there is not distant from his Christ-centered message to the Corinthians here.

239. The ESV and the NRSV inexplicably omit the quantitative relative pronoun and substitute "all," thereby missing Paul's emphasis on the multiplicity of God's promises and somewhat obscuring the hermeneutical implications of his affirmation.

240. I owe this predication to Edward Kim.

In a letter to Eberhard Bethge written from the Tegel prison on August 21, 1944, Dietrich Bonhoeffer reflects on this verse. His thoughts capture much of what Paul is saying here:

> Everything depends on the "in him." Everything that we rightly may expect from God, everything for which we may ask is to be found in Jesus Christ. Everything that a "God," according to the way that *we* conceive him, must and can do, has nothing to do with the God of Jesus Christ. We must sink ourselves ever again, taking much time and without haste into the living, speaking, acting, suffering, and dying of Jesus in order to discover what God promises and what God fulfills. It is certain that we are allowed to live constantly in the nearness and presence of God, and that this life is for us an entirely new life. Nothing is impossible for us, because nothing is impossible for God. No earthly power can touch us apart from God's will. Danger and distress only drive us closer to God. It is certain that we have nothing to which we may lay claim, and yet everything for which we may ask. It is certain that our joy is hidden in suffering, our life is hidden in dying. It is certain that in all things we stand in a community that bears and carries us. To all this, God has said "Yes," and "Amen" in Jesus. This "Yes" and "Amen" is the solid ground on which we stand.[241]

Bonhoeffer, in the midst of his own troubles, profoundly grasps the way in which Paul speaks to the Corinthians of God's promises as operating "in Christ" contrary to all appearances and all human expectations. Paul's naming Jesus "God's Son" implies such a story. That God's Yes has come about in Jesus means nothing other than the entrance of the final, decisive deliverance from evil into the present age. Its localization in Jesus means that God's ways remain hidden in the present, fallen world. This faithfulness of God has been established not only in Jesus' resurrection but also in the faith of the Corinthians that was created through the proclamation of Jesus Christ in their midst. This Yes of God in Christ will carry the Corinthians until the time when the eschaton, which has arrived already in Jesus, shall arrive for the world. Paul makes this announcement already in 1 Cor 1:8: "who shall confirm you until the end, blameless in the day of our Lord, Jesus Christ."

There is another small but significant element of Paul's thought in this verse: "Therefore also through him is the 'Amen' to God for [the] glory [that comes about] through us."[242] This "Amen" is not God's word in Jesus. It is

241. Bonhoeffer, *Widerstand und Ergebung*, 209-10.

242. Bonhoeffer misses this dimension of the verse, as do the ESV, NIV, and NRSV, which misconstrue the closing δι' ἡμῶν as expressing agency, rather than instrumentality. Paul does not speak of his own pronouncement of "Amen" but of the "Amen" that must echo from the Corinthians to God for the glory of the new covenant worked through the apostle.

the verbal response that arises from those who have been given the gift of salvation. It is a word of faith and hope in the glory that is yet to be revealed. God's saving Yes in the crucified and risen Christ does not return to him empty but creates its own reception and thus brings the fruit of thanksgiving and faith. This "Amen" reflects the liturgy of the earliest church, which had been borrowed from the synagogue. In 1 Cor 14:16 it appears as the church's participatory response to a benediction or thanksgiving that had been spoken in worship. The apostle already has given thanks to God in his benediction in vv. 3-7. He awaits the thanksgiving that will arise from the Corinthians. As an invitation to that thanksgiving, he will again offer thanks for God's work through him in his trials (2:14). He does so once again in his hope that the Corinthians will fulfill *their* promise to participate in the gift for the saints in Jerusalem (9:15; see also 8:16). In more than one way in this letter, then, Paul invites the Corinthians to utter "Amen" to God through Jesus Christ. The "Amen" to which Paul invites the Corinthians is a thankful affirmation of "the glory [that comes about] through us." The Corinthians are to enter into thanksgiving to God for Paul's mission as an apostle of Christ, the very mission that they question. Their worship of God cannot take place without their thankful reception of Paul as their apostle.

21 Paul now returns to speak of his confidence in the saving work of God that binds him and the Corinthians together as apostle and church (cf. v. 15), recalling their boast in one another (v. 14). His own trustworthiness is comprehended within that work (v. 17). It is none other than God who "establishes" the apostle together with the Corinthians "unto Christ" and who has "sealed" him with the down payment of the Spirit. Paul's affirmation of God's saving work in Christ takes an incipiently trinitarian form. Despite his apparent instability and inconstancy, it is *God* who confirms the apostle and, with him, the Corinthians.

Paul thus directs all attention away from himself, characterizing God in two parallel statements in vv. 21-22 that reinforce one another:

> 21The One who establishes us with you for Christ and who anointed us is God.
>
> 22He is the One who also sealed us and gave us the Spirit in our hearts as a guarantee.

It is God and God alone who "establishes" Paul, making his apostolic "message" preached in word and life trustworthy, despite the Corinthians' suspicions about his constancy. The apostle is the vehicle of God's Yes in Christ (vv. 19-20). It is God likewise who performs his work in the Corinthians, "establishing" them and securing their salvation along with that of Paul. The present tense of the verb "establish" *(bebaioō)* stands apart from the following aorists, signaling that this work of God is not yet complete. The hope of the apostle is nevertheless "firm" *(bebaios)*.

God establishes the Corinthians and the apostle together "unto" or "for" Christ. Already here Paul presents himself in the secondary role that he ascribes to himself in 11:2. As apostle, Paul has betrothed the Corinthians to Another.[243] Although their bond with the apostle is essential to their salvation, the Corinthian church is the bride of Christ, and not of the apostle.

Both the pairing and parallelism of Paul's statements are of significance. Each statement characterizes God in such a way that the second member of each pair further explains and defines the first. God's "establishing" Paul with the Corinthians is bound up with God's anointing him.[244] Likewise, God's "having sealed" Paul signals the effective completion of his task and the divine recognition of his apostolic work.[245] This remarkable note of finality corresponds to the gift of the Spirit as a "down payment," namely, the entrance of the eschaton into the present.

The parallelism of the pairs is also semantically operative. The first member of each of the statements focuses on *God* and the certainty of God's saving work in and through the apostle: God's "establishing" the apostle corresponds to God's having "sealed" him, marking him and his work as complete and acceptable. The second member of each pair focuses on *the apostle* in whom God performs his work. "Being anointed" thus corresponds to "being given the guarantee of the Spirit."

A chiastic pattern is also apparent. The exterior elements of the confession emphasize *the salvation of the apostle*. The internal elements have to do with *his apostolic calling*. Paul's apostolic calling is thus formally "contained" within the salvation granted him in Christ and cannot be extracted from that salvation. His labor is given *within* his life in Christ. It is neither a way to life that he must fulfill, nor does it consist in merely external duties that may be exercised without the engagement of his person. His salvation and his calling are one. What Paul expresses formally in this chiasm also comes to expression materially in his first word in v. 21: God is the One who "establishes" him *with* the Corinthians in Christ.

In a number of contexts, the verb *bebaioō* ("establish") speaks metaphorically of "validation" or "making certain or true" as a "giving stability."[246] In First Corinthians Paul thanks God that the "testimony of Christ" has been

243. Here again Bonhoeffer's reflections in *Life Together* apply. See p. 16 above.

244. Here the durative aspect of the present participle βεβαιῶν ("the one who *establishes*") corresponds to his continuing apostolic ministry in the present time.

245. See below on v. 22.

246. The same is true of the *nip'al* of אמן in the Hebrew Scriptures, which is reflected in Paul's expectation of "the Amen" to the glory worked by God through him (v. 20).

"established" among the Corinthians (1 Cor 1:6). In Romans he describes Christ as having been a servant of the circumcision in order to "establish" the promises given to the fathers, i.e., to effect them and bring them to fulfillment (Rom 15:8). The promise to all Abraham's seed likewise had to be "firm" and valid (Rom 4:16). As Paul writes to the Philippians, his imprisonment and impending trial are to serve the "establishment" or "validation" of the Gospel (Phil 1:7). Already in this letter Paul has indicated that his hope for the Corinthians is "firm" and "validated," since (he trusts) they share in sufferings with him (1:7). In all these instances, it is a word or promise (or the hope based on that word) that is "established" by an event that fulfills that which was spoken and announced. In this context, however, as also in the thanksgiving of 1:8, Paul speaks of *persons* being "established." There it is the Corinthians; here it is the apostle himself. Their persons have been taken up into the Gospel. They have been encompassed and are carried by God's word of promise and effective call. God's "establishing" Paul is nothing other than God's making his Yes in Christ effective in the apostle.[247]

God establishes Paul and the Corinthians "unto" or "for" Christ. They are thus Christ's possession[248] and are indwelt by Christ, so that they share both corporately and individually in his resurrected life.[249] The "establishing" that Paul has in view is thus obviously oriented to the eschaton, even though the action takes place here and now.[250] Both the apostle and the Corinthians belong to the crucified and risen Christ, in whom God's decisive Yes is found.[251] This announcement of the entrance of eschatological realities into the present suggests that Paul associates God's work of "establishing" him and the Corinthians with the gift of the Spirit, of which he speaks in the final element of his confession. His thought here comes remarkably close to 1 Cor 1:4-9, where he thanks God for God's work in "establishing" the Corinthians. In the present context, his emphasis has shifted to God's work through him as apostle. His

247. See also LXX Pss 40:13 (41:12); 118(119):28.

248. Thus their members are members of Christ (1 Cor 6:15). They are "of Christ" and exist under his saving lordship (1 Cor 15:23). They have been betrothed to Christ (2 Cor 11:2).

249. They have been called into fellowship with Christ (1 Cor 1:9). Thus Christ is not to be "divided" by disputes within the church (1 Cor 1:12; cf. 12:12). Their new identity is found in Christ (2 Cor 6:15). Indeed, the decisive test as to whether they share in salvation is whether Christ indwells them or not (2 Cor 13:5).

250. In 1 Corinthians 1:4-9 Paul speaks of the "testimony" of Christ having been established among them as they wait for the revelation of Christ (1:7). God shall "establish" them until the end, so that they are blameless in Christ's "day" (1:8). "Establishing" is given in relation to the Lord and his coming.

251. The reference to being confirmed points back to the assurance that Paul has regarding the Corinthians (2 Cor 1:7). As in the earlier passage, the salvation of Paul and that of the Corinthians is inescapably linked.

affirmation here obviously anticipates his presentation of the mission of the "new covenant," which is "of the Spirit" (3:1-18).

Again in this verse, then, Paul returns to a fundamental theme of the letter, the bond between the church and the apostle worked by the Gospel, a bond that remains fundamental to their reception and continuing grasp of the Gospel and the communicative relation with God that constitutes salvation. The distinction between "us" and "you" in this context indicates that the "we" language in these verses refers to the apostle. Yet Paul does not speak of God's work in him without in the same breath speaking of God's work in the Corinthians. God "establishes" Paul by "establishing" him *with* the Corinthians. On the one hand, the salvation of the apostle cannot be separated from God's work through him in the salvation of the Corinthians. On the other hand, the Corinthians' doubts about the apostle only place their own salvation in jeopardy. Paul already has reminded them that they share in salvation as they share with him in sufferings (1:7). He is their boast in the day of Christ, just as they are his (1:14).

With the metaphor of "anointing," Paul signals that he has been commissioned by God for apostolic service. He quite likely echoes the anointing of priests and prophets in Scripture.[252] Before all else, however, the "anointing" of the apostle identifies him and his mission with Christ, "the Anointed One" *(Christos)*. As we have seen, Paul bears the message of Jesus not only in his words but in his person. The giving of the Spirit is depicted in metaphors of fluidity in Scripture, so that it is likely that "anointing" here indirectly speaks of the gift of the Spirit, as it does in biblical tradition.[253]

22 A "seal" is a visible mark that signifies that a person or object is under the authority and protection of another. Among its other functions "sealing" may signify the confirmation or approval of a person or the completion of an action, as for example in Romans 4:11, where Paul describes Abraham's circumcision as a "seal" of his uncircumcised faith. Later in Romans he characterizes his delivery of the contribution for the saints in Jerusalem in the same way: it is a completion and "sealing" of the "fruit" of the Gentiles and their gift (Rom 15:28). Already in 1 Cor 9:2 Paul questions the Corinthians rhetorically, "Are you not the seal of my apostleship in the Lord?" They are the visible mark of authentication, the confirmation of Paul's apostolic calling. Paul makes the same point in the present context. This "sealing" corresponds, moreover, to God's "establishing" Paul and the Corinthians for Christ. It makes good sense, then, to understand Paul's speaking of God's "sealing" him as referring to God's confirmation of him as apostle.

Here Paul associates the "sealing" with the "guarantee," "deposit," or "down payment" *(arrabōn)* of the Spirit in his heart (v. 22b).[254] All three ele-

252. E.g., Exod 29:7; 1 Sam 16:13; Isa 61:1-3.

253. E.g., 1 Sam 16:13; Luke 4:18; Acts 10:38.

254. The term ἀρραβών is a Semitic loanword, the rather broad usage of which generally

ments of Paul's confession have pointed forward to this final one, especially the immediately preceding reference to "sealing."[255] As is clear from his description of the gift of the Spirit as a "deposit," this final statement is distinctly eschatological in orientation. This is also clear in 2 Cor 5, where Paul describes the very purpose and end of God's work in him as "that which is mortal" being "swallowed up by life" (5:4). There again he speaks of the Spirit as the *arrabōn,* the "guarantee," "deposit," or "down payment" of this hope (5:5). This "deposit" constitutes the present possession of that which is to come; the gift of the Spirit is nothing other than the new creation as it is present within the fallen world.[256] The utter confidence with which Paul speaks in vv. 15-22 is the work of the Spirit of faith (4:13), the in-breaking of the eschaton into this fallen world. At the same time, by speaking of the Spirit as a down payment, Paul expresses an eschatological reserve. Over against the excesses of the Corinthians, which are all too apparent in First Corinthians, Paul binds the work and presence of the Spirit to the apostolic mission. He thus introduces here the central theme of 2 Cor 3, the apostolic mission and message as the communication of the Spirit, who rewrites and remakes the human heart.

Recalling his expression of confidence as apostle at the beginning of this section (v. 15), Paul stresses that the gift of the Spirit has been given "within our hearts." The confession again speaks of God's saving work taking place *sub contrario:* God hides salvation under contrary appearance.[257] Paul's call to the Corinthians to accept his apostolic ministry of comfort through suffering has intimated this paradox already (1:3-7, 8-11). He will shortly make clear that his "commendation" as apostle rests finally in the work of the Spirit in the hearts of the Corinthians, not in the outward and superficial evidence they seek (3:3). The apostolic ministry of the Spirit and life comes with a glory that far transcends Moses' ministry of death (3:8). Indeed, it calls forth an apostolic openness that stands in contrast with Moses' veiling his face (3:12-18). Nevertheless, while Moses' glory was outward and visible, the glory of the new

---

signifies a first installment or deposit that secures a claim to a subsequent completion of a contract or claim. See BDAG, "ἀρραβών," 134.

255. See Eph 1:13-14, where "sealing" takes place by the Spirit, who is the guarantee (ἀρραβών) of "our" inheritance.

256. *Pace* F. W. Horn, *Das Angeld des Geistes: Studien zur paulinischen Pneumatologie* (FRLANT 154; Göttingen: Vandenhoeck & Ruprecht, 1992), 393-94, the Spirit is the gift of the eschaton, albeit in the form that it is given within the present world. Furthermore, both here and in 5:5, Paul, in the first instance, affirms his hope as apostle. Baptism does not come directly into view.

257. This paradoxical juxtaposition appears prominently at the opening of 1 Corinthians. The word of the cross is foolishness to those who are perishing. In working salvation, God destroys human wisdom and understanding (1 Cor 1:18-19). God must reveal his gifts to us, otherwise they remain mere foolishness to us (1 Cor 2:6-15).

covenant found in the Gospel remains hidden to those who are perishing (4:1-6). It is "seen," not outwardly, but in the heart. It is "seen" by being spoken and heard (4:6, 13-15). Paul thus warns the Corinthians against those who boast in personal presence and not "in heart" (5:12). Indeed, he charges them with looking at matters according to outward appearance (10:7).

In speaking of the Spirit as down payment, Paul makes explicit the means by which God distributes Christ's saving comfort. It comes through the new life of the Spirit given within Paul's heart. The Spirit who creates faith within the heart of the apostle does so as well in those who hear his apostolic message (4:13). The marks of an apostle are thus *God's work,* which is not subject to human judgments.

c. Paul's Failure to Visit and His Love for the Corinthians (1:23–2:4)

23*But I call God to witness against me — it was to spare you that I*
refrained from coming again to Corinth. 24*Not that we lord it over your*
faith, but we work with you for your joy, for you stand firm in your faith.
21*For I made up my mind not to make another painful visit to you.* 2*For if*
I cause you pain, who is there to make me glad but the one whom I have
pained? 3*And I wrote as I did, so that when I came I might not suffer pain*
from those who should have made me rejoice, for I felt sure of all of you,
that my joy would be the joy of you all. 4*For I wrote to you out of much*
affliction and anguish of heart and with many tears, not to cause you pain
but to let you know the abundant love that I have for you.

Only after his theological explication of God's work through him does Paul defend his failure to complete his promised visit to Corinth. God's work does not exclude, but includes, the heart and life of the apostle. Paul now unfolds this human element of his relationship with the Corinthians, which provides the frame for his theological exposition in the body of the letter. Both his failure to visit them and the letter that he sent in place of that visit have come between him and the church. Both are in view here. When Paul returns to speak of his relations with the Corinthians again in 7:5-16, the letter he had sent them stands at the center of his attention. In both instances, his intense love and concern for the Corinthians provide the thematic center of the narrative. Paul's personal relationship with the church is not a secondary matter but springs from the Gospel itself (1:14). As the apostle of Christ, he participates in Christ's love for the Corinthians (5:14).

His framing of the body of the letter around his relationship with the Corinthians makes it clear that this bond between apostle and church constitutes the drama of the letter. The apostolic claimants who have made their way to the church come into view only insofar as they have endangered that bond and thereby have jeopardized the relationship between the Corinthians and Christ. Already within this brief section, we find an indication that it is not an open theological error that Paul attacks in this letter but the *practical judgments* of the Corinthians concerning the legitimation of an apostle.[258] Paul's decision not to visit Corinth followed a confrontation in which a leader within the church challenged his apostolic authority — an anticipation of the troubles that now have arrived in Corinth. This figure apparently enjoyed the backing of the church, which took no immediate action against him. Yet Paul makes no mention whatsoever of a doctrinal controversy at stake in the confrontation. The problem apparently did not lie in openly false teaching but in the response of the Corinthians to the challenge to Paul's apostolic authority. To be sure, the Gospel itself was at stake in this practical judgment, just as it was in Antioch in the question of table fellowship with the Gentiles, and in Galatia and elsewhere with respect to Judaizing. But in none of these instances did anyone imagine that they were changing the Gospel or offering a different gospel, at least not at the outset. Paul had to make clear to them that they were doing so. Likewise, his later charge in this letter that the Corinthians happily accept "another Jesus, another s/Spirit and another g/Gospel" is not a description of events as the Corinthians perceived them (11:4). It is a diagnosis of a spiritual condition of which they were unaware.

23 Paul's own person suddenly comes fully into view in his emphatic, "I call upon God as witness on my life *[psychē]*."[259] While this oath introduces Paul's explanation for his failure to complete his promised visit to Corinth, it need not indicate that he is directly responding to charges against him. Rather, he is allaying suspicions and affirming his love for the Corinthians, despite the contrary appearance. As we have observed, Paul's oath here is not unique. Elsewhere he declares his love for churches with a similar appeal to God as his witness, when he is distant from them and for one reason or another has been unable to visit them.[260]

It was "to spare" the Corinthians that Paul did not come to Corinth.[261]

258. See the excursus "Paul's Opponents in Corinth and the Purpose of the Letter," pp. 100-110.

259. Against the ESV and NRSV, Paul calls upon God, not as a (potential) witness against himself, but as one who will confirm that (ὅτι) which he says. On the usage, see LXX Num 35:30; LXX Deut 19:15; 1 Macc 2:37; 2 Cor 13:1. Rightly (in part) the NIV: "I call God as my witness."

260. See Rom 1:9-10; Phil 1:8, and also 1 Thess 2:5, 10, where he recalls his conduct while he was with the Thessalonian church.

261. More precisely, in order to spare the Corinthians, Paul "no longer" (οὐκέτι) came to Corinth. Not surprisingly, the unexpected temporal statement has called forth scribal "corrections," esp. in the Western text. Most likely Paul presupposes the unexpected, intervening visit to Corinth of which he speaks in 2:1. After that grievous encounter, in which some leading

This note of severity, which Paul "corrects" in his following statement, is an expression of his apostolic authority. He assumes a parental role in his relationship with the Corinthian church, a role that also comes to expression in First Corinthians.[262] In the conclusion of Second Corinthians, he threatens that "if" he comes to them again (and finds them disobedient), he will not spare them (13:2).[263] His delay in taking this tone is an expression of the nature of apostolic authority, according to which he is a servant of the church, not its lord (v. 24). The delay in severity in the letter follows the pattern of his delayed visit.

24 The authority of the apostle ends where the faith of the Corinthians begins. He does not speak here of a mere "believing" without content. Paul knows of no absolute faith, only faith as it is determined by Jesus Christ and God's work in him, and which thus has definite form and content. Over this faith, the apostle is no lord but merely a "co-worker." As in the thanksgiving and again in 1:12-14, Paul shifts his self-reference to the plural: "We do not lord over your faith but are co-workers of your joy." Perhaps we can detect here a subtle charge against Paul's opponents in Corinth, whom Paul later charges with abusing the Corinthians (11:19-21). Or perhaps Paul quietly warns the Corinthians against a false dependency on the human leaders whom they themselves would choose. It is not Paul's person but the calling as apostle that is at stake in his contention with the Corinthians. Paul's thought here comes very close to his correction of the Corinthian overestimation of Christian leaders in 1 Cor 3:1-15, where he likewise speaks of himself and Apollos as God's co-workers. The division of labor in that relationship remains uneven: they plant and water, but God causes the growth. They have their earthly tasks, but the creation, preservation, and extension of life is God's work. Paul will likewise speak of himself as working together with God in this letter (6:1). Here his focus differs: God is not lost from sight, but Paul now describes himself as a co-worker with the Corinthians, or more precisely, "a co-worker of their joy." The unusual genitive "of your joy" expresses "with whom" the apostle works, as do genitives elsewhere with such compound terms.[264] But it is not a person that appears here. Paul does not speak of the Corinthians directly, as they are in themselves, but indirectly, as they are in their experience in Jesus Christ. He does so because at this moment they cannot rightly see who they are, or how he labors for them. His self-description implicitly announces the reason he has failed to visit them and anticipates his response to their reception of his letter (7:8-13a).

---

figure within the church resisted Paul's authority (2:5-11), Paul "no longer" held to his plan of visiting the church on his way to Macedonia (1:15).

262. 1 Cor 3:1-4; 4:14-21.

263. See also 11:1-4, where he takes the role of a parent who betroths a daughter to a husband, and 12:14-18, where as a "parent" Paul is ready to "spend" himself for his children.

264. See Rom 16:3, 9, 21; 1 Cor 3:9; Phil 2:25; 1 Thess 3:2; Phlm 1, 24.

The apostle is a co-worker of *the joy* of the Corinthians. For this reason he has sought to avoid bringing them sorrow (2:1-4), and he later expresses his joy that he grieved them only "unto repentance," which brings salvation and no regrets (7:10). His bringing them sorrow had their joy as its sole aim. Indeed, it is his calling to bring them comfort in the midst of affliction (1:3-7). The joy of the Corinthians is interwoven with the joy of the apostle (2:3), just as their salvation is intertwined with his (1:12-14). Accordingly, Paul later expresses his joy at their reconciliation to him through Titus (7:4, 7, 13).

By faith, the Corinthians "stand." This metaphor appears elsewhere as an expression of the certain possession of salvation,[265] or as a call to remain in the salvation already received.[266] It is obviously related to Paul's confidence that God will "establish" the Corinthians with him for Christ (v. 21). To fail to "stand" is to "fall."[267] The imagery implies legal contention or battle in which testing and trial take place. To "stand" is to prevail; to "fall" is to suffer condemnation, defeat, and even death.[268] Paul's affirmation to the Corinthians that they "stand" by faith is a reminder that they remain in a contention and battle on this earth. It remains a question as to whether they will stand before the Lord.[269] Unless they stand by faith — and not by their own gifts or powers — they will not stand at all.[270]

2:1 Paul's decision not to travel to Corinth on the way to Macedonia was prompted by an intervening visit. Even before that visit, at the writing of First Corinthians, considerable confusion and problems in the church are already evident. When writing that letter, Paul hoped to send Timothy to them to help resolve the situation (1 Cor 4:17; 16:10). If Timothy in fact completed that trip (and Paul's co-workers had considerable freedom), it apparently failed. Paul himself subsequently traveled to Corinth with rather unhappy results: he came to them "in grief." As Paul's following statement in v. 2 makes clear, this meant grief for the Corinthians, as well as for Paul.

After having made and announced his plans to visit the church, Paul decided to cancel the first leg of his travel to Corinth. Intervening news of problems in the church might well have prompted this decision, although Paul makes no report of it. Paul's later description of the situation he found on his "emergency" visit to Corinth reflects much the same situation that is apparent in First Corinthians: strife, disorder, and immorality (12:20-21). He

265. Rom 5:2; 11:20; 14:4; 1 Cor 10:12; 15:1; Eph 6:11, 13-14; Col 4:12.

266. 1 Cor 10:12; 16:13; Gal 5:1; Phil 1:27; 4:1.

267. Rom 11:11, 22; 14:4; 1 Cor 10:12.

268. Paul likely draws on biblical language, e.g., Pss 20:7-8; 91:7-8; 1 Sam 1:19. The imagery appears relatively frequently in the Qumran literature: e.g., 1QM XIV, 4; 11QMelch II, 9; 1QH XV, 29-31; 1QH XVIII, 6, 11; 1QH XX, 28, 30.

269. Cf. Rom 11:20; 14:4, 10; 1 Cor 10:12; 15:1; Gal 5:1; Pss. 1:5; 76:7; 130:3.

270. The language of Isa 7:9 differs slightly, but the issue is the same.

fears that he will find the same on his pending, third visit. The challenge of the apostolic claimants obviously remains a crucial concern to him in this letter. But his reference to the moral failures of the church makes it clear that a larger drama is playing itself out.

2 This larger drama, as we have seen, is the relationship between the church and its apostle. Paul does not want to grieve them, because they are the very ones who bring him joy.[271] To grieve them is to grieve himself. He is bound to the church in weal and in woe.

3 In place of his visit, Paul wrote a letter to the Corinthians. In now referring to this letter, the apostle underscores the bond between him and the church: it is not only the Corinthians who were spared grief, but the apostle himself: "I wrote this very thing" (namely, that he had decided not to come to Corinth),[272] "lest coming,[273] I should have grief from those [over whom] I should[274] have rejoiced."[275] In apostolic boldness and charming rhetoric, he then expresses his confidence that "my joy is the joy of *all* of you." Paul's repetition is emphatic. As we have noted, the Gospel binds, not

271. It is clear that Paul here describes emotional distress and not physical pain. It is therefore preferable to render λυπεῖν and λύπη as "to grieve" and "grief," rather than as "pain" (ESV, NRSV; the NIV alternates). All three versions render the terms as "grief" and "sorrow" in 7:8-13. It is unfortunate that they did not maintain continuity in usage between the two passages, which obviously correspond to one another.

272. Against the ESV, NIV, and NRSV ("I wrote as I did"), the verb ἔγραψα takes τοῦτο αὐτό as its object, the antecedent of which is surely his opening statment in v. 1, that he had determined not to visit Corinth again in grief.

273. Although ἵνα μή commonly introduces a statement of a negative purpose or fear, the English versions (ESV, NIV, NRSV) interpret the negation μὴ in relation to the verb σχῶ, not in relation to the entire construction (ἵνα μὴ ἐλθὼν λύπην σχῶ). This is odd, not only in that one would have expected μὴ to be postponed if Paul intended this sense (μὴ σχῶ), but also because Paul has just referred to his decision *not* to come to Corinth. It is rather strange to think that he would jump immediately to speak about a plan to visit them that he has not announced up to this point in the letter. The matter at hand is his failure to visit, not what he might yet do. In all probability, he did not reach the decision to visit them again until he had received news of their reception of Titus, which he has not yet recounted (7:5-7). As is clear from the immediate context, Paul is here taking up the statement of his decision not to visit Corinth in v. 1, explaining it further in the light of his expression of love for the Corinthians in v. 2, which he interjects as an explanation of his decision. V. 3a implicitly recalls the decision of v. 1: "I determined not to come," which Paul then elaborates in terms of his legitimate fear, "lest coming, I should have grief from those (about whom) I should have rejoiced."

274. The imperfect form ἔδει expresses an unreal condition: Paul did not come and have grief from those over whom *it would have been necessary* for him to rejoice.

275. Against the ESV, NIV, and NRSV, χαίρειν does not bear a causative sense ("those who should have made me rejoice"), as is reinforced by Paul's use of the alternative causative verb εὐφραίνω in v. 2. Had Paul come to Corinth, it would have been necessary for him to rejoice over those who provided him with grief, a situation he found impossible.

only the apostle with heart and life to the Corinthians, but the Corinthians to the apostle. In his love for them, their grief is his grief and their joy is his joy. Paul likewise trusts (*pepoithōs;* cf. 1:15, 3:4) that his joy is theirs. This confidence does not rest in the inconstant Corinthians; it rests, rather, in God's work through the Gospel in their hearts, to which Paul here calls them back.

4 Not merely Paul's failure to visit the Corinthians has damaged their relationship. It is also the letter that he sent in the place of that visit. His declaration here that he did *not* write to them in order to grieve them is already an indication that his letter had precisely this effect. When he later returns to speak of the letter, he acknowledges that his letter did in fact bring them grief (7:8-13a). But he remains glad about it, since the letter grieved the Corinthians "for repentance" (7:9).

Paul does not *state* that the Corinthians had grieved him, although they obviously had done so. This would have been a mere retaliatory response, which would have added further injury to their relationship. He does, however, describe the sorrow with which he wrote to them: "out of great affliction and anguish of heart . . . through many tears." He presents his sorrow in the language of trial and suffering. Alongside his trial in Asia (1:8) he must face his trial with the Corinthians, which fills out the content of the letter. After a few more lines of the letter, Paul will go on to speak of how his concern for them paralyzed him in Troas (2:12-13). He returns to his description of this burden in his recounting of Titus's report to him about the Corinthians (7:5-16). He suffers under his daily concern for all his churches (11:28-29), and at this moment, especially for them.

Above all else, he wants them to know of the "exceeding love" that he has for them. Paul wants the Corinthians to know that, before all else, his "tough love" for them is genuine love. Twice more, at crucial points in his appeals to them, he addresses them as his "beloved ones" (7:1; 12:19). The anguish — or better, "constraint" *(synochē)* — of heart with which he formerly wrote to them is a reflection of the love of Christ that constrains *(synechei)* him as apostle (5:14). He protests to them, in fact, that he has carried out his apostolic ministry among them with "love without pretense" (6:6) and later asserts that, despite appearances, God knows that Paul loves them (11:11). He is ready to love them the more, even if they love him less (12:15). Just as God's Yes is hidden in Christ, Paul's love for the Corinthian church is hidden in the trials of their stormy relationship.

d. Forgiveness for the Offender (2:5-11)

5*Now if anyone has caused pain, he has caused it not to me, but in some measure — not to put it too severely — to all of you.* 6*For such a one, this* *punishment by the majority is enough, [7]so you should rather turn to forgive and comfort him, or he may be overwhelmed by excessive sorrow. [8]So I beg you to reaffirm your love for him. [9]For this is why I wrote, that I might test you and know whether you are obedient in everything. [10]Anyone whom you forgive, I also forgive. Indeed, what I have forgiven, if I have forgiven anything, has been for your sake in the presence of Christ, [11]so that we would not be outwitted by Satan; for we are not ignorant of his designs.*

Apparently on Paul's second, sorrowful visit to Corinth (v. 1), a leader within the Corinthian church had resisted his authority as apostle. The church itself failed to take any action initially, thus implicitly providing this person support. It is hardly surprising that this incident should have taken place. Already when Paul wrote First Corinthians, the church was divided into factions, most of which aligned themselves against the apostle (1 Cor 1:10-17). His apostolic authority had been contested for a long time, even before the other apostolic claimants arrived (1 Cor 9:1-18). Indeed, the outsiders most likely would not have been so well received had it not been for the problems that made the church ripe for further trouble.

Although nearly all ancient commentators, and some modern ones, identify the offender here as the immoral person of 1 Cor 5:1-6, it is unlikely that the same person or incident is in view. Paul would not have expressed any reservation about the grief that the offender caused the church ("I do not wish to overbear"), had the immoral conduct of this person been the cause of the conflict.[276] It is clear from Paul's careful language that someone had affronted him, questioning and resisting his apostolic authority. When he returns to speak of his relationship with the Corinthians later in the letter, he frames the matter in personal terms, albeit indirectly (7:12).

Nevertheless, it is likely that the conduct of a number of persons within the Corinthian church lay in the background to the conflict. In the closing of the letter, Paul expresses his fear that, on his upcoming third visit, God will again humble him as on the previous visit, and he will mourn those who previously sinned and had not repented of their "impurity, immorality, and licentiousness" (12:21; cf. 13:2). As we have noted, the church earlier had taken pride in its tolerance of an immoral relationship in which one of its members was engaged (1 Cor 5:2, 6). While it is improbable that this person was the one who openly resisted Paul's authority, it is quite likely that this situation — and others like it, unhappily frequent, but perhaps somewhat less outrageous — provided the background to the confrontation that took place during Paul's second visit to Corinth. Tolerance of immorality was a manifestation of one

276. Other problems in Corinth might well have led to a confrontation with the apostle, such as the question of the exercise of tongues and prophecy in 1 Cor 14:37-39.

way in which the Gospel was being distorted there.[277] The various distortions of the Gospel had their representatives.[278] The figure who resisted Paul was one of them.

Out of this situation Paul wrote his "tearful letter" to the Corinthian church. Whatever other issues were at stake (and it was likely that immorality was one of them), the confrontation in Corinth finally had to do with the authority of the apostle. This was the fundamental issue, and the one that remains in contention throughout the present letter. Although the Corinthians *now* have affirmed the authority of the apostle and rebuked the one who insulted him, they did not respond in this way when the confrontation took place. Their present response to the situation is an overresponse, which Paul must now correct.

5 Paul immediately deflects the matter from himself: "If someone has caused grief, he has not grieved me." Although the offense clearly had to do with Paul, he removes his person entirely from the incident. The grief has been inflicted instead on the entire congregation: "but, rather, all of you." Someone in the church had done damage to the relationship between the apostle and the church. Damage therefore had been inflicted on the whole church.

Paul's reserve — the church has been grieved only "in a certain respect" *(apo merous)*[279] — reinforces the distinction between his calling as apostle and his person. He correspondingly expresses his wish "that I might not overbear." He does not want to overstep his authority as apostle by suggesting that a *personal* injury to him is an injury to the whole church.[280]

6 Paul in v. 5 apparently repeated a judgment that he had already rendered on the matter, through the "tearful letter" and Titus who bore it. In this verse it becomes clear that the Corinthian church has accepted this judgment and responded accordingly. The offending person has received a "rebuke from the many," which most likely included exclusion from the church and the life of its members (cf. 1 Cor 5:11-13). This rebuke already is sufficient.

7 Much as Paul himself does with the Corinthians later in this letter (7:5-16), Paul urges them "to forgive and to comfort" the offender. Their rebuke is to be merely the way to forgiveness and comfort for him. The Corinthian handling of the matter is like that of a drunken person, who lurches side-to-side as they go. If before they responded to the insult with unwar-

277. 1 Cor 15:30-34.

278. As is evident, e.g., in Paul's comment in 11:4.

279. Here the phrase ἀπὸ μέρους clearly means "in a respect" (as in Rom 15:15), since it is the *whole* church that has been grieved.

280. See 1 Thess 2:9 and 2 Thess 3:8, where Paul describes the reason for his self-supporting labor among the Thessalonians using the same verb (ἐπιβαρεῖν): he did not wish to "weigh upon" anyone in the church financially. This idea corresponds with his aim with them of not making use of his "weight" or authority as apostle (1 Thess 2:6; 2 Thess 3:9).

ranted leniency,[281] now they are in danger of an unwarranted severity. There is a danger that the rebuked offender might be "swallowed up" *(katapinō)*, consumed by grief. The grief that has been brought upon him is not to be final and ultimate, like the "grief of the world" that brings death (7:10). As Alan Jones, former dean of Grace Cathedral has observed, we live in a time in which *everything* is permitted and *nothing* is forgiven.[282] This is the way of the world, the way of the flesh, the way of Satan himself. This is the way that the Corinthians had been responding to the matter. There must be discipline in the life of the church. Yet that discipline must always be aimed at restoration and comfort. The Corinthians must be to the offender what Christ and Christ's apostle have been to them. The grief that Paul has caused them is meant only for their joy.

8 Paul thus exhorts the church, "Affirm [your] love toward him." He does not suppose that the love of the Corinthians for the offender was to cease at the point of their rebuke. It was merely hidden within the discipline they had to exercise. They are therefore now merely to "affirm" or "confirm" *(kyroō)* their love, to show it openly, as God has done for us in Christ. Nothing is more important for any human being than to know that he or she is unconditionally loved by another, and finally by God himself. It is this love that the Corinthians are to affirm to the former offender.

While it is clear that Paul is asking the Corinthians to affirm *their* love, he does not word the exhortation in that way. The Corinthians are simply to affirm *love* for the former offender *(kyrōsai eis auton agapē)*. The apostle does not have in view mere human affections, transient and fickle as they are. Love is a gift from God, indeed, *the* ultimate gift from God given in and through Jesus Christ, the new reality that is present within the church (1 Cor 13:1-13; 16:14). The love that is present with the church is nothing other than the love of God, no matter that it is also living and active in each member. For the Corinthians to affirm love to the one who offended is to affirm *God's* love for him in which they themselves share. Only in that unconditional way can he truly receive *comfort*.

9 Paul here indicates that he wrote to the Corinthians in order to test their genuineness, to see if they are "obedient in all things." This demand for unconditional obedience transcends the limits of any legitimate call for loyalty to Paul. He is no fanatic, seeking to establish a sect around his person. It is his calling as apostle that is at stake. It is not, of course, merely a cold command that the Corinthians follow his orders. His purpose, as he has just claimed in v. 4, is not to grieve the Corinthians but to make them know the love he has for

281. They responded similarly to the case of immorality in the church, 1 Cor 5:1-13.

282. Cited by G. O. Forde, *On Being a Theologian of the Cross: Reflections on Luther's Heidelberg Disputation, 1518* (Grand Rapids: Eerdmans, 1997), x.

them. Paul offers yet another perspective in 7:12. In the larger purpose of God, the purpose of his previous letter was to make the Corinthians aware of their own zeal for the apostle. Their allegiance is to be a spontaneous outworking of the Gospel that the apostle bears.

In the closing of the letter, Paul speaks as if the Corinthians have not yet fully recognized his authority. He is ready to punish all disobedience among them, "as soon as [their] obedience has been made complete" (10:6). The two assessments of the situation need not be played off against one another. On the one hand, the hard-won reconciliation between the Corinthians and the apostle, mediated by Titus, was undoubtedly fragile. The long history of their stormy relationship could not be erased by a recent moment of repentance and a declaration of love. The unbounded joy and confidence that Paul declares in 7:5-16 is in some measure rhetorical. His effusive praise communicates his unreserved love for the Corinthians and his welcome of their action. It is intended to encourage them to abiding fidelity, even if it is also rooted in his confidence in the power of the Gospel. Paul's reserve in 10:6 should likewise be taken with a grain of salt. His severity is to some extent based on the hope and expectation that the Corinthians will prove obedient.

10 While in v. 9 Paul asserts his authority, he here underscores the paradoxical freedom of the Corinthians and the implicit limits of that authority (cf. 1:24). Whomever they forgive, Paul has forgiven as well, on account of their being in the presence of Christ. The apostle and his church are so bound together in Christ that their action is his action. Indeed, he is present with them. In their faith, they do not stand under the apostle but together with him (1:24).

Again Paul excludes any personal judgment of his own about the matter, by interjecting: "If I have something to forgive." It is obedience to the Gospel that is at stake. The church itself bears the authority of the apostle to pronounce forgiveness in such matters, which include the rejection of any apostolic teaching and instruction and all immoral behavior (1 Cor 5:1-13). This forgiveness can be given and received only where guilt has been recognized. By deflecting attention from any personal injury he might have suffered, Paul calls the Corinthian church to recognize the grief that disobedience to the Gospel has inflicted on the church, and thus to forgive the one who had offended. Earlier they had failed to discipline an immoral church member (1 Cor 5:1-13). Now they are in danger of exercising a vengeance that is no longer restorative.

The word that Paul uses here for "forgiveness" *(charizomai)* is significant. In place of the more frequent term *aphiēmi*, which communicates forgiveness through the metaphor of release, *charizomai* normally signifies "giving," the free giving of gifts.[283] Paul implicitly describes "for-give-ness" as an act of giving. The Corinthians are to "give" forgiveness to the offender, as Paul has

283. See, e.g., Rom 8:32; 1 Cor 2:12; Phil 1:29; Phlm 22; cf. Eph 4:32; Col 2:13.

done on their account as well. His language here anticipates his profound treatment of giving in 8:1–9:15.

11 The contention over the legitimation of the apostle is no mere human drama. Where the Gospel is at stake, greater and hidden powers battle one another. While the Corinthians might have regarded the situation as a mere human affair to be decided by their own judgments, Paul warns them that they stand in jeopardy of being mere pawns of Satan, subject to his tricks. As he does elsewhere, Paul refers to the hidden, angelic agent of evil with the loanword from the Aramaic (or Hebrew), "(the) Satan," i.e., "(the) Adversary." As the adversary of God and God's saving purpose, Satan is their adversary as well. This *personal* power of evil is real for the apostle, active in thwarting his plans,[284] in misleading both the world and his churches,[285] in inflicting sickness and injury[286] — and yet not finally to be feared. He has been defeated.[287] As Paul's later attack on the false apostles makes clear, the real opponent of the apostle in the church makes his appearance here (11:12-15).

Paul makes the clever Corinthians aware that there is another one who is yet cleverer than they are, to whose power they are subject apart from the Gospel. If they do not grant forgiveness but continue to treat the offender harshly, in a false party spirit on Paul's behalf, they will do nothing but further Satan's purposes.[288] Together with the apostle, the Corinthians know — or should know — Satan's schemes *(noēmata).* He wishes to rob them of the gift of forgiveness and thereby to further factions in the church. The Gospel has removed them from the power of the "rulers of this age," who have not understood the wisdom of God and thus crucified the "Lord of glory" (1 Cor 2:8). Now the Corinthians know the Gospel — unless perhaps "the god of this age" has "blinded their minds" (2 Cor 4:4).

e. Paul's Concern for the Corinthians (2:12-13)

> [12]*When I came to Troas to preach the gospel of Christ, even though a door was opened for me in the Lord,* [13]*my spirit was not at rest because I did not find my brother Titus there. So I took leave of them and went on to Macedonia.*

Paul now returns to the narrative of his activities. Having decided not to visit the Corinthians, he is making his way to Macedonia. He is not merely traveling

284. 1 Thess 2:18.
285. 2 Thess 2:9; 2 Cor 11:11.
286. 1 Cor 5:5; 2 Cor 12:7.
287. Rom 16:20.
288. Cf. 1 Cor 1:13.

but is engaged in apostolic ministry on his way. The Corinthians most likely were aware from their contact with Titus that Paul was to meet him in Troas. They are also aware that the two finally met, otherwise Paul would not have written to them again. Paul is filling in the details for them.

Although he leaves it unstated, the Corinthians are well aware that Paul's "great affliction and anguish of heart" concerning *them* (v. 4) is the cause of his distress in Troas. By recounting his experience, he effectively reaffirms his deep love for them. Indeed, he breaks off the narrative without reporting the conclusive meeting with Titus that the Corinthians expect. Only in 7:5-16 does he return to the story and recount its happy ending. As a result, the Corinthian readers are kept in a certain narrative suspense with the apostle throughout the body of the letter (3:1–7:16). His teaching on the calling of an apostle is set within the context of his experience as their apostle. Paul's trouble with the Corinthians is the fundamental trouble of the letter. The burden of his concern for all his churches is the greatest burden he bears (11:28-29). The breaking off of the narrative serves to drive home the true nature of apostolic ministry as that of suffering and comfort, especially that of Paul's suffering with the Corinthians.

12 Paul here emphasizes *Christ,* the crucified and risen Lord, as the content of the Gospel, as his following thanksgiving in v. 14 makes clear.[289] His description of the Gospel as "the Gospel of Christ" prepares for his description of his experience as its bearer in the following verses.

Paul came into Troas "for the Gospel of Christ." Against the English versions (ESV, NIV, NRSV), Paul does not say explicitly that he came to Troas for the proclamation of Christ. As he is about to make clear to the Corinthians, he bears the Gospel not merely in his mouth but also in his body and life. And it is of his body and life that he speaks. His opportunity for proclamation was thwarted by his paralyzing concern for the Corinthians, just as the same concern had caused him to cancel his announced visit to them. Nevertheless, just as God manifests the aroma of Christ in every place through the apostle, God did so in Troas as well. When Paul arrived in Troas, there was in fact "a door that had been opened" for him "in the Lord." The figure of speech obviously signifies an opportunity that can be given by God alone, who opens or closes doorways of opportunity according to his own purposes. The key to the door rests with God. It is not opened to those who stand without, except as God wills.[290]

13 The hindrance to ministry in this instance came through the apostle

289. 2 Cor 4:4; 9:13; 10:14. See also Rom 1:9; 15:19; 1 Cor 9:12; Gal 1:7; Phil 1:27; 2 Thess 1:8.

290. Paul uses the same image in 1 Cor 16:9, where it also becomes clear that a divinely given opportunity does not necessarily appear without opposition or trouble. The figure has biblical roots (Job 12:14; Isa 22:22), appears elsewhere in the New Testament (Rev 3:7-8; 4:1; cf. Matt 16:19!), and was likewise taken up in rabbinic literature (see Str-B 3:484-85).

himself. Although there was "an open door" for him in the Lord, he was so taken up with worry over the Corinthians that he was paralyzed, unable to make use of the *God-given* opportunity that lay before him. We should not overlook this admission of weakness. Not only his strategic aims but his ability to respond to the very work of God fail him here. Paul is no hero of faith. His life, his weaknesses, and his failures — which he is not ashamed to confess — all rest in the hand of Another, who displays his strength in the apostle's weakness. Bonhoeffer likewise expresses his faith: "I believe that also our mistakes and errors are not without purpose, and that it is not more difficult for God to deal with them than with our supposed good deeds."[291] So much for the Corinthians' adoration of leaders and their powers! It is no wonder that the apostle did not fit their taste for glory.

Paul "had no rest in his spirit" when he did not find Titus his brother. At the conclusion of his statement, the main verb finally appears: "having come to Troas, a door having been opened, *I had no rest in my spirit.*" As is the case in 1:9, the verb *eschēka* is no mere "aoristic perfect" but undoubtedly expresses the continuing effect of a prior event.[292] Here it is the conflict with the Corinthians that lies in the background. Furthermore, it is not certain that the verb *eschēka* itself expresses past time: it may well function as something like a "historical present," making the narrative vivid and close to the readers: "I have no rest." The decisive marker of past time comes only in the following clause: "I departed for Macedonia." The same verbal structure appears in 7:5, where Paul resumes the story of his concern for the Corinthians. There, too, Paul's use of the perfect *eschēka* does not simply replace an aorist form but adds vividness to the narrative. The juxtaposition of 2:12-13 and 7:5 suggests that this is the case. As we have noted, Paul frames the body of the letter with reference to his troubles with the Corinthians. A vivid use of the perfect to describe his distress at the opening and closing of his theological argument communicates the tension that continues to run through their relationship.

It is important to note, however, that Paul's focus shifts in the transition from 2:13 to 7:5. His trouble here is the relationship with the Corinthians: he has no rest "in [his] spirit." There, as he announces his joy over the reconciliation that took place through Titus, he includes all the trials he bears and develops his statement theologically: when he came into Macedonia, he says, "*we* had no rest in our *flesh.*" The restored relationship with the Corinthians becomes God's comfort to him in all his other troubles that fill out the whole of his earthly existence. He speaks of himself there, moreover, no longer directly in singular form, but as one who receives comfort, among all others.

According to the Lukan report in Acts, Paul already had visited Troas

291. Bonhoeffer, *Widerstand und Ergebung,* 19.

292. See the discussion above at 1:9, pp. 36-37.

— albeit briefly — where he was led by a vision to travel on to Macedonia (Acts 16:8-10). It appears that he left a small church there according to Luke, since during his travel to Jerusalem, he met his traveling companions in Troas (Acts 20:1-12). In v. 13 Paul speaks of his "taking leave *of them*," which indicates the presence of a church in Troas and thus indirectly corroborates the Lukan report. It is worth remembering that, although Paul aims at the proclamation of the Gospel where Christ is not yet named,[293] he does not use the term "evangelize" merely for the initial announcement of the Gospel but for the entire ministry of the Gospel, including the ministry of it to believers.[294] As this present context again makes clear, those who confess Christ must themselves be "evangelized" again and again. Here, however, Paul failed to minister the Gospel, despite his God-given opportunity. Outwardly judged, this visit was a failure. Paul arrived and departed in distress. The life of the apostle does not run in a straight line. It is filled with weakness and failure, and yet it is charged with the triumph of God, who accomplishes his untraceable purposes in Christ. Paul will take up the narrative of God's wondrous and indescribable ways at the conclusion of the letter's body (7:2-16).

f. Paul's Thanksgiving to God (2:14-17)

> [14]*But thanks be to God, who in Christ always leads us in triumphal procession, and through us spreads the fragrance of the knowledge of him everywhere.* [15]*For we are the aroma of Christ to God among those who are being saved and among those who are perishing,* [16]*to one a fragrance from death to death, to the other a fragrance from life to life. Who is sufficient for these things?* [17]*For we are not, like so many, peddlers of God's word, but as men of sincerity, as commissioned by God, in the sight of God we speak in Christ.*

In this transition to the body of the letter, Paul describes his experience as apostle in the radically extrinsic terms that constitute his message to the Corinthians in this letter. Both Paul and the Corinthians understand that Christ is present in power in his apostles. The Corinthians imagine that this power is made inherent to an apostle, so that the power of an apostle manifests the power of Christ. Paul must teach them that the power of Christ remains radically extrinsic: Christ's power is present only in the *weakness* of an apostle.[295] Thus the gift of salvation is not a matter of receiving a private possession, but the gift and grace of a relationship of communication and

293. Rom 15:20-21; 2 Cor 10:15.

294. In addition to this verse, see Rom 1:15 and even Rom 15:20 itself; Gal 1:8-9; 4:13.

295. See 12:9-10.

exchange.[296] Our weakness, in which the crucified Jesus has shared to the ultimate extent, is met by his power. It is not thereby removed from us but is overcome *in him,* the risen Lord. Our salvation remains abidingly outside of us. We are thereby removed from our false hopes and idols and, indeed, from ourselves, so that we live in faith in the true God. This relationship of communication of weakness and power (12:9-10), poverty and wealth (8:9), sin and righteousness (5:21), death and life (4:10-12) necessarily takes the form of hope: it reaches its fulfillment in us only in the resurrection from the dead (4:16–5:5). This is the essence of Paul's message to the Corinthians, which he introduces here in his dramatic portrayal of his apostolic mission as a Roman triumph in which God alone is the triumphant conqueror. His mission does not consist in his doing (and especially not as his performance of deeds of power) but in his "suffering" the work of God in him, by which the power of Christ is manifested and savingly distributed within the world.

This communication of life in death that constitutes the nature of salvation bears profound hermeneutical implications, which are irreducibly material and theological in nature. Second Corinthians is nothing other than an explication of "the word of the cross" that Paul announces in First Corinthians (1 Cor 1:18). Already in 1:12-14 Paul has spoken in hermeneutical terms of the Corinthians' "recognition" of him and his words. In the present passage the rich vocabulary of perception and understanding that characterizes the body of the letter, and especially 2 Cor 3, makes its appearance in the unusual form of the perception of an odor. A whole series of terms and figures will follow: looking, seeing in a mirror, being blinded, beholding, being manifest, illumination, the image of God, light shining out of darkness, keeping in view, knowing, and recognizing.

The missing thanksgiving for God's work among the Corinthians receives its full compensation here. Just as God receives the first word of blessing in the opening of the letter, God here receives the last word of thanksgiving at the close of the opening. In a beautiful interweaving of themes, a contrast thus emerges between the opening blessing and this closing thanksgiving. In the opening blessing Paul describes God as fully and entirely engaged in the comfort of human suffering and need (1:3-7). The thanksgiving and its recounting of benefits would normally be found where Paul has placed his benediction of God. It has been postponed until this point. Rather than speaking of God's work in the Corinthians, it is taken up with the suffering of the apostle and God's victory in him. This unexpected inversion of blessing and thanksgiving reinforces one of the fundamental themes of the Corinthian correspondence: in the face of the Corinthian obsession with power and of their failure to receive their many benefits as God's gifts, Paul insists on their recognition of God the Giver.

296. See 13:4.

The shift in topic from the plans and activities of the apostle to those of God is anticipated already in the opening benediction (1:3-7), in the report of deliverance in Asia (1:8-11), and in Paul's theological explanation of his failure to visit Corinth (1:15-22). This description of the relationship between God and the apostle continues throughout the body of the letter. God's work in the apostle has priority over God's work through the apostle and thereby determines its form. Paul's activity is encompassed by his passivity, not in such a way that it is obviated, but in such a way that his own work is contained within the larger work of God in Christ that he "suffers." Despite his plans and purposes, he does not lead a "purpose-driven" life but a "God-driven" life. His life and his works are not in his own hands but in the hands of Another, who forms it according to the pattern of the crucified and risen Christ. Paul's thanksgiving in 2:14-17 thus introduces the fundamental theme that Paul develops in the following body of the letter (3:1–7:16).

14a In an abrupt transition from his report of distress in Troas, Paul breaks into a thanksgiving to God that must have been utterly unanticipated and jarring to the Corinthians. The thanksgiving itself is of significance. The apostle has blessed God for his work in and with him as an invitation to the Corinthians to join the same thanksgiving (1:3-7). He likewise has invited them to work together on his behalf in prayer, "in order that thanksgiving might be made for us by many persons for the gift given to us through [those] many" (1:11). Again in this verse Paul implicitly invites the Corinthians to give thanks for God's dealings with him. Their thanksgiving will bind them not only to God but, once again, as we have observed, to the apostle whom God sent to them. As we have noted, the theme of God's gift-giving and the "thanks-giving" to God in the reception of the gift is at the core of Paul's message in this letter. In the thanksgiving of the Corinthians for which Paul hopes, God's gifts *are received as free gifts,* not as benefits that belong to them by luck, nature, or worthiness. In thanksgiving, God's giving retains its priority and freedom, unbound and unconditioned. Even in our response, we remain receivers, who in "thanks-giving" receive *the Giver,* who in Christ gives life to the dead.

Paul's thanksgiving is one of faith and hope, contrary to outward appearance and human reason: God *always* leads the apostle to death as a captive in triumph. This is clearly the meaning of the verb *thriambeuō* in this context. The term is drawn from the Roman custom of celebrating the triumph of a general in battle by allowing him to lead the captives before his chariot in an elaborate public procession through the city.[297] The ritual included not only the burning of incense along the way but the sacrificial offering of bulls and

297. See Josephus's description of Titus's *triumph* (celebrated with Domitian and Vespasian) after the conquest of Judea, in *J.W.* 7.115-57.

finally — in tradition and memory, if not always in practice — the execution of the captives, or at least the most prominent among them.[298]

The apostle of Christ is thus led to shame and death, as was his crucified Lord. The shame and open humiliation of the victims of the *triumph* was well known and abhorred in antiquity.[299] For some, suicide was preferable.[300] As we have noted, moreover, the *triumph* did not merely bring humiliation, it traditionally ended in the execution of the most prominent victims, who were prisoners of war.[301] Paul includes this dimension of the triumph in his thanksgiving, as he describes God's work as spreading the "odor of the knowledge of [Christ]" (v. 14) and himself as "the fragrance of Christ" (v. 15) and — for some — "an odor from death, unto death" (v. 16).

Paul's statement was jarring not only for the Corinthians. It also has been so for many, if not most, translators and interpreters. It is unique not only among Paul's thanksgivings, but also among all those in Scripture, which without exception recount God's *benefits*.[302] The causative sense given in the KJV, "which causeth us to triumph," is unattested. The positive translation of the verb, "always leads us in triumph [*or* gives us the triumph] in Christ," which Schlatter adopts, along with other versions and older interpreters, is likewise to be rejected.[303] The verb was not used to describe victorious troops but defeated prisoners who had been brought to Rome to be paraded as the

298. See esp. M. Beard, *The Roman Triumph* (Cambridge, Mass.: Harvard University Press, Belknap Press, 2007), 107-42; also S. J. Hafemann, *Suffering and Ministry in the Spirit* (Grand Rapids: Eerdmans, 1990), 16-34. H. S. Versnel is more interested in showing the origins of the practice. See his *Triumphus: An Inquiry into the Origin, Development, and Meaning of the Roman Triumph* (Leiden: Brill, 1970).

299. See esp. P. Marshall, "A Metaphor of Social Shame: ΘΡΙΑΜΒΕΥΕΙΝ in 2 Cor. 2:14," *NovT* 25 (1983): 302-17; Beard, *The Roman Triumph,* 107-42.

300. See Beard's description of what she calls the "Cleopatran Solution," in *The Roman Triumph,* 114-17.

301. Beard underplays the frequency of the executions. Whether or not her reservations are warranted, others must decide. It is clear, however, that, in the mind of the public, the image of the *triumph* included the execution of the vanquished, as for example in Seneca's portrayal of the complaint of one who was saved from death by a benefactor, only to be reminded of it constantly: "How long will you parade me? How long will you refuse to let me forget my misfortune? In a triumph, I should have had to march but once!" (*On Benefits* 2.11.1, in Seneca, *Moral Essays,* vol. 3 [LCL; trans. John W. Basore]).

302. The juxtaposition of death and life likewise appears in Romans 7:24-25 and in 1 Cor 15:57, which are oriented respectively to the risen Lord and the hope of the resurrection. Here, in contrast, the life and deliverance that Paul's thanksgiving presupposes is hidden in God's work in Christ. Paul is calling his readers to follow the trace of that mysterious and wonderful work.

303. See Schlatter, *Paulus, der Bote Jesu,* 495. See further G. Dautzenberg, "θριαμβεύω," *EDNT* 2:155.

spoils of war. The neutral rendering, "always puts us on display" (HCSB) or "make known,"[304] is also inadequate, since the allusion to the Roman triumph is quite clear in context.[305] Even the rendering of the ESV and NSRV, "who in Christ always leads us in triumphal procession," leaves the verb under-interpreted, as does the similar reading of the NIV. The NIV captures the sense of the verb properly but then misinterprets Paul's language by making Christ into a triumphant general: "But thanks be to God, who always leads us as captives in Christ's triumphal procession." It is God, not Christ, who is the subject and *triumphator.*[306] Like the apostle who follows him, Christ is the prisoner and victim led to slaughter; the risen Christ remains the Crucified One (13:4).

The "word of the cross" thus determines the life of the apostle (1 Cor 1:18). This expression, which Paul introduces at the very beginning of First Corinthians, captures the essence of his message in both letters. As is well known, Luther has taken it up into his description of the "theology of the cross" (or, more properly, the "theologian of the cross"). Luther thereby seeks to correct the abuse of God's power, glory, and majesty, namely, "the invisible things of God" that we turn into idols in our self-love.[307] As is the case with Paul, for Luther the cross of Christ, in which God's power is hidden within suffering and death, serves a saving, hermeneutical function. The cross deconstructs us

304. Dautzenberg, "θριαμβεύω," *EDNT* 2:155.

305. Against Furnish, *II Corinthians,* 175.

306. So, rightly, G. Delling, "θριαμβεύω," *TDNT* 3:159-60. As we shall see, in 2 Corinthians 10 he inverts the imagery, taking the role of a general and making the Corinthians the object of his conquest (2 Cor 10:1-6). The NIV is obviously influenced by Col 2:15, which speaks of God making public display of "the rulers and authorities, leading them as captives in triumph in Christ." But even this text does not support the NIV rendering. Although Christ appears as the "head of all rule and authority" in Col 2:10 (see also 1:16), it is nevertheless *God* who is the subject of the action in Col 2:15, where the focus rests on Christ's cross, to which "the handwritten decree that was against us" was nailed and thus removed. Not in his resurrection, but *in Christ's crucifixion* "the rulers and authorities" are unclothed, shamed, and led captive. Whether we regard them as political powers or spiritual ones or both, they are paradoxically undone by the passivity and death of Christ, in which the apostle shares (Col 1:24).

307. Luther, *LW* 31:52 (Heidelberg Disputation, Thesis 20; see also Theses 19, 21-22 and Thesis 4): "The 'back' and visible things of God are placed in opposition to the invisible, namely, (the visible things of) his human nature, weakness, foolishness. . . . Now it is not sufficient for anyone, and it does him no good to recognize God in his glory and majesty, unless he recognizes him in the humility and shame of the cross. Thus God destroys the wisdom of the wise, as Isa. [45:15] says, 'Truly, thou art a God who hidest thyself.' "

Neither Paul's "word of the cross" nor Luther's "theology of the cross" may rightly be made to serve as a general description of human experience. Both speak of God's concrete, specific, and localized work in Jesus.

and all our pretensions, bringing us to ourselves — and to God's mercy and comfort in Christ.

Neither "the word of the cross" nor Paul's dramatic statement about his being led as a captive in God's triumph is a glorification of suffering. The apostle does not have a martyr complex, as might be said of Ignatius and other, later Christian leaders. Nor can his statements here or elsewhere rightly be turned into a principle concerning the course of human events and prescription for human action. Paul offers no "natural theology of the cross."[308] God so acts with the apostle "in Christ." Paul's phrase critically *localizes* his sufferings. God leads him as a captive in the Crucified One, *who is risen,* in whom the apostle, too, has life. We must not read v. 14a without v. 14b, in which Paul celebrates the manifestation of the knowledge of Christ through his being led as a captive. He preaches "the word of the cross" as *Good News* (1 Cor 1:17-18). Indeed, it is precisely this inconceivable juxtaposition of death and life, evil and good that makes Paul's statement in v. 14 so jarring and so difficult for interpreters: he gives *thanks* to God that God leads him as *a captive in a triumph.* It is impossible to "see through" this paradox, to make it comprehensible to practical reason. One can only hear and believe the Gospel it announces. In this verse Paul is doing what he later describes in the words of the psalmist: "I believed, therefore I spoke" (4:13; Ps 116:10). In *faith* he knows that the One who raised Jesus shall also raise him with the Corinthians (4:14). According to this faith, in leading the apostle as a captive, God *even now* "manifests through [him] the knowledge of Christ in every place" (v. 14b).[309] This knowledge of Christ manifest through the apostle is life, freedom, and glory, as Paul will shortly make clear in 3:1-18. Verse 14 thus expresses the profound paradox that is fundamental to God's saving work in Christ: *in him alone* God turns death into life, and shame into glory.

In effecting salvation, God judges the world, setting aside its wisdom, strength, and honor (1 Cor 1:18-31). There is no salvation without this judgment of Christ's cross, into which Christ's apostle now has been thrust. The life of the Spirit is given only through death, as Paul will make clear to the Corinthians

308. Oswald Bayer has warned that, from Hegel onward, modern theology has been in danger of adopting a "natural theology of the cross," in precisely the sense we have described above. See O. Bayer, *Theology the Lutheran Way* (Lutheran Quarterly Books; ed. and trans. J. G. Silcock and M. C. Mattes; Grand Rapids: Eerdmans, 2007), 193-98; further O. Bayer, *Gott als Autor: Zu einer poietologischen Theologie* (Tübingen: Mohr Siebeck, 1999), 258-59. In contrast, J. Moltmann, *The Crucified God: The Cross of Christ as the Foundation and Criticism of Christian Theology* (trans. R. A. Wilson and J. Bowden; New York: Harper & Row, 1974), 267-338, seems to succumb to this danger in the latter part of his work.

309. The natural antecedent to the pronoun "[knowledge] of him," is Christ, whom Paul names in the preceding phrase ("in Christ"). This identity is confirmed by the following verse, where Paul speaks of being "the aroma of Christ" (v. 15).

shortly (3:6). In Christ's cross the world has been crucified, and so has the apostle (Gal 6:14). The continuity of the Creator's purpose notwithstanding, the old, fallen world must be done away with in order for the new creation to come (5:14-17).

This drama of salvation is being played out before the eyes of the Corinthians in the body and life of the apostle. The sufferings of Christ overflow to him in abundance (1:5). Already in First Corinthians, Paul describes his apostolic experience in such terms:

> For, I think, God has designated us apostles to be last of all, as ones condemned to death; we have become a spectacle [*theatron*] for the world, and angels, and humanity" (1 Cor 4:9).[310]

Apostles are not the revered and esteemed preachers that the Corinthians imagined but men condemned to a shameful death, paraded about in dishonor and subject to all forms of suffering.[311] They are the offscouring and scum of the earth (1 Cor 4:13). In the present letter, Paul goes on to describe his apostolic experience as "always carrying about in the body the dying [*or* deadness] of Jesus" (4:10).[312] The question is whether the Corinthians have understood and grasped the salvation given them in the Gospel and portrayed for them in the apostle, or whether they have unwittingly substituted for it a cheap and false promise of earthly power and pleasure. A substitution of this kind is not so much an "overrealized eschatology" (as it has often been named)[313] as it is a jettisoning of biblical eschatology, according to which there is no Christ without a cross and no kingdom without judgment.[314] Above all else, this substitution is manifest in the Corinthian attraction to the apostolic claimants who have made their way to the congregation. We are known by our heroes.

310. Although this portrayal of apostolic life as a "being led to death in the *theater*" does not quite fit the procession of the Roman *triumph,* it does match the related practices in the provinces. The metonymic usage of θέατρον for the event that takes place in the theater is attested elsewhere. See BDAG, "θέατρον," 446; G. Kittel, "θέατρον," *TDNT* 3:42-44. Obviously, Paul further speaks figuratively of the apostles themselves as the "spectacle." On the *triumph* and the provincial theaters as an alternative for prisoners of lesser stature, see Josephus, *J.W.* 6.417-18.

311. See the list of hardships that follows in 1 Cor 4:10-13.

312. This description of apostolic experience serves as the summary of a list of hardships (4:8-9) and corresponds to the lists of 6:4-10 and 11:23-33, where Paul describes in greater detail the suffering and dishonor to which he was subject as apostle.

313. See A. Thiselton, "Realized Eschatology at Corinth," *NTS* 24 (1978): 510-26.

314. Thus H. Richard Niebuhr's characterization of liberal Christianity: "A God without wrath brought men without sin into a kingdom without judgment through the ministrations of a Christ without a cross" (*The Kingdom of God in America* [New York: Harper & Row, 1959], 193).

In the unhappy drama that is before their eyes, the Corinthians are to "see" the risen Christ, who secures the apostle and his salvation and, with it, theirs as well. Paul already has reported his deliverance from death in Asia, which he presents as an anticipation of the resurrection. Even more, the Corinthians *already know* of God's deliverance of the apostle from his distress over them in Troas, since they have responded positively to Titus, his emissary (2 Cor 7:5-16). At this moment they have been granted a privileged perspective on the drama of apostolic life.

We must not forget that, even as Paul summarizes the whole of his life and ministry here, he refers most immediately to his distress over the Corinthians. As we have noted, the concern for the churches is the greatest burden on the apostle (11:28-29). In describing his experience, Paul has in view, not merely outward sufferings, but inward battles and personal weaknesses, which he "suffers" as an apostle of Christ.

14b Through the captive apostle, God "manifests the odor" of the knowledge of Christ in every place.[315] Paul's confident affirmation is based on the participation in Christ that has been given to all Christians, and especially to him as apostle: both sufferings and comfort overflow to him, as he has made clear from the very beginning of this letter (1:3-7).

The synesthetic metaphor "to manifest [*or* make visible: *phaneroō*] an odor" underscores the contrary appearance of the apostle through which God distributes the saving knowledge of Christ. The crucified and risen Christ cannot be *seen* in the apostle. Only the "scent of Christ" is present in him. By use of this olfactory imagery, Paul makes clear that recognition of God's saving work in the world is not a matter of perceiving events and then forming judgments about them. We are not, and cannot be, neutral observers. Our judgments are already formed in the act of perception itself: the crucified Christ is to us either the fragrance of life or the stench of death, and that immediately, without reflection. The metaphor of "odor," which displaces "sight," thus explains the twofold response to the manifestation of the saving knowledge of Christ in the apostle: faith detects the fragrance of life, unbelief can smell only the stench of death. Paul later will use the figure of "sight" and "blindness" to express this reality. This later metaphor, however, attributes "blindness" to the actions of external powers: Moses and his veil and "the god of this age" (3:13-14; 4:3-4). With his metaphor of "odor" Paul locates the failure to perceive the saving work of God in human beings themselves.

315. Against the ESV and NRSV, which translate ὀσμή both here and in v. 16 as "fragrance," the term is to be rendered "odor" (which in fact is related etymologically to ὀσμή). It bears a neutral sense, signifying a smell that might be either bad or good. Esp. in v. 16, in which the twofold nature of the "odor" comes to expression, the neutral sense is required. The NIV likewise fails here, rendering ὀσμή (and also εὐωδία, v. 15) as "aroma."

The reference to "odor" recalls the Roman *triumph,* which was accompanied by the burning of incense and the offering of sacrifices, and also the biblical context of sacrificial offerings, in which God receives that which had been sacrificed as a burnt offering as a "fragrant aroma."[316] Indeed, in v. 15, Paul will speak of himself as a "fragrance" for *God.* One must be granted the divine perspective in order to perceive savingly what takes place in the apostle.

Paul splits the usual biblical idiom "fragrant odor" (LXX: *osmē euōdias*) into its two distinct terms, "odor" (vv. 14, 16) and "fragrance" (v. 15). This allows him to speak — in a warning to the Corinthians — of the twofold effect of his being paraded in God's *triumph.* Through him God works not only salvation and life but also judgment and death, and does so *in every place.* Paul is aware that what is transpiring in him as apostle has universal significance, small, local, and despised though it may be. The apostles are a spectacle to the world, angels, and all human beings (1 Cor 4:9).

15 It is "in Christ" that God leads Paul as a captive. The phrase expresses the participation of the apostle in Christ that he now unfolds further.[317] The apostle is "the fragrance [*euōdia*] of Christ *for* God." Although most English versions interpret the dative of the biblical idiom as a dative of reference ("the fragrance of Christ *to* God"), it is better understood as a dative of advantage. The antecedent usage is probably best understood as speaking of burnt offerings as a fragrant (or soothing) aroma *for the benefit of the Lord.*[318] Verse 16 makes it clear that Paul has in view the effect of the aroma on human beings. He is a fragrance of Christ *for God* — with respect to some an aroma of death, with respect to others an aroma of life. In other words, it is for God and for God's purposes that the apostle has been made to be the fragrance of Christ.

There is, then, a shift in imagery from v. 14 to v. 15. The context of the Roman *triumph* is not displaced, but it is superseded by Paul's use of the biblical image of an offering by fire, which was "a soothing aroma for the Lord." The traditional outcome of the Roman *triumph* now becomes a sacrifice to God. Just as Paul understands Christ's death on a Roman cross as a divine sacrifice, so his experience of Christ's sufferings is an aroma or odor of Christ for God. In the Corinthian correspondence, reference to the Passover, which traditionally included burnt offerings,[319] is prominent[320] and is likely included in the image that Paul presents here.

It is the *saving* purpose of God that is effected in the apostle; he has been

316. E.g., Gen 8:21; Exod 29:18; Lev 1:13; Num 15:3.

317. See again 1:5, 19, 21, where Paul likewise describes his participation in Christ.

318. The Hebrew uses the preposition ־לְ, while the LXX has the simple dative, as Paul does here.

319. See 2 Chr 30:15; 35:16.

320. Esp. 1 Cor 5:7-8; 11:23-26.

made to be the *fragrance* of Christ. Offerings by fire, with "a soothing [fragrant] aroma to the Lord," to which Paul makes reference, have an implicitly salvific overtone and are sometimes explicitly described in this way.[321] It is *of Christ* that Paul is the fragrance.[322]

Nevertheless, God's work through the apostle has two outcomes. He is the "fragrance of Christ for God" among both "those being saved" *and* "among those who are perishing." For some he is a delightful fragrance, for others the stench of death. The "word of the cross" is the point of division (1 Cor 1:18). Those who cannot perceive the risen Christ in Paul cannot do so because they cannot see beyond the judgment of the world as it is displayed in the suffering apostle. Salvation arrives only where this judgment has fallen. Everything depends on one's response to the apostle and the Gospel that he bears in his body and life.[323]

The present tense forms that Paul employs are also of significance.[324] The durative aspect they express must be given its force. Paul speaks of those who *"are being saved"* and those who *"are perishing."* The drama of salvation is taking place here and now. It is taking place before the eyes of the Corinthians. Things are not the way they seem, neither for the Corinthians nor for us. God is doing away with "the things that are," replacing them with "the things that are not" (1 Cor 1:28). The rulers of this age and the lords of this world are passing away, and our Lord comes (1 Cor 2:6; 16:22).[325] Yet all this is taking place in a way that is not subject to human discernment or judgment.

16 In his description of the twofold effect of God's work in him, Paul returns to the neutral term "odor" *(osmē)*. For some, the apostle is nothing other than "the odor from death unto death." For others, he is "the odor from life unto life" (v. 16a). Just as the apostle is the fragrance of Christ for God, he is the odor of death and life within the world. He has become the vehicle of communication between God and the world, whether it responds in faith to

321. See, e.g., Gen 8:20-22; Exod 29:38-46; Lev 4:27-31.

322. Our appearance before his judgment seat notwithstanding, Christ for Paul is, before all else, the Savior, whom he proclaims as sheer Good News. See 1:19-20; 2:12; 3:3; 4:4-6; 5:14-21.

323. The effect of the apostle, we should note, is *not* like that of Law. As we shall see afresh in 2 Cor 3, the *purpose* of the Law was to bring death, and that not as an end in itself, but as the way to life. God's purpose with the Gospel is to bring *life* to those who live in death. It is not the reception of the Gospel but blindness to it and the failure to grasp it that bring judgment and death.

324. See also 1 Cor 1:18 and 2 Cor 4:3.

325. In 1950 Gustav Heinemann, a leading member of the Confessing Church during Nazi rule and later president of the Federal Republic of Germany, declared at the general meeting of the Protestant church (EKD) in Essen, Germany, "Let us answer the world, when it wants to make us fearful, 'Your lords are passing away, but our Lord comes!' "

the life given in Christ, or whether it encounters the condemnation and death to which it already belongs in its unbelief.

God's saving work in Christ, communicated through the apostle, bears both judgment and salvation. Nevertheless, the work of God in Christ is not ambivalent. God's unconditional saving Yes is in him (1:20). The fundamental question is whether our eyes have been opened to see through the suffering and death of Christ to the gift of life and glory that is wrapped within this contrary, outward form. As Paul implicitly has indicated and later makes clear, this capacity to see is not within the power of human reason but is a saving work of God the Creator (4:4-6). "The peace of God passes all understanding, and so does God's plan of salvation."[326]

The prepositional pairings should not be overlooked: the odor arises "*from* death, *unto* death; *from* life, *unto* life." The apostle knows nothing but "Jesus Christ crucified" (1 Cor 2:2). He bears the death of Jesus in his body (4:10). He *proclaims* the "word of the cross" in a paradox as *Good News* (1 Cor 1:18). Life is at work in the Corinthians through the death at work in the apostle (2 Cor 4:12). Correspondingly, just as death is at work in the apostle, so death is effected in those who cannot see beyond mere outward appearances.

The last clause of v. 16 properly belongs with v. 17. The break in subject is clear and is marked by Paul's use of *kai* in v. 16b (rather than a continuative *de*). His question nevertheless arises from the drama he has just described: "Who is sufficient for these things?" It represents more than a mere jab at his opponents in Corinth. In this jarring thanksgiving, Paul expresses to the Corinthians the fundamental theme of the letter: the legitimation and sufficiency of an apostle. He immediately goes on to deny that he now is commending himself "again" to the Corinthians (3:1). His battle is larger than a mere skirmish over his person with his opponents. He is fighting for the hearts and minds of the Corinthians, whom he seeks to instruct in the *theology* of the apostolic calling, a theology that cannot be separated from the Gospel and from the cross.

If apostolic ministry is more than persuasive preaching, if it is more than the display of gifts and powers,[327] and if it is the effecting of the final judgment and the creation of the new life of the age to come, the question as to who is sufficient for it applies not only to Paul's opponents but to all apostles, including Paul himself. Here the radical "eccentricity" of Paul's understanding of life and ministry again comes to expression. He is and *remains* insufficient for the apostolic ministry to which he is called, as he expressly says in 1 Cor 15:9. His sufficiency is located abidingly outside himself in God and in the Gospel, as

326. E. Käsemann, "Justification and Salvation History," in *Perspectives on Paul* (trans. M. Kohl; Philadelphia: Fortress, 1971), 63.

327. It does not matter what those powers and gifts might be apart from love (1 Cor 13:1-13).

he indicates shortly in the following chapter (3:5-6). Both his account of his trial in Asia and (even more) his account of his distress in Troas make clear that the display of Christ's strength in Paul's weakness is not an accidental or transient characteristic of his ministry but is essential to it. Within that weakness, contrary to all appearances, he is called to speak out of faith (4:13).

17 All that Paul has said in this section (1:12–2:17), including the thanksgiving he has offered to God, is an assertion of his "simplicity and purity" in his dealings with the Corinthians. He now completes the inclusio begun at 1:12. If he were merely peddling the word of God — the Gospel — others might well be regarded as more sufficient for the task than he (v. 17). True ministry of the Gospel is the exception, not the rule: "For we are not peddling the word of God as many do." Paul's reference to "the many," which may well signify "most" (if not "all"), suggests that while he has hardly forgotten the present situation, he intentionally sets it in a larger context. The apostolic claimants in Corinth are nothing special. They are merely part of a larger group of wandering teachers who peddled the Gospel like wares to be sold.[328] Their theology operated according to a business model. In contrast, the work *of God,* the imparting of life and death, takes place through the apostle. The breadth of Paul's statement makes its edge all the sharper. Faith cannot be sold as a commodity but must be communicated, and that *indirectly,* not in the advertisement of our work but in the open and public confession of *God's work:*

> Faith is not everyone's concern, and likewise is not communicable as a piece of merchandise, but is the kingdom of heaven, and hell within us.[329]

This is precisely what takes place in Paul, Christ's apostle, contrary to all the expectations of the Corinthians. The cross does not sell well in Corinth. Nor does it do any better in our world. Paul nevertheless turns the Corinthian suspicions concerning his refusal to accept remuneration into an argument for his authority as apostle, much as he does again later in the letter.[330] Already at this point, without a direct statement, he effectively disarms this long-standing complaint.[331]

328. Paul is aware of the danger to his other churches. See Phil 3:17-21; 2 Thess 2:1-17, and already 1 Cor 4:14-21, which takes up the instruction of 3:1-17 and the factions named in 1:10-17.

329. Johann Georg Hamann, in reference to his activity as an author, in his *Briefwechsel,* vol. 7 (ed. Arthur Henkel; Frankfurt: Insel-Verlag, 1979), 176.6-8, letter to F. H. Jacobi, April, 30, 1787; quoted in O. Bayer, *Contemporary in Dissent: Johann Georg Hamann as Radical Enlightener* (trans. R. A. Harrisville and M. C. Mattes; Grand Rapids: Eerdmans, 2012), 64; O. Bayer, *Autorität und Kritik: Zu Hermeneutik und Wissenschaftstheorie* (Tübingen: Mohr Siebeck, 1991), 108-9.

330. 11:7-12.

331. Paul addresses the issue already in 1 Cor 9:1-27.

Despite his charge that many have turned the Gospel into a business scheme, Paul does not reject all compensation as illegitimate. He earlier has affirmed the right of those who proclaim the Gospel to obtain their living from it (1 Cor 9:5-14). Yet where there is a right, there will always be abuse. Paul regards the abuse as having become the rule. The term he employs *(kapēleuō)* was used for the activities of street peddlers who hawked their wares. It had been used already in the same type of criticism of the Sophists by Plato.[332] Not surprisingly, it also appears in Philo's judgment concerning popular Hellenistic philosophers of his time.[333] It naturally bore negative connotations, especially that of offering adulterated commodities or defective goods. Paul probably makes use of the image he introduces here when he later denies that he adulterates the word of God (4:2). The term itself, however, simply signifies "peddling."[334] Any other associations have to be drawn from the context. In this case, Paul obviously associates peddling with duplicitous motives, contrasting it with his own claim to sincerity.

Paul continues to seek to win over the hearts and minds of the Corinthians to a proper understanding of apostolic ministry. His refusal to accept support from them *facilitates* his claim to sincerity and makes it persuasive: he can hardly be a peddler of God's word, since he will not accept remuneration for delivering it. Already in 1 Cor 9:15 he speaks of this practice as his boast. He would rather die than surrender it. Later in this letter, he returns to this boast as an evidence of his love and as a means of removing any claim or boasting of his opponents that they too are apostles (11:5-15). They have not been ashamed to take funds from the Corinthians. His "self-defense" here is necessarily also an accusation against them, even if it has a broader scope.

In claiming sincerity, Paul returns to his boast concerning his conduct with respect to the Corinthians, rounding it off and concluding his attempt to allay their suspicions about his failure to visit them. He thus repeats his claim to have dealt with them (and all others) "out of sincerity."[335] As the associations of the term suggest, he is prepared to stand in the judgment of pure sunlight. The practice of self-support that lies behind Paul's words gives them remarkable weight.

Paul's second claim, that he speaks "as from God," is less a claim of per-

332. Plato, *Protagoras* 311b-311e.

333. Philo, *Gig.* 39.

334. See esp. Hafemann, *Suffering and Ministry in the Spirit,* 101-25.

335. Paul's use of the comparative particle ὡς here and in his following claim obviously does not express irreality. The usage follows and corresponds to his denial of acting as (ὡς) those who peddle the word of God. Nevertheless, by using the ὡς, Paul distances himself slightly from the pattern that he follows: he speaks *as* from sincerity, and *as* from God. He partakes in God and in the eschatological reality of sincerity and yet does not identify himself with either.

sonal empowerment than it is a dramatic assertion of the source of his words. The claim to sincerity prepares the way for this radical claim to apostolic authority. The authority does not rest in him. He does not speak from himself but is the mere instrument of God's speech. The sincerity of the apostle is the channel through which God's word arrives.

The expression of empowerment, and not only empowerment but responsibility, comes in the following phrase: "we speak in Christ." On the one hand, the phrase again communicates the "eccentricity" of apostolic ministry. It is not finally Paul but Christ, who speaks and works in him. Paul speaks not in his own person but "in Christ." This is not to say that Paul has no identity. Rather, Paul's own identity rests entirely in Christ and in the new person Christ makes Paul to be.

On the other hand, "to speak in Christ" implies conscious, intentional action. It is to have the Spirit and to speak in faith, as Paul subsequently makes clear (4:13).[336] In the conclusion of the letter, Paul once again returns to the formulation that he uses here: "before God, in Christ we speak" (12:19). There, too, he makes a claim to sincerity, even if it is implicit. There, too, he recalls his good conscience and the anticipation of the judgment in which he will be manifest to God (cf. 5:11), as well as the presence of Christ in him, who grants him faith and the power to speak (cf. 13:3, 5). There, too, he makes clear that he is not defending *himself* but, rather, "upbuilding" the Corinthians (12:19). His aim both there and here is that they understand the true ministry of an apostle and in what the legitimation of an apostle lies. He speaks and acts not merely for them, nor merely in their presence, but in the presence of God.[337] The situation is very much like the "devotional address" that Kierkegaard describes: it is not the case that the apostle is an actor and that the Corinthians are theatergoers who are to judge what he says. It is rather the case that Paul is the prompter, who whispers the proper lines to the Corinthian actors, whose sole duty it is to listen properly. Consequently: "In the most earnest sense, God is the critical theatergoer, who looks on to see how the lines are spoken and how they are listened to."[338] Contrary to what the Corinthians imagine, they are not the audience. It is God, in whose presence the apostle speaks, who is the audience of both of them.

336. What he speaks he speaks in faith, in God's presence with the awareness of the judgment to come (5:11).

337. 2:17; 4:2; 5:11.

338. S. Kierkegaard, *Purity of Heart Is to Will One Thing* (trans. D. V. Steere; New York: Harper & Row, 1948), 181.

II. THE BODY OF THE LETTER: THE APOSTOLIC MISSION AND THE APOSTLE IN MISSION (3:1–7:16)

The transition to the body of a Pauline letter is marked by the shift from Paul's report of his apostolic labors to his theological concern for his addressees.[1] This transition is unusual in Second Corinthians, even if it is clearly marked. The apostle himself remains the focus of the argument. Yet it is not simply the apostle who stands at the center of interest. As we have seen, Paul cannot speak of himself or his salvation without in the same breath speaking of the Corinthians and their salvation.[2] The apostle and his church are bound together by the Gospel that he bears. This bond is threatened by the false apostolic claimants, who now appear briefly and indirectly in the argument.[3] The real drama remains centered on the threatened relationship between the Corinthians and Christ, who is present in his suffering apostle.

The apostle is nothing other than an agent and emissary *(diakonos)*[4] of Christ and of a new covenant (3:6). This agency and the form that it takes in life constitute Paul's defense of the apostolic ministry with which he has been entrusted. He introduces this theme at the opening of his discourse (3:3) and builds on it throughout the entire body of the letter.[5] His defense recalls the argument of 1 Cor 3:1–4:5, where he insists that he and Apollos are mere emissaries of the Lord (*diakonoi,* 3:5),[6] mere assistants of Christ (*hypēretai Christou,* 4:1), and mere stewards of the mysteries of God (*oikonomoi mystēriōn theou,* 4:1). The controversy concerning the legitimating marks of an apostle was

1. Schnider and Stenger, *Studien,* 52-54.

2. 1:6-7, 14, 21-22.

3. 3:1; 5:11-12; 6:14–7:1.

4. J. N. Collins has shown that the standard interpretation of the διακον- word group as primarily related to waiting on tables or mere service is misguided. The relevant terms function within the semantic field of agency or mediation and have to do with such actions as the conveying of messages, the performance of errands, or, more generally, the doing of the bidding of another. If one could set aside the negative connotations that it has accrued, "lackey" might be the best rendering of the Gk. διάκονος. Probably "agent," "attendant," or "steward" now best communicates the sense. See, e.g., Josephus, *Ant.* 7.224; 8.354; 9.54; 11.228. The same understanding is present in Matt. 20:26 par. Mark 9:35; Matt 23:11 par. Mark 10:43-45. The ideas of agency, acting as an envoy, and mission are primary in the Pauline contexts. See J. N. Collins, *Diakonia: Re-interpreting the Ancient Resources* (New York: Oxford University Press, 1990); BDAG, "διακονέω, διακονία, διάκονος," 229-31.

5. 4:1; 5:18; 6:3-4.

6. See Collins, *Diakonia,* 196-97.

present already at the beginning of Paul's troubles with the Corinthian church. It now has become the focal issue. The Corinthians suppose that apostles have been endowed with powers of their own. Paul insists that he is a mere agent of the Crucified One, who lives.

The body of the letter falls into two distinct sections (3:1-18; 4:1–7:16). In the first of these, in true audacity, Paul announces the confidence that places him beyond any need for legitimation by the Corinthians. As the letter of Christ, whose hearts have been rewritten and transformed by the Spirit of God, they themselves are the legitimation of his apostolic ministry. His following description of the new covenant — which receives its definition in relation to the old — is thus fundamental to his defense of apostolic ministry. As we shall argue shortly, it does not introduce the question of Judaizing as a second front in his battle with the Corinthians. The opening section of the letter's body (3:1-18) serves instead as a sort of prologue, not unlike that of John's Gospel or the book of Job, in which the drama that lies behind the argument is unveiled. God gives the gift of the Spirit, life, and righteousness only where death and condemnation are present. Paul's appeal to the Exodus narrative in 2 Cor 3 discloses the pattern of God's work that lies behind the experience of comfort in affliction for which he already has given thanks (1:3-7). God's work in "letter" and "Spirit" is characteristic of all true apostolic ministry, as Paul already has made clear in the conclusion of his thanksgiving and the apostolic report (1:7; 1:8–2:17). It appears therefore again as a fundamental motif within his defense of apostolic mission in the following section of the body, disclosing the deeper structure of that ministry (4:1–7:16). The mission of the new covenant of the Spirit — which takes place only in the context of the death and condemnation — supplies the theological interpretation of Paul's apostolic experience of suffering and deliverance. The deadness of Jesus, which the apostle bears in his body, is that of the One who was "made into sin on our behalf, that we might be made the righteousness of God in him" (4:7; 5:21). The exchange of "sin" and "righteousness" in Christ of which Paul speaks in 5:21 has its background and basis in the communication of condemnation that came through Moses (3:9).[7] Indeed, Paul's succinct summary of God's saving work in Christ in 5:21 may be regarded as a complement to 3:1-18 that fills in its christological "deficit." Participation in Christ and the transformation of the human being — a primary theme in the body of the letter — takes place in communication and *exchange,* namely, the exchange of identity between fallen humanity and Christ, in life and in death, that has taken place in Christ's cross and resurrection. The "grammar" of that exchange is determined by the condemnation delivered by Moses, on the one hand, and, on the other, by God's work in Christ. As the opening section of the body, 3:1-18 supplies this "grammar." This is its argumentative function.

7. "Sin" is nearly a *hapax* in the letter, appearing otherwise only in 11:7.

The "grammar" of the letter and the Spirit, and thus of Moses and of Christ, supplies the underlying motif of the second section of the body (4:1–7:16). As we have observed, God's saving work takes place under the form and appearance of its opposite: God gives life only through death, righteousness only through condemnation, glory only through dishonor. Paul's argument that the Spirit brings a glory that transcends that of Moses' face is not merely an assertion of the finality of God's saving work in Christ. It also defines the form of God's saving work as taking place *sub contrario,* a definition that then informs the following argument. Paul thus does not speak at all of the Law, circumcision, or "works" in 3:1-18, nor, for that matter, in the letter as a whole.[8] He employs instead the categories of old and new covenants, Moses and Christ,[9] drawing a contrast between outward, visible glory that is merely temporary and the eternal glory that is yet unseen. With considerable irony, he makes the point that the letters of attestation (3:1) and signs (12:12) that the Corinthians seek have their epitome in Moses' ministry of death. The abiding glory of the Gospel presently remains hidden under its opposite and can be grasped by faith alone. *All* visible glory is subject to the glory of the "letter" that brings condemnation and death. As quickly becomes clear in the following context (4:1-6), the story of "the sons of Israel" is paradigmatic for all of humanity, including the Corinthians. God's way with Israel discloses the forces at work in the fallen world. All human efforts to attain power and glory — which amount to self-justification — lie under the condemnation and death that the Law worked on Israel (cf. Rom 3:19-20).

Correspondingly, as Paul already has made clear to the Corinthians, not only they but he himself has been given a passive role in God's saving work. He is not primarily an actor but one who is acted upon by God. What has been savingly done for him and what he must suffer have priority over anything that he does, including his own service (4:7-15). His hope in the Gospel is passive in orientation: before all else, he is a recipient of salvation (4:16–5:10). His apostolic service is determined by the crucified and risen Christ, who is present and made manifest by the Spirit. In the midst of trial and suffering, the apostle lives and speaks in hope by the Spirit, who is at work in him.

Within this passivity, Paul is highly active. He is an ambassador for Christ who calls the Corinthians to be reconciled with God (5:11-21), a reconciliation that necessarily includes their reconciliation with the apostle, who as a servant of God has lived and spoken to them in sincerity and openness (6:3-13; 6:14–7:1). According to Titus's report, that reconciliation has come about, at least temporarily (7:5-16). The renewed desire of the Corinthians for Paul is a confirmation of his boasting in them, a boasting that is nothing other than his faith in God's work through the Gospel.

8. He once refers to "lawlessness," in 6:14.

9. See, however, Rom 10:1-13.

Paul's vivid and emotional response to Titus's report in 7:5-16 completes the narrative of his anxious experience in Troas, which he dramatically broke off in 2:12-13, and brings the body of the letter to a conclusion. In suspending that story, he underscored his deep love and concern for the Corinthians. As we have noted, the argument of the letter is not a distant or theoretical legitimation of apostolic ministry. It is the legitimation of *Paul's* apostolic ministry to the *Corinthians.* Neither he nor they can be abstracted from the argument. His rejoicing over their reconciliation to him — impermanent and fragile though it may be — is the necessary completion of his argument. The trouble with the Corinthians outweighs all Paul's outward troubles. Their reconciliation to him is nothing other than a joyful instance of comfort that God has granted him in his trials (7:6).

A. The Apostolic Mission: The New Covenant as the Audacity of Apostolic Hope (3:1-18)

The opening rhetorical question "Are we beginning *again* to commend ourselves?" challenges the Corinthians' perception of the apostle (3:1).[10] They have misjudged him, and their relationship with him. As the following question shows, Paul anticipates a negative response: "We don't need — as do certain ones — letters to you or from you, do we?" (3:1). Later, at a critical juncture in the second section of his argument, he "again" denies that he is defending himself (5:12). In his confrontative argument in the closing of the letter, he charges, "I ought to have been commended by *you*" (12:11). Yet once more in the conclusion of the letter, he clarifies the situation: "For a long time you have supposed that we are defending ourselves to you. In the presence of God, in Christ, we speak all these things, beloved, for your edification" (12:19; cf. 4:2; 6:4). The Corinthians imagine that Paul has somehow wronged and, indeed, defrauded them.

That Paul "again" might be commending himself likely recalls an earlier confrontation, which almost certainly is to be identified with the grievous visit to which he refers in 1:23–2:11. Yet the problem has deeper roots: the Corinthians have *long* supposed that he is defending himself. At an earlier stage in his troubled relationship with them, Paul used the language of self-defense (1 Cor 9:3). The issue is not merely that of his establishing his apostolic credentials. He is under suspicion as a fraud. Even Paul's earlier "defense," however, had to do with the authority of an apostle and not with his own person. Already at that point, he refused to submit himself to the judgment of the Corinthians

10. Paul's apostolic audacity outstrips any earthly vision! Cf. B. Obama, *The Audacity of Hope: Thoughts on Reclaiming the American Dream* (New York: Crown Publishers, 2006).

or to that of any human court. As a steward of divine mysteries, he is accountable to the Lord alone (1 Cor 4:1-5). Consequently, it is clear that, when Paul uses the particle "again" in 2 Cor 3:1, he recalls his preceding conflict with the Corinthians *ironically.* He is not commending himself "again"; indeed, he has never done so in the terms they require. Only after making it clear that he is not commending himself is he free to commend himself. He does so in terms that the Corinthians do not request or expect. He appeals to the Corinthians — and, indeed to every human being — as apostle, commending himself by his conscience and transparency of life and heart (4:1-2; 5:11-13; 6:4). Paul's "self-commendation" is paradoxical also because it is not a *self*-commendation but the commendation of the Gospel and of the work of God that takes place in him. He thus commends himself in everything that the Corinthians do not expect or seek: in perseverance, in afflictions, in experiences of need and distress (6:4-10). The apostolic calling is "eccentric," therefore its commendation also must be "eccentric."

EXCURSUS: PAUL'S OPPONENTS IN CORINTH AND THE PURPOSE OF THE LETTER

In 2 Cor 3 Paul continues to deal with the controversy between him and the Corinthian church over the legitimation of an apostle.[11] This construal of the purpose of the letter is preferable to the highly problematic attempt to identify Paul's adversaries as advocates of Judaizing and representatives of the Jerusalem church or, alternatively, as Hellenistic divine-men of a Jewish variety. Paul describes his apostolic service in 2 Cor 3:1-18 in terms of the Spirit as opposed to the letter, the new covenant as opposed to the old, and Christ as opposed to Moses. The appearance of these themes has been thought to indicate that he is combating familiar opponents, the advocates of Judaizing who caused trouble for him in Galatia and elsewhere. But this thesis is unlikely. This is also the case for the attempt to ascribe a developed Hellenistic theology to the adversaries.

In the first place, to read Paul as speaking either to the question of Gentile Judaizing or refuting the claims of Hellenistic "divine-men" is to ignore Paul's explicit expressions of concern for the Corinthians throughout the let-

11. For similar judgments, see T. Schmeller, *Der zweite Brief an die Korinther* (EKK 8/1; Neukirchen-Vluyn: Neukirchener Theologie/Patmos Verlag, 2010), 1:179-80; M. E. Thrall, *A Critical and Exegetical Commentary on the Second Epistle to the Corinthians* (ICC 47; Edinburgh: T&T Clark, 1994), 1:227-29; and esp. J. L. Sumney, *Identifying Paul's Opponents: The Question of Method in 2 Corinthians* (JSNTSupp 40; Sheffield: JSOT, 1990), 128-91; J. L. Sumney, *"Servants of Satan," "False Brothers," and Other Opponents of Paul* (JSNTSupp 188; Sheffield: Sheffield Academic, 1999), 79-133.

ter.[12] Once these are set aside or overlooked, the attempt is made to recover the theology of the opponents from hidden clues. The "mirror-reading" of the views of opponents from Paul's statements remains a necessary, albeit precarious, element of interpretation. When, however, as in this instance, it remains based on mere supposition and guesswork, it is likely to reveal more about the interpreter than about Paul or his opponents. This is especially the case in relation to 2 Cor 3.[13] All that we may legitimately draw from Paul's explicit statements concerning the theology of his opponents has to do with their claims to apostolic authority and their attempt to discredit Paul with the Corinthians.[14] This information is highly significant, but it does not provide any indication of a theological program on their part. It is questionable, in fact, whether they presented a united front. The apostolic claimants who formed the opposition to Paul were not in agreement with one another. Each one sought to establish his own claim to authority in Corinth.[15] Corinth had been a destination for itinerant Christian preachers for some time. This dynamic is evident already in First Corinthians. Even if they have only one "father" in Christ, the Corinthians have *countless* "instructors" (*paidagōgoi*, 1 Cor 4:15). In their allegiance to various leaders, the Corinthians have split into factions that accorded their leaders apostolic status: only an apostle can supplant an apostle (1 Cor 1:10-13). Indeed, the claim to being "of Christ" almost certainly constitutes a claim to apostolic status.[16] The arrival of the Jewish apostolic claimants in Corinth by no means introduced a new problem; it only brought the existing problem to a critical phase.

12. See 1:23–2:11; 5:12; 6:11–7:16; 10:7-11; 11:1-21; 12:11–13:10. The same applies to the quest for a background in a Hellenistic "theology of glory," as with D. Georgi, *The Opponents of Paul in Second Corinthians* (Philadelphia: Fortress, 1986).

13. This sort of mirror-reading (and here "mirror-reading" may be too generous a designation) characterizes Dieter Georgi's description of Paul's opponents as Jewish "divine-men" who appealed to Moses and Christ (*The Opponents of Paul*, 229-83).

14. 10:1-11; 11:5-33.

15. See also 2 Cor 10:12.

16. It is therefore understandable that Paul's apostolic credentials came into question even before the writing of First Corinthians (1 Cor 9:1-12, esp. v. 3). Indeed, the unhappy confrontation that took place on Paul's second visit to Corinth almost certainly had to do with an implicit apostolic claim: as we have noted, it takes an apostle to supplant an apostle (2 Cor 2:5-11). For this reason, the idea that Paul's attack on the Jewish apostolic claimants in 2 Cor 10–13 is a response to a new problem is entirely unpersuasive. It may well be that these "superapostles" (11:5; 12:11) are new arrivals in Corinth. But they exploited a situation that already existed. The factions that Paul describes in his first word on the matter are all centered on Jewish leaders: Paul, Apollos, Cephas, and, of course, Christ (1 Cor 1:12). This observation works against all those who adopt a partition theory, and also against the moderating position that, during the composition of the letter, Paul had to address a new crisis, e.g., Harris, *The Second Epistle to the Corinthians*, 51-54; R. P. Martin, *2 Corinthians* (WBC 40; Waco, Tex.: Word Books, 1985), li.

Paul's silence with regard to Judaizing in Corinth should not be overlooked either. The question of Gentile circumcision appears only briefly and secondarily in the Corinthian correspondence. In Paul's one brief mention of circumcision in 1 Corinthians, he first addresses the interest of some Jewish believers in removing the mark of their circumcision. Only then does he instruct those who had been "called in uncircumcision" not to be circumcised (1 Cor 7:18-19). Admittedly, the Corinthian church is sharply divided. Some Gentiles were tempted to accept circumcision. Yet where Jews are tempted to Hellenize, there can hardly be a strong tendency for Gentiles to Judaize. This is so, even though the Corinthian church wanted a Jewish apostle. The Jewish claimants to that role apparently made no demands upon the Corinthians to Judaize. Just the opposite: they sought to conform to the Hellenistic tastes of the Corinthians. Paul nowhere takes up the question of obedience to the Law or "the works of the Law" in the Corinthian correspondence, not even in 2 Cor 3. His silence is again telling. Paul instead appeals to Moses, the letter, and the old covenant as a manifestation of divine judgment on the hearts of human beings. His retelling of the story of the giving of the Law is merely one form of the theme of the cross as God's judgment on human wisdom, which runs through the entire letter. The argument in 2 Cor 3 is addressed to the entire church. At best, any Judaizing would have been limited to a mere faction. Those who wish to find advocates of Judaizing in Corinth must read them into the text.

Of course, Paul's opponents were Jewish, even Aramaic speaking.[17] They claimed that they had encountered Jesus, either during his earthly ministry or, more likely, in a postresurrection apparition.[18] In some measure, the story of Moses and "the sons of Israel" may serve to deflate those claims. The opponents also made claims to having displayed apostolic signs (12:12). It is unlikely that they appealed to the authority of the Jerusalem apostles in order to undermine Paul. In the improbable event that Paul had lost the confidence of Jerusalem completely — he still names Cephas, along with others, positively in 1 Cor 9:5 — he would almost certainly have presented his own version of his relationship to Jerusalem if the opponents had challenged him on this basis.[19] Paul in no way qualifies the authority of the Jerusalem apostles in the letter, as he does decisively in Gal 1:6–2:21. In his boasting, which obviously parallels the claims of his opponents, he makes no reference to Jerusalem

17. 11:22.

18. 5:16; 12:3; cf. 1 Cor 9:1-3; 15:8.

19. Despite the obvious misunderstandings and tension that followed his meeting with the leaders in Jerusalem, Paul elsewhere openly recounts their having extended "the right hand of fellowship" to him and Barnabas (Gal 2:1-10). Even if there had been problems between him and the Jerusalem apostles, one would have expected some sort of defense, had his opponents attempted to use the authority of Jerusalem against him.

(11:22-23). There is no good reason to interpret Paul's ironic naming of his adversaries as "super-apostles" as a reference to the Jerusalem leaders (11:5). It is primarily the rhetorical powers and knowledge of the apostolic claimants that he challenges, not their authorization by Jerusalem (11:6). The reference to "the one who comes proclaiming another Jesus" (11:4) is hardly to be taken as a reference to the arrival of a representative of Jerusalem, for which there is no other evidence in the letter.[20] If the Jewish apostolic claimants, who have arrived on the scene late in the drama, did make appeal to Jerusalem, they would have had to contend with an already existing faction that claimed to follow Cephas. The situation in Corinth argues against any appeal to external authority, even if Jewish origin and an encounter with Jesus were held in esteem. Varying judgments as to who should be the leader of the church had led to factions (1 Cor 1:10-17). Not even Cephas enjoyed the confidence of the entire church. The Corinthians were ready, at least for a time, to tolerate or even support *someone from within the church* who rejected Paul's authority (2 Cor 1:23–2:10). Indeed, the Corinthian church not only requires letters of support for any apostle. It also sends them.[21] Any church that can itself approve and recommend apostles has little or no need for the authority of Jerusalem.[22] It is Paul himself who must urge the church to complete its promised gift for "the saints" in Jerusalem (8:1–9:15). Their sluggishness is hardly a mark of respect, let alone submission to the authority of Jerusalem.

Finally, as we have noted, aside from chapters 10–13, Paul's adversaries do not appear prominently in the letter. Even in those chapters, it is the judgment of the Corinthians that remains the target of his argument, not the theology of the opponents.[23] Paul battles for the minds and hearts of the Corinthians, who appear to be much more attracted to Hellenistic rhetoric than they are to Judaizing.

The Hellenistic orientation of Paul's opponents is evident in the letter, an orientation that, given their Jewish heritage, has caused considerable confusion and debate among interpreters concerning their identity. The adversaries regard powerful rhetoric *(logos)* as a prime mark of apostolic authority and derisively point out Paul's lack of ability: "His letters, they say, are weighty and powerful, but the presence of his body is weak and his rhetoric is contemptible" (10:10).[24] It is likewise clear that they regard a charismatic appearance and a powerful

20. See Käsemann in response to Schlatter: *Die Legitimität des Apostels,* 14-16; Schlatter, *Paulus, der Bote Jesu,* 631-32.

21. 3:1; 1 Cor 4:1-5.

22. Paul's instruction concerning women and head coverings likewise makes it clear that the church in Corinth was not inclined to follow the instructions of Jerusalem or any other church (1 Cor 11:2-16).

23. 10:4-6, 7; 12:19-21.

24. See also 11:6; 1 Cor 1:18–2:5.

personal presence as an essential mark of apostolic authority. As we have noted, the opponents also appeal to heavenly revelations and works of power that they have been able to perform as signs of their authority (12:1, 12). How else would one represent the risen Christ? The single indication of the theological criterion by which the Corinthians formed their judgments, and by which the apostolic claimants presumably made their claims, was evidence of the presence of Christ in the apostle (13:3). It is noteworthy that Paul has nothing to say about the content of the revelations the adversaries claimed to have received or the nature of any signs they claim to have performed. Even when he charges the Corinthians with gladly enduring someone who comes proclaiming "another Jesus" and bringing "another s/Spirit" and "another Gospel," he does not describe the content of the preaching he rejects (11:4). Either Paul intentionally overlooks the objectionable substance of their preaching — which is hardly likely — or we must suppose that his response is to be found in the explicit polemic of the letter.[25] It is surely not irrelevant that Paul rejects any knowledge of Christ "according to the flesh," i.e., according to the standards of human judgment (5:16). All parties agreed that the presence of Christ served as the criterion of apostolic authority (13:3). Paul's opponents and the Corinthians measured that presence by the standard of power, charisma, and success. Once separated from the crucified and risen Jesus, the gifts of the Spirit and the hope of the resurrection would have been distorted in the same way. It is Paul's pitiful *parousia* that the opponents have derided and that has alienated the Corinthians from him. His failure to appear as promised in Corinth has contributed to their suspicions about him as well (1:15–2:4). Even more, Paul's *praxis* of refusing to accept support from the church — which sets him apart from the other apostolic claimants — repeatedly appears as a matter of contention.[26] The issue appears already in First Corinthians.[27] The fundamental matters of contention that appear within the letter are thus the *parousia* and *praxis* of the apostle. To attempt to read another theology of the opponents off of 2 Cor 3 is more than a little speculative, not least because there is no good reason to suppose that they were one mind with one another, even if they were united against Paul.

The fundamental error of the Corinthians, according to Paul, lies in their assumption that the legitimation of an apostle — and therewith the Gospel itself — is subject to human judgment.[28] Everything is to be judged accord-

25. We must not forget that Christ, the Spirit, and the Gospel had been distorted in Corinth already when Paul wrote First Corinthians. See 1 Cor 1:13; 12:1-3; 15:12. Paul's opening instruction on the Spirit (12:1-3) sounds ominous in the light of 2 Cor 11:4.

26. I am again borrowing this fitting language in part from Mitchell, *The Birth of Christian Hermeneutics,* 81.

27. 1 Cor 9:1-27.

28. As we have noted, Ernst Käsemann's thesis in *Die Legitimität des Apostels* that 2 Cor 10–13 is Paul's defense of apostolic ministry may be applied to the entire letter.

ing to appearance.[29] Throughout the letter, Paul is dealing with the practical *reasoning* of the Corinthians, which is blind and misdirected. The Gospel is at stake: it is not the Corinthians who are to judge the Gospel, but the Gospel that is to judge them. We need not suppose, however, that the false judgments of the Corinthians were based upon a developed theological program. An articulated theology need not precede such judgments; it may well follow them. This apparently was the case in Paul's confrontation of Cephas in Antioch. Even without words, Cephas's withdrawal from table fellowship with Gentiles sent a theological message.[30] Paul found himself compelled to expose the theological significance of what was taking place. As we have observed, the advocates of Judaizing in Galatia likewise by no means imagined that they were setting aside the Gospel but imagined that they were dealing properly with the new situation of Gentile conversion. All the evidence suggests that something similar had taken place in Corinth. The series of seemingly disparate issues that Paul addresses in First Corinthians grows out of the same theological problem with which he must deal in Second Corinthians. The radicalization of the situation brings Paul's response that goes to the root of the problem. At the outset of that earlier letter, Paul deals with God's overturning of human reasoning, especially its practical judgments, in the crucified Christ (1 Cor 1:18-31). He does so, moreover, precisely in relation to the question as to the standard by which apostles are to be judged (1 Cor 3:1–4:21). Already in the first letter he had to defend his apostolic calling (1 Cor 9:1-27). The list of problems with which Paul had to deal in First Corinthians had not vanished when he wrote Second Corinthians. Or at least Paul fears that they had not (2 Cor 12:20-21). All of these failures have their root in the more fundamental failure of the Corinthians to understand the Gospel as "the word of the cross," which pronounces and, indeed, effects judgment upon the present world. They cannot imagine that life is to be found only in death, wisdom only in foolishness, and glory only in shame. They thought that the Gospel came to deliver them from all the latter things. And it did, of course, but only by working their death, exposing their foolishness, and doing away with their glory. If grace is to be grace, it must be costly grace.[31] Salvation is God's deliverance of us from ourselves through the foolishness of the cross.[32] Otherwise we live in the love of self and of the

29. 10:7, 8-12.

30. Thus Paul reports, "When I saw that they were not *rightly walking,* with respect to the truth of the Gospel, I said . . ." (Gal 2:14). Often it is supposed that the "ones from James" (Gal 2:12) arrived with the message that table fellowship with Gentiles was not permissible. But Paul makes no mention of any demands that they brought. He characterizes the situation in the terms given above. He addresses the situation as it appeared in practical terms before his eyes.

31. D. Bonhoeffer, *The Cost of Discipleship* (New York: Simon & Schuster, 1995 [orig. 1939]), 43-46.

32. Cf. Gal 6:14-16.

present world. The Corinthian misunderstanding of the Gospel thus manifests itself in their loss of the horizon of the eschaton and in their jettisoning of the hope of the resurrection.[33] It likewise displays itself in their misconception and misuse of the gifts of the Spirit. As Paul makes clear again and again in Second Corinthians, faith does not bring a personal endowment with power; rather, an abiding communication with God in the crucified and risen Christ. For Paul this communication, in the proclaimed word and the response of faith, is the essence of salvation. It is the exchange of sin and righteousness, death and life, weakness and power that first took place in the incarnate Christ and now takes place in us in faith. The gifts of God are given solely in this communication and thus are accompanied by difficulties, trials, and trouble. Comfort is ours only in affliction. The power of the crucified Christ is manifest only in weakness. This weakness is not a quality to be acquired by self-humiliation or a perverse glorification of suffering. Such thinking would merely repeat the error of the Corinthians in an inverted form. Weakness — and in this context, the weakness of the apostle in particular — serves a material hermeneutical function: it exposes us for what we are before God (12:9-10). The Corinthians imagine that salvation means that they will be made like God. They do not realize that in salvation God has been made like them and has come to them in their foolishness, sin, and weakness.[34] The Corinthian wish to be free from weakness is the secret wish to save that which cannot be saved. It is the attempt to separate the gifts from the Giver.

It was unavoidable that the Corinthian misunderstanding of the Gospel finally came to a head in the question of the marks of an apostle. Paul was the thorn in the flesh of the Corinthians. They could not easily withdraw from their relationship with the one who had first brought the Gospel to Corinth. But his weak bodily appearance, apparent lack of gifts, and constant experience of trouble contradicted all that they imagined Christ and salvation to be. The question at stake in the apostle is the mark of Christ's presence within the world. Paul's answer, simply put, is to point to the nail prints in the hands of the risen Lord, who "was put to death in weakness, but lives by the power of God" (13:4). As the apostle of Christ, Paul bears the "deadness of Jesus" (4:10) in his body in order that the life of the risen Jesus might also be manifest in him. This apostolic existence is merely Christian existence written large. The

33. It is worth noting that Paul's first word on the matter is not his description of their theology but his own theological judgment, which he draws from their conduct: 1 Cor 4:8. Quite understandably, then, there was an impulse to deny, or more precisely, to reinterpret the resurrection. But this view, although it was present in Corinth, had not yet been adopted by the entire church (1 Cor 15:1-58).

34. See Luther WA 5:128.39–129.1: "Because we in Adam ascended to being like God, he has descended into our likeness in order to bring us to the knowledge of ourselves . . . to make out of unhappy and proud gods, true human beings, namely, miserable mortals and sinners."

Corinthians realize this truth, at least intuitively. For this very reason, Paul has become an embarrassment to them. They put up with him but are not yet ready to embrace him (11:1). The Corinthians have failed to see that the Gospel bears a definite form within the world. The lesson of Second Corinthians is that the Gospel may be lost not merely by bad doctrine but by bad living, and not merely by the "bad living" of immorality — which was certainly present in Corinth — but by the decision to measure the work of the Gospel and the presence of Christ by the standards of power, success, and popularity. According to Paul, this practical judgment, which above all else values charisma, wealth, and numbers, is heresy.

Furthermore, to suppose that we may read the position of Paul's opponents out of 2 Cor 3 because Paul there appeals to Moses and the giving of the Law is to overlook the apostle's understanding of the role of Scripture in forming the identity of the church.[35] The remarkable knowledge of Scripture that Paul presupposes within the Corinthian church has long been recognized. It has been perceived less clearly, however, that he expects from them much more than a mere knowledge of the text or formal commitment to its authority. According to Paul, the Scriptures "figure out" the Corinthians, reveal their identity, and make it new in Jesus Christ (vv. 12-18). In him, the wisdom of the world has been done away with, just as the Lord once swept away the wisdom of the wise in Israel (1 Cor 1:19; Isa 29:14). Because Christ is now their wisdom, the Corinthians are to boast in the Lord, just as the Lord called the wise in Jerusalem to do (1 Cor 1:31; Jer 9:23-24). Christ is their Passover lamb. They are a new, unleavened bread (1 Cor 5:7). The children of Israel are their "fathers," in whom they discover their own course of life and its dangers (1 Cor 10:1).[36]

It is of fundamental importance that Paul characterizes his argument concerning apostolic ministry as a reminder of "not going beyond what is written" (1 Cor 4:6). Already in his use of agricultural imagery he draws on the Scriptures, transferring (*metaschēmatizein,* 1 Cor 4:6) to Apollos and to himself the image of planting and watering, a figure that acknowledges that the growth and maturing of the church belongs to God alone (1 Cor 3:6). Paul thus finds himself and his mission in Scripture. The image of temple construction likewise corresponds to this hermeneutic (1 Cor 3:10-17). The Scriptures reveal the world as the creation cared for by God, in which human activity, including the apostolic mission, has its limited place. As we have noted, Paul finds the defining pattern of Christian experience in the story of Moses, the exodus, and Israel's sojourn in the wilderness (1 Cor 10:1-13). We need not suppose, then,

35. On this point, see F. M. Young and D. Ford, *Meaning and Truth in 2 Corinthians* (Grand Rapids: Eerdmans, 1988), 80-84.

36. See further 1 Cor 3:19-20 (Job 5:12; Ps 94:11); 1 Cor 6:16 (Gen 2:24); 1 Cor 9:8-10 (Deut 25:4); 1 Cor 14:20 (Isa 28:11); 1 Cor 15:54-55 (Isa 25:8; Hos 13:14).

that Paul's appeal to the story of Moses in 2 Cor 3 is directed against adversaries promoting Judaizing, nor even against the apostolic claimants who have made their way to Corinth. Paul sets forth the apostolic mission as he finds it in Scripture and directs this exposition to the Corinthians, whose hearts he seeks to win. Paul's identity and role as an apostle is given to him in the Scriptures. Its narratives provide him with his theology. His appeal to the story of the giving of the Law is not contingent upon the presence of particular adversaries. It is fundamental to his Gospel. In Moses and the giving of the Law, he finds a pattern of judgment and grace that speaks to all the world, and especially to the closed minds and hearts of the Corinthians.

Paul's appeal to Scripture in 2 Cor 3 is therefore no abstract typology, theoretical and detached from life. His ministry of the Gospel finds its definition in antithesis to the ministry of Moses. This is nowhere more evident than it is in this chapter. While he elsewhere argues against Gentile Judaizing by defining the place and purpose of the Law, works, and circumcision in relation to Christ and faith and to the gift of the Spirit, all these terms fall away here. Paul speaks instead of "the letter" in relation to the Spirit, the old covenant in relation to the new, Moses in relation to Christ.[37] This antithesis between the two different ways in which God relates to human beings — in demand and promise, in judgment and mercy — enduringly remains within the present world. Its significance is now concentrated upon the question of human understanding, the mind and heart of the fallen human creature: Paul's "theological grammar" expresses itself here in the opposition between the visible, outward, and temporal, and the invisible, inward, and eternal; between "the letter" and "the Spirit." This distinction is one of *theological* hermeneutics, and by no means a Platonic contrast between a world of things and a world of ideas. Paul's "grammar" arises from the crucified and risen Christ. The outward and visible glory of this present world, in which human beings boast and trust, lies under the judgment of the cross; the invisible and inward glory of the age to come, which is present in the risen Lord, is hidden under weakness and suffering. The invisible is concretely and materially present in the world, as is the visible. Moreover, the visible requires revelation just as much as does the invisible. Human wisdom, which falsely estimates both the world and the cross, must be manifest for what it is and destroyed in order for faith and the Spirit to arrive. God's judgments and work always differ from our own, and they take a form that is contrary to all our reasoning.[38] The Scriptures supply Paul with the "theological grammar" by which he parses the Corinthians and

37. On the latter, see the near parallel in Rom 10:1-13.

38. Thus it is the hidden Jew, whose circumcision is of the heart by the Spirit, who is finally a Jew (Rom 2:14:29; cf. Phil 3:1-11). The children born of promise, whose mother is the Jerusalem above, are free (Gal 4:21-31; cf. 5:1-6).

their false judgments in 2 Cor 3, in much the same way as he does in his appeal to the story of the exodus in 1 Cor 10:1-13. His use of the figure of Moses naturally anticipates and dethrones his adversaries' claim to be representatives of Jewish tradition (11:22). Perhaps, too, he is undermining their claim to knowledge of Jesus (5:16). But Paul's attention is focused more fundamentally on the Corinthians and their understanding of God. The contrast between the visible and invisible reflects the larger issue that drives the letter, namely, the legitimation of the apostle and salvation of the Corinthians, which has been jeopardized in their misunderstanding of him. The apostolic claimants are only a part of this drama, as is apparent from 1 Corinthians, where the same issues are in play, even though the intruders had not yet arrived on the scene. Paul's remarkable concentration on the hermeneutical implications of the Gospel is an indication that he is not combating Judaizing opponents or merely Jewish-Hellenistic spiritualists. He is dealing with the Corinthians themselves.

The contrast between the visible and invisible in 2 Cor 3 is matched by Paul's preceding, theological interpretation of his experience in Troas (2:12-17). Paul is the odor of Christ for some "from death to death," for others "from life to life" (2:16). Everything depends on how one perceives the sufferings of the apostle. As with the sense of smell, these perceptions are preformed: either one has been given the "nose" to sense the salvation present in the apostle, or one finds only the stench of death. Similarly, in the following context, Paul speaks of the "god of this age" who has "blinded the minds of the unbelieving, so that they cannot see the light of the Gospel of the glory of Christ" (4:4). Within his argument in 2 Cor 3, he recalls Moses' placing a veil over his face so that the "sons of Israel" could not see its glory and thus not look upon the "goal" of "that which is done away" (3:13). Not only has the apostle been "figured out" in the story of Moses, the Corinthians have been "figured out" with him.[39] Indeed, the whole of unbelieving humanity has been "figured out" within the story of Moses' dealings with the "sons of Israel." The temporary glory of Moses' mission was visible. The eternal glory of the apostolic mission, although it vastly transcends that of Moses, is hidden with the cross, the suffering and death of Christ. Moses' mission belongs to the present age and its glory, across which the shadow of death is cast. The Corinthian attraction to strength and wisdom is a perverse and foolish substitution of the ephemeral and dying for that which is weighted with eternal glory (4:17-18). "You are looking at things according to appearance!" (10:7). The "apostles" who offer such attractions are ministers of Satan — the god of this age — who clothes himself as an angel of light (11:12-15). The story of the giving of the Law through Moses lays bare the truth about the present world and points to the decisive and eternal hope

39. I have borrowed this language from C. R. Seitz, *Figured Out: Typology and Providence in Christian Scripture* (Louisville, Ky.: Westminster John Knox Press, 2001).

given in the Gospel. The mission of "the letter" that works death has its end in the Spirit, who brings life. The visible glory of the old covenant that appeared in Moses' face is eclipsed by the glory of the crucified Christ. This glory, as Paul expressly tells the Corinthians, can be perceived only where the Spirit is present. There alone the veil that rests on the human heart is removed.

---

1. *The Corinthians as Paul's Commendation (3:1-3)*

> 3[1]*Are we beginning to commend ourselves again? Or do we need, as some do, letters of recommendation to you, or from you?* [2]*You yourselves are our letter of recommendation, written on our hearts, to be known and read by all.* [3]*And you show that you are a letter from Christ delivered by us, written not with ink but with the Spirit of the living God, not on tablets of stone but on tablets of human hearts.*

1 As we have noted, Paul's language here is ironic. When he asks, "Are we again commending ourselves?" he is speaking to the Corinthians' perception of the situation. In his lengthy rehearsal of his experiences, actions, decisions, and motives, he has not been commending himself to the Corinthians *in their terms* (1:8–2:17). In that sense, his commendation is no commendation. Everything that he says is for their edification, however, as he later expressly affirms (12:19).

In his second rhetorical question, Paul brings the false apostolic claimants briefly into view. Unlike "certain ones," he does not need letters to or from the Corinthian church. The mercenary interest of "the many" (2:17) now becomes focused on certain unnamed persons.

Although Paul's adversaries claim a Jewish heritage (11:22) and may well have brought letters of commendation, it is not at all clear that they brought letters purporting to come from the Jerusalem church. Paul's lack of specificity here argues against that assumption. If they had appealed to the authority of the Jerusalem church, one would have expected a direct response from the apostle, along the lines of that in Galatians 2:1-21. Furthermore, as we have observed, Paul speaks of letters not only to the church but also *from* the church in Corinth. The Corinthians regard *themselves* as sufficient to judge the legitimacy of apostolic claimants.

The use of letters of commendation was common among the scattered congregations of earliest Christianity (Acts 18:27), as it also was within Diaspora Judaism (Acts 9:2; 22:5). We know, in fact, that the church in Corinth received such a letter of commendation for Apollos (Acts 18:27). Paul himself commends Phoebe, a prominent member of the church in Cenchreae, to the church at Rome (Rom 16:1-2). He obviously had no difficulty with the practice of sending and receiving letters of commendation. The problem with the Corinthians lay in their assumption that *apostles* should be subject to the judgment of the churches. While Paul certainly does not regard his own person as anything special, the Gospel that he bears stands above the church, to which it has given life.

Paul's wording here prepares for his claim to boldness in the following context. One might render his question, "Or do we *use [chraomai]* . . . letters of commendation?" He picks up this language in 3:12 when he affirms, "Therefore, having this hope, we *use* [again, *chraomai*] great boldness."

2 The legitimation of the apostle rests in the Corinthians themselves: "You are our letter." As the legitimation of apostolic ministry, they are not in a position to legitimate that ministry by their own judgments. Paul's apostolic credentials lie in them and their faith, which has its boast in God's work in and through Christ.[40] As he indicates at an earlier stage in the conflict, the Corinthians themselves are "the seal" of his apostleship, the confirmation of its validity (1 Cor 9:2). In a profound and tragic irony, the Corinthians are seeking the signs of an apostle in the weak and suffering Paul (12:12). They have not yet realized that they themselves are the proof of God's power that is also at work in him (1 Cor 2:5).

This letter, Paul says, "is written in our hearts."[41] Just as he cannot speak of himself and his apostolic calling apart from the Corinthians, he cannot speak of the Corinthians and their faith apart from himself. As we have observed repeatedly, the drama of the letter is the relationship between the apostle of Christ and his church, or more precisely, the fresh communication of Paul's love in Christ to a church that has rejected it. The previous letter, written with tears, had precisely the same aim (2:4). Paul's expression of distress in Troas and joy at the good news from Titus of the Corinthians' "zeal" for him (7:5-16) serve to reaffirm that love (cf. 11:11). His open statement of his love for them here likewise anticipates his appeal in 6:11-13 ("our mouth is open to you, Corinthians") and especially in 7:2-4 (v. 3, "You are in our hearts to die together and live together!"). At this moment, the Corinthians weigh especially heavily in his daily burden of concern for the churches (11:28-29).

That the Corinthians are "written in [his] heart," entails much more, however, than Paul's love for them. His passive wording signals that, before all else, he participates in and remains a recipient of the new covenant that he describes in the remainder of this chapter. Contrary to the Corinthians' ex-

40. 1:12-14, 20-24.

41. Despite the attestation of ℵ and 33 to ἐν ταῖς καρδίαις *ὑμῶν* ("[written] in your hearts"), the reading "[written] in our hearts" (ἐν ταῖς καρδίαις *ἡμῶν*) is to be preferred, not least because it is the *lectio difficilior.*

pectations, Paul does not speak first of something that he has done. He begins with what has been done in him. Even in his apostolic activity, he is a recipient of God's work in Christ. His calling as apostle is an outflow of the salvation given to him and cannot be separated from it. His love for the Corinthians is thus no mere fallible, human commitment. It is by the work of God that the Corinthians are "in [his] heart."

The letter of the Corinthians, written within his heart, is "known and read" by everyone. Paul's claim that his love for the Corinthians is a matter of open and public knowledge is an assertion of his integrity and, in fact, pregnantly echoes his earlier claim concerning his letters: just as those letters contain nothing other than what the Corinthians "read and know" (1:13), so all the world knows that he has them "written in his heart." Paul's love for the Corinthians is a matter of record: he boasts of his cost-free ministry among them.[42] His distress in Troas and joy in Macedonia over them were likewise known to others.[43] He also has boasted about them ("Achaia") to the Macedonians in their commitment to the collection for Jerusalem (9:1-2). His claim here that this love letter is "known and read *by all*" is hyperbolic. Or perhaps it is not: the apostles have been made a spectacle to "humanity and to angels." They bear the drama of Christ in their bodies and lives (1 Cor 4:9). Paul carries the treasure of the Gospel in an earthen vessel so that the life of Jesus may be manifest in his flesh (4:7-12). He has been made manifest to God and thus, he hopes, to the conscience of the Corinthians (5:11). In his suffering and deliverance, and in the sincerity that is his through the Gospel, his apostolic life has become a prolepsis of the final judgment, when all human beings shall be made manifest before Christ's seat of judgment (5:10). That all persons know and read the love letter written in Paul's heart is his claim to the final and decisive significance of his apostolic life and mission. The eschaton, which has broken into the world in Christ, is present in Christ's apostle and servant.

3 The eschaton is also present in the Corinthians. Although English translations generally do not make it apparent, Paul here speaks of *the Corinthians* being manifest as a letter of Christ.

Paul thus continues the metaphor of v. 2 but transposes his description of his apostolic ministry to an active sense: "[you] are manifest as a letter of Christ administered by us." The knowledge of Christ that is manifest in the apostle (2:14) — his passivity includes his activity — is manifest in the Corinthians as well. This "odor" has been communicated to them through him, "from life unto life" (2:16).

Contrary to what the Corinthians suppose, Paul plays only a subordinate role in his apostolic labors. He is the mere agent of Another, an emissary of

42. 11:5-11; 1 Cor 9:15.

43. 2:14-17; 7:5-16.

Christ. As we have noted, Paul here introduces the fundamental theme upon which he builds throughout the body of the letter.[44] He responds afresh to the long-standing misunderstanding of apostolic mission within the Corinthian church that has now reached a critical point, taking up the argument of 1 Cor 3:1–4:5 in a new form.

The Corinthians are "a letter of Christ." Genitive relations are semantically productive and not to be pigeon-holed.[45] In what ways, then, are the Corinthians "Christ's letter"? The context itself invites the question. The genitive relation in the first instance is probably that of possession, as in Paul's preceding reference to the Corinthians as "our letter." Yet the idea of Christ's authorship is also surely present: the Corinthians are "Christ's letter" *communicated* (or, indeed, "delivered"; RSV, ESV) by the apostle.[46] They are thus not Paul's commendation but a commendation of Christ, who has sent the apostle as his agent and envoy. Furthermore, it is likely that the idea of *content* is also present in the genitive relation "of Christ." The Corinthians are a letter in which Christ is present. This reading of the genitive corresponds to Paul's immediately preceding description of God, who makes Paul to be "the odor of Christ among both those being saved and the perishing." Through him the crucified and risen Lord is *communicated* to the world, whether it responds in faith or in unbelief (2:15-16). A genitive of content likewise matches Paul's following description of himself as a "minister of a new covenant" through whom God imparts the Spirit and righteousness (3:8-9; cf. 1 Cor 11:23-26). The "administration" of Christ's letter is nothing other than the "administration of the new covenant," which imparts a new relation to God. The Spirit — given through the apostolic mission — communicates the glory of the Lord to those in Christ, a glory that is found solely in the crucified and risen Christ (3:17-18; cf. 4:4-6). Indeed, the fundamental theme of the letter is the presence of Christ in the apostle, a presence that is *communicated* to the believing Corinthians.[47] The Corinthians thus are not merely a letter written by Christ. They have been made to share in Christ. They are Christ's letter in that Christ himself is present in and among them. For this reason, too, Paul is able to say, as he does already in v. 2, that the Corinthians have been written as a letter *in his own heart.*

As the letter of Christ, the Corinthians are "written not by [means of] ink but by the Spirit of the living God."[48] That the Corinthians are so "written"

44. 4:1; 5:18; 6:3-4.

45. Against the ESV and NIV, which interpret the genitive simply as an expression of source: "a letter from Christ."

46. Paul's usage in this context is best understood within the field of meaning of communication and agency. See Collins, *Diakonia,* 203-4.

47. 1:3-7, 19-22; 2:14-17; 5:17; 10:7; 11:2, 10; 13:3, 5.

48. The Greek datives (οὐ μέλανι ἀλλὰ πνεύματι θεοῦ ζῶντος) likely shift subtly from instrumentality to agency, without disrupting the parallelism. It is possible that Paul here

implies an unqualified remaking, a rewriting of their person and life by God the Creator. As Paul later says expressly, "If someone is in Christ, there is a new creation" (5:17).

Paul here speaks of the saving work of God as simultaneously fixed and yet dynamic, complete and yet in progress. The medium of God's writing is not mere ink but "the Spirit of the living God," the God who, according to name and title, is powerful and active in the hearts and lives of the Corinthians. Paul thus contrasts the inert and dead medium of "ink" with the agency of the Spirit: "written not *with* ink but *by* the Spirit of the living God."[49] Nevertheless, in that the Corinthians are a *written* letter, God's work in them is complete and *fixed,* as is all writing. They are, moreover, "a letter of Christ," who has been communicated to them by the Gospel that Paul must defend against all misunderstanding. The fixity of the epistle does not exclude, but includes, the incessant work of "the Spirit of the living God," in ever new, living, and fresh ways. As Paul will make clear in the following context, the Spirit establishes an active, saving *communication* between the fallen human being and God, a communication that does not end, not even with death itself (vv. 17-18). This communication is both determinate and yet unendingly new.

In the immediate context, the contrast between "the living God" and the inactive and lifeless black ink of a letter may also recall the scriptural contrast between Yahweh and the idols.[50] The Corinthian requirement that *apostles* have letters of approval is at root idolatrous. It is not that letters of commendation are wrong. Paul himself has written them. But the authority of an apostle is of a different order than that of normal human affairs: God is present and at work in Christ's apostle. Thus, while Paul here speaks of the work of salvation as having been completed in the hearts of the Corinthians, he still must battle for their hearts and, indeed, call them afresh to receive the Gospel and to be reconciled with God. There is no escaping this paradox of Christian faith and life. The Corinthians are to grow into that which they have been given and have received. They must be called back again and again to accept that which is already theirs through Jesus Christ.

Paul's reference to the *written* work of "the Spirit of the living God" prepares for a sudden shift of imagery. The medium upon which the external writing might have taken place is not papyrus, as one might expect, but "plates

---

speaks of the "living God" as the agent and the Spirit as the means, since he speaks of the "administration of the Spirit" (3:8). Yet Paul clearly speaks of the Spirit as an agent elsewhere in context (3:6, 18) and identifies the Spirit with "the Lord" (3:17).

49. The Greek datives may be read either way.

50. E.g., Josh 3:10; 1 Sam 17:26, 36; Jer 10:10; Dan 6:10; Acts 14:15; 1 Thess 1:9. See also Bel 5-25.

of stone." Letters of abiding, public significance in antiquity did not remain on papyrus; they were displayed as inscriptions. And of course the Law was written on plates of stone. As Paul underscores, the letter of Christ is not written there, but instead "in plates [that are] fleshly hearts." This immediate juxtaposition of letters of commendation with "plates of stone" reinforces the conclusion that we have drawn already. Paul is not combating the threat of Gentile Judaizing as he describes Moses' mission. Rather, he is exposing and challenging the Corinthians' insistence on signs of apostolic authority and especially, at this point, on letters of commendation. In presupposing that they may judge God's work in the apostle, the Corinthians have misunderstood everything. Insofar as they believe, they themselves *are* that work: the Spirit of God has written Christ upon their hearts through the apostle and the Gospel that he bears.[51]

Mere letters presuppose the lack of direct, personal communication. The Spirit of the living God, in contrast, transcends all distance as he performs his work on the hearts of the Corinthians. In their desire for letters of commendation, they overlook the work of the Spirit and thus set a distance between themselves and God. This distance marks the human encounter with God in the Law; there God addresses the human being from a distance, through a mediator, in written letters.[52]

Initially, Israel received the Decalogue as the *spoken* words of God at Sinai (Exod 20:1-26). But the people, who could not bear to hear God's voice, appealed to Moses to act as God's spokesperson: not God, but Moses was to speak to them and deliver God's words (Exod 20:19). Indeed, it is not clear in the Exodus narrative that the people actually heard the words of the Decalogue. They seem to have heard only the thunder and trumpet associated with the Lord's speaking.[53] The Lord subsequently instructs Moses to ascend the mountain to receive "the tablets of stone, and the Law and commandment that I have *written* for their instruction" (Exod 24:12).[54] The giving of the Law in written form, even at the start, signals Israel's rebellious heart and distance

51. Indeed, the Spirit binds the apostle and the Corinthians to one another; as "the letter of Christ," the Corinthians are written in Paul's heart (v. 2). The distance between them remains and yet is overcome.

52. Paul elsewhere emphasizes that the Law was delivered through a mediator, whose presence signals distance from God (Gal 3:20).

53. Exod 19:18-19; 20:18.

54. The giving of the written Law takes place immediately after the conclusion of the covenant ceremony, with its sacrifices and the idyllic covenant meal of the elders of Israel with God — a fleeting moment of peace. The intervening event reinforces the reading presented here, since it finalizes the relation between God and Israel *based on the spoken words of the Lord's voice*. The fresh word to Moses to receive written instruction indicates that this relationship already was imperfect and damaged, just as it was in Israel's inability to hear the Lord.

from God. Not only in its inability to listen to God's voice but also in its disobedience and grumbling in the wilderness, Israel has shown itself unwilling to follow the Law.[55] The turn to idolatry in the worship of the golden calf, as dramatic as it is, represents only a fresh manifestation of a rebellion that was already present.[56] The giving of the Law as commandments *written in stone* signals the distance between wayward Israel and the God who nevertheless wills to live in communion with his people. In shifting his imagery in v. 3, Paul thus implies a basic correspondence between epistles of commendation and the letters of the Law written in stone, which cannot change the rebellious human heart or bring communion with God. Both communicate from a distance and imply a disrupted relationship.

Paul's language in the final clause of v. 3 obviously is highly allusive. Not only does he recall the giving of the Law on plates of stone at Sinai,[57] but also he alludes to the Jeremianic promise of a new covenant, as is clear in his characterization of the work of the Spirit as a *writing* upon the human heart (Jer 31:31-34). He goes on to define apostolic ministry in precisely this way in v. 6. The promised new covenant is the Lord's work that effects true obedience within the hearts of rebels; it is fulfilled in the apostolic mission.

At the end of v. 3, Paul fills out his allusion to the new covenant with yet another allusion. The letter of Christ is written on "plates [that are] fleshly hearts," and *not,* as most English translations have it, "human hearts."[58] The adjective *sarkinos* is to be understood here as "fleshly," not merely "human." Paul describes the human being as fallen, given over to sin and death.[59] His

55. Exod 15:26; 16:4; cf. 19:5-6. According to Deuteronomy, Israel's fundamental unwillingness to follow the Lord's commandments continues to manifest itself throughout the forty years in the wilderness (Deut 8:1-3; 9:7-29).

56. In a form of "corporate solidarity," the book of Deuteronomy places the new generation of Israel back at "Horeb" itself, so that they themselves "heard the voice out of the darkness" (Deut 5:23). The Lord came to Israel in this way in order to discipline them, in order to secure their obedience (4:9-14, 33-40). The experience at Horeb is to remain a living memory that instills the keeping of the (written) commandments, which is nothing other than obedience to "the voice of the Lord" (Deut 13:18; 15:5; 28:1-2, 15). The theological emphasis differs from Exodus, but the distance between Israel and the Lord signaled by the written form of the divine commands remains. It is even accentuated: Moses himself is not sufficient. Israel's inability to hear God's voice at Horeb becomes the basis of God's promise to raise up another prophet like Moses, in whose *mouth* he will place his words (18:15-19).

57. See Exod 31:18; 32:15-19; 34:1-4, 28-29 ("plates of the covenant"; likewise Deut 9:9-11).

58. Thus, wrongly, ESV, NIV, NRSV.

59. The same sense is present in Paul's two other uses of the adjective "fleshly" (σάρκινος), which he likewise applies to human beings in contrast with the work of the Spirit (Rom 7:14; 1 Cor 3:1). The alternative adjective (σαρκικός), which Paul uses for the realities of the fallen world (Rom 15:27; 1 Cor 9:11; 2 Cor 1:12; 10:4), itself denotes that which is external and lesser, or fallen (2 Cor 1:12). It may be that Paul elsewhere uses this alternative form to signify

language in v. 3 recalls Jer 17:1,[60] which speaks of the sin of Judah, "engraved on the plate of their heart with a diamond point."[61] He thus takes up this image of the *rebellious* human heart as a stone "plate" or "tablet," hardened in opposition to the words engraved by God's finger on the stone tablets of the Law.[62] In his subsequent reference to Moses' veil, he speaks correspondingly of the minds of the sons of Israel "being turned into stone."[63] Paul does not address warm and loving "human" hearts here, but the wayward and hardened hearts of the Corinthians. They are Christ's palimpsest: upon the very hardened hearts into which sin and rebellion have been inscribed, the Spirit of the living God makes his own, fresh inscription, an inscription that creates them anew. The proverbial admonition of a father to his son "write my commandments on the tablet of your heart" is here performed by God himself (Prov 7:3).[64] Yet in contrast to Jer 31:33, Paul does not speak of the Law being written on the heart. It is Christ, the Law's goal *(telos)*, who is written there (v. 13; cf. Rom 10:4). The fundamental conflict between "flesh" and "Spirit," which is characteristic of Paul's understanding of the work of the Gospel in the world, is present here.[65] The Creator triumphs in the midst of sin and death, and saves the wretched and miserable.

In v. 3 there is probably also an allusion to the "fleshly hearts" of Ezek 11:19 and 36:26, although not in the direct sense that nearly all interpreters suppose.[66] In these passages God promises to remove "the heart of stone" from his people and to give them "a heart of flesh," placing his Spirit within them and causing them to walk in his commandments. In Ezekiel the "hearts of flesh" are the *result* of God's saving work. Paul, in contrast, speaks of "fleshly hearts" as the place of human fallenness *upon which* God performs his saving work.[67] Over against the stony plates of the Law are the stony plates of "fleshly hearts." It is upon these that the Spirit savingly writes. They are the place of re-

---

the mere "worldliness" of the Corinthians, i.e., their belonging merely to the elements of the fallen world, speaking of them more as creaturely things (1 Cor 3:3; cf. 1 Cor 3:1).

60. The verse is admittedly lacking in the LXX, which hardly makes a difference. See, however, *Tg. Neb.* at Jer 17:1. See Robert Hayward, trans., *The Targum of Jeremiah* (The Aramaic Bible 12; Wilmington, Del.: Michael Glazier, 1987), 97.

61. Cf. Zech 7:12, "They made their heart as hard as diamond."

62. In fact, Paul speaks shortly of the minds of the "sons of Israel" being hardened (3:14) and of a veil lying upon their heart (3:15).

63. He uses πωρόω instead of σκληρύνω ("to harden"), which is usual in the LXX.

64. See also LXX Prov 22:20.

65. See Rom 2:28-29; 7:5-6; 8:4-13; Gal 3:3; 4:29; 5:16-17, 24; 6:8.

66. The parallelism of the language (καρδίαι σάρκιναι) seems to have blinded interpreters to the difference in thought between Paul and these passages in the book of Ezekiel.

67. See, in contrast, *Barn.* 6:14, which cites Ezek 11:19; 36:26 directly in reference to the re-creation of the human being by God the Spirit, who is incarnate in Christ and comes to indwell "us."

bellion and sin to which salvation comes. Paul here anticipates his subsequent description of "the sons of Israel," whose minds and thoughts were *turned to stone* (3:14; cf. 4:4). Although his language in v. 3 is noticeably close to that of Ezekiel, the imagery is inverted. He reconfigures the text and incorporates it into his allusion to the stony heart of Judah upon which the Lord promises to inscribe his Law (Jer 17:1; 31:31-34). Perhaps the basis of this inversion can be found in Ezek 11, where the promise of a "heart of flesh" first appears.[68] In this context, "flesh" connotes subjection to condemnation and death. The officials in Jerusalem who "devise iniquity and give wicked counsel" advise against building houses, since "the city is the pot and we are the flesh" (Ezek 11:3).[69] The Lord instructs the prophet to tell them that, not they, but the many whom these officials have slain are the "flesh" within the pot of the city. God will execute judgment on them by the sword, yet not in the city, as they expect, but "at the border of Israel." The city will not be "the pot." And they will not be the "flesh" within it (Ezek 11:10-12). They instead shall go into exile and suffer death there. Only at this point does the promise to the exiles that God will bring them back to the land of Israel appear (Ezek 11:16-20). God will remove the heart of stone from their flesh and give them a heart of flesh, so that they may keep his ordinances and walk in his ways. In this context, the "heart of flesh" represents not merely obedience to God's commandments but also *the recognition and acceptance of the divine judgment on the nation.* In receiving the "heart of flesh," the people come to see and confess their own guilt, as is evident in the parallel passage in Ezek 36:31:

> Then you shall remember your evil ways, and your dealings that were not good; and you shall loathe yourselves for your iniquities and your abominable deeds.

Insofar as Paul recalls the language of Ezekiel, he does so in order to communicate the self-knowledge effected by the work of Christ within the human heart. It is God's purpose to bring the Corinthians back to themselves so that they recognize what they are: mere mortals given over to sin and death. The allusion thus corresponds to the fundamental issue at stake in Corinth. The treasure of the Gospel is ever only contained in earthen vessels. This is true not only for the apostle but also for the Corinthians. God's saving work takes place only on the "fleshly hearts" of sinful people. The godly need not apply. Indeed, they refuse to do so.

68. Ezek 11:19; also 36:26.

69. Admittedly, the LXX breaks up the linguistic connection, since it renders בָּשָׂר as κρέα in Ezek 11:3, 11, while describing God's saving work as effecting a καρδία σαρκίνη in Ezek 11:19.

2. The New Covenant as Paul's Sufficiency (3:4-11)

> 4*Such is the confidence that we have through Christ toward God.* 5*Not that we are sufficient in ourselves to claim anything as coming from us, but our sufficiency is from God,* 6*who has made us sufficient to be ministers of a new covenant, not of the letter but of the Spirit. For the letter kills, but the Spirit gives life.* 7*Now if the ministry of death, carved in letters on stone, came with such glory that the Israelites could not gaze at Moses' face because of its glory, which was being brought to an end,* 8*will not the ministry of the Spirit have even more glory?* 9*For if there was glory in the ministry of condemnation, the ministry of righteousness must far exceed it in glory.* 10*Indeed, in this case, what once had glory has come to have no glory at all, because of the glory that surpasses it.* 11*For if what was being brought to an end came with glory, much more will what is permanent have glory.*

4 As apostle, Paul requires no letters of commendation. He has no need to commend himself. The Corinthians themselves are his letter of commendation — or rather, not his but that of Christ, who works in and through him to rewrite the hearts of fallen human beings. This is a claim of unheard-of audacity, as Paul himself recognizes: "And *such* confidence we have through Christ toward God." As we have noted, the term *pepoithēsis* ("confidence") bears an essentially passive meaning. It is oriented to the object of trust rather than to the act of trusting.[70] Paul's "confidence" does not consist in his own courage or conviction. It is a confidence that has been given to him and that rests outside of him in Christ's work — a work that includes the Corinthians themselves. As it is spoken and told, Paul's confidence is a boasting[71] that is a hope fixed on unseen realities, as he will make clear shortly (3:12).[72]

Paul's little phrase "through Christ" is crucial. The crucified and risen Christ is the vehicle of his empowerment. His confidence is thus a confidence that life is given in and through death — not just any death, but the death of Christ in which he shares. This is the mission and ministry of the new covenant that Paul unfolds in vv. 4-11: the *newness* of the covenant of the Spirit is the life and righteousness that it brings out of the death and condemnation worked by the old covenant.

5 Paul immediately qualifies and defines the confidence given to him through Christ. He remains inadequate and insufficient in himself and thus cannot suppose that anything in his service comes from him. Nevertheless, his rhetorical question "Who is sufficient for these things?" (2:16) — namely, the

70. See the comment on 1:15, p. 56.

71. 1:12-14; cf. 1:15; 5:12; 10:2, 8.

72. See also 1:7, 13.

impartation of death and life — does not end in an aporia. Nor is the Corinthian requirement of commendation of the apostle justified. The sufficiency of the apostle remains God's sufficiency and in no way becomes a strength, quality, or virtue of his own. Nothing comes from Paul, yet life and death are enacted through him. Paul has been torn away from himself. His life and identity, calling and work have been determined outside him. His boasting is a boasting in the Lord and decidedly *not* in himself, his powers, and his abilities.[73] His confidence is a confidence in the God who raises the dead: this theme, which Paul introduces at the beginning of the letter, continues throughout.[74] As we have seen more than once, the "eccentricity" of the apostle is not accidental but essential to his apostolic calling, and indeed to salvation itself.

6a God, who remains the subject of the discourse, has *also* made Paul sufficient as apostle, that is, as "an emissary of a new covenant."[75] Paul does not act out of his own powers, as the Corinthians imagine. As apostle, he is nothing other than a *diakonos,* an agent of another, a representative on mission. In using the adverb "also" *(kai)* and the plural form "us," Paul implicitly places himself alongside other apostles. He here defines the nature of the apostolic calling in a manner reminiscent of his argument in 1 Cor 3:1–4:5, where he similarly sets himself alongside Apollos as an "agent on mission" (*diakonos,* 1 Cor 3:5).[76] Now, however, he refers directly to the Scriptures, rather than merely borrowing its agricultural imagery.[77] His unusual language should not be overlooked. One was not normally judged as "sufficient" or "competent" as an "emissary" or "agent" of another. As he already has reminded the Corinthians, "stewards" and "underlings" are examined not for their adequacy but for their *faithfulness* (1 Cor 4:1-5).

Paul here describes his role as an emissary of "*a* new covenant," not "*the* new covenant." In introducing this expression, he clearly refers to the Lord's Supper tradition that he himself delivered to the Corinthians and, through the

73. See 10:17-18, where Paul again appeals to Jer 9:23-24, as he has already done in 1 Cor 1:30-31. Significantly, he now cites (or strongly alludes to) the text in reference to apostolic ministry, which has become the point of contention. On "boasting," see above, pp. 48-49.

74. See 1:9; 4:7; 10:17-18; 12:9-10; 13:4.

75. The term "emissary" expresses more directly the communicative role of the apostle signified by the term διάκονος than does the usual translation "minister" (ESV, NRSV, NIV). On the usage in this context, see again Collins, *Diakonia,* 197-98. The language clearly anticipates his more formal description of himself as acting as Christ's ambassador (ὑπὲρ Χριστοῦ . . . πρεσβεύομεν, 5:20).

76. In 1 Cor 3, however, he is not yet defending his apostolic calling but only defining the differing ministries that had been given to him and to Apollos. The issues that were already at work in the Corinthians' attraction to various leaders have now come to a head in the question of the legitimation of the apostle.

77. See n. 110, p. 127.

"cup-word" of that tradition, to the Jeremianic promise of a new covenant.[78] Yet his anarthrous usage emphasizes the significance rather than the referent of his words. Paul describes what it *means* to serve a new covenant, rather than pointing to "the new covenant," with which the Corinthians already were familiar. He does not recall the "cup-word" here, at least not directly, nor does he have in view simply the celebration of the Supper, but the whole of his apostolic mission, including his life as an apostle. It is very likely that Paul's focus on his apostolic mission calls forth his usage of the term "covenant" here. Whether it is old or new, a covenant establishes a relationship between God and human beings. The nature of that relation is determined by the divine word that establishes the covenant, whether it is conditioned by demands or given by unconditioned promise.[79]

Paul is an emissary of a "*new* covenant." His description of this covenant as "new" is already an indication that he does not conceive of God's saving dealings with the world in terms of a single, overarching covenant with Israel.[80] His following description of the new covenant excludes that possibility; the new covenant is *not* of the letter *but* of the Spirit. The genitive relations "of the letter" and "of the Spirit" express the differing contents of the covenants, i.e., that which is delivered and dispensed by each of them.[81] This distinction between demand and gift, which we shall consider in greater detail below, is already present in the "new covenant" of Jer 31:31-34. to which Paul alludes. There the Lord promises that he will make a new covenant "with the house of Israel and with the house of Judah," *not like* the covenant he made with their ancestors when he brought them out of Egypt (Jer 31:32). The new covenant will be different from the covenant made at Sinai, which Israel broke. The Lord now will place his Law *within* them and shall write it on their heart (Jer 31:33).[82] They thus will belong to him as his people, and he will belong to them as their God (Jer 31:33; cf. Ezek 11:20); the *communicative* relation that Paul describes in vv. 16-18 is constituted in this new covenant. No longer will there be any need for anyone to admonish and instruct another. The written Law, the very purpose

78. See 1 Cor 11:23-26, esp. 11:25: "This cup is the new covenant in my blood." Cf. Jer 31:31-34, esp. 31:31. It is likely that the Lukan form of this tradition reflects the form that Paul has adopted and employed.

79. For the same reason, Paul turns to covenant language in Gal 4:21-31.

80. This idea has a long history. On the current scene it is represented in new form by N. T. Wright, *The New Testament and the People of God* (Christian Origins and the Question of God 1; Minneapolis: Fortress, 1992), 259-79; S. J. Hafemann, *Paul, Moses, and the History of Israel: The Letter/Spirit Contrast and the Argument from Scripture in 2 Corinthians 3* (WUNT 81; Tübingen: Mohr Siebeck, 1995), 438-44.

81. The genitive relation functions in this way in Num 18:19; 25:12-13; 2 Chr 13:5; Isa 54:10; Ezek 34:25-26.

82. Cf. Ezek 11:19-20; 36:26-27.

of which is to provide the basis of instruction, no longer shall be necessary (cf. Exod 24:12).[83] All shall know the Lord and obey him with the spontaneity that marks true obedience (Jer 31:34).[84] All of these blessings are predicated and based on the forgiveness of sins: the new covenant arrives only where the old covenant has worked transgression and condemnation.[85] Indeed, the very naming of this covenant as "new" means that it is defined in contrast with the "old." The recipients of the "new covenant" know themselves to be nothing more than forgiven sinners. The covenant made at Sinai is constituted by the Law, which remains outside the human being as divine moral instruction, requirement, and demand.[86] The new covenant is no longer demand but an unqualified promise and gift. It is purely and simply the work of God the Creator, who through the Gospel enters into and savingly re-creates the human heart, thereby establishing a relationship with the rebellious human being.[87] The former commandment thus is displaced by the fulfilled promise — which endures forever, as Paul emphasizes in context (v. 11).[88] In all probability, it is the announcement of the "new covenant" in Jer 31:31 that prompts Paul to speak of "the old covenant" in v. 14.[89] The claim that the old and new covenants are somehow the same because the "content" of the Law is communicated or imparted by both of them is built upon a flawed and fatal abstraction.[90] God's communication with fallen humanity cannot legitimately be abstracted from its form, so as to become a higher idea or concept.[91] This would be equivalent to saying that, because two statements have to do with the amount of one thousand dollars, it makes no difference that one comes in the form of a bill of demand and the other in the form of a gift. Just as the form of the new covenant differs from the covenant made at Sinai, so its content radically differs from the old covenant.

83. See the comments on the written Law on pp. 115-16 above.

84. Instruction remains necessary insofar as the Corinthians (and, with them, all believers) must grow in faith and grasp Christ more fully. In themselves they remain sinners; in Christ they have been made new. Not even the apostle stands above them with respect to their faith, as Paul has affirmed already (1:24).

85. In the parallel passages in Ezek 11:14-22; 36:22-28, the Lord promises blessing in the face of Israel's sin and rebellion.

86. Esp. in the book of Deuteronomy, the "covenant" made at Horeb is identified as the Decalogue, or the Law (Deut 4:13; 5:1-22; 9:9-11, 15; 29:9).

87. The demand "Do this and you shall live" (cf. Lev 18:5) has been transcended by the apostolic proclamation, through which the Spirit is given freely (cf. Gal 3:1-4).

88. As O. Hofius observes, the abiding nature of the new covenant also appears in the corresponding contexts in the Scriptures; see Jer 32:40 and Ezek 16:60; 37:26 ("Gesetz und Evangelium nach 2. Korinther 3," in *Paulusstudien* [WUNT 51; Tübingen: Mohr Siebeck, 1989], 86).

89. So, rightly, Hofius, "Gesetz und Evangelium nach 2. Korinther 3," 81.

90. Against Wright, *Paul in Fresh Perspective,* 123-25.

91. On this topic, see Bayer, *Theology,* 144-48.

They differ as much as a demand differs from a promise, condemnation differs from righteousness, and death from life.[92]

Correspondingly, as we have seen already, in v. 3 the apostle echoes Jer 31:33 in the form of a sharp contrast: Christ's letter is written, "*not* in plates of stone, *but* in plates of fleshly hearts." Paul speaks of the Lord's "writing of the Law on the heart" promised in Jeremiah as *a replacing* of the Law. This contrast becomes even clearer in his following contrast between the mission of the "letter" as bringing death and condemnation and the mission of the Spirit bringing life and righteousness. In Jesus Christ "the letter" has been done away with.[93] Shortly, in a striking statement, unique within the New Testament, Paul describes the Law as "the *old* covenant" (3:14; cf. Heb 8:13). Moses, who is read in the synagogue, gives way to Christ and to the Spirit, who is present in the apostolic proclamation (3:15-18).[94]

EXCURSUS: PAUL'S UNDERSTANDING OF "COVENANT"

Paul's use of the term "covenant" *(diathēkē)* is infrequent and, even in that infrequency, varied. In his massive exposition of his Gospel in Romans, he employs the term only twice. In one of these instances, in a nearly rabbinic delight in particularity, he speaks of a *plurality* of covenants given to Israel (Rom 9:4; cf. Eph 2:12).[95] In his other use of the term "covenant" in Romans, he announces

92. Already in the earliest church, this distinction became a point of controversy, the test case of which was the question of Gentile circumcision. Does the gift of salvation in Jesus Christ reinforce the requirement of the Law? That was the position of those who advocated Gentile Judaizing. Paul, in contrast, understood that the Law requires immediate, unconditioned obedience from the heart, a requirement that the fallen human being will not and cannot fulfill (Gal 3:11-12; 5:3; Rom 7:7-13). The saving work of God in Christ answers this demand of the Law, bringing it to fulfillment. Circumcision of the heart by the Spirit thus transcends the outward circumcision demanded by the written Law (Rom 2:25-29).

93. 3:7, 11, 13, 14.

94. Elsewhere Paul elaborates this transcendent work of the Spirit more concretely. According to Paul, outward circumcision has been displaced by the circumcision of the heart, the promise of which has come to reality in Jesus Christ (Rom 2:25-29). Believers in Christ have *died* to the Law, *so that* they may live to Christ (Gal 2:19-21). Those who belong to Christ are free *from* the Law, and thus free from condemnation and death, *so that* they are free *for* Christ and the new life of obedience that God has given to them in him (Rom 7:1-5; Gal 5:1-6, 13-14).

95. The significance of the plural should not be overlooked. Within the Hebrew Scriptures there is no plurality of covenants: בְּרִית appears only in the singular. The plural form that appears in rabbinic literature — which in a certain respect reflects a delight in the words of the text of Scripture — is obviously a later development, in which Paul already shares. In the Qumran writings, however, one still finds only the singular form.

the hope of a *future* covenant that God will make with Israel, when as Redeemer the Lord goes forth from Zion (see Isa 59:20-21). Even if one happily grants that the idea of a covenant might well be present where the language is not, the infrequency and particularity of Paul's usage of the term "covenant" in Romans do everything other than suggest that the concept of covenant is fundamental to his thought. Either he is a very poor communicator, or he intentionally formulates his message in the terms of "Gospel" and "promise."

In Galatians Paul draws a sharp distinction between the covenant given to Abraham as *promise* (Gal 3:15, 17), and the covenant made at Sinai, which consists in *Law* (Gal 4:21-31). The latter brings slavery, the former brings freedom. The term "covenant" is thus not univocal for Paul but refers to two radically different divine orders: Law and promise, demand and gift.

Elsewhere within the Corinthian correspondence Paul refers to "covenant" in his tradition of the words of institution of the Lord's Supper, where, as we have noted, Jesus' cup-word has been interpreted as effecting the new covenant promised in Jeremiah (1 Cor 11:25; also Luke 22:20). Here again, this new covenant brings about a new, saving relationship with God in the face of the condemnation brought by the Sinai covenant.

The same may be said for the Markan form of the words of institution, according to which Jesus speaks of his saving death as a replacement of the sacrifices associated with the Sinai covenant.[96] The Pauline tradition makes this replacement explicit by associating it with the Jeremianic promise. The setting of this tradition within the life and worship of the early church indicates that Jesus' death was widely understood as effecting the Jeremianic new covenant and that such understanding was fundamental to the life and thought of earliest Christianity.[97] In the celebration of the Lord's Supper, the churches were reminded of their origin and identity. This new identity was based on a decisive break with God's dealings with his people through the Law, a break that brought the fulfillment of God's promises.[98]

It is instructive to compare this understanding of the new covenant

96. Mark 14:24 (par. Matt 26:28): "This is my blood of the covenant, shed on behalf on many." Cf. Exod 24:8.

97. It is likely that the alteration of the text of Exod 24:8 in Heb 9:20 that brings it into conformity with the Lord's Supper tradition reflects the fundamental character of the Lord's Supper tradition within the life of the churches. LXX Exod 24:8, reflecting the Hebrew text, reads: Ἰδοὺ τὸ αἷμα τῆς διαθήκης. In contrast, Heb 9:20 reads: Τοῦτο τὸ αἷμα τῆς διαθήκης, in correspondence to the Markan tradition (Τοῦτό ἐστιν τὸ αἷμά μου τῆς διαθήκης, Mark 14:24).

98. The two occurrences of the term "covenant" in the book of Acts fall into the same pattern. Both references are associated with Abraham — the first with the promise that in his seed the nations would be blessed (Acts 3:25), the other with the covenant of circumcision (Acts 7:8). This practice is taken up in the "custom of Moses," i.e., the Law (Acts 15:1), which is no longer binding on the disciples.

(or, respectively, in Markan tradition, the replacement of the Sinai covenant), which formed the identity of the earliest church, with the vocabulary by which the church proclaimed God's saving work in the crucified and risen Jesus. In the New Testament the term "covenant" appears as an element of proclamation only where it is directed to Jewish hearers and defined in terms of God's promises to Abraham. An appeal to the "sons of the covenant" appears in the context of Peter's proclamation in the temple: this covenant is not the Sinai covenant but, instead, God's word of promise to Abraham (Acts 3:25). Peter's entire address is cast in terms of God's fulfillment of the words of the prophets in Jesus (Acts 3:17-26). Likewise, in Stephen's speech, "the covenant of circumcision" is associated with God's promises to Abraham (Acts 7:8). The same is true of the Benedictus (Luke 1:72-73).[99] According to the Lukan witness, the hope of Israel's final salvation remained alive within the first generation of believers in Jesus as Messiah and came to expression in this recollection of God's promise. It thus appears that the dissociation of "covenant" from Law was an essential element of the earliest proclamation of faith in Jesus as Messiah among Jews; otherwise within early Judaism "covenant" (along with circumcision) was associated especially with the Law.[100]

Matters were different in the proclamation to the Gentiles, who, although they are included within the larger implications of the promises to the patriarchs, are not the direct recipients of those promises and could not be expected to see themselves as such. The Lukan report in Acts, together with the letters of Paul, makes it clear that the earliest church used other categories, such as "Gospel," "faith," "promise," and "fulfillment" to communicate the salvation that God had worked in Jesus to Gentile hearers. It is no wonder that the term "covenant" did not come into prominent usage in the proclamation to the pagans. Indeed, its significance with respect to the Law had to be clarified for Jewish believers in Jesus — a clarification that led to considerable controversy within earliest Christianity.

There is a contrast, then, between the earliest proclamation of the church and its intramural celebration of the Lord's Supper as the enactment of a new covenant. In its worship, the identity of the believing community, which retained its Jewish heritage, was *defined* by God's new work in Jesus, in *contrast* with the former covenant at Sinai.[101] This definition, which an-

99. God's covenant is "the oath he swore to Abraham" (Luke 1:73).

100. F. Avemarie, "Bund als Gabe und Recht," in *Bund und Tora: Zur theologischen Begriffsgeschichte in alttestamentlicher, frühjüdischer und urchristlicher Tradition* (WUNT 92; ed. F. Avemarie and H. Lichtenberger; Tübingen: Mohr Siebeck, 1996), 163-216. *Mutatis mutandis,* this association of "covenant" with "Law" applies esp. to the Qumran writings, including references to the new covenant (CD VI, 19; XIV, 21).

101. It is worth remembering that, aside from Luke 1:72, it is *only* in the words of institution that we find reference to a divine "covenant" in the Gospels.

nounced Jesus' saving death and resurrection as the fulfillment of Israel's Scriptures, set the earliest believers apart from their Jewish contemporaries. In this regard, the difference between the Markan and Pauline traditions of the Lord's Supper is probably significant. The language of the former, which only indirectly speaks of the setting aside of the Sinai covenant, may well have required further definition as Gentiles entered into the believing community in increasing numbers. The explicit appeal to the "new covenant" of Jeremiah in the Pauline tradition is very likely an interpretive reformulation of the Markan tradition.

As we have noted, it is only in the letter to the Hebrews, which contains more than half the references to "covenant" in the entire New Testament, that the significance of the term "covenant" becomes a matter of extended theological argument.[102] Here the conception of covenant is oriented entirely to the cultic dimension of the Sinai legislation. We meet again in Hebrews the same definition of Christian faith with respect to the Law and Jewish tradition that we find in the Lord's Supper. Jesus has become the guarantor and mediator of a "new covenant,"[103] namely the new covenant promised by Jeremiah.[104] In contrast with the covenant commanded at Sinai, this covenant is eternal. The former covenant, like the present creation itself, now has been made old and is passing away.[105] The basic pattern of thought is the same as that found in the Lord's Supper tradition, even if it is developed in terms of the cult rather than in terms of "works," as in the Pauline letters.[106]

In light of the preceding observations, we may say that the relative silence of the earliest church with respect to the term "covenant" — there are only sixteen references outside of Hebrews, all of which are cited above — raises enormous questions about the assumption that the idea of a single, ongoing covenant with Israel, now inherited by the church, was widely assumed within its life and thought.[107] The unique and extensive theological reflection given to the contrasting divine covenants in the letter to the Hebrews indicates that the opposite was the case. It is not that Christ was understood within the context of "covenant," but that the old and new covenants, i.e., demand and

102. Seventeen of the thirty-three occurences of διαθήκη in the New Testament appear in Hebrews, and these only within the last half of the letter, from 7:22 to 13:20.

103. Heb 7:22; 9:15-28; 12:24.

104. Heb 8:6-13; 10:15-18.

105. Heb 8:13; 13:20. Hebrews is unique in that it interprets the Law primarily in terms of its cultic regulations, and not in terms of its ethical requirements.

106. This original orientation may well have to do with the addressees of the letter, Jewish believers who are tempted to retreat from open confession of their faith under the pressure of persecution.

107. Against, *inter alia,* Wright, *The New Testament and the People of God,* 259-79; Hafemann, *Paul, Moses, and the History of Israel,* 438-44.

promise, were understood within the context of Christ and God's work in him. What appears in the opening of Hebrews is true for Paul and the rest of the New Testament: God's word in his Son is definitive. In that final word all the fragmentary and partial words to "the fathers" and "the prophets" have their place.[108]

Despite the obvious difference in audience and argument, Paul's references to a "new" and "old covenant" here in v. 6 and v. 14 appear as something of a parallel phenomenon to the theology of the letter to the Hebrews, as is also the case for his distinction between two radically different "covenants" in Galatians 3–4.[109] The argument in 2 Cor 3 differs in that Paul here appeals to God's dealings with Israel as revealing fundamental realities about fallen humanity, apart from any controversy with adversaries or definition of faith in Jesus over against early Judaism. The distinction between the Corinthian believers and "the sons of Israel" is left unexplored. Indeed, rather than distinguishing the Corinthians from "the sons of Israel," Paul's argument presupposes the ways in which they are fundamentally the same. Much as he has done already in his recollection of Israel's idolatry after the exodus (1 Cor 10:1-13), Paul finds the identity of believers in Christ within the story of Israel.[110] As we have noted, in Moses and the giving of the Law, apostolic calling, faith, and unbelief are "figured out."[111] The contrast that Paul finds between new and old covenants illumines the distinction between (1) outward, temporal human standards and (2) the unseen work of God that creates the human heart eternally new, through the crucified Christ, by the Spirit. It is this distinction that the Corinthians have failed to learn.

6b As we have noted, Paul's anarthrous usage places emphasis on the meaning and quality of the "new covenant." He now describes that covenant in remarkable brevity. It is not "of the letter, but of the Spirit." With this sharp

108. Within the Hebrew Scriptures the giving of "covenants" and "oaths," with which "covenant" is associated, appears as a strictly postlapsarian phenomenon; the covenants and oaths guarantee fidelity (and respectively, promises) in a world full of infidelity.

109. Gal 3:15, 17; 4:24.

110. As we have noted above (p. 107), it is in this sense that we are to understand Paul's warning to the Corinthians "not to go beyond that which is written" (1 Cor 4:6). He has transferred the form (μετασχηματίζειν) and imagery of agriculture and temple-construction to himself and Apollos in order to teach the Corinthians this very lesson: their identity, together with that of the apostle, is given in Scripture, which places them within creation in anticipation of consummation in the life beyond the coming judgment.

111. Yet again, I am using the language of Seitz, *Figured Out: Typology and Providence in Christian Scripture.*

contrast Paul defines the new covenant — and at the same time, implicitly, the covenant made at Sinai, which he is about to name "old" (v. 14). The antithesis between "letter" and "Spirit," which also appears in the letter to Rome,[112] thus stands out as an essential element of Paul's theological grammar. But what sort of a distinction does Paul make here?

This question, which has left a long and significant history of interpretation, has at least three dimensions.[113] First, Paul does not use the antithetical pairing "letter" and "Spirit" to describe *mere* hermeneutical principles, but the difference between (1) the encounter with God in the Law and its demand and (2) the saving encounter with God that takes place in Christ. As is clear from Paul's usage here and elsewhere, "letter" refers to the Law and signifies it as "written code," thus emphasizing its externality. It is likely that the remarkable absence of the term "Law" in this context, in which Paul describes the various aspects of the giving of the Law, including its inscription on tablets, is due to his focus on the question of external standards, especially the letters that the Corinthians require. The distinction between "the letter" and "the Spirit" is the difference between Moses in action and Christ in action.[114] In these terms Paul signals the decisive events in and through which God's promises come to fulfillment.

Second, although "letter" and "Spirit" are material, theological terms for Paul, they have hermeneutical implications, which are relevant to the very question of human understanding, as Paul has indicated in other terms in 1 Cor 2:6-16 and as becomes clear in vv. 12-18. As in the other instances of his use of the term "letter," Paul has in view the broken and distant communication between God and the fallen human being that takes place through the Law. "The Spirit," in contrast, speaks of the decisive renewal of communication with God that takes place by the Spirit, who re-creates the human heart.[115]

Finally, although Paul sets "letter" and "Spirit" in an antithetical relation, he joins them together in a paradoxical unity. This unity becomes clear in his explanatory statement in v. 6: "For the letter puts to death, but the Spirit makes alive."[116] Only that which has been put to death can be made alive. This coincidence of opposites can be described only as a paradox, one that scandalizes human reason in its practical judgments concerning God, especially that of the Corinthians. Paul does not offer here a dialectical opposition that might be resolved in a higher,

112. Rom 2:27, 29; 7:6.

113. On the history of interpretation, see G. Ebeling, "Geist und Buchstabe," *RGG3*, 2:1290-96; J. von Lüpke, "Geist und Buchstabe," *RGG4*, 3:578-82.

114. Thus Ebeling, "Geist und Buchstabe," *RGG3*, 2:1291.

115. See also Rom 2:17-29; 7:4-6.

116. Already the "grammar" of Paul's usage indicates that the relation as it is expressed by the particle δέ is one of coordination; the giving of life can take place only in death.

abstract unity such as the concept of grace or that of God's self-revelation to us.[117] Paul instead describes the ways of the Lord, who "kills and makes alive, brings down to the dead and raises again" (1 Sam 2:6).[118] Paul here echoes not merely the text of First Samuel but, even more directly, the Deuteronomic Song of Moses, which recounts the Lord's work of putting to death and making alive, wounding and healing, in the history of Israel's experience with the Law (Deut 32:39).[119] The antithesis of letter and Spirit is resolved, not in an idea or principle, but in the event of Christ's cross and resurrection, which, although it can be definitively articulated and proclaimed, cannot be reduced to an intellectual construct. It is, rather, an event that calls forth constant wonder, amazement, and thanksgiving, as Paul himself underscores later in this letter (9:15).

Paul does not here speak immediately of Christ, in whom life is given in death. He is instead explaining the apostolic mission, in which glory is hidden under suffering, and thus concentrates on the coincidence of death and life. This "christological deficit" nevertheless implicitly points the readers to the crucified and risen Christ, who is the author of their new life (3:3) and the image of God, with whom they have been brought into saving communication by the Spirit (3:17-18; 4:6). Paul will fill out this "deficit" in 5:21.

"For the letter puts to death, *but* the Spirit makes alive." Just as God gives comfort only to those in affliction (1:7), the Spirit gives life only to that which the letter has put to death. This theological grammar of deliverance, found especially in the Psalms,[120] is prominent in the Pauline letters and appears elsewhere in the New Testament as the definition of the saving power of the Creator that is displayed in the rebellious human creature.[121] Paul does not speak of sin and transgression in salvation-historical categories, as if they were

117. This was the proposal of Karl Barth, who argued that the Law is the necessary form of the grace of the Gospel, and the Gospel is the hidden content of the Law. See his classic essay "Evangelium und Gesetz," in *Gesetz und Evangelium: Beiträge zur gegenwärtigen theologischen Diskussion* (WdF 142; ed. Ernst Kinder and Klaus Haendler; Darmstadt: Wissenschaftliche Buchgesellschaft, 1968), 1-29. Barth then must make the condemning "office" of the Law to be a result of its *misuse* by the human being in unbelief and self-justification: see Barth, "Evangelium und Gesetz," 23. Paul, in contrast, interprets Moses' placing a veil over his face as *effecting* the hardening of the hearts of "the sons of Israel" (3:13-14). This action, which recalls Paul's prior reference to their inability to gaze upon the glorified face of Moses (v. 7), is clearly a symbolic act of judgment (v. 9). For Paul, the misuse of the Law is *the result* of its condemning work, and not the other way around.

118. Luther, "Thus when God makes alive he does it by killing, when he justifies he does it by making men guilty, when he exalts to heaven he does it by bringing down to hell," *LW* 33:62 ("The Bondage of the Will").

119. Indeed, LXX Deut 32:39 stands closer to Paul's language in v. 6 than does LXX 1 Kgdms 2:6. I thank Dr. Beth Langstaff for this observation.

120. See 1 Sam 2:6; Pss 30:3; 71:20; 138:7; 143:11.

121. See Rom 4:17; 8:11; 1 Cor 15:22, 36; Eph 2:5; Col 2:13; 1 Pet 3:18; John 5:21.

now behind us. Rather, he describes the intersection of the new creation with the fallen world. Insofar as unbelief and disobedience remain, the Corinthians need written instruction, including that of the Law. This instruction from the Law is no abstract expression of God's moral will but one of concrete demands that bring condemnation and death. The "letter" itself is an effective word that, in its own way, performs what God intends. Only where the Law has arrived is it possible to hear the Gospel rightly.[122]

Paul's concluding affirmation, that "the Spirit makes alive," provides the basis for his following argument in vv. 7-11 concerning the transcendent glory given to the apostolic mission. This argument culminates in a return to his affirmation in v. 6. The glory of Moses' mission has been done away with. The unseen glory of the gift of the Spirit and righteousness abides without end: the Spirit who makes alive, makes alive eternally.

EXCURSUS: THE LETTER AND THE SPIRIT IN RECENT INTERPRETATION

Interpreters have not readily come to terms with the paradoxical relation of "the letter" and "the Spirit," by which Paul defines his apostolic mission. The history of interpretation may be understood as a record of attempts to tame the "letter" that kills in order to liberate the Spirit that gives life.[123] God's saving work in human history then comes to be subsumed within a larger scheme of spiritual, moral, or intellectual progress. The work of God in Christ is then reduced to a spiritual or moral principle, or perhaps to a rhetorical strategy. This reduction is evident, for example, in Origen's appropriation of Philo's allegorical method, by which he interprets "letter" and "spirit" as the distinction between the material and the ideational. Despite the broad, lengthy, and continuing influence of this reading of the text, it is clear from the context that Paul is *not* contrasting literal and figurative interpretation of the Scripture. Origen's interpretive move, as well as others like it, runs the danger of offering a "covert soteriology" in which the attempt is made to *escape* the death that the letter effects.[124] Augustine's interpretation of "letter" as "Law without grace" has served as a healthy corrective to this misstep.[125]

122. Cf. Gal 3:22; Rom 3:19-20.

123. In this respect, Gerhard Forde rightly connects the Platonic tradition with the Enlightenment, and specifically with Lessing, in his *Justification by Faith: A Matter of Death and Life* (Philadelphia: Fortress Press, 1982), 14-15.

124. Forde, *Justification by Faith*, 14.

125. Augustine also accepted the allegorical model. See the collection of statements by Augustine on the "letter and the Spirit" in G. L. Bray, ed., *1-2 Corinthians* (ACCS 7; Downers

As Augustine rightly perceived, the antithesis between "letter" and "Spirit" that Paul presents is material. The ongoing discourse of 2 Cor 3 makes clear that it is rooted in Moses and in Christ. Paul does not give priority to meanings behind the text, and certainly not to the "certain" truths of reason as opposed to the "accidental" truths of history, as G. E. Lessing, along with other thinkers of the Enlightenment, supposed.[126] Neither the Law given through Moses nor the crucified and risen Lord can be stripped of their historical particularity and retain their significance. The events on which Paul bases his distinction are no mere hulls that can be removed from the kernels of deeper truth or hermeneutical insight. Nor is the opposition between "letter" and "Spirit" one of external authority over against individual conscience, as it was with Kant. The gift and work of the Spirit are inseparable from the apostolic proclamation of the Gospel. This Gospel, although it is properly a spoken word, may itself be written in letters, as Paul does in this very letter to the Corinthians (1:18-20; 4:3-5). In the thought of the Enlightenment the paradoxical relation between "letter" and "Spirit" is undone by a "chemical" dissolution of reason from history, just as in Origen's allegory it was dissolved by a progression away from the material world into the world of ideas.[127] In contrast, Paul's distinction between "letter" and "Spirit" is bound to the message of the crucified Christ, who lives and is therefore inherently tied to history. Indeed, it is a history that is being replayed in the life of the apostle and the Corinthian church.

Current interpretation has not escaped the tendency to dissolve the Pauline paradox. A prominent example of it appears within Richard Hays's valuable and influential work on Paul and his use of Scripture. While Origen takes flight *from* the corporeal, Richard Hays takes flight *into* the corporeal. For him, the new covenant effects the embodiment of "text."[128] Paul's ministry is one of Spirit-empowered transformation, the enactment of Scripture within

---

Grove, Ill.: InterVarsity Press, 1999), 216-18. Luther later filled out Augustine's reading: "The letter is nothing but THE LAW WITHOUT GRACE. We on the other hand, may say that the Spirit is nothing but GRACE WITHOUT LAW," *LW* 39:189 ("Concerning the Letter and the Spirit").

126. See esp. G. E. Lessing, "Über den Beweis des Geistes und der Kraft," in *Gotthold Ephraim Lessing Werke, 1774-1778* (ed. A. Schilson; Frankfurt: Deutscher Klassiker Verlag, 1989), 8:437-45, esp. 441-42: "the accidental truths of history can never become the proof of the necessary truths of reason."

127. On the Kantian dissolution, see O. Bayer, "Scheidekunst und Ehekunst: Glaube und Geschichte bei Kant und Hamann," in *Heil und Geschichte: Die Geschichtsbezogenheit des Heils und das Problem der Heilsgeschichte in der biblischen Tradition und in der theologischen Deutung* (WUNT 248; ed. J. Frey, S. Krauter, and H. Lichtenberger; Tübingen: Mohr Siebeck, 2009), 611-32.

128. R. B. Hays, *Echoes of Scripture in the Letters of Paul* (New Haven: Yale University Press, 1989), 122-53.

Christian community. Indeed, only those who participate in that enactment can understand the text. There is something that rings true in Hays's reading, as is clear from Paul's metaphor of the Corinthians as a "letter written [by the Spirit] upon fleshly hearts" (3:3).[129] It nevertheless requires qualification or correction in at least two respects: first, in that it overruns the distinction between the arrival of the eschaton in Christ and the arrival of the eschaton for the fallen world; second, in that it misses the relationship of communication between God and the human being worked by the apostolic mission, which for Paul constitutes the essence of salvation.

Concerning the first qualification: in another context, Hays would have been correct in his assessment that "the problem with the old covenant lies precisely in its character as a written thing," which (because it is *merely* written) is unable to give life.[130] Paul speaks elsewhere of the "weakness" and "inability" of the Law (Rom 8:3), which cannot "make alive" (Gal 3:21). In the present context, however, Paul does not describe the Law as weak but precisely the opposite. The "letter" is a living power. It is not dead, nor is it a mere witness to our condemnation.[131] It delivers death. It is our executioner. Indeed, this strange mission of Moses bears the very glory of God. The "letter," as the written demand of God, cannot be regarded as a mere problem to be overcome. It serves the purpose of God, one which is alien and yet strangely necessary to God's saving work.

It is too simple, then, to speak as Hays does of the Corinthians as the "breathing instantiation of the word of God."[132] As Paul makes clear in this very context, the "word of God" has been given in a twofold way, as both "letter" and promise. The first is necessary to the second. The crucified Jesus is the risen Lord, and the risen Lord is none other than the crucified Jesus. Indeed, in contrast to Hays's reading, for Paul the "enfleshment" of Scripture — the

129. Nevertheless, as we have noted, σάρκινος is to be rendered here as "fleshly" hearts, not "fleshy" hearts, as Hays and others would like to do. See Hays, *Echoes,* 128-29.

130. Hays, *Echoes,* 131. In context, Hays rightly qualifies the statement we have cited by indicating that the problem with the old covenant "is precisely that it is (only) written." This qualification, slight though it may be, already calls into question his larger thesis concerning the apostolic mission as the embodiment of the text. There are texts that remain written texts and as such have the power to impart life, including this very letter of Paul to the Corinthians. That is to say, the distinction between "letter" and "Spirit" corresponds to that between Law and Gospel.

131. Hays, *Echoes,* 131 This misreading of the text leads to confusion in Hays's response to J. Christiaan Beker's criticism that, in his reading, the word of Scripture loses its critical function. This critical function is nothing other than its living power to put to death, and not merely the showing up of our faults. Scripture speaks to us, not in the space of our silence, but in the face of our spoken lies in thought, word, and deed. See R. B. Hays, *The Conversion of the Imagination: Paul as Interpreter of Israel's Scripture* (Grand Rapids: Eerdmans, 2005), 188-89.

132. Hays, *Echoes,* 131.

incarnation of the Word — has taken place in the first instance not in the community but in the crucified and risen Christ. Of course, it has taken place in Christ *for the community,* but it remains "in" Christ. The church has been called outside of itself. Its life remains just as "eccentric" as that of the apostle.[133] Despite Paul's affirmation that the Corinthians are a "letter of Christ" (v. 2), it is by no means apparent that this is so, especially not to the apostle, who can see very well the strife, jealousy, factions, and immorality that continue to stain the life of the church (12:20-21). It is only *in the faith of the apostle* that Corinthians are a "letter of Christ, known and read by all" (3:2; 5:14-16). Paul does not describe the Corinthians as they are in themselves. He speaks out of the certainty of Christ's work that he trusts will have its triumph in them.

Concerning the second qualification: as Paul makes clear from the very start of the letter, Christ's gift of comfort and salvation is inseparable from participation in Christ's sufferings in the present time (1:3-7). The life of the apostle, in whom the experience of all believers is written large, is one of suffering and deliverance: "Thanks be to God, who always leads us in his triumph in Christ!" (2:14). The new covenant is much more than moral transformation, even if the good conscience and blameless conduct of the apostle are included within it.[134] What goes missing in Hays's reading, or at least threatens to do so, is the relationship of communication with God into which the Corinthians have been placed, a communication between the human being under the power of death and the God who gives life in Christ. The removal of the veil that Paul describes later in this chapter effects this communication and, thus, "freedom" (v. 18). If, as Hays concludes, the hope of the new covenant is that "Scripture will have become a self-consuming artifact; the power of the word will have subsumed itself into the life of the community, embodied itself without remainder,"[135] there seems to be no place left for the communication with God that for Paul constitutes the essence of salvation. In fact, it is precisely this communicative relation, as it has been manifest in the apostle, that the Corinthians have failed to comprehend. Paul has been thrust into trial in Asia so that he might not trust in himself, but in God (1:8-9). He bears the deadness of Jesus in his body so that Jesus' life might be manifest in him (4:10). The Lord's power is perfected in his weakness (12:9-10). He is weak in

133. Hays wants to maintain an ecclesiocentric hermeneutic built on a christocentric foundation. See his *Conversion of the Imagination,* 186-87. It is hard to see, however, how Hays does not end up with a verticalized form of the Ritschlean ellipse, unless he wishes to identify Christ and the church without remainder — as he rightly seems unwilling to do. One cannot have two centers: either the center is Christ, or it is the church.

134. 3:3; cf. 1:12-14; 6:3-10.

135. Hays, *Echoes,* 129. At the resurrection the need for Scripture will be surpassed, of course, but not the communicative relation with God. One therefore cannot properly speak of "the power of the word" being "subsumed into the life of the community."

Christ and yet lives with Christ by the power of God (13:4). For their part, the Corinthians are called to petition, thanksgiving, lament, and praise on behalf of the apostle. Nowhere outside of the Psalms and the Passion Narratives of the Gospels does one find such dramatic expression and communication of emotion as one finds with the apostle in Second Corinthians and Galatians.[136] If one follows Hays's reading to its conclusion (it is not clear that Hays himself does so), there finally can be no need for any apostle or Scripture that stands over against the community, judging it, giving it life, calling it to prayer, praise, and thanks.[137] The community itself becomes the revelation of God.[138] There is a danger here of a modern subjectivity that seeks to consume and absorb into itself all that is external.[139] As we have observed already, the relationship between "letter" and "Spirit" is not dialectical, as Hays suggests, but strictly paradoxical: through sin and death, God the Creator works life and righteousness.[140] Scripture cannot be reduced to a metaphor that illumines the Gospel.[141] The eclipse of the old covenant by the new does not mean that sin, death, and condemnation have been left behind. They remain with us as long as the present, fallen world continues.[142] The arrival of the new covenant is the *intersection* of the new creation with the fallen world, which has its specific *locus* "in Christ" (5:17). *Where* the Spirit of the Lord is, there is freedom (3:17). The ministry of the Spirit is nothing other than the apostolic proclamation of Christ, who himself is present in that word (1:19). God's Yes to his promises is given *in the Son of God,* not in the community, which for its part is called to a believing "Amen," in response to the divine address (1:20).

Admittedly, the removal of Moses' veil brings a vision of the glory of the Lord that transcends what our words presently can express. Nonetheless, this eschatological vision of the Lord's glory is bound to the apostolic proclamation. The apostle will not be a lord over the faith of the Corinthians, even if he has heard unutterable utterances in paradise (1:24; 12:4). As Paul makes clear, the vision given to us is localized "in Christ" (v. 14). The Spirit is present in him alone, just as the Lord was present only in the inner tabernacle (v. 17b). Our vision of the divine glory is given only in a mirror (v. 18; cf. 1 Cor 13:12).

136. See 1:23; 2:14; 6:11-13; 7:2-16; 9:15.

137. Admittedly, Hays does not see this conclusion. See n. 133.

138. Hays, *Echoes,* 144.

139. See the discussions of Hegel and Schleiermacher in Bayer, *Theology,* 144-59.

140. Hays, *Echoes,* 133, 138, 142, 149. Such a dialectic can be only a sort of Hegelian dialectic in which the community so completely consumes the text that it has no need any longer for an external word.

141. Hays, *Echoes,* 149.

142. Against Hays (*Conversion of the Imagination,* 187-88), the "unrealized" eschatology of the apostle cannot be reduced to a dialectic that is progressively reduced. It is a paradox, in which we progress into that which we already have been given and possess.

We thus "see" through our ears: it is only in the *proclamation* of the apostolic Gospel that Christ's glory can be discerned (4:4). The Spirit remains bound to the apostolic word of Christ. We are called not merely to a new perception of God but to a new relationship with God in Christ. The glory of God is given to the human creature in an exchange of life and death, righteousness and condemnation, weakness and strength (v. 18; cf. 1 Cor 13:13). Just as Christ remains for Paul the Crucified One, who lives, the *communication* established by God's work in Christ may be regarded as characteristic of the eschaton itself. We are and shall remain those under condemnation and death who finally have been delivered from it all by the love of Christ. The end of the world is not the end of the Word. The fullness of the eschaton will not end, but rather will establish, the abiding relationship of saving communication between God and the human creature in Christ.

In stark contrast to Hays, Scott Hafemann wants to preserve the externality of the Law by interpreting the contrast between "letter" and "Spirit" as that of stages of divine revelation.[143] In this way, Hafemann attempts to dissolve the Pauline antithesis into a scheme of salvation-historical progress. For Hafemann, "letter" signifies Law apart from the gift of the Spirit, "Spirit" signifies a gift added to the Law that enables the performance of its demands. As with Hays's work, there is something that rings true in Hafemann's proposal, and much that requires revision.

Hafemann is surely right to insist that Paul, in using the term "letter," speaks of the Law from a limited perspective.[144] "The letter" for Paul is a metaphorical description of the Law. More precisely, it is a synecdoche by which he describes the message or content of the Law in terms of the *form* by which it is communicated. The apostle's figural location of message in form calls into question Hafemann's attempt to separate the two. The synecdoche appears in only three contexts, in which the "letter" always stands in contrast with the Spirit (see also Rom 2:27-29; 7:5-6). As is apparent from the word itself, "letter" signifies Law as the *written commandments* of God. Paul thus speaks in the following context of 2 Cor 3 of "the mission of death" as "engraved with letters in stones" (v. 7). In Rom 2:27-29, he likewise associates "the letter" with circumcision "in the flesh," and he sets over against it the circumcision of the heart effected by the Spirit. The contrast entails the difference between the *outward* address of the Law as demand and *inward* re-creation by the Spirit as a gift. It presupposes the fallen and rebellious heart of the human being, which

143. In a qualification of this salvation history, Hafemann allows that some within Israel possessed the Spirit prior to Christ (*2 Corinthians* [NIV Application Commentary; Grand Rapids: Zondervan, 2000], 133).

144. Hafemann, *2 Corinthians*, 131; Hafemann, *Paul, Moses, and the History of Israel*, 167-68.

cannot be changed, but only removed, as the promissory texts of Scripture echoed in Rom 2 directly announce.[145] As Paul makes clear in Rom 7:5-6, through the power of sin, the Law provokes our rebellion against God and thus "bears fruit for death." In the crucified Christ, those who believe have been removed from the Law. They have been joined to the risen Lord; their service to God takes place in the eschatological "newness of the Spirit," *not* in "the oldness of the letter." Here the meaning of "letter" becomes clear: it signifies the Law as it comes to the human being as an external demand, bringing about condemnation and death.[146] Nevertheless, as becomes apparent in 2 Cor 3:7-18 (where the term "Law" admittedly is lacking), the condemning Law *itself* bears witness to Christ, in whom its fulfillment is given.[147] In this function as witness to Christ, Paul no longer speaks of the "letter," but, here, of "the old covenant" (v. 14) and, elsewhere, simply of "the Law," or "Scripture."

Hafemann is surely correct also when he claims that "letter" signifies Law apart from the Spirit.[148] Can one, however, rightly speak, as Hafemann wishes to do, of the Law *with the Spirit?* Here again there is a misguided attempt to separate the content of the Law from its form as demand.[149] As we have noted, in describing the Law in synecdoche as "letter," and thus as a body of written commandments, Paul expresses the inseparability of its message from its form. He never speaks of "Law" in abstraction as a bare expression of God's will, to which no threats or demands are attached.[150] Furthermore, the distinction between "letter" and "Law" that Hafemann proposes violates the "theological grammar" of "letter" and "Spirit" that appears explicitly in Rom 7:1-6. Those who belong to Christ have *died* to the *Law,* so that they might be joined to him as risen Lord. To be alive to the Law is to be separated from

145. See Deut 30:6; cf. Ezek 11:19; 36:26-27.

146. This understanding of the Law, which corresponds closely to that of the book of Deuteronomy, is apparent in Paul's following description of the effect of the commandments in vv. 4-11, and it may be filled out by his statements concerning the Law elsewhere (Gal 3:10-14; Rom 3:9-20; 4:13-15; 7:1-25). It is no surprise, therefore, that in other contexts Paul speaks not merely of the "letter" but of the Law itself as bringing wrath and condemnation (Rom 3:19-20; 4:15; 1 Cor 15:56). Indeed, Paul is able to ascribe the work of condemnation to the whole of "Scripture," which imprisons "all things under sin" (Gal 3:22).

147. See also Rom 3:21, 31; 10:4.

148. Hafemann, perhaps unconsciously, follows Augustine, who understands the Spirit to give life by causing the letter to be fulfilled, so that it no longer kills. See n. 125, above.

149. See pp. 122-23 above.

150. Hafemann, *Paul, Moses, and the History of Israel,* 179. This is so even when Paul speaks of keeping or completing the Law (Rom 2:26-27) or of "keeping the commandments of God" (1 Cor 7:19). The promise of God's eschatological re-creation of the human heart (cf. Deut 30:6), in which true obedience is present, is prefigured in the literal requirement of circumcision and cannot be understood apart from that prefigurement. Fulfillment has nothing in common with abstraction.

Christ. To be joined to Christ is to be dead to the Law (7:4-5).[151] In Paul's words: "We have been removed from the Law, having died by that by which we were held, so that we serve in the newness of the Spirit and not in the oldness of the letter" (Rom 7:6).[152] It is clear that *the referent* of the term "letter" is the "Law," which it signifies as "written code." The new covenant and the apostolic mission of it is "*not* of the letter, *but* of the Spirit." The distinction between the two is the distinction between "demand" and "gift."

The driving concern behind Hafemann's attempt to overcome the Pauline antithesis is the attempt to establish a single, undifferentiated divine covenant within Scripture. For Hafemann, the new covenant brings the widespread distribution of the Spirit, who enables obedience to the will of God revealed in the Law, the substance of which does not differ from the Gospel.[153] Yet precisely because the new covenant does not differ from the old, in Hafemann's thought, it brings the gift of the Spirit in an undefined way. The saving work of God is loosed from its definition by the condemning work of God in the Law and thus finally from the Gospel, too, which does not differ from the Law in content. The influence of Barth's joining of Law and Gospel, which has been mediated to Hafemann through the work of Daniel Fuller, is apparent here.[154] The problems with the proposal are significant. In the first place, in order to establish an interpretation of Scripture that may be drawn into a single, unbroken line, Hafemann must set aside the divine purpose that Paul explicitly ascribes to the Law. According to Hafemann, "As the expression of God's abiding will, it is not the law *per se* that kills, or any aspect or perversion of it, but the law *without the Spirit*" (emphasis his).[155] Much like Hays, Hafemann views the Law in terms of its powerlessness to effect obedience.[156] For Hafemann, "The law without the Spirit remains a mere *lifeless* 'letter.'"[157] But that is not what Paul says. The letter is not "lifeless" but has the right and power

151. In order to avoid this clear statement, Hafemann must bifurcate Paul's usage of "the Law" into "condemnation" and "the expression of God's will" (*Paul, Moses, and the History of Israel*, 179). The question is whether it is true to Paul and to Scripture to abstract the Law from its given form.

152. If we should read Gal 5:18 in the way that Hafemann proposes, we would land in pure confusion: "If you are led by the Spirit *(and the Law)*, then you are not under the Law."

153. Yet once more, see above, pp. 122-23.

154. D. P. Fuller, *Gospel and Law: Contrast or Continuum? The Hermeneutics of Dispensationalism and Covenant Theology* (Grand Rapids: Eerdmans, 1980); D. P. Fuller, *The Unity of the Bible: Unfolding God's Plan for Humanity* (Grand Rapids: Zondervan, 1992).

155. Hafemann, *2 Corinthians*, 132. Here there may be some confusion, since one would think that "the law per se" is precisely "the law without the Spirit," according to Hafemann's proposal.

156. Hafemann, *2 Corinthians*, 132.

157. Hafemann, *2 Corinthians*, 133.

to kill.[158] It is, again, our executioner. For Hafemann, the death that Moses administered through the Law is to be avoided.[159] Paul, in contrast, speaks of death and condemnation as the mission and very glory of the Law (3:7, 9, 11).[160]

Hafemann does not seem to realize the difficulties he creates by stripping the Law of its condemning function, the *usus elenchticus*. If the Law is the mere expression of "the election and salvation of Israel," as Hafemann suggests, why would God "allow" the letter to kill, as Hafemann affirms?[161] On the one hand, if "the call for obedience is given entirely within the provisions of the sacrificial system," as Hafemann claims, *why* should the Law bring death?[162] Any and all disobedience may be overcome by the sacrifices for which the Law makes provision. Is there a need for Christ? On the other hand, if the divine demand for obedience transcends the sacrificial system, and if Israel was unable to keep the Law, as Hafemann concedes, it is hard to see why God did not from the very start grant the obedience-working Spirit to Israel.[163] If the new covenant is a continuation of the old and is not strictly bound to the word of Christ, why would God withhold this good gift? Was he playing some cruel, salvation-historical game? Is it not rather the case that the Spirit gives life only where the Law first has put to death? It is not clear within Hafemann's scheme why and how the gift of the Spirit is bound to the proclamation of the crucified and risen Lord.

In dismissing the divine purpose Paul ascribes to the Law in 2 Cor 3,

158. Against Hafemann, *2 Corinthians*, 132, the letter brings condemnation and death where it is received, while the Gospel brings condemnation and judgment where it is rejected.

159. Hafemann, *2 Corinthians*, 144-47. Here the "covert soteriology" that Forde discerns makes its appearance (see p. 130). According to Luther, no one should flee from "this blessed death." Such a flight is equivalent to not allowing "Moses' face [to] shine clearly": "Therefore, it is impossible for someone who does not first hear the law and let himself be killed by the letter, to hear the Gospel and let the grace of the Spirit bring him to life. Grace is only given to those who long for it. Life is a help only to those who are dead, grace only to sin, the Spirit only to the letter. No one can have one without the other" (*LW* 39:185).

160. See also Rom 3:19-20; 4:15; 7:13-25.

161. Hafemann, *2 Corinthians*, 131.

162. Hafemann, *2 Corinthians*, 131. One might well speak of the sacrificial system as creating the framework or space in which flawed obedience is to take place. But human rebellion — including that of Israel — will not stay within this space: we seek other gods. The sacrifices do not provide forgiveness *ex opere operato*. The prophetic attack on this false understanding goes well beyond the charge of hypocrisy to announce the end of the cult (e.g., 1 Sam 15:22; Jer 7:22-23; Hos 6:6; Amos 5:21-23; Mic 6:6-8; Ps 40:6-7). The author of Hebrews picks up this critique in terms for which Hafemann does not give account: "It is impossible for the blood of bulls and goats to remove sins" (Heb 10:4).

163. Unlike Barth, Hafemann does not attribute the "death-dealing" effect of the Law to a misuse of the Law by the self-justifying human being; rather, he points to a weakness in the Law itself.

Hafemann thus misses the work of the Spirit. Where Hafemann speaks of the Spirit empowering the human being, the apostle speaks of the Spirit as raising us from the dead and creating us anew (v. 6; cf. 5:17). It is a problem for Hafemann that divine glory brings death. For him, Israel thus must be shielded from that death.[164] But to do so would be to act as Moses did; to cut off Israel from death is to cut off Israel from the life of the resurrection that follows. God, the Creator, brings righteousness only out of sin, and life only out of death. Only those who have died to the Law through the crucified Christ have been joined to the risen Lord and serve in the newness of the Spirit (Rom 7:4-6).

Perhaps the fundamental problem with Hafemann's program is that he seems to conceive of "sin" merely in terms of human acts of transgression. For Paul, the problem of sin is far deeper: we have been possessed by "sin" in such a way that we live in simultaneous powerlessness and guilt. The fundamental sin, "sin in its utter sinfulness" (Rom 7:13), is that we will not hear and do God's good will for us, because we do not want God to be God, but we wish to be God in God's place.[165] We thus are not sinners because we sin, but we sin because we are sinners. Because Hafemann misses this dimension of Paul's thought, he adopts an unrealistic conception of the human being. For him, Paul is called as apostle to "mediate the Spirit to a transformed people who are being empowered to keep the law as appropriated under the new covenant."[166] There is a "changed condition of God's people" and a "resultant obedience to the covenant."[167] No one would have been more surprised than the apostle to hear this description of the Corinthians! He is sent to those with hearts of stone (3:3). His expressions of confidence notwithstanding, the Corinthians have acted for the most part in raw unbelief. They have brought him far more grief than joy (1:23–2:4). Their heart remains closed to him, and attached to his opponents (6:11-13). They remain "yoked with unbelievers" (6:14). Paul must wage war, destroying their proud reasoning before the work of edification can truly begin (10:3-6). He asks them directly if they are in the faith and urges them to test themselves (13:5).

If God has fundamentally transformed the rebellious nature of the Corinthians, as Hafemann affirms, how is such radical disobedience possible? In Hafemann's thought, while God's act of redemption is unconditional,[168] the

164. Hafemann, *2 Corinthians*, 143-44.

165. Luther, *Disputation against Scholastic Theology*, "Non potest homo naturaliter velle deum esse deum. Immo vellet se esse deum et deum non esse deum" (WA 1:225, thesis 17). See M. A. Seifrid, "Romans 7: The Voice of the Law, the Cry of Lament, and the Shout of Thanksgiving," in *Perspectives on Our Struggle with Sin* (ed. T. L. Wilder; Nashville, Tenn.: B&H, 2011), 111-65.

166. Hafemann, *2 Corinthians*, 133.

167. Hafemann, *2 Corinthians*, 136.

168. Hafemann, *2 Corinthians*, 137.

maintenance of that relationship is conditioned upon Spirit-empowered, human obedience.[169] It is hard to see how this claim fits the message of the apostle, for whom the new covenant, precisely in its *newness,* depends, not on the human being, but solely on the Spirit who brings the life of the resurrection. Christ inscribes himself on the human heart, making it anew.[170] Where the heart is re-created, unbelief and rebellion are no longer possible. Obedience must of necessity flow forth from the new creature, just as the sun necessarily shines, and a good tree necessarily bears good fruit. This remains true, even though we remain sinners.[171] How else is one to explain Paul's simultaneous, unqualified confidence in the Corinthians? To make our relationship with God finally dependent on our actions is to remove it from its location in Jesus Christ and the apostolic proclamation of him. Indeed, if the "new creation" is brought about by obedience to covenantal stipulations, we are "co-creators" of our own life and salvation, Hafemann's insistence on divine monergism notwithstanding. Christ, who, according to the apostle, has been written on the hearts of the Corinthians, then becomes a distant goal to which they must attain (3:3). Faith and obedience then become human qualities that span the gap between God's past work and future promises.

Furthermore, as we have noted, with Hafemann these qualities are given through an undefined work of the Spirit. The relationship between the human being and God threatens to become one of mute empowerment. What goes missing here, as it does with Hays, is Paul's understanding of salvation as a *verbal* exchange that constitutes *communication* between the fallen human being and the God who addresses us in the condemning voice of the Law and then, decisively, in the Gospel of Christ. The *response* of repentance and faith in the heart to the divine word of the Gospel is *not mute but spoken* in words of confession, petition, lament, and thanksgiving, which, despite their spontaneity, are not arbitrary or self-chosen but defined by the unconditioned word of promise from which they arise.

To raise these objections does not force one into the untenable thesis that Paul adopted a perfectionistic theology. It rather directs attention to the paradox of v. 6: "the letter kills, but the Spirit makes alive." As we have noted, Paul locates this distinction in Christ, in whom the old covenant has been done away with (3:14); "*where* the Spirit of the Lord is, there is freedom" (3:17). The new creation has not yet arrived universally in the fallen world. It has intersected it at one, fixed place: if anyone is *in Christ,* there is a new creation" (5:17). Outside of the crucified and risen Christ, the written code of the old covenant continues in force, along with sin and death. We Christians live in the

169. Hafemann, *2 Corinthians,* 136-40.

170. Hafemann, *2 Corinthians,* 134-36.

171. I am borrowing these figures from Luther. See, e.g., *LW* 31:360.

intersection of the times.[172] To the extent that we live in unbelief, we remain sinners along with the rest of the world. To the extent that we possess Christ and his work by faith, we are saints. Indeed, as Paul shortly makes clear, it is Christ who first possesses us.[173] Christ is not remote from us but is given to us in the definite and unconditional word of the Gospel. This astounding word appears at the very opening of Paul's argument to the wayward Corinthians: "you are a letter of Christ!" (3:3). This apostolic announcement is *not* a diagnosis of the conduct of the Corinthians. Rather, it is Paul's "confidence through Christ toward God" (3:4). He does not speak of the Corinthians for what they are in themselves, but for what God has made them to be in Christ, just as he judges no one "according to the flesh" (5:16). No scheme of salvation-historical progress can explain the expressions of absolute confidence and wrenching concern, unbounded joy, and abject despair over the Corinthians that are inextricably intertwined in this letter.[174] The apostle does not address "transformed hearts" empowered by the Spirit for obedience.[175] He addresses those who are wayward, rebellious, and foolish, whose salvation is found solely in the crucified and risen Christ, to whom the apostle again must call them back.

It is not the case, either, that Paul's antithesis results in an ambivalent understanding of Scripture, as if it finally bore two messages and taught two ways of salvation.[176] He presents a paradox, not a contradiction. The relationship between "the letter" and "the Spirit" is ordered. The mission of death and condemnation is done away with in Christ (vv. 7, 11, 13, 14). It belongs to the present, fallen creation. The new covenant and the ministry of the Spirit remain and abide (v. 11). They belong to the new creation, which endures forever. As Paul makes clear elsewhere, the Law has the power to put to death but not to raise to life (Gal 3:21). It is "holy, righteous, and good," but it cannot make anyone holy, righteous, or good (Rom 7:12). It performs its strange work of condemnation in preparation for God's final work in Jesus Christ. God grants righteousness only to the condemned, and resurrection only to the dead. The two "words" of God do not meet in a higher idea that might lead to a rational synthesis. This is to be freely admitted! But they do meet in the crucified and risen Christ. God's unconditioned and unqualified Yes is found in him (1:20).

The material relationship between the requirements of the old covenant and the gift of the Spirit in the new covenant does not come to explicit expression in 2 Cor 3. It is nevertheless implicit in the contrast between the tablets of stone and the tablets of hearts. As we have noted, the term "letter" serves as

172. I have borrowed this image from Bayer, *Luther's Theology,* 116-19.

173. See 5:14-15.

174. E.g., 2 Cor 1:6-7, 14, 21-22; 4:12-15; 6:11-13; 7:2-4, 14-16; 10:1-11; 11:1-11.

175. Hafemann, *2 Corinthians,* 133.

176. Hafemann, *2 Corinthians,* 131; Hafemann, *Paul, Moses, and the History of Israel,* 140.

a synecdoche, in which the message of the Law is identified with the medium by which it is communicated. It is the *form* of the divine communication that determines the difference between demand and gift, between death and life: in this respect, the medium is the message.[177] If the Law is written on the heart, one no longer needs instruction in it by one's neighbor, as the promissory text of Jeremiah itself makes clear (Jer 31:34). *Where* the demands of the Law are fulfilled, the Law no longer has any place (Gal 5:22-23).[178] Those who are led by the Spirit are not under the Law (Gal 5:18). The whole Law is fulfilled in the love of neighbor (Gal 5:14; Rom 13:8-10). In these contexts, Paul does not speak of "love" as a virtue that must be cultivated or as an abstract ideal, which would be subject to the distortions of the human imagination. He, rather, speaks of it as a *reality* that has entered into the world in Jesus Christ and that bears the definite contours that he describes in 1 Cor 13. Where this reality is present, the prohibitions "do not commit adultery, do not murder, do not steal, do not covet" (Rom 13:9) have been fulfilled and are no longer necessary. For this reason, Paul is able to speak of "keeping the commandments of God" as more important than circumcision (1 Cor 7:19). He likewise can point to an uncircumcised person as keeping the righteous requirements of the Law (Rom 2:26). The unqualified love of the neighbor marks the arrival of the fulfillment of the Law by the greater reality of eschatological life. Where the Law is fulfilled, it is neither necessary nor in force.

Finally, another, much more traditional attempt to revise the Pauline antithesis comes from Margaret Mitchell, who reads the distinction between "letter" and "Spirit" as the expression of a dilemma of communication in which Paul finds himself.[179] In his continuing conflict with the Corinthian church, Paul finds it necessary to insist on the straightforwardness of his statements to them and to call for their literal interpretation.[180] At the same time, his desire to instruct the Corinthians requires him to use language symbolically and to direct attention to the depths of his allegorical intent. He thus becomes the inaugurator of a hermeneutic of clarity *and* obscurity, one that runs along a "veil scale" between "agonistic" insistence on literal interpretation and "apocalyptic" deployment of the allegorical. The place at which Paul operated on this scale depended on the need of his recipients and on his judgment as to how he might best benefit them at the moment.[181] This

177. I borrow here the language of Marshall McLuhan.

178. Conversely, if the Law were still binding, it would have to be kept as a whole (Gal 5:3). The requirement of circumcision, the transcending of which is a boundary marker between the present age and the age to come, would still be in force (Gal 6:14-16). The apostle knows no distinction between moral and civil (or ceremonial) Law.

179. Mitchell, *The Birth of Christian Hermeneutics.*

180. Mitchell, *The Birth of Christian Hermeneutics,* 59.

181. Mitchell, *The Birth of Christian Hermeneutics,* 70-71.

strategy led to difficulties with the Corinthians, who regarded Paul's letters as "veiled" and hard to understand.[182] Indeed, Mitchell insists that in all written communication there is a collision between words and intentionality, or meaning: Paul's claim that the text of his former letter required "no digestion" is belied by both the fact and substance of his subsequent letter(s).[183] Paul's "veil scale" shaped subsequent Christian interpretation of Scripture, especially patristic hermeneutics; Origen and Gregory of Nyssa are of particular interest to Mitchell.[184]

Is it the case, however, that the miscommunication between Paul and the Corinthians corresponds to the way in which Mitchell describes it? It is obvious that there have been serious misunderstandings between them. But were they the result of written communication? They had arisen already prior to Paul's writing of 1 Corinthians and came about not merely from the misreading of letters but from the "misreading" of Paul's person and proclamation, as is clear from his lengthy discourse concerning the apostolic mission in 1 Cor 1:10–4:21. Furthermore, it is not at all apparent that the Corinthians regard Paul's letters as difficult to decipher or that their doubts about the apostle have to do with a perceived obscurity of his writing. Where they have misread him, as in his instruction not to associate with immoral persons (1 Cor 5:9-11), they have supposed that they read him rightly. Indeed, why would they ask for fresh, written instruction from him if they regarded his teaching as indecipherable (1 Cor 7:1)? As even his adversaries concede, Paul's letters are his strong point: "his letters are weighty and powerful" (10:10). What troubles the Corinthians is the discrepancy between the weakness of Paul's person and the power of his proclamation, or as Mitchell herself nicely puts it, the discrepancy between Paul's *parrēsia* and his *parousia*.[185]

There is no doubt, of course, that the distance and incomplete nature of written communication may engender misunderstanding. This has taken place between Paul and the Corinthians. As substitutes for presence, letters cannot deliver the *communion* between persons that is inherent to full communication.[186] It remains a question, however, as to whether it is the "writtenness" of written communication that is the cause of misunderstanding, and not distance itself that prevents full communication. Even if we grant that it is only with determined effort that we can prevent the misinterpretation of what we write, the very fact that we *do* write betrays a confidence that it is possible for

182. Mitchell, *The Birth of Christian Hermeneutics*, 98, 145 n. 49.

183. Mitchell, *The Birth of Christian Hermeneutics*, 98.

184. Mitchell's interaction with patriarchal interpretation stops short of Augustine, for whom the distinction between "letter" and "Spirit" takes on material significance.

185. Mitchell, *The Birth of Christian Hermeneutics*, 81. We might again add that Paul's *praxis*, esp. his refusal to accept support, likewise stands in contrast with his *parrēsia*.

186. See 1 Cor 13:12; cf. 2 John 12; 3 John 13-14.

writing to communicate our thought, if not fully, at least sufficiently.[187] In a world full of text-messaging, this point seems apparent.

More fundamentally, it is not clear that a scale or gradient aptly characterizes the relationship between the literal and the figurative, or the nature of human understanding.[188] Paul's earlier reminder to the Corinthians of the dictum "not going beyond that which is written" (1 Cor 4:6) obviously appeals to the "literal" or "written" meaning of the text of Scripture. Yet, as Mitchell observes, Paul issues this warning in the very context of indicating that he has transposed "figures" on to himself and Apollos.[189] This conjunction of the literal and the figurative need not signal a tension or conflict. In this instance, the "written" (and in this sense "literal") sense of Scripture itself is figural. Indeed, it is precisely the figural sense of the literal text that Paul has in mind in his transposition.[190] He has planted, Apollos has watered, but God has caused the growth of the Corinthian church, which is God's field (1 Cor 3:9). Paul takes up the familiar, biblical imagery of Israel as the cultivated vineyard of the Lord

187. For Mitchell, since texts don't just mean things but must be judged and argued, one may truly speak of a "scale" or gradient that runs between the "literal" and the "figurative" (*The Birth of Christian Hermeneutics*, 72, 109). One imagines, however, that Mitchell hopes and supposes that what she has written means something and can be understood in some significant measure. Even if one grants the obvious possibility of miscommunication and disagreement, one wonders how this applies to paychecks, instructions for the operation of equipment, military commands, and, in a certain measure, contracts and the like, in which the *immediate* intent of the author may be fixed sufficiently apart from debate, admittedly in terse and literal form. This fixity of meaning and its literal form are determined by the definite and limited context in which such writing operates. The matter changes in literature, of course, in which the more fundamental question of the meaning and nature of human life is examined. Here the context has been expanded to include larger and, indeed, ultimate issues. Scripture operates in such a context and does so radically: it places the rebellious and fallen human being in the presence of God.

188. Mitchell's presentation of the distinction between "literal" and "figurative" as that of definite (and argumentative) versus imaginary (and revelatory) seems to reflect the modern assumption that literal discourse (itself a figural expression) must be granted the last word in the communication of truth. One indication of the tenuous nature of this assumption is the frequency of common metaphors in everyday language, the meaning of which is nearly always evident: bringing owls to Athens, David and Goliath, silk purses and sows' ears, mountains and molehills, all belong here. For a further critique of this assumption, see C. Gunton, *The Actuality of the Atonement: A Study of Metaphor, Rationality, and the Christian Tradition* (Edinburgh: T&T Clark, 1988), 27-52; M. Johnson, "Philosophy's Debt to Metaphor," in *The Cambridge Handbook of Metaphor and Thought* (ed. R. W. Gibbs, Jr.; Cambridge: Cambridge University Press, 2008), 39-52. In anticipation of our following argument, we may suggest that figural speech is fundamental to language. Purely "literal" discourse is secondary, derivative, and difficult, if not impossible, to attain.

189. Mitchell, *The Birth of Christian Hermeneutics*, 64.

190. One might equally well say that Paul appeals to the "literal" sense of a figural text.

and applies it to himself and the Corinthians.[191] As we have observed, the figural meaning is literally present in the antecedent texts to which Paul appeals. Furthermore, the figures cannot in themselves provoke misunderstanding. The Corinthians could hardly imagine that they were a field, or that Paul and Apollos were farmhands. What is required of the Corinthians is that *they see themselves* in the picture that Paul draws for them from the storybook of Scripture. In this picture, they are not finally actors, agents, or judges as they imagined. They are, instead, the objects of God's care. Nor are they an Edenic garden, but the cursed ground, which yields its produce only by the sweat of the brow of the apostle. Moreover, and to Paul's point in this context, those who have been sent to them are mere hirelings of another, who have performed their appointed tasks and who therefore are not to be judged by the Corinthians.[192] As we have noted more than once, both Paul and the Corinthians are "figured out" in Scripture.[193] The metaphors that Paul employs are not directed to bare intellects that must merely decipher them. They are directed to the wayward hearts of the Corinthians that are filled with false pictures and stories. In his use of biblical imagery, Paul is combating the idols of the Corinthian hearts.

We may go a step further and argue that figurative language, rather than literal discourse, is the fundamental form of human communication.[194] All human communication may be regarded as an answer in one way or another to God the Creator, who sends his address "to the creature through the creature."[195] That is to say, God's communication to us always comes in the form

191. E.g., Isa 5:1-7; Ps 80:8-13.

192. It is significant that Paul shifts to the imagery of the human endeavor of construction, which will have its end in judgment (1 Cor 3:10-15).

193. Again I am alluding to Seitz, *Figured Out: Typology and Providence in Christian Scripture.*

194. The irony that the expression "literal discourse" is figurative in both terms should not go unnoticed. Our letters run to and fro, without our noticing it.

195. Johann Georg Hamann, *Aesthetica in Nuce,* N II, 198.29. More than any other, Oswald Bayer has drawn out the theological implications of Hamann's insight. See his *Schöpfung als Anrede: Zu einer Hermeneutik der Schöpfung* (Tübingen: Mohr Siebeck, 1990), esp. 9-32; also *Gott als Autor,* 1-40; and *Contemporary in Dissent.* Bare, analytic description entails the removal of the evocative figures through which the Creator addresses us. Thus Hamann, in the same context, drawing on Francis Bacon, claims, "Poetry is the mother tongue of the human race, as gardening is older than the farm-field, painting than writing, song than declamation, parables than argumentative conclusions, barter than commerce" (*Aesthetica in Nuce,* N II, 197.15-17). For a full discussion of Hamann's "metacriticism" of Kant's preference for mathematical precision in place of the original, pictorial nature of human language, see O. Bayer, *Vernunft ist Sprache: Hamanns Metakritik Kants* (Spekulation und Erfahrung: Untersuchungen 50; Stuttgart-Bad Cannstatt: Frommann-Holzboog, 2002), 280-361. See also Gunton, *The Actuality of the Atonement,* 36-38. On the larger philosophical context of Hamann's claim and its reception, see G. Figal, "Metapher III: Religionsphilosophisch," *RGG4,* 5:1166-67.

of figures and masks.[196] Our birth and upbringing, our daily bread, the gifts that we richly and daily enjoy — all come to us in this way. Admittedly, in the fallen world this communication is distorted and broken. Within us and without us, God's name is not sanctified. But the heavens continue to declare the glory of God. Whether in faith or in unbelief, our speech, in word and deed, is our response to the divine address. Just as God's address arrives in figures, our response, like that of a child to its mother, is likewise fundamentally poetic and figural. This figural response inherently bears a surplus of meaning that transcends the mere transmission of data. In our speech, we address not only God but also other persons, with whom we wish to share in our wit and whimsy, joys and sorrows, satisfaction and outrage. Indeed, the creation and loss of metaphors is part of the development of language: we invent new, living metaphors that in time become "dead metaphors" as their connection with life is obscured. We remove figural usage from our speech only partially, only with the greatest effort, and only for special purposes such as providing directions or securing legal rights. It is no accident that the stories of the creation and consummation of the world appear in Scripture in the form of pictures. This pictorial form of speech, not that of literal or scientific discourse, is fundamental to us as human creatures.

Consequently, especially in the face of human rebellion against God, the communication of truth about God is *always* agonistic in its apocalyptic intent, and *always* apocalyptic in its agonistic intent. It is necessarily figurative, since its first purpose is to do away with the false figures that capture the human heart. Paul must first destroy fortresses in Corinth (10:4) before he builds up the church (13:10). In this context at least — we need not consider the wider range of literature — a "veil scale" with a literal endpoint and a figural endpoint is a mirage. Moses' veil has no scale. Furthermore, while the figures of Scripture do contain hidden meaning that may result in miscommunication, that hiddenness is not the final cause of miscommunication. It is, rather, the *surplus* of meaning in the figures that works misunderstanding. By its provocative re-interpretation of the world, the storybook of Scripture exposes us in our rebellion. For this reason, we require an interpreter to tell us the truth about ourselves that we cannot imagine and otherwise will not hear. The Emmaus road was necessary. David needs Nathan's interpretive word: "You are the one!" (2 Sam 12:7). Matthew likewise summarizes Jesus' teaching in parables by underscoring their revelatory power, "I shall open my mouth in parables, I shall spew forth things hidden from the foundation of the world" (Matt 13:35;

196. Thus "wisdom" is the elucidation and understanding of the riddles through which God speaks to us in and through creation as it is opened to us by Scripture. These riddles call us outside of ourselves into communication with and worship of the Creator: "The fear of the Lord is the beginning of knowledge" (Prov 1:7; cf. Ps 111:10).

Ps 78:2).[197] Jesus' parables are hard to understand, *not* primarily because they contain *hidden* meaning (as they certainly do), but because their figures *reveal* truths about Jesus' hearers that these hearers are not ready or able to receive.[198] As Paul already has instructed the Corinthians, God hides himself in "the word of the cross" in order to reveal himself to fallen human creatures, whose own wisdom first must be destroyed in order for saving wisdom to arrive (1 Cor 1:18-31). It is this "word of the cross" that Paul unfolds in Second Corinthians.

If, then, Paul's language is obscure to the Corinthians, it is *not* because they cannot intellectually fathom his figures or follow his allusions. While ignorance of antecedent literature upon which allusions play may well precipitate misunderstanding, Paul expects that the Corinthians will know or at least learn the Scriptures to which he alludes.[199] The Corinthians misunderstand the apostle because, in their unbelief, they are *unwilling* and thus unable to follow his figures. They are in danger of being hardened with Israel and blinded with unbelievers. Paul calls for a response of self-judgment and faith that entails a new heart and understanding. It is often the case in Scripture that the hearers are unable to understand because they in some way or another will not follow the judgments that understanding requires. The Synoptic parables and the Johannine misunderstandings are classic examples of this phenomenon. Misun-

197. The psalmist recounts stories that his generation has known and heard, so that they may be told to the following generation. The stories are known and open to all; nevertheless, they must be retold. The retelling takes place in a parable (מָשָׁל) and in riddles (חִידוֹת) from the past. The retelling is thus not merely a reminding but also a revealing of that which is hidden within the Lord's dealings with Israel. This revelatory retelling must take place from generation to generation. The wonder of what the Lord has done for Israel is never exhausted in the telling but remains a wonder. Matthew takes up this thought explicitly in his witness to Jesus, the son of David, in whom is found the fulfillment of this Scripture (Ps 78:67-72). As is the case in the psalm itself, the fulfillment that takes place in Jesus' parables does not do away with the hiddenness of God's work, even though it decisively reveals it. Indeed, that hiddenness takes on its full dimensions with Jesus. Matthew radicalizes the biblical language. While the psalmist speaks of things known "from of old," Jesus speaks of things "hidden from the foundation of the world." He does so, moreover, *not* by recounting the history of God's dealings with Israel, but by telling parables of God's work in pictures drawn from everyday life. In Jesus' final revelatory act, Israel's story is set aside in favor of a picture book of the world as the place of the saving works of the Creator, who establishes the kingdom through Jesus. Just as the stories of the psalmist, which expose the truth about Israel, require interpretation, so these parables, which expose the truth about Jesus' hearers, require interpretation. This interpretation is given by Jesus himself (Matt 13:18-23, 36-43).

198. See Matt 13:10-17; Mark 4:10-12; Luke 8:9-10. In the Fourth Gospel, contrary to what the disciples suppose, Jesus promises to cease the use of figures only at the arrival of the eschaton and in the gift of the Spirit, which is its prolepsis (John 16:25-33).

199. As Kierkegaard would remind us (in "Of the Difference between a Genius and an Apostle"), Paul is not a genius, for whom aesthetics and intellect are of primary importance, but an apostle, who is sent to communicate.

derstanding, it should be noted, is not limited to the use of figurative language. The disciples misinterpret Jesus' figurative warning about the "leaven of the Pharisees" by taking it literally (Mark 8:14-21). But they also misunderstand his literal statement about the "Son of man rising from the dead" by taking it figuratively: it did not fit into their picture of the world (Mark 9:9-10).[200] There is, then, no scale of clarity that runs between the literal and the figurative.[201] Misunderstanding may take place in response to either mode of discourse, since it does not arise from the nature of the discourse, but from the challenge to the pictures and stories that capture the human heart.[202]

The problem between Paul and the Corinthians, then, is not *merely* hermeneutical. It is irreducibly and profoundly theological. The miscommunication that has taken place between them has to do with the cross, which is present not only in the "word" that Paul proclaims (1 Cor 1:18) but also in his own body and life (2 Cor 4:10). Paul thus does not suggest that "the sons of Israel" did not understand the immediate sense of the individual commandments (as if they could not comprehend the words "You shall not murder!"). He tells the Corinthians that Israel could not perceive how those commandments serve the divine purpose and thus finally could not comprehend them at all. Only the Spirit can remove the veil so that we may see that the Law, which brings death, fulfills its purpose in Christ, who brings life.

A disjunction between "meaning" and "intent" here emerges that Mitchell rightly perceives. Again, however, this disjunction is not merely formal. Nor does it have to do merely with intellectual perception.[203] The break in communication in Corinth is bound up with the strangeness of God's dealings, in which he puts to death in order to make alive, and judges in order to justify. Thus the Corinthians, although they have understood Paul in part (1:14), are in danger of misunderstanding him, because they judge what God is up to in the apostle according to human standards. The saving wisdom of God remains

200. Some of the Corinthians also found it difficult to accept a literal resurrection from the dead and likewise engaged in figural reinterpretation (1 Cor 15:12-58).

201. As Gunton rightly argues, understanding is dependent, not on a scale between literal and figurative, but rather on observing how a word is used in context (*The Actuality of the Atonement*, 35). In a biblical context, this will mean that readiness of the hearer or reader to see the world in a new way, in self-judgment, is fundamental to understanding.

202. Admittedly, figural language may well be misunderstood if one is uncertain as to whether or not an allusion is present, or precisely what sort of allusion might be in play. Did Paul die daily? Did he fight with wild beasts at Ephesus (1 Cor 15:31-32)? The first question is easier to decide than the second, unless, perhaps, one asks what precisely constitutes "death."

203. Apart from special contexts, speech and writing may be understood as action intended *to do something*, rather than merely impart information. See J. L. Austin, *How to Do Things with Words* (William James Lectures; Cambridge, Mass.: Harvard University Press, 1962).

"hidden in a mystery" (1 Cor 2:7), although it is precisely this wisdom that Paul openly proclaims (1 Cor 1:18-25).[204] Admittedly, the hiddenness of God's saving work allows place in the world for the "god of this age" to work blindness and deception (4:3-4). The apostle is the odor not only of life but also of death (2 Cor 2:15-16). But here it is once again clear that the Corinthian misunderstanding does not arise from Paul or *his* hermeneutical strategy, but from the saving strategy of *God,* who in working salvation hides himself in Christ's cross and likewise in the suffering of the apostle. Only through the "eschatological reserve" of God's hiddenness may the human being — who lives in unbelief and idolatry — be brought into the self-judgment of faith and thus be saved.

Paul's actions as apostle are bound up with God's work in Christ: just as the Yes to all of God's promises is found in the crucified Jesus, so Paul's word to the Corinthians is not Yes and No, the outward appearance of his failure to visit notwithstanding.[205] The apostle is finally not acting but being acted upon by God. He is led in God's triumph in Christ (2:14). He bears the deadness of Jesus in his body (4:10-11). His very speaking — he describes his writing as *speaking* — is given to him by the "Spirit of faith" (4:13; LXX Ps 115:1 [116:10]). The "simplicity and purity" of his conduct is fundamental to his apostolic mission (1:12-14). To practice guile would be to adulterate the word of God. He commends himself only through the "manifestation of the truth" (4:1-2). Transparency is essential to him, since the life and work of Another are being displayed in his life. For his part, Paul wants nothing more than that the Corinthians open their heart to him, just as he has opened his heart to them (6:11-13). His life and salvation is bound to theirs, just as theirs is to his.[206] As we have noted, the Corinthians are not the final interpreters of Paul, despite what they imagine. Nor are we. Both we and they have been interpreted by God, who is present in the suffering apostle of Christ. In the end, contrary to what Mitchell supposes, Paul *does* rely on textual evidence to confirm his apostolic calling: the Corinthians themselves are that text — to which we might be regarded as a footnote.[207] Not merely the interpretation of words but the interpretation of human beings is at stake in Paul's communication with the Corinthians. Yet it is not the case, either, that the Corinthians have become the sort of embodiment of the text that might allow the Scripture to be left behind as an artifact, as Hays proposes. The Spirit, who is given through the apostolic proclamation of Christ — a proclamation that, we should remind ourselves, stood before the

204. The apostle does not speak in "words taught by human wisdom" but in those "taught by the Spirit," which only those who are spiritual can receive (1 Cor 2:12-16).

205. According to Paul's account, his failure to complete his promised visit, which apparently has caused doubts to arise among the Corinthians, is the result of his love for them and desire to spare them grief (1:23–2:4).

206. 1:14, 21-22; 2:1-4; 7:2-16; 12:14-18.

207. Cf. Mitchell, *The Birth of Christian Hermeneutics,* 70.

Corinthians as a written letter — brings life and righteousness only where the letter brings death and condemnation. The Corinthians are living witnesses of that twofold work, as is, in another way, the suffering apostle. Justification comes through condemnation, life through death, wisdom through the foolishness of the cross. It is this material relation that Paul communicates in his antithetical paradox "letter" and "Spirit." And it is this material relation that is fundamental to the Corinthian misunderstanding of the apostle.

---

7 Having asserted his audacity and confidence in v. 4, and having announced its basis in vv. 5-6, Paul now argues for that confidence in vv. 7-11 by recounting the initial encounter between "the sons of Israel" and Moses at the (second) inscription of the Ten Commandments at Mount Sinai (Exod 34:29-32). Here Paul is not so much defending his assertion that "the letter kills, but the Spirit gives life" (v. 6) as he is *proceeding* from that assertion.[208] Only Paul's reference to the inability of "the sons of Israel" to look upon the glory of Moses' face — his interpretation of their fear (Exod 34:30) — provides the connection to his claim that "the letter" brings condemnation and death.[209] This inability has its counterpart in Moses' placement of a veil over his face, which Paul subsequently interprets as an act of judgment (v. 13). It is especially this noetic dimension of condemnation and death that he has in view here and throughout the letter: the *noēmata,* i.e., "the thoughts and minds" of "the sons of Israel," were "hardened" (v. 14a). The apostle deals with the Corinthian misunderstanding of God's work in the world. As he does elsewhere, Paul calls the Corinthians to engage in self-judgment by his appeal to Scripture.[210] Only the blind may receive sight. He asks them to see themselves within the

208. So, rightly, C. K. Stockhausen, *Moses' Veil and the Glory of the New Covenant: The Exegetical Substructure of II Cor. 3,1–4,6* (Analecta biblica 116; Rome: Editrice Pontifico Istituto Biblico, 1989), 111, 114-15.

209. This assertive form of argument, which may be regarded as an *apostolic* form, is not unusual for Paul. See, e.g., Rom 3:9-20; Gal 3:10, 19-22. Paul's testimony that the Law brings condemnation and death calls for a confession of failure that can be answered only in the first person, as in Rom 7:7-25.

210. As we have noted, the understanding of the Law that appears in the paradoxical antithesis of v. 6 is characteristic of Paul: the Law that was given for *life* effects *death* (Rom 7:6; cf. Rom 4:15; Gal 3:10-12, 21-22). Paul is not ignorant of the offer of life in the Law, nor is he unaware of the anthropological optimism that characterized most of his Jewish contemporaries, who supposed that life could be possessed through the Law. Here, however, he is not engaging them in argument but unmasking the similarly false presuppositions of the Corinthians, who, in their misunderstanding, suppose that *they* are competent to judge the marks of an apostle. The word of the cross is a scandal to both Jew and Greek.

Exodus story, first in "the sons of Israel" (vv. 7-11), and then in the figure of Moses (vv. 12-18).

Paul's entire argument in the first unit (vv. 7-11) appears in summary in vv. 7-8. If the mission of death came about in glory, the mission of the Spirit also shall be in glory. The following two movements of thought in vv. 9-10 and v. 11 merely elaborate *(gar)* what is already implicit in Paul's reference to the Exodus narrative: the mission of the new covenant is encompassed by a *greater* (vv. 9-10) and *enduring* (v. 11) glory.

We should not overlook the significance of the obvious here: Paul *argues,* or indeed *asserts,* that there is a glory to the apostolic mission. The outward and visible glory that appeared on Moses' face is transcended by the glory of the apostolic mission, which is presently inward and unseen, the knowledge of which can be imparted only by the apostolic word of the Gospel. Paul now goes to the heart of the controversy between him and the Corinthians. Contrary to what they imagine, the Corinthians are not competent to judge the apostle. Rather, it is they who are judged in God's dealings with them in him. While the Corinthians themselves live in honor and suppose that the world is to be so measured, the apostle lives in dishonor (1 Cor 4:10). Through Jesus Christ, not through the Corinthians' own wisdom, their "Amen" arises to God for the glory displayed in the apostle (1:20). The eternal weight of glory is not yet manifest, only the afflictions that prepare it (4:17). The glory of the apostolic mission is not one seen with the eyes but is perceived with the ears alone. Paul subsequently underscores the priority of hearing over seeing in a metaphor that again takes on a synesthetic quality: the light of the knowledge of God's glory in the face of Christ shines *in the heart* of the apostles (2 Cor 4:6; cf. 2:14b). Having the "Spirit of faith," they *speak* (2 Cor 4:13). God's glory in Christ cannot be seen presently. It is manifest in the world only indirectly, in distress and deliverance. It must be heard, believed, and spoken.

As Paul's language makes clear, the Law itself brings death, and not merely Moses' deficient administration of it.[211] The "mission of death" is engraved — ineffaceably — with letters in stones *(diakonia . . . entetypōmenē).* The very content of the Law, its requirements and threats, appears here as "the *diakonia* of death," i.e., the *communication* of death. The message cannot be abstracted from the form in which it is communicated. Neither can the messenger be separated from the message that he bears. The divine "emis-

211. Against Hafemann, *2 Corinthians,* 146-47. See again the discussion of the διακονία word group and the work of Collins, *Diakonia,* mentioned above in n. 4, p. 96. In the discussion of the following verses, we will vary in rendering διακονία as "mission," "ministry," or "administration" according to context. The term, in contexts such as these, signifies agency or communication on behalf of another.

saries" are identified with the covenants they administer: Moses is *read* and thus, according to Paul's metonym, is inseparable from "the letter" that brings death (3:15).

This communication of death "came about in glory, so that the sons of Israel were not able to look upon the face of Moses, on account of the glory of his face." Paul here recalls the reception of Moses after the giving of the written Law in Exod 34:29-35. More precisely, the initial moment of Israel's response to Moses stands at the center of his attention. According to the Exodus narrative, as Moses descended the mountain with the two tablets of the Law in his hands, he did not realize that "the skin of his face shone, because he had spoken with God" (v. 29). Seeing Moses' face, Aaron and the sons of Israel were afraid to come near to him (v. 30). After their flight (which remains implicit in the narrative), Moses called them back to himself: first Aaron and the leaders, to whom he spoke, then all "the sons of Israel." He then enjoined upon them all that the Lord had spoken to him on the mountain, mediating to them the Law written on stone tablets (vv. 31-32). Afterward, he placed a veil over his face (v. 33). When he entered into the wilderness tabernacle to speak with the Lord, he removed the veil (v. 34). This action became Moses' practice: he would speak with the Lord in the tabernacle with an unveiled face; then, with unveiled face, he would recount the Lord's commands to the sons of Israel; afterward, he would place the veil on his face until he again entered the tabernacle to speak with the Lord (v. 35).

As we have noted, Paul's attention is focused on the initial moment of encounter between Moses and "the sons of Israel." Here he interprets their initial fear as an *inability* to look at Moses' face, "on account of the *glory* of his face." The narrative of this event corresponds to the prior account in Exodus of Israel's encounter with God when the Lord spoke his commandments to them.[212] Now a mediator stands between Israel and God, just as they had requested. Yet even the reflected glory of the mediator's face strikes fear in their heart, so that they are afraid to approach him. Nevertheless, Moses performs his mediatorial service. He calls the sons of Israel to himself, so that first Aaron and the leaders, and then all the sons of Israel, return to him, *despite the glory of his face* that they continue to see (Exod 34:31-33). Only when he has finished speaking does he again place the veil on his face (v. 33). *The veil comes after the word of the Law.* It is quite clear, then, that, once their fears were overcome, the sons of Israel saw the glory of Moses' face. Indeed, they did so repeatedly, as Moses delivered divine instruction to them.[213] The text of Exodus is quite clear about this pattern (v. 35).

212. See the account of Israel's fear in Deut 5:22-27, 28-33, which meets with the Lord's approval; likewise Heb 12:18-21.

213. Hafemann's claim that Moses veiled himself to protect Israel from the divine glory is at odds with Hafemann's own interpretation. The text of Exodus makes it clear that Israel saw

Consequently, it must be said that Israel's worship of the golden calf — as significant as this idolatry is in the course of the Lord's dealings with Israel — does not hold the place in the Exodus narrative that Hafemann and Hahn assign to it.[214] Hafemann understands the Law to have been life-giving and transforming prior to Israel's idolatry, but death-dealing afterward because of Israel's rebellion. It is certainly not the case, however, that the worship of the golden calf is the first instance of Israel's rebellion against the Lord in the Exodus narrative. As we have noted, already in the provision of manna in the wilderness, Israel fails the Lord's test as to whether or not they would follow his Torah (Exod 16:4). The same story continues at Horeb, where the Lord brings water from a rock for them (Exod 17:1-7). The very distance that Israel must maintain from the Lord at the giving of the Law speaks of their state of rebellion. Already at this point, they must be warned against "breaking through to look at the Lord" (Exod 19:16-25).[215] Likewise, in the narrative of Deuteronomy (which equally would have stood in the scriptural background to which Paul alludes), Moses accuses Israel of having been rebellious against the Lord from the day they came out of Egypt (Deut 9:7, 24). The incident of the golden calf figures largely in Moses' warning to Israel there, but it certainly does not stand alone (Deut 9:1-29). The Lord's stern word to Israel that he will not "go up" with them to the promised land but merely send his angel before them (Exod 33:1-3), which figures largely in Hafemann's reading, is in fact a repetition of an earlier warning, given prior to Israel's idolatry (Exod 23:20-22). Furthermore, just as Moses' intercession overcame the Lord's wrath against Israel in its idolatry, his fresh petition in this later context secures the Lord's

---

the glory of Moses' face *as he gave them divine instruction.* Only *afterward* did he veil himself. In other words, Israel sees Moses' face as he delivers the Law in its deadly force. They do not see Christ, who comes after the Law as its fulfillment. Against Hafemann, *2 Corinthians,* 144; Hafemann, *Paul, Moses, and the History of Israel,* 223.

214. Hafemann, *2 Corinthians,* 142-44; Hafemann, *Paul, Moses, and the History of Israel,* 225-31; S. Hahn, *Kinship by Covenant: A Canonical Approach to the Fulfillment of God's Saving Promises* (New Haven: Yale University Press, 2009), 142-53. While Israel's sin with the golden calf understandably holds a prominent place in early Jewish tradition (e.g., *Midr. Num* 11.3; *Midr. Song* 3.18; *LAB* 12:1-10), it is not clear that this one transgression surpasses all others, since (1) rabbinic tradition elsewhere points to the serious results of other sins (e.g., *Midr. Num* 10.2; *Midr. Deut* 2.22; 10.4; *Midr. Esth* 1.13; *Midr. Lam* 1.35); (2) the event also becomes an example of the power of Moses' intercession and the Lord's mercy (e.g., *Midr. Exod* 15.26; 46.1; *Midr. Num* 18.6; *Midr. Deut* 1.2). Furthermore, as Schmeller notes (*Der zweite Brief an die Korinther,* 201), the rabbinic traditions that connect the sin with the golden calf and the inability to bear God's glory are later than Paul. See also L. L. Belleville, *Reflections of Glory: Paul's Polemical Use of the Moses-Doxa Tradition in 2 Corinthians 3.1-18* (JSNT 52; Sheffield: JSOT Press, 1991), 66, 75.

215. R. Otto, *The Idea of the Holy: An Inquiry into the Non-rational Factor in the Idea of the Divine and Its Relation to the Rational* (trans. J. W. Harvey; London: Oxford University Press, 1958).

presence with his people, despite the fact that they remain "stiff-necked" (Exod 33:14-17). The presence of God will give "rest" to Moses and, by virtue of his intercession, to Israel as well. God promises to grant Moses' petition and thus to be with Israel in blessing, not judgment.[216] The Lord dwells with sinners and rebels.

The shift in the Exodus story from God's direct address to Israel by his own voice (Exod 19:16–20:21) to the mediation of God's words through Moses (20:22–24:8) and finally to the commandments written on stone tablets (24:12-18) is of far greater significance to Paul's account than is the story of Israel's idolatry. This fundamental change in the Lord's dealings with Israel is not precipitated by any particular event. Indeed, it follows the high point of Israel's relation with the Lord, the idyllic covenant-meal at which the elders of Israel see Israel's God and live (24:9-11). As is quite clear from the surrounding narrative, the giving of the commandments in written form is necessary because of the inability of the people to endure the voice of God (20:19). Moses' words of encouragement to them are of no avail: "Don't be afraid, for God has drawn near only in order to test you, and to put the fear of God upon you, so that you will not sin" (20:20). Israel, which has already failed the Lord's tests, is not able to endure his voice. Consequently, the Law is mediated in the final form of commandments written in stone. It is precisely this element of the narrative that Paul takes up explicitly and emphatically (vv. 3, 7). He says nothing of the golden calf. That the commandments are given in *written* form signals Israel's distance from God and the broken communication between them.

According to Paul, "the sons of Israel" were unable "to look upon" Moses' face on account of its glory. The verb that Paul uses *(atenizō)* signifies "directing one's gaze" or "giving one's attention" to someone or something. The sense of the verb is that of "looking intentionally" and not that of "prolonging one's gaze," although, of course, duration may be incidental to such a beholding.[217]

216. The claim that the priesthood passed from the people of Israel (or their firstborn) to the Levites upon Israel's idolatry runs into conflict with the text. Already in Exod 6:16-25 the lineage of the Levites is set forth. Likewise, at the first giving of the Law at Sinai, the priests are distinguished from the people, as is Aaron from the priests (19:21-24). The instructions for the inner sanctuary, where Moses alone enters to receive divine instruction (34:34) and where Aaron alone is to make annual atonement (30:10), are given *before* Israel's idolatry, as are likewise the instructions for the tabernacle where the priests are to serve (28:1-43). Most significantly, it is Aaron who instigates the worship of the golden calf, and who in fact formed it (32:1-6). Yet he retains his priesthood! Against Hafemann, *2 Corinthians*, 142-43; Hahn, *Kinship by Covenant: A Canonical Approach to the Fulfillment of God's Saving Promises*, 139-47.

217. The Greek ἀτενίζειν, with its intensifying ἀ- added to the verbal stem τείνω (to stretch, draw tight), lies in the background of the Latinate terms "attention" and "attend." Thus also the adjective ἀτενής, "strained tight, tense, or intense." See LSJM, ἀτενίζω, 269. Paul uses the verb ἀτενίζειν only here and in v. 13. It appears 12x in Luke-Acts (Luke 4:20; 22:56; Acts

In the present context, Paul speaks of "the sons of Israel" as being unable *to direct their gaze* to Moses' face and its glory. The moment of fear, when "the sons of Israel" first encountered Moses as he returned from Sinai, becomes for Paul the crucial point of the narrative (Exod 34:30).[218] He draws his reference to "the glory of Moses' face" from the concluding statement of the passage that, as Moses gave instruction, "the sons of Israel would see Moses' face, that the skin of his face was radiant" (34:35). Their initial fear having been overcome by Moses' appeal, they come to listen to him and see his face. Paul's attention, however, is focused on their moment of fear and flight. Just as they are unable to endure God's voice, they are unable to endure his nearness as it is reflected in Moses' face. Paul's retelling of the event prepares for his following interpretative reading — which stands in obvious tension with the first — according to which Moses' veiling of his face was an act of judgment that prevented the sons of Israel from looking upon *(atenizō)* its glory (v. 13).

The glory of Moses' face "is done away with" *(katargoumenēn)*. The verb *katargeō* does not mean "to fade away," but rather "to do away with," "to bring to nothing,"[219] or, when it is used in reference to persons or agents in action, "to render idle."[220] In Pauline usage, which is the most frequent in the New Testament, *powers* are almost always the logical subject of the verb, especially the power of God or Christ, but also the powers of evil.[221] In most instances, Paul uses the passive form of the verb (15x), so that the nature of the divine agency or that of opposing powers remains unexpressed. In these contexts, human beings appear, not as agents in action, but as the objects of the saving work of the Creator or, conversely, the showplace of evil powers. Correspondingly, in these same contexts, *katargeō* does not signify that an object or thing has been rendered ineffective, but rather that such a thing has been done away with, brought to nothing, or abrogated.[222] This sense is apparent in Paul's usage in 2 Cor 3, particularly in v. 11, where he contrasts "that which abides"

1:10; 3:4, 12; 6:15; 7:55; 10:4; 11:6; 13:9; 14:9; 23:1), 3x in the LXX (1 Esd 6:27; 3 Macc 2:26; Odes 12:10), and 2x in Josephus (*Ant.* 19.345; *J.W.* 5.517).

218. Paul's interpretive move has precedents in early Jewish tradition, which likewise spoke of Israel's inability to look upon Moses' face (Philo, *Mos.* 1.70; *Pesiq. Rab.* 10.6) because of the sin of the golden calf (*Midr. Num* 11.3).

219. Hafemann, *Paul, Moses, and the History of Israel,* 301-9.

220. The verb, which is built on the nominal stem ϝεργ-, may thus express the two possible senses of "work" that are also present in English: either the active idea of working or the passive idea of something that has been worked (as in "a work of art"). It may signify either the rendering of an action ineffective or the abolition of a thing.

221. The sole exception is 1 Cor 13:11, which itself is a figure of God's work. On the powers of evil, see Gal 5:4, 11.

222. E.g., Rom 7:2, 6; Gal 5:4. Against Hafemann, *2 Corinthians,* 144; Hafemann, *Paul, Moses, and the History of Israel,* 305-6.

with the substantival participle *katargoumenon:* it is naturally to be rendered "that which is done away with." Of course, in v. 6 Paul speaks of "the letter" as a power that kills — indeed, a personified power. But here and elsewhere in this context, where he uses the verb *katargeō,* he does not speak of the *actions* of agents that have been halted or rendered idle. He presents *realities* that have been abrogated in Christ: the glory of Moses' face (v. 7), the entire mission of Moses (vv. 11, 13), and the old covenant itself (v. 14). The old covenant and its glory do not fade away of themselves.[223] The glory of the new covenant eclipses that of the old.

In this last word in v. 7, then, Paul recalls the work of the Spirit "who makes alive" (v. 6) and prepares for his description of the contrast between the old covenant and God's work in Christ (vv. 12-18). He thus signals at the very outset of his description of Moses' mission that this mission is *now* done away with by something greater.[224] Again in vv. 11, 13 he will speak of Moses' mission and its glory as having been done away with, before he finally *locates* the end of the old covenant in Christ (v. 14). As we have noted, this conjunction of the temporal and the local is characteristic of Paul: he understands the new creation as having intersected the fallen world in the crucified and risen Jesus (5:17).[225] It is only in him, and not within the world at large (or in some salvation-historical scheme), that the mission of death has been brought to an end.

8 "How shall not the mission of the Spirit even more be in glory?" The opposition that Paul presents in vv. 7-8 is imbalanced: he does not set the mission of *life* over against that of death, but rather against that "of *the Spirit.*" As Paul's appeal to the figure of Moses already makes clear, the gift of life is no mere possession of the human being that can be isolated from the Giver. Life and salvation are found in the *communicative* relation between the human being and God established by the Spirit. Paul takes up this theme in vv. 12-18.

As interpreters regularly observe, in vv. 8-9 Paul argues from the lesser to the greater *(qal wahomer; a minore ad maius).* His argument does not rest, however, on a natural or logical deduction. It is not immediately apparent that

223. Against the NIV, "glory, transitory though it was." *Pace* Hofius, "Gesetz und Evangelium nach 2. Korinther 3," 96-99; Belleville, *Reflections of Glory: Paul's Polemical Use of the Moses-Doxa Tradition in 2 Corinthians 3.1-18,* 203-8.

224. Against the ESV ("glory, which was being brought to an end"). Here as well as in vv. 11 13, 14, the durative aspect of the present tense should be understood as expressing not an ongoing action but a state of affairs, and not one in the past but in the present. V. 14, where Paul speaks of the old covenant as having been done away with "in Christ," esp. makes this sense clear. Rightly, the NSRV: "a glory now set aside."

225. Cf. 1:20; Gal 6:14-16. Paul is thus able to affirm paradoxically that he does *not* "do away with the Law through faith" but rather "establishes the Law" (Rom 3:31), and yet that in Christ the old covenant — which is nothing but the written Law — is done away with (v. 14).

the work of the Spirit is larger and greater than that of the letter. The finality of the gift of the Spirit and of life is bound up with the new covenant, which Paul *asserts* as the essence of his mission in v. 6. As we have noted, the argument of vv. 7-11, rather than being merely logical in nature, is fundamentally assertive — based on apostolic authority — as becomes apparent in vv. 9-11, where Paul shifts away from the rhetoric of deduction to straightforward assertions of the greater and enduring glory of the Spirit and life.

The question that Paul puts in v. 8, "How shall not the ministry of the Spirit even more be in glory?" does not call for a mere logical conclusion, but for an affirmation of the Gospel. The future form *estai* (How *shall* not . . .) is to be understood as a real future, and not *merely* as a logical one. The glory of the apostolic ministry of the Spirit is not yet manifest. It presently remains hidden under its opposite. The wisdom of God, which has the glory of believers as its end, remains hidden: the Lord of glory was crucified by the rulers of this age (1 Cor 2:7-8). Just as there was a glory to the mission of Moses, there is a glory that belongs to the mission of the apostle but that is visible only to the eyes of faith. The paradoxical unity of "the letter" and "the Spirit" thus bears not only an anthropological dimension but also a theological one. We presently encounter God's glory in two forms: the glory of God that accompanies the mission of Moses and brings death, and the glory of God that belongs to the distribution of the Spirit and brings life. The difference between these two ways of encounter with God cannot be resolved in a higher, abstract conception of the divine glory. They have met and have been resolved in the crucified Christ, who is now risen. We cannot yet see how the condemnation of the Law has been swallowed up. We only hear it in the Gospel. Our vision of their unity must await the light of glory. Presently we walk by faith, not by appearance.

9 The argument shifts to an assertion that explains and reinforces the preceding rhetorical question: "For if there [was] a glory to the mission of condemnation, the mission of righteousness shall abound by much more with glory." Paul here unfolds the significance of the paradoxical relation of "letter" and "Spirit" in new terms. He now contrasts "condemnation" and "righteousness." The forensic dimension of God's saving work thus becomes apparent: the judgment of the fallen human being takes place within that saving work. Furthermore, the contrast is now heightened; the unseen glory of the ministry of righteousness "abounds much more in glory" than that of condemnation.

The term Paul uses for "condemnation" *(katakrisis)* signifies the act of effecting condemnation. It is the death worked by the "letter," expressed in forensic terms. Correspondingly, "righteousness" *(dikaiosynē)* expresses the concrete effect or result of the divine judgment. It is the life that the Spirit works, likewise forensically conceived. There is a hint here of the subsequent contrast Paul draws between the temporary work of the letter and the abiding work of the Spirit (v. 11).

In both instances, Paul speaks not of bare decisions but of operative statements, judgments that enact what they say (as in the pronouncement of sentences in the modern courtroom).[226] The act of condemnation brings death (v. 7). "Righteousness" corresponds to the gift of the Spirit (v. 8). Paul's language here matches his declarations to the Corinthians elsewhere that the crucified Christ has become righteousness "for us" (1 Cor 1:30) and that "we" have become the righteousness of God in him (5:21). In these instances, "righteousness" is neither a mere status nor a process of transformation. It is the reality of the new creation that is present in the risen Lord and that is given to us in him (5:17). In his association of "righteousness" with "glory" Paul faintly echoes the book of Isaiah, where "righteousness" is associated with "light," namely, the radiance of the Lord's saving work.[227]

As we have noted, the gift of the Spirit is nothing other than the "down payment" *(arrabōn)* of the resurrection, its intersection with the fallen world, as Paul twice announces to the Corinthians in this letter (1:22, 5:5). This gift of life is located in Christ, as Paul makes clear in this very passage (vv. 3, 14).[228] Indeed, Paul explicitly identifies Christ with the Spirit in 1 Cor 15:45. This connection between v. 8 and v. 9, between the Spirit and "righteousness," is characteristic of Paul's theology. It corresponds to biblical language concerning righteousness and justification elsewhere; in forensic contexts, the Scriptures consistently speak of justice *done* and righteousness *effected.*[229]

It is the *apostolic* mission that Paul here describes as the "mission of righteousness." He subsequently charges his opponents as being "false apostles" and, in fact, "emissaries of Satan," who disguise themselves as "emissaries of righteousness" (11:15). Outward appearances, which are the basis of human judgments, are always deceptive (cf. 5:12). God's work in Christ overturns all such false estimations. Those who seem to be apostles are not. The one who seems *not* to be an apostle is the true apostle sent to the Corinthians. The glory of the mission of righteousness, although it is transcendent, presently remains hidden.

10 Paul now underscores the significance of the greater glory of the gift of righteousness. The heightened glory of the mission of righteousness so transcends the former glory that "by this measure that which has been glorified has not been glorified, on account of the surpassing greatness of glory." The glory of the ministry of the Spirit and righteousness so outshines the glory of

226. See Austin, *How to Do Things with Words,* 152-53.

227. See, e.g., Isa 42:6-7; 49:1-7; 51:4-5; 53:11; 59:9; 62:1.

228. See also 1 Cor 2:4, 6:11; Gal 3:2, 5, 14.

229. E.g., 1 Kgs 10:9; 2 Chr 9:8; Pss 17:2; 24:5; 35:27; 37:6; 98:2; 99:4; 103:6; Isa 33:5; 54:17; 62:1-2; 63:1; Jer 33:15. It is rulers who judge; their pronouncements are enacted. See, e.g., Abraham's question to the Lord (Gen 18:25) or Solomon's famous judgment (1 Kgs 3:16-28); likewise, the petition for the king in Ps 72:1-4. The same is all the more true of God, the Creator.

Moses' mission that the former glory is no glory at all. Barth's characterization of the arrival of the eschaton is apt in this context: "Because the sun rises, all lights are extinguished."[230] Paul uses similar imagery in his description of the eschaton in 1 Cor 15:40-44: there are differing glories, earthly and heavenly; the sun differs from the moon in glory, and the stars differ from one another in glory. It is the same way in the resurrection of the dead, Paul continues: the body is sown in dishonor and raised in glory. The contrast between the sun and the moon obviously plays a central role in 1 Cor 15 and corresponds to that between the glory of Moses' mission and that of the apostle in 2 Cor 3; the brightness of the latter so outshines the former that it has no glory. The greater light rules the bright day of the new creation. The lesser light rules only the present darkness and night of sin, death, and condemnation (cf. Gen 1:16).

The paradoxical relationship between the letter and the Spirit continues here. The contrast that Paul sets between them is so radical and difficult that most, if not all, translations do away with it: "that which has been glorified *has not been glorified*, on account of the surpassing greatness of glory."[231] On account of the glory of the apostolic mission, the former glory is made no glory at all. It has been done away with. Yet it is to this very glory that Paul makes appeal as a confirmation of the glory of the ministry of the Spirit and righteousness. Negation and affirmation are juxtaposed, as are death and life. The glory associated with the letter prepares for that of the Spirit. Only those under condemnation may receive the gift of righteousness. Yet the glory of the mission of righteousness is so bright that it eclipses and eliminates the former glory. There is no line of continuity that may be drawn between them. They meet in the crucified and risen Lord alone.

In this verse Paul shifts his language slightly, yet significantly. In vv. 7-9 he has spoken of the glories of the two differing ministries or missions. Here his reference broadens to the neuter form "that which has been glorified," encompassing Moses within Moses' mission. The emissary belongs to the mission entrusted to him. This is true not only for the apostle but also for Moses. In broadening his reference (as he continues to do in vv. 11-13), Paul brings into view the figure of Moses, whom he has introduced in v. 7. In vv. 12-18, he will draw a contrast between his mission and that of Moses.

11 In his final formulation of the letter-Spirit antithesis, Paul returns to the final word of v. 7: the glory of Moses' face and of the mission of death

230. K. Barth, *The Resurrection of the Dead* (trans. H. J. Stenning; New York: Fleming H. Revell, 1933), 81.

231. The ESV splits its rendering of Paul's twofold use of the perfect form of δοξάζω into past and present — without sufficient warrant ("what once had glory has come to have no glory at all"). The NSRV is similar. The NIV simply transposes the second usage to present time, again without warrant ("what was glorious has no glory now").

has been done away with. It has been abrogated. Here again he anticipates his argument in vv. 12-18, and at the same time he returns to his original claim that divine glory attends the ministry of the Spirit: "for if that which is done away with [came about] through glory, how much more [does] that which abides [do so] in glory."[232] Now he has developed the letter-Spirit paradox in such a way that the contrast between abrogation and permanence itself supports his opening assertion that "the letter kills, but the Spirit gives life." The former is temporal, the latter is eternal.

Paul's description of the divine glory that is attendant upon the two missions now changes slightly. That which has been abrogated came about "through glory." That which abides does so "in glory." Although there was a divine glory to Moses' mission of death, that glory did not properly belong to it but only came *through* it. It was thus an "alien" glory. In contrast, the abiding ministry of the Spirit and righteousness remains enveloped *in* the bright, divine glory that properly belongs to it.

This final contrast between "that which is done away" and "that which abides" has a deep connection to Paul's larger argument in the letter. This connection is especially apparent in Paul's later affirmation of the contrast between his present afflictions and the "eternal weight of glory" that they effect. As one who shares in the Spirit of faith (4:13), he looks not at the things that are seen but at the things that are unseen, "for the things that are seen are temporal, but the things that are unseen are eternal" (4:18). Moses' mission and the condemning work of the letter, with its outward, visible glory, belong to the present, fallen age. This work has been gathered up into the deadness of Jesus, which manifests itself in the apostle, who constantly bears it in his body (1:5; 4:10). In contrast, the Spirit, given in and by the risen Christ, is the guarantee of the age to come and brings its presently unseen glory into the world (1:22; 5:5). The Spirit works faith (4:13).

3. *The Apostle and the Church in the Freedom of the Spirit* (3:12-18)

> [12]*Since we have such a hope, we are very bold,* [13]*not like Moses, who would put a veil over his face so that the Israelites might not gaze at the outcome of what was being brought to an end.* [14]*But their minds were hardened. For to this day, when they read the old covenant, that same veil remains unlifted, because only through Christ is it taken away.* [15]*Yes, to this day whenever Moses is read a veil lies over their hearts.* [16]*But when one turns to the Lord, the veil is removed.* [17]*Now the Lord is the Spirit, and where the Spirit of the Lord is, there is freedom.* [18]*And we all, with*

232. The distinction is not fully captured by the ESV, NIV, or NRSV.

unveiled face, beholding the glory of the Lord, are being transformed into the same image from one degree of glory to another. For this comes from the Lord who is the Spirit.

Paul's focus shifts from mission to messenger. He now explains and defends the audacity of his apostolic hope that he has described in vv. 1-3 and that he has expressed in v. 4: "*such* confidence we have through Christ toward God." This audacity is a *spoken audacity:* "the great boldness" that Paul employs is the unqualified confidence that righteousness and life are imparted within the world through the word he proclaims: "Who is sufficient for these things?" (2:16). The boldness and free speech *(parrēsia)* of the apostle effect the freedom of the Spirit's presence (v. 18).[233] His confidence is the utter confidence that the Corinthians are "a letter of Christ," in whom Christ himself is present, despite all outward appearance. Through the new covenant, the Spirit is present with them. They have been granted a vision of the very glory of God. Consequently, as an apostle of Christ, Paul stands above any need of confirmation or commendation. His audacity is unparalleled. It springs from the hope of the new covenant, which of itself moves and compels him to speak. This opening of Paul's mouth is also the opening of Paul's heart to the Corinthians, as he will later declare to them (6:11).

This audacity belongs to Paul precisely in the weakness and suffering to which he is subject as an apostle, which is so repulsive to the Corinthians. Paul has already spoken of that suffering (1:3-11) and will do so shortly again (4:7-15). As we have seen, he suffers most of all with his churches, and especially with the wayward Corinthians.

As a messenger of the new covenant, Paul contrasts his "boldness born of hope" with Moses' practice of veiling his face before "the sons of Israel" (vv. 12-18). As we have observed, his appeal to the narrative of Exodus 34 does not serve to ward off the threat of Judaizing. It is rather that Paul finds his story, together with that of the Corinthians, within the stories of Scripture. The argument of vv. 12-18 is a continuing interpretation of the Exodus story of the giving of the written Law, to which Paul already has appealed in v. 7. Now, however, there is a decisive turn. Not only were the sons of Israel unable to look on the glory of Moses' face, Moses prevented them from doing so. His veil hid the divine glory that was the goal of the Law. Moses, the minister of the Law, *enacts* the condemnation brought by the Law. Moses' veil, Paul furthermore announces, remains until the present day. It continues to rest on the reading of the Law and on the hearts of the "sons of Israel," so that they

233. For reflections on this theme, see W. C. v. Unnik, "The Christian's Freedom of Speech in the New Testament," *BJRL* 44 (1962): 466-88. I thank Jeffrey Oschwald for this reference.

cannot see that the Law has been done away with in Christ. Yet that blindness does not end the story. It takes a surprising turn. Those "in Christ" know the freedom of Moses and, with an unveiled face, behold the glory of the Lord.

Verses 12-18 thus describe Paul's apostolic audacity, first (v. 12) in contrast with Moses' practice of veiling his face (vv. 13-15), and then in connection with Moses' removal of the veil as he "turned to" the Lord in the tent of meeting (v. 16; Exod 33:7). This new element of the narrative in v. 16 becomes the focus of a relatively lengthy series of interpretive statements in vv. 17-18, in which Paul again describes his boldness as an apostle. The three focal points of the passage thus are (1) Paul's declaration of boldness in vv. 12-13; (2) his interpretive declaration concerning the effect of Moses' veil in hardening of "the sons of Israel" in vv. 14-15; and (3) his final interpretive elaboration of Moses' removal of the veil in the presence of the Lord in vv. 16-18, which surprisingly appears as a continuation of the narrative.[234] The first and third points are fundamentally connected to one another. When Paul affirms that "we all . . . behold in a mirror the glory of the Lord" (v. 18), he describes the common salvation in which he and the Corinthians share, through the new covenant, of which he is an emissary. This is his hope and the basis of his audacity (v. 12). This apostolic audacity embraces the Corinthians as a "letter of Christ" administered through him (v. 3) and written in his own heart (v. 2). As he repeatedly makes clear to the Corinthians, he cannot speak of himself without speaking of them. His salvation and theirs are bound together (1:12-14, 21-22).

12 The opening statement in v. 12 is consequential (*oun;* "therefore"), building on Paul's preceding assertion of the transcendent and enduring glory of the new covenant. This glory is Paul's hope, and it brings about his boldness. The hope and boldness of v. 12 thus anticipate the vision of the divine glory that Paul describes in vv. 17-18. It should be no surprise that this boldness includes the Corinthians' participation in the vision of the divine glory.

Paul's phrasing "having such hope" corresponds to his preceding claim of "having such confidence" (v. 4). This confidence, as we have observed, is fundamentally objective and corresponds to Paul's expression of hope here. In his following description of himself as apostle, he speaks of his present affliction as preparing "an eternal weight of glory" (4:17), a hope that is obviously bound up with "being clothed" with the dwelling from heaven, in which that which is mortal shall be swallowed up by life (5:4). His hope is that of the life of the resurrection, of which the Spirit is the down payment (5:5).

Having such hope, Paul "uses much boldness." He continues to explain the unparalleled audacity that places him above the Corinthians' questions and judgments. His apostolic mission is the channel through which God has recreated them and given them righteousness and life and thus freedom (v. 17).

234. Verse 16 is introduced by the particle δέ, as are vv. 17 and 18.

The "confidence" that Paul "has," he employs in his words and actions. In all likelihood, the semantic motivation of the term for boldness, *parrēsia (pas-rhēsis),* "open" or "free speech," is connoted here. Paul's boldness, after all, has to do with his open claim to apostolic authority; the freedom of the Corinthians, the freedom of the presence of the Spirit, is worked by his freedom of speech. It is his word to the Corinthians that has come into question, which he defends (1:18). His mission is a *speaking* ministry of "the word of God" (2:17) and the new covenant (3:6). He proclaims the Gospel, namely, that the crucified Christ is Lord (4:3-5). In the midst of trial, he *speaks* as the psalmist did because he has been given the same "Spirit of faith" (4:13). He *persuades* people (5:11). He *makes appeal* as Christ's ambassador (5:20). He has opened wide his mouth and heart to the Corinthians (6:11). His boldness is a *speaking* boldness.

13 Paul immediately contrasts his apostolic mission with the mission of Moses. Just as the ministry of the new covenant is antithetical to the ministry of the letter, the practices of their respective emissaries are opposed to one another. Moses acts as the Law does and effects condemnation and death: his veil cuts off access to the glory of the Lord. With his free speech, in contrast, Paul effects the freedom that Moses' veil barred. The "not *just as* Moses did" has its counterpart in the "*just as* the Lord who is the Spirit does" (v. 18).

Paul now moves beyond his recollection of the initial moment of fear on the part of the "sons of Israel" in v. 7 (Exod 34:30) to Moses' action, picking up the continuing narrative of Exodus 34 and drawing on vv. 33-35. After Moses had commanded Israel all that the Lord had spoken to him on Sinai, Moses placed a veil (or cover) over his face (v. 33). This practice became the pattern: Moses would enter the tent of meeting to speak with the Lord. He would then come forth and announce to "the sons of Israel" what the Lord had commanded him (v. 34). As he did so, they would see Moses' face, and its radiance. Afterward, Moses would cover his face until he went in to speak with the Lord (v. 35).

Paul understands Moses' action as an effective parable, much like the prophetic signs performed by Jeremiah or Ezekiel. What Moses does to himself comes upon "the sons of Israel." The story of Moses thus anticipates the story of Israel. The narrative dynamic correspondingly now shifts: whereas Paul earlier interprets Israel's fear as the inability of the sons of Israel to gaze at the glory of Moses' face, he now indicates that Moses placed the veil on his face so that they would not be able to gaze at "the goal of that which is done away with."[235]

235. Paul may well have drawn upon the narrative of Exodus 34:29-35 in formulating the theological statement that concludes his recounting of that narrative. Both ancient and modern translations, including the LXX and the Vulgate, read the opening verb in v. 33 as a *qal* form: "And when Moses *ceased* [וַיְּכֵל; LXX κατέπαυσεν] speaking to them. . . ." But the MT points the verb as a *pi'el:* "And when Moses *brought to completion* [וַיְכַל] speaking to them, he placed

These two interpretive moves, while they stand in obvious tension, are not finally at odds with one another. As we have seen, Israel's fear is a manifestation of its inability to encounter the Lord or hear his voice. In v. 14, Paul goes on to describe Moses' veil as bringing about the *hardening* of the minds of "the sons of Israel." He thus brings into view the biblical motif of "hardening," according to which the Lord surrenders human beings to their own waywardness. Moses' placement of this covering was not only a response to Israel's fear; it was also an act of judgment on the rebellion that spawned that fear.

Moses prevented the "sons of Israel" from looking upon "the goal of that which is done away with." Paul here theologically interprets the "glory of Moses' face" (v. 7) as a figure of his theology of "the letter and the Spirit." The glory of Moses' face was the glory associated with "the letter," which brought death and condemnation. This glory has been made to be no glory at all by the brilliance of the glory of the new covenant, which brings the Spirit and righteousness (v. 10). The glory of Moses' face thus holds the promise of something greater. Yet, as Paul makes clear, the connection between the two "glories" becomes apparent only in Christ (v. 14). One cannot see through God's work from without; one can only find oneself within God's work, as one guilty and condemned and yet granted the Spirit and righteousness.

Paul underscores the fundamental discontinuity between "the letter" and "the Spirit" by speaking of the goal *of that which is done away with.*[236] As in v. 11 he again uses the neuter form to describe the former glory, encompassing "the letter" and its work within the glory with which it came. In Christ, not only the glory of the "old covenant," but the very covenant itself has been done away with, as Paul is about to make clear (v. 14).

Paul's reference to "the sons of Israel" is drawn from the text of Exodus itself,[237] in which the title is frequent, concentrated, and prominent, appearing in the very opening words of the book ("these are the names of the sons of Israel, who came to Egypt with Jacob").[238] Paul's use of the title, which otherwise

---

a veil. . . ." Nine out of the ten occurrences of the verb in Exodus take the *pi'el* form. Even this one exception might well be pointed as a *pi'el,* since it clearly conveys the sense of bringing a task to completion (Exod 39:32). The closest parallel to the usage of Exod 34:33 is that of Exod 40:33, which speaks of Moses *completing* the work of the tabernacle. If we follow the MT pointing in Exod 34:33, the text stands in close relation to Paul's theological description of Moses' deed: he reads the text as saying that Moses placed a veil on his face so that the sons of Israel might not see the *completion* (τέλος) of that which he had just communicated to them. In fact, several of the related uses of the *pi'el* form in Exodus are translated in the LXX by συντελεῖν.

236. Again, Paul speaks not of "what was being brought to an end" (ESV) in the past but of the "goal of that which is done away with" in the present, in Christ.

237. Exod 34:30, 32, 34, 35.

238. The Hebrew title of the book is thus אֵלֶּה שְׁמוֹת, "these are the names." The "sons of Israel" came to Egypt with Jacob.

appears only once in his letters,[239] is another indication that his argument here is oriented to the text of Scripture, and specifically to the figures and patterns of God's ways with Israel. He is not responding to advocates of Judaizing. In contexts in which he deals with that issue, he naturally speaks of "Jews" and "Gentiles" (or "Greeks") and of "Judaism." Along with the names "Israel" and "Israelites," the title "sons of Israel" is honorific and allusive. Just as these terms are often bound to the particular text of Scripture with which Paul deals, this is also the case here.[240] Although Paul does not in this context develop the promissory associations of the title, his interpretive citation of Exod 34:34 — according to which Moses paradigmatically "turns to the Lord" — strongly suggests that Israel does not serve as a mere negative foil in this passage. Just as God's purpose was not completed with the Law, so his purpose for Israel is not ended in the hardening that came to it through Moses.[241]

14a "Instead their minds were hardened."[242] As we have noted, this assertion is pivotal to the passage. Just as Paul theologically interprets the divine glory in the last clause of v. 13 as the goal of the abrogated Law, he now provides his theological interpretation of Moses' veil. This act of covering his face, according to Paul, was an effective sign: what Moses performed upon himself was enacted on the sons of Israel. The same is true of his unveiling his face, which Paul recounts in v. 16. The apostolic mission of the new covenant that Paul is defending is efficacious and has its counterpart in the efficacious act of Moses.

The term *noēmata,* which is rendered "minds" in the English versions, represents an unusual usage on Paul's part. The usage of the term in the Scriptures is relatively infrequent. Aside from two instances in the Septuagint, the term appears only with Paul. Five of the six appearances of the term with Paul appear in this very letter.[243] The term *noēma* normally signifies a "concept" or "plan" formed by one's thought and disposition (which, in turn, is often expressed by the term *nous,* which is often itself rendered "mind").[244] Paul has used the term in that sense in reference to the "schemes of Satan" (2:11). In the present context, however, it is clear that the *noēmata* of the sons of Israel correspond to their "heart" *(kardia),* of which Paul speaks in v. 15 (see also

239. Rom 9:27 in citation of Isa 10:22, which he alters from "people of Israel" to "sons of Israel," very likely introducing honorific and promissory connotations.

240. See, e.g., Rom 9:4; 11:1; 2 Cor 11:22 (Israelites); Rom 9:6, 27, 31; 10:19; 11:2, 7, 25, 26; Gal 6:16 (Israel). The honorific nature of the title "Israel" becomes esp. apparent when Paul redirects his reference by speaking of "Israel according to the flesh" (1 Cor 10:18; cf. Gal 6:16).

241. Cf. Rom 11:25-27.

242. Here, as well as in v. 15, the ἀλλά is to be understood as contrastive, rather than adversative. See BDAG, "ἀλλά," 45.

243. 2:11; 3:14; 4:4; 10:5; 11:3; Phil 4:7.

244. T. Krischer, "Νόος, νοεῖν, νόημα," *Glotta* 62 (1984): 141-49; J. Behm, "νοέω, νοῦς, νόημα," *TDNT* 4:960-67; BDAG, "νόημα," 675.

v. 3).[245] Paul thus implicitly identifies the "plans and purposes" of the heart with the heart itself.[246] As we think in our heart, so are we (Prov 23:7)! From this perspective, the "heart" is not faculty or power within the human being that exists beyond what we think and do. We *are* what we plan, think, and conceive. Our persons are found in our works. This usage, which may well be unique to Paul,[247] corresponds to his expectation of final judgment, at which the purposes of hearts will be exposed (1 Cor 4:5) and our persons will be manifest in our works (2 Cor 5:10). It likewise corresponds to his fundamental concern in the letter, the false and blind practical reasoning of the Corinthians.

Paul uses a distributive plural here, just as he will employ a collective singular ("heart") in v. 15: "the minds" of the sons of Israel were turned to stone. Paul's use of *noēma* and *kardia* in this context suggests the biblical understanding of the "heart" as the whole of the inner life, and not merely the intellectual life, as *kardia* tended to signify in Hellenistic thought.[248] It is not merely the "intellects" of "the sons of Israel" that were hardened, according to Paul, but also their affections, judgments, and purposes (their *noēmata*). Conversely, when the Hebrew Scriptures speak of the hardening of the *heart,* this hardening includes an intellectual dimension, the failure to listen, perceive, see, and understand.[249]

In speaking of the "hardening" of "the sons of Israel," Paul takes up a biblical motif that appears especially in the Lord's dealings with Pharaoh, and also in Isaiah's throne-room vision.[250] In these and similar contexts, the Septuagint uses the term *sklērynō* for "hardening." Paul instead employs *pōroō,* "become as stone." There may have been a shift in usage in the Hellenistic period. The Gospels likewise employ the latter term.[251] But since Paul still uses *sklērynō* (Rom 9:18), the appearance of *pōroō* here may be regarded as a semantic choice: the thoughts, purposes, and thus "the minds" of "the sons of Israel" were *turned to stone.* Paul here recalls the "*tablets* of fleshly hearts," upon which

245. Here, as well as in 4:4-6 and in Phil 4:7, Paul closely associates *noēmata* with the heart *(kardia).* The latter usage is likely a hendiadys.

246. Paul likewise sometimes uses the term νοῦς to signify the faculty of thought and disposition, while in other instances he uses the term to signify the disposition itself (e.g., 1 Cor 1:10; 2:16; Phil 4:7; 2 Thess 2:2).

247. Philo uses the term relatively often (42x) but always in the conventional sense of "conceptions" or "plans."

248. J. Behm, "καρδία, κτλ.," *TDNT* 3:609-16.

249. E.g., Exod 7:3, 13, 22; 8:19; 9:12; Ps 95:7b-11; and likewise Isa 6:8-10, although the expression "harden the heart" does not appear there.

250. With respect to the latter, as we have noted already, it is unlikely that Paul regards the hardening of Israel as permanent. Just as there is an end to Isaiah's mission when the divine judgment is complete (Isa 6:11-13), so there will be an end to the hardening of Israel.

251. Mark 6:52; 8:17; John 12:40.

the Spirit performs his work (v. 3). As the story of Pharaoh makes clear, the motif of divine hardening is a display of God's judgment on human beings in rebellion against his word: God entraps them in their very defiance. The divine act of judgment and the human act of rebellion cannot be separated from one another, even if they can be distinguished.[252] Paul's recounting of the narrative of Israel's encounter with Moses at the giving of the Law takes the same form. The inability of "the sons of Israel" to look at Moses' face corresponds to their inability to endure God's voice and thus reveals their wayward hearts.[253] The "sons of Israel" were granted "the letter" but were neither able nor permitted to perceive that its outward glory served a larger end.

God's dealings with Israel reveal the pattern of his work with all the world. Already in the opening chapter of First Corinthians, Paul deals with the same issue, building his argument to the Corinthians on the Lord's judgment upon Israel found in the book of Isaiah: "I will destroy the wisdom of the wise, and the understanding of the understanding I will set aside" (1 Cor 1:19; Isa 29:14). In the Isaianic context, the Lord announces that he is bringing blindness on Israel and its prophets, making them drunk, and thus surrendering them to their own wisdom (Isa 29:9-12; cf. 6:6-10). He shall overthrow the plans and purposes of the rebellious, who as mere clay seek to take the place of the potter (Isa 29:15-16). Only the blind receive sight. Only those who are themselves foolish find God's wisdom in Christ.

14b Paul follows his brief assertion with a lengthy explanation *(gar)*. Moses' act of judgment extends "until the present day," according to Paul. As we have observed, Moses' veil thus takes on the character of an effective sign: not only did the veil bring judgment on Moses' immediate hearers, *the very same veil* lies upon the reading of the old covenant "until today." Paul obviously has in view not the veil in itself but the veil in action, as it brings hardening on the hearers of the "letter." The "reading" to which Paul refers is not the private reading of the text but its public reading in the synagogue. Despite this open reading of the Law, the meaning of the Law remains closed and hidden to "the sons of Israel." God's dealings with Israel are thus no mere figure from the past that the Corinthians merely read. Paul's words concerning "the sons of Israel" open the world to their eyes. The pattern stands before them: the Corinthians are well aware of the refusal of the synagogue to believe in Christ and thus to see the goal of the Law.[254] Moses' veil remains. Paul's shift from speaking of the thinking of "the sons of Israel" to the "reading" of the Law shows that his

252. Thus in the Exodus narrative of the hardening of Pharaoh, the text varies from ascribing the hardening of Pharaoh's heart to God to ascribing it to Pharaoh himself (e.g., Exod 4:21; 8:15, 32; 9:12, 34).

253. See above, p. 152.

254. Cf. Acts 18:1-17.

focus rests not on individual Jews but on the *event* of encounter with the Law, one that is simultaneously individual and corporate. This encounter brings condemnation and death, including blindness to the goal of the condemning Law in the life-giving Christ.

Here, for the only time in the New Testament, Paul describes the Law as "the old covenant." His language is clearly prompted by his earlier reference to a "new covenant," through which he allusively links the promise of Jeremiah with the Gospel (v. 6).[255] The Sinai covenant is made "old" by the "new." The adjective *palaios* here takes on the significance of "antiquation" through Paul's statement that this covenant has been abrogated.[256] Yet Paul's description is not salvation-historical. It is not that a new era has dawned *within* human history. Otherwise, the veil that "remains to this day" would have long since fallen away from the reading of the old covenant. It is rather that *in Christ* the new creation has *intersected* the fallen world. Only here, in this new creation, where the new covenant has been given, has the Sinai covenant been made old.

The major English translations have handled the translation of this verse rather badly. In the first place, they shift the meaning of the negated participle *anakalyptomenon* beyond its normal usage. We find with them: "[not] removed" (NIV); "unlifted" (ESV); "still there" (NRSV).[257] But the verb *anakalyptō* signifies "to uncover" (or, less frequently, in metaphor, "to reveal)."[258] The motivation for this change from the normal sense most likely rests in the false assumption that "the veil" *(to kalymma)* is the subject of the participle *anakalyptomenon* ("[not] being uncovered [or revealed]").[259] We shall consider the alternative to this decision in a moment. Given this assumption, if one translates the participle according to its usual sense, one lands in a reading that is nearly tautologous: "the covering has not been uncovered." No one can uncover a cover, unless, perhaps, one first covers it with yet another cover![260]

255. Quite independently, the letter to the Hebrews makes nearly the same twofold, theological move (Heb 8:7-13). The Pauline interpretation of the Markan cup-word tradition likewise contains the same implicit theology (Mark 14:24; 1 Cor 11:25).

256. See LSJM, "παλαιός," 1290. Paul's thought is thus close to that of the author of Hebrews: "In speaking of a new (covenant, God) makes old [πεπαλαίωκεν] the first covenant. And that which has been made old [τὸ παλαιούμενον] also is aged and about to pass away" (8:13).

257. The versions likewise shift the translations of καταργεῖται outside its normal range, so that it more or less corresponds to the rendering of ἀνακαλυπτόμενον that they offer.

258. See LSJM, "ἀνακαλύπτω," 908; BDAG, "ἀνακαλύπτω," 525. The metaphorical use appears in LXX Dan 2:28; Tob 12:7; *Pss. Sol.* 2:17; 4:8; 8:8. The verb thus overlaps with the more frequently metaphorical ἀποκαλύπτειν. On the various ways in which interpreters have rendered the verbs in v. 14, see Schmeller, *Der zweite Brief an die Korinther,* 216-18.

259. The decision is likely prompted by correspondence in gender between the neuter noun τὸ κάλυμμα and the neuter form of the participle ἀνακαλυπτόμενον. But that correspondence is by no means decisive.

260. The Lutherbibel (1984), which makes the same mistakes as the English versions,

The questionable decision of making "the veil" the subject of the participle *anakalyptomenon* ("uncovered") is thus accommodated by attributing an unattested meaning to the verb.

Furthermore, because "the veil" is assumed to be the subject of the participle, the following *hoti* clause must be interpreted as causal. The ESV is representative of the other English versions: "that same veil remains unlifted, *because* only through Christ is it taken away."[261] The difficulties this decision presents are obscured only by the unwarranted shift in the meaning of the participle and verb. The decision also disrupts the syntax of the clause: the *hoti* that follows *anakalyptomenon* ("[not] being uncovered [or revealed]") is most naturally taken as introducing the object of revelation, as would be the case after any verb of revelation or manifestation.[262]

The problematic renderings of the English versions arise from their reading of the neuter participle *anakalyptomenon,* which either must be taken as an absolute usage or must be given "the veil" *(to kalymma)* as its subject, as takes place in the English versions. As we have seen, the decision to make "the veil" the subject of the participle both disrupts the normally expected syntax and introduces unacceptable translations of the verbs. Absolute usage of a participle, while not frequent, is by no means lacking, especially with passive, impersonal verbs. The recognition of this usage here is surely the preferable interpretive decision. Verbs of revelation often have a *hoti* clause as either a grammatical or logical object. This clause takes the neuter gender. When a verb of revelation takes the passive form, the logical object of the action appears as the grammatical subject of the verb. This is precisely what takes place here. The grammatical subject of the neuter, passive participle *mē anakalyptomenon* is not "the veil" *(to kalymma)* but the following nominal clause (revealed *that . . .* [*hoti*]), as is regularly the case after passive verbs of saying, communication, or revelation.[263] The last clause in v. 14 thus should be read: "it not having been

---

speaks admittedly of a "cover that has not been uncovered" ("diese Decke [bleibt] unaufgedeckt"), but this rendering implies in the end the removal of the veil, through the extended sense of the German verb "aufdecken." This extended sense does not apply to the Greek. In contrast, the Einheitsübersetzung (1979) reads the text correctly: ". . . und es bleibt verhüllt, daß [der alte Bund] in Christus ein Ende nimmt."

261. If one takes the ὅτι as causal, one runs into difficulties so long as one recognizes the proper sense of ἀνακαλύπτω.

262. Here the verb is passive, so that the object of revelation is the *grammatical* subject of the verb. The unexpressed logical subject is surely God.

263. Thus, for example, γέγραπται ὅτι (Rom 3:10; 4:17; 8:36; 1 Cor 14:21), ἐγράφη ὅτι (1 Cor 9:10); γεγραμμένον in periphrasis (Luke 4:17-18; John 2:17; 6:31, 45; 10:34 [with ὅτι]; 12:14; 19:19, 20); τὸ εἰρημένον (Luke 2:24; Acts 2:16-21; 13:40-41; Rom 4:18); τὸ ῥηθέν (Matt 2:23 [with ὅτι]; 24:15); Verbs that take a double accusative in the active voice may then take a double predicate in the passive: κηρύσσεται ὅτι (1 Cor 15:12); μεθερμηνευόμενον (Matt 1:23; Mark 5:41; 15:22, 34; John 1:38, 41; Acts 4:36).

revealed [*or* uncovered] that in Christ it [namely, the old covenant] is done away with."[264] Paul plays upon the figure of the veil or "covering" *(to kalymma)* in his use of *anakalyptō*. He might instead have used the verb *apokalyptō* ("reveal"). But the verb *anakalyptō* frequently bears a literal, physical sense and thus plays upon the veil that lies upon the reading of the Law. By this use of the passive participle, Paul maintains the role of Moses as the agent of God through whom the veiling takes place. A finite verb would have disrupted the allusion to the veil, which continues through vv. 14-18.

For the reasons we have noted already, the English versions also shift the meaning of the verb *katargeitai* in the direction of their chosen rendering of the participle. Indeed, these versions must do so, since the decision to make "the veil" the subject of the participle spills over into the rendering of the main verb. Thus both the ESV and NIV speak of the veil, which is also supposed to be the subject of *katargeitai,* as "taken away," while the NRSV describes it as having been "set aside." But *katargeō* signifies either "to abrogate" or, when used in reference to action, "to render idle."[265] The former sense is obviously present here. As is the case with the negated participle *mē anakalyptomenon,* the verb *katargeitai* is a *passivum divinum.* God is the logical subject of both verbs.

The "old covenant" is the grammatical subject of the verb *katargeitai.* The context makes it clear that Paul speaks of God doing away with the "old covenant" in Christ. God has abrogated the Law, which is given as nothing other than "letter." It is for this very reason that Paul names the Sinai covenant "old," i.e., antiquated and abrogated. How else is one to explain Paul's designation of the Sinai covenant as *old,* a description that is unparalleled in his letters? The anticipatory statements that the glory of Moses' face has been done away with (v. 7), together with the mission of Moses that brought it (vv. 11, 13), have their culmination here. Paul is bringing his argument to its conclusion: the arrival of the new covenant renders the former covenant "old." The contrast between "the letter" and "the Spirit" that Paul asserts at the opening of his argument in v. 6 thus has its resolution in Christ. The opposition does not present a contradiction, but the profound paradox of God's saving work.

264. With Grindheim, then, the impersonal participle is to be regarded as an accusative absolute, or perhaps as a nominative absolute. On the latter, see John 1:38 and the periphrastic usage of verbs of revelation: Mark 5:41; 15:22, 34; John 1:41; 6:45; Acts 4:36. Cf. S. Grindheim, "The Law Kills, but the Gospel Gives Life: The Letter-Spirit Dualism in 2 Corinthians 3:5-18," *JSNT* 84 [2001]: 97-115; see further, *Smyth* §2076; BDF §424. Schmeller's objections to this reading (*Der zweite Brief an die Korinther,* 216-18) may be set aside: (1) the participle μὴ ἀνακαλυπτόμενον does not have the covering as its object but interprets it; (2) the veil is not abrogated, it is removed: it is instead the glory of Moses' face and that of the old covenant that are done away with (vv. 7, 11, 13).

265. See pp. 155-56.

The negated participle *mē anakalyptomenon,* "it not being uncovered," serves as an adverbial modifier, *interpreting* the figure of the veil that lies on the reading of the old covenant. God has not (yet!) uncovered (or revealed) to "the sons of Israel" that the old covenant has been abrogated in Christ. God's inaction has taken place through Moses, whose act of covering his face with the veil effects divine judgment. This simple reading of v. 14b corresponds to Paul's series of statements that the glory of Moses' face (v. 7), together with his entire mission (vv. 11, 13), has been done away with. This final affirmation of the abrogation of the Law makes explicit the meaning of Paul's preceding statements. The localization of this abrogation, "in Christ," prepares for Paul's following allusion to the tent of meeting and to his localization of the freedom to the place "where" the Spirit is present. The continuity of Paul's argument is disrupted if the *hoti* clause is not read as the subject of the participle.

15 "Instead, until the present day, as often as Moses is read, a veil lies on their heart."[266] As the parallel repetition makes clear, Paul's statement resumes and restates v. 14b. The prior participial clause ("it not being uncovered that in Christ it is done away with") serves as an interjection that prepares for the turn in discourse in v. 16. As we have noted, it represents the last in the series of declarations concerning the abrogation of the Law extending back to the beginning of Paul's argument in v. 7 (see vv. 11, 13). Just as the adversative "instead" *(alla)* in v. 14a is focused on the final phrase of v. 13 ("[looking upon] the goal of that which is abrogated"), so the adversative "instead" *(alla)* in 15a is focused on the final clause of v. 14 ("[it being uncovered/revealed] that in Christ it is done away with").[267] Paul thus says that, rather than it having been revealed that in Christ the old covenant has been done away with, "up until this day, whenever Moses is read, a veil lies on their heart," namely, that of the sons of Israel.

Paul now changes the terms found in v. 14b in a twofold manner, speaking of Moses rather than the old covenant, and of a veil lying on the heart rather than on the reading of that covenant. In the first shift of terms, Paul identifies the old covenant with its emissary. The old covenant is nothing other than Moses, who conversely is nothing other than the covenant he administers. Paul thus concludes his contrast between himself and Moses by focusing on the figure of Moses, who now has been defined by the old covenant. The second shift should be regarded as individualizing. Paul continues to speak

266. Once again, in parallelism to v. 14, the ἀλλά here is contrastive, not adversative. See BDAG, "ἀλλά," 45.

267. "Christ" thus corresponds to the "goal" of Moses' mission that has been abrogated. Here, too, the simple reading of v. 14b offered above is corroborated, as it also is by the obvious connection between Moses and the old covenant. In Christ "Moses" with his entire mission finds its goal and is done away with.

about the practice of reading Moses in the synagogue. Yet he now speaks of the veil as lying upon "their heart." The corporate dimension is obvious, but the singular "heart" speaks of individual reception — or rather, in this case, the absence of it. Paul returns to the emphasis on *individual persons* in encounter with Moses that he described in his recounting of the Exodus narrative in vv. 13-14a, where he speaks of "the minds" of the many.

Paul's description of the regular reading of Moses in the synagogue with the temporal adverb "as often as" not only recalls Moses' practice in the Exodus narrative (Exod 34:34) but it also prepares for the following contrast with Moses' "turning" to the Lord. According to the biblical narrative, "as often as" he did so, he removed the veil.

16 Paul concludes his appeal to the Exodus narrative by finally citing the text, or at least alluding to it strongly: "And as often as he turned to the Lord, he removed the veil." As we have noted, Paul's recounting of the Exodus narrative takes a sharp turn, even as he presents it as bearing continuity.[268] The apostle and his church ("we all") share in the experience of Moses, who knew the freedom of speaking with the Lord face-to-face.

In contrast with the Septuagint and the underlying Hebrew text, Paul describes Moses as "turning to the Lord," rather than "entering to speak with the Lord."[269] The expression "turn to the Lord" appears frequently in the Scriptures, especially the prophets, as a description of Israel's repentance.[270] This usage extends into the New Testament, especially into the Lukan writings, first as a description of repentance (Luke 1:16, cf. 22:32), and then of the conversion of Jews[271] and Gentiles[272] to faith in the Messiah. It is likely, then, that Paul alludes to conversion here. But in what way?

Most, if not all, English versions remove the reference to Moses: "But when one turns to the Lord, the veil is removed" (ESV, similarly, NIV, NSRV). This reading is influenced not only by Paul's interpretive alteration of Exod 34:34 but also by Paul's preceding statement that a veil lies on Israel's heart. "Conversion" is thus understood as an act of the individual,

268. He introduces v. 16 with the continuative particle δέ, which can express a reserved contrast.

269. The MT at Exod 34:34 is fairly simple: וּבְבֹא מֹשֶׁה לִפְנֵי יְהוָה לְדַבֵּר אִתּוֹ יָסִיר אֶת־הַמַּסְוֶה ("When he entered to speak with him, he removed the veil"). The LXX elaborates slightly: ἡνίκα δ' ἂν εἰσεπορεύετο Μωυσῆς ἔναντι κυρίου λαλεῖν αὐτῷ, περιῃρεῖτο τὸ κάλυμμα ("As often as Moses entered in before the Lord to speak with him, he removed the veil").

270. See the LXX of Deut 4:30; 30:2; 1 Kgdms 7:3; 4 Kgdms 23:25; 2 Chr 15:4; 19:4; 24:19; 36:13; Neh 1:9; Ps 21:28 (22:27); Isa 19:22; 44:22; 45:22; 55:7; Jer 3:7, 10, 14; 4:1; 24:7; 38(31):18; Lam 3:40; 5:21; Hos 6:1; 7:10; 14:2-3; Joel 2:12, 13; Amos 4:6, 8, 9, 11; Hag 2:17; Zech 1:3; Mal 3:7.

271. See Acts 3:19; 9:35.

272. See Acts 11:21; 15:19; 26:18, 20; Cf. LXX Ps 21:28 (22:27); Isa 45:22; see further 1 Thess 1:9; Jas 5:19; 1 Pet 2:25.

for whom the veil is removed in conversion. The references to "turning to the Lord" in the Hebrew Scriptures count somewhat against this reading, since the great majority of them speak of the conversion of the nation as a whole. One also must remember that "conversion" is a metaphorical usage of *epistrephō,* which frequently means simply "to turn." This sense fits the description of Moses' action in Exod 34:34 quite well: he turns to the Lord, away from the people.[273]

There are more fundamental reasons why the usual English translation is highly unlikely. In the first place, Moses, who appears in v. 15, is the natural and most likely subject of the verb in v. 16. Second, the form of v. 15 parallels that of v. 16 ("as often as . . . as often as"), providing all the more reason to suppose that Moses continues to be the subject of the verb in v. 16. Furthermore, Paul obviously cites or strongly alludes to Exod 34:34 (in which Moses is the subject), making it even more likely that Moses is the subject of his citation. Finally, and most significantly, Paul understands Moses' action of placing a veil over his face as an effective sign (vv. 13-14). It is likely, then, that he likewise regards Moses' turn to the Lord and the removal of the veil in the same way. What Moses performs upon himself takes place for others.

The verb *peraireitai* in v. 16b should be taken as a middle form, not the passive, and translated actively: "As often as he turned to the Lord, *he removed the veil.*" The corresponding imperfect form in LXX Exod 34:34 is a middle form that is to be translated actively,[274] just as the *hip'il* form *yasir* in the MT bears an active sense. The usual English translation of the verb as a passive (which itself is questionable) is prompted by the prior decision to interpret v. 16a as a reference to conversion.

Paul, then, refers to Moses' action of removing the veil when he "turned" or entered in to speak with the Lord.[275] Yet he words his description in terms of conversion, a "turning to the Lord." As we have noted, Paul presents Moses' action as an effective sign, just as he does with the placement of the veil in vv. 13-14a.[276] In this regard, the *locality* of Moses' action, which Paul himself takes up, is significant: *where* there is the Spirit of the Lord, there is freedom (v. 17). Despite Paul's alteration of the language of Exodus, it is clear that Moses' "turning" is an entrance into the tent of meeting. Just as Moses encountered

273. Cf. the usage at Exod 5:22, in which the LXX ἐπέστρεψεν δὲ Μωυσῆς πρὸς κύριον reflects the MT: וַיָּשָׁב מֹשֶׁה אֶל־יְהוָה.

274. In Septuagintal usage, the passive voice of περιαιρέω appears only in the future tense. Most occurrences are either active or middle in form.

275. Although Paul does not extend his citation to include Moses' activity of speaking with the Lord, the thought lies subtly in the background.

276. It is possible, even likely, that Paul here hints at a future "turning" of Israel to the Lord (cf. Rom 11:25-27). Similarly, Schmeller, *Der zweite Brief an die Korinther,* 210-11.

the Lord there, so the fallen human being savingly encounters God only where the Spirit is present, namely, in Christ and the new covenant (vv. 6, 14).

Although he obviously appeals to Moses' return from Sinai in v. 7, Paul here describes the communication between the Lord and Moses as taking place in the tent of meeting (Exod 33:7). The Exodus narrative points in both directions (Exod 34:29-35). In contrast with Jewish tradition that focused on Moses' ascent to God, Paul points to the condescension of the Lord to speak with Moses.[277]

17 While in v. 16 Paul is content to cite the Exodus narrative (or at least to allude to it strongly), in vv. 17-18 he elaborates the text for his Corinthian hearers. The transition, especially his abrupt identification of "the Lord" as "the Spirit," is surprising, and understandably it has provided difficulties for interpreters. Paul's bold interpretation of the text — he warned us that he speaks with apostolic audacity! — undoubtedly results from the very confession that he offers here: the decisive interpretation of Scripture is given in Christ (v. 14), by the Spirit (v. 17). The similarities to the Qumran writings, and particularly to *Pesher Habakkuk,* are not accidental; in both instances, the direct identification of the biblical text with contemporary events arises from the conviction that those events are eschatological and definitive. Paul's treatment of the text goes well beyond what would be described as historical-grammatical or historical-critical exegesis. The same is true in another way for the Qumran writings. Their interpretive moves do not reflect hermeneutical methods or rules that one might follow. Each of them represents a theological hermeneutic, one that is not general and abstract, but highly particular. For Qumran, this hermeneutic is determined by the Teacher of Righteousness and Torah as it was interpreted and practiced in the rule of the community. Paul's hermeneutic is determined by Christ and the new covenant, or more precisely, by the distinction between "the letter" and "the Spirit" that Paul describes in this passage. His jarring use of Scripture here should not be perceived so much as a problem than as a warning against regarding interpretation as reducible to a set of rules that might be mastered. Paul's very point in this passage is that the meaning of Scripture must be *given:* where and only where the Spirit is present is there freedom. Nevertheless, as his knowledge of the biblical text shows, here and elsewhere, that gift of understanding does not exclude, but includes, the labor of studying, reading, and learning the text.

Paul's earlier elaboration of Moses' placement of the veil in vv. 14-15 also sheds light on the apparent problems with his interpretation of Moses' removal of the veil in vv. 17-18. In the first place, we must remember that Paul introduces a similar, and indeed, parallel transition into his discourse in

277. E.g., Philo, *Mos.* 1.69-70; *4 Ezra* 14:4; *L.A.B.* 12:1; *Deut. Rab.* 11.4.

v. 14, when he indicates that the minds of "the sons of Israel" were hardened. He follows that interpretive statement with an explanatory, contemporizing restatement of it in vv. 14b-15. Something similar happens in vv. 17-18. Despite Paul's obvious eschatological perspective, he does not contemporize the text of Exodus in v. 17 but merely interprets it theologically: "The Lord is the Spirit. And where there is the Spirit of the Lord, there is freedom." This reading of the text corresponds to the opposing interpretive statement of v. 14a: "Instead their thoughts and minds were hardened to stone." Just as Paul follows that interpretive statement with a contemporizing explanation (v. 14b-15), so he goes on to contemporize his theological interpretation of Exodus 34:34 in v. 18: "And we all, with unveiled face. . . ." As drastic as his reading of the text may seem, Paul already has performed the same operation in the earlier context. His identification of the Lord as the Spirit stands out more sharply only because it is a *theo*-logical statement, and strikingly pneumatological. Christological definition follows in 4:1-6.

What, then, does Paul mean when he says that "the Lord is the Spirit"? He clearly draws the subject of his predication from his preceding citation of Exod 34:34: the Lord to whom he refers is the One who spoke with Moses in the tent of meeting. Paul likewise draws his predicate from his earlier description of his apostolic mission: he is an emissary of a new covenant of the Spirit (v. 6), the Spirit of the living God, who writes Christ upon hardened hearts (v. 3). The Spirit given through the apostolic mission is none other than the Lord himself. Yet that is not quite how Paul puts the matter here. He affirms that *the Lord* is the Spirit. This identification is obviously not absolute, since Paul distinguishes the Lord from the Spirit in the following clause when he speaks of "the Spirit of the Lord." It is, nevertheless, an identification.[278] Paul thus identifies God as essentially communicative and self-giving. The Lord who spoke with Moses is the Spirit of whom the Scriptures speak, and who in speaking gives himself through the apostle to the Corinthians. The predication especially recalls Paul's instruction to the Corinthians in 1 Cor 2:9-16. The Spirit's work is to make known to us God's free gifts to us, gifts of love that otherwise remain beyond our comprehension (1 Cor 2:9, 12). Just as no one is able to know the thoughts of a human person except the spirit of that person, so only the Spirit of God, who searches out the depths of God, can make known to us "the things of God" (1 Cor 2:10-11).

The Lord not only speaks *to* human beings, he speaks *with* them. In identifying the Lord as Spirit, Paul interprets the Exodus narrative, which explains that Moses' face was shining because he had spoken *with* God on Sinai (Exod

278. There is thus here identification with distinction, and distinction with identification. Cf. 1 Cor 8:6, in which Paul in other terms identifies God, the Father, and the Lord, Jesus Christ, while also distinguishing them.

34:29), and that Moses entered the tent of meeting in order to speak *with* the Lord (Exod 34:34). Indeed, according to the book of Numbers it is direct, verbal communication and exchange, "mouth to mouth" between the Lord and Moses, that sets him apart from all other prophets (Num 12:8; cf. Exod 33:11). The narratives of Moses' remarkable verbal exchanges with the Lord, which often are taken up with intercession for Israel but also include complaint and petition, make audible what otherwise transpired in secret.[279] Those who belong to Christ have entered into the same relationship with the Lord. Moses' desire that the Lord place his Spirit on all the people of God has been fulfilled in Christ (Num 11:29). We are thus called into a communicative relation with God in which we hear God's voice through the apostolic word that opens the Scripture to us. We then respond to God in petition, thanksgiving, lament, and praise, as Paul calls the Corinthians to do.[280]

"Where there is the Spirit of the Lord. . . ." As we have noted, the reference to "the Spirit of the Lord" distinguishes the Lord from the Spirit, even as Paul has just identified them. His localization of the Spirit corresponds to the narrative of Moses' encounter with the Lord in the tent of meeting, and it likewise matches the biblical pattern of the Spirit of the Lord coming upon certain persons, who then acted as judges or prophets.[281] The gift of the Spirit is likewise "localized" within the apostolic mission of the new covenant (v. 6) and is distinct from the Law. *Only* in Christ has the veil been done away with. Yet *all* in Christ are judges and prophets.

"Where there is the Spirit of the Lord: *freedom.*" Paul simply presents and announces *eleutheria,* "freedom," as a "hanging nominative," just as he does with *kainē ktisis,* "a new creation," in 5:17.[282] Here, for the only time in the letter, Paul describes salvation as *freedom,* which necessarily finds its definition in opposition to slavery to condemnation and death, as is clear in Paul's use of this metaphor in his other letters, especially Galatians and Romans.[283] His "localization" of the Spirit and freedom presupposes that the human being is *not* inherently free, but bound. Rather than living in the freedom of communication with God, we, in our rebellion, are slaves to sin, condemnation, and death. This slavery includes the hardening that came upon "the sons of Israel" and the blindness worked by "the god of this age" (4:4). Not only in 2 Cor 3 *but in the entire letter,* this thematic of condemnation and righteousness, death and life is pointedly focused on the question of *human (mis-)understanding.* Only where the Spirit of God is present are

279. E.g., Exod 32:7-14, 30-34; 33:12-23; Num 14:11-25.

280. E.g., 2 Cor 1:11, 20; 2:15; 9:15.

281. E.g., Judg 11:29; 13:25; 14:6, 19; 15:14; 1 Sam 16:13; 1 Kgs 22:24; Isa 61:1.

282. I owe this observation to Nate Collins.

283. Rom 6:12-23; 8:18-30; Gal 4:1-11, 21-31.

we granted this freedom to see ourselves and God rightly, that is, to see ourselves as fallen and condemned and God as our justifier and savior.[284] The "freedom" of which Paul speaks is unconditioned. It is no inherent or natural possession of the human being that we must actualize. It is not a potential that we must realize by our effort. It is a *liberation* from a heart turned in on itself. It is a liberation from a self-imposed legalism. Freedom is the gift of response to God's goodness, a gift that is unqualified and unconditioned.[285] Paul's message to the Corinthians — that human thinking and perception lie in bondage — was no less scandalous to them than it is to our (post)modern contemporaries.

"Freedom" for Paul is furthermore not a mere inward intellectual, psychological, or spiritual state that brings detachment from suffering, sin, and death. Paul is no Stoic. Quite the contrary, as he makes clear to the Corinthians in this letter: the sufferings of Christ are his in abundance. As we have just noted, the freedom of the Spirit is a freedom of hearing and responding to God, which is found in the "place" into which the human being is placed by the Gospel that Paul proclaims. Freedom is not a freedom of autonomy, as it is usually understood, but a freedom of communication. It is not found in the isolation of the person from the world. It is "located" within a relationship of verbal communication and exchange with God that encompasses the whole of life, including the petition and lament that arise from suffering and need. Paul thus describes freedom from sin and death as a slavery for righteousness and for God (Rom 6:15-23).[286] There is no absolute freedom, according to the apostle; we all have one Lord or another.[287] "Freedom from" is always "freedom for." Our liberation, furthermore, is not limited to exchange and communication with God but extends to communication with our neighbor, whom we in our freedom paradoxically are called to serve, and from whom we also receive. Thus Paul, in the immediate context of his declaration of freedom in 2 Cor 3, announces to the Corinthians that, as he proclaims Jesus Christ as Lord, he is their slave for Jesus' sake (4:5), echoing the language of Gal 5:13: "Do not let your freedom become a launching point of attack by the flesh; instead through love serve one another." Only one who is free and who does not need to secure their own life and salvation — or even the assurance of that salvation — can

284. See Luther's comments on Ps 51 concerning the true knowledge of God, *LW* 12:311.

285. On this theme, see O. Bayer, *Freedom in Response: Lutheran Ethics; Sources and Controversies* (Oxford Studies in Theological Ethics; Oxford: Oxford University Press, 2007), 1-12.

286. It is important to note that he uses this "human" language only on account of the enduring reality of our "flesh" in its weakness (Rom 6:19). "Slavery" to God is no slavery; rather, it is true freedom.

287. See E. Käsemann, *Commentary on Romans* (trans. G. W. Bromiley; Grand Rapids: Eerdmans, 1980), 178-80.

become the servant of another.[288] Otherwise our "service" always turns out to be self-serving.

Paul's declaration of freedom undoubtedly recalls the Lord's liberation of Israel from Egypt, which was no program of improvement but an immediate triumph within the world. As we have noted, Paul does not announce a freedom that is to be actualized (as if *we* had to turn faith into works), but an eschatological reality that has arrived in the world by the Gospel. Although it has its visible marks within the world, it remains fundamentally hidden under the cross and suffering. The confession of this freedom is already a mark of its presence.

18 In his final elaboration of the Exodus narrative, Paul returns to the claim of vv. 7-11, that the mission of the new covenant is accompanied by glory, despite all contrary appearance, and thus completes his argument that the Corinthians themselves constitute his apostolic letter of commendation. It is not merely the apostle who appears in contrast with Moses here, but also the Corinthians who are joined to him in his mission: "we all . . . are transformed from glory to glory." Unlike the glory of the old covenant that was given to Moses alone, the glory of the new is communicated to all those in Christ. Nevertheless, the common vision of the Lord's glory does not do away with Paul's authority as an emissary of the new covenant. It is for this authority that he contends in this letter.[289]

As we have noted, Moses' meeting with the Lord is presented in Exodus fundamentally as a *verbal exchange,* even if it includes a visual encounter. It is from this verbal communication with the Lord that Moses' face shone (Exod 34:29, 35). Moses' speaking with the Lord may well correspond to the earlier description of Moses' encounter with the Lord in the tent of meeting: "the Lord would speak to Moses *face-to-face,* as one speaks to a friend" (Exod 33:11). Verbal exchange between the Lord and Moses remains primary, but the narrative presents this exchange as including, or at least nearly including, a visual dimension.[290] A similar tradition appears in Num 12:6-8, in which Moses is distinguished from the prophets by the Lord's speaking with him "mouth to mouth, *as a vision,* not in riddles."[291] To this description the text adds: "and he

288. See Bayer, *Luther's Theology,* 288-90.

289. See the discussion of Paul as co-worker at 1:24, pp. 71-72 above. All Christian ministry — indeed, all human relations — is to be characterized by this simultaneity of *authority* and submission with *equality,* which must express itself in visible and audible ways, not only the relations of pastors and churches, but also those of parents and children, husbands and wives, and so on. See O. Bayer, *Freiheit als Antwort: Zur theologischen Ethik* (Tübingen: Mohr Siebeck, 1995), 55-59.

290. Admittedly, the text stands in some tension with Moses' following request to see the Lord's glory, a request that the Lord denies (Exod 33:20).

291. The wording of the Hebrew text is admittedly difficult, since "and a vision" (וּמַרְאֶה)

beholds the image [*or* form] of the Lord." Speech again remains the fundamental mode of encounter, even as it is taken up in seeing. Here again, even more pronouncedly, hearing and speaking encompass "seeing."[292] Deuteronomy 34:10 appears to fit this pattern as well: "There has not arisen in Israel another *prophet* like Moses, whom the Lord knew face-to-face." In biblical tradition, hearing presently has priority over seeing and itself constitutes "seeing."

Paul, in contrast, presents the encounter of believers with the Lord as a visual encounter, contrasting it with the distance of "the letter." Throughout the chapter, and especially in vv. 12-18, he is setting forth the noetic effects of judgment and salvation, which are naturally expressed in a visual metaphor. Yet Paul is not ignoring or inverting the emphasis of the Exodus text. His claim to an unhindered vision of the divine glory is a defense of the mission of the new covenant, i.e., the apostolic proclamation of the Gospel. He refuses to corrupt the *word* of God (4:2). In 4:1-6 he goes on to describe that proclamation as a gift of light and illumination, to which only unbelievers are blind. Already in v. 14 he has interpreted "seeing" as "hearing." The veil that prevented the vision of divine glory rests on the *reading* of the old covenant. The visual language of v. 18 likewise participates in this synesthetic metaphor and recalls the similar visual-olfactory metaphor of 2:14-15. In both instances, the mixing of the senses expresses the radical failure of human understanding — which always is determined by what is outward and visible — to properly "see" and know God. In Christ, God hides comfort, life, and righteousness behind suffering and the cross. This work of God can be perceived only by faith that is born of hearing the apostolic word. Paul is not circumventing his apostolic proclamation with the visual metaphor he draws from the book of Exodus. He is describing it. His equality with the Corinthians as one who perceives the Lord's glory does not do away with the authority of his apostolic message. Rather, it establishes it.

The "localization" that Paul emphasizes in v. 17 continues implicitly in v. 18: "We all *with an unveiled face. . . .*" The vision of the Lord's glory is not given to all the world but is found in Christ alone, in whom the old covenant is done away with. That the faces of those who believe are now unveiled recalls Moses' unveiling himself as he "turned" to the Lord (v. 16). Where the Spirit is present, Moses' prophetic actions now have come to reality. *Only that which once was veiled can be unveiled.* The Spirit gives life only to the dead. To see with an unveiled face is to be freed from the hardening that is God's judgment on our rebellion. Our blindness to the Lord and his goodness has been overcome in Christ.

---

is unexpectedly conjoined to the Lord's speaking with Moses. The pattern of the following clauses strongly suggests that, in the Lord's verbal exchange with him, he receives a vision that transcends that of (other) prophets.

292. That is so, unless perhaps the verbal exchange itself is here characterized as a vision.

"We all with unveiled face *behold in a mirror* the glory of the Lord."[293] The closest and most relevant parallel to this statement from extrabiblical literature appears in Philo's discussion of how human beings obtain their conceptions of the deity. In a manner that is obviously reminiscent of Plato, Philo distinguishes between knowledge that is gained through created things and knowledge that arises from a direct perception of the Creator. According to Philo, it is this latter kind of knowledge for which Moses makes request in Exod 33:11. Moses does not want God to reveal himself to him through heaven, earth, water, air, or anything else that has come into being. He does

293. A number of interpreters have advocated taking the verb κατοπτριζόμενοι in the active sense, as "reflecting (the glory of the Lord)," e.g., N. T. Wright, *The Climax of the Covenant: Christ and the Law in Pauline Theology* (Minneapolis: Fortress, 1992), 188-89; Belleville, *Reflections of Glory: Paul's Polemical Use of the Moses-Doxa Tradition in 2 Corinthians 3.1-18*, 279-82; Schlatter, *Paulus, der Bote Jesu*, 519-20. This interpretation introduces an ethic that is close to that of Eastern Orthodoxy — closer than it is to that of the Reformation. The reading is unlikely for a number of reasons. In the first place, it disrupts Paul's interpretive appropriation of the pattern of Moses' veiling his face before "the sons of Israel" and unveiling it in his encounter with the Lord. The veiling and the unveiling are paradigmatic acts that perform their work on "the sons of Israel." Moses does not remove his veil before "the sons of Israel" but only before the Lord. Paul takes up this pattern in v. 18: "we all with unveiled face. . . ." He thus pictures believers as encountering the Lord directly, as Moses did, not as reflecting God's glory to one another. The idea that v. 18 speaks of *believers* reflecting God's glory to one another obscures the decisive locus of the Spirit's presence that Paul emphasizes in v. 17 (cf. v. 14). Only *in Christ* has the veil been done away (v. 14). It is from the Gospel of Christ's glory, not from believers, that light shines forth, just as it is the crucified and risen Christ alone who is the image of God (4:6). The question that stands before the Corinthians is whether they can see through the suffering apostle to the Christ who is present in him (2:14-17; 13:3-4). Therewith the question is answered as to whether this Christ is present in them as well (13:5-6). As true as it is that the Corinthians are a letter of Christ, written by the Spirit (3:3), this reality remains hidden behind their unbelief and disobedience. To read Paul as speaking of believers directly reflecting the glory of God thus also obscures the way in which God's glory is displayed *sub contrario* in the present world. Furthermore, the *source* of the transformation of believers thereby becomes diffuse. We surely do not simply transform one another. How, then, is the work of the Spirit by which we are transformed to be defined? Is it merely one of mute empowerment? The irreducibly *verbal* nature of communication between the human being and God, which is integral both to Paul's reading of the story of Moses and to Paul's mission (3:6; 4:1-6), goes missing if one reads v. 18a as speaking of our reflecting God's glory. The visual image then overruns the verbal revelation that is fundamental to Paul's thought here. Finally, and decisively, the closest parallel to Paul's usage of the infrequent middle form of the rather infrequent verb κατοπτρίζω is that of Philo, *Leg.* 3.101, who, discussing very nearly the same passage in Exodus, clearly uses the verb with an active sense of "perceiving in a mirror." This reading of κατοπτριζόμενοι as active likewise matches the figure of a mirror as Paul uses it in 1 Cor 13:12 to describe our present vision and knowledge of God. It is in the incarnate, crucified, and risen Christ and in the Gospel that we behold the glory of the Lord (4:3-6), not in any moral transformation of our persons.

not wish *to view God's image in a mirror in anything other than in God himself.*[294]

Obviously, there are decisive conceptual differences between Paul and Philo. Philo wishes to see beyond the "shadows" of created things, which he understands in terms of Plato's cave. He wants to apprehend the uncreated and eternal deity. Paul, in contrast, understands God to have revealed himself savingly in the creature, namely, the crucified Christ.[295] Indeed, he is engaged in battle with the Corinthians over precisely this confession: in the suffering apostle, whom the Corinthians are in danger of rejecting, Christ is present.[296] For Paul, the creature is not an obstacle to divine revelation but, in Christ, has become the very vehicle of it.[297]

Nevertheless, there is a certain linguistic and conceptual proximity of Philo and Paul. Both of them understand the vision of God to involve viewing God in a mirror. Philo understands this mirror image to consist in ideas that are eternal and unchangeable, in contrast with those that come through impermanent, created things. He thus speaks of viewing God in a mirror in a twofold way: one might view God in the mirror of created things, or in the mirror of God in God himself.[298]

For Philo it is important to transcend the former and attain to the latter. Paul, in contrast, understands the vision of God in a mirror as the one vision given to us in the present time. The arrival of the eschaton will bring this indirect vision to an end: we shall then see face-to-face and know God fully, just as we now already are fully known. He anticipates a direct, personal encounter with God that transcends the Platonic idealism that shapes Philo's thought. The vision of the Lord in the mirror thus expresses Paul's eschatological reserve, and corresponds to his similar reservation in 1 Cor 13:12: "Presently we see by

294. Philo, *Leg.* 3.101: μὴ γὰρ ἐμφανισθείης μοι δι᾽ οὐρανοῦ ἢ γῆς ἢ ὕδατος ἢ ἀέρος ἤ τινος ἁπλῶς τῶν ἐν γενέσει, μηδὲ κατοπτρισαίμην ἐν ἄλλῳ τινὶ τὴν σὴν ἰδέαν ἢ ἐν σοὶ τῷ θεῷ. The translation by Yonge is flawed at this point. See Colson and Whitaker, LCL, "Nor would I find the reflection of Thy being in aught else than in Thee Who art God."

295. 1 Cor 1:18–2:16; 2 Cor 5:18; 13:4.

296. 2 Cor 2:14-17; 13:3-6.

297. Indeed, with Johann Georg Hamann, one may confess that the Creator's glory is manifest and known only as it is given "to the creature, through the creature" (*Aesthetica in nuce,* N II, 198.28-30). On this topic, see Bayer, *Schöpfung als Anrede: Zu einer Hermeneutik der Schöpfung,* 9-32; C. Gestrich, *The Return of Splendor in the World: The Christian Doctrine of Sin and Forgiveness* (Grand Rapids: Eerdmans, 1997), 1-28.

298. For Philo, then, the mirror is not an indirect means of viewing. On "looking in a mirror" in antiquity, which includes the act of reception by the viewer, see A. Weissenrieder, "Der Blick in den Spiegel: II Kor 3,18 vor dem Hintergrund antiker Spiegeltheorien und ikonographischer Abbildungen," in *Picturing the New Testament: Studies in Ancient Visual Images* (WUNT 2/193; ed. A. Weissenrieder, F. Wendt, and P. v. Gemünden; Tübingen: Mohr Siebeck, 2005), 313-43.

means of a mirror, in a riddle." As he twice states expressly in this letter, the Spirit is given presently as a "down payment" (1:22; 5:5). More precisely stated, the "vision in a mirror" serves in context to indicate that "seeing" serves as a synesthetic metaphor: our present "seeing" is "hearing." Location counts for everything; the mirror is the crucified Christ. Hearing and believing the apostolic proclamation is the opening of the heart, mind, and "eyes" to "the light of the Gospel of the glory of Christ, who is the image of God" (4:4).[299] We walk by faith, not by appearance (5:7). Presently we see only through our ears. In the light of glory we shall see with our eyes.

"We behold . . . *the glory of the Lord.*"[300] Believers in Christ behold God's fundamental goodness (Exod 33:19). This vision of the divine glory takes place according to the pattern of Moses' encounter with the Lord, and yet with decisive changes. Christ, in whom the Spirit is present, displaces the tent of meeting, and likewise displaces Moses, the mediator through whom judgment and condemnation arrived. Neither the apostle nor other Christians stand in the place of Moses. We *all* behold the glory of the Lord. Our vision of the divine glory is unmediated, even if it is presently indirect. His eschatological reserve notwithstanding, Paul emphasizes that the vision of the Lord's glory has been granted to all those who believe. His language at this point remains oriented to the text of Exodus, which he interprets in terms of the gift of the Spirit. The "Lord" here refers to the God of Israel, whom Moses encountered and who communicates himself to believers in Christ.[301] Paul's appeal to the Exodus narrative prepares for the christological turn of his thought in 4:1-6. This turn has not yet taken place.

Despite Paul's bold speech (cf. v. 12), he understands that the glory of the Lord remains hidden. He is arguing — or more precisely, asserting — the glory of the apostolic mission of the new covenant, to which the Corinthians are blind. This is the thrust of vv. 7-11, which he elaborates in vv. 12-18. The apostle *trusts* that there will be an "Amen" from the Corinthians to the glory of God that comes about through his apostolic mission (1:20). This "Amen" has not yet resounded, despite Titus's successful visit. All that Paul says in 2 Cor 3 stands under "the word of the cross" (1 Cor 1:18–2:16). The god of this age has blinded unbelievers, so that they cannot "see" the light of the Gospel (4:4). The

299. Rightly J. Jervell, *Imago Dei: Gen. 1,26f. im Spätjudentum, in der Gnosis und in den paulinischen Briefen* (FRLANT 58; Göttingen: Vandenhoeck & Ruprecht, 1960), 186; Furnish, *II Corinthians*, 242; F. Back, *Verwandlung durch Offenbarung bei Paulus: Eine religionsgeschichtlich-exegetische Untersuchung zu 2 Kor 2,14–4,6* (WUNT 2/153; Tübingen: Mohr Siebeck, 2002), 141-42.

300. Cf. John 1:18.

301. Many, if not most, interpreters take "Lord" as a reference to Christ. This decision is a bit premature. It obscures Paul's pneumatological statement, which draws directly from the Exodus narrative; furthermore, it renders his reference to looking in a mirror quite difficult.

glory of the Lord is revealed *sub contrario,* hidden under its opposite.[302] The revealed glory of God that appeared in Moses' face was hidden from Israel within the tent of meeting. The glory of God in the person of Jesus Christ has been revealed to all who hear the Gospel and believe.

The vision of the Lord's glory is transforming. This statement constitutes the core of Paul's lengthy sentence in v. 18: "we are transformed into the same image from glory to glory." The double prepositional phrases that modify the verb are crucial to its interpretation. They are not to be understood as signifying linear progress of some sort, as if Paul spoke of movement from one degree of glory to another. This reading might conform to the Corinthians' expectations, but it certainly does not conform to the experience of the apostle, who bears the deadness of Jesus in his body. The pairing of the phrases corresponds instead to the related pairings in 2:16 ("death to death" and "life to life), which likewise signify "communication."[303] The vision of the Lord's glory imparts that glory to inglorious and weak human beings subject to sin, suffering, and death. Our transformation is an exchange in which we are removed from ourselves.

It is this claim of the presence of hidden, yet abiding glory that lies behind Paul's earlier argument that the new covenant brings a glory that transcends that of the old (vv. 7-11). The glory of the crucified Christ is nothing other than the glory of the eschaton,[304] which has broken into the present age.[305] The transformation it brings is the projection of the eschaton into the present, fallen world.[306] Correspondingly, within biblical tradition, the Lord's display of light and glory upon his people is a mark of *their deliverance from evil and suffering.*[307] It is not a moral quality within them but God's favor and comfort given to those in need and distress, including the distress of their sin and rebellion. Moses' transforming communion with the Lord, verbal though it was, included the vision of the Lord's goodness and the Lord's comforting

302. See 4:7-15; 6:3-10.

303. Although it is often read otherwise, the same is true of Rom 1:17.

304. See Rom 5:2; 6:4; 8:18, 21; 9:23; 2 Cor 5:17; but cf. Rom 9:4.

305. Rom 6:4; cf. 4:20; 15:7; 2 Cor 1:20; 3:7-11.

306. This thought is present in Rom 6:4, even if the language of transformation is lacking there. Christ's brothers and sisters shall be conformed to his image at the eschaton (Rom 8:29). Paul's thought in Rom 12:2 is likewise clearly and decisively eschatological in nature, even if interpreters rarely take note of it: the transformation of the mind removes us from the form of *the present age.* In Phil 3:21 Paul speaks directly of the coming of the Lord Jesus as effecting the transformation of our "body of humiliation" into the form of "the body of his glory." His description of the resurrection obviously centers upon change in form, even if the terminology differs (1 Cor 15:35-58).

307. See LXX Ps 33:6 (34:5); Isa 60:1-5; and Num 6:24-26 in connection with Pss 4:6; 31:16; 80:3. The Isaianic Servant is a "light to the nations," not as a moral beacon, but as a sufferer who has been delivered by the Lord, who alone creates light (Isa 42:6; 49:6).

pronouncement (Exod 34:6-7).[308] It, too, communicated deliverance from all trouble, including the trouble of Israel's sin.

Believers "behold in a mirror" the glory of the Lord and thus are transformed into "the same image." Paul's reference to "the *same* image" is drawn from the immediately preceding verb "behold in a mirror" *(katoptrizō)*, which implies a reflected vision.[309] At this point (and not in reference to the "glory of the Lord") Paul implicitly introduces the christology that he will develop in 4:1-6. According to the Hebrew Scriptures, every human being bears the image of God in which Adam was made (Gen 1:26-27; 9:6). In the New Testament, in contrast, God's image is ascribed in the first instance to Christ alone.[310] The common possession of humanity is now christologically concentrated. We share in the divine image only as we share in Christ.[311] In one respect, this concentration obviously has to do with the reality of human sin and fallenness, through which the divine image has been distorted and, in a certain sense, lost.[312] Yet Paul also speaks of our sharing in the image of Christ as the larger purpose of God the Creator: Adam was an anticipation of Christ — yet a mere anticipation.[313] Paul's striking language of "beholding in a mirror" thus contains an implicit reference to the proclaimed Christ. He is the image of God and the "same" image into which we are transformed.[314] The image is that of deliverance and comfort given in suffering and distress, life given in death itself.

308. Frances Back's argument (*Verwandlung durch Offenbarung*, 24-76) that Paul understood a transforming vision as the reception of a divine message and prophetic inspiration, as it was in Hellenistic Judaism, therefore may be just slightly off the mark.

309. Although "image of God" and "glory of God" are obviously related, they are not equivalent. An image is always a representation, even if it participates in the reality it reflects, and thus may communicate distance (Ezek 1:28). This is tragically the case in Paul's description of "the fall" in Rom 1:23, in which the "image," even of the human being created in God's image, is false. Conversely, while Paul speaks of the woman as the glory of the husband, he does not go on to say that she is the husband's image (1 Cor 11:7). Against Jervell, *Imago Dei*, 174-75.

310. 2 Cor 4:4; Col 1:15. See also 1 Cor 11:7.

311. Col 3:10-11; cf. Eph 4:24.

312. Paul's statements concerning the human being in Rom 1:23; 3:23 are directly related to this issue. Cf. Wis 2:23-24.

313. Rom 8:29; 1 Cor 15:45-49. Cf. Gal 3:28, which intimates this larger dimension of the divine purpose in that Paul here speaks of the transcending of the created distinction between male and female.

314. Paul here may echo Gen 1:26-27, as his following allusions to creation and fall in 4:2-6 also suggest: the image and glory of God lost in the fall is now restored in Christ. It is not at all clear, however, that Paul is here battling an early Jewish tradition that associated Adam's glory with Moses (which is in some measure reflected in 1QS IV, 28; CD III, 20; 1QH IV, 15). Paul gives no clues of such a controversy here and may recall the story of Adam apart from such a dispute. In the following argument, he does not connect the story of Moses' veil with contemporary Judaism; rather, with the blindness of all unbelievers (4:4). Against Jervell, *Imago Dei*, 176.

This transformation is thus larger and greater than moral improvement, even if it includes a moral dimension. The removal of Moses' veil brings a communication of glory that carries fallen human beings from death to life, and from condemnation to righteousness. The visual imagery, it should be remembered, is a synesthetic metaphor, in which "hearing" constitutes "seeing." The glory of the Lord is found in the crucified and risen Christ, in whom all God's promises are an audible Yes. Faith is the responsive "Amen" to the glory of God worked through the apostle (1:20). To be transformed by that glory and to share in it is to share in the resurrection from the dead. This resurrection necessarily projects itself into the present in the form of the new obedience of believers (cf. Rom 6:4). In this respect, it is important to remind ourselves once again that Paul here *asserts* that transformation takes place in Christ. He does so in the face of outward behavior on the part of the Corinthians that flatly contradicts that claim.

Yet the transformation that he affirms is no less real for its being hidden behind human weakness and failure. It is precisely this lesson that Paul seeks to drive home to the Corinthians, who before all else are attracted to the outward and visible power of the "super-apostles." Just as Satan transforms himself into an angel of light, so his messengers transform themselves into apostles of Christ and messengers of righteousness (11:12-15). Appearance is everything. The transformation of believers takes the opposite form: the treasure of the knowledge of God's glory is contained in earthen vessels (4:7); power is present within weakness (12:9); the word of the cross remains foolishness to the world (1 Cor 1:18). Christ is not yet openly seen in the apostle or his church: they are not yet raised from the dead. In all the wrong ways, and according to human standards, the Corinthians seek proof of the crucified and risen Christ, who speaks in the apostle (13:3-4). The transformation worked by the glory of the Lord is manifest presently in the form of faith, as Paul, appealing to a psalm, makes clear in his following argument: "we believe, therefore we speak" (4:13).[315] It is faith that receives the divine communication in the Gospel and responds in petition, thanksgiving, lament, and praise.

In his following argument, Paul correspondingly emphasizes the distinction between the "outer person" and the "inner person," who is made new day by day, and who "sees" the things that are unseen and eternal (4:16-18). He does not thereby fall into a sort of Platonic idealism. Faith lives from God's words of promise, which have their Yes in the crucified and risen Christ. Paul thus elaborates his affirmation of faith: "knowing that the one who raised the Lord Jesus also shall raise us with Jesus" (4:14). As we just have noted, this inherent connection between the act of believing and the content of faith comes to ex-

315. It is likewise manifest in love, as Paul will make clear from the example of the Macedonians (8:1-15).

pression in the visual imagery of v. 18: it is in beholding the mirror-image of the crucified and risen Christ that we are transformed. The glory of the Lord that is thereby imparted to us is not a mere imitative participation in God's faithfulness. It is a reflection of the power of the Creator to call light out of darkness and life out of death.

It is not at all clear, then, that the present tense form *metamorphoumetha* should be translated, as it usually is, as a continuing event, i.e., "we are being transformed" (ESV, NIV, NRSV). The durative aspect expressed by the present tense can just as well signify immediacy and vividness, as it surely does here. Moses, who provides the pattern for Paul's claim, did not undergo a process of transformation by which his face gradually came to shine. The act of creation by which Paul describes the illumination of the human heart is no process but an event (4:6). In the face of the obviously inglorious state of Christians in the world, translators and interpreters have tended to opt for the ideal of progress rather than recognizing that the apostle speaks of an undiminished glory that is anything but manifest in the present. The gift of life is given only where there is death. Transforming power is present only where there is weakness.

As the final comparative clause makes clear, Paul is here still unfolding Exod 34:34 in terms of the gift of the Spirit given through the new covenant. The compressed, anarthrous phrase provides some difficulty in interpretation. Out of the various possibilities, it is most likely that Paul speaks of "the Lord who is the Spirit."[316] He thus first names the Lord as the one who communicates his glory and then adds the predication: "[he is] the Spirit." This reading corresponds to Paul's initial predication in v. 17, thus rounding off his interpretive statements with an inclusio. It likewise matches the pattern of the Exodus narrative upon which Paul draws: we are transformed, *just as from the Lord,* who so imparted his glory to Moses. The interpretive predication then follows. Furthermore, it conforms to the significance of Paul's rather frequent anarthrous usage "Lord Jesus," which bears the implicit predication that the Lord is Jesus,[317] and his similar phrasing "God, our Father," which likewise contains an unexpressed predication.[318]

The Lord is the Spirit . . . the Lord who is Spirit. Paul concludes his interpretation of the Exodus narrative with this predication. While the predication implies the deity of the Spirit, it is in the first instance a predication about the Lord. Paul announces a profound truth about the God who thundered at Sinai and who met with Moses in the tent of meeting. As with Elijah after

316. On the possibilities, see Thrall, *The Second Epistle to the Corinthians,* 1:287; Schmeller, *Der zweite Brief an die Korinther,* 229.

317. See, e.g., the similar usage in prepositional phrases: Rom 1:7; 14:14; 1 Cor 1:3; 2 Cor 1:2; Gal 1:3; Phil 2:19; 1 Thess 1:1; 4:1; 2 Thess 3:12; Phlm 3.

318. E.g., Rom 1:7; 1 Cor 1:3; 2 Cor 1:2; Gal 1:3; Phil 1:2; 1 Thess 1:1; Phlm 3.

the storm, earthquake, and fire of God's wrath, there comes only a still, small voice. The Lord wills to speak with us face-to-face, as he did with Moses. It is this relationship of communication and giving, in which the gift is the Giver himself, that constitutes our salvation. The condemnation and disruption of communication worked by our rebellion and Moses' veil (v. 13) is overcome by that which "the Lord who is the Spirit" works.

B. The Apostle in Mission: God's Agent as the Bearer of God's Saving Work (4:1–7:16)

The apostolic mission is defined by the new covenant given to Paul by God. Only after he has set forth that mission does Paul provide a description of his person and work that fills out the rest of the letter's body. The inner connection between the message of Christ and the messenger of Christ is clear, not only from the verbal links to 2 Cor 3 that appear in 4:1-6, but also from the larger structure of Paul's thought in 4:1–7:16.

The brief opening section of this unit (4:1-15) falls into two parts. In the first of these (4:1-6), Paul describes afresh the mission that has been given to him. While in 3:4-18 he presents this mission in terms of its saving work in the communication of the Spirit, here in 4:1-6 he describes the saving work of God in him, as well as the broader effect of his mission in the world. The question at stake is the legitimation of the apostle. Paul's conduct is determined by the mission and mercy that have been given to him: as an apostle, he is nothing but a vessel of the Gospel. The hermeneutical dimensions of God's work in the world stand at the center of Paul's interest. The *perception* of the apostolic mission determines the reception or rejection of "the Gospel of the glory of Christ, who is the image of God." Paul here recalls his introductory description of his mission in 2:14-17. Life and death are determined by what one perceives in him.

In the following section (4:7-15), Paul's discourse shifts dramatically from his Gospel to his experience as an apostle. His bodily life within the fallen world stands in the sharpest contrast to the "treasure" of the knowledge of God's glory that he bears. As the apostle of Christ, he bears the whole Gospel of the *crucified* and risen Christ, in the whole of his body and life.[319] Out of

319. Several significant witnesses omit the word "Jesus" here (A B 33, Tertullian). Esp. in the Western tradition, the order is transposed: "Christ Jesus" (D F G, Ambrosiaster). Yet there is strong external support for the reading "Jesus Christ" ($\mathfrak{p}^{46}$ א C). It is possible that Paul's profound Christology offended scribal sensibilities: Who can speak of God's glory being found in Jesus, the one who walked on earth and was crucified? The ascription of glory to the title of exaltation, "Christ," would have been easier to swallow.

this living, verbal, and visual proclamation of the Gospel, salvation comes to the Corinthians. They must yet learn that salvation is nothing other than power at work in weakness. The power of Christ manifests itself in the spoken word of faith in the face of opposite appearances. Together with the trials that accompany and call forth this word, the apostolic mission is for the benefit of others, especially the Corinthians. As is clear from his summary statement in 4:15 ("all these things are for your sake"), in 4:1-15 Paul provides a full description of himself as apostle in mission: in word *and* life, he proclaims the crucified and risen Christ.

As is typical of his writing, in the following sections (4:16–5:10 and 5:11-21) he elaborates what he already has said in fresh perspective. The elaboration comes in a chiastic pattern corresponding to the twofold form of his description of his mission in 4:1-15. In 4:16–5:10, Paul continues to speak of his bodily experience. While in 4:1-15 he describes the eschaton as it has entered the present world in his mission and person, in 4:16–5:10 he describes the life of faith in light of the eschaton, namely, the resurrection of the dead and the judgment to come. The eschatological reserve of his preceding self-description in 4:7-15 prepares for his presentation of himself as one possessed by the hope of the resurrection (4:16–5:10). He thus corrects the Corinthians, who, in judging the apostle by present and visible standards, are at risk of abandoning that hope.

Again in 5:11-21, Paul provides a description of his apostolic mission, completing the chiasm that begins in 4:1-6. While in 4:1-6 he describes the *effect* of his mission on him and on the world, in 5:11-21 he presents the saving *purpose* of Christ and of God that is the content and substance of his mission. As we have noted, in the former passage he speaks of the eschaton as it has entered into the present. In the latter he speaks of his present in the light of the eschaton. It is in this context, then, that we hear the Gospel as Paul articulates it for the Corinthians. As we have noted, the passage fills in the "christological deficit" of his description of his mission in 3:12-18.[320] Only at this point, when it has become clear that his participation in the Gospel determines his ministry of the Gospel, does Paul describe his active mission in the world. His life and labor flow out of the salvation granted to him and are shaped by the content and form of that salvation. The love of Christ and the reconciling work of God determine his judgment and understanding of the world to which he ministers. This world includes the Corinthians, to whom he directly appeals to grasp the grace that has been granted them (6:1-10).

This appeal to the Corinthians to be reconciled to God brings with it the appeal that they be reconciled to him, their apostle (6:13–7:16). The two events of reconciliation are inseparable. To embrace Paul and the God who sent him, the Corinthians will have to break with others — namely, the other apostolic claim-

320. See p. 97 above.

ants — whom Paul here describes in severe terms (6:14–7:1).[321] His final appeal to the Corinthians is nevertheless positive: he builds on the Corinthians' positive reception of Titus, his messenger, and makes it a matter of boasting (7:5-16).

1. *The Apostle as Proclaimer of Christ (4:1-15)*

Paul's attention shifts here from the saving work of the new covenant to its immediate effect in him and in the world. He thus appears in a fundamentally passive role, even in the act of proclamation (4:1-6), and even more so in the sufferings that accompany it (4:7-15).

a. The Light of the Gospel in the Heart of the Apostle (4:1-6)

1Therefore, having this ministry by the mercy of God, we do not lose heart. 2But we have renounced disgraceful, underhanded ways. We refuse to practice cunning or to tamper with God's word, but by the open statement of the truth we would commend ourselves to everyone's conscience in the sight of God. 3And even if our gospel is veiled, it is veiled to those who are perishing. 4In their case the god of this world has blinded the minds of the unbelievers, to keep them from seeing the light of the gospel of the glory of Christ, who is the image of God. 5For what we proclaim is not ourselves, but Jesus Christ as Lord, with ourselves as your servants for Jesus' sake. 6For God, who said, "Let light shine out of darkness," has shone in our hearts to give the light of the knowledge of the glory of God in the face of Jesus Christ.

The mission that Paul has been given defines him as a person and as an apostle. He is here allaying suspicions about himself. Yet his description of his mission is not in the first instance a defense against accusations of impropriety. It is before all else a presentation of the effect of the Gospel within the world that in its twofold outcome serves as a warning to the Corinthians.

1 Paul returns to the assertion that concludes his thanksgiving in 2:17. He is not lacking or insufficient as an apostle. He does not fail. The first-person plural that Paul expanded to include all believers in 3:18 ("we *all* with unveiled face . . .") now is reduced to a reference to Paul, or more precisely, to Paul as apostle. Despite this individual reference, Paul's continuing use of the plural allows him to invite the Corinthians to see themselves reflected in his experience. Apostles are not essentially different from other Christians, even if they bear the sufferings of Christ in special measure. In them Christian existence is written large.

321. Paul thus anticipates the judgments of 11:12-15.

Although nearly all translations (including NRSV, NIV, ESV) translate *enkakoumen* as "lose heart," it is more likely in this context that this (negated) verb should be rendered "not failing" (including moral failure, i.e., "not acting wrongly").[322] The verb, which is rather infrequent,[323] may in some instances bear the former sense.[324] In other contexts it bears the latter sense,[325] which is to be preferred here because it more closely fits Paul's following assertion of integrity (v. 2), as well as the defense of apostolic mission that constitutes his larger argument. He is under suspicion as a fraud (12:16, 19). In the face of such suspicion, he insists that he does not act wrongly *but* has renounced the hidden things of shame. The contextually opposing assertion determines the sense of the term *enkakeō*. Paul recalls his earlier claims to integrity,[326] and he asserts his sufficiency as apostle, just as he does in 3:1-6. Here he does so in a new way. He employs the infrequent term *enkakeō* again in 4:16 — albeit no longer in the sense of moral failure — at the beginning of his lengthy elaboration of his apostolic mission that completes the body of the letter. There, however, it is not moral failure that he denies but mortal failure. God's power in Christ overcomes the weakness of his earthly existence. It is thus clear that *enkakeō* signals the fundamental point of his argument: contrary to what the Corinthians suppose, as the apostle of Christ, Paul is not a failure or a fraud.

As he does in 3:4-6, Paul here again attributes his sufficiency as apostle to the saving relationship of communication with fallen human beings that God brought about in Christ: "On account of this . . . we do not fail." Paul's integrity as an apostle is not his own work, but that of God. This work of God *includes* the striving and labor of the apostle. The work of God thus provides the boundary and criterion for Paul's own work, as well as its inner drive and source of strength. He has not "conducted himself in fleshly wisdom, but *in the grace of God*" (1:12).[327] As we have noted already, his exposition of the new

322. See the Vulgate "non deficimus," which, although it is somewhat ambiguous, probably is to be understood as "not failing, not wanting."

323. The verb ἐγκακέω competes with ἐκκακέω (which bears the same sense) and yields to it by the third or fourth century A.D. See the v.l. ἐκκακοῦμεν at 2 Cor 4:1, represented by C D² Ψ and the Byzantine tradition.

324. Probably Eph 3:13, perhaps Luke 18:1; Gal 6:9; 2 Thess 3:13; See the lexicographer Hesychius (fifth century): ἐγκακοῦμεν· ἀψυχοῦμεν.

325. See Polybius, *Histories* 4.19.10. It is worth considering whether the translations of Luke 18:1, Gal 6:9, and 2 Thess 3:13 should be revised, even if the church fathers tend to use the verb in the sense of "lose heart." See, however, *Herm. Vis.* 9:8, where ἐκκακέω most likely bears the sense "fail."

326. See 1:12-14, 24; 2:17.

327. Grace, for Paul, is not conditioned by one's own effort, striving, or doing — otherwise, it is not grace (Rom 11:6).

covenant, of which he is an emissary, provides the basis for all that follows in the body of the letter.

"Having this mission according to our having received mercy, we do not fail." Paul's calling as an apostle is nothing other than the mercy of God granted to him. Paul's calling does not elevate him above the Corinthians (1:24) but, paradoxically, makes him their equal even in difference. Indeed, it makes him their slave (v. 5). The mercy of God thus provides "the space" in which Paul exercises his calling as apostle. "Mercy" cannot be attained by discipline, strength, virtue, or works. Nor is it a mere divine attribute to which one mentally assents. The mercy of God "works" in the apostle, just as Paul elsewhere announces concerning God's grace toward him (1 Cor 15:10). Paul thus describes himself as fundamentally one upon whom God has had pity, a mere recipient of mercy, together with all who belong to God through Christ. In speaking in this way, he obviously recalls his opening thanksgiving, in which he names God as the "Father of mercies and God of all comfort" (1:3-7).[328] Behind and before all Paul's sufferings as an apostle of Christ stands the mercy of God given to him through *Christ's* sufferings. Paul knows God as absolute and unqualified Giver, as a God of sheer mercy, who meets the distress and misery that belongs to *Paul* in his own distance from and rebellion against God. His own death and condemnation have been overcome in Christ (3:7, 9). His understanding of his apostolic calling thus corresponds to the well-known definition of evangelism by D. T. Niles: It is "simply one beggar telling another beggar where to find bread."

2 "But [we] have renounced the hidden things of shame." Paul returns to his claim to integrity, taking up again the assertions of 1:12-14 and 2:17. Not only God has hidden things, but so, too, have human beings. Yet while God presently hides his glory, human beings hide their shame. Both will be revealed together.

There are undoubtedly suspicions about the apostle within the church, fueled by both his refusal to accept support from the Corinthians and his failure to visit them as promised (1:15-22; 12:14-18). But these suspicions have to do with God's work and Christ's presence in the apostle, rather than Paul's own person.[329] The question of Paul's integrity goes to the heart of his legitimacy as an apostle and cannot be settled by human judgments, as he has indicated to the Corinthians in an earlier letter (1 Cor 4:1-5). Indeed, the fundamental

328. The distinction between the verb ἐλεέω that appears in 4:1 and the noun οἰκτιρμός is inconsequential. Terms built on the root of the former generally signal an emphasis on the effect or action, while terms related to the latter tend to focus on feelings of compassion. The word groups are obviously closely related and appear elsewhere in connection with one another, as in Rom 11:30-32; 12:1.

329. As we have seen, the same is the case in 1:12-14, 1:15-22, and 2:17.

issue is the false assumption of the Corinthians that they are competent to judge the apostle (3:1-3). The visible and outward standards that they bring to the matter prevent them from seeing that they themselves are being judged in their response to the suffering apostle. Appearances are deceptive.

"We have renounced the hidden things of shame." As in his previous assertions, Paul lays claim to an essentially *verbal* integrity, which includes the whole of his conduct. He immediately describes it as not *walking* in guile. Here "walking" is "talking," just as "talking" is "walking." Integrity is found in the Gospel, where word and deed are bound together in the truth about the human being that it makes manifest. In the context of divine mercy, this renunciation of "hidden things of shame" implies that Paul himself once participated in them. As his following expansion of this statement makes clear, he refers to deeds performed in guile and deceit. In the expression "hidden things of shame," various genitive relations are possible, none of which excludes the others: source, possession, quality, or perhaps epexegesis (i.e., things hidden because of shame, hidden things belonging to shame, hidden things that are shameful, hidden things that consist in shame).[330] The expression very likely recalls the Genesis story of Adam and Eve hiding themselves from the Lord God after eating the forbidden fruit, although they formerly were naked without shame (Gen 2:25; 3:8, 10). At the same time, Paul's language also anticipates the coming of the Lord, who will "bring to light the hidden things of darkness" (1 Cor 4:5).[331] The theme of the manifestation of the human being at the final judgment is an essential element of Paul's argument in this section of the letter.[332] Paul's renunciation of "the hidden things of shame" implies the undoing of the fall and the presence of the new creation. It implies confidence in the coming judgment, at which the legitimacy of the apostle will be truly tested.

Paul then follows with a descriptive clause: "not walking in guile, nor corrupting the word of God." The "word of God" in this context clearly refers to the Gospel. Paul returns to the assertion of 2:17: "we do not peddle the word of God." He thus stresses that the Gospel is not his word, nor that of any other human being. It remains God's word and God's alone. As the bearer of this word, Paul does not operate with treachery or deception. His not "corrupting the word" includes his conduct as well as his speech: that is his integrity. The term that Paul uses for "guile" *(panourgia; pas-ergeō)* implies not only trickery, but the readiness to do anything, even that which is underhanded, in order to achieve one's aims. Paul later uses the term in reference to the wiles of the

330. Cf. Heb 12:2: "the cross of shame."

331. The parallel genitive construction suggests that "darkness" here signifies evil, just as "shame" does in the present context.

332. See 4:6; 5:10, 11, 17.

serpent in the deception of Eve, and therefore, by implication, in reference to the apostolic claimants who have arrived in Corinth.[333] His claim to integrity serves also as an indirect charge against his opponents.

Rather than acting in deceit, Paul, through "the manifestation of the truth," commends himself "to every human conscience before God." Here again it becomes apparent that the setting of apostolic ministry is very much like that of Kierkegaard's devotional address, in which speaker and audience are assigned their roles in the presence of God.[334] The apostle does not stand on the stage so that the Corinthians may assess and judge him, as they wrongly suppose. This correction of the Corinthians' conception of the "audience" helps to explain how Paul here is able to speak of his "commending himself," while in 3:1 he denies that he is doing so. The ministry of the apostle is a prolepsis of the last day, which brings judgment and salvation into the present time. This prolepsis is apparent already in 2:14-17, where Paul describes himself as an odor of Christ among both the saved and the perishing. It likewise appears in 5:11, where he describes himself as *already* having been manifest to God, even though he must yet appear before Christ's judgment seat (5:10). The same — nearly Johannine[335] — thought appears here. It is for this reason that Paul oddly doubles the prepositional phrases and speaks of his mission as taking place in the presence of all humanity. He commends himself *to* all human consciences, *in* the presence of God. The scene is that of the final judgment, into which *all* human beings are placed by "the word of God" as they hear it from the apostle and see it in him.

More precisely, it is "by the manifestation of the truth" that Paul commends himself. This "manifestation," too, likely implies the setting of eschatological judgment, given Paul's similar statements in both Corinthian letters.[336] In this context it is clear that truth is not merely cognitive. It is not mere knowledge that the human being can grasp and assess, as the Corinthians might imagine. It is not the Corinthians who assess the truth. It is the truth that assesses them. Their "hidden things of shame," their darkness and lies, are exposed by it. The truth is not merely spoken by the apostle but is embodied in the apostle, and not merely in his integrity, but in the suffering and deliverance that he experiences. Of course, the cognitive element is not missing: truth entails knowledge. Paul describes the Gospel as "the word of truth" (6:7). But he also pairs it with "integrity" and contrasts it with "evil," "immorality," and "unrighteousness" (1 Cor 5:8; 13:6). Truth is larger than human cognition. The apostle is not the judge of the truth but a vehicle for it, not merely in his

333. 11:3, 12-15.

334. See p. 95.

335. See, e.g., John 3:18-21; 5:24-30; 12:29-33.

336. See 1 Cor 3:13; 4:5; 14:25; 2 Cor 5:10.

head, but in his body and life, where it is manifest in such a way that all human beings are called to account.

It is not to human beings that Paul commends himself by the manifestation of the truth but to "every *conscience* of human beings." Just as he — by the grace of God — lives in transparency and thus appeals to his conscience (1:12), he appeals to every conscience and goes on to appeal directly to the Corinthians (5:11). Behind the idols and false judgments that have captured human hearts, Paul understands that a faculty of moral judgment remains within them. This faculty is obviously not infallible. It may well approve what is wrong and reject what is right. It is certainly not sufficient to deliver the human being from the blindness of unbelief and idolatry, as Paul makes clear in this very context (4:4-6).[337] Despite its limitations and perversions, however, the moral faculty of the conscience remains. As human beings, we may well be immoral, but we can never be amoral. The apostle appeals to the conscience, just as he does when he subsequently denies that he is commending himself, yet he offers the Corinthians an alternative "boasting," in contrast to those "who boast in appearance and not in heart" (5:12). He goes to the heart of the matter. In doing so, he refuses to pander to the tastes, opinions, and judgments that otherwise determine human life. He sees beyond all human pretensions and speaks to human beings as they appear by the light of the Gospel in the presence of God.

3 If Paul's Gospel is "veiled" or hidden, it is not so on account of him and his conduct. This is Paul's claim. Obviously, there has been misunderstanding of Paul's Gospel within the Corinthian church.[338] But the apostle does not speak merely defensively here. Indeed, he provides provocation. He insists that his person and conduct have provided no obstacle to his message; he has been open and transparent with the Corinthians in all his dealings with them. The ability of the apostle to communicate has not come into question in Corinth. It is rather, as we have noted, the stark difference between his *parrēsia* and his *parousia* and *praxis* that has become an offense for the Corinthians. His failure to visit Corinth as he had promised (1:15–2:4) has raised the question of his reliability. His refusal to accept financial support from the church remains an ongoing issue (11:5-11). To those who are perishing, the Gospel is hidden not only in the cross, but also in the life of the apostle.

The provocative question that Paul implicitly raises here is whether *the Corinthians* are among the perishing. It is again clear that he is recalling his summary description of apostolic mission in 2:14-17: he is the "odor of death" among those who are perishing (2:15-16). Is he so to the Corinthians? In their ambivalence toward the apostle and their attraction to his opponents, their

337. Indeed, Paul's understanding of the conscience arguably appears in Rom 7:14-25, where, in the presence of the Law, it serves only to establish human guilt.

338. See the discussion of the misunderstanding of Paul, pp. 142-50.

very salvation is at stake. The question is whether his Gospel is veiled to them. We may remind ourselves once more that it is Paul who, in a more positive tone in the opening of the letter, indicates that the Corinthians have understood him only in part, and that this understanding is essential to their salvation (1:13-14). They are in danger of fulfilling the pattern of hardening and blindness that came upon "the sons of Israel" who were prevented from seeing through Moses to Christ (3:14-15). In a manner very similar to his admonitions in 1 Cor 10:1-13, Paul's figural interpretation of Israel's history reappears here. The narrative of the biblical text is not thereby surpassed or set aside. Quite the opposite. Paul invites his present readers to find themselves, and the dangers and temptations they face, within Scripture, as those upon whom "the ends of the ages have arrived" (1 Cor 10:11). Despite the difference in time, their times remain the same. Paul's readers do not interpret the text. The text interprets them.[339]

Paul's reference to "veiling" or "hiding" the Gospel makes it clear that he employs the visual imagery of 2 Cor 3:18 metaphorically: seeing is hearing. He likewise immediately speaks in the present context of "blinding" as the cause of unbelief (v. 4). Everything depends on our perceptions and prejudgments, which, contrary to what the Corinthians suppose, do not lie within our powers. As Paul already has warned them, "the word of the cross is foolishness to those who are perishing" (1 Cor 1:18). In that word, God destroys all human wisdom, which in its practical judgments always overreaches its proper place by attempting to judge and rule the world and the God who made it. Salvation thus arrives only where this perverted human wisdom has been destroyed (1 Cor 1:19; Isa 29:14). The apostolic proclamation of the crucified Christ is *Good News,* which is and must remain foolishness to the world (1 Cor 1:17, 20-25). The story of the cross defies all the stories that humans tell themselves. Correspondingly, the conditional form of Paul's statement ("If our Gospel is veiled . . .") does not hide the naive hope that all human beings might grasp the Gospel. As his open declarations in 1 Corinthians make clear, Paul well understands that the saving power of God is hidden from the wisdom of the world in the cross of Christ. His conditional statement is instead a prodding of the Corinthians to examine themselves. As the visual imagery already makes clear, however, grasping the Gospel is not a matter of human insight or intuition, and certainly not a matter of human decision. Hearing, seeing, and thus believing itself must be worked by God the Creator.

339. In a corresponding way, Johann Georg Hamann rightly regards Johann Albrecht Bengel's well-known dictum — "te totum applica ad textum, rem totam applica ad te" (apply yourself totally to the text, apply the text totally to yourself) — as describing the interpretation of Scripture *precisely backwards.* See Bayer, *Autorität und Kritik: Zu Hermeneutik und Wissenschaftstheorie,* 19-26.

4 We are determined by powers beyond ourselves. Paul expresses this matter in one of the most provocative statements of all of Scripture: "the god of this age [*aiōn*] has blinded the minds of unbelievers, so that they might not behold the light of the Gospel." His language anticipates his later description of Satan as one who clothes himself as "an angel of light" (11:14). It likewise anticipates his appeal to the Genesis narrative of the serpent's deception of Eve (11:3). Yet his characterization of Satan here is unparalleled in its boldness: "the god of this world." He obviously means it ironically.[340] Satan is finally no god at all. Paul here describes him as ruling over "this age" in that he blinds human beings and binds them in unbelief under his rule.

It is the "minds" of unbelievers that Satan blinds. Here again, as in 3:14 (and 2:11), Paul employs the term *noēma*, which generally signifies "the mind in action."[341] These "thoughts, plans, and conceptions" of unbelievers, or "minds in action," obviously entail their practical judgments about the world — and about the cross. It is "the light of the Gospel" that unbelievers cannot "behold."[342] Paul emphasizes the blinding work of Satan by contrasting it with the *light-giving* character of the Gospel. He does not employ the usual term for "light" *(phōs)* here, but *phōtismos*, "illumination." He furthermore uses here a rather infrequent term for "seeing" or "beholding" *(augazō)* that is itself related to light, illumination, and brightness, which in contexts such as this one signifies "contemplation," "beholding," or "grasping," perhaps picturing it as the capturing of light in the eye of the mind.[343] It is Satan who has prevented unbelievers from grasping the stunning brightness of the Gospel that is there for all to see. The blinding of those who do not believe obviously recalls the effect of Moses' veiling himself on the sons of Israel (3:14). Just as Moses' act of judgment delivered Israel over to condemnation, so Satan has blinded unbelievers. Yet just as Moses' veil was not the end of the story for Israel, so the "god of this age" is not the end of the story for the world. The apostolic proclamation continues.

It is "the Gospel of the glory of Christ" to which "the god of this world" blinds unbelievers. Paul frequently characterizes his proclamation as the "Gospel of Christ," underscoring that the story of the incarnate, crucified, and risen One is the essence of the Gospel.[344] Here his defining words are even more

340. Paul elsewhere voices for the Corinthians (1 Cor 8:6) Israel's confession of the Lord as one. He does so emphatically in Rom 3:30 as well.

341. See the brief discussion of the term *noēma* above, pp. 165-66.

342. As we have noted, in this synesthetic context one "sees" through one's ears, in the hearing of the Gospel.

343. In the Hellenistic period, it is Philo who uses this verb most frequently. See, e.g., *Fug.* 136.4; *Somn.* 2.1.3; *Ios.* 68.2; *Spec.* 4.60.6; *Prov.* 2.35.7. The verb appears in LXX Lev 13:24, 25, 26, 28, 38, 39; 14:56 as an intransitive that signifies "shining."

344. Rom 1:9 (cf. 16:25); 1 Cor 9:12; 2 Cor 2:12; 9:13; 10:14; Gal 1:7; Phil 1:27; 1 Thess 3:2; 2 Thess 1:8; 2:14.

pointed: the glory of Christ is the glory of the Crucified One, whom God has raised. He is the One in whose sufferings Paul shares (1:5), and in whom is found God's Yes, in utter contradiction to all human expectations. He is the One in whom Paul is led to his death as a captive, and yet in whom life is present and given to the world (2:14). The "glory of Christ" is the glory of the *crucified* Christ, whom Paul proclaims, and who is an offense to the world — and the wisdom and power of God to those who believe.[345] Christ's glory is not merely a display of moral excellence; it is the display of power in weakness (cf. 13:4).[346] To speak of the glory of Christ is to speak in paradox.

Paul goes further: Christ is the image of God. As we have noted, Paul inserts an element of eschatological reserve into 3:18 by speaking of our "beholding in a mirror" the glory of the Lord. Now he exploits the christological potential of that (properly) theo-logical statement. The mirror in which we see the reflection of "the glory of the Lord" is the crucified and risen Christ, who is the image of God. We have observed already that, in contrast to the Old Testament, in the New Testament it is Christ who is described as "the image of God."[347] It is furthermore clear that Paul does not conceive of the "image of God" as being a mere copy or something less than God. In recalling the vision of the glory of the Lord from 3:18, he here implicitly identifies Christ with the God of Israel. He likewise goes on in v. 5 to speak of his proclaiming "Jesus Christ as Lord," which likewise implies the identification of Christ as Israel's God. In v. 6 he inverts the formulation that he employs here and announces that, in his own heart, God has given "the light of the knowledge of the glory of God in the face of Jesus Christ." The glory of Christ, God's image, is the glory of God found in Jesus. The inversion now implies the identification of God with Christ, just as Paul has identified Christ with God. This conception of an "image" as participating in the reality that it makes visible was already present in Hellenistic Judaism.[348] Paul's thought is therefore not alien to his time and place, even if his ascription of deity to Jesus is unparalleled.

As we have noted, Christ is not for Paul merely a moral image or figure. Of course the goodness of God is displayed in him! But that goodness is not merely a moral ideal or vision.[349] In speaking of Christ as the image

345. 1 Cor 1:23-24, 30; 2:2.

346. As we have noted in the discussion of 3:18, within biblical tradition the display of God's glory is redemption and deliverance from suffering. See above, pp. 183-84.

347. See p. 184 above.

348. J. Eckert, "Christus als Bild Gottes und die Gottebenbildlichkeit des Menschen in der paulinischen Theologie," in *Vom Urchristentum zu Jesus: Für Joachim Gnilka* (ed. H. Frankemölle and K. Kertelge; Basel: Herder, 1989), 337-57, esp. 347. See Wis 7:25-26; Philo, *Deus* 4.5; *Spec.* 1.81.3; *Her.* 56.6.

349. At various points, the work of N. T. Wright tends in this direction. See his *Jesus and the Victory of God* (Christian Origins and the Question of God 2; Minneapolis: Fortress,

of God, it is not simply Jesus' earthly ministry that Paul has in view but also the incarnation, cross, and resurrection. The display of divine glory is the manifestation of deliverance from distress and death, into which God himself has entered in Jesus. Again Paul echoes faintly the Isaianic association of light and righteousness.[350] Paul's picture and understanding of God is determined by God's entrance into and involvement with the world in Jesus. God, for Paul, is defined in Christ, the image of God: Christ is the crucified God.[351] In Christ's love, God shows himself to be the self-giving God, who empties himself to death at our hands in order to break us of our idols and give us life (5:14). He is likewise the God who triumphs over our suffering and death by entering into them for us. If it is true to say that, after Paul, one cannot speak of Christ without speaking of God, it is truer to say that one cannot speak of God without speaking of Christ.[352] The suffering of God in Christ has long been problematic for Christian theology. Paul presents it as fundamental to his mission and message.

5 Paul now explains *(gar)* the transparency of his ministry (v. 3) and underscores the brilliant clarity of Christ's glory by describing his proclamation in terms that speak to the Corinthian situation: "For we do not proclaim ourselves, but Jesus Christ as Lord." In so defining his proclamation, Paul both instructs the Corinthians and calls into question the motives and practices of his adversaries. Like much of contemporary Christianity, the Corinthians had long been enamored of gifted leaders, just as they had idolized God's gifts. Already at the beginning of First Corinthians Paul addresses the problem: "Each one of you says, 'I am of Paul, and I of Apollos, and I of Cephas, and I of Christ . . .'" (1 Cor 1:12). The hero-worship to which the Corinthians fell prey had been cultivated by Paul's opponents, who had become the objects of the Corinthians' adoration. The comparisons that the opponents drew between one another, and especially between themselves and Paul, entailed the implicit "self-proclamation" that Paul rejects (10:12). Something of their claims

---

1996), 133-44, 659-62; Wright, *The New Testament and the People of God,* 467-76; N. T. Wright, *What Saint Paul Really Said: Was Paul of Tarsus the Real Founder of Christianity?* (Grand Rapids: Eerdmans, 1997), 177-80.

350. See above, n. 307, p. 183.

351. See Luther, "A theologian of glory does not recognize, along with the apostle, the crucified and hidden God alone," in *LW* 31:227 (Disputation concerning the value of indulgences); Moltmann, *The Crucified God: The Cross of Christ as the Foundation and Criticism of Christian Theology,* 267-338, seems in the latter part of his work to turn the truth of the cross into a general human experience, so that it loses its specificity and force.

352. See J. Gnilka, *Der Kolosserbrief* (HTKNT; Freiburg: Herder, 1980), 61 (on Col 1:15): "If one draws the conclusion — which in itself is true — that one can no longer speak of God without having to speak of Christ, it would be more fitting to formulate the matter inversely and positively: the one who speaks of Christ speaks of God."

appears in the opening of his "fool's speech" (11:22–12:10). Their disdain of Paul's weak physical presence and rhetoric is likewise indicative of their self-estimation (10:10). Appearance counted for everything, as it often does today. Paul counters those who boast in "face" *(prosōpon)* and not in heart (5:12). One wonders how Paul would have fit into today's Facebook culture. At this point, there were few in Corinth who "liked" his message, and fewer still who were willing to "friend" him.

Paul nevertheless includes himself in his proclamation: "and [we proclaim] ourselves as your slaves on account of Jesus." The concluding causal clause, *dia Iēsoun,* might be taken retrospectively as in the rendering here, or prospectively ("for Jesus' sake"), as is often done (ESV, NIV, NRSV). The former reading is more likely, since in v. 1, and again in the following explanatory statement in v. 6, Paul describes himself in a passive role. His service is fundamentally passive, even as he is remarkably active. Before all else he is a recipient of mercy and one in whose heart God, the Creator, caused his glory to shine. *Jesus'* glory has shone in Paul's heart (v. 4), just as the glory of God is found in Jesus (v. 6). Taken in this way, Paul's concluding statement again bears the profound christology that characterizes the whole of vv. 1-6: the apostle identifies the crucified and risen Jesus with God, even as he obviously distinguishes between them.

Paul proclaims Jesus as Lord, and himself as *the slave* of the Corinthians, on account of Jesus. While in 1:24 he places himself next to them, here he presents himself beneath them. This is not what they expected in a leader, nor what most leaders deliver. As Paul later comments ironically, the Corinthians are happy when someone enslaves them, eats them up, takes them in, exalts themselves, and strikes them in the face (11:20). As fallen human beings, they strangely desire abusive leaders and despise as weak those who would serve them.

The stronger rendering "slave" is to be preferred to that of "servant" (ESV; NIV). In modern English, the latter term tends to connote self-chosen service. Paul here speaks instead of his belonging to the Corinthians "body and soul," and that "on account of Jesus." He describes his slavery as a work of God and not any choice of his own, even if he speaks otherwise elsewhere.[353] It is only here and in 1 Cor 9:19 that Paul describes himself as a "slave" of those to whom he ministers. He is first and foremost a "slave of [Jesus] Christ."[354] In the context of his dealings with the Corinthians, it is clear that his slavery to them is an enactment of God's saving work in Jesus and is defined by it. All things belong to the Corinthians, including Paul, Apollos, Cephas, the world, life and

353. See, however, 1 Cor 9:19: "Being free from all, I have enslaved myself to all, that I might gain the many."

354. Rom 1:1; Gal 1:10; Phil 1:1; cf. Titus 1:1, "slave of God."

death, both things present and things to come (1 Cor 3:22). Paul is thus their slave. Nevertheless, as Paul goes on to remind them, "And you are of Christ, and Christ is of God" (1 Cor 3:23). As Paul puts it in the present context, it is "on account of Christ" that he is their "slave." As was the case in Galatia, Paul does not seek to please people: otherwise he would not be Christ's slave (Gal 1:10). He works with the Corinthians for their joy (1:24) and seeks to build them up, even if that work first requires the destruction of their idols (10:8; 12:19). His servitude to the Corinthians thus means that he must confront and contradict them.

6 Paul closes this section with a dense and abrupt causal statement that, together with v. 5, recalls his introductory words in v. 1. Just as he there speaks of the ministry given to him as an outflow of the mercy granted to him, he here indicates that his proclamation (v. 5) has its cause and basis in God's saving work within him. He thus becomes quite concrete. His heart, in which God caused light to shine, *was* darkness. The statement is ontological. The darkness of night was inherent to his very being. Paul — and implicitly all others — was among those who have been blinded by "the god of this age." Only the "light" of the Gospel, God's effective word, has brought him the knowledge of God's glory.

According to the apostle, God the Savior is none other than God the Creator, and vice versa.[355] In v. 6 "saying" is obviously "commanding":[356] God *said,* "Out of darkness let light shine."[357] The spoken word of God creates light, just as it does in the first word of creation that appears in the text of Genesis (Gen 1:3). In identifying God by his works, Paul simultaneously defines salvation as an act of creation and presents creation as an act of salvation. They are bound together not only in their like action but also in their form: just as the creation of light is the work of the word of God, so the Gospel is God's effective word that creates light in the darkness of the human heart. In this effective word, which performs what it says, God's person and work are revealed. Salvation is coming to know and confess God as the creator of our life.

In citing this first word of creation — given its form, there is no doubt

355. The missing antecedent to the relative pronoun ("*who* shone in our hearts"), which, correspondingly is an implicit predicate in the preceding clause, must be supplied: "God, who said, 'Let light shine out of darkness' *is the one* who shone in our hearts. . . ."

356. Cf. Matt 4:3, "Εἰ υἱὸς εἶ τοῦ θεοῦ, εἰπὲ ἵνα οἱ λίθοι οὗτοι ἄρτοι γένωνται."

357. The future form λάμψει is obviously to be taken as imperative. Another textual tradition offers the infinitive λάμψαι as a variant reading. It is mainly Western but also includes the majority text and some impressive witnesses, e.g., $\aleph^2$ C D^2 F G 33. This tradition recognizes the divine command but shifts it to indirect discourse ("God who said that light should shine . . ."). Perhaps because εἶπον does not often bear imperatival force, it was not recognized here.

it is a citation — Paul reads it theologically. His interpretation of Scripture is integrative and synthetic, to the point that he is prepared to alter the wording in order to highlight the theological significance of the text within the larger context of Scripture. Understanding has priority over verbatim repetition.

In his interpretive reading, Paul draws on the opening description of chaos in Genesis, according to which the earth was *tohu wabohu,* and "darkness" rested "on the deep" (Gen 1:2).[358] It is "out of darkness" that God caused light to shine. Not only does Paul draw the immediate context into his citation of the first word of creation, he also recalls at least two lines of biblical tradition. First, his reading of the text obviously corresponds to the depiction of creation elsewhere in Scripture as the subjugation of the forces of chaos. In the book of Isaiah and the Psalms, in an act of creation, Yahweh crushes Rahab or the heads of Leviathan in order to subdue the chaotic forces in the sea.[359] These passages of Scripture present creation as an act of salvation, just as Paul does here.[360] "Darkness" and "light" do not merely represent "ignorance" and "knowledge," although these are obviously included in the figure. "Darkness" also signifies "evil" (whether physical or moral), just as "light" is a symbol for "blessing" and "good" (again, whether physical or moral).[361] It is "out of darkness" that God causes light to shine: out of evil, God creates good; out of nothingness and death, God brings forth life. Paul thus, second, recalls the biblical tradition of the form and nature of God's works: the Lord turns a rock into water (Ps 114:8), makes the wilderness a pool of water (Isa 41:18-19), turns mourning into dancing (Ps 30:11), turns sorrow into joy (John 16:20), out of death brings forth life (Rev 1:18). As Paul earlier reminded the Corinthians, God has made the wisdom of the world folly, and has made the folly of the cross wisdom and power (1 Cor 1:18-25). The same dynamic is at work in the benediction with which Paul opens Second Corinthians: God has the power to bring comfort, not merely apart from affliction, but within it (1:3-7). The works of the Creator have not ceased within the world. Indeed, according to Paul's word here, we cannot know God unless we know God as the Creator who performs these unfathomable, saving acts.

The Creator who out of darkness brought forth light is the one who has illuminated the heart of the apostle. It is he "who has shone in our hearts in order to give the light of the knowledge of the glory of God in the face of

358. The opening wording of Gen 1:2 (וְהָאָרֶץ הָיְתָה תֹהוּ וָבֹהוּ) itself suggests that the copula is to be taken as a verb of action: "the earth *became* nothing and emptiness." Paul obviously interprets the act of creation in this way.

359. See Pss 74:12-17; 89:8-10; Isa 51:9-10.

360. Creation thus appears as a complex event that harbors the mystery of the origin of evil, into which neither Paul nor the biblical traditions that he echoes inquire.

361. E.g., Pss 18:28; 112:4; Job 18:18; 30:26; Isa 9:2; 42:16; 45:7; 50:10; 58:10; 60:1-7; John 1:5-9; 3:19-21; 8:12; 12:35-36, 46.

Jesus Christ."[362] Through the parallel form of his descriptions, Paul draws an implicit contrast between "the god of this age" and God the Creator. In the crucified and risen Christ, the true God works in a way that is contrary to all appearance and expectation. The "god of this world" rules by the deceit of outward appearance. It is God's *speaking* that has created light in the heart of the apostle, just as in v. 4 it is the *Gospel* that bears the brightness of Christ's glory. The word of the Gospel, which bears all the promises of God, remains hidden under its opposite, in the crucified Jesus and the apostle who proclaims him. As the word of the Creator, it nevertheless has the power to create light in the heart of the apostle.

The other elements of Paul's statement in v. 6 are also set in parallelism with v. 4. He shifts from speaking of the blinded "minds" (or "thoughts") of unbelievers to the light given in his "heart," thus making clear that the "heart" finds its identity in its affections and aims.

In place of "the light of the Gospel," he now speaks of "the light of knowledge," as he moves from the message of Good News to its work within the heart. The genitive "of the knowledge" is almost certainly epexegetic: God has created in Paul the illumination *that is* the knowledge of God's glory. The following genitive relation is, then, that of content, as is clear from this rendering. The closing local clause is not limiting but defining. Paul does not speak of "the glory of God in Jesus Christ," as if there were another glory of God that is manifest elsewhere. The glory of God is manifest to us only in the crucified Jesus, who is proclaimed and borne by the apostle. This is the occasion of stumbling for the Corinthians and for all the world.

As we have noted, in a noteworthy criss-crossing of language between v. 4 and v. 6, Paul expresses a profound christology in which he identifies Christ with God and God with Christ. The Gospel communicates the glory of Christ (v. 4). Yet Paul speaks in v. 6 of the glory of God. In v. 4 Paul describes Christ as the image of God. He now asserts that God's glory is made known in the face, or person, of Christ. Christ's glory is nothing other than God's glory manifest in him; God's glory is visible nowhere but in Christ. In so speaking, Paul is not engaging in theological play, nor is he providing abstract theological instruction. His language is directed to the immediate situation in Corinth. He is dealing with the cause of their stumbling. The glory of Christ and of God is not visible in the world, as was the glory of Moses. The glory of Christ is the glory of the new covenant, which is manifest in the Gospel solely to the ears and eyes of faith.

The glory of God is known in "the face of Jesus Christ."[363] In speaking

362. The first-person plural form continues to refer to Paul as a representative of all apostles, as the causal relation to v. 5 makes clear.

363. Several significant witnesses omit the word "Jesus" (A B 33 Tertullian). Esp. in the

of the *prosōpon,* or "face," of Jesus, Paul recalls the encounter with God that takes place where the Spirit is present (3:18). Just as all believers behold the glory of the Lord in the freedom of an unveiled face (cf. 4:3), so the glory of God is known in the "face" of Jesus.

The translation of *prosōpon* as "face" is nevertheless somewhat problematic; one might well render it "person." Paul uses the term in varying ways within Second Corinthians itself. It may signify "persons" (1:11), "[personal] presence" (2:10; 8:24; 10:1), or "[mere] appearance" (5:12; 10:7).[364]

In a fundamental way, v. 6 recalls the blessing that the Lord charged Aaron and his sons to pronounce upon Israel, so that his "name," and thus his person, would rest on them:

> The Lord bless you [sg.] and keep you [sg.].
> The Lord make his face to shine upon you [sg.] and be gracious unto you [sg.].
> The Lord lift up his countenance upon you [sg.] and give you [sg.] peace (Num 6:24-26).

The blessing spoken to the nation is given in the form of address to individual persons. Each one of us, no matter that we might pretend otherwise, needs and seeks "a gracious God." It is this blessing that Aaron is called to pronounce. That he must pronounce the blessing presupposes that it may not be taken for granted or regarded as automatic. The Scriptures also know the reality of God's hiding his face, which calls forth lament. Blessing is constantly under threat in the world and must again and again be pronounced and received afresh. It is not merely the guarantee of good things or the promise of success. As this text makes clear, blessing must be *spoken.* It brings the knowledge that we are recognized, accepted, and loved by God. It is the assurance that, behind and beyond the course of events in this world and in our lives, there is a God who loves us and welcomes us into his presence. The "comfort" that Paul announces in 1:4 is not merely external help but the love and concern of Another. It is this that all human beings seek and that God has given in Jesus Christ.

It is the *word* of the Creator that has created light in Paul's heart, just as it is the light of the *Gospel* to which unbelievers are blind. Even if Paul here

---

Western tradition, there was a tendency to transpose the order to "Christ Jesus." Nevertheless, the reading "Jesus Christ" has strong external support ($\mathfrak{p}^{46}$ א C). Perhaps the name "Jesus," which implicitly refers to the lowly Crucified One, presented something of an offense to copyists, in the face of Paul's profound Christology. Who could speak of God's glory being manifest in Jesus? It was, perhaps, easier to employ the honorific title "Christ."

364. The rather transparent etymology (πρός + ὤψ: "toward or with respect to the face") may be present semantically in all this varying usage.

distinguishes the apostolic encounter with God from that of other Christians, this encounter remains fundamentally *verbal* — in this respect, the same as theirs. Furthermore, his use of the plural form in the description of his "enlightenment" extends the significance of his language to others, who did not encounter the risen Christ on the Damascus road as he did.[365] Paul undoubtedly refers to his own experience of conversion here and thus indirectly recounts his vision of the risen Christ.[366] But he only indirectly alludes to this outward vision, for he no longer knows Christ according to the flesh (5:16).[367] His point here is that the word of the Creator alone can create light in the darkness of the human heart. It is significant that, in the Lukan account of Paul's conversion, Paul did not receive a bare vision, but an audition. This audition was essential to his coming to faith: "Lord, who are you?" — "I am Jesus, whom you are persecuting" (Acts 9:5; 22:8; 26:15).

One might, then, render Paul as speaking of "the glory of God *in the person* of Jesus Christ." The connection with 3:18 would then be obscured, but Paul's thought would be communicated more clearly. It is in the person of the crucified and risen Jesus that God's glory — against all outward appearance — is displayed. The vision of God's glory, unhindered though it is, remains indirect and subject to an eschatological reserve. We do not yet see "face-to-face" (1 Cor 13:12). The light of the Gospel and of God's glory in Christ comes to us through our ears.

b. The Earthen Vessel and the Word of Faith (4:7-15)

7But we have this treasure in jars of clay, to show that the surpassing power belongs to God and not to us. 8We are afflicted in every way, but not crushed; perplexed, but not driven to despair; 9persecuted, but not forsaken; struck down, but not destroyed; 10always carrying in the body the death of Jesus, so that the life of Jesus may also be manifested in our bodies. 11For we who live are always being given over to death for Jesus' sake, so that the life of Jesus also may be manifested in our mortal flesh. 12So death is at work in us, but life in you. 13Since we have the same spirit of faith according to what has been written, "I believed, and so I spoke," we also believe, and so we also speak, 14knowing that he who raised the Lord Jesus will raise us also with Jesus and bring us with you into his presence. 15For it is all for your sake, so that as grace extends to more and more people it may increase thanksgiving, to the glory of God.

365. Acts 9:1-9; 22:3-21; 26:9-20.

366. Cf. 1 Cor 9:1.

367. Insofar as Paul here alludes to his own vision of the risen Lord, it remains a prolepsis of the day of the Lord.

Paul's mission as apostle, in both word and deed, is determined by the mercy granted to him: God the Creator has spoken the light of his glory in Christ into Paul's heart. The messenger himself is *made new* by the message he bears. The medium is thus the message.[368] This newness, however, is not yet visible but remains hidden under trials and suffering. Even if his conduct is beyond reproach, the apostle is *not* transformed outwardly but remains in weakness so that the power of God might be displayed in him. The communication between God and the human being that constitutes salvation takes place by means of the word and faith. The essence of apostolic ministry is speaking in faith, doing so out of situations that contain no earthly hope.

7 "We have this treasure in earthen vessels." The coincidence of opposites present in the crucified and risen Christ has been communicated to the apostle. The knowledge of God's glory within Paul's heart does not manifest itself immediately in his earthly life. His outward life bears the contrary appearance.

Knowledge, especially the knowledge of God's glory, is power. Paul shifts quickly from the metaphor of riches to that of power.[369] The power that is manifest in him in "superabundance" remains *God's* power and must be manifest as such.

The "earthen vessel" that bears the treasure is the *whole* of Paul's bodily life.[370] The "body" is not merely an external, dispensable part of him. He speaks immediately of his bodily life as encompassing the whole of his existence: the superabundance of power is of God and not of *Paul* (v. 7).[371] Nevertheless, Paul draws a distinction between his person and his body, and he goes on to describe that distinction as one between his "inner" and "outer" person (or "human being": *anthrōpos,* 4:16-18). Yet, as Paul's statement in v. 7 makes clear, this distinction is not absolute. It does not imply that the inner life or soul is superior to the body, or that it is somehow *intrinsically* eternal. Paul does not announce the hope of a disembodied state (as some of the Corinthians might well have imagined), but the hope that our earthly "dwelling" and body might be clothed with one from heaven, so that our mortality is swallowed up by life (5:4).[372] The new existence is a heavenly one, but it is also a bodily one. The distinction that Paul draws between person and body is therefore not a distinction of "substance" or "material" but a distinction between personal existence and bodily life, one that is established by God's

368. Again I am echoing Marshall McLuhan.

369. The same transition appears in Paul's presentation of the "word of the cross" (1 Cor 1:18, 24-25; 2:4-5).

370. LXX Pss 2:9; 30:13 (31:12); Acts 9:15; Rom 9:21-23; 1 Pet 3:7, probably also 1 Thess 4:4, in reference to a wife. But see LXX 1 Kgdms 2:15.

371. Likewise, life is at work in the Corinthians, while death is at work in Paul (v. 12).

372. See also 1 Cor 15:12-58.

address to (and claim upon) each of us. This address is inherent to our earthly life but also transcends it.[373]

That Paul is an "*earthen* vessel" in the first instance signifies his intrinsic lack of worth; earthenware pots were inexpensive, common, and impermanent. Power is perfected in weakness (12:9). God places the riches of his presence only in cheapware. Paul does not preach himself, but Jesus Christ as Lord (v. 5).

8-9 The reality of power in weakness that Paul describes with the image of a treasure in an earthen vessel is not static but dynamic. He now expands that image in five dramatic pairings that present his existence as apostle.

It is difficult to render adequately the paradoxes that Paul presents. He is pressed but somehow not constrained, at a despairing loss and yet not despairing, persecuted yet somehow not abandoned by God,[374] overthrown — and thus destroyed — yet not destroyed.[375] His life is full of afflictions, yet his afflictions are, or rather shall be, overcome by the comfort and deliverance granted him in Christ. Paul here returns to the theme that he introduces in his opening benediction (1:3-7) and apostolic report (esp. 1:8-11; 2:12-17). Apostolic existence is one of affliction and comfort, trouble and deliverance.[376] Yet the life of the apostle does not differ essentially from that of others. It is believing existence written large: "A theologian is made by living, or rather by dying and being damned, not by thinking, reading, or speculating."[377] The Corinthians wish to deny this reality and have embraced the false ideal of a life of power elevated above trouble. They expect their leaders to reflect this ideal.

The list of hardships that Paul presents recalls the list in 1 Cor 4:9-13 and anticipates the one yet to appear in the present letter in 6:4-10. His juxtaposition of deliverance with distress recalls similar contexts in Scripture, especially the thanksgiving Psalms.[378] The psalmists are in distress, pursued by enemies, given over to death, and yet are delivered.[379] The apostolic experience

373. C. Gestrich, "Luther mit Leib und Seele: Impulse für die christliche Eschatologie," in *Denkraum Katechismus: Festgabe für Oswald Bayer zum 70. Geburtstag* (ed. J. von Lüpke and E. Thaidigsmann; Tübingen: Mohr Siebeck, 2009), 289-314.

374. To be "abandoned" in biblical idiom is to be abandoned by God (e.g., LXX Pss 9:11[10]; 21:2 [22:1]; 37:22 [38:21]; 70[71]:11). Like the psalmists, the apostle practices the theological art of distinguishing between outward circumstances and the stance of God toward him.

375. The verb καταβάλλω in contexts of battle or in reference to persons generally implies destruction; see, e.g., LXX Pss 36(37):14; 72(73):18; LXX Isa 26:5; LXX Jer 19:7; Josephus, *Ant.* 8.284.

376. At this point, Paul differs decisively from the Stoic tradition. The contrastive pairings do not have to do with the distinction between "body" and "soul" but with the suffering and deliverance of the whole person (4:16-18 notwithstanding).

377. Luther, "Vivendo, immo moriendo et damnando fit theologus, non intelligendo, legendo aut speculando," WA 5:163.28-29.

378. One might question whether vv. 8-9 may rightly be described as a "list of hardships."

379. E.g., Ps 3; 7; 9; 13; 18:1-19; 22; 71. See also *T. Jos.* 1:4-7.

corresponds to that of the psalmists. Again and again Paul is delivered from danger and death, and yet under the condition of eschatological reserve. The final deliverance, in which he hopes and trusts that the Corinthians will share as well, is yet to come. This eschatological reserve defines his existence. The apostle is like one condemned to death, whose life has been made into a theater for the world (1 Cor 4:9-13). He is led to his death in a triumphal procession (2:14-17). The same assessment of apostolic life appears in the present context: "Death is at work in us, but life is at work in you" (v. 12). As is clear from his report of his experience in Asia, Paul does not dismiss or forget God's present acts of deliverance (1:8-11). Yet none of them endure. One trouble is replaced by another. All present deliverance is a partial and temporary sign of the final deliverance that is to come in the resurrection, for which Paul hopes (vv. 14-15). The paradoxical pairings in vv. 8-10 thus may be read as referring either to immediate deliverance or to the life of the resurrection. Paul leaves the matter open. He by no means paints a dark and gloomy picture of life. Indeed, his life takes the form of trouble and deliverance in order that the Corinthians might know life (v. 12). In all of his troubles, he hopes for God's saving help. But he does not name a time, place, or manner in which that help must come. He recognizes that God may grant him "only" the final deliverance. It is this deliverance for which he hopes and for which all else is a mere anticipation.

10 Paul concludes his list of the paradoxical experiences of an apostle by describing it christologically.[380] At all times he carries "the deadness [*nekrōsis*] of Jesus" in his body in order that the life of Jesus also might be manifest in his body. The term *nekrōsis* is best translated "deadness," expressing an enduring state, rather than as "death" (ESV, NIV, NRSV), which might be taken to signify merely a past event. Paul chooses this rather infrequent term over the usual word for "death," *thanatos*, which appears in the next verse (v. 11). In his only other use of the term *nekrōsis*, in Rom 4:19, he employs it in this same sense of "deadness." Already in the opening of the letter it is apparent that Paul's understanding of Christ's death overturns normal chronology. While he understands it as a unique event in a specific time and space, he also speaks of Christ's death as an enduring reality: the sufferings of Christ are his in abundance, even as comfort is his through Christ (1:5). Jesus, crucified in weakness, lives — even now — by the power of God (13:4). Paul's thought is not essentially different in Romans and Galatians, where he reminds his readers that they have been crucified with Christ.[381] The enduring reality of Jesus' death means that the world has been crucified to Paul, and Paul to the world (Gal 6:14). Jesus' resurrection

380. It is here that Schlatter comments, "As the herald of Jesus, he recounted the history of Jesus' passion, but he not only recounted it, he experienced it as well" (*Paulus, der Bote Jesu*, 533).

381. Rom 6:1-11; Gal 2:19-21.

does not *undo* his death: it *overcomes* it. Jesus is the Crucified One, who lives. It is this understanding of Jesus' death that Paul presents here; the afflictions and hardships that Paul endures are a manifestation of the "deadness" of Jesus that he bears. Just as the enduring "deadness" of Jesus is overcome in Jesus' resurrected life, so the apostle again and again is delivered from danger and death; "the life of Jesus" is thus manifest in his body.[382]

11 Paul now transposes his christological description of apostolic existence in v. 10 into an explanatory statement. The repetitive form and content of the statement make it clear that his preceding christological description of his paradoxical experience itself provides the explanation for the marks of an apostle. At the same time, Paul changes his wording in more than one way, shedding light on his preceding statement.

Jesus' life is manifest in the apostle through a life-and-death drama. The present earthly life of the apostle is "ever again"[383] brought to an end by the presence of the crucified Jesus. Only in this way may the resurrected life of Jesus be displayed in him. Paul speaks of himself and all other apostles as "we, who live." They possess the life of this age. On account of the crucified Jesus, who is present in them, they are delivered over to death.[384] The earthly life of the apostle is thereby transcended by "the life of Jesus," that is, the life of the risen Lord, which is manifest in him. The sufferings of Jesus are reenacted in his apostles, and so is his resurrection.

More precisely, the life of Jesus is manifest in Paul's "mortal flesh." In the previous verse, Paul speaks of "the body." Now he sets bodily life within the context of the present age: it is nothing but life in mortal flesh. God wills to manifest Jesus' life, the life of the age to come, in the weak and transitory flesh, body, and life of the apostle — that is, within "an earthen vessel." This "resurrection of the dead" has been put on display before the eyes of the Corinthians in order that they, too, might share in life. Just as an exchange of life and death has taken place in Jesus, so because of Jesus an exchange of life and death takes place through the apostle. Paul presents Christ to the church.

Paul makes it clear, however, that this display remains a mere anticipation. He *constantly* bears the deadness of Jesus and *ever again* is delivered over to death. Death is at work in him so that life might be at work in the Corinthi-

382. Note the height of the paradox: immortality is manifest in the suffering and death of mortal flesh.

383. The shift from πάντοτε (v. 10) to ἀεί (v. 11) is of little semantic significance. The causal phrase διὰ Ἰησοῦν again is most likely retrospective, in light of the parallel statement in v. 10.

384. Paul uses the language of the Synoptics, which itself at times suggests that Jesus' being delivered up is an act of God, definitely in this sense in Rom 4:25 and 8:32. See also Gal 2:20. See 1 Cor 11:23, which stands close to the Synoptics in its ambiguity as to whether it is a human act or that of God.

ans (v. 12). God's acts of deliverance of the apostle notwithstanding, the final manifestation of "the life of Jesus" in Paul's "mortal flesh" awaits the resurrection of the dead. The purpose clause of v. 11 has not reached its fulfillment but remains open. Paul goes on to announce that hope of fulfillment in vv. 13-15.

12 "Therefore death is at work in us, and life [is at work] in you." It is again clear that the distinction Paul draws between his "person" and his body is not absolute. Although he spoke of death at work in his "body" and "mortal flesh" in the preceding verses, he now speaks of his person ("us") as the place in which death is operative. He here identifies himself with his body. At the same time, the apostle presents the work of God within him as essentially extrinsic: the life of Jesus that is manifest in his "body" or "mortal flesh" does not belong to him. That "life" is at work in the Corinthians, while death is at work in him. The "yet not I" of Gal 2:20 appears here emphatically. The "treasure" remains distinct from "the earthen vessel" in which it is contained. This "treasure," we may recall, is the saving knowledge of God's glory in the person of Christ (v. 6). It is manifest in Paul's "mortal flesh," not only in the impossible rescues from danger and trouble that have been granted him, but also in the gift of the Spirit, who works faith in him and brings it to word.

13 Paul's self-description now shifts from his passive experience of God's work in him to his own activity as apostle. In vv. 13-15 he returns to his opening claim of sincerity and transparency (v. 2), rounding off his characterization of apostolic ministry.

"And having the same Spirit of faith. . . ." It is clear from these opening words of v. 13 that Paul is not introducing a new topic but continuing his preceding description of apostolic existence.[385] The mission and action of the apostle are included within his passivity as an "earthen vessel." First and foremost, he suffers God's work in him. This fundamental passivity establishes the framework and nature of his mission.

Correspondingly, Paul describes the basis of his mission as resting in the gift of the Spirit. He "has" the same Spirit of faith as the one who appears in Scripture. This correlation makes it clear that Paul is not speaking of his own spirit, but of God's Spirit, and that, although he "has" the Spirit, he has the Spirit as a *gift* that remains *extrinsic* to him, and not as an inherent dimension of his person. The fundamental passivity of the apostle again comes to expression here. His faith is not his own but is the work of "the Spirit of faith."[386] His faith in the midst of all his trials is no heroic faith that is to serve

385. Note the parallel form and transition in 3:4, 12, which also appears in 4:1, even if Paul here clearly introduces the topic of his apostolic mission.

386. The genitive relation here (πνεῦμα τῆς πίστεως) is surely one of source and quality, as in Rom 1:4 (πνεῦμα ἁγιωσύνης), Rom 8:2 (πνεῦμα τῆς ζωῆς), and Rom 8:15 (πνεῦμα δουλείας . . . πνεῦμα υἱοθεσίας).

as a moral example for others. It is purely and simply the gift and work of the Spirit.

In speaking of his "having" the Spirit, Paul obviously recalls his description of apostolic ministry as a mission of the new covenant and of the Spirit. That which has been given to the apostle is not for the apostle alone but is for all, including the Corinthians, who, along with all Christians, behold the glory of the Lord in the freedom of the Spirit (3:18). In the present context it again becomes clear that the visual language Paul employs in 3:18 is metaphorical. He here deals with the fundamental stumbling block for the Corinthians: the dramatic difference between his *parrēsia* and his *parousia,* between his speech and his presence. Paul is an earthen vessel that bears the treasure of the knowledge of God's glory. The Corinthians cannot look into his face and discern the presence of the Spirit, as they suppose that they can. The Spirit is hidden under the sufferings of the apostle and is finally "seen" only in his speaking. The Corinthians must learn to see through their ears.

The contours of the relationship between "the letter" and "the Spirit" (3:6) become apparent here.[387] It is the Law as the written *demand* of Scripture that Paul regards as antithetical to the Spirit, not the Scripture as it is *written.* He now appeals to "that which has been written" as a witness to the Spirit and, in this sense, bearing the Spirit. Of course, it is in the living voice of the psalmist, who himself speaks of his speaking, that the Spirit is manifest. Yet the inherently spoken form of the Spirit's work and presence does not hinder Paul from locating it in the written word. Indeed, he suppresses any direct reference to the psalmist and introduces the words of the psalm as "that which has been written." The living voice of faith, in which the Spirit is present, speaks in the written words of Scripture.

Paul takes up only a brief statement from LXX Ps 115:1 (116:10). While the reading that he offers is certainly possible in the Hebrew text, it is clear that he follows the Septuagintal rendering, which interprets the Hebrew *kî* as explicative and correspondingly takes the verb *dibber* to express the act of speaking *(laleō):* "I believed, therefore I spoke."[388] The brevity of the citation is remarkable in that the following clause in the text corresponds remarkably to his theme: "I am greatly afflicted."[389] Paul undoubtedly expected his Corinthian readers to detect this contextual echo, as well as that of the larger context in which the psalmist gives thanks to the Lord for delivering him from death

387. See the discussion at pp. 127-30.

388. Paul's reading of the text thus stands at odds with most translations of Ps 116:10, which take the כִּי as temporal or temporal-concessive and interpret the verb as introducing the content of the speech, e.g., "I believed even when I spoke, 'I am greatly afflicted'" (ESV; similarly NRSV; see also NIV).

389. LXX Ps 115:1 (116:10), "I am exceedingly brought low" (ἐγὼ δὲ ἐταπεινώθην σφόδρα).

and goes on to complain that "all humans are liars" (Ps 116:11).[390] Just as the psalmist speaks in the face of affliction, so does the apostle. And just as the psalmist gives thanks for deliverance from death, so the apostle looks forward in hope to the resurrection. Yet the succinctness of Paul's citation should not be overlooked. His appeal to the text is concentrated on the words that he cites. His point is that he has been given the Spirit of faith, who is a *speaking* Spirit. Therefore he speaks out of the midst of his trials, in defiance of all outward appearance. That his *parrēsia* is at odds with his *parousia* is God's purpose and work. The apostolic message sounds forth from the unimpressive, weak, and powerless — not as a heroic act, but as the work of the Spirit alone. The faith of the Corinthians is not to rest in the wisdom of human beings, but in the power of God (1 Cor 2:4-5).

14 The faith and speech that the Spirit works is not a mere feeling or wishing but entails knowledge and certainty.[391] What brings Paul to speak and fills out his message is the knowledge that "the One who raised the Lord Jesus[392] from the dead shall also raise us with Jesus and shall present us with you." As Paul has made clear from the beginning of the letter, his life and, with it, that of the Corinthians is bound to the death and resurrection of Jesus. He shares in comfort only as he shares in Christ's sufferings. Yet as he shares in Christ's sufferings, he shares in the gift of comfort that includes the resurrection (1:3-7).[393] The Yes to all of God's promises is found in the crucified and risen Jesus (1:20).

As we have seen, Paul cannot speak of his own salvation without speaking of that of the Corinthians. His salvation has its necessary outworking in his calling as apostle. The mercy that he has received has given him his apostolic mission (v. 1). The authenticity of that mission is now being tested in the Corinthians. Paul's confidence in this testing rests *not* in the Corinthians but in the One who raised Jesus from the dead. Only that One can "present" the apostle with the Corinthians. This "presentation" is obviously not for the purpose of judgment, even though Paul shortly will speak of our being manifest before the throne of Christ (5:10). Rather, it signifies the arrival in the presence of God that constitutes salvation. The "mirror," through which we presently experience God's presence (3:18), will no longer be present there. In the resurrection of the body, communion between God and redeemed humanity comes to fulfillment. Paul here anticipates the hope he later expresses of his

390. See Rom 3:4.

391. "The Holy Spirit is no Skeptic, and it is not doubts or mere opinions that he has written on our hearts, but assertions more sure and certain than life itself and all experience" (Luther, *LW* 33:24 ["The Bondage of the Will"]).

392. Jesus or the Lord Jesus? Cf. Metzger, *Textual Commentary,* 510-11, who argues that the shorter reading has broad support and that the greater probability is that pious scribes added "Lord" than the alternative of supposing an assimilation to Rom 8:11.

393. The same thought appears elsewhere in Paul's letters, e.g., Rom 6:1-11; 8:1-11.

presenting the Corinthians as a bride to Christ (11:3).[394] God is the one who shall present the apostle and his church together.

15 Paul closes the initial explication of his person and work as apostle with a word of explanation *(gar)* directed to the Corinthians. "All things" are for their sake: Paul's trials and deliverance, his bearing Jesus' "deadness," the manifestation of Jesus' life in him, and the work of the Spirit, who grants him faith and speech. All these things are for the sake of the Corinthians — and for us who still read the apostle today. Most likely, the Corinthians also could hear an echo of Paul's words from an earlier letter in these words, "Do not boast in human beings, for all things are yours, whether Paul, or Apollos, or Cephas . . ." (1 Cor 3:21-22). All things work for the good of the Corinthians (Rom 8:28). Grace has been given to the apostle to be "multiplied" so that "the many" share in it. Paul's wording points well beyond the Corinthians, even though he obviously directs this statement to them.

Yet Paul does not here speak of grace being multiplied *to* the many, but *through* the many, so that it "might cause thanksgiving to abound to the glory of God."[395] That grace has a *purpose* does not diminish or deflect Paul's affirmation that "all things" are for the sake of the Corinthians. This is clear from Paul's formulation itself: it is *grace itself,* multiplied through the many, that causes thanksgiving to abound. The return of thanksgiving to God does not nullify or empty God's favor and giving.[396] Quite the contrary; in thanksgiving, God's giving comes to its fulfillment.[397] It is clear already in this verse that Paul understands the act of reception itself as worked by God. It is not in the first instance the Corinthians who are thanks-givers, but grace itself, which, as it is "multiplied through the many," causes thanksgiving to abound to God's glory.[398] God's glory is thus not abstract, cold, and distant, but the glory of the one Giver of all good gifts, including the gift of thanksgiving in which all good gifts are received. Paul will take up this theme in his encouragement to the Corinthians to complete their participation in the collection for Jerusalem.[399]

394. Cf. Eph 5:27; Col 1:22.

395. Wrongly, ESV and NRSV "to more and more people"; NIV "that is reaching more and more people."

396. See below, pp. 316-67, for Paul's encouragement and instruction of the Corinthians concerning the collection for Jerusalem.

397. On this question see esp., O. Bayer, "The Ethics of Gift," *Lutheran Quarterly* 24 (2010): 447-68.

398. God's grace and giving have other dimensions for the life of the Corinthians. Paul has already invited them to enter into intercession for him, in order that thanks might arise to God for him from "many" (1:11). He likewise will invite them to "the grace of giving" (8:7) in the collection for Jerusalem (8:1–9:15), in which God's giving elevates them to the role of givers rather than debasing or shaming them.

399. See esp. 9:6-15.

The mercy of God granted to Paul has its goal in the multiplication of grace and the abounding of thanksgiving. Paul concludes his first description of his person and work in an affirmation of his hope for the salvation of the Corinthians, much as he does in his first explanation of his failure to visit them (1:21-22). The apostle and his church are bound together by God's work in Christ.

2. *The Apostle as Bearer of Hope (4:16–5:10)*

We find here the second part of the x-pattern, or chiasm, in which Paul takes up his immediately preceding presentation of his mission, shifting his perspective from the entrance of the eschaton into the world in the Gospel to his continuing life and labor in the hope of that coming eschaton. He thus continues his discussion of his certitude of the resurrection begun in 4:13-15, now placing it within the horizon of hope. His emphasis now shifts from the knowledge of God and the certainty of faith to the corresponding material hope of the resurrection from the dead. This hope of the resurrection (4:16–5:10) is bound up with the reconciliation to God that constitutes the message and mission of the apostle (5:11-21). The expectation that all human beings will be "manifest" before the judgment seat of Christ is the pivotal point of Paul's presentation of his mission in this section (5:10). The confidence with which Paul anticipates this event springs from the hope of the resurrection that he already possesses. The prospect of this judgment nevertheless calls for "the fear of the Lord" (5:11), and it brings the pressing invitation to the Corinthians and the world to be reconciled with God (5:20).

Paul's adversaries in Corinth now come into view somewhat more directly than they did in 2:17. Once more he affirms to the Corinthians that he is "not again defending" himself, most likely taking up their words about him (5:12).[400] He is not and has not defended himself, but in Christ he speaks in the presence of God for their edification (12:19). In reality, he is defending the apostolic mission with which he has been entrusted, and here he seeks to instruct the Corinthians so that they themselves may have an adequate response to the opponents.

The Corinthians have supposed that the salvation that is present in Christ is manifest outwardly in power, wealth, and honor; before all else, Christ's apostles should manifest such blessing. Paul instructs the Corinthians that just the opposite is the case. In this section, Paul develops and explains the contrast between the treasure of the knowledge of God and the earthen vessel that contains it. As he has indicated already, the glory of the new covenant en-

400. See the discussion at 3:1, pp. 99-100.

dures into eternity, and with that glory, the hope of the resurrection (3:11). His explication of this hope necessarily entails a description of the human being, a description that is determined by this hope of the eschaton. The apostolic understanding of the human being and human existence consequently cannot be contained within static, ontological categories but is bound to the promise of salvation found in the Gospel. We cannot analyze ourselves, not even by the most profound philosophical or psychological analysis. We must be told by God who we are and what we shall be.

Paul's eschatologically oriented anthropology is contained in a series of metaphors that run through this section: the inner and outward human being (4:16-18), the earthly and heavenly habitations (5:1-4), the clothing of mortality with life (5:4), the present life as absence from the Lord (5:8-9). In all of these the Corinthians' understanding of themselves is being overturned by the hope of the Gospel, in which the truth about ourselves and the world is manifest (4:2).

a. The Eternal Weight of Glory (4:16-18)

> [16]*So we do not lose heart. Though our outer self is wasting away, our inner self is being renewed day by day.* [17]*For this light momentary affliction is preparing for us an eternal weight of glory beyond all comparison,* [18]*as we look not to the things that are seen but to the things that are unseen. For the things that are seen are transient, but the things that are unseen are eternal.*

Paul's distinction between the "treasure" of the knowledge of God and the earthen vessel that contains it issues here in an anthropological distinction between the "inner" and "outer" human being. He also takes up the issue of "seeing" (or "not seeing") that he introduced in 4:1-6, now contrasting the things seen (to which the Corinthians are all too ready to give their attention) and those not seen, by which the apostle and all Christians with him live. It here becomes apparent that the glory of the new covenant and the apostolic mission is the glory of the eschaton, which is presently unseen, hidden under weakness and suffering.

16 Paul's repetition of his claim "we do not fail" marks the transition to his second elaboration of his apostolic ministry. As in 4:1, the verb *enkakeō* here should be translated "not failing," rather than in the usual way as "not losing heart."[401] Now it is not the question of his possible moral failure that he addresses, but that of his possible mortal failure, namely, his weakness, suffering, and death. Paul continues to address the question of his legitimacy as an

401. See the discussion at 4:1 on p. 190.

apostle.[402] This is the purpose and aim of his discourse. He is not in the first instance reporting his psychological state to the Corinthians. Nor is his claim to competency based on the Corinthian standards. As he will subsequently indicate, he persuades people, but has been manifest to God (5:11). Paul's "not failing" rests not in himself but in God, by whom he is "made new day by day." Out of this work of God flows the certitude of the faith by which he speaks (4:13) and by which he "walks" (5:7). Admittedly, in this context his "not failing" includes his courage (5:6). But he is affirming much more than a upbeat disposition here. While in v. 1 Paul had in view the question of his moral failure as an apostle, he speaks here of the possible failure of his entire person and existence. These are finally not two different conceptions of "failure" but Paul's single understanding of apostolic (and thus human) life as the new creation of God in Christ. The life of the apostle, who bears the deadness of Jesus in his body (v. 10), thus displays the pattern of the Isaianic Servant, who does not "grow dim" or "become crushed," despite adversity and rejection.[403]

Paul now develops the distinction between "the treasure" of the knowledge of God's glory and "the earthen vessel" in which it is contained. He speaks in fundamental anthropological terms of the inner and outer "person," or, better, the inner and outer "human being." The terms are Platonic and already had been taken up by Philo and the author of 4 Maccabees.[404] They were most likely familiar to Paul's readers in Corinth.[405] Paul's further affirmation in v. 18 ("while we do not look upon the things seen, but on the things unseen") also sounds Platonic at first hearing. Yet Paul does not take over this language without recasting it in his own mold.[406] Paul does not juxtapose differing parts of the human being, the reason and the animal impulses, as did Plato, but, paradoxically, two whole human beings, the outer and the inner. This is possible for him because he does not draw a contrast between the material world and the world of ideas, but between the present age and the age to come. The outer human being belongs to the former, the inner human being to the latter. Both are irreducibly material. The eschaton, which has broken into the present time, is hidden in Jesus Christ, in the word of the Gospel, and in the gift of the

402. See 3:1-3 and 4:1.

403. Isa 42:1-9, esp. v. 4, the opening verbs of which often are rendered improperly in psychological terms in English translation; also Isa 49:1-6. See the discussion at n. 307, p. 183.

404. See T. K. Heckel, *Der innere Mensch: Die paulinische Verarbeitung eines platonischen Motivs* (WUNT 2/53; Tübingen: Mohr Siebeck, 1993), 11-79. See esp. Plato, *Republic* 9.588-89; and, e.g., Philo, *Fug.* 68.1–72.3; 4 Macc 7:11-15.

405. It is not clear that Paul is taking up the vocabulary of adversaries. It appears much more likely throughout this section of the letter that he is using language and concepts familiar to his readers, and yet unmistakably recasting their meaning and taking possession of them for his own purposes.

406. He likewise does so in Rom 7:22.

Spirit.[407] The Platonic language that Paul borrows allows him to speak of this hidden presence of the eschaton in the world in the ontological terms that are necessary to express its full reality. The "inner person" (or, again, "inner human being") is the new person, who by the gift of the Spirit is present in the heart of the apostle. Obviously, the present form of the new creation (5:10) is not the same as the resurrection from the dead that must still come. The Spirit, nevertheless, is the "down payment" of the resurrection, its actual presence within the fallen world. For the apostle, then, there is a *homo absconditus* who encounters the *Deus revelatus* in Christ, just as the *homo foris* encounters the *Deus absconditus* in suffering and affliction.

Paul's "outer person" is "being destroyed." This rendering is to be preferred to "wasting away" (ESV, NIV, NRSV), which seems to ignore the usual sense of *diaphtheirō*,[408] Paul's apostolic self-reference to his sufferings, and the immediate context of his argument. The present tense is probably to be taken as iterative, given Paul's following statement that "we are made new again *day by day*." As the opening connective ("*Therefore* we do not fail, but even if . . .") makes clear, both statements recall the preceding section, especially Paul's "list of hardships" (4:8-10), according to which he is thrust again and again into suffering and death, in order that Jesus' resurrected life might be manifest in him. The conjunction of destruction and deliverance that Paul presents here is a summary of the paradoxes he describes there. Paul has been in numerous hopeless situations, including the recent experience in Asia (1:8-11), in which he was as good as dead. He has protested already to the Corinthians, "I die daily" (1 Cor 15:31).

"But even if our outward person is destroyed, *our inner person is made new day by day*." Paul once more recalls the list of hardships in 4:8-10, as well as the deliverance that he has received. Even in that earlier context, Paul leaves open the form that deliverance might take. Here he speaks not of a removal of the trouble but of a deliverance from the trouble "in the inner human being," namely, in faith and hope. God thus "removes the person from the evil, and not the evil from the person."[409] Nevertheless, this inward "transfer" or

407. Similarly, Heckel, *Der innere Mensch*, 116.

408. See LSJM, "διαφθείρω," 418.

409. Paul's thought is close to the reflection that Luther offers on John 14:27 in a sermon on Pentecost Sunday 1523 (WA 12:576.20-29): "The world regards it as peace when evil is torn away and separated from the person. That is so when one is poor, and thus thinks that he has great unrest with his poverty, and seeks to find a way to lay it aside, and supposes that, if it were done away with, he would have peace and be rich. It is the same with someone who is dying, and death lies upon him. He thinks thus, 'If I could be rid of death, then I would have peace and remain alive.' But Christ does not give such a peace. He rather allows the evil to lie there so that it presses the person and does not take it away but uses another art and makes the person different and removes the person from the evil, and not the evil from the person."

"being-made-new" is no mere psychological state. It is a foretaste of the eschaton. This work of God corresponds to Paul's preceding reference to the gift of "the Spirit of faith," who creates faith and gives the apostle words in the face of distress and death itself. The work of the Spirit is not a once-in-a-lifetime event but a daily experience for the apostle. Day after day, according to Paul's need, he is "made new." God does not grant him strength in advance — lest, perhaps, he should trust in that strength — but removes him from trouble only as trouble comes to him.[410] Comfort arrives only with the sufferings of Christ, not beforehand.

As with all of Paul's "newness" language, this "being-made-new" is to be understood in eschatological terms, as the repeated experience of the life of the new creation.[411] This interpretation of the text is confirmed by Paul's following reference to the eternal weight of glory that is presently being worked by his sufferings (v. 17), and likewise his description of the hope of the resurrection that follows as an explanation (5:1-6). The "inner person" participates in that which is yet to come, by the Spirit, who effects a faith that speaks (vv. 13-15) and who is a "down payment" of the final gift of the resurrection (5:5).[412]

17 Paul now explains *(gar)* his preceding statement. "Being-made-new" implies a participation here and now in the eternal weight of glory that affliction works for him. It is clear that Paul here is thinking of faith and the gift of the Spirit, by which he has been given eyes to see the unseen hope of the eschaton.

Paul here dramatically understates his affliction and juxtaposes it to a climactic description of the glory to come, emphasizing the incomparable difference between the two. His striking wordplay accentuates the contrast. He sets eternity over against the moment, juxtaposing weight, gravity, and consequence to that which is light, trivial, and banal.

He describes his affliction as a "light thing" that is "present" or "momentary." As we have noted, the term *thlipsis* usually bears the sense of "pressure," "constraint," or "burden, even though it is frequently used in the LXX and the NT metaphorically in the sense of "affliction."[413] Yet Paul's burden is no burden at all, but a light matter in his estimation. Furthermore, the "deadness of Jesus," which he bears about in his body at all times, is a mere "momentary" matter. Everything depends on one's perspective, or, more precisely, on being given an eye for the things unseen.

410. See Bonhoeffer, *Widerstand und Ergebung,* 19.

411. Here the translation of the ESV, NIV, and NRSV of ἀνακαινοῦται as "being renewed" is misleading, in that it suggests a mere strengthening or refreshing, missing Paul's eschatological orientation.

412. For Paul, then, faith is something more than a human decision or disposition. Faith is itself the presence of the eschaton.

413. See above, p. 23.

It is obvious that Paul plays upon not only this Greek term for "burden" but also the Hebrew term *kābôd* ("glory"), which may also connote the idea of "weight" or "heaviness." The momentary weight of affliction (which is pure lightness) works an eternal weight *(baros)* of glory for Paul. It does so in a manner that is so surpassing that it can hardly be described: it surpasses even that which is surpassing *(kath' hyperbolēn eis hyperbolēn).*

Present suffering and affliction is thus not vain and pointless. To the contrary, in God's hand it works an "eternal weight of glory" beyond all measure. The thought parallels that of Rom 8:18: present sufferings are not worthy to be compared with the glory that is to be revealed "to us." One must not misunderstand the apostle here. It is not the case that we by our patient endurance win or acquire an eternal weight of glory. Nor do we gain this glory by working through our grief and loss and "making sense" of it. The apostle's statement is far bolder: the affliction *itself,* apart from any work of our own, works an eternal weight of glory. From the very start of the letter he makes it clear that his afflictions are nothing other than the sufferings of Christ. These sufferings, although they have been completed in time and space, transcend these boundaries and come to the apostle — and to all true Christians. Likewise, the mercy and comfort that he experiences come to him through Christ, crucified and risen (1:5). As he reminds the Corinthians, we share in Christ's comfort only as we share in Christ's sufferings.[414] The connection between present affliction and eternal glory is found in Christ, *into whom* Paul, along with all Christians, is driven in faith and hope by afflictions, so that they work for him "an eternal weight of glory."

Correspondingly, the *glory* that is being worked for the apostle through his sufferings is not properly his own glory, but the glory of God and of Christ in which he shares. "Glory" remains the glory of God alone. Nevertheless, the human being, who is called into a saving relationship of communication with God, paradoxically shares in it. This line of thought is apparent in Romans[415] and comes to expression elsewhere in the Corinthian correspondence. The hidden wisdom of God has been prepared for our glory (1 Cor 2:7), a glory that will be manifest in the resurrection (1 Cor 15:43). In the present letter Paul thus describes his apostolic ministry as the effecting of glory (1:20). His entire discussion of the mission of the new covenant turns upon the greater, life-giving, and abiding glory that is communicated through it to the human being (3:7-8, 9-10, 11). This glory is nothing other than the "glory of the Lord," into which they are transformed (3:18). Here the presently hidden nature of that glory, for which Paul must argue in 3:7-18, becomes apparent. Likewise Paul here emphatically underscores the "how much more," that is, the transcendence, of that glory (3:9-11).

414. He makes the same point in Rom 8:17.

415. See Rom 1:23; 3:23; 5:2; 6:4; 8:18, 21; 9:23.

18 Paul already participates in the coming glory and already is renewed through the vision of faith: "while we look not upon the things that are seen, but on the things that are unseen." He thus draws a fundamental contrast between human perception (that sees only matters that can be estimated, calculated, and brought under human control) and God's work in Jesus. Only those who have been liberated from "the god of this age" by the work of the Creator in Christ have eyes to see the unseen. The "word of the cross" teaches them that "things that are seen are temporary, but the things that are unseen are eternal." Through God's power in Christ, our afflictions work an eternal weight of glory for us, apart from any work of our own. Within this work of God, we have the "task" of looking away from the things that are visible — both the joyful and the sorrowful, the pleasant and the painful — and looking upon the things that God has worked in Christ, which remain unseen in the present, fallen world. Yet even this "work" is not our own but the gift of God in Christ.

Again here, Paul should not be understood as speaking in Platonic terms. In his distinction between "the seen" and "the unseen," he is not making a generalized contrast between the material world and the world of ideas. His differentiation is eschatologically grounded and specific. The "things seen" are those of the present, fallen world. The "things unseen" are God's promises, which find their Yes in Jesus and the hope of the resurrection that is yet to come. The "things unseen" are the eternal dwelling that we have from God.

b. The Dwelling from Heaven (5:1-5)

5 [1]*For we know that if the tent that is our earthly home is destroyed, we*
have a building from God, a house not made with hands, eternal in the
heavens. [2]*For in this tent we groan, longing to put on our heavenly dwell-*
ing, [3]*if indeed by putting it on we may not be found naked.* [4]*For while we*
are still in this tent, we groan, being burdened — not that we would be
unclothed, but that we would be further clothed, so that what is mortal
may be swallowed up by life. [5]*He who has prepared us for this very thing*
is God, who has given us the Spirit as a guarantee.

The apostle lives *out of* unqualified assurance of salvation, and not *into* it. He does not seek assurance from his works, but he lives and works out of the assurance already given him in Christ. The certainty that afflictions work and *increase* an eternal weight of glory is grounded *(gar)* in the certainty of the house and home from heaven, which is already prepared and complete. Paul thus again speaks paradoxically, shifting from the image of the inner and outer human being to that of heavenly and earthly "habitations," or dwelling places. The inner person is the presence of the new creation within the present order, who gives attention to the things not seen. The image of the heavenly "habitation" presents the eschaton as a matter of hope that nevertheless is present as a down payment in the gift of the Spirit. The two images are thus complementary. The first emphasizes the new vision and perception of the world given by the Spirit; the second underscores the physicality of Christian hope in the resurrection of the dead. While the distinction between an "inner" and "outer" person presupposes *discontinuity* between this life and the one to come, the image of a dwelling from heaven affirms the *continuity* of personal identity between the present life and the life of the resurrection. Paul's language legitimates the call for a place for the "soul" in modern theology, which has tended toward a monistic understanding of the human being. Our identity is found *finally* in an embodied existence. Yet our identity is not found in *mere* bodily life, but in a communication with God that penetrates and defines bodily life. In the present context Paul describes himself as possessing a conscious existence that transcends bodily life, even as it is fulfilled in that life. This qualified dualistic (or even tripartite) anthropology is grounded, not finally in an ontology of substance, but in God's word of address to us that creates us anew in Jesus Christ.

1 Paul's vision is directed to "the things unseen" out of *(gar)* the unqualified assurance that he possesses an eternal dwelling in heaven. As is the case elsewhere, Paul's use of the plural, "We know that . . . ," introduces a confessional statement to which he invites his readers.[416] The first-person plural continues to refer to Paul as apostle, but his confession invites the Corinthians to see themselves in him. In v. 10, then, Paul explicitly includes them in the expectation of standing before Christ's judgment seat.

Present life in the body is not a permanent residence but a mere dwelling in a tent.[417] The apostle is only a guest on this earth.[418] The image of a "tent" as a metaphor for the body was well known in the Hellenistic world. This imagery, however, set the body over against the mind.[419] Paul uses the figure but takes it in an entirely new direction. He recalls Israel's wandering in the wilderness and the hope of an abiding home. If this "tent" should be brought to an end, we know that we have a building from God. His hope is entirely

416. See esp. Rom 7:14; 8:22, 24, 26; 1 Cor 8:1, 4.

417. The genitive in the expression ἡ ἐπίγειος ἡμῶν οἰκία τοῦ σκήνους ("earthly house of a tent") is clearly epexegetic: "our earthly house, which is a tent."

418. Thus the wonderful hymn by Paul Gerhardt: "I am a guest on earth and have here no place to stand; heaven is my home, there is my fatherland. Here I journey until the grave; there in eternal rest is God's gracious gift, which brings all labor to an end" (author's translation).

419. See, e.g., Wis 9:15; Philo, *Gig.* 54.2. The language of Isa 38:12 ("my dwelling place is pulled up and uncovered like a shepherd's tent. . . . I have woven my life to an end like a weaver") is closer to that of Paul, since the text speaks of the whole person who faces death. Cf. Thrall, *The Second Epistle to the Corinthians,* 1:357-58.

material. The body is not set over against the mind. The earthly body is set over against the body of the resurrection.

As is the case with *diaphtheirō* in 4:16, the verb *kataluō* signifies destruction or dissolution. Despite the wider reference of the first-person plural usage here, Paul still refers to the potential of a violent end to his life as an apostle. The hope that he bears, however, is the comfort of all Christians. If his present life in his earthly body ends, Paul is confident that he has a building from God, a house "not made with hands."

The contrast between the present dwelling in a tent and the eternal "building" from God recalls the replacement of the wilderness tabernacle by the temple.[420] Earthly pilgrimage ends only with the *construction* of a permanent dwelling, a place of communion with God.[421] In a manner that is characteristic of Paul's eschatology, he announces that this construction is already complete: "we have a building from God." The glory (and thus salvation) that is presently worked by affliction is thus paradoxically grounded in the work of God that has already been accomplished. The confessional statement of the apostle is unqualified, the prepositional phrase emphatic: "We have a building *from God,* not made with hands, eternal, in the heavens."

The elaboration "not made with hands" is in the first place a warning against the attempt to establish one's life and obtain blessing by works. It is a form of Paul's teaching on justification as it is directed to the secularized Corinthians, who, in their estimation of letters of recommendation (3:1) and attraction to outward appearance (5:12), have set aside the work of God mediated by the apostle. The Corinthians have long been tempted to worship wisdom, power, and status (1 Cor 1:26-31) and thus to boast in persons and their works (1 Cor 3:21). Naturally, comparisons with others are necessary (1 Cor 4:6-7). The opponents of Paul, to whom the Corinthians are so strongly attracted, likewise separate the gifts from the Giver and base their claims to superiority on personal powers and works.[422] It is this secularized form of "works righteousness" that we most often encounter in our (post)modern world. Our contemporaries have not escaped the question of how to find "a gracious God" simply because they no longer have contact any contact with churches. To the contrary, in their antinomianism they plunge themselves ever more deeply into a "works righteousness." It is definitely not a "works righteousness" of the pious. Rather, it is the "works righteousness" of the secularized, the type that

420. See Furnish, *II Corinthians,* 294-95, who, however, wrongly emphasizes the corporate dimension of the image at the expense of the individual.

421. Paul's presentation of our present communion with the Lord, "who is Spirit," according to the pattern of Moses' encounter with the Lord in the tabernacle *itself,* expresses his eschatological reserve (3:18).

422. 10:12, 18; 11:5-6; cf. 11:22-33.

we find here with the Corinthians. Once God is set aside, the entire burden for establishing life, happiness, and indeed one's own self falls on human beings themselves, who by cleverness and luck must *construct* their life.[423] Paul's simple word "we have a house . . . not made with hands" is the profound and comforting announcement that our life, happiness, and future have been secured for us by God, in Christ.

Paul shortly also reminds the Corinthians of the coming judgment, at which they and all their works will be manifest before Christ (v. 10). That the Corinthians have succumbed to this secularized "works righteousness" is an admonition for much of contemporary Christianity, which also in large measure has lost the horizon of the final judgment.

Paul's warning against "works" is effectively a warning against idolatry, as is apparent from its connection to biblical tradition. Idolatry always entails the human attempt to "construct" life and blessing. There are no unnecessary gods; all of them satisfy one human need or another.[424] One of the fundamental elements of the prophetic critique of idolatry centers on this truth. Idols are lifeless projections of the human imagination, things "made with hands" that not only must be constructed but also must be maintained by human effort: thus the derisive and decisive Isaianic critique.[425] Correspondingly, in a number of contexts the Septuagint translates the term *elîlim* ("nothings," in reference to idols) with *cheiropoiētos* ("things made with hands").[426]

The warning against idolizing the temple, which is "made with hands," appears already in the Old Testament Scriptures. Even in 2 Sam 7, David's plan to build a house for the Lord is surpassed by the Lord's promise to build a "house" for David (2 Sam 7:11).[427] The narrative of Solomon's prayer of dedication in 1 Kings likewise contains a decided reserve: "But can God really dwell on earth? Behold, the heaven and the heaven of the heavens cannot contain you. How then could a house that I build do so?" (1 Kgs 8:27). The critique becomes pointed with Jeremiah: the hope that "the temple of the Lord" will provide protection is a deception.[428] When the temple is regarded *eo ipso* as a guarantee of security and blessing, it is nothing more than a human work

423. For further reflections on this matter, see O. Bayer, "Rupture of Times: Luther's Relevance for Today," *Lutheran Quarterly* 13 (1999): 35-50.

424. I gained this insight from an unpublished lecture on faith given by Oswald Bayer.

425. Isa 40:18-20; 44:9-20; 46:6-7.

426. Lev 26:1; Isa 2:18; 10:11; 19:1; 31:7. See also Wis 14:8. Cf. Isa 21:9; 46:6; Jdt 8:18; Bel (Theodotion) 1:5; Dan (Old Greek) 5:5, 23; 6:28.

427. The Lord's promise is given in a metaphor. The "house" that he promises to build for David is that of a continuing dynasty and kingdom. This figure nevertheless corresponds to Paul's usage in a fundamental way, since the "house" that he awaits is the bodily life of the resurrection.

428. Jer 7:1-15.

that takes the place of the work of God.[429] A critique of "temple idolatry," fraught with significance, is implicit in the words attributed to Jesus by the "false witnesses" in Mark's gospel: "I shall destroy this temple made with hands, and after three days I shall build another temple not made with hands" (Mark 14:58).[430] John's gospel takes up the element of truth in this witness: the risen Jesus replaces the temple "made with hands."[431] Paul's thought in the present context is remarkably close to these traditions of Jesus' words.

In all these instances, the fundamental issue is the false estimation of the "works of (human) hands." All our attempts at building God a house or at establishing or working for God's kingdom on earth are corrupted by our idolatry. We cannot free ourselves from the desire, mostly unconscious, to instrumentalize God, to put God in a box and use him, and therewith to use others for our own desires and ends. The greatest scandal for us, along with Jesus' first disciples, is that God must establish his own dwelling with us and his own kingdom among us.

The same critique of "temple idolatry" stands behind Paul's metaphor of the "building from God, *not made with hands.*" With his elaborative description of the "building from heaven," Paul not only sets the heavenly dwelling over against the earthly tent, but also over against all human attempts to construct and secure life or to "build the kingdom." These attempts are nothing other than the vain effort to secure the future by our works.[432] Here the inherent connection between secularized (yet pious) "works" (or giftedness) and eschatology again becomes clear.[433]

The building made without hands is "eternal, in the heavens." Its future is unshakeable because it is God's work, not our own. Paul recalls his immediately preceding reference to the certain hope of "an eternal weight of glory" and the unseen things that "are eternal."[434] The house that we have from God endures into eternity.

429. Isa 66:1-2.

430. The Markan report itself suggests that there is an element of truth to this witness: "*not even in this way* was their witness consistent." Jesus' prediction of the destruction of the temple appears in Mark 13:1-2. The critique of the temple likewise becomes explicit in Stephen's speech, which may be regarded as representative of at least one element of earliest Jewish Christianity (Acts 7:48; Isa 66:1). Luke presents the same critique of idolatry in Paul's Areopagus speech (Acts 17:24), and thus draws a parallel between the idolization of the temple and the pagan temples.

431. John 2:18-22.

432. In a different way, the author of Hebrews understands the former high-priestly service of the wilderness tabernacle to be transcended in Jesus' exaltation to God's right hand (Heb 9:11, 24).

433. See esp. 1 Cor 4:6-13; also 1:18-25.

434. The language also corresponds to Paul's affirmation of hope of "eternal life" (Rom 2:7; 5:21; 6:22-23; Gal 6:8).

In another way, too, Paul's thought is close to the tradition of Jesus' words. Even if it is only implicit in his thought at this point, it is "the life of Jesus" (4:10) that stands at the center of Paul's hope, in whom "the building from God" may be found.

The building from God is "in the heavens." With this description, Paul underscores the "otherness" of the resurrected body and the life to come. He by no means speaks of an immaterial home in heaven. His language especially recalls his defense of the hope of the resurrection in 1 Cor 15:44b-58, where he likewise stresses the incompatibility of our present body and life with that which is yet to come. Just as we have borne the image of Adam, the earthly human, so we shall bear the image of Christ, the human from heaven (1 Cor 15:46-49). That which is corruptible and mortal must be clothed with incorruptibility and immortality (1 Cor 15:53-54). Paul there uses the language of "being clothed" for the arrival of the life of the resurrection, just as he goes on to do in the present context in vv. 2-4. The location of the house built by God "in the heavens" presupposes its present hiddenness. It belongs to the "things unseen" (4:18), to which the attention of the apostle is directed.

Paul's affirmation that he already "has" a building from God has caused unnecessary problems for interpreters.[435] He is not speaking of some sort of "spiritual" resurrection body that he expects to receive immediately at his death. As his continuing confession shows, he reckons with an "interim" state in which he is "absent from the body, but present with the Lord" (v. 8).[436] Nor is he speaking of some sort of spiritual habitation that is something less than the resurrected body. The "building" from God is the abiding counterpart to our present bodily life, which Paul likens to dwelling in a tent. It can hardly be the case, then, that "the house made without hands" is some mere spiritual body, worn like a garment beneath our outward self. He is not speaking of a heavenly dimension of earthly existence. His discourse in 5:1-10 is a complement to that of 4:16-18, which provides its eschatological framework: the contrast between the "inner" and "outer" person is not final and definitive but has reference to the eschaton, in which our persons will be revealed (5:10). A

435. See Thrall, *The Second Epistle to the Corinthians,* 1:363-68, who lists nine interpretive positions and who opts for a reference to the individual body of the resurrection. This view is not to be rejected entirely, but it cannot do justice to Paul's language, as her solution for Paul's present tense "have" as an expression of the immediacy of a resurrection body makes clear. See further Harris, *The Second Epistle to the Corinthians,* 375-80, who outlines five possibilities and opts for a "future acquisition of the spiritual body at death as an ideal possession actualized at the parousia" (p. 378). This interpretation remains insufficiently defined and misses the christological center of Paul's thought.

436. See also 12:2. On the interpretation of this passage, see A. T. Lincoln, *Paradise Now and Not Yet: Studies in the Role of the Heavenly Dimension in Paul's Thought, with Special Reference to His Eschatology* (SNTSMS 43; Cambridge: Cambridge University Press, 1981), 59-71.

corporate solution to the problem of the present possession of a "building from God," especially the appeal to the idea of the possession of a heavenly temple, is likewise inadequate. Not only does it overrun Paul's individualistic language, it also fails to explain how Paul both has the building from God and yet longs "to be clothed" with it. The paradoxical character of Paul's hope cannot be dismissed so simply.

All such attempts to decipher Paul's language fail to recognize that the certainty of Paul's hope is grounded in Christ, and in the Spirit given through Christ as a "down payment" of the resurrection. Not only does Paul share in the "deadness" of Jesus, he also really shares in Jesus' resurrected life here and now, as he has just affirmed (4:10-11). This participation in the risen Lord obviously does not obliterate the distinction between him and the apostle, who is still subject to suffering and death. Nevertheless, because he shares in Jesus, who "lives by the power of God" (13:4), he *has* a building from God, a house "made without hands, eternal, in the heavens." The dwelling is his, even if he possesses it presently *in spe non in re* ("in hope, not in substance"). God's Yes to all his promises is found in the risen Son of God (1:20). We have that Yes in hope. This hope is something much greater than mere human wishing or imagination. According to Paul, the very longing for and awaiting this dwelling from heaven is the work of God, who "remade us" for this purpose and, in so doing, gave us the Spirit, who is the guarantee and down payment of the resurrected body that is our eternal dwelling (5:5). Although our resurrection remains in the future, it has entered the present in the resurrected Lord and in the Spirit given through him.[437]

Paul's language is obviously individual, yet it cannot be reduced to individual terms but is joined to a corporate conception. Paul confesses his own hope in a way that it includes all Christians. The individual and corporate are simultaneous in this hope fixed on God's work in Christ.

2 The certainty of hope does not bring Paul rest, but unrest. It is no mere quiet confidence. Just as the Spirit of faith causes the apostle to speak (4:13), so the assurance of a heavenly dwelling drives him to prayer, which arises from the very depths of his being. Indeed, he explains his certainty by appealing to this longing: "*For* in this tent we also groan, longing to be clothed with our dwelling from heaven."

Even if this desire remains inarticulate in "groaning," it nevertheless constitutes prayer that God hears, understands, and answers.[438] Paul's thought is not distant from that of Rom 8:23-27, where he speaks of the Spirit as inter-

437. See Schmeller, *Der zweite Brief an die Korinther,* 288-90, who rightly sees that the hope of the resurrection explains Paul's language here, and that other options, including the corporate reading, are in themselves inadequate.

438. E.g., Pss 12:5; 38:9; 79:11; 102:20.

ceding for us as the interpreter of our groaning in the hope of the "redemption of the body." Here as well as in Romans, our groaning recalls the groaning of the children of Israel in slavery in Egypt; the resurrection is thus simultaneously our redemption from slavery and our arrival in the promised land.[439] Yet Paul's recollection of the "groaning" of Israel before the exodus does not exclude allusion to the psalmists or to the other hardships that Israel had to face in the course of its history.[440] In the "son of God" *all* the promises of God find their Yes.

We groan, "longing to be clothed with our dwelling from heaven." Paul quickly moves from the metaphor of a temple to that of clothing. While the former emphasizes the happy difference between this life and the one to come, the latter communicates the continuity of our personal existence and self-consciousness. The compound form *ependysasthai* ("being clothed") that appears here and in v. 4 probably signifies putting on one garment over another.[441] Paul does not, however, thereby express the hope of escaping death or of an immediate postmortal possession of a resurrection body.[442] The apostle, who bears the deadness of Jesus and who reckons with the destruction of his "earthly tent," is not fixed upon the hope of escaping death or an intermediate state through an immediate transformation of his body.[443] He hopes instead that "the mortal" will be "overclothed" with life, even though it has been given over into death. Especially his subsequent language of the "swallowing up of the mortal by life" (v. 4) suggests that the double verbal prefix *(epen-)* bears semantic force. Being "overclothed" does not exclude, but includes, the resurrection of the dead. Paul speaks in the same manner of mortality being "swallowed up" by life in 1 Cor 15:50-57, where he includes both those who are living at "the last trumpet" and those who have died. The "overclothing" of mortality with life thus presupposes the resurrection, which is Paul's sole interest here.

3 The exceedingly difficult question of the variant readings "being unclothed" or "being clothed" is to be resolved in favor of the latter: "If we are clothed, we shall not be found naked." External evidence clearly favors this reading. The former may be readily understood as a scribal attempt to avoid an apparent tautology, and perhaps also a borrowing from v. 4, where the term "to be unclothed" *(ekdysasthai)* appears.[444]

439. Exod 2:24; 6:5.

440. E.g., Judg 2:18.

441. See Josephus, *Ant.* 3.152; 5.37. Perhaps, too, LXX 2 Kgdms 13:18.

442. Against Harris, *The Second Epistle to the Corinthians*, 382. The distinction between an "ideal" possession of this resurrection body at death and the "real" possession of it at the last day only obscures Paul's confession.

443. Cf. 1 Cor 15:50-52.

444. See Metzger, *Textual Commentary*, 511.

To read this statement as a tautology is to miss Paul's metaphor. "To be found naked" is to be separated from one's bodily life. As Paul's elaborative repetition of v. 2 in v. 4 makes clear, he is reminding the Corinthians that the hope of the Gospel is a resurrected body, and not the bodiless existence of the naked soul. Paul's reference to "not being found naked" does not have to do with a fear of existence apart from the body, which he, in fact, prefers to bodily existence in the present life (v. 8).[445] It is, rather, a biblical idiom for shame, which here has particular reference to the final judgment, as becomes quite clear in v. 10. "Not being found naked" at the judgment is to share in the life of the resurrection and thus to be delivered from all shame.[446] "To be found naked" is the shame of being exposed for what we are as children of Adam; the final judgment recalls the first judgment.[447] Salvation, according to the apostle, lies in being clothed with Christ.[448] Paul develops this metaphor further in v. 10, when he speaks of our being made manifest before "the judgment seat of Christ," where we will be recompensed according to our bodily deeds.[449] The distinction between our persons and our works implies the paradox of the moment of nakedness before God in judgment, which Paul understands to have been overcome in Christ. Paul's language and thought remarkably parallel a passage from Plato's *Gorgias,* in which Zeus determines that, in judgment, souls must be separated from the body and judged as "naked souls."[450] They enter as such into their final state, with blessing or punishment. While Paul also affirms that our persons will be exposed for what they have done in the body at the judgment, he words his confession of hope and expectation of judgment in an anti-Platonic manner. Our hope is that we will be clothed. We shall be delivered from judgment by the risen Christ, in whom we share. Our salvation is the bodily existence of resurrected life; this life differs from our present "sojourn in a tent," but it is not the end of bodily existence. Indeed, it is the fulfillment of bodily life. It is not unlikely that the Platonic tradition was known to the Corinthians, who already were inclined to reject the resurrection. Paul seems to be responding to it, or to something very much like it.[451]

4 Paul here repeats the thought of vv. 2-3, rewording it, expanding, and

445. Cf. Phil 1:21-23.

446. See Phil 3:9; 2 Pet 3:10; cf. Gal 2:17.

447. See, e.g., Gen 2:25; 3:7-11; Mic 1:11; Nah 3:5; Rev 3:17-18; 16:15.

448. E.g., Rom 13:14; Gal 3:27.

449. There is thus a paradoxical relationship between the certainty of being clothed (and possessing the dwelling from heaven) and the reality of the final judgment. We shall discuss this paradox further in connection with v. 10.

450. Plato, *Gorgias* 523a-526d. See also the brief discussion in Heckel, *Der innere Mensch,* 112-13.

451. The imagery had been taken up by Philo. Once more, see Heckel, *Der innere Mensch,* 113-14 n. 86.

interpreting his statements there, so as to leave no misunderstanding.[452] The dwelling from heaven for which he groans is not some immaterial existence of the soul but the immortal life of the resurrection.

Paul now confesses that he is presently burdened, in contrast to his description of his present affliction as a "light matter" (4:17). Nevertheless, his point here is the same as in the earlier context. As is already clear from vv. 2-3, and as he reiterates in v. 4b, our "being burdened" *(baroumenoi)* arises from our longing to be clothed with the dwelling from heaven. The weight *(baros)* of heavenly glory that Paul awaits (4:17) already rests on him. The promise of the dwelling from heaven, the life of the resurrection, weighs upon him, burdening his present life with unstillable longing and restlessness. The hope of the resurrection is no narcotic that leaves its possessors passive, listless, and dormant. On the contrary, it makes them restless pilgrims. Paul's thought thus radically differs from Wis 9:15, which speaks of the corruptible body weighing down the mind, and the earthly body hindering the mind with its many thoughts. He makes it clear that he does not seek an escape from the body — just the opposite: the fulfillment of bodily life in the resurrection.

In the second part of v. 4 Paul elaborates the nature of his burden, clarifying the hope of the resurrection. The phrase *eph' hō,* often interpreted as causal, is best understood as introducing the conditions under which the preceding statement holds.[453] Paul's "being burdened" is not a condition of longing to be unclothed, but rather one of longing to be clothed. That is to say, he longs for the resurrection.

In the last clause of v. 4, Paul expresses his hope of the resurrection, yet again in fresh terms, now echoing his own language in 1 Cor 15:53-54, where he cites Isa 25:8: "Death is swallowed up in victory." There he likewise describes his hope as the clothing of "the corruptible with incorruption," and the clothing of "the mortal with immortality" (1 Cor 15:53). "Being clothed" obviously corresponds to the "swallowing up of death." "Death," or here in v. 4 "that which is mortal," shall be consumed by a larger reality.[454] The well-known poem of John Donne "Death Be Not Proud" fits Paul's confession well, even if Donne too quickly slides past the reality of death in the earlier part of the poem. Its conclusion corresponds well to Paul's thought: "One short sleepe past, wee wake eternally, And death shall be no more; death, thou shalt die." The "swallowing up" of death by life, which corresponds to our "being clothed,"

452. The parallelism of wording to v. 2 is apparent in the first clause of v. 4, which then diverges from the former already at the end of the clause.

453. See the similar metaphorical, prepositional usage in Phil 3:12; 4:10; Rom 5:12; T. Zahn, *Der Brief des Paulus an die Römer* (Kommentar zum Neuen Testament 6/3; 3rd ed.; Leipzig/Erlangen: A. Deichertsche Verlagsbuchhandlung, 1925), 265-69.

454. "Being swallowed up," a figure for ultimate defeat in battle, implicitly signals death itself (e.g., Pss 35:25; 69:15; 124:3).

implies a certain continuity. Death is not erased but conquered. The memory of God's victory over it shall remain to be celebrated. This is implied in the taunt of Isa 25:8 that Paul cites in 1 Cor 15:54 and echoes here. His "earthly house" that is a mere tent may be destroyed, but the end of the mortal lies in its "being swallowed up" by life. Donne likewise takes up this theme.

5 Paul concludes his confession by naming God as the source of his hope, not only in the objective sense that he raised Jesus from the dead, but also in the subjective sense that he has made Paul — that is, created him anew — for that resurrection and has thus created hope in his heart. The scope of his statement now broadens. While in v. 1 he ascribes the construction of his eternal dwelling to God, he now describes God as the one who has made him for the very purpose of life and immortality. Paul thus speaks of God as Creator, the One who works a new creation (5:17). Already in his earthly sojourn, Paul has been remade, "worked by God" *(katergasamenos)* for the life of the resurrection. The certainty of his hope, his longing, and his "being burdened" do not come from him. He "suffers" this work of God in him. Just as he plays upon the theme of the "burden" of glory in v. 3, indicating that it has been projected into the present time, so he here plays upon the theme of "working," or "effecting." Paul's affliction "works" an eternal weight of glory for him (4:17), but this effect is encompassed within the larger work of God, who has "worked" (and thus created) Paul for life. This is God's end and purpose for him. What the apostle confesses about himself here applies to all Christians. His confession is an invitation to share in that affirmation.

Paul follows this identification of God with a second, which echoes the similar twofold expression of confidence found in 1:21-22. Here, as well as there, Paul names God as "the One who has given the Spirit to us as a down payment." These identifying statements are not to be overlooked or taken lightly. In them Paul teaches the Corinthians how they are to know and understand who God is, and how he deals with them.[455] God is the One who gives the Spirit to the apostle and, through the word of the apostle (4:13), to the Corinthians. This gift of the Spirit, moreover, is the down payment of the resurrection, the eschaton, as it has broken into the present. Just as God has "worked" and made the apostle for the life of the resurrection, God wills to work through the apostle for the Corinthians as well. This thought is implicit here and explicit in the earlier passage, where Paul identifies God in the same way (1:21-22).

c. The Confidence of Faith (5:6-10)

[6]So we are always of good courage. We know that while we are at home in the body we are away from the Lord, [7]for we walk by faith, not by sight.

455. See also 4:6; 7:6; 11:31; 13:11.

> [8]*Yes, we are of good courage, and we would rather be away from the body and at home with the Lord.* [9]*So whether we are at home or away, we make it our aim to please him.* [10]*For we must all appear before the judgment seat of Christ, so that each one may receive what is due for what he has done in the body, whether good or evil.*

The apostle has confidence "at all times," even in the face of the greatest adversity. He is not, however, claiming to possess a heroic faith. It is God who has (re)made him for the life of the resurrection and who has given him the Spirit, as a down payment and gift. *Therefore* he has confidence. He knows that he is being carried by Another. For this reason his future is secure. This confidence includes the expectation of the final judgment before Christ, where his person and works will be manifest. In a way that has been difficult for interpreters to comprehend, Paul's anticipation of the final judgment entails a paradox. On the one hand, he possesses an unqualified confidence that his true home is with the Lord, in both communion with him and in the eternal dwelling of a resurrected body. This hope, moreover, rests in the work of God, who has made Paul for this end, apart from any works or worthiness in him. On the other hand, this certainty does not exclude, but includes, his expectation of a final judgment, at which his person will be manifest in his works.

6 Paul, speaking of matters of life and death, communicates their fundamental existential relevance for him to the Corinthians by breaking off his thought in this verse (i.e., an aposiopesis), interjecting an explanatory statement (v. 7) and then resuming his statement in slightly altered grammatical form (an anacoluthon). Paul thus completes the thought of v. 6 in v. 8. What he says here anticipates his stated preference there of being absent from his present bodily life and present with the Lord.

"Confidence" for the apostle is not *being* confident but *having* confidence. Confidence is given to him from without, not mustered from within. It is given as the hope of the resurrection, a hope that encompasses the subject — Paul himself. God has made *us* for this end and has given *us* the down payment of the Spirit. The apostle's self-reference in v. 5 is clear. Yet the plural form here signals that his *pro me* is not reserved for him alone. It is an invitation to the Corinthians and, through them, to us to know that God's work in Christ is given to us with the same certainty that it was given to Paul.

Paul nevertheless speaks in the first instance of his apostolic confidence, the confidence with which he speaks of the Corinthians as a letter of Christ (3:1-4) and which he practices in his bold speech (3:12). He will again in this letter speak of his confidence in the Corinthians *(tharreō),* as a result of their reception of Titus (7:16). He later ironically confesses to being "confident" (or "bold," again *tharreō*) toward them while absent and similarly asks their permission to be bold in the present letter (10:1-2). Paul's apostolic confidence includes the Corinthians, whether in encouragement or in rebuke. His salvation is bound up with theirs, as theirs is with his.

He *knows* that being at home in the body is to be absent from the Lord. In speaking in this way, Paul does not set aside his preceding affirmations concerning the dwelling from heaven and the clothing of immortality, which express the hope of the resurrection. As the remainder of this section makes clear, Paul reckons with an intermediate state between his death and the resurrection, as well as an "unclothed" appearance before Christ, the judge of all humanity. "To be absent from the body" and "present with the Lord" is not the *final* state of the human being, but it is now the real and present state of the apostle and countless others with him.

Paul's description of what has been traditionally called "the intermediate state" therefore complements his affirmation of the resurrection. The converse is also true. Paul certainly does not imagine that the possession of the resurrected body will bring a fresh exile from the Lord's presence! The very image of the temple that he employs communicates the opposite: the resurrected body will be the place of eternal communion with God. Paul's characterization of the intermediate state thus significantly qualifies his presentation of the resurrection. The life of the resurrection is no mere extension of physical life in the body. It includes the communion "with the Lord" that has entered the world in Christ. In speaking in this way, Paul recalls the work of the Spirit, who brings the freedom of communication with God, the vision of the Lord's glory (3:18). This aural "vision," it may be recalled, entails an eschatological reservation. It is only in a mirror that we presently behold that glory. "To be at home in the body is to be absent from the Lord." Thus, while the intermediate state does not contain the fullness of the eschaton, it brings an essential element of it: our being present with the Lord.

As we have observed, Paul's reference to "the Lord" in 3:18 remains properly "theo-logical." He speaks of the God of Israel, now present as Spirit. Paul develops that reference christologically in 4:4, where he describes Christ as the image of God. He thus goes on to characterize his message as the proclamation of "Jesus Christ as Lord," thus implicitly identifying Jesus with the God of Israel (4:5). The glory of God is found in the person of Jesus Christ (4:6). Paul follows these affirmations of Jesus' participation in the divine identity with a series of statements that express Jesus' true humanity: he is the dead one who lives (4:10-11). Paul is confident that the One who raised "the Lord Jesus" shall also raise "us" with Jesus (4:14). This final reference to "the Lord" prior to the present verse significantly informs Paul's thought here. In the earlier context, he describes his hope of the resurrection as a "being raised with Jesus." Despite the temporal distance between his coming resurrection and that of Jesus, he understands his resurrection as a participation in Jesus' life.[456] In all likelihood, his description of the resurrection

456. See also 4:10-11.

as a "being clothed" (vv. 2-4) is bound up with his understanding that believers have been "clothed with Christ" and yet still must be "clothed" with him.[457] Paul here is making it clear that participation in Christ entails communication and communion with him; to be home in the body is to be absent from the Lord. The thought is not distant from that of Phil 1:21 ("For me to live is Christ, and to die is gain."), where Paul faces the prospect of execution. In the present verse as well as in Philippians, the *beneficia Christi* are bound up with personal communion with him, and vice versa.[458] Indeed, participation in Christ, understood in this way, helps us to understand the inner connection between Paul's hope of the resurrection and Paul's preference for the intermediate state over against present life in the body. God not only raised the Lord Jesus but shall also raise "us" *with him* (4:14). Paul knows of no other communion with Christ than that which is found in Christ's saving death and resurrection. The Lord in whose presence he longs to be is none other than the crucified and *risen* Christ, in whose resurrection lies the promise of the resurrection of all those who belong to him.

This personal dimension of the apostolic hope, the communion of our person with Christ and thus with God, mediated by the apostolic word, is not to be confused with an inward-looking individualism. Current theological interest is so narrowly focused on the resurrection that it threatens to lose the personal dimension — and perhaps "the soul" — of Paul's hope.[459] Human beings need something more than the meeting of the physical needs and the healing of their wounds. In, with, and beyond these goods, we need compassion and comfort. More precisely, we need to know that there is a person, One who not only has the power to help us but also cares for us and loves us. This is the theme of divine comfort with which Paul introduces the letter (1:3-7). It reappears profoundly here.

7 Paul's brief explanatory interjection is of fundamental importance. It contains the argument of the entire letter: "For we walk by faith, not by appearance."[460] "Walking," a common biblical metaphor for the conduct of one's life, naturally implies the path or way to be traveled.[461] Our present, earthly path has its end.

457. E.g., Gal 3:28; Rom 13:14.

458. See also Phil 3:10.

459. This weakness appears in N. T. Wright, *Surprised by Hope: Rethinking Heaven, the Resurrection, and the Mission of the Church* (New York: Harper One, 2008). The concomitant minimizing of the intermediate state is the result of an overemphasis upon material and physical good. If liberal Christianity and existentialism tended to reduce the human being to a mere soul, the current tendency is to reduce the human being to a mere body.

460. The preposition διά, which expresses the means by which we "walk," may imply the distinction between person and body that is operative in this context. In contrast, in some contexts Paul uses διά to express agency or source (e.g., 2 Cor 1:1; Gal 1:1, 15; 2:16). See BDF §223.4.

461. E.g., Gen 17:1; Lev 18:3-4; Deut 8:6; 1 Sam 8:3; Ps 1:1. See 2 Cor 4:2; 10:2-3; 12:18.

The terms that Paul uses to describe his "walk" are defined in certain measure by their opposition: to walk by faith is not to walk by appearance. Faith lives from God's spoken word of promise; to this word God has been faithful in the crucified and risen Son of God and Lord whom Paul proclaims (1:18-20). This is true even for Paul, although he has seen the risen Lord. It is the speaking God and Creator who has shone in the heart of the apostle (4:6). He has been given the Spirit of faith, who speaks in hope in the face of all contrary appearance (4:13-15).

Paul therefore does not walk by "appearance." Although the term *eidos* is usually translated here as "sight" (ESV; NIV; NRSV), this rendering tends to give the false impression that Paul is speaking of "faith" and "sight" as differing human faculties. But the apostle is not speaking of mere human faculties. He describes "things seen" and "things unseen" (4:18). Just as "faith" is not a mere faculty or sense but includes the content and hope of the Gospel, so *eidos* does not signify the act of seeing but the object and content of sight, namely, the outward and visible present world.[462] Paul walks by faith, not by appearance. This certainly does not mean that he has no regard for practical matters, that he closes his eyes to the problems that stand before him, or that he refuses to make plans (as the Corinthians suspected that he did). The entire letter speaks against such a reading of this verse. Nevertheless, as his dealings with the Corinthians make clear, he does not accept outward appearance as final. Nor are his own plans in the end decisive.[463] Paul possesses the inestimable gift of being able to distinguish between the trouble that comes to him and God's unchanging love for him in Christ. Like the psalmists, he hopes and trusts in God's good purposes for him, despite the "accusations" of external circumstances. Just as the sufferings of Christ abound to him, so his comfort abounds through Christ (1:5).[464] He "sees through" such things, not because of cleverness, but by the gift of the Spirit and faith. In relation to God's saving purposes, Paul does not look at "the things seen," but at "those that are not seen" (4:18). The former are mere *eidos,* mere appearance. The latter have to do with realities that "eye has not seen, and ear has not heard, and which have not entered into the human heart." They are the things that God has prepared for those who love him, which transcend all human reasoning, thought, and estimation (1 Cor 2:9-10). They are already "heard" and received, but not yet "seen."

The Corinthians, for their part, are in danger of succumbing to the temptation of measuring all things by appearance. For this reason, Paul is now suspect in their eyes and the opponents are attractive. As Paul later informs

462. It may often be translated "form," e.g., Luke 3:22; John 5:37. See LSJM, "εἶδος," 482; BDAG, "εἶδος," 280.

463. This is esp. clear in his thanksgiving in 2:14-17.

464. See also Rom 8:18-39.

them, even "Satan disguises himself as an angel of light" (11:13). The apostle, for his part, is trying to provide them with a response to those who boast in appearance (*prosōpon,* 5:12). As the basis for the practical judgments of human reason, "appearance" includes all human estimations of wisdom, strength, and honor, or, conversely, weakness and suffering. Although Paul speaks of himself in this verse, this parenthetical statement, like the rest of the passage, is in the first instance an invitation to the Corinthians to see things differently.

8 As we have noted, Paul here takes up his opening statement, reformulating it so that there is a slight break in the grammar. He thus signals that the weighty matters that he is discussing are by no means mere theory for him but affect him profoundly. It likewise becomes clear that his preceding parenthetical statement in v. 7 is no mere aside, but of fundamental importance.

He now completes the thought that he introduces in v. 6: "We have confidence and are pleased instead[465] to be absent from the body and to be present with the Lord." The indicative form and actuality of his statement communicate the reality of death to which he is exposed.[466] His final hope rests in "a dwelling from heaven," the body of the resurrection with which he shall be clothed (vv. 1-4). Nevertheless, he would be happy to be in the presence of the Lord rather than continuing life in his earthly body. He is looking for something more than a new and better house. Material repair or a fountain of youth would be insufficient. He is awaiting his true home, from which he remains absent during the whole of his earthly sojourn. What makes "the house from God" a *home* is the presence of the Lord, with whom Paul longs to live. This dimension of Paul's understanding of salvation is already evident in the temple imagery that he employs in v. 1. While communion with God will be complete only at our resurrection, it is this very communion present here and now through Christ that constitutes and effects the new creation. Over his present life, Paul thus prefers the *better* life of the intermediate state, which in turn contains the promise of the *best* life, the life of the resurrection.

9 Before all else, the apostle is a bearer of hope and witness to a salvation yet unseen. In the first instance, he is not one who works but one who has been worked upon by God, just as he explicitly indicates in v. 5. With respect to God, his role is fundamentally passive. Yet this passivity does not render Paul indolent or idle. Just the opposite, it works the greatest effort and activity in him. As Paul earlier informed the Corinthians, "I labored more than all of them" (1 Cor 15:10). It is only consistent, then, that he concludes his opening presentation of his passive role as apostle with a reference to his ambitions

465. In this context, in which the two modes of existence are contrasted, μᾶλλον should probably be taken as expressing Paul's preference in contrast: "much more," "rather," or "instead."

466. See 4:10-12, 16.

and to the expectation of a judgment according to works. This conclusion provides the transition to his labors as God's agent of reconciliation (5:11-21), yet it remains within the framework of his presentation of God's work upon him. Not only materially, but in the very form of his argument, Paul presents his apostolic work as encompassed within the larger work of God in Christ.

As we have noted, Paul's hope does not make him quiet and content with the world but makes him restless and fills him with longing for the world that is to come. The certainty of salvation does not morally lame him. It empowers his "walk." To fail to comprehend, or to lose from sight this paradoxical relation between God's work and our work, between the Gospel and ethics, is to lose both elements of the calculus. There is no faith without works. Nor are there *truly* good works apart from a faith that remains unconditioned by them. They otherwise turn out to be self-serving attempts to gain the good or to assure oneself of it.

This paradox belongs to Paul's theological grammar, apart from which he cannot be understood. It appears in his first word in v. 9: *Therefore* also we have as our ambition, whether at home or absent, to be pleasing to him. Communion entails mutual joy in the presence of one another; just as Paul would be very pleased to be present with the Lord, he wants to be pleasing to him. This ambition of being pleasing to the Lord includes the expectation of having to appear before him in judgment, as Paul makes clear in the following verse.

There is irony in Paul's announcement of his ambition. He otherwise does not seek honor from others and, in fact, regularly faces dishonor from them.[467] It is the opponents, with their gifts and powers, who clamor for the attention of the Corinthians and seek to win honor from them.[468] Above all else, however, Paul's expression of *ambition* is paradoxical. The certain hope of the eschaton, namely, of being home with the Lord and thus being pleasing to him, forms and determines Paul's present. He strives after that which he already possesses.[469]

It is important to see, too, that Paul does not describe himself as seeking to please the Lord by his works. His ambition is greater and deeper. He seeks *to be* pleasing to the Lord. His ambition includes the whole of his person and being. He is not in a position to remake himself so that he might be pleasing to the Lord. Nor need he do so. God has already remade him for the life of the resurrection and his home with the Lord (v. 5). Paul seeks to be what God has made him to be in Christ. He walks by faith, not by appearance. Prior to the eschaton, when the purposes of human hearts are revealed, appearance is all that works can offer.

467. 6:8; cf. 1 Thess 2:6.

468. 5:12; 11:5-10, 21b-23; 12:1.

469. See Phil 3:12.

10 The hope of the resurrection does not bypass the final judgment but necessarily runs through it. As we have noted, Paul now broadens his first-person language to include the Corinthians and, with them implicitly, all human beings. All of us must be manifest before the judgment seat of Christ. Strikingly, Paul presents the event of judgment in the form of a divine passive. Neither God nor Christ appears in an active role in Paul's statement. This indirectness stands in contrast to Paul's open statements about God's love and saving work in Christ.[470] God's "proper work" is that of salvation. Yet that "proper work" does not exclude, but includes, God's work of judgment. Neither of the affirmations may be allowed to overrun the other. The love of Christ and his death for all do not eliminate the final judgment, with its double outcome. Yet the reality of the final judgment does not qualify God's unconditional and ultimate love in Christ. Paul does not provide a resolution to the questions raised by this asymmetric, twofold affirmation. This is good. If we could figure out this relationship, faith would no longer be necessary. In Christ we have been given an eternal home with God, the life of the resurrection. The prospect of final judgment does not condition this hope for the apostle, nor should it for us. Yet this confidence does not eliminate the prospect of the final judgment.

In accord with a broad witness of the New Testament, Paul understands that Christ will be the final judge of humanity.[471] Paul presupposes the scene of public judgment by a ruler. The *bēma* is most likely the seat on the raised platform that was used for public judgments and declarations.[472] Although the ESV, NIV, and NRSV have retained the traditional rendering "judgment seat," it is possible that Paul means to refer simply to "the step" *(bēma)* or raised platform upon which this seat stood.[473] The scene is clear in any case. Paul understands that "we all," namely the Corinthians and, beyond them, all human beings, will be "manifest" publicly before Christ, the Ruler and Judge.

That "we" shall be manifest implies the exposure of our persons, and especially the plans and intentions of our hearts. These include not only the motives of which we are aware but also "the hidden things of darkness," our innermost affections and thoughts, which we are unable to examine or understand (1 Cor 4:4-5).[474] All that we are shall be made open and public before us, before the world, and before Christ. In this judgment our works will be manifest, not for what they presently appear to be, but for what they are in

470. E.g., 1:3-4; 2:14; 4:6; 5:14, 18-21.

471. Matt 25:31-46; John 5:22-29; Acts 10:42; 17:31; 1 Cor 4:4; 2 Tim 4:1, 8; Rev 19:11; likely also Rom 14:10-12.

472. E.g., Matt 27:19; John 19:13; Acts 12:21.

473. Perhaps Acts 18:12, 16, 17; 25:6, 10, 17.

474. See also Rom 2:16.

reality. All unbelief, coveting, self-seeking, pride, greed, envy, and lust that now indwell our works in a hidden way will be exposed.

Paul's expectation of a judgment according to works ("the things done through the body")[475] does not contradict his rejection of justification by works.[476] As this latter formulation itself makes clear, the desire to be justified *by* works implies the attempt to secure one's person by one's works, to "make" oneself by one's works, and thus to hide oneself behind fig leaves. We thereby attempt to deny the reality of our fallen hearts and to act as our own creators. God does not want mere works from us. God wants our hearts and lives. Only through God's work in Christ, in which we are created anew, can our rebellious hearts be reconciled to God. All other efforts to do so entail a blindness to the truth.

We are to be manifest for who we are before Christ's judgment seat in order that we "might receive back again the things done through the body." Paul describes the final judgment as the return of deeds to the doer: what goes around comes around. His indirect and indeed impersonal description of the final judgment continues here. It is clear that he understands God, and even Christ, to stand behind this work of judgment. The Scriptures, especially the biblical psalms, announce and even celebrate this supreme, divine justice, by which the Lord causes evil to turn back upon itself, thus bringing its own punishment. The Creator governs the fallen world by maintaining this connection between "deed" and "recompense." Paul expresses the same understanding elsewhere when describing the final judgment: "What a person sows, they shall also reap" (Gal 6:7). He thus understands the final judgment not merely as a declaration but as an effected declaration, a word in action. The same is true, as we shall see, of his understanding of the final judgment as it has entered the world in Christ.

Here the paradoxical relation between the certainty of salvation and the prospect of judgment is pushed to its limit. The claim that the ultimate question of salvation (or condemnation) does not come into view here does an injustice to the text and to the apostle himself. He is able to speak in a differentiated way about the judgment and can well imagine that someone might be saved, even while their faulty attempts to edify the church are destroyed. But even in the context in which he voices this understanding, he ends his discussion with a solemn warning concerning final condemnation on the basis of works (1 Cor 3:13-17). In the present context, moreover, he is speaking of all our bodily deeds and provides no qualification to the undivided standard of "good or evil" that he presents as constituting the final judgment. A differentiation in judgment is implicit in that our deeds differ from one another. But

475. See also, e.g., Rom 2:16; Gal 6:7-8; 2 Cor 11:15.

476. See, e.g., Rom 3:20, 27-28; 4:2, 6; 9:12, 32; Gal 2:16; 3:2, 5, 10.

condemnation and justification are not thereby excluded. Indeed, that is the very matter that is at stake with the Corinthians, and in all the world, where the mission of the apostle takes place.[477] Paul summarizes the matter in the singular form, speaking of a simple either-or. The "things done through the body" will be recompensed, "whether good or evil," i.e., as a comprehensive reality. This summary implies what Paul states explicitly at the beginning of this verse. It is not merely that our deeds shall be judged, but that *we* then shall be made manifest in our deeds. Our person and life, unseen motives and aims, found in our deeds, "whether good or evil," shall come into judgment.

There is probably significance in Paul's use of the adjective *phaulos* as opposed to the more frequent *kakos*. Both signify "evil." But while the latter tends to signify "evil" as that which is harmful and damaging, the former often signifies "evil" as that which is despicable and contemptible.[478] It names "evil" as reprehensible, heinous, and abhorrent. Not surprisingly, it appears in other contexts that speak of judgment.[479]

Thank God, our lives are not in our own hands! We have "a building, not made with hands, eternal in the heavens," as Paul has just made clear to the Corinthians (5:1). Faith itself is nothing other than the work and presence of the Spirit, who creates the confession of the one who speaks (4:13). Paul goes on shortly to describe God's work in Christ as effecting the new creation (5:17). What "the letter" condemns and kills, the new covenant and the Spirit "make alive" (3:6). In Christ, we have been made new persons. His risen life shall carry us through the final judgment. We do not, however, possess that life in ourselves. It remains in the word of the Gospel, by which Christ is given to us. Everything depends on holding fast the apostolic word, as Paul himself later reminds the Corinthians (13:5).

3. The Apostle as Agent of Reconciliation (5:11-21)

As we have noted, Paul's description of his ambition of pleasing the Lord and his reminder of the reality of the final judgment in the presence of Christ serve as a pivot within his exposition of his apostolic mission (4:1–5:21). In the opening sections (4:1-15; 4:16–5:10), he presents himself in fundamentally passive terms as the recipient of light and life, an earthen vessel, and the object of the Creator's work of renewal. His apostolic work is not in the first instance his

477. 2:14-17; 4:7-15; 6:1-2; 11:12-15; 13:5.

478. Thus the verb κακόω signifies treating badly, harming or destroying, while the verb φαυλίζω signifies despising, abhorring, disparaging. See also LXX Prov 22:8a: ὁ σπείρων φαῦλα θερίσει κακά (MT: זוֹרֵעַ עַוְלָה יִקְצָור־אָוֶן).

479. E.g., John 3:20; 5:29; Rom 9:11.

own, but the work of God upon him, in him, and through him. This passivity does not stifle his activity but creates it and provides the "space" in which it takes place. In this third section (5:11-21), then, Paul turns to a description of his own work as an apostle, within the larger framework of God's work. It is in this section that we hear Paul's apostolic message as he formulates it for the Corinthians. While in 2 Cor 3 his attention is focused on the hidden glory of the new covenant and on the life and communion with God that it brings, here he presents the content of the new covenant, the Gospel, in the form that is most relevant for the needs of the Corinthians at this moment: they must be reconciled afresh to God.

a. The Apostle as the Opportunity for Corinthian Boasting (5:11-13)

> [11]*Therefore, knowing the fear of the Lord, we persuade others. But what we are is known to God, and I hope it is known also to your conscience.* [12]*We are not commending ourselves to you again but giving you cause to boast about us, so that you may be able to answer those who boast about outward appearance and not about what is in the heart.* [13]*For if we are beside ourselves, it is for God; if we are in our right mind, it is for you.*

Paul's discourse obviously does not take place in a vacuum. He is seeking to win the hearts and minds of the Corinthians, who long have had doubts about the apostle and now are being seduced by rival "apostles." It is entirely fitting that, as he begins to describe his own apostolic activity, he addresses this problem. His words here are transitional. In the first instance he characterizes theologically what he has just done in describing his own person and experience as apostle in 4:1–5:10. At the same time, as his language makes clear, he now speaks more directly about his work. As we have noted, he likewise speaks more explicitly about his adversaries than he has done before, even if he does so only briefly.[480] If the problem in Corinth is to be resolved, it must be resolved in and by the Corinthians themselves. Throughout the entire presentation of his apostolic mission (4:1–5:21), he seeks to provide them with the theological response they need.

11 Paul joins his fresh description of his apostolic mission directly to his expectation of the final judgment: "*Therefore,* knowing the fear of the Lord, we persuade people." In speaking of "the fear of the Lord," he obviously echoes biblical language that carries associations of faith, obedience, and reverence. Yet, as the very connection with the prospect of final judgment makes clear, the "fear of the Lord" is no mere respect or reverence. The apostle reckons with standing before the Lord in judgment. His assurance of his salvation does not

480. Cf. 2:17.

rest in some sort of calculus he might perform. It rests in Christ, in whom the apostle finds God's Yes. He lives, then, in fear that is overcome in faith. On the one hand, the "fear of the Lord" involves the knowledge of God as a *mysterium tremendum*, a mystery that brings fear and trembling (cf. Phil 2:12). On the other hand, the Lord before whom Paul must appear is the crucified and risen Christ, in whom comfort abounds, and who has secured Paul's life and salvation. It is the latter faith that allows the former fear. Otherwise the human being flees from God in a fear born of hatred: just as there are two kinds of grief, there are two kinds of fear of God (cf. 7:10). Paul might say, as does the psalmist, "There is forgiveness with you, in order that you might be feared" (Ps 130:4).

Knowing the fear of the Lord, Paul persuades people. As is apparent from his similar statement in Gal 1:10, "persuasion" was regarded not only with admiration but often also with suspicion in the ancient world.[481] Rhetoric can be used to deceive and manipulate. This is the very suspicion that the Corinthians have harbored against Paul.[482] He now openly and confidently admits that he "persuades people." This is his aim. He does so, however, "knowing the fear of the Lord." This knowledge frees him from any final concern about human opinions.[483] Yet it also binds him to service. The fear of the Lord includes the recognition that he must be manifest before Christ in order to be judged for what he does and says. The Corinthians have no reasons to hold persuasion such as this in suspicion.

As Paul now tells the Corinthians, he persuades people, but he has been made manifest to God. His thought here is remarkably close to that of 4:2, where he speaks of his own action and life: he bears the truth and manifests it to every human conscience in God's presence by his transparency. Here, in contrast, he presents himself as passive, borrowing from his description of the final judgment in v. 10 as a "being manifest" before the judgment seat of Christ. Paul thus speaks of himself as already having passed through that judgment, even though he must yet face judgment. His own life as an apostle is a prolepsis of the last day; his outer person is destroyed, but his inner person is created anew day by day (4:16). In that he belongs to Christ, the judgment has taken place in him. His person is exposed before all the world. As he tells the Corinthians elsewhere: "We [apostles] have been made a theater-show for the world, both for angels and for human beings" (1 Cor 4:9).

Paul hopes that he is also manifest in the consciences of the Corinthians. Out of his good conscience (1:12), he appeals to the consciences of the Corinthians, just as he appeals to the conscience of every human being

481. See also Acts 26:28.

482. 10:10-11; 11:7-10; and esp. 12:14-18.

483. Cf. 1 Cor 4:1-5.

(4:2). He seeks to draw the Corinthians into looking beyond appearances and then to act on the basis of this God-given faculty. We should remember that he does not regard the conscience as an infallible guide. It is a mere human faculty.[484] Here, as well as in Paul's preceding averments, the saving work of God provides the final basis of Paul's appeal. Yet Paul obviously does not reject the faculty of the human conscience. For him the human being remains a creature addressed by God, even in blindness and rebellion. Paul thus has an earthly, human responsibility. He seeks to persuade the Corinthians. In persuading them, he appeals to their conscience. His persuasive recounting of his apostolic mission is a laying bare of his person and life before the eyes of the Corinthians. His language here anticipates the appeal of 6:11, "Our hearts are open to you, O Corinthians, our heart has opened wide." Everything now depends on their response to the apostle, who as the odor of Christ brings not only life but also death.

12 As in 3:1, Paul denies that he is "again" commending himself to the Corinthians. It is likely that in both cases he refers to the unhappy confrontation that took place on the earlier visit, when he "came to [them] in grief" (2:1). As v. 13 makes clear, this "commendation" was no real commendation but a speaking out of character forced on him by the unusual circumstance of the challenge to his apostolic calling. Paul here clarifies that he is up to something other than self-commendation (cf. 12:19), just as in 3:1 he rejects the very requirement that he do so.

Paul nevertheless does commend himself, as we have seen in 4:2. He does so, however, in a way that overturns the expectations of the Corinthians. Rather than appealing to their standards and requirements, he appeals to their consciences (v. 11). His commendation, moreover, is not a self-commendation, but a commendation of the saving work of God that takes place in him and through him. His commendation rests in his "having been manifest," in God's work in him through Christ. Just as he has boasted in the witness of his conscience (1:12), he now wants to provide them with an opportunity for "eccentric" boasting "on [his] behalf." It is not Paul's boasting in himself, as the Corinthians would expect in a self-commendation, but a boast in God's work in Paul.[485]

Paul presents the Corinthians with this occasion and basis for boasting in the face of his adversaries, whom he mentions here for the first time in the letter.[486] Yet even this reference to the opponents remains more or less indirect; Paul merely characterizes them as "those who boast in appearance [*prosōpon*]

484. Cf. 1 Cor 10:28-29. On this topic, see again Eckstein, *Der Begriff Syneidesis bei Paulus.*

485. See the discussion of boasting above, pp. 48-49.

486. They are also likely included in the larger number of the "many" who "peddle the word of God" (2:17).

and not in heart." He contrasts the outward with the inward, where God alone can see, and where God performs the work of salvation that re-creates the heart. "Boasting in appearance" means judging matters according to visible, external standards (10:7). It includes claims to a powerful and impressive personal presence (10:1). The weak apostle and his "underwhelming" *parousia* fail to measure up. God's saving work in Christ is not found in the outward and visible, as the Corinthians are tempted to suppose. It is hidden in the wisdom of the cross and sufferings of Christ, in which the apostle shares. God's glory is revealed in the person *(prosōpon)* of the crucified Christ (4:6).[487] In the face of the claims of adversaries, Paul seeks to arm the Corinthians with the proper theological weapons. They themselves must know how to respond to the challenge.

13 Paul here explains *(gar)* his "not-commending" himself again. If he "was beside himself," i.e., if he spoke as one insane, it was for God and God's purposes with the Corinthians.[488] The language corresponds to that of the "fool's speech" (11:16–12:10), in which Paul speaks out of character, "in a state of boasting" (11:17). Just as he there engages in foolishness (*aphrōn,* 11:16-21), he normally acts with prudence *(sōphroneō)* for the sake of the Corinthians. In view of his claim that he is not commending himself *again,* Paul's statement likewise suggests that on an earlier occasion he has spoken as a "fool," or as he puts it here, as one "insane."[489] This occasion was almost certainly the confrontation that took place in Corinth.[490] Presently he speaks to the Corinthians properly. They themselves are to respond to the adversaries.

Paul's statement is therefore not to be interpreted as a reference to an ecstatic experience, nor does it have reference to ecstatic experiences of his opponents. The connection with the "fool's speech" is close both conceptually and linguistically. It is highly unlikely that Paul is speaking here of the ecstasy of a vision; the verb *existēmi* does not normally bear this sense, nor does Paul give any indication of amazement or visible ecstasy on his part in his report of his vision, even if he was transported to heaven (12:1-10). The introduction of this event here would hardly be germane to the argument.[491]

487. It is again clear that Paul understands apostolic ministry as taking place in the form of the "devotional address" that Kierkegaard describes: God is the true audience, not human beings. See p. 95.

488. The aorist ἐξέστημεν might be taken to represent present time (as in the ESV), but (1) its combination with the present tense σωφρονοῦμεν (2) and Paul's preceding affirmation, "We are not *again* [πάλιν] commending ourselves," mark it as expressing past time. Paul is referring to the earlier confrontation in Corinth.

489. On this usage of ἐξίστημι, see Mark 3:21; BDAG, "ἐξίστημι," 350.

490. 2:1, 5; 12:20-21.

491. Wrongly, e.g., Harris, *The Second Epistle to the Corinthians,* 417-18; Thrall, *The Second Epistle to the Corinthians,* 1:405-6. Cf. Sumney, *Identifying Paul's Opponents,* 144-45.

b. The Love of Christ in the Reckoning of the Apostle (5:14-17)

> [14]*For the love of Christ controls us, because we have concluded this: that one has died for all, therefore all have died;* [15]*and he died for all, that those who live might no longer live for themselves but for him who for their sake died and was raised.* [16]*From now on, therefore, we regard no one according to the flesh. Even though we once regarded Christ according to the flesh, we regard him thus no longer.* [17]*Therefore, if anyone is in Christ, he is a new creation. The old has passed away; behold, the new has come.*

Paul finally describes his motivation as apostle. This motivation is not goal-oriented. As we have noted, the apostle does not live a purpose-driven life. His life is a Christ-driven life, one driven, not by what he must do and accomplish, but by what God has done for him and yet does in him. Contrary to all our usual reasoning, the completed work of God in Christ does not lame or paralyze the apostle. Just the opposite: it frees him for service. It is not the case, either, that he makes no plans and has no goals. But his goals and plans are not ultimate, and therefore they do not ultimately burden him. His motivation is reasoned (v. 14), but behind and before that reasoning the work of Christ constrains and drives him. It is this work, which includes him, his life, and his thinking, that he elaborates in these verses.

14 As he often does, Paul adds a further explanatory statement here: "for the love of Christ constrains us." The explanation unfolds his final statement in v. 13: whether Paul foolishly "commends himself" or speaks with a sound mind, he does so under the constraint of the love of Christ, for the benefit of the Corinthians.

Paul is constrained by the love of Christ. This constraint explains his varying conduct with respect to the Corinthians. One died for all, therefore all died. The love of Christ, manifest in his death, is a love in which Christ savingly possesses human beings and makes them new (vv. 15-17). Paul is not speaking here of his love for Christ, but of the love of Christ that encompasses all human beings, including Paul himself (v. 16). This love of Christ overpowers the apostle and determines his life and actions. It nevertheless does not make him a robot, but rather creates the space for his own critical judgments: "judging this, that One died on behalf of all." The constraint of Christ's love is not a compulsion. It brings the freedom of a sound mind (v. 13).

Paul judges that "One died on behalf of all, therefore all died." As the conclusion in the second clause makes clear, as a benefit for all *(hyper pantōn)*, Christ's death was his "place-taking" for all. It was, moreover, an *exclusive* place-taking. Christ did not merely come to share the lot of humanity, but to fill their place in their stead. He died that they might live.[492] Paul thus regards Christ's death as substitutionary. Yet his description of Christ's death is broader and deeper. According to the judgment of the apostle, *if* One died on behalf of all, *then* all died. Substitution (or exclusive place-taking) implies for Paul an inclusive place-taking. Christ was not merely a representative. In his self-giving death, he also incorporated "all," so that all humanity was really present in him. His death was their death. In Christ's death, all died.[493] This is Paul's conclusion. For this reason he judges no one according to the flesh but sees all human beings with new eyes.

Paul here describes the work of salvation entirely in terms of Christ's love and purpose. God does not directly enter the picture, except in Paul's reference to Christ "having been raised" (v. 15).[494] Paul presents Christ's saving death as *Christ's* act of power and lordship, performed out of Christ's love for all humanity. In his free act of giving, Christ acts as the God who conquers death and brings life through his own suffering and weakness. In so doing, he lays claim to all human beings, who are now to belong to him.

Paul's simple words concerning the scope of Christ's saving work should not be overlooked: One died for all, therefore all died.[495] This atoning event is universal. At the same time, it is quite clear that Paul by no means envisions a universal salvation. As the fragrance of Christ for God, the apostle is the odor of both *death* and life (2:14-16). The "god of this age" has blinded the minds of those who are perishing, so that they might not see the light of the Gospel (4:4).[496] There is thus an interruption between Christ's accomplishment of salvation and its distribution by the Gospel, an interruption that remains unexplored and unexplained by the apostle. It cannot be bridged by any rational formula, at least not in the present time, during which we see only in a mirror in a riddle.

15 Paul continues his thought. Christ's love has a purpose not only *for* the human being but *in* the human being, a purpose that is essential to the salvation Christ has effected. He died that "those who live might no longer live for themselves, but for the One who died and was raised on their behalf." In other words, Christ died in order to deliver human beings from their fatal

492. Cf. 4:12.

493. Cf. Gal 6:14-15.

494. In the following verses, Paul presents the event of salvation as the work of God through Christ (5:18-21).

495. One can hardly claim that the "all" is a hyperbolic reference to "many," since Paul goes on to describe the result of Christ's work as bringing him to regard *no one* according to the flesh (v. 16). If someone is in Christ, there is a *new creation* (v. 17). God was in Christ reconciling *the world* to himself (v. 19), namely, the world that lives in the blindness of rebellion (1 Cor 1:20-21, 27-28).

496. See also 6:1-2; 12:15.

bondage to themselves. It is this deadly narcissism of the Corinthians that Paul deals with throughout the letter. They suppose that they are competent in themselves to judge the apostle.[497] The opponents judge that they are competent in themselves to replace him.[498] Both base their judgments on powers and abilities that they imagine that they possess. Christ wills to free them from this boasting. He died in order that "they might no longer live for themselves, but for him who died and rose again on their behalf." What Paul here describes as "possession" by Christ, he subsequently characterizes as "reconciliation with God" (vv. 18-21). Salvation is found in a relationship of communication.

Paul's thought here is *not* that of Zinzendorf: "All this I did for you. What have you done for me?"[499] The reality of discipleship is present within Paul's confession, yet not as a demand but as a gift. It is present as an "indicative" moment within Christ's work. The apostle is not speaking here of dedication *to Christ,* but of liberation *by Christ,* the joyous reality of being possessed savingly by Christ as Lord. This is clear from his own indication that he is constrained by Christ's love (v. 14), his reference to Christ's resurrection (v. 15), and his continuing description of Christ's work as creating new persons and reconciling them to God (v. 17, 19). Human beings, who by their very nature "live for themselves," *have died* in Christ's death. Obedience to God requires something more than a new motivation or a fresh dedication of ourselves. It requires a new creation of the human being. We have been *given* Christ as Lord. We cannot make him Lord by our own decisions, which remain inherently self-seeking, whether we recognize it or not.

In this respect, Paul's subtle interweaving of references to "life" in v. 15b is significant. As he already has made clear, "those who live" have died with Christ (v. 14). Their (former) "life" was the earthly life of the world under the power of sin and death.[500] One died for those who live in order that they might live for "the One who died and was raised" for them. Their life now is a participation in Christ. They have been liberated from their being-turned-in-upon-themselves and have been given the freedom of abiding communication with "the One who died and rose again on their behalf." Their death is conquered in his death. Their life is found in his life. Christ remains to them an unqualified Giver. A life *for* Christ, the concern of Zinzendorf, is contained

497. E.g., 3:1.

498. E.g., 10:7-11.

499. Zinzendorf was moved by his viewing of the *Ecce Homo* by Domenico Feti in the Düsseldorf gallery of art, which bears the script, "Ego pro te haec passus sum. Tu vero, quid fecisti pro me?" Frances Havergal, perhaps inspired by Zinzendorf, wrote a quite similar hymn, the first verse of which runs: "I gave My life for thee, / My precious blood I shed, / That thou might'st ransomed be, / And quickened from the dead; / I gave, I gave My life for thee, / What hast thou given for Me?"

500. Cf. 1 Cor 15:47-49.

within the new life *from* Christ that Paul describes here. A life in service to Christ is nothing other than the ongoing reception of Christ's gift of himself. It does not constitute a "return gift," which would be nothing other than a fresh self-assertion, an isolation of one's self and life from Christ. Knowingly or unknowingly, we would thereby seek to pay off our debt and to bring Christ under obligation to us. Gifts are given to be received, not to be repaid. They thereby establish and define relationships. In the presence of Christ, we may happily remain beggars.

Christ was raised for us. This is Paul's final word on redemption here. He does not speak of Christ's death apart from Christ's resurrection. Christ does not save by his mere "faithfulness" and mere obedience to God. Christ's act of weakness is an act of power by which he comes to his saving lordship and possesses humanity: he is the one who died and was raised *on our behalf.*

16 In two parallel statements, in this verse and the next, Paul elaborates his "acting with sound mind" for the sake of the Corinthians. The conjunction with which he introduces both of these results *(hōste)* may signify a logical conclusion ("therefore") and is usually translated in this way in this context. It is more likely, however, that in both these instances Paul is expressing the *result* of Christ's love that claims human beings as Christ's own. In the present verse, Paul again speaks of how he "reckons" or "judges" the saving work of Christ in its effect on human beings, just as he does in v. 14. *Because* Christ died for all, no one is to be regarded "according to the flesh," i.e., by outward appearance.

In the first instance Paul here describes the constraining power of Christ's love, which brings Paul himself a radically new understanding of others. Already Paul's opening description of his apostolic mission in 4:1-6 makes it clear that, where the Gospel is at work, it brings an entirely new understanding of God and of the world. It brings light to the darkness and gives sight to the blind. This new understanding of the world remains Paul's topic. "In Christ," human minds, hearts, and thinking are made new and different. They are created anew.

Paul thus first of all includes himself among those for whom Christ died, who no longer live for themselves but for Christ. The "we" *(hēmeis)* at the opening of the verse is emphatic: "*we* . . . know no one according to the flesh." The deadly narcissism of a life turned in on itself has been broken for Paul by the power of Christ. The *pro me* of the Gospel does not further an autonomous individualism. It brings it to an end.

In his self-reference, Paul continues to instruct and correct the Corinthians, elaborating the reason why he is not "commending himself to them again" (v. 12). To submit to this requirement would be to acknowledge an authority that the Corinthians do not possess. They are not in a position to judge the apostle or the Gospel that he bears. It is the Gospel that judges them. They have died. Their life now belongs to Christ, the crucified and risen Lord. Just as Paul "knows no one according to the flesh," so he does not seek to commend himself to them.

To "know according to the flesh" is to know according to the practical judgments of human reasoning. It is to know according to the human wisdom that regards the cross, together with the apostle who bears it, as foolishness (1 Cor 1:18-25). Human knowledge and judgment, based as they are on outward appearance, cannot see into the "heart" where God works through the Gospel (v. 12). "Knowing according to the flesh" correspondingly entails an estimation of others that furthers personal advantage. These two aspects of "knowing according to the flesh" — the insufficiency of human knowledge and its self-seeking nature — are bound together. We require a word from without to interpret the world to us. In the rebellion of unbelief, human beings reject that word and are thrown back upon their own constructions of reality, their own interpretations of the world. These stories that we tell ourselves are conditioned not merely by our time and place but also, and more fundamentally, by the self-seeking that is inherent to our rebellion against God. In our weakness, we are sinners. In our sinfulness, we are weak.

Paul earlier has boasted that he has not conducted himself toward the Corinthians "with fleshly wisdom" (1:12), and he rejects the suspicion that he "walks" or makes his plans "according to the flesh," i.e., in a duplicitous way, for his own benefit (1:17; 10:2-3). In admonishing the Corinthians, Paul encourages them to resist those who "boast in appearance and not in heart" (5:12). He charges them later with "looking at things according to appearance" (10:7). The opponents "boast according to the flesh" (11:18), just as Paul ironically does in his "fool's speech" (11:22–12:10).

Paul elaborates his first statement by broadening it in the latter part of the verse: "Even if we have known Christ according to the flesh, now, in contrast, we no longer know [him so]."[501] What does he mean when he speaks of "knowing Christ according to the flesh"? The prepositional phrase "according to the flesh" is undoubtedly adverbial, as becomes clear in the following clause, in which Paul omits the object of the verb altogether. His emphasis rests on "knowing according to the flesh." Here as well as elsewhere in the letter, his concern is to explicate the work of Christ on human thinking and judgment.

Nevertheless, he speaks of "knowing *Christ* according to the flesh." The question remains as to what he means by the expression as a whole. It is highly unlikely that he is describing his former, negative judgment concerning the message of the cross.[502] In the present context he is warning the Corinthians

501. The εἰ καί introduces a concessive clause, not a "hypothetical" (yet real) condition. Cf. 2 Cor 4:16; 7:8, 12; 12:11. Against R. Bultmann, *Der Zweite Brief an die Korinther* (KEK 6; Göttingen: Vandenhoeck & Ruprecht, 1976), 157-58.

502. E.g., Gal 1:13; 1 Cor 15:9; Acts 9:1-5.

against holding in regard "those who boast in appearance" (v. 12). "To know someone" here signifies not merely acquaintance but affirmation and recognition. [503] This is the sense in which Paul, in the preceding clause, denies that he now "knows anyone according to the flesh." It is clear, moreover, that the name "Christ" was held in high regard in Corinth. Already at the outset of the trouble in Corinth, there were those within the church who claimed to be "of Christ" (1 Cor 1:12).[504] The opponents likewise claim to be "of Christ" and thus to be Christ's apostles.[505] The Corinthians are seeking evidence of the presence of "Christ" in Paul (2 Cor 13:3). In 1 Corinthians Paul had to qualify his reference to Christ in order to make his point: he solely proclaims and wants to know "Christ *crucified*" (1 Cor 1:23; 2:2). It is obvious that "Christ" was honored and worshipped in Corinth. The question was *which* "Christ" received this acclaim.

In all probability, then, Paul here addresses the claim of his opponents that they had direct, personal knowledge of Christ and, with it, a commission from him. They claimed either to have encountered Christ already during his earthly mission or to have encountered him in a postresurrection appearance. The latter is more likely. As we have noted, the phrase "according to the flesh" functions adverbially. Paul does not refer to "Christ according to the flesh," but to "knowing according to the flesh," i.e., a knowledge based on human capacities of perception and judgment. In one way or another, in representing themselves as apostles,[506] the opponents must have made the claim to have encountered Christ, as is clear from Paul's earlier protest to the Corinthians that he is an apostle who has seen "Jesus, our Lord" (1 Cor 9:1). Paul likewise places himself among those to whom the risen Christ appeared and associates that appearance to him with the appearance of Christ to "all the apostles" (1 Cor 15:7-8). This latter context hints at the possibility that the opponents made claims of postresurrection encounters with Christ. This suspicion is strengthened later in the present letter when Paul, in the "fool's speech," compares his own experience to their claims of having had "apparitions and revelations of the Lord" (12:1). It remains possible that the present verse serves to counter claims of contact with the earthly Jesus. But Paul's boasting in the "fool's speech" serves as a counterpoint to the apostolic claims of his opponents. In that boasting, he makes no mention there of any contact they were supposed to have had with the earthly Jesus, only of their claims to have had apparitions of the risen Lord. This supports the conclusion that Paul here has in view postresurrection

503. E.g., 1 Cor 1:21; 2:2; 8:3; 13:12; 16:15; 2 Cor 12:2-3; Gal 4:8-9; 1 Thess 4:5; 2 Thess 1:8; cf. Gal 2:9.

504. It is possible that those who claimed "to be of Christ," in contrast to being of Paul, Apollos, or Cephas, were making their own claim to be apostles.

505. 2 Cor 10:7; 11:13.

506. 10:7; 11:13.

appearances of Christ. Yet these postresurrection appearances involve only a "knowing according to the flesh." In this respect, they do not differ from a claim to have known "the earthly Jesus." They are not yet the vision of the glory of the Lord with an unveiled face, which is given by the Spirit (3:18).

Paul here employs the first-person plural: "If . . . *we* have known Christ according to the flesh." He implicitly includes himself among all those who had known Christ in this way. The plural form here marks Paul's place as one apostle among all of Christ's apostles. As is clear from the preceding reflections, it is almost certainly wrong to understand Paul as speaking in a narrow sense of an otherwise unknown contact he had with Jesus during the time of Jesus' earthly ministry. He more likely refers to his encounter with the risen Christ, to which he appeals in substantiation of his apostolic claim (1 Cor 9:1; 15:8). As dramatic as that encounter was for Paul's life (cf. Gal 1:15-24), it was nevertheless an earthly vision of the risen Lord.[507] Paul does not contest the claim of the opponents to have known Christ, but here with his first-person plural, he indicates that he is their equal. His point here, however, is that such knowledge of Christ has been transcended by another. The story line of earthly life has been broken into by the age to come: "*Now* we know no one according to the flesh . . . *now* we *no longer* know [Christ so]."[508] Whether the opponents presented Christ as a great miracle-worker or powerful leader or wise teacher or, as was likely, all these at once, Paul nevertheless counters: "We know him thus no longer."[509] His focus rests on our reception of Christ, our knowledge of him. By the power of his saving work, we no longer know Christ as a mere teacher or miracle-worker, nor as a mere moral ideal and example. We know him as the One who died for us that we might live for him (vv. 14-15). For Paul, the true knowledge of Christ consists in the knowledge of Christ's saving benefits.[510] These saving benefits include the overturning of our understanding of the world: we are not those who may see and judge, but the blind who have been judged and yet have been granted sight. The work of God in Christ calls

507. As we have seen, Paul describes his conversion in this letter as the illumination of his heart by the word of the Creator (4:6). In this respect, he does not differ from others in the least. It should also be recalled that, according to the Lukan report, Paul's companions had the same encounter with Christ, without the opening of eyes and ears that was necessary to faith (Acts 9:7; 22:9).

508. At this point, Paul comes perceptibly close to the Johannine witness, according to which the gift of the Spirit is absolutely essential for the disciples themselves to see and understand (e.g., John 16:25-33).

509. 1 Cor 2:6-16; 3:18-20; with respect to the Corinthian perception of the apostle himself, see 2 Cor 10:10-11; 12:11-13.

510. As is well known, this formulation belongs to Melanchthon's 1521 *Loci Communes:* "hoc est Christum cognoscere, beneficia eius cognoscere." That it has been taken to extremes in Ritschlean theology and elsewhere does not rob it of its validity.

into question our capacity to know and understand God, the world, and our own hearts. In the wisdom of God, the world through wisdom did not know God (1 Cor 1:21). We require a word from God, an *effective* word, that tells us who Christ is — and who we are — in such a way that we are transformed by the light of the first day of creation. Contrary to what the Corinthians imagine, "having known Christ according to the flesh" cannot in itself confer any authority, wisdom, or power.

This new knowledge of Christ includes "the earthly Jesus" and all his works and words. Paul's affirmation stands at odds with the assertion of Rudolf Bultmann that Paul had no interest in "the earthly Jesus."[511] In a certain sense, Bultmann was right. For him "the earthly Jesus" was the object of historical investigation. All that could be known of him was what modern, historical-critical investigation could discover about him. Paul would have had no interest in the sort of Jesus who could be discovered by the cleverness of historical method. Yet Paul understands what Bultmann in his naive modernism could not see, namely, that all our intellectual work is conditioned both by our limited perspective and also, more fundamentally, by our perverted self-interest. As Albert Schweitzer recognized, the nineteenth-century research into the historical Jesus ended in portraits that were mere reflections of their authors.[512] The same is true of all portraits of Jesus, and in another way true of Bultmann, who sought in radical criticism to burn away the earthly Jesus in favor of an immediate knowledge of Christ. His modernistic overconfidence is apparent to us now. Paul would never have accepted Bultmann's equation of the earthly Jesus with the "historical Jesus." Precisely in the present context, it is clear that for Paul the earthly Jesus, who willingly gave himself into death for us, is the risen Lord and Christ. Furthermore, as is apparent in his instruction to the Corinthians concerning the Lord's Supper, Paul accepts and affirms *the tradition* that communicated to him the words and deeds of Jesus of which he himself had no direct knowledge (1 Cor 11:23-26). Bultmann remains subject to the autonomous individualism of the Enlightenment, which must construct the world for itself out of its own thought and labor, and which remains blind to the reality that we cannot *extract* ourselves from the traditions into which we are placed. We can only engage the world in critical reception of these traditions.[513] For that critical reception, Paul offers the word of the Gospel, which has the power to judge all things.

17 Paul again announces the effect of Christ's love at work: "As a result,

511. Bultmann, *Der Zweite Brief an die Korinther,* 156. He speaks here of Christ's "being discoverable in the world," in which manner, Paul says, we are no longer to know Christ.

512. A. Schweitzer, *The Quest of the Historical Jesus: A Critical Study of Its Progress from Reimarus to Wrede* (ed. J. M. Robinson; trans. W. B. D. Montgomery; New York: Macmillan, 1968).

513. See Bayer, *Autorität und Kritik: Zu Hermeneutik und Wissenschaftstheorie,* 59-82.

if anyone is in Christ, [there is] a new creation." Both the unusual, immediate repetition of the consecutive conjunction *(hōste)* and the repeated reference to the in-breaking of the eschaton (which Paul now identifies as the "new creation") indicate that he here returns to the thought of vv. 14-15, describing its result in a statement parallel to v. 16. He moves from a description of the effect of Christ's love on *his* judgment and perception of the world, to the work of that love within the world. As v. 18 makes clear, however, he has not ceased to speak about himself and his apostolic mission. Paul includes himself within his universal condition "if anyone is in Christ." The new creation includes the apostle. He thereby rejects any distinction between himself and any other Christian, and, indeed, any other human being. In v. 17 Paul applies the declaration of v. 16 to himself: no one is to be regarded according to what they seem to be outwardly, not even the apostle Paul himself.[514] Yet the verse obviously has broader import: all human beings are included with the apostle in the condition "if *anyone* is in Christ." Verse 17 serves as a pivot upon which Paul turns from describing himself and his conduct as an apostle (vv. 11-16) to his apostolic mission (vv. 18-21). His apostolic labor flows out of the understanding that the ground at the foot of the cross is entirely level.

The conditional "if" indicates that (1) the salvation that has been accomplished by Christ's love must be distributed to the world (this is the apostolic mission) and (2) this distribution is not universally received. The localization of salvation that we have seen elsewhere (e.g., 3:14-18) thus reappears here. The new creation has broken into the world, but not universally. It is found "in" Christ alone, namely, in the apostolic proclamation of Christ and the faith that receives that proclamation.

The thought here complements that of v. 16: Paul's knowing "no one" according to the flesh has its counterpart in his affirmation concerning "anyone" who is in Christ. Just as God was to Abraham "the One who makes alive the dead, and calls into existence that which is not," so he must be to all Christians as well (Rom 4:17). We find here a variation on the theme of Galatians: the cross and resurrection, which bring the eschaton into the world, overturn all human estimations of others.[515] In Galatians, these judgments are based on the mark of circumcision and the "works of the Law" (Gal 6:15). In Second Corinthians, these judgments are based on claims of rhetorical ability, power, and proximity to Christ. That "in Christ" there is a new creation implies that all the wisdom, power, and prestige that belong to the old creation have been judged and done away with.[516] The old must be done away

514. In Gal 2:6, 9, he correspondingly speaks of "those who seemed to be [something]."

515. Indeed, "in Christ Jesus" not only is there no longer "Jew nor Greek, slave nor free," there is no longer "male and female" (Gal 3:28).

516. Cf. 1 Cor 1:26-31.

with in order for the new to arrive. With the new, the promise of salvation arrives, setting aside the old order in its entirety, including the old covenant and its demands (3:14).[517]

The emphatic brevity of Paul's statement that is somewhat obscured in translation should not be overlooked: "If anyone is in Christ, a new creation." The abruptness of Paul's wording marks the unqualified and undiminished entrance of the eschaton into the present world. The declaration is all the more startling, given the eschatological reserve that Paul otherwise communicates to the Corinthians.[518] Even here, though, there is an implicit reserve: "*If anyone is in Christ,* [there is] a new creation." As we have noted, the inbreaking eschaton is localized. It is not found everywhere in the world. It is found in Christ, the crucified and risen Lord alone. This defining localization corresponds to Paul's abrupt declaration concerning the Spirit in 3:17: "*Where* the Spirit of the Lord is, *there* is freedom." Yet *within* this sphere of God's work in Christ, the eschaton has arrived in full force. Thus God the Creator has brought light to the apostle's heart (4:6). The "inner person" of the apostle is being renewed day by day, even if his outer person is destroyed (4:16). He has been given the Spirit, who as a "down payment" is nothing other than the reality of the eschaton in its present form (5:5). If anyone is in Christ, *(there is) a new creation,* which is known and experienced even within the present age. That this experience arrives hidden under the cross and suffering does not mean that it is not real.

Not only the brevity of Paul's statement startles, but also his remarkable juxtaposition of "person" and "creation."[519] How can it be that, if *someone* is in Christ, there is *new creation?* The predication is jarring, not only for individualistic readings of Paul, but also for all those that give priority to community or cosmology. What we tend to separate, the apostle joins. The basis of Paul's statement lies in the death and resurrection of Christ, or more precisely, in the crucified and risen Christ, who by his love possesses human beings as his own and, in re-creating them, creates his own community. In the first instance, Paul's striking juxtaposition puts us human beings in our place: we are mere "created things," mere pieces of clay into which the Creator has breathed life — and has made anew in Christ. At the same time, the re-creation of the human being implies the re-creation of all things, as the echo of the book of Isaiah in Paul's words implies. In Christ, the divine

517. Esp. Augustine and Luther emphasize the break with God's dealings with humanity in the Law. See Schmeller, *Der zweite Brief an die Korinther,* 328. Paul's corresponding statements in Gal 3:28 and 6:15 confirm this judgment.

518. E.g., 1 Cor 4:1-13; 15:12-19.

519. Thus the New Living Translation ("anyone who belongs to Christ has become a new person") does away with Paul's reference to creation. Although it retains the word "creation," the ESV makes the same reduction: "if anyone is in Christ, he is a new creation."

purpose for the human being to be ruler over creation is fulfilled; this is implicit in Paul's description of the longing of all creation for the revelation of God's "sons" in Rom 8:18-27. In that context, too, Paul describes these "sons" as those who groan for "the redemption of the body" in the hope of a new creation (Rom 8:22-23). In the present context, his focus rests on the re-creation of the human being, with whom Christ in love wills to establish a relationship of communication (vv. 14-15). This communicative relationship of persons is real. We have died with Christ. Our life is now bound to him as crucified and risen Lord in such a way that his resurrected life is ours. In the present verse, Paul describes the implications of Christ's possessing us: we already share, here and now, in the new creation that is present in him. This participation is personal, but certainly not privatistic. We share in the One who died for all. The "for me" of Christ's work is an essential dimension of the "for us," and not only of the "for us" (and thus the "for the church"), but also of the "for the creation."

Paul reinforces the startling realism of his declaration in an elaborative allusion to the book of Isaiah: "The former things have passed away, behold, new things have come to be!" The language is reminiscent of various passages in Isaiah,[520] especially Isa 43:18-19, where the Lord announces to Israel the promise of deliverance:

> Do not recall the first things, and do not contemplate the former things. Behold, One making something new! Now it springs up. Do you not recognize it? I am making a way in the wilderness, and streams in the desert.

This promise of the Creator's wondrous provision of Israel's need recalls the deliverance from Egypt, and yet it marks a decisive break in Israel's history. It announces a *new* work of God that separates Israel from its past. The Lord acts as Creator, who makes a people for himself afresh, just as he did in the exodus.[521] It should be noted that the Isaianic promise speaks only indirectly of the return from exile. It is focused on the Lord's marvelous deed of making "a way in the wilderness and streams in the desert." The lonely beasts of the wilderness thus praise him, as shall his people, to whom he shall give drink (43:20-21). The promise of return from exile does not appear as a continuous story in the book of Isaiah, but is subsumed within a series of vignettes that announce the Lord's work as Creator.[522] The same is true of Paul's varying

520. See also Isa 42:9; 48:6.

521. The past acts of the Creator thus anticipate his present work, both in the passage from Isaiah and for Paul. The "former things" (τὰ ἀρχαῖα) are not "old" (παλαιός). Rather, they serve as signs, figures, and anticipations of what the Creator now creates.

522. The Lord appears thus as a ruler (Isa 40:10; 42:10-17), the shepherd who gathers and brings his people (40:11), the one who supplies them with drink (41:17-20; 43:18-21), the

appeals to the images of return from exile in this letter (and elsewhere). All of them are subsumed within the work of God in Christ.[523] The work of the Creator determines the story of deliverance, and not the other way around.

The reference to a "new creation" also echoes the conclusion of the book of Isaiah, where the promise of something "new" appears as the promise of a new heavens and a new earth (Isa 65:17-25; 66:22). This promise, together with its entirely unexpected fulfillment, prevents Israel from imagining and saying that its idols were responsible for its salvation (Isa 48:3-8).[524] By this word of promise and its unexpected fulfillment, the Lord strips his people of their idols and establishes a new, saving relationship with them. He thus calls Israel to faith, just as Paul calls the Corinthians to reconciliation with God in the present context.

Paul underscores the radical break with the past announced in the book of Isaiah: the Lord establishes a new relationship with his people in his fresh work as Creator, a relationship in which their sin and idolatry are overcome, sorrow is done away with, and the entire order of the world is changed.[525] Paul's elaboration of the prophetic word is absolute, even more emphatic than that of Isaiah: "the old has passed away, behold new things have come to be." As we have noted, his language stands especially close to that of Isa 43:18-19, where the Lord speaks of the new realities as already present. According to Paul, the Yes to this promise, and to all the promises of God, is found in Jesus Christ, crucified and risen (1:20). The moment of fulfillment has come. The apostle marks the times by Christ's work: "from now on we know no one according to the flesh" (v. 16). Yet even for the apostle the promise fulfilled in Christ remains in the form of promise. It is not thereby reduced to some vision or ideal to which we are called to attain. As Paul's startling declaration makes clear, the new creation is present in an unqualified way in the risen Lord. The new creation thus presently takes the form of faith and hope. This does not diminish its reality in the least. As the life of the apostle makes clear, it does not thereby become a mere inward sentiment or a private contentment that may be separated from life lived. The re-created human being has been granted the capacity in Christ to see beyond the visible things of this life to those things that are invisible and eternal (4:16-18). Those who see the world in this new way "do not fail," no matter what comes to them, and in the midst of

---

one who causes them to grow as plants (44:1-5), or, conversely, the one who dries up the land and the deep (42:15; 44:27; 50:2; 51:10). The only constant in the varying images is the work of the Creator, who, contrary to all human calculations, promises, fulfills, and saves.

523. See esp. 6:2, 16-18.

524. The new thing that the Lord is doing arrives first in the form of promise: before it happens, the Lord announces it (Isa 42:9).

525. Rev 21:4-5 recalls this same complex of texts from the book of Isaiah as the voice from the throne announces the abolition of death, sorrow, lament, and pain: "The first things are past. . . . Behold, I am making all things new!"

the most contrary circumstances, they speak forth faith and hope by the Spirit who possesses them (4:13). As the apostle's battle with the Corinthians makes clear, the reality of the new creation, unseen though it is, marks the outward life of Christians. It marks all their judgments concerning others, plus all their decisions about life. Where there is a new creation, there is a new relation with God. The idols of the human heart have been stripped away, just as the Lord announces in the book of Isaiah. This new relationship with God is the new covenant, of which Paul has been made an emissary.

c. The Ministry of Reconciliation (5:18-21)

> 18 *All this is from God, who through Christ reconciled us to himself and gave us the ministry of reconciliation;* 19 *that is, in Christ*[526] *God was reconciling the world to himself, not counting their trespasses against them, and entrusting to us the message of reconciliation.* 20 *Therefore, we are ambassadors for Christ, God making his appeal through us. We implore you on behalf of Christ, be reconciled to God.* 21 *For our sake he made him to be sin who knew no sin, so that in him we might become the righteousness of God.*

At the end of a lengthy, theological description of his apostolic calling that began in 4:1, Paul now finally comes to describe his apostolic labor. It is no wonder that he takes such care in doing so. He deals in matters of ultimate significance. Through him, God works death and life itself in the world; Paul is no peddler of God's word (2:17).

Paul now speaks of himself as an agent of God. He already has made it clear that he is one called to proclaim the Gospel, the word of God, which he also bears in his person (4:1-15). This word is not idle. It performs its work in the apostle, who is therefore an occasion for "boasting" on the part of the Corinthians (5:11-13). He is not a mere spectator to God's work but a participant in it alongside the Corinthians: the love of Christ performs its work not only in the world but also in him (5:14-17).

After this long introduction, Paul now speaks of his *work*, the *mission* he has been given by God in the world, and especially with the Corinthians. This work is nothing other than the reconciliation of sinful and self-centered human beings to God. It takes place through the "word of reconciliation," the

526. There has been debate as to whether to understand the verbal form that Paul employs here as predication ("God was in Christ") or as paraphrasis ("God was reconciling the world to himself in Christ"). The latter is far more likely. This interpretation is clear, given Paul's immediately preceding periphrastic use of καταλλάξαντος in relation to God, and his following coordinate, periphrastic use of the participle θέμενος. See also the usage in 2:17 and 4:3, and probably also 5:4, 9:12.

announcement of God's work in Christ, which has been given to the apostle. As we noted earlier, here, for the first time in the letter, Paul articulates the Gospel that he proclaims, thus filling in the "christological deficit" of 2 Cor 3. His delay is indicative of the problem in Corinth and the purpose of the letter. The Corinthians continue to live within the reasoning of the world, which measures all things by visible power, success, and glory. This false reasoning, has been overcome in Christ, in whom our blindness has been conquered by the light of the Gospel. Paul has emphasized to the Corinthians the fundamental hermeneutical implications of the Gospel. This hermeneutical function of the Gospel is necessarily material in nature. It cannot be separated from the message of Christ crucified and risen. Already with his announcement that in Christ there is a new creation (v. 17), Paul has given indication that the hermeneutical effect of the Gospel has a material basis. Now he spells out that material basis more fully: God made Christ to be "sin" so that, in Christ, we might become the righteousness of God.

18 Paul again describes his coming to faith as an act of God the Creator: "all things are from God." It is God who remains constant, not "all things." They are done away with and created anew. Paul has already described God's work in salvation as that of the Creator, who causes light to shine forth from the darkness of the human heart (2 Cor 4:6). This saving Creator chooses "the things that are not, so that he might bring to nothing the things that are" (1 Cor 1:28). Nothing runs in a straight line.

Paul here characterizes, confesses, and identifies God. All things are "from the God who reconciled us to himself to through Christ." The Creator, who does away with the old and establishes the new, is God, who has reconciled "us" to himself in Christ.[527] In normal Greek usage, it is the (personal) object of the active voice form of the verb *katallassō* ("reconcile") whose enmity is done away with.[528] In other words, Paul is not speaking here of the overcoming of God's enmity against humanity, but that of the fallen humanity

527. The "us" refers to the apostle, as is clear from Paul's immediately following reference to his mission.

528. Conversely, it is the subject of the passive voice form, whose enmity is done away with, as is apparent from Paul's appeal to the Corinthians in v. 20. See also Rom 5:10; 1 Cor 7:11. On the question of the usage, see S. E. Porter, *Καταλλάσσω in Ancient Greek Literature, with Reference to the Pauline Writings* (Estudios de Filologia Neotestamentaria 5; Cordoba: El Almendro, 1994), 145-62; S. E. Porter, "Reconciliation and 2 Corinthians 5,18-21," in *Studies on 2 Corinthians* (ed. R. Bieringer and J. Lambrecht; Leuven: Leuven University Press, 1996), 693-705. *Pace* Porter (and others), however, to suppose that Paul's usage here breaks the usual pattern would require univocal and decisive evidence, which is simply lacking here. The thematic background to Paul's usage is present already in his description of Christ's death (vv. 14-15) and the arrival of the new creation (v. 17). It appears again in his summary statement about God's work of "exchange" in Christ (v. 21). Furthermore, Paul in context speaks directly of the reconciliation of the Corinthians: he acts as God's ambassador toward them (v. 20).

against God. More precisely, he is speaking of his *own* enmity against God, his "living for himself" (v. 15) that has been overcome in Christ's death and resurrection.[529] Our blindness (4:4-6) is our hatred of God, and vice versa.

Here and in the following verse, Paul speaks of God's action "through" and "in" Christ. Yet his first word concerning the cross, in vv. 14-15, was of *Christ's* love and self-giving. God's action is thus implicitly identified with Christ's action, and Christ's action is identified with that of God.

God's reconciling work through Christ on the apostle is inseparable from the mission given to the apostle, as we have seen repeatedly in the letter: God has reconciled Paul to himself *and* has given him the mission *(diakonia)* of reconciliation. Paul acts out of that which he has received. He accomplishes in the world only that which has been accomplished for the world by God in Christ.

Paul here "translates" his description of the mission of the new covenant in 2 Cor 3:7-11 into the terms of ambassadorial service. This "translation" lies at hand, since, as we have noted, *diakonia* ("mission") already signifies agency on behalf of another. The shift in terms is not merely an attempt to communicate the truth to a Hellenistic audience, but it belongs inherently to Paul's understanding and defense of the apostolic calling. His "translation" does represent, however, a shift in focus from the work of God to the work of the apostle, through whom God communicates and effects his reconciling work in Christ.

19 This verse is not repetitive, although it may seem to be so. The scope of Paul's statement broadens, as he now describes his mission. He no longer speaks directly of himself as apostle, but of the world as the object of God's reconciling work in Christ.

The difficult opening wording is to be understood as Paul's signal that he is describing his mission in a form that approximates indirect discourse or citation.[530] His statement is to be taken as a whole: the mission of reconciliation includes both (1) the announcement of the work of God in Christ and (2) the claim to apostolic authority by which it is "distributed" in word.[531] Paul has already spoken in this way: "we do not proclaim ourselves, but Jesus Christ as

529. Paul says the same in Rom 5:10: God reconciled us to himself through the *death* of his Son.

530. The ὡς ὅτι signals an indirect communication of content or indirect discourse. See 2 Cor 11:21; 2 Thess 2:2; LXX Esth 4:14; see further the examples in BDAG, "ὅτι 5b," 732.

531. *Pace* Hofius, who regards v. 19c ("and he has established in us the word of reconciliation") as a counterpart to v. 19a-b. Vv. 19b-c are to be read together ("not reckoning their trespasses . . . and establishing in us the word of reconciliation"). The distinction that Hofius wants to maintain between God's word in the act of reconciliation and the message of the apostle is established by the way in which the whole of v. 19 unpacks v. 18c ("and giving to us the mission of reconciliation"). See O. Hofius, "'Gott hat unter uns aufgerichtet das Wort von der Versöhnung' (2 Kor 5:19)," *Paulusstudien* (WUNT 51; Tübingen: Mohr Siebeck, 1989), 16-17.

Lord, and ourselves as your slaves, on account of Jesus" (4:5). The definition of the apostolic mission is included within that apostolic mission.

The issues that appear in vv. 14-15 reappear here: God was in Christ reconciling *the world* to himself. While "the world" remains God's creation, it is presently the world in rebellion against God.[532] It is that world, without exclusion or exception, that God was reconciling to himself in Christ. The enmity of this world against God has been done away with in Christ's cross and resurrection. There is thus no "condition" for the world to fulfill. In its rebellion against its Creator, it could not do so in any case. Yet it is clear that Paul does not imagine that all the world is saved. Indeed, he immediately raises the question as to whether the Corinthians themselves know the reconciling work of God. The "interruption" between God's saving work in Christ and its effect in the world that we saw in vv. 14-15 is implicit here as well.

In reconciling the world to himself, God "was not reckoning their trespasses to them." Our hostility against God manifests itself in our deeds in the world. Paul here recalls his expectation of the judgment before Christ, in which each one will receive recompense for what has been done in this life (vv. 9-10). It is significant in this conext that Paul introduces the category of "transgressions," since he otherwise, in vv. 14-15, 16-17, 21, speaks of persons. He does not speak simply of "sins." Transgressions can take place only where God's will is made known, especially as it is made known in the Law.[533] His reference to transgressions thus recalls his description of the mission of the "letter" in 2 Cor 3:7-11. It likewise makes clear that the act of reconciliation is nothing other than the act of final judgment brought into the present time in Christ. In the wonder of God's grace, this judgment in Christ does not bring our condemnation, but our reconciliation to God, in which we are made new.

As we have noted, Paul's description of his mission is to be read as a whole: "God was in Christ reconciling the world to himself, not reckoning to them their transgressions, *and placing in us the word of reconciliation.*" The mission of the apostle has been included already within the reconciling work of God in Christ. Paul here explicitly locates his word of proclamation within the completed work of God in Christ. Correspondingly, the "placement" of the word of reconciliation "in" the apostle is inherent to the mission of reconciliation. The work of God in Christ would remain isolated and distant if it were not communicated in a definite "word" *(logos)* that effects reconciliation. This "word" has been placed "in" the apostle. In the first instance, this "placement" is a commissioning of the apostle and an entrusting of this

532. See, e.g., 1 Cor 1:20, 21, 27, 28; 2 Cor 7:10.

533. Paul's infrequent use of the term παράπτωμα is largely clustered around his description of the entrance of the Law into the world in his letter to Rome (Rom 4:25; 5:15-20). See also the use of the related term παράβασις in Rom 2:23; 4:15; 5:14; Gal 3:19.

message to him.[534] For the apostle, however, to bear the message of Jesus is to bear the dying and life of Jesus in his body (4:7-15). The Gospel is to be found nowhere but in an earthen vessel (4:7). It is therefore altogether likely that, in speaking of God "placing the word in him," Paul communicates to the Corinthians that he bears the message not only in his mouth but also in his body and life. This is the central matter of the contention between them. Paul continues to speak of this embodiment of the message in his person in the following verse.

20 The apostle has been sent forth as Christ's ambassador, bearing "the word of reconciliation." The work of Christ is communicated to the world through the word given to the apostle. Again it is clear that the apostle understands the cross as an event of substitution that is simultaneously exclusive and inclusive. Paul speaks *on behalf* of the crucified and risen Christ.[535] In so speaking, *God* entreats the world through him.[536] The apostle thus serves as Christ to the world, without, of course, replacing or supplanting Christ. As in vv. 18-19, God's action is identified with Christ's action, so that Christ is implicitly identified with God.

Paul's message is simple yet profound: We appeal, on behalf of Christ, "Be reconciled to God!" The main English versions (ESV, NIV, NRSV), by the use of direct address in the second person ("We appeal *to you*"), suggest that Paul here speaks to the Corinthians. But he turns to them explicitly only in 6:1. It is far more likely that he here presents his message to all the world.

The crucified and risen Lord makes appeal through Paul, communicating his *work* to the world through the *word* of his ambassador.[537] The apostolic appeal is no call for a decision upon which everything depends. It is the communication of that which is already done and accomplished, including the decision itself.

That Paul is sent in ambassadorial service implies that a state of enmity and conflict otherwise exists between God — or indeed Christ — and the world.[538] The announcement of peace here anticipates the state of war that Paul announces in 10:3-6.

534. See, e.g., 1 Cor 9:17; Gal 2:7; 1 Thess 2:4. Rightly, Hofius, "Das Wort von der Versöhnung."

535. 4:10-11; 13:3-6.

536. The NIV wrongly interprets the particle ὡς as marking irreality rather than manner or (contemporaneous) time. It is not "as though" God were entreating through the apostle, but precisely the case that God does so, just as God has worked salvation in the crucified and risen Christ.

537. *Pace* Hofius ("Das Wort von der Versöhnung," 22), Paul simultaneously represents Christ *and* Christ speaks in him (cf. 13:3).

538. On the work of an ambassador in the Greco-Roman world, see G. Bornkamm, "πρεσβεία," *TDNT* 6:681-83; D. E. Garland, 2 *Corinthians* (NAC 29; Nashville, Tenn.: Broad-

21 Correspondingly, the apostolic announcement of the Gospel here is no mere objective report that brings salvation no matter what the response to it might be. It is bound to the apostolic appeal that precedes it ("We ask on behalf of Christ: be reconciled to God"). God's saving work in the crucified Christ overturns the false values and judgments that have captured the hearts of the Corinthians. The "word of the cross" has been at the center of the contention between the apostle and the Corinthians, at least since the writing of First Corinthians (1 Cor 1:18-25). There Paul instructs the Corinthians that, as often as they celebrate the Lord's Supper, they "proclaim the *death* of the Lord" until he comes (1 Cor 11:26). The apostle bears in his body Christ's scandalous death and — the greatest scandal of all — proclaims this death as "good news." It is this death he now interprets for the Corinthians.

Paul's declaration that God, in his work in Christ, was "not reckoning the trespasses" of the world (v. 19a) makes clear that Paul understands the reconciliation of the world to God as a forensic event. In it, the final judgment enters into the present time.[539] Paul now unfolds that event christologically, filling the "christological gap" of 2 Cor 3 in epigrammatic form:

> He made the one who did not know sin to be sin,
> in order that we might become the righteousness of God in him.

Here we find the only instance in which Paul speaks of "sin" soteriologically within the letter.[540] According to the apostle, God has effected a saving exchange in Christ, one that is irreducibly ontological: God made Christ *to be* sin, so that we might *become* the righteousness of God in him.[541] Paul's declaration of the Gospel here cannot be reduced rightly to a mere work of

---

man & Holman, 1999), 295-98; R. Vorholt, *Der Dienst der Versöhnung: Studien zur Apostolatstheologie bei Paulus* (WMANT 118; Neukirchen-Vluyn: Neukirchener Verlag, 2008), 379-84; C. Breytenbach, *Versöhnung: Eine Studie zur paulinischen Soteriologie* (WMANT 60; Neukirchen-Vluyn: Neukirchener Verlag, 1989), 65-68.

539. In this context "reconciliation" and "justification" refer to the same *event,* namely the cross and resurrection of Christ. But they bring out its significance in differing ways. The former has to do with the effecting of harmony between persons; the latter, with establishing justice and proper order within the world.

540. In 11:7 and 13:2 he speaks of committing sin.

541. Paul's language at Gal 3:13 has a remarkably similar ontological orientation, "Christ redeemed us from the curse of the Law, *having become a curse on our behalf.*" In this connection one cannot help but think of Luther's explication of Gal 3:13, in which he describes Christ as having become "the maximal sinner" *(peccator maximus):* the greatest thief, adulterer, murderer. Of course, it is not that he was such a person in himself, but he "put on our clothing and mask" — i.e., he took upon himself our sinful person in order to give us his innocent and victorious person (*LW* 26:276-80). See also Luther's description of Christ as "transferred" sin, and "the sin of God" (2 Cor 5:21), in "Contra Latomus," *LW* 32:206.

Christ.[542] Indeed, the exchange of "sin" and "righteousness" is the work of *God*, who has acted in and through Christ. Furthermore, it entails something more than *work*. It involves the very person of Christ, who, in his suffering and death, "was made sin" for us. Paul has not lost sight here of the hermeneutical function of the Gospel in overturning human perceptions and judgments, even as he presents the Gospel in material terms.[543]

This is not the first time that the Corinthians have heard Paul speak this way about God's justifying work in Christ. He announces "the word of the cross" to them in similar terms in First Corinthians. By God's doing, the Corinthians are "in" Christ Jesus, "who became for us wisdom from God, and righteousness, and sanctification, and redemption" (1 Cor 1:30).

Likewise, in 1 Cor 6:11, Paul reminds the Corinthians of God's redeeming work in related terms: ". . . but you were washed, but you were sanctified, but you were justified in the name of the Lord Jesus, and in the Spirit of our God" (1 Cor 6:11).

God's justifying work appears in these two passages as *a new existence* that is present in Christ (1 Cor 1:30), and *as an event* that has taken place for the Corinthians (1 Cor 6:11). In the present context, Paul takes up both of these perspectives, speaking of the *event* of God's work in Christ that brings our transfer into a new *existence* in Christ. It can hardly be accidental that Paul speaks in this manner about justification in the Corinthian correspondence. He is countering the false judgments of the Corinthians with the judgment of God that has taken place in the crucified and risen Christ. His appeal to God's justifying work does not have to do with mere Jewish concerns, or merely with the entrance of the Gentiles into the church. It has to do with life, death, and the judgment of the world.

According to Paul, God made Christ, "the One who knew no sin," to be sin. The reference to the cross is unmistakable. Nevertheless, in telling silence, Paul does not explicitly *name* the cross here. He instead "unveils" the cross for the Corinthians, describing the mystery of God's work that lies there. In God's saving action, Christ was put in our place. Yet Christ did not take our place in the sense of becoming merely one more sinner among other sinners. Paul is emphatic: "*the*

542. Here we should also remember that, in this context, Paul presents Christ's work as an act of love toward rebellious, self-seeking human beings, and not in the first instance as an act of obedience toward God. Of course, he also understands it as the latter (e.g., Rom 5:19). But it should not go unnoticed that here he presents Christ's redeeming act of love as a parallel to God's work in and through him (vv. 14-15, cf. 18-19). Christ acts, not merely as a human being in relation to God, but as God in relation to human beings.

543. Christ who was made sin, and in whom we become righteousness, is thus the "earnest mirror" in which we see the glory of the Lord and in which we are judged and saved. See Luther, "This earnest mirror, Christ, will not lie or trifle," *LW* 42:9 ("A Meditation on Christ's Passion," 1519).

One who knew no sin, God made to be sin on our behalf." Christ thus became the "sinless sinner."[544] In this sense, Christ's "place-taking" was exclusive and substitutionary. It is likely, in fact, that Paul's identification of Christ with sin recalls the usage of Leviticus in which the sacrificial offering for sin is identified *with the people* in their sin. The Levitical sacrifice was not merely an action or work, but entailed an identification of "being."[545] This thought is clear in Paul's words. He speaks of God making "the One who knew no sin" *to be sin.*[546] This defining description of Christ makes clear the ontological nature of the saving event.[547] It is not merely Christ's work that God offered in our place, but it is Christ himself: "God made him to *be* sin."[548]

In this verse Paul does not describe "sin" as a mere act, or even as mere guilt, but as the guilt and power of evil that have taken up residence in the human being.[549] He speaks not merely of sin as an act of transgression, but as a reality that has *possessed* the human being and has become inseparable from our person, much like the instances of demon possession that we find in the Synoptic Gospels. "Sin" has to do not merely with our *works,* but with our whole *person* in guilt and rebellion, condemned and enslaved.[550] Paul's thought here has to do with what has been traditionally called "original sin." Our salvation of necessity includes death and resurrection to new life.

Paul here describes the reality of the new creation in a manner that emphasizes the transfer and exchange that takes place in salvation. God made Christ to be what we are in order that we might "become" the righteousness of God "in him." Paul thus follows his opening allusion to Christ's cross with an allusion to Christ's resurrection. God's setting Christ in our place, namely, in condemnation and death, has as its end our being set in Christ's place in righteousness and

544. I have borrowed this expression from Michael Cameron, *Christ Meets Me Everywhere: Augustine's Early Figurative Exegesis* (New York: Oxford University Press, 2012), 143, 145.

545. See esp. Lev 16:1-34; 17:12-14. Cf. P. Stuhlmacher, *Biblische Theologie des Neuen Testaments,* vol. 1: *Grundlegung: Von Jesus zu Paulus* (Göttingen: Vandenhoeck & Ruprecht, 1992), 290-95; B. Janowski, *Sühne als Heilsgeschehen: Studien zur Sühnetheologie der Priesterschrift und zur Wurzel KPR im Alten Orient und im Alten Testament* (WMANT 55; Neukirchen: Neukirchener Verlag, 1982), 242-48, 265-71, 355-62.

546. As is well known, Paul's language here parallels that in Gal 3:13, where he speaks of Christ *becoming* a curse for us (and not merely *bearing* a curse).

547. Cf. Rom 3:20; 7:7-13.

548. It is likewise clear in Paul's following appeal to the Isaianic Servant that he has in view Christ's *person,* not merely his work (6:2; Isa 49:8). See Isa 53:10, where the Servant is identified with guilt or a guilt offering.

549. He does the same in Rom 7:7-25 and 8:3 ("[God] sending his own son . . . condemned sin in the flesh"). His language parallels the reports of demon possession in the Gospels. See esp. the story of the Gerasene demoniac (Mark 5:1-20 par. Matt 8:28-34 and Luke 8:26-39).

550. Again, the similarity to the language and thought of Rom 7:7-25 is evident.

life. Salvation takes a twofold form. In his work in Christ, God meets us where we are in "sin" and carries us into the "place" of the risen Christ, who is God's righteousness. As Paul's formulation also makes clear, this "transfer" entails a change of being. Christ was made what we *are* — in order that we might become what he *is* in his resurrected life.[551] Indeed, as we have noted, the ontological description of salvation is fundamental. Paul's first statement, that "God made him who knew no sin to be sin," announces a change of being. This action on God's part brings our transfer from within ourselves to Christ: "in order that we might become the righteousness of God in him." Salvation consists in the translation of our being from the reality of "sin" that has possessed us, to the reality of God's righteousness in Christ. God, with his "placement" of Christ into our being, picks us up in Christ's death and sweeps us up into Christ's life. The communication, or exchange, between God and the human being that constitutes salvation begins here, in Christ's taking our place, not in our seeking God.

The purpose clause "in order that we might become the righteousness of God in him" contains the productive ambiguity that runs through the entire passage. On the one hand, from the perspective of God's work in Christ, the purpose has been fulfilled. God has reconciled the world to himself in Christ (v. 19). Paul goes on to describe the Corinthians themselves as "righteousness" and to identify them with Christ (6:14-15). At the same time, the work of God is distributed through the word given to the apostle, who calls the Corinthians afresh to be reconciled with God (v. 20). The purpose clause thus contains an implicit call to this reconciliation. The Corinthians are to "become the righteousness of God" in Christ, not by any work or moral endeavor of their own, but simply by receiving the grace of God given to them in Christ, as Paul exhorts them to do in the following passage (6:2). We cannot remake ourselves. We must be remade by God in Christ.

Paul here describes the new life given in Christ as "the righteousness of God," echoing his description of the new covenant that brings life and righteousness (3:6-11). In so speaking, he obviously refers to the new creation that has broken into the world in Christ, which he has already announced in v. 17. The themes of creation and righteousness are likewise connected in the book of Isaiah.[552] In identifying this "new creation" as "the righteousness of God," Paul recalls the context of the Lord's announcement of a "new creation" in the book of Isaiah, which celebrates "God's righteousness" as an act of judgment and deliverance granted to God's people and, indeed, to all creation.[553] In this act of judgment, the Lord reveals *what* is right and, in so doing, reveals that

551. Cf. Rom 8:29-30.

552. See Isa 42:1, 3, 9; 43:18-19, 26; 48:1, 6, 18.

553. See esp. Isa 42:6; 43:26; 45:8, 13, 19, 21, 23, 24; 50:8; 51:4-8; 53:11. Similar usage appears in the Psalms. Some examples appear in the following footnote.

he is right, over against all unbelief and idolatry. The Lord is the one true God, Ruler and Creator, who fulfills his promises for his people and for the world, in saving judgment.[554] The "righteousness of God" is thus simultaneously God's act of judgment and the justification of God. This sense of the expression is clear in the present context, where Paul speaks of "sin," not merely as the work of human beings, but as their identity, and correspondingly speaks of "the righteousness of God," not merely as God's act, but also as *God's identity.* This identity, which both calls for and effects the recognition of God, has been manifest in the crucified and risen Christ. There we meet God savingly and participate in a relationship of exchange and communication, in which there is no confusion of Creator and creature.

Paul's use of the expression "righteousness of God" thus presupposes an act of judgment and revelation that establishes *saving communication* between God and humanity. As we have noted, this communication appears here in the form of transfer and exchange: just as Christ was made to be sin, fallen human beings *become* the righteousness of God in Christ. They are made new in such a way that *their very being* is an announcement of God as the one, true saving Creator and Lord. Paul takes up this thought shortly in 6:14, when he warns the Corinthians to break with unbelievers: there can be no sharing between "righteousness" and "lawlessness." By virtue of God's work in Christ, the Corinthians *are* "righteousness." Even their faith is the work of God and not their own work. This new reality does not entail an "infusion" or "impartation" of righteousness, nor an "essential" indwelling of divine righteousness. It is best described as a transfer, a relocation of our persons to a "place" outside ourselves: the righteousness of God is found "in Christ." As is more than obvious in this letter, the Corinthians do not have this righteousness in themselves, but in Christ, in whom the exchange of life and death has taken place. Paul calls them to be reconciled to God afresh in this very context (5:18-21). His description of God's justifying work here corresponds to his message to the Corinthians throughout the letter: God's saving work in Christ cannot be separated from the person of Christ — incarnate, crucified, and risen.

Paul's language concerning justification here varies from the way that Protestants generally speak of justification as Christ's righteousness as imputed to believers.[555] This is not to say that this Protestant terminology is entirely at

554. Pss 7:17; 35:28; 40:9-10; 71:2; 98:2; Isa 42:4; 43:8-13; 45:22-25; 51:4-8.

555. Although Melanchthon developed the description of justification as "the imputation of Christ's righteousness" in the 1530s, it was the internal Protestant debate with Andreas Osiander (who understood justification as based upon the divine presence of Christ indwelling the believer) that brought it into its enduring prominence. That formulation was a change over against Luther, who speaks instead of God's imputing righteousness (or not imputing sin) on account of faith, or on account of Christ, who is present within faith. Luther understands "justification" as a forensic *act* of God by which he creates the human being anew in Christ

odds with Paul. As we have seen, he understands the righteousness given to believers as located in Christ and thus abidingly extrinsic to them. Furthermore, he understands Christ's cross and resurrection as a forensic event: just as "the letter" effects our condemnation and death, so God effects our righteousness and life in Christ. As a *forensic* event, it entails an act of imputation. Indeed, Paul's language of "God's reckoning [*or* imputing] righteousness," which appears elsewhere, and especially prominently in Rom 4, underscores the personal dimension of God's justifying work; by his word of promise, now fulfilled in Christ, God receives and accepts us just as we are. Nevertheless, Paul here obviously does not speak of a bare declaration. He speaks of a forensic *event*. Furthermore, he does not merely speak of the work of salvation; he "locates" salvation in the person of the crucified and risen Christ. What the apostle says in the present verse cannot rightly be reduced to the idea of an imputed righteousness. He speaks of the human being created anew *in Christ*.[556]

At least two observations are of importance in this matter. First, as we have noted, Paul's understanding of justification is decidedly forensic and extrinsic, as Protestants are concerned to insist. We do not have our righteousness in ourselves, but only in relation to the crucified and risen Christ, who has made us his own. Against its own intention, however, the traditional Protestant understanding can lead to the false assumption that "justification" has become an inherent possession of the Christian. Once justification is understood simply as a bare imputation or declaration, the righteousness credited to the believer may be regarded wrongly as "money in the bank." It may become a sort of intrinsic possession, even if it is not based on an intrinsic moral quality. The very concern to affirm the extrinsic nature of justification may then be undermined. It was in response to such a misunderstanding that Bonhoeffer wrote his *Cost of Discipleship*:

> The essence of grace, we suppose, is that the account has been paid in advance; and, because it has been paid, everything can be had for nothing. Since the cost was infinite, the possibilities of using and spending it are infinite. What would grace be if it were not cheap?[557]

---

by the word of the Gospel. Correspondingly, "faith" for Luther is not finally a performance of the human being but a performance of God within the human being, an act of creation. On this topic, see F. Nüssel, *Allein aus Glauben: Zur Entwicklung der Rechtfertigungslehre in der konkordistischen und frühen nachkonkordistischen Theologie* (Forschungen zur systematischen und ökumenischen Theologie 95; Göttingen: Vandenhoeck & Ruprecht, 2000), 20-61.

556. If the usual Protestant terminology presupposes a legal framework of "righteousness" understood as distributive justice, within which God's love brings salvation, the apostle operates from a framework constituted by God's saving righteousness, which by no means overlooks human sin and guilt but judges it and overcomes it in Christ.

557. Bonhoeffer, *The Cost of Discipleship*, 43.

According to Paul, in contrast, our righteousness is found only in an abiding relationship of communication with Christ. Paul thus calls the Corinthians to be reconciled afresh to God (v. 20) and warns them against "receiving" the announcement of the Gospel, i.e. "the grace of God," in vain (6:1-2). Justification is not found in a *bare* declaration (which must be believed to be effective, in any case) but in a relation, an apprehension or grasping of the crucified and risen Christ.[558] Or in terms closer to those of Paul here, justification is found in the "transfer" of our person into Christ, through the exchange that has taken place in him. God's justifying declaration remains, so to speak, clothed in the crucified and risen Christ and is not to be found outside of him.[559] Because Christ has taken on our identity, we have been given his, not in a merging or mixing of persons or beings, but in a relationship of communication.[560] To be justified *by* faith is to be justified *in* the very form of faith.[561] This communication takes the form of the paradox that we have seen already. The faith that grasps the word is a work of that word: Paul says as much when he announces that God has reconciled the world to himself in Christ, and then he calls the Corinthians to be reconciled to God. In Paul's understanding, then, justification is fully forensic and declaratory. As an *event*, however, it includes the reality of the new creation that has been effected by God in Christ, apart from any work or quality in us — indeed, in spite of who we are and what we continue to do in our unbelief.

Second, the usual understanding of "justification by faith" must be grounded in one way or another within a more comprehensive understanding

558. Luther's image of faith as a ring that clasps Christ as a gem is useful here. See *LW* 40:89, 132.

559. Luther's picture of our marriage as a "poor harlot" to Christ, the rich bridegroom, comes close to Paul's thought. See Luther, *LW* 31:351-52 ("The Freedom of a Christian").

560. Luther's note, added to a letter of Melanchthon to Johannes Brenz on May 12, 1531, is indicative of his understanding of justification and of the distance of his thought from that of Melanchthon. It is worth citing here because Luther appeals to our very text:

> I, too, in order to grasp this matter better, picture for myself that there is nothing in my heart of this quality, which might be called faith or love, but rather in its place, I set Christ himself, and say: this is my righteousness, he himself is the quality and my formal righteousness (as they say), in order that I free myself from looking upon the Law and works, and even from looking at the object itself, Christ, insofar as he is understood as a teacher or giver of gifts. But I want him to be for me the gift and teaching in himself, in order that I might have all things in him. Thus he says, "I am the way, the truth, and the life." He does not say, "I give you the way, the truth, and the life," as if it were at work within me from without. It is necessary for him to be, to live, and to speak, not through me, but in me (εἰς ἐμέ) 2 Cor 6[5]: in order that we might become righteousness in him, not in love or in the gifts that follow (sc. faith). (*Corpus Reformatorum* 2:501)

561. See Nüssel, *Allein aus Glauben,* 50.

of salvation. It does not in itself answer the question of the origin, basis, and nature of faith, or that of the new obedience of the Christian. The interpretation of "justification by faith" as the imputation of Christ's righteousness through the instrument of faith requires supplementation. It does not finally answer the question as to why and how "faith" is not to be regarded as a human performance (or work) upon which salvation is contingent.[562] The same is true of the question of the obedience of the Christian, which we have touched on above.[563] Traditionally, both of these questions have been addressed by the construction of an *ordo salutis* into which "justification" is then embedded. The alternative, which has been taken up in varying ways and measures within Protestant tradition, is to locate "justification" *within* a "union" with Christ.[564] These are the two simple interpretive choices that present themselves: justification either is to be defined in terms of *God's work* in *Christ,* or it is to be defined in terms of the *individual recipient* of salvation and thus described within an *ordo salutis.* Although the appeal to "union with Christ" is not without its dangers, to the extent that it is founded on explicit biblical language, it is surely to be preferred to logical constructions that do not appear explicitly in the biblical text. The construction of an *ordo salutis* around the individual human being is especially fraught with difficulty in that Paul here and elsewhere does not present the human being as a "constant" in salvation, but as one who is put to death and made alive in Christ.

Finally, it may be noted that Protestant understandings of justification often are based simply on the obedience of Jesus as a human being over against God. Jesus' deity comes into view only as it helps his humanity, and it gives his act of obedience sufficient depth to answer human guilt in God's presence. The current tendency to interpret Paul's Gospel in terms of "the faith(fulness) of Jesus" or the image of God (as it has appeared in Jesus' obedience) may be re-

562. As is esp. clear in Romans, Paul understands faith as the fundamental obedience of the human being, and unbelief as the fundamental sin (Rom 1:5; 3:3, 31; 6:17; 10:16; 14:23; 15:18; 16:19, 26). To describe faith as a mere "instrument" is to risk overlooking its primacy. Luther, in contrast, whose understanding of justification is determined by union with Christ through faith, is able to appropriate this essential dimension of Paul's thought, since he understands faith as the reality of the new creation worked by the word of the Gospel. He does not need to relegate "faith" to an instrumental role, because he proceeds from God's work in Christ, not from the human being. Indeed, Luther speaks of Christ as instrumental to faith (see, e.g., *LW* 26:133-34, 274), and of faith as the one true obedience to God (see, e.g., his exposition of the First Commandment in the Large Catechism, WA 30/1:400-401).

563. On these questions and the development of Lutheran thought in the later sixteenth and seventeenth centuries, see again Nüssel, *Allein aus Glauben,* 20-61.

564. Here it is critical to note that, for Paul, the exchange with Christ that constitutes justification is nothing other than the faith that "receives" this grace of God. "Union" with Christ does not take place prior to a pronouncement of justification (as it did with Osiander). Nor does it take place subsequent to the justification of the sinner, as it did in most of the *ordines salutis* constructed by Protestants.

garded as a reaction against this traditional understanding.[565] As we have seen, however, Paul speaks here (and elsewhere) of the effecting of righteousness as *God's work,* just as he earlier has described salvation as an act of *Christ's love* toward fallen humanity (vv. 14-15). As is recognized widely, justification for Paul is not merely a transaction directed toward God. It is also God's action toward us, namely, the overcoming of our sin and the communication of God's righteousness to us in Christ.[566] Justification is the whole of the Christian life, viewed from the perspective of our relationship with God; or more precisely, the triumph of the saving God in his contention with us.[567] We remain Christ's sin, since he has none of his own; Christ remains our righteousness, since we have none of our own. Paul's way of describing justification here (and elsewhere) tells us *where* we are to find help, comfort, and assurance in a way that otherwise often is obscured.

4. *The Appeal to the Corinthians (6:1–7:16)*

As we have noted, Paul builds the body of the letter around his failed visit to the Corinthians, which prompted his decision not to complete his promised visit but to send Titus to them instead.[568] The framework of the body itself, with Paul's interruption of his account of his distress over the Corinthians while in Troas (2:12-13) and with his closing resumption of his narrative of

565. See, e.g., Wright, *Jesus and the Victory of God,* 608-11. Wright correspondingly reads Paul as speaking of himself being made into "the righteousness of God," i.e., an embodiment of God's covenant faithfulness in his apostolic work. This reading of the "we" in v. 21 entails, however, an unwarranted deflection from the apostolic appeal to the world that Paul voices in v. 20: "we ask on behalf of Christ, be reconciled to God." V. 21 does not turn attention to the apostle but instead supplies the content of the proclamation that brings that appeal. It is clear, moreover, that the "righteousness" of the apostle is not that which he works but that which he "suffers" by God's work in him. Indeed, Wright's linking of "righteousness" to "faithfulness" means that, while all believers are righteous, some are more righteous than others (N. T. Wright, "On Becoming the Righteousness of God," in *Pauline Theology,* vol. 2: *1 and 2 Corinthians* [ed. D. M. Hay; Minneapolis: Fortress, 1993], 206-8).

566. As is apparent from the current debate, the former understanding of justification is problematic insofar as "faith" becomes a minimal performance on the part of the human being that is necessary for salvation. This problem is accentuated when, as is now common, "faith" is understood as "faithfulness," namely, "the faithfulness of Christ," in which we share. Justification then becomes dependent on the change worked in us, and the question must arise: "How much change is enough?"

567. "Sanctification" is likewise the whole of salvation, viewed from the perspective of our relationship with the world — or more precisely, our recognition of the claim of the transcendent God upon our body and life.

568. See pp. 69-82.

Titus's visit with them (7:2-16), shows how fully his argument is directed to his immediate relationship with the Corinthians.

Paul's closing appeal, a summary of the argument of the letter up to this point, is to be understood in this light. His rejoicing over the Corinthians' positive reception of Titus is to be seen in the light of the immediate tensions between Paul and the church; it by no means signals that the troubles within the church had been overcome. This is clear from Paul's appeal to the Corinthians to receive him (6:11-13). He addresses them here as if nothing at all had been resolved in their relationship and supposes that the false alliances that the Corinthians had formed still remained. Already here Paul's language about the opponents is critical and condemning, even if they appear only indirectly and briefly within his appeal (6:14–7:1). The apostle knows that one swallow does not a summer make. He praises the Corinthians for their response to Titus in the highest terms, and does so not merely for rhetorical effect but out of confidence in the Gospel and genuine love for them, which he also wishes to communicate (7:2-16). He knows that much remains to be resolved, and he reserves his most pointed rhetoric for the closing of the letter (10:1–13:10). In the present context it is more important for him to build upon that which he is able to build. Construction, not demolition, constitutes his true work as apostle (13:10).

His first appeal to the Corinthians is nothing other than his apostolic call to be reconciled to God, expressed in terms of their present need (6:1-10). This reconciliation to God and reception of the apostolic proclamation cannot take place, however, without the reconciliation of the Corinthians to the apostle himself. In this context, Paul commends himself to the Corinthians at length (6:3-10). As is apparent from his very grammar, however, this "self-commendation" is subordinate to God's work through the Gospel, of which Paul is a messenger not only in word but also in body and life. The commendation comes in terms that the Corinthians do not request or expect.

a. The Appeal to Receive God's Grace (6:1-10)

6 1 *Working together with him, then, we appeal to you not to receive the*
grace of God in vain. 2 *For he says,*

> *In a favorable time I listened to you,*
> *and in a day of salvation I have helped you.*

Behold, now is the favorable time; behold, now is the day of salvation.
3 *We put no obstacle in anyone's way, so that no fault may be found with*
our ministry, 4 *but as servants of God we commend ourselves in every way:*
by great endurance, in afflictions, hardships, calamities, 5 *beatings, impris-*

onments, riots, labors, sleepless nights, hunger; [6]by purity, knowledge, patience, kindness, the Holy Spirit, genuine love; [7]by truthful speech, and the power of God; with the weapons of righteousness for the right hand and for the left; [8]through honor and dishonor, through slander and praise. We are treated as impostors, and yet are true; [9]as unknown, and yet well known; as dying, and behold, we live; as punished, and yet not killed; [10]as sorrowful, yet always rejoicing; as poor, yet making many rich; as having nothing, yet possessing everything.

6:1 God's work in the apostle does not leave the apostle idle, but brings him to action: "And working together [with God] we appeal." Paul's work corresponds to the work of God, who makes appeal through him (5:20). Just as God reconciled the world to himself through Christ, God now makes appeal through the apostle.

Up to this point, Paul has been describing his apostolic mission within the world. With his adverbial modifier, Paul emphatically now turns to the Corinthians: "we *also* appeal that *you* not receive the grace of God in vain." Even though he quite clearly refers to himself, he continues to employ the plural form in self-reference throughout his defense of his apostolic ministry. He thus sets himself among all those who serve the Gospel, especially other apostles. Only when the matter becomes quite specific, in his praise for the Corinthians in their reception of Titus, does he shift to the singular form of self-reference (7:2-16).

The apostle is not afraid to address the Corinthians as unbelievers, even though he appeals to them explicitly as believers within a few lines (6:14–7:1). The turn away from the world and toward God is not behind them once and for all. It still lies before them.

"Grace" here is the gift of God in Christ, including the Gospel, which the Corinthians have heard from the apostle and, in this sense, have received.[569] The question that remains is whether or not they have believed the Gospel that they have received. In which Christ do they believe? Is it the crucified Christ, whom the apostle proclaims, or another Christ?[570] In addressing the Corinthians as unbelievers, Paul is not setting a condition to God's grace. This is clear from his description of Christ's effective, saving work (5:14-15) and from his earlier paradigmatic description of his conversion as an act of God the Creator (4:6). It is instead the case that the effective work of God in Christ and its uneven distribution meet in the Corinthians. From the perspective of

569. While Paul is able to distinguish between "gift" and "grace," he also speaks concretely of χάρις as a gift (in which the act of giving is included and emphasized). See, e.g., Rom 1:5; 12:3, 6; 1 Cor 1:4; 2 Cor 1:15; 8:1, 4, 6, 7, 19. See also the discussion at 8:1, p. 319 below.

570. See 11:4.

the work of God, Paul is confident of their salvation.[571] Their recent response to Titus provides him an occasion to express his confidence in them (7:4). In the face of their betrayal of the Gospel and allegiance to the opposing apostolic claimants, Paul questions their salvation.

2 Paul explains his apostolic "co-operation" with God *christologically* by citing the book of Isaiah, specifically, the second Servant Song (Isa 49:8). Paul interprets the text in reference to Christ, who also appealed to God and was delivered — yet not apart from his death on the cross.[572] The pattern of Christ's experience reappears in the apostle, who bears the deadness of Jesus in his body (6:3-10).

It is probably best to understand the formula by which Paul introduces the citation as referring to God himself (and not indirectly to Scripture), since Paul has just spoken of God in v. 1. It is the voice of the Lord that speaks in the Isaiah citation. Paul thus omits the Isaianic introductory formula "thus says the Lord" but retains its sense: "for *he* [namely, the Lord] says. . . ."

The citation presents the Lord's response to the lament of the Servant that all his labor and effort have been in vain, even though his justice *(mishpat)* and recompense lie with "his God." The Servant's complaint corresponds to the leitmotif of Isa 40–54: the Lord's promise shall have its fulfillment in the wondrous deliverance of Israel from exile and oppression, which arrives as a new creation contrary to all human possibilities and expectations.[573] Out of hopelessness, darkness, and death, the Lord brings forth salvation, light, and

571. E.g., 1:3-7, 21-22.

572. Against, e.g., Harris, *The Second Epistle to the Corinthians,* 461-63, and Thrall, *The Second Epistle to the Corinthians,* 1:452-53, the citation does not refer to the Corinthians, at least not in the first instance. Against W. J. Webb, *Returning Home: New Covenant and Second Exodus as the Context for 2 Corinthians 6.14–7.1* (JSNTSupp 85; Sheffield: JSOT Press, 1993), 138, Paul does not identify the Isaianic Servant with himself, but with Christ. The citation of Isa 49:8 ("in an acceptable time I heard you") does not explain the mission of the apostle ("working together [with God,] we also appeal . . ."; v. 1a); rather, Paul here speaks of the "grace of God" (6:1b), which is found in Christ, crucified and risen (5:21). The reference to Christ is esp. clear in 6:2, where Paul announces, "*Now* is the acceptable time, *now* is the day of salvation." The fulfillment of the Lord's word has taken place in the resurrection of Christ (see 5:21b), not in the apostle, who remains subject to suffering and death (6:3-10).

573. See p. 253. The Servant announces and brings deliverance as the recipient of deliverance; the Servant's gathering of Israel arises from the salvation that has arrived for the Servant himself in the wake of his failed labor (Isa 49:1-12). For this reason the Servant himself is a "covenant" for the people (v. 8). Indeed, the Servant's word, like the word of the Lord itself, is an "effective word" that performs what it says; the call to the prisoner to come forth (49:9) has its counterpart in the Servant's *bringing forth* the prisoners (42:7). The return from exile is a work of the Creator, in which human creatures are mere objects. This is first true of the Servant, and then of Israel. It is not Israel's return from exile that is the controlling paradigm in Isaiah, but the works of the Creator in promise and fulfillment. Correspondingly, for Paul, the

life. In the immediate context of the book of Isaiah, the Lord responds to the lament of his Servant with a lengthy promise that contains the words that Paul cites: "At an accepted time I heard you, and in a day of salvation, I helped you" (Isa 49:8).[574] These opening words of the Lord's response assert the fundamental significance and, indeed, the crucial timing of the Lord's work: salvation requires waiting in patience and hope.

The expression "time of acceptance" contains a play upon the word "acceptance" *(dektos)*, facilitated by the Greek usage of the Septuagint. On the one hand, the term expresses the idea that the "time" or "moment" is the one that is pleasing and acceptable to the Lord.[575] Time here is of the essence. On the other hand, the parallelism of the expressions "time of acceptance" and "day of salvation" signals the sense found in the Hebrew text: the "time of acceptance" is the time in which God accepts the Servant and his lament, shows him favor, and delivers him.[576] The two conceptions are, in fact, bound together. Because the Lord rescues the Servant out of — and not prior to — despair, defeat, and death, salvation truly arrives for the Servant. Against all appearance and expectation, the Lord promises and fulfills, creating light out of darkness, making streams in the desert and a path in the sea.[577] Otherwise, as the Lord admonishes, Israel would say to itself that its idol, the work of its hands, had brought it deliverance.[578] This pattern of God's work likewise appears in the Psalms: the "when" and "how" of deliverance and grace lies in God's hands, not ours.[579] God works joy in sorrow, hope in hopelessness, life in death. In this way our idolatry is overcome, and we are granted the knowledge of God.

Another decisive dimension of God's work appears in Paul's use of the text. In the original context, the word of the Lord to his Servant takes the form of a "prophetic perfect." Out of the certainty of the promise, what the Lord announces is spoken of as if it has already taken place.[580] In the apostolic proclamation the moment of fulfillment has arrived. What the Lord promised

---

story of the crucified and risen Christ is the interpretive pattern for all of Scripture, including the return from exile.

574. The wording of Paul's citation does not vary from the Septuagintal rendering, which, in turn, corresponds closely to the Hebrew text.

575. Even if the wordplay is not present in the Hebrew text, the understanding that the time in which the Lord acts is one of the Lord's own choosing is essential to the thought found in the text.

576. See the parallel usage in Isa 61:1-2.

577. See Isa 41:17-20; 42:16; 43:16; 45:7; 51:10.

578. Isa 48:3-5.

579. See, e.g., Ps 69:13, "time of acceptance"; 102:13; 105:19, and the similar descriptions of the creation waiting for the good gifts of the Creator (104:27; 145:15).

580. The Hebrew perfect forms are thus taken up by the Septuagintal reading and by Paul as aorists with the temporal markers inherent to the utterance.

his Servant has *now* come to pass in Christ. Again, time is of the essence. Paul thus announces with breathtaking boldness: "Behold, *now* is the well-accepted time! Behold, *now* is the day of salvation!" The apostle thereby recalls the decisive "now" of the new creation that God has effected in Christ, the entrance of "the righteousness of God" into the present. *Now* is the time of salvation — the sufferings of the apostle, those of all the oppressed in this world, the rebellion of the Corinthians, and that of the entire world notwithstanding.

Paul thus strikingly explains his appeal to the Corinthians (second-person plural) not to receive God's grace in vain by means of the Lord's promise to his Servant (second-person singular). Indeed, in the Isaianic context, the Lord names the Servant himself as a "covenant of [*or* for] the people" (Isa 42:6; 49:6). The salvation that comes to the Servant is a sign of salvation for all Israel. Paul's implicit reference to the crucified and risen Christ is evident. Christ, whose justice rested with God, is the one whose labor appeared to be in vain. Paul's earlier allusive reference to "the new creation" announced by the Lord to Israel in exile[581] and his identification of the risen Christ as "the righteousness of God" (5:21)[582] express the thematic that now becomes explicit in this citation. Paul points to the promise of "the righteousness of God," the deliverance from enemies, and the bringing about of justice, as it now has been fulfilled in the crucified and risen Christ. The Corinthians are to find their life, identity, and future in him. Just as the Servant appears within the book of Isaiah as a figure who is simultaneously individual and yet embodies Israel, so Christ remains distinct and yet incorporates within himself all who believe and belong to him. The salvation of the Corinthians is found solely in the help and deliverance that God has granted to Jesus.

Jesus, the Servant, was placed within a relationship of saving communication with God. The promise of justice for which he waited lay hidden and appeared vain, despite all his labors. He made his lament known to God, who *heard* him and answered him with salvation.[583] Paul thus invites the Corinthians to enter into the relationship of saving communication with God that has been worked for them in the crucified and risen Christ. In his person, their sin has been overcome and done away with. In his person, they have been granted righteousness, life, and salvation. The theme of saving communication that we have seen elsewhere in the letter appears here in full force. In order to enter into that communication, the Corinthians must close their eyes to the outward and visible suffering of Christ and his apostle, and against all appearance they must open their ears to the apostolic message: "*Now* is the day of salvation!"

581. See 5:17; cf. Isa 43:18-19; 51:16.

582. Cf. Isa 42:6; 45:8-25; 46:12-13; 50:8; 51:5-8.

583. The Gospel tradition recalls the cry of dereliction, in which Jesus out of the depths of misery echoes the words of the psalmist. See Mark 15:34 (Ps 22:1).

In a way that does not appear readily in English translation, Paul's wording itself suggests this relationship of communication and exchange. His appeal to the Corinthians in v. 1 might be rendered, "We appeal to you not *to accept* the grace of God in vain." Here "accept" is to be understood in the sense of "receive" or "experience the arrival of." The same word-root appears in the text of Isaiah that Paul cites. The Lord promises an "acceptable time." And Paul correspondingly announces that "now is the well-accepted time." God's saving work of reconciliation effects communication with the fallen human being. Just as God has granted salvation in the time acceptable to him in the deliverance of the crucified Christ — and not before the crucifixion — so Paul calls the Corinthians not to "experience the arrival of" this grace of God in vain. In the crucified and risen Christ, God has established the place in which he accepts and receives fallen humanity, and where the enmity and rebellion of humanity have been overcome. In Christ we meet and accept God in his grace.

It is important to see that Paul does not here present Jesus, the Servant, as a *mere* moral example, to which we are to be conformed. Both in the book of Isaiah and in Paul's identification of Jesus with the Servant, the Servant is before all else the object of divine deliverance. The Isaianic drama centers upon the promises of the Lord that have seemingly come to nothing for the Servant. The time of *waiting,* to which Paul points, is essential to the story. Out of emptiness and vanity, out of nothingness, the Lord creates life and salvation. He delivers his Servant out of oppression, injustice, and death itself. It is as the object of deliverance and salvation — and not as a moral exemplar — that the Lord makes his Servant a "light to the nations" (Isa 42:6; 49:6). In this very same sense, light arises upon Israel and Jerusalem, so that the nations are drawn to them (60:1-3). The crucified and risen Christ is our deliverance, the "place" where we, in all our misery and failures, savingly meet God.

EXCURSUS: PAUL'S LIST OF HARDSHIPS — AND THE WORKS OF GOD

What follows in vv. 3-10 is Paul's "self-commendation," not in terms of his person or gifts as the Corinthians would have expected, but as an agent of reconciliation and an emissary of God. Paul expresses the subordination of his person to his mission grammatically: vv. 4-10 contain a series of participles that parallel his opening use of the participle "working together [with God]" and that are thus likewise subordinate to the main verb in v. 1: "we appeal to you." Paul's self-commendation lies in his "co-operation" with God, a co-operation in which the work of God determines Paul's life and work. In this co-operation, the apostle "suffers" rather than accomplishes God's work. This "suffering" co-operation is his mission, his *diakonia* (vv. 1, 4).

Paul's commendation correspondingly takes the unique form of a list that combines hardships, "virtues," and expressions of God's power.[584] Whether we should speak of "virtues" in this list remains a question, since the qualities Paul names are neither acquired nor infused habits but the presence of Christ himself, as Paul's reference to the Spirit and the power and work of God make clear.[585] All of these qualities, hardships, and references to God's power that Paul names serve his appeal to the Corinthians not to receive the grace of God in vain (v. 1), and they correspondingly prepare for his appeal that they open their hearts to him (vv. 11-13). The reception of God's grace in Christ and the reception of the suffering apostle cannot be separated.

The hardships that Paul names here recalls the list of 4:7-15 and prepares for the following list of hardships within the "fool's speech" (11:22–12:10). In the former passage, he stresses the paradoxical nature of God's work in his weakness and suffering, especially the bringing forth of life out of death. In the latter passage, he counters the apostolic claim of his opponents by recounting his labors, trials, and sufferings. In the present text the two forms meet: Paul closes the list by underscoring the twofold experience of the work of God in his suffering and labor, which likewise brings a twofold reception within the world.[586] The pairings in vv. 8-10 subtly recall the twofold work of God through the apostle within the world, which bring not only life but also death

584. The combination is clearly unique to Paul. It stands apart from the Stoic lists that consisted either of virtues or of hardships, even though Stoics associated virtues closely with the endurance of hardships. See M. Ebner, *Leidenslisten und Apostelbrief: Untersuchungen zu Form, Motivik und Funktion der Peristasenkataloge bei Paulus* (FB 66; Würzburg: Echter, 1991), 297. In this way, J. T. Fitzgerald's comparison of Paul's lists and those of the Stoics must be qualified, as he himself recognizes, even if he does explore the significance of this profound difference (*Cracks in an Earthen Vessel: An Examination of the Catalogues of Hardships in the Corinthian Correspondence* [SBLDS 99; Atlanta: Scholars Press, 1988], 206). See further a critique of Fitzgerald's reading of Paul as similar to Stoic thought: W. Shi, *Paul's Message of the Cross as Body Language* (WUNT 2/254; Tübingen: Mohr Siebeck, 2008), 187-224.

585. Also in this way, Paul's list differs decisively from the Stoic lists of virtues, despite formal similarities. Its content reflects the experience of Christ and thereby of God's suffering people, including the Suffering Servant of the book of Isaiah. See K. T. Kleinknecht, *Der leidende Gerechtfertigte: Die alttestamentlich-jüdische Tradition vom "leidenden Gerechten" und ihre Rezeption bei Paulus* (WUNT 13; Tübingen: Mohr Siebeck, 1984), 263-68, 365-76.

586. The list likewise recalls the one that appears in 1 Cor 4:9-13 and, in fact, comes close to it in the paradoxical form with which it closes. The references to Paul's personal qualities and the operation of the Gospel are lacking in this earlier list. Paul furthermore here contrasts his experience with that of the Corinthians in his paradoxical pairings. The argument is much the same but more sharply put in this earlier text.

(2:15-16). Everything depends on the reception of the apostolic message borne by the messenger in both word and life.

Verses 3-10 fall into three units marked by three differing introductory terms ("in," "through," and "as"). The first unit (vv. 3-6), the lengthiest of the three, contains a two-part introductory statement that provides the interpretation of all that follows (vv. 3-4a) and thus explains Paul's unique joining of hardships, "virtues," and references to God's power within his list.

This first unit of the list, with its eighteen elements, begins with the quality of "perseverance" and then presents a ninefold description of the apostle's labors and sufferings in plural forms (vv. 4c-5). Paul then returns to name four qualities of his conduct (v. 6a-d), interrupting the list with a reference to the Holy Spirit (v. 6e) and completing it with the quality of "love without hypocrisy" (v. 6f). He then concludes the list with reference to "the word of truth" and "the power of God" (v. 7a-b). The nine hardships are thus sandwiched unevenly between six references to qualities of Paul's person. The three final, emphatic references to the Spirit, Word, and power of God overlap these qualities. Paul thereby stresses the work of God in him that not only subjects him to danger and trouble but also keeps him from "failing" (4:1, 16). Just as the sufferings of Christ overflow to the apostle, so does comfort (1:5).

The second unit of the list, the briefest, picks up the references to God's power as it is operative in the Gospel (vv. 7c-8). Paul now introduces three descriptions of his *activity* by use of the preposition "through," underscoring his own role in seeking to avoid causing offense at the apostolic mission. These descriptions take the form of paradoxical pairings, which emphasize the battle for the Gospel within the world and the unexpected form that battle takes.

Paul then closes the list with seven pairs of references to his own person, introduced by the adverbial conjunction "as." He remains at the center of the contention, but his self-descriptions go well beyond his own person and powers. The apostle is the battleground for the Gospel. It is not he who is being tested, but the Gospel that is being tested in him. The Gospel provides its own occasions for offense within the world, which the apostle cannot, and will not, hinder.

---

3 This verse is a direct continuation of Paul's preceding statements: the participles in vv. 3-4 correspond to the opening participle in v. 1. Paul provides no occasion for "stumbling," lest the mission entrusted to him come into reproach. He here recalls his opening "boast" that he has conducted himself "in simplicity and purity" in the world (1:12-14). At the same time, his claim is highly ironic. The Corinthians have, in fact, taken offense at Paul and his mission. Paul himself underscores this offense in the paradoxical pairings that make up the second half of his list (vv. 7c-10). The Gospel manifest in his life and hardships remains hidden to those who are perishing (4:1-3).

4 Paul's summary "self-commendation" again takes the form of the traditional biblical contrast between "two ways."[587] These "two ways" run courses that are entirely unexpected by the Corinthians: the way of salvation turns out to be, not a path of unchanging blessing, but one of difficulty and suffering.[588] Paul does nothing in any way to bring reproach to that mission, *but,* in contrast, commends himself as "God's agent." The "as" *(hōs)* of the comparative clause anticipates the concluding elements of Paul's list, also introduced by *hōs,* in which the person of the apostle stands at the center of interest (6:8c-10).[589] The question, of course, is what an emissary or agent of God should look like. Paul's answer to the Corinthians overturns all their expectations: God's agent appears in weakness and distress, the form of the crucified Christ.

Paul thus here begins his list of hardships that he brackets and interweaves with the work of God. Now we have his opening blessing of God made concrete (1:3-7).[590] The first element expresses the work of God in the apostle: "perseverance." This work stands in paradoxical relation to that which Paul has just announced in v. 2: "Now is the well-accepted time! Now is the day of salvation!" Salvation has come. Yet the first mark of an apostle, and thereby of all Christians, is a life of perseverance, of waiting for salvation yet to come. The new creation has *intersected* the fallen world in the crucified and risen Christ, but it has not yet arrived for the fallen world with its sufferings, terrors, and wrongdoing. For this salvation the apostle waits.

We have observed already that the qualities that Paul names in his list of hardships are not properly virtues but, rather, the manifestations of God's work in him. This work includes his perseverance in his numerous trials. As Paul indicates later to the Corinthians, this perseverance is an essential mark of an apostle: the "signs" of an apostle come only through perseverance (12:12). The Corinthians' unwillingness to embrace Paul as their apostle is thus an expression of unbelief, a refusal to accept the suffering that must come to all Christians. The Corinthians stand to lose in their rejection of Paul. As he informs them at the opening of the letter, the comfort given to them through him is active and dynamic, effecting their endurance of the same sufferings that he bears as an apostle (1:6).[591] Comfort is given only to those who know trouble.

587. See 1:12-14; 4:1-3.

588. Cf., e.g., Ps 1:1-6.

589. The comparative ὡς θεοῦ διάκονοι stands in place of the expected predicate accusative.

590. See esp. 1:6, "the endurance of the same sufferings that we also suffer" (ἐν ὑπομονῇ τῶν αὐτῶν παθημάτων ὧν καὶ ἡμεῖς πάσχομεν).

591. See also Rom 5:3-5, where Paul announces without qualification that "tribulation

Now the hardships appear in the list. Paul commends himself as an emissary of God, "in tribulations, in pressing needs, in straitened circumstances." In differing ways, all three of the terms with which Paul begins present hardship as a burden or pressure that one must endure. We have already commented on his use of the term *thlipsis,* or "affliction," which in biblical usage carries the overtones of a "burden."[592] The following term, *anankē,* expresses the idea of pressing or compelling need. Paul will use it again in his short list of trials in 12:10, as he also does the third term. This third term, *stenochōria,* signifies a straitened circumstance, a tight spot. In his earlier list Paul describes himself as, paradoxically, "in every way afflicted, yet not in straitened circumstances" (4:8). Now Paul expresses the nature of God's work in him. The understatement falls away. Paul describes the full force of his trials: he has been repeatedly placed in tight spots, and not merely the one in Asia that he has reported in this letter.[593] He is given "much perseverance" in numerous afflictions, needs, and pressures.

5 Paul's description of the hardships he has endured now becomes concrete. He commends himself "in beatings, in imprisonments, in riots, in labors, in times of sleeplessness, in times of fasting." What Paul has experienced goes well beyond what Luke reports. This is also apparent in the "fool's speech" (11:22–12:10). There, too, he names "imprisonments" and "beatings," and he makes the latter even more precise by speaking of five lashings, three beatings with rods, and one stoning that he has endured (11:23-25b; cf. Acts 14:19). That Paul's hardships extended well beyond what we find in Acts is likewise implicit in his earlier admonition and protest to the Corinthians (1 Cor 4:9; 15:30-31). In the narrative of Acts, we hear of only one beating and one imprisonment at this point in Paul's mission, those that took place in Philippi.[594] Likewise, from the Lukan report we know of only one riot (in Ephesus) at the time Paul writes the present letter.[595] Luke also reports a later riot and beating during Paul's final visit to Jerusalem, which were followed by imprisonment (Acts 21:30-36). But these hardships are yet to come for Paul.

The first three hardships express sufferings inflicted on the apostle from without, by other persons. The next three, "toils, times of sleeplessness, times of fasting," are sufferings that come from the rigors of the apostolic mission. Paul names these trials, too, in his "fool's speech" (11:27). The experiences of

---

effects perseverance." This certain knowledge and "boast" belongs to all Christians through Christ (5:1-2). See further Rom 12:12; 15:4; 1 Cor 13:7.

592. On the sense of θλίψις, see above, p. 23.

593. See 1:8-11.

594. Acts 16:22-33; cf. 1 Thess 2:2.

595. Acts 19:23–20:1. As we have noted, that commotion might itself have been followed by an imprisonment. See pp. 39-40.

"fasting" are not acts of self-chosen adherence to Jewish fasts but times of want and need.[596] Such is the life of God's agents!

6 The list continues with moral qualities, into which Paul inserts a reference to the gift of the Spirit: "in purity, in knowledge, in patience, in kindness, in the Holy Spirit, in love without hypocrisy."

Aside from the variant reading at 11:3, the abstract term "purity" *(hagnotēs)* appears here as a *hapax* not only for Paul but also for the entire New Testament and the Septuagint. It is also otherwise quite infrequent.[597] It bears overtones of devotion to God and of morality, both of which are likely operative in this context.[598] Paul acts in purity both in relation to God and in his dealings with the Corinthians. His language again recalls his opening "boast of his conscience" that he has acted in "the simplicity and sincerity of God" in the world and toward the Corinthians (1:12-14).

It is no accident, then, that Paul follows the claim to purity with the claim to "knowledge." Purity is not a mystical experience, nor is it simply inward. It is present only in communication. For Paul, apart from the knowledge of Christ and of God, there can be no purity. Paul's claim to his own gift of knowledge in 11:6 likewise follows his expression of concern for the Corinthians, whom he has betrothed to Christ, as a *pure* virgin (11:1-4). Paul thus binds the gift of knowledge, to which the Corinthians attached considerable importance, to the crucified and risen Christ.[599]

Paul likewise binds knowledge to love. The following qualities of "patience" and "kindness" recall the two opening elements of the profound description of love that appears in 1 Cor 13:4-13. The former quality, "patience," is fundamentally passive in nature. The Greek term *(makrothymia)* is composite and relatively transparent semantically: it is "slowness to anger." The term signifies tolerance and long-suffering with the weaknesses, difficulties, insults, and injuries that come from others. This is precisely what Paul has had to do with the Corinthians, although he nowhere says it explicitly. "Kindness" complements "patience" here, just as it does in 1 Cor 13:4. Bearing with the faults of others has its counterpart in actively doing them good. Again, this is precisely what the apostle has done, and continues to seek to do, for the Corinthians.

Now comes the interjection "in the Holy Spirit." Paul makes it unmistakably clear that the endurance, patience, and kindness, and all other "virtues" displayed in him do not have their basis in him, but in the gift of the Spirit

596. See 11:27.

597. Even the corresponding adjective ἁγνός is relatively infrequent in the NT, LXX, and Hellenistic literature in general.

598. See esp. the usage of the adjective ἁγνός in 7:11 and 11:2.

599. On the Corinthian concern with knowledge, see 1 Cor 1:5; 8:1-11; 13:2, 8; 2 Cor 8:7. On the knowledge of the crucified Christ, see 1 Cor 2:2; 2 Cor 2:14; 4:6.

given to him. The apostle's patience and kindness are the fruit of the Spirit (Gal 5:22-23). Indeed, he has been made an agent and missionary of "the new covenant," through which the Spirit is being distributed within the world. Paul's embedding his reference to the Spirit at this point within this list makes clear in what the mark of the Spirit within the world consists. He again recalls his description of love as it has entered the world in Christ (1 Cor 13:4-13).

Paul brings his list of moral qualities to a conclusion with a twofold form, "unhypocritical love," which corresponds to his opening claim to "much perseverance," his preceding reference to the "Holy Spirit," and his following claims concerning Word and power. The twofold form is thus emphatic, marking the conclusion of the claim to moral qualities within the list and linking those claims to the work of God by the Spirit, in the Word and power. The love of the apostle is unfeigned and without hypocrisy because it is the work and fruit of the Spirit given to him. Such love is a mark not only of the apostle but of all Christians. Paul calls for the same genuine love in his exhortations to the church at Rome (Rom 12:9) and also calls the Corinthians to this highest gift (1 Cor 13:1-13). He will insist more than once in what follows that he truly and deeply loves the Corinthians, no matter what they might suppose.[600] It is the love of Christ that constrains him (5:14).

7 Having named four qualities of his life and conduct, Paul takes up and expands his prior reference to the Holy Spirit: "in the word of truth, in the power of God." The "word of truth" is the Gospel that has been entrusted to the apostle. Paul already has sworn to the Corinthians that he has not "walked in guile" or "corrupted the word of God." He has, rather, "manifested the truth," which is hidden only to those blinded by the "god of this world" (4:2-4). As the "word of truth," the Gospel has invaded the world that is ruled by deceit. It is not accidental that Paul here immediately also lays claim to the very "power of God," almost certainly in reference to the "word of truth" itself.[601] As the bearer of the word, the apostle himself is the battleground for the truth. As he goes on to declare, he is regarded as a deceiver, yet he remains true (6:8). The "truth of Christ" is in him (11:10). The apostle can do nothing against the truth, but only for it (13:8). In this battle for the truth, the Corinthians themselves are at stake. Paul fears that they might be deceived, just as the serpent deceived Eve (11:1-4). The opponents are false apostles, deceitful workers, who, as Satan's agents, disguise themselves as Christ's apostles, just as Satan transforms himself into an angel of light (11:12-15).

The list now takes a turn, which is obscured somewhat by the traditional division of the verses. The first eighteen elements of the list (vv. 4-7b) describe

600. See 8:7; 11:11; 12:15, 19.

601. He uses the same description of the Gospel at the beginning of his letter to Rome (Rom 1:16-17).

hardships and qualities that Paul experiences *passively.* The work of God that the apostle *suffers* is fundamental. In the framework and space of this experience, his own work takes place. He now goes on to name and describe that work, shifting from the preposition *en* ("in" or "by") to *dia* ("through") in a threefold list (vv. 7c-8b).

In this brief list the apostle speaks of the weapons given to him in the battle that he must wage: "through the weapons of righteousness of the right hand and the left." As we have seen already, Paul understands "righteousness" not merely as a "word" or declaration from God but as an effective word of judgment and work of God within the world.[602] By its very nature, that word of judgment and righteousness arrives in the context of contention. One of the fundamental images for the establishing of righteousness is that of the Lord (or his chosen agent) girding himself with a shield and sword, or directing his arrows at his enemies, and contending for righteousness.[603] These weapons have been placed in the hands of the apostle as the bearer of the Gospel in his body and life.[604] They are not "fleshly" but have divine power. With them Paul "destroys fortresses" (10:4-6).

In referring to weapons "of the right hand and the left," Paul almost certainly appeals to the image of a sword and shield, offensive and defensive weapons, wielded on the right and left respectively.[605]

8 The "weapons" given to the apostle are inseparable from the message of Christ that he bears in his own person: "through glory and dishonor, through slander and praise" With the first pairing, Paul obviously recalls the hidden glory of the new covenant, of which he is an agent (2 Cor 3:7-11, 18). The Lord of glory was crucified (1 Cor 2:8). His apostle must likewise bear dishonor and scorn, and that in contrast to the Corinthians whom he serves (1 Cor 4:10).[606]

Paul inverts the order of the third pairing, placing the negative before the positive. He thus forms a chiasmus, an x-pattern, in the list: "through *glory* and **dishonor**, through **slander** and *praise.*" He thereby underscores the offense of the "word of the cross" that he bears, as well as the blindness of the world to the apostolic mission. Like his Lord, the apostle faces slander and criticism, no

602. See 3:9; 5:21.

603. See, e.g., Pss 7; 18; 35; 45:1-5; Isa 41:1-7; 51:4-8; 54:14-17; 59:17-20; 63:1-6; further, Wis 5:15-23. As is apparent both in the Psalms and the book of Isaiah, this work of effecting righteousness belongs to the Lord alone, who in bringing judgment fulfills his words of promise. For him and this word the psalmists wait. And where no one waits for him, he acts on his own behalf.

604. Ebner points to the similarity between Paul's language and that of the Stoic and Cynic "mirrors" of virtues for rulers *(Regentenspiegeln), Leidenslisten und Apostelbrief,* 271-80.

605. Cf. Eph 6:10-17, esp. vv. 14, 17.

606. See also 1 Cor 1:28; 2 Cor 10:10.

matter what measure of praise might come to him. The inversion of the terms bespeaks the nature of the battle. Slander and disgrace, including that of the cross, are themselves offensive weapons; the glory of God is manifest in the suffering apostle and the Gospel of the crucified Christ he bears.

Again within v. 8, there is a shift in Paul's list that is not well represented in the traditional division of verses. He already has made the point that his "weapons" are not separable from his person. He now underscores the irreducibly paradoxical nature of apostolic experience, which, we should remind ourselves, is nothing but Christian experience written large. As is the case throughout this section, he continues to use the plural in self-reference, locating himself among all other apostles. The conjunction "as" *(hōs)* bears a twofold sense. On the one hand, it may signify the way in which the apostle appears and is perceived by others. On the other hand, it may signify the apostle "as" he really is within the world. The former sense is surely present, especially in the first elements of the list. But Paul here describes something more than the way he is perceived. He presents the work of God that he "suffers," which constitutes the apostolic experience. Especially in the latter elements of the list, it is clear that he is describing realities that are at work in him.

One dimension of his experience is the twofold reception of the apostles within the world. They are "regarded as deceivers, and [yet] true." Paul has just claimed that he bears "the word of truth." He has likewise made clear more than once to the Corinthians that his life and person are determined by that word.[607] The reception of the Gospel is the reception of the apostle, and vice versa. The same is true of the rejection of them. What the Gospel offers as truth, the world calls deception. What the world offers as truth, the Gospel shows to be deception.

9 The inverted order of the pairings, with the negative element placed first, continues throughout the remaining six pairs (vv. 9-10). The apostles are those who are "unknown and known, dying and behold, we live! punished and not put to death."

The pairing "as unknown and known" does not merely have to do with knowledge, but with the recognition and acceptance of the apostles. It might well be rendered, "as unaccepted and accepted." Paul has already expressed the hope that the Corinthians "know" and thus accept him, as well as what he has written to them, even if at the moment this remains questionable (1:13-14). Whether they do or not, Paul, along with all apostles, remains recognized and accepted by God.[608] His unshakable hope is that his acceptance by God in Christ shall bring with it the acceptance of his mission and message by the Corinthians.[609]

607. See 1:12-14; 4:1-3.

608. Cf. 1 Cor 13:12, where the idea of acceptance is likely also in play.

609. See 4:13-15; 5:1-10.

The apostle is found "dying," yet, he exclaims, "Behold, we live!" He interrupts the series of self-descriptive participles with the announcement of God's wondrous and unexpected work. He again recalls the surprising acts of deliverance that God has performed for him, not merely in Asia (1:8-11), but repeatedly in the course of his mission. He bears the deadness of Jesus in order that the life of Jesus might be manifest in him (4:10-11). Yet these experiences of deliverance are but mere anticipations of the resurrection, which Paul implicitly includes in the contrastive pair. Just as the crucified Christ lives by the power of God, so the apostle lives in hope, one that includes the salvation of the Corinthians (13:4).

The apostles are "punished" *(paideuomenoi)* and "not given over to death." The term *paideuomenoi* generally signifies "education" or the "discipline" of a child. But it may also express the idea of punishment, including that of criminal justice,[610] as it likely does in this context, given the stark contrast of each of the pairings in context. Severe punishment, including scourging, could be included in the concept.[611] The "educative" dimension of the term is not lost thereby but is expanded to include the larger public that observed the sentence. The wording of the pairing stands especially close to the language of Ps 118:18 (LXX 117:18): "The Lord has disciplined me severely, but he has not given me over to death." Within his thanksgiving, the psalmist recounts how he has been placed in the danger of death, yet has been delivered by the Lord (Ps 118:17). The apostle shares in the experience of the psalmist, and that of Christ. Indeed, one may wonder here whether Paul does not recall the tradition of Jesus' trial before Pilate, as it is found in Luke. There Pilate suggests to the crowd that he might "punish" Jesus *(paideuein)* and release him. The punishment of scourging takes place, but only as a prelude to the cross.[612] In a corresponding way, it is entirely possible that the term for Paul serves as a meiosis, understating the measure of his experience of death, in much the same way as does his language in 4:8-9. It is likely, too, that the term still expresses the educative function of the "punishment." In the apostles, and especially in Paul, the Corinthians, together with all others, are to learn of God's ways in Christ. Paul himself is "disciplined" in his sufferings: in them he learns of Christ and Christ's comfort.

10 The apostle exists "as grieving but always rejoicing, as poor but making many rich, as having nothing and possessing all things." The final elements of the list focus on the paradoxical existence of the apostle. He underscores that paradox by shifting from the connective "and" to the adversative "but." Grief and joy are present simultaneously in his life: he does not always grieve,

610. The same is true of the Hebrew equivalent יִסַּר, e.g., Lev 26:18, 28; Deut 22:18.

611. See further LXX Deut 22:18; 2 Kgdms 22:48; 3 Kgdms 12:11; Prov 3:12; also Heb 12:6.

612. See Luke 23:16.

but he always rejoices. What he calls the Philippian church to do, he does himself: he rejoices in the Lord *always.*[613] Sorrow that comes from God, unlike that of the world, works salvation (7:10). This is true for the repentance of the Corinthians,[614] but it has a wider significance. To rejoice *in the Lord* is not to pretend that suffering has been banished from the world or that there should be no place for lament. To rejoice in the Lord is to see our sufferings in the light of God's promises fulfilled in Jesus Christ. It is to live in the hope that God the Creator shall yet turn our "mourning into dancing" (Ps 30:11).

The apostles are those who are "poor *but* making many rich." Again Paul emphasizes the paradox by using the adversative. His life corresponds to the picture of Peter we find in Acts: "Silver and gold, I do not have [even the little that might help a beggar], but what I have, I give" (Acts 3:6). Paul's life likewise is conformed to that of Jesus, who, he later reminds the Corinthians, "became poor on account of you, in order that you, through his poverty, might become rich" (8:9). He is still teaching a church focused on wisdom, power, and wealth that true riches are to be found only in the "word of the cross" that he bears (1 Cor 1:18, 26-31).

He concludes the list on this same note: "as having nothing *and* possessing all things." He now drops the adversative, implicitly expressing the hope of the eschaton. He has already warned the Corinthians against boasting in people. To do so is to seek one's identity in allegiance to others who seem to possess wealth, power, or wisdom. There is no need to do so! Indeed, the adoration of Christian leaders is idolatry. "All things are yours," Paul tells the Corinthians. This includes not only Paul or Apollos or Cephas, to whom various allegiances had formed within the church. It includes all the world itself, life and death, the present age and the one to come. All things have been given to us. And we belong to the crucified and risen Christ, who in turn belongs to God (1 Cor 3:18-23). The apostle has nothing, and yet he possesses all things.

b. The Appeal to Receive Paul as Apostle (6:11–7:16)

The body of the letter now comes to its close. The apostle is nothing more than the agent of Another, the emissary of the new covenant (3:1-18). He is the bearer of God's saving work, not only in his proclamation, but in his body and life, in which the crucified and risen Christ is manifest. Out of his own participation in Christ's redeeming love and God's reconciling work in him, Paul is an agent of reconciliation. He is an ambassador of Christ (4:1–5:21). To receive the apostolic appeal to be reconciled to God, and also to receive God's

613. Phil 4:4; also 1:18; 2:18; 3:1; likewise 1 Thess 5:16.

614. See 2 Cor 2:2-5; 7:8-10.

grace, requires the Corinthians to be reconciled to the suffering apostle as well. Their salvation is bound up in him and his salvation, as he makes clear to them in the very opening of the letter (1:12-14). He has argued that he merely "co-operates" with God. He gives no occasion for offense, so that the Gospel may provide its own offense. A final turn in the argument is necessary: he now directly calls the Corinthians to be reconciled to him.

His appeal falls into three distinct units. Paul begins with a brief, emotional word to the Corinthians (6:11-13). He then abruptly admonishes them to break their ties with unbelievers (6:14–7:1). This rather lengthy exhortation includes a lengthy, composite citation from the Scriptures. Paul's language is also allusive and theologically rich. This deviation from the discourse and vocabulary of the letter has caused a number of interpreters to suggest that the unit represents an interpolation that is not original to the letter. It is likely, however, that Paul continues to speak directly to his conflict with the Corinthians. He has already alluded to his opponents in Corinth (5:12), and now he "names" them in much the same way that he will do in 11:12-15. They are unbelievers and, indeed, belong to "Beliar." The similarity of Paul's language to that of the Qumran community should not surprise us. Just as the Qumran community used such terms in inner-Jewish polemics, Paul now does so in inner-Christian polemics. The earliest church had not yet lost its Jewish roots, not even in Corinth, and certainly not in Paul.

The third unit is quite concrete. Paul recounts to the Corinthians his meeting with Titus, in which he received the news of Titus's visit with the Corinthians and their reconciliation with Paul. Taking up this good news, Paul seeks to build on it and secure the fidelity of the Corinthians to his apostolic mission (7:2-16). As we have observed, Paul earlier in his apostolic report postponed any mention of his meeting with Titus, breaking off his narrative in the midst of his anxiety over the Corinthians (2:12-13). The Corinthians, although they have received Paul's co-worker, up to this point do not know what Paul's response to them might be. Paul's long delay in reporting his response to them underscores his anxiety over them and his unbounded joy over their repentance (see 7:5-6). The whole of his argument in the body of the letter is framed within his relationship with the Corinthians. He is *their* apostle, and he seeks to win *their* hearts. The aim of the letter is quite specific. It is an apostolic word on target. It speaks to us today, not despite of its specific and personal nature, but in and through it.

(1) The Appeal for Reciprocation from the Corinthians (6:11-13)

11 We have spoken freely to you, Corinthians; our heart is wide open.
12 You are not restricted by us, but you are restricted in your own affections.
13 In return (I speak as to children) widen your hearts also.

11 Paul's letter has been remarkably personal and self-descriptive. The unveiled face of the apostle and the church in the presence of the Lord is to have its counterpart in their open hearts toward one another. The apostle has been open with the Corinthians and has made himself even more vulnerable than he has been before. Now he speaks directly and emotionally to them. For the moment, the distance between the writer and recipients of the letter disappears. He has spoken to them, and now speaks to them, as if they were in one another's presence.

He has made it clear that they are close to his heart. Now he makes his heart close to them. He has opened it up wide to them. This image probably bears a twofold sense, just as it does in English. The apostle has bared his soul to the Corinthians. If they know him at all, they know him now, as they have never known him before. This is obviously the sense of his first statement, which informs this second description as well. At the same time, he goes on to appeal to the Corinthians to "open wide" to him as well. Here it is clear that he is asking them to welcome him, just as he has opened his heart to welcome them.[615]

12 It is no secret that the Corinthians have harbored suspicions about Paul, suspicions that have been fed by his failure to visit them as promised and also, perhaps, by his opponents.[616] The former especially has affected their relationship recently. Paul has already explained the reasons for his decision. As he has just emotionally exclaimed, he has bared his soul to them. Sincerity and transparency are fundamental to his mission; they are his boast and the basis of his good conscience.[617] Thus he charges the Corinthians here: "You are not constrained by us. You are constrained by your own inward affections." Paul is now bold to say that the problem in his relationship with the Corinthians does not lie with him but with them. He tells the truth in the most direct way.

13 Paul's directness continues in the last word of this appeal. He asks them to reciprocate his openness by opening their hearts, to make an equal return to him, for what he has given to them. He asks them to play fair, which he should hardly need to do. He makes it clear to the Corinthians that they are behaving like children. This tone is to be seen against the background of the Corinthian presumption that they were the benefactors, and perhaps even patrons, of the apostles, who had the right to judge them. Paul is challenging Corinthian pride, in the very context of expressing his love. Apostolic love is tough love. Paul's language here has larger implications: in that Paul addresses the Corinthians as children, he assumes the role of their parent. This figure will appear again indirectly in 11:1-4 and explicitly in Paul's concluding words

615. In a negative sense of "opening wide" to receive, see LXX Isa 5:14; Hab 2:5. It is unlikely that Ps 119:32 constitutes a parallel to Paul's language here.

616. See 1:15-22; 1:23–2:4; 12:14-18.

617. See 1:12-14; 4:1-3.

in 12:14-15. Paul's claim of the role of parent is nothing other than a claim to apostolic authority, an authority grounded in the Gospel.[618]

(2) The Appeal to Break with the Opponents (6:14–7:1)

[14]*Do not be unequally yoked with unbelievers. For what partnership has righteousness with lawlessness? Or what fellowship has light with darkness?*
[15]*What accord has Christ with Belial? Or what portion does a believer share with an unbeliever?* [16]*What agreement has the temple of God with idols? For we are the temple of the living God; as God said,*

I will make my dwelling among them and walk among them,
and I will be their God,
and they shall be my people.
[17]*Therefore go out from their midst,*
and be separate from them, says the Lord,
and touch no unclean thing;
then I will welcome you,
[18]*and I will be a father to you,*
and you shall be sons and daughters to me,
says the Lord Almighty.

7[1]*Since we have these promises, beloved, let us cleanse ourselves from every defilement of body and spirit, bringing holiness to completion in the fear of God.*

Paul's second appeal seems to break with the argument of the letter up to this point. Not only new language but new patterns of thought appear in the discourse. It is understandable that the originality of the unit has been called into question. Nevertheless, this section in all probability comes from Paul himself and is original to this letter. Paul's warning makes use of contemporary early Jewish vocabulary that is rich in biblical allusions. The composite citation that he presents here is the lengthiest of the Corinthian correspondence (vv. 16b-18). The entire appeal is oriented to Scripture. These characteristics of the argument should not surprise us and are certainly not atypical of Paul. Nor would they have been alien to the Corinthian church, which apparently knows the Scriptures quite well. Paul not only expects the Corinthians to be familiar with the Scriptures, but also that they will be able to follow his allusions and arguments drawn from the biblical text.[619] He furthermore remains oriented

618. 1 Cor 4:14-15. See the further discussion at 12:14.

619. See esp. 1 Cor 4:6, which follows the allusions and citations of 1 Cor 3:1-23; likewise, 1 Cor 10:1-13.

to the thought, practice, and needs of the earliest believing community in Judea, as becomes clear at decisive points of his argument in the Corinthian correspondence.[620] The Corinthians expect their apostles to be thoroughly Jewish. In this respect, at least, Paul does not disappoint them (11:22).

The introduction of this very Jewish and biblical argument comes after Paul has concluded his defense of his apostolic mission. A break and change in thought at this point in the letter are to be expected. His first appeal to them, in vv. 11-13, itself marks a break in the argument. It is not strange that it is followed by a second appeal that introduces new forms and thought. The entire letter, in fact, is marked by breaks: Paul breaks his narration of his experience after 2:12-13 and takes it up again in 7:2-16; the collection appeal appears (but only appears) to be an interruption in the closing of the letter (8:1–9:15); Paul's combative tone in 10:1–13:14 is likewise thought to be at odds with what precedes. Each one of these interruptions in the flow of thought has been thought to mark the insertion of letter fragments or secondary material. But each of these breaks within the letter reflects the broken relationship between Paul and the Corinthians that he seeks to repair. Perhaps interpreters have come to suppose that the letter to Rome is the standard by which all of Paul's letters are to be measured and judged. Second Corinthians does not fit that pattern.

The opening of Paul's admonition is colored by the language of early Jewish polemics and comes particularly close to the usage of the Qumran writings. There is no need to imagine a direct dependence here, although it cannot be excluded. It is more likely that the similarity in thought and form is to be attributed to commonalities in early Jewish polemics: this is how one addressed one's adversaries who had departed from the truth. Paul's particular proximity to the thought of the Qumran writings is likely also due to their common eschatological stance; both imagined final salvation to have arrived, the former in the community itself, the latter in Christ. It is at this point, too, that the distinctiveness of Paul's thought is evident. It is he who draws the contrast between Christ and Beliar (v. 15). His eschatology is also more radical than that of the Qumran community, which still hoped for the restoration of the temple in Jerusalem. Despite, or rather because of, Paul's christocentric thought, he understands the believing community itself to be the temple of God (v. 16).[621] He likewise understands the believing community itself to embody righteousness in a way that the Qumran sect did not.[622] Likewise, while

620. See, e.g., 1 Cor 11:2-16; 11:17-34; 14:36; 16:22. This orientation again becomes evident in the appeal for the collection for Jerusalem in 8:1–9:15.

621. The same thought is fundamental to Paul's ecclesiology in 1 Cor 3:10-17, and to his ethics in 1 Cor 6:12-20.

622. 4Q548, 7 speaks of the "sons of righteousness." But this phrase is likely due to their faithfulness and obedience to the Teacher of Righteousness.

the Community Rule and other Qumran writings draw a contrast between "the sons of light" and the "sons of darkness," they do not name the community members "light" (or others "darkness") as Paul does. For Paul, even though Christ remains decisively extrinsic, all believers really participate in Christ. At Qumran, in contrast, participation in "light" corresponded to the measure of knowledge and practice.[623] The similarities between Paul and Qumran are remarkable, but so are the differences. It should not go unnoticed, either, that Paul does not speak of "Belial" ("worthlessness") in the original Hebrew form as the Qumran texts and the Talmud do,[624] but of "Beliar," in correspondence to Hellenistic Jewish tradition.[625] It is unlikely, but not impossible, that Paul draws directly on the Qumran writings. If he does so, he certainly alters their thought.

The essentially Jewish character of the material speaks for its originality. An insertion by another hand would have to have taken place later. But by the end of the first century, the church had become basically Gentile in composition. It is easier to suppose that a very Jewish Paul wrote the section as part of the letter than it is to imagine that a later Gentile hand added this material. The appeal to Scripture identifies believers with Israel directly and without qualification. With time, such use of Scripture became increasingly alien.

Paul's admonition is not a general statement against association with unbelievers or pagan idolaters (which, in the Corinthian context, amount to the same persons). It is specifically directed against his adversaries in Corinth.[626] This reading of the text corresponds to the thrust of Paul's argument in context: he first calls upon them to open their hearts to him (6:11-13), and now calls upon them to break their ties with his opponents (6:14–7:1). He subsequently reinforces the reconciliation that has taken place through Titus (7:2-16). He has already alluded to the opponents, with whom the Corinthians will have to break, if they are to maintain their allegiance to the apostle (5:12). He goes on to name these opponents with nearly the same terms he uses here: they are agents of Satan, who disguise themselves as apostles of Christ, just as Satan

623. This is true, even though "the sons of light" and "sons of darkness" were understood to be led by different angelic powers. See, e.g., 1QS I, 9-10; III, 3-5, 18-26.

624. E.g., *b. Ber.* 31b; *b. Sanh.* 11b; 1QS I, 18-24; II, 4-5; X, 21.

625. E.g., *T. Reu.* 2:2; 4:7, 11; 6:3; *Jub.* 1:20; 15:34.

626. Admittedly, the majority of interpreters come to the former conclusion. Quite understandably, therefore, many regard 6:14–7:1 as an interpolation. Nevertheless, a good number of interpreters regard the passage to be addressed against Paul's opponents. Beyond the arguments offered here, see J.-F. Collange, *Énigmes de la Deuxième Épître de Paul aux Corinthiens: Étude Exégétique de 2 Cor. 2:14–7:4* (SNTSMS 18; Cambridge: Cambridge University Press, 1972), 302-17; D. Rensberger, "2 Corinthians 6:14–7:1 — a Fresh Examination," *Studia Biblica et Theologica* 8 (1978): 25-49; and esp., D. I. Starling, *Not My People: Gentiles as Exiles in Pauline Hermeneutics* (BZNW 184; New York: Walter de Gruyter, 2011), 71-73.

clothes himself as an angel of light (11:12-15). The interpretation of the warning as directed against idolatry is undermined considerably by the entirely personal nature of his appeal: it is not a *practice,* but *persons,* from which the Corinthians are to separate themselves.[627] Nor can his appeal be understood rightly as a general warning.[628] To read it in this way would mean that one must break off any and all contact with unbelievers. The Corinthians would then have to retreat to Qumran, or indeed to depart from the world, as Paul himself observes in his correction of their misunderstanding of an earlier letter.[629] Paul need not repeat that earlier instruction here. It already informs his statements and the Corinthians' understanding of them. They could hardly have forgotten what he said. Here, in a new way, he calls the Corinthians to separate themselves from unbelievers who masquerade as believers. This was the message of Paul's earlier letter to Corinth: they were to refrain from joining or mixing together with unbelievers. It is reflected in his corrective statement in 1 Cor 5:9-11.[630] Only in the context of his correction of Corinthian misunderstanding of his letter, and of the problem of the immoral man within the Corinthian church, does Paul alter the image of withdrawal and separation to that of expulsion. In that context he appeals to the image of the celebration of Passover, rather than the return from Babylonian exile.[631] In all probability, the exhortation contained in the original letter matches the pattern of Paul's thought here.

The immediate context signals clearly that Paul has his opponents in view. The Corinthians instantly would have grasped the import of his words. Indeed, it is highly probable that he is alluding to his early letter in which he originally gave this instruction. It would be strange if he did not do so. He may even be citing that letter.[632] The Corinthians will now read that letter in

627. Furthermore, Paul makes no mention of idolatry or idolaters in Second Corinthians; he would surely have done so had idolatry been an ongoing problem within the church (cf. 1 Cor 10:1–11:1). His call to separate from idolaters (1 Cor 5:11) is not repeated here. Nor does he refer to idolatry as one of the transgressions that he fears he must deal with in his upcoming visit to Corinth (2 Cor 12:19-21).

628. Nor does the passage speak directly to the question of a believer marrying an unbeliever, as it often has been interpreted at least since the beginning of the third century. See Cyprian, *Treatises* III, 62.

629. Already in First Corinthians, Paul had to clarify an earlier letter to Corinth, in which he instructed them not to be associated with unbelievers. They misunderstood him fundamentally. What he meant, he tells them, is that they are not to associate with a so-called brother or sister who lives in open violation of the Gospel. He does not have in view unbelievers in general, but those who pretend or imagine that they are believers when they are not (1 Cor 5:9-13).

630. See LXX Hos 7:8; 2 Thess 3:14.

631. 1 Cor 5:2, 6-8, 13.

632. Admittedly, the language of the earlier letter apparently varies from the appeal here. If in the earlier letter he called the Corinthians to separate themselves from "immoral persons"

the light of the clarification that Paul provides in 1 Cor 5:9-11. This clarification only sharpens the point of his attack on the opponents. Of course, Paul remains silent about this allusion to earlier correspondence. But that silence only drives home his message to his audience: the Corinthians themselves are to make the connection between his earlier instruction and the apostolic claimants. It is their hearts for which Paul battles.

The argument in 6:14–7:1 begins with an exhortation (6:14a). Paul grounds the exhortation in a series of five rhetorical questions that contrast the identity of believers with that of unbelievers (6:14b-16a). Paul then supplies his own affirmation, namely, that the believing community is "the temple of the living God" (6:16b). He explains that affirmation by appealing to a composite citation of Scripture (6:16c-18). The citation begins with unconditioned promises (6:16c) and then concludes with exhortations and conditioned promises (6:17-18). Paul concludes the appeal with a self-inclusive exhortation based on these promises (7:1).

The composite citation presents at least three different images. In the first place the people of God appear as a temple in which the Lord dwells, following Paul's own characterization of believers (6:16). This image is followed by the call to the priests to remove the vessels of the Lord from Babylon, a call that Paul expands to believers separating themselves from unbelievers (6:17). The return from exile obviously stands in the background. The chain of citations finally turns to the divine promise to be a father to David's son, a promise that is now expanded to the whole people of God (6:18). Paul thus moves from the image of the presence of the Lord in the temple, to the return of priests from exile, to that of the Lord as father. These images might be regarded as having their unity in the prophetic promises concerning the return from exile, since it is here that the various dimensions of promised salvation come together in Scripture. But that is already true of the exodus. Indeed, within the Scriptures the return from exile is presented as a new exodus. The latter provides the pattern for the former. The return from exile is no mere progress in salvation history; it is a return to the exodus.[633] Furthermore, within this passage the paradoxical intersection of fulfilled promise and the demands upon which

---

(πόρνοι, 1 Cor 5:9), he here calls them to separate from "unbelievers" (2 Cor 6:14). Yet Paul's statement in 1 Cor 5:9 appears to be a summary directed to the immediate problem of immorality in Corinth (1 Cor 5:1). He goes on to describe his earlier instruction as a warning against association with persons subject to various vices (1 Cor 5:10-11). It is possible that he used the term "unbelievers" in the earlier letter as well. Indeed, it is likely, given the Corinthian misunderstanding, which seems to appear in the question of unbelieving spouses (1 Cor 7:10-16).

633. This is true even with respect to kingship: the return from exile re-establishes the Lord as Israel's king after the failed monarchy, and it "distributes" kingship to the people, according to the pattern of the exodus (e.g., Deut 33:5; Exod 19:6; cf., e.g., Isa 6:1-6; 44:6).

salvation is conditioned disrupts any story line, including that of return from exile.[634]

14 The exhortation "Do not be unequally yoked with unbelievers" bears a biblical allusion that does not appear in its counterpart in 1 Cor 5:9. It recalls the prohibition against plowing with an ox and a donkey yoked together (Deut 22:10; Lev 19:19). It may well also recall the description of Israel's idolatry in Numbers 25:3, "Israel yoked itself to the Baal of Peor." The image of being yoked appears in the New Testament and rabbinic writings as a description of service to God.[635] The warning against being unequally yoked is thus an admonition against common *labor* with unbelievers; it likely bears a special significance with respect to Paul's opponents in Corinth.

The five explanatory, rhetorical questions follow, with their opposing pairs. The first three pairs describe God's saving work in its contrast to the world (vv. 14b-15a). In the fourth, Paul makes it clear that he continues to speak of believers and unbelievers: "Or what portion does a believer have with an unbeliever?" (v. 15b). In the fifth pair, Paul summarizes his point in the image of the temple, making apparent that his appeal bears both a corporate and individual dimension.[636]

In the first pairing, Paul draws on his preceding argument: "For what participation is there between righteousness and lawlessness?" The Corinthians have been made to be "the righteousness of God" in Christ (5:21). They do not possess this righteousness in themselves, but in relation to Christ. Nevertheless, this relation effects a new reality within the present world. Paul's question implies this reality, presenting it in stark terms: despite all appearances, the Corinthians *are* righteousness. They therefore have no share, no participation in "lawlessness," in which the entire world outside of Christ lies. In all likelihood, Paul does not thereby have in view "law" in general, but speaks specifically of the Law of Moses. The "righteousness" effected by God in Christ is the abrogation of that Law as its fulfillment and goal.[637]

Paul then moves to creational language, echoing his earlier argument: "Or what does light have in common with darkness?" God's saving work in Christ brings a new creation, including the re-creation of the human being (5:17). Paul has made this point already, and he recalls it here. He even more directly recalls his description of his own conversion as God creating light out of darkness within his heart (4:6). The same is true of all believers: they,

634. These reflections qualify the thesis of Webb, *Returning Home,* who sees Paul's citation as driven by exile theology.

635. Matt 11:29-30; Acts 15:10; Gal 5:1; Phil 4:3; *m. 'Abot* 3.5; *b. Ber.* 12b, 13a-b, 14b.

636. Paul's thought here thus corresponds to the correction he provides in 1 Cor 5:9-13.

637. See Gal 5:14, 22-24; Rom 10:4; 13:8-14.

too have been made to be "light."[638] The image belongs to Jewish tradition, as we have noted, and especially recalls the language of the book of Isaiah. Yet Paul differs from Jewish tradition, as well as from the thought of the Qumran community: "being light" is not a matter of following the Law or of imitating goodness, as Paul himself makes clear in his dialogue partner in Rom 2:19. "Becoming light" is being the recipient of deliverance and the saving work of the Lord, who is Creator.[639]

15 Participation in salvation is not merely a matter of morality or "substance," it is a matter of personal relation. The third question deepens the first two: "Or what harmony is there between Christ and Beliar?" Paul certainly does not imagine that the Corinthians or anyone else has lost their personal identity in salvation, in a sort of mystical merging with Christ. Nevertheless, he identifies them with Christ, just as he has done in his description of salvation in 5:14-15 and as he does in other contexts.[640] They live in a relationship of communication with Christ, in which an exchange of identities has taken place, the exchange that Paul describes in 5:21. They are Christ's sin; Christ is their righteousness. The same understanding is implicit in 1 Cor 1:30.

In contrast, Paul identifies unbelievers and the world with "Beliar." The Hebrew form *belial* appears twenty-seven times in the Scriptures, signifying "worthlessness" or "nothingness."[641] As we have noted, in early Jewish literature the term (whether in Greek or Hebrew form) came to refer to Satan.[642] Paul does the same. He has already explained that "the god of this age" has blinded the minds (and thoughts) of unbelievers (4:4). He goes on to identify the opposing apostles at Corinth as "agents of Satan" (11:15). It is unclear whether the meaning of the term "Beliar" would have been transparent to the Corinthians. Nevertheless, Paul implicitly names as "worthless" and "nothing" that which the Corinthians prized and that which the opponents offered as the highest value. Although Satan appears as an angel of light, his promises are empty. Although God appears to have given empty promises, in the risen Christ he has shown himself to be faithful.[643]

638. See 1 Thess 5:5; Eph 5:8-9, 13-14; cf. Rom 13:12.

639. See esp. Isa 42:6; 45:7; 49:6; 51:4; 60:1-3.

640. See, e.g., Rom 8:10; 13:14; Gal 2:15-21; 3:27-28; 5:24.

641. See, e.g., MT Deut 13:14(13); 15:9. It appears in the construction "son [daughter] of Belial" (e.g., Judg 19:22; 20:13; 1 Sam 1:16), or also independently as a description of a "worthless" or immoral person (e.g., 1 Sam 25:25; 30:22; 2 Sam 16:7; 20:1). There are two related etymological interpretations of the term בְּלִיַּעַל in the Talmud (*b. Sanh.* 111b): the children of Belial are those who have lost their share in the age to come and thus will "not ascend" (בלי יעל), or those who have thrown off the yoke of heaven and thus are "without yoke" (בלי עול).

642. See above, p. 289.

643. Thus Luther: "God's faithfulness and truth always must first become a great lie before it becomes truth. The world calls this truth heresy. And we, too, are constantly tempted

Having shifted his rhetoric to the category of persons, Paul returns to the terms of the opening admonition: "Or what portion does a believer have with an unbeliever?"[644] The obvious answer is "none." It is clear, however, that Paul is not only directing these words to the situation in Corinth; he is also thinking in eschatological terms. Only then, at the eschaton, will the division within humanity appear. It should not go unnoticed that, within about twenty-five lines, Paul moves from calling the Corinthians to faith and reconciliation with God (6:1-2) to addressing them as believers. The power of the Gospel and the infidelity of human beings set the terms of his argument.

16 Having effectively rounded off his admonition by returning to the contrast between believers and unbelievers, Paul now opens it again in a fresh summary that encapsulates the theology of all that precedes: "Or what agreement is there between the temple of God and idols?" Paul has more than once identified the Corinthian church as the temple of God, both corporately (1 Cor 3:10-18) and individually (1 Cor 6:19). Earlier in the letter, he made use of the image of the wilderness tabernacle (3:12-18). He has also used the imagery of the temple in the transition from the earthly existence "in a tent" to the "building" we "have" from God (5:1-2).[645] In the present context, he speaks without eschatological reserve in language that is unique to earliest Christianity: already here and now, believers are the temple of God.[646] The prior rhetorical questions are gathered up in this final picture: righteousness, light, and the presence of God are all associated with the temple.[647] Conversely, the image of the temple is to be understood in these terms. It informs the preceding imagery by the promise of saving communion with God that is the very reason for its existence.

In contrast to his preceding questions, Paul now supplies his own affirmative answer, which then leads to his lengthy appeal to Scripture that undergirds and explains his claim: "For we are the temple of the living God" (v. 16b). The description of the Lord as "the living God" implies a contrast with the dead idols and with all who defy his power.[648] He is the God who is

---

to believe that God would abandon us and not keep His Word; and in our hearts He begins to become a liar. In short, God cannot be God unless He first becomes a devil . . . , the devil does not become and is not a devil without first having been God. He does not become an angel of darkness unless he has first been an angel of light" (*LW* 31:14).

644. The possessive dative πιστῷ is somewhat unexpected. It is not too surprising that the genitive form πιστοῦ appears (B 33). But the dative has better attestation and is the *lectio difficilior.*

645. The image of the believing community as the temple of God has roots in Paul's thought and beyond in early Christian tradition. See Rom 15:20; Eph 2:19-22; 1 Pet 2:4-10.

646. See Eph 2:21; 1 Pet 2:5-6; Rev 21:22. Cf. John 2:19-21, in which the christological basis of this identification becomes apparent.

647. See, e.g., Pss 89:14; 97:2 (righteousness), and Ps 43:3; Isa 60:1-3 (light).

648. E.g., 1 Sam 17:26, 36; 2 Kgs 19:4, 6 (Isa 37:4, 17).

constantly active within the world, who not only intervenes in human affairs but also guides and directs all of them. The name "living God" also implies his communication and communion with his people, as Paul will make clear in his following citation of Scripture.[649]

Paul's affirmation that "we *are* the temple of the living God" defines his appeal to Scripture, particularly the words of promise with which it opens. What is given to Israel in promise has now been fulfilled. The promise has come to reality, just as all of God's promises have their Yes in the crucified and risen Christ (1:20). It has taken place, "just as God said."

The quotation of Scripture follows. As we have noted, it is a lengthy composite of texts of Scripture that (most likely) Paul has joined together into a seamless whole.[650] The merging of scriptural texts in citation is not unusual for Paul or for earliest Christianity, even if the citations are not usually so lengthy.[651] This merged citation is more than a cut-and-paste operation. It constitutes an act of interpretation. The exhortations that appear in the citation are paradoxically based upon the unconditioned promise of God to dwell and walk among his people and to be their God; they thus are to separate themselves so that God will be their father, and they his sons and daughters.[652] The appeals of the apostle that frame the citation bear the same form: the "imperative" (7:1) is paradoxically found within the "indicative" of God's work (6:14-16a). This typically Pauline pattern suggests that the composite citation is the work of the apostle, who reads the Scriptures with the remarkable confidence that all of God's words, ways, and promises find their fulfillment and interpretation in the crucified and risen Christ.

As we have noted, the first elements of the citation support and explain Paul's claim that the believing community is nothing other than the temple of God: "I shall dwell in them and walk among them. And I shall be their God, and they shall be my people."

Paul draws on the Lord's promise to his people in Lev 26:12[653] that, if they walk in his statutes and keep his commandments, he will walk among them and be their God.[654] They shall be his people. Despite Israel's failure to

649. See, e.g., Deut 5:26; Josh 3:10; Hos 1:10.

650. It thus differs from the Scripture citation in Rom 3:10-18, in which Paul merely places the texts in a lengthy chain. Even there, however, his collection of texts is interpretive and bears a coherent message.

651. See, e.g., Rom 9:24-26 (Hos 2:25[23]; Hos 2:1 [1:10]); Rom 9:27-28 (Hos 2:1 [1:10]; Isa 10:22-23); Rom 9:33 (Isa 28:16; Isa 8:14).

652. See esp. the διό ("therefore") that opens the exhortations (v. 17).

653. See also 1 Kgs 6:13. LXX Lev 26:3 replaces the promise of the Lord's placing his "dwelling place" among them with his placing his "covenant" among them, perhaps emphasizing the call to obedience.

654. See Lev 26:3.

obey the Lord and the subsequent punishment of exile that came upon it, the prophets, especially the temple-oriented prophets Ezekiel and Zechariah, take up the promise afresh. They take it up, moreover, in new form: no longer is the promise of God's dwelling among his people contingent on their obedience. The Lord himself will restore them in such a way that he will dwell among them.[655] They will truly have him as God and be his people; the wording recalls the promise of the Jeremianic new covenant, to which Paul already has made appeal.[656] According to Paul, this promise has now come to fulfillment: "We are the temple of the living God."

The twofold imagery of "dwelling in [*or* among] them and walking among [them]," which appears in Lev 26:11-12, reflects the period of the tabernacle, even if the context anticipates the temple. The second element of the promise falls away in the announcements of the prophets.[657] Paul thus "relocates" the Leviticus text to the context of the prophets, and especially Ezek 37:27. Nevertheless, by appealing to Leviticus and the sojourn in the wilderness, Paul communicates the paradoxical nature of Christian life even in his appeal to Scripture. On the one hand, he makes it clear that the unconditional promise of the prophets has been fulfilled: in Christ we have arrived at the journey's end, and already here and now we are the temple of God. On the other hand, Paul also makes it clear that we remain the wandering people of God, whom God accompanies on our entire earthly journey.

It is likely, too, that the pairing "dwelling in and walking among" signals both individual and corporate realities. God both indwells each one of his people and "walks" within their midst.[658]

That "God has become our God, and we have become his people" is something larger than a mere formal arrangement. As the promises of God's dwelling among his people make clear, it entails the remaking of our heart, in such a way that we truly "have" God as our God and "hang our heart" on the true God.[659] The prophet Hosea speaks of this new relation as a true marriage, in which the spouses give their hearts to one another (Hos 2:19-20). This promise is fulfilled in Christ, in whom God has taken possession of the human heart.

17 Paul now shifts from his elaboration of the fulfilled promise to the exhortation with which he began his appeal (v. 14). He makes an interpretive

655. See esp. Ezek 37:27; 43:7-9; Zech 2:14-15(10-11).

656. See esp. Jer 24:7; 30:22; 31:1, 31-34; 32:38; Ezek 11:19-20; 36:26-28; 37:27; Zech 8:8.

657. See 1 Kgs 6:13; Ezek 37:27; 43:7-9; Zech 2:14-15(10-11).

658. See 1 Cor 14:24-25, where Paul envisions an unbeliever overwhelmed by the exposure of his heart within the prophesying community and declaring, "God really dwells among you" (Isa 45:14).

659. Luther, "For these two belong together, faith and God. That to which your heart clings and entrusts itself is, I say, really your God" (Large Catechism: The First Commandment).

insertion into his citation, "'*Therefore,* come out from their midst, and be separate,' says the Lord, 'and do not touch that which is unclean.'" Paul juxtaposes the call and demand of God, upon which God's acceptance of us is conditioned in the text, to the promise of God that is now fulfilled in Christ. Paul is not thereby contradicting himself. Rather, he is expressing the fundamental paradox of Christian living that already appears in his relocation of Lev 26:11-12, which speaks of the wilderness wanderings, into the context of the temple. God's call for us to act proceeds from what he has accomplished and enacted for us in Christ. The same pattern appears in the Isaianic context of the citation: the call to depart from Babylon comes in the wake of the announcement of Jerusalem's salvation (Isa 52:7-10). This paradoxical relation is not to be regarded as a puzzle to be solved. The fulfillment of promise creates the "space" in which our obedience takes place. It is not the case that our being accepted by God remains finally contingent upon our withdrawal and separation from evil — as if we could accomplish such a thing! It is rather that, *precisely because* that work has been accomplished for us, we therefore are to so act and do. This paradox is nothing other than what the Scriptures call faith. One thinks here of Bonhoeffer's word that "only the one who believes, obeys," and conversely that "only the one who obeys, believes."[660]

Paul here makes use of the exhortation that emerges from the promise of return from exile in Isa 52:11. The passage that he cites displays the same relationship of the "indicative" and the "imperative" that he employs. The "Good News" of salvation is being proclaimed. The Lord has revealed his arm, displaying his salvation before the nations (Isa 52:7-10). *Therefore* the priests of Israel are called to remove the holy vessels of the Lord from Babylon.[661] They are not to touch what is unclean (v. 17c; Isa 52:11).[662]

At the same time, Paul alters the citation significantly. In Isa 52:11 it is from Babylon that the priests and Levites are to go forth. They are to depart from "it." In contrast, Paul has "go forth from *their midst.*" The city is naturally associated with its people. The redirection of the citation also recalls the exodus from Egypt, when God brought his people forth "from them."[663] God in Christ calls for himself a new people. Paul's alteration of the text serves to direct the citation against "unbelievers" (v. 15). He points, implicitly, to the apostolic claimants in Corinth.

660. Bonhoeffer, *The Cost of Discipleship,* 63.

661. See 2 Chr 36:10, 18-19, and the book of Ezra.

662. Here one might find the barest hint of a warning against idolatry. Yet the Pauline form of the citation, with its shift to "come out from *the midst of them,*" again suggests a fundamentally personal reference. One wonders, in fact, if the Corinthians who were withholding conjugal rights from their spouses misinterpreted a similar, earlier statement by Paul (1 Cor 7:1).

663. Exod 7:5; Ps 136:11.

Paul omits any reference to "those who bear the vessels of the Lord" and thus implicitly expands the priestly role to include the whole people. The promise of Exod 19:5-6, that the entire people would be priestly, finds its fulfillment in Christ. Paul makes the same theological point in relation to kingship in his alteration of the Davidic promise in v. 18.

The final word of v. 17 shifts the form of the citation to that of a conditional promise: "[Go forth, and be separate, and do not touch the unclean], and I shall welcome you." Again, the traditional versification is misleading. The promise properly belongs with v. 18, in which Paul provides an elaborative promise and concludes with a scriptural citation formula. Paul draws this final word in v. 17, "I shall welcome you," not from Isaiah, but from elsewhere in the prophets, where it appears as an unconditioned word of redemption.[664] Despite Israel's rebellion and transgression, the Lord promises that he will savingly receive his people. These echoes of the "indicative," which anticipate the work that God has performed for us in Christ, resound within Paul's "imperative." The "imperative" is not thereby done away with; rather, it is placed in a larger context that limits and defines it. We who belong to Christ are those who have been accepted by God, not because of who we are, but despite who we are. The relationship of communication, which Paul regards as the essence of salvation, reappears here with full force: God accepts us, and he welcomes us as his sons and daughters. The image of the temple now gives way to that of royalty and family.

We must remind ourselves of Paul's earlier instruction to the Corinthians concerning what it means to "separate oneself," as it appears in the exhortation from the book of Isaiah (1 Cor 5:9-13). It does not mean that Christians are to avoid all contact with unbelievers. They certainly are not to separate from their unbelieving spouses (1 Cor 7:1-16). The Corinthians are to remain in the world and enjoy the fruits of the creation, even if they are not of the world, and even if the fallen creation is coming to its end. Paul's appeal to the Scripture reinforces the argument that his exhortation is directed against his opponents. The Corinthians, informed as they were by Paul's previous letters, would have understood the significance of Paul's usage of the term "unbelievers" as a reference to those who made a claim to be believers but lived otherwise.

18 As we have noted, v. 17d-18 form a single unit. Paul's citation thus begins with an unconditioned promise (v. 16c), moves to exhortation (v. 17a-c), and concludes with a promise in conditional form (v. 17d-18).

The numinous presence of the transcendent God in the temple now receives its counterpart in the comforting presence of the God who is father. Paul supplements the priestly imagery of Isa 52:11 with the royal imagery

664. LXX Jer 23:3; LXX Ezek 11:17; 20:41; LXX Mic 4:6; LXX Zeph 3:19-20; LXX Zech 10:8-10.

drawn from the Lord's promise to David concerning David's "house." The Lord sets aside David's desire to build the Lord a house and instead promises to build David a house by giving him "seed," i.e., a descendant, and a series of descendants, who will sit on David's throne. The Lord then promises, "I will be a father to him, and he shall be a son to me" (2 Sam 7:14). In the context of the book of Samuel, the promise is unconditioned, as it also is in Ps 89:29-37. Rebellion will meet with discipline, but not rejection. In contrast, Ps 132:11-18 makes the promise conditioned upon fidelity. In the present context, Paul echoes the latter, but the original, unconditioned form of the promise could hardly be forgotten and likely stands in the background as well. "As many as may be" the promises of God, whether conditioned or not, they all find their fulfillment in Christ, according to Paul (1:20).

Quite naturally, this promise was understood in earliest Christianity to find its fulfillment in the crucified and risen Christ, who was marked out as God's Son, the very ascription that Paul uses in his early and defining reference to Christ.[665] Paul interprets the promise in terms of the participation of believers in Christ, just as he has already identified them with him in v. 15. He thus expands the royal promise to include all believers, just as he expanded the priestly promise of Isa 52:11 to include them as well. As we have noted, the fulfillment of Exod 19:5-6, in the kingship and priesthood of believers, plays in the background of Paul's citation.

Paul alters the citation not only by giving it a plural form but by making it explicitly gender-inclusive: "And I shall be a father to you, and you shall be my sons and daughters, says the Lord Almighty." He thus picks up the universalism of hope found in the book of Isaiah: "Bring my sons from afar, and my daughters from the ends of the earth!" (Isa 43:6). Just as in Gal 3:28 he understands participation in Christ to be participation in the eschaton in which gender distinctions have been transcended, so here the promise of a son to David implicitly finds its fulfillment in the resurrection of Jesus from the dead.[666] Paul thus indicates that both "sons and daughters" share in this new relationship with God.[667] Despite the dangers of excess in the Corinthian church,[668] he makes an open assertion of equality!

The lengthy citation that began with a formula also closes with a formula: "says the Lord Almighty." The term that Paul uses for "Almighty" *(pantokratōr)*

665. E.g., Rom 1:3-4; Acts 13:33; Heb 1:5; 5:5.

666. Notice that Paul does not imagine that the distinctions of the present creation, including those between husband and wife, have been undone. Two dangers face us in contemporary Christianity. On the one side, there is the danger of seeking to realize the eschaton in the present. On the other side, there is the danger of ignoring the eschaton and elevating the life of the family to God's highest aim.

667. See also Isa 43:6, where a similar inclusiveness appears.

668. See 1 Cor 11:2-16; 14:33-35.

was used in the Septuagint to translate "Lord of hosts" *(YHWH-Sebaoth),* a name of God that generally appears in petitions, promises, or announcements of judgment. The Greek term, a *hapax* in Paul, and indeed the entire New Testament aside from the Apocalypse, stresses the invincible power that belongs to God. This name of God often serves to underscore the certainty of his word and correspondingly appears in the context of his promise to David (2 Sam 7:8), from which Paul may draw it for his conclusion.[669]

7:1 Paul concludes his appeal with an exhortation, echoing his opening words (v. 14) and the Isaianic text (v. 17). Here he broadens the scope of his appeal to include "all defilement of flesh and spirit." His tone likewise changes, mostly like in connection with his inclusive citation of 2 Sam 7:14: just as all believers are "sons and daughters" of God, so Paul includes himself as a mere member of the family of God within the exhortation: "beloved, let us cleanse ourselves. . . ." He has not lost sight of the adversaries against which he warns the Corinthians. In conclusion, he is simply setting the appeal in the larger context that the promises he cites themselves imply. His authority as apostle is limited to the Gospel. Beyond this authority, he will not stand over them, but only alongside them in their faith (1:24).

Paul now names the words of Scripture that he has cited as "promises," making no distinction between the unconditional promise with which he opens the composite citation and the conditional promises with which he closes it. As we have noted, it makes no difference to him: *all* the promises of God, no matter how many they are or what form they may take, find their Yes in Jesus, the Son of God (1:20). Those who belong to Christ live out of that fulfillment in him.

God has done everything that belongs to our salvation. Yet, as we have observed, the work of God does not exclude our action. It defines its "place." We are thereby prevented from taking burdens upon ourselves that we cannot bear. Progress thereby loses the seductive charm that leads to idealism and self-deception. We progress within what already has been done for us.

The wording of the exhortation is unusual for Paul: "Let us cleanse ourselves from all defilement of flesh and spirit." The language is likely called forth in part by the priestly tradition to which he appeals in v. 17, and in part by the situation with the opponents that he must address. It is also remarkably one-sided, calling the Corinthians to do for themselves what properly belongs to salvation itself: they are to cleanse themselves of defilement.[670] Paul frames the matter in this way only because he has set it in the context of God's promises.

669. The formula λέγει κύριος παντοκράτωρ (יְהוָה צְבָאוֹת) is also common in the prophetic literature (Jeremiah, Nahum, Haggai, Zechariah, Malachi), which Paul may likewise echo (see, e.g., LXX Zech 2:15[11]).

670. Cf. Phil 2:12.

He elsewhere has made it clear to the Corinthians that their "washing" and "sanctification" has taken place in Christ's name (1 Cor 6:11). His thought here comes close to that of 1 Cor 5:7, in which he calls them to "clean out the old leaven" because we *are* a new loaf: Christ, our Passover, has been sacrificed for us. Our doing comes out of what God has done in Christ.

We are to cleanse ourselves of "all defilement of flesh and spirit." The usage of "flesh" and "spirit" as correlated (and not opposing) anthropological terms is somewhat infrequent for Paul, but certainly not alien to him.[671] Paul uses the former not only to refer to fallen existence within the world, but also to our (bodily) existence in the fallen world: he himself thus "walks in the flesh," even if he does not "war according to the flesh" (10:3). In his accounts of his concern for the Corinthians that frame the body of the letter, he likewise contrasts his "having no rest in [his] spirit" (2:13) with his "having no rest in [his] flesh" (7:5). The distinction should not be pressed into a dualistic anthropology. In such usage it is fairly clear that Paul speaks, as he does elsewhere, of the whole person as "flesh" or as "spirit."[672] Indeed, in the case of the latter, it is not always clear whether the spirit of the person or the indwelling Spirit of God is in view, or both.[673] Something of that thought may be present here as well, since Paul begins his composite citation with the Lord's promise to indwell his people, a promise that corresponds not only to the preceding exhortations but also to Paul's description of the apostolic mission of the new covenant.

In the present context, it is likely that Paul's exhortation is called forth by both the texts to which he has appealed and by the danger of the adversaries. He does not want the Corinthians again to suppose that purity might be attained by mere physical withdrawal from the world. The adversaries, furthermore, present a real spiritual danger to the Corinthians. Yet they, too, are "in the flesh" and are to be avoided, just as their claims to apostolic status are to be rejected.

Paul then puts the matter positively. In so cleansing themselves, the Corinthians will be "perfecting holiness in the fear of God." Once again the paradoxical nature of God's work in Christ comes into view. The Corinthians already have been "sanctified" in Christ (1 Cor 6:11). Indeed, the crucified and risen Christ himself is their sanctification (1 Cor 1:30). No less than justification, sanctification has been accomplished for us once and for all in Christ. The Corinthians are to grasp in life and experience that which has been done

671. E.g., 1 Cor 2:11; 5:5; 6:17; 7:34. See J. Kremer, "πνεῦμα," *EDNT* 3:117-20.

672. See, e.g., Rom 1:3 and, further, 1 Cor 5:5. The warning in 1 Cor 6:15 concerning uniting Christ with a prostitute reflects the same anthropology, even if in that context he speaks of the body, rather than the "flesh." In this connection, see also 1 Cor 7:34. The *totus homo* anthropology, according to which the believer is entirely flesh and yet entirely spirit, appears classically, e.g., in Gal 5:17.

673. E.g., Rom 8:10, 15; 12:11; 1 Cor 5:5.

for them. They, along with the apostle, are to "perfect" the holiness that already has been accomplished and given to them in Christ "in the fear of God" (cf. 5:11). As the present context makes clear, this "fear of God" includes reverence for his words of promise fulfilled in Christ. Neither the Corinthians nor we may dare set these promises aside.

(3) The Appeal from the Reception of Titus (7:2-16)

The chapter begins with an appeal to the Corinthians (7:2-4). Paul continues the exhortation that he begins in 6:11-13. The rest of the chapter is to be read as an elaboration of this appeal: the troubles with the Corinthians have not been overcome, even if a temporary victory has been achieved in the Corinthian reception of Titus, Paul's messenger.

Nevertheless, the tone of the chapter is entirely positive, as Paul seeks to build upon this victory. Paul now closes the circle of the argument of the body of the letter. He again takes up the narrative of his concern for the Corinthians that he broke off at 2:11-13. The themes and questions of that narrative now reappear, as Paul recalls the drama that called forth this letter. He earlier left off the story with his departure for Macedonia (2:13), and he takes it up again with his arrival and meeting there with Titus, whom he had sought in Troas in his concern for the Corinthians (7:5). Paul, who had been thrust into distress over the Corinthians, has been comforted by God through them. He therefore rejoices (7:5-7). The themes of joy and sorrow in relationship to the Corinthians that Paul introduces in 1:23–2:4 come to expression again here, signaling the closure of the argument (7:8-13a). Paul underscores Titus's joy over the response of the Corinthians to his mission to them (7:13b-16). The fidelity of the Corinthians to the apostle is no private matter, and it does not have to do with Paul's person. It has to do with their fidelity to the Gospel, which binds them to Christ, and thereby to Titus and to all other Christians. Paul's concluding words prepare for his appeal to the Corinthians to complete their promised contribution for Jerusalem, which will serve as an expression of their acceptance of the apostolic Gospel (8:1–9:15).

The closure of the body of the letter makes clear again that this letter to the Corinthians was entirely occasional, called forth by the confrontation that took place in Corinth, Paul's decision not to visit the Corinthians, and the "tearful letter" that caused them so much grief. The occasion calls forth from Paul a profound and remarkable defense of the apostolic mission, the meaning of which transcends these particular circumstances without ever leaving them behind. Basic questions about Christian life, the interpretation of Scripture, and the significance of the apostolic message are answered in Paul's response to the Corinthian defection.

As we have noted, Paul by no means regards the Corinthians' positive response to Titus as the end of the story. Their relationship with one another remains fragile. This is already clear from his personal appeal prior to his happy report. The drama of the letter centers upon the threatened relationship of love that exists between the apostle and his church. More precisely stated, it is the relationship of love between Christ and the church, to whom the apostle has betrothed them (11:2). Yet the church does not have independent access to Christ but may come to him only through the apostolic word. Their temptation and weakness, as we hear from Paul in the closing of the letter, is that they gladly accept "another Jesus" (11:4). In one way or another, every church will have its Christ. The question is whether it will have the Christ of the apostolic proclamation, or another.

(a) Paul's Appeal and Joy (7:2-4)

> [2]*Make room in your hearts for us. We have wronged no one, we have corrupted no one, we have taken advantage of no one.* [3]*I do not say this to condemn you, for I said before that you are in our hearts, to die together and to live together.* [4]*I am acting with great boldness toward you; I have great pride in you; I am filled with comfort. In all our affliction, I am overflowing with joy.*

2 Paul returns to the appeal he has made to the Corinthians: they are to receive him. They are to make room for him, just as they are to open their hearts to him. His tone changes for a moment, adumbrating his sharp words in 10:1–13:10. A contention exists between Paul and the Corinthians, a question of who is in the right: "We have done no one injustice. We have corrupted no one. We have taken advantage of no one." Paul's failure to visit Corinth has sharpened the distrust and suspicions about him in the church. He clearly regards this distrust as without ground and dismisses it with a few brief words. He will later in an ironic manner ask the Corinthians to forgive the injustice he has done to them in refusing to accept support from them (12:13).[674] Indeed, it is Paul who has been done an injustice by the one who openly resisted his authority within the church. But he quickly brushes this injury aside (7:12).

The second protest has an edge to it: in protesting that he has "corrupted no one," Paul intimates his concern that others will seduce the church from its simple devotion to Christ (11:3).[675] He has warned long before of the weighty consequences for anyone who corrupts "the church of God" (1 Cor 3:17).

674. Of course, this practice is long-standing with Paul (1 Cor 9:1-27). He will not allow the church to become his patron, and himself their client.

675. It is likely that Paul uses the verb φθείρω in the sense of "corruption" of their spiritual life. But the usual sense of seduction or moral corruption may well play in the background.

He likewise insists that he has taken advantage of no one. Even though it is hardly possible that he has done so, it is clear that he is responding to suspicions about him that may have been fed by his failure to visit. He is supposed somehow to have tricked and taken in the Corinthians (12:16). But here he points to his refusal to receive funds from them and to his willingness to spend himself for them (12:13, 14-15). His co-workers have conducted themselves in the same way (12:17-18).

3 Just as God acts in Christ in judgment and salvation, Paul, having contended for himself briefly, now changes tone and becomes a reconciler. He does not seek the condemnation of the Corinthians! They are "in his heart," which echoes one of the fundamental themes of the letter.[676] He does not play a game of winners and losers. To do so would be a loss for both of them. From the depths of his heart he seeks the fellowship with them that is found in Christ alone. This fellowship in Christ comes to expression in the purpose clause with which Paul fills out his expression of love: "you are in our hearts to die together and to live together." Life comes after death, not before it! This is true only in the crucified and risen Christ. In him alone the apostle and his church have their fellowship.

4 Paul continues his positive tone in a remarkable expression of confidence and boasting in the Corinthians. His upbeat words about them obviously anticipate his response to their welcome of Titus that appears in the following sections (7:5-16, esp. v. 14). When he later builds on that reception of his messenger in his appeal for the completion of the Jerusalem collection, he again speaks of his boasting on behalf of them before others. There, as well as here, he communicates his boasting about the Corinthians to them in order to encourage them to verify and vindicate it.[677] Of course, this confidence and boasting in the Corinthians, like all boasting, is not properly a boast in them as they are in themselves. It is a boast in God's work in Christ in and among them.[678] Again in this boasting, the apostle and his church are bound together in Christ: he is their boast, just as they are his at the day of Christ (1:14).

Not only does Paul boast in the Corinthians, he is "filled with comfort." He immediately goes on to describe the comfort that he received in Titus's positive report about the Corinthians. Yet he first ascribes that comfort to God, and only subsequently to them (7:5-7). This fits his message: God is the God of *all comfort* (1:3). Although God uses human agents and messengers, all comfort that is given and received finally comes from God alone.

676. See 1:7, 14 and 1:23–2:4, and esp. Paul's account of his paralyzing concern for the Corinthians in Troas, 2:12-13.

677. See 8:24; 9:2-3.

678. 1 Cor 1:30-31; 2 Cor 10:17.

Nevertheless, in the present context, with Paul's words of praise for the Corinthians, something remarkable has taken place. The apostle and his church have exchanged roles. Normally, it is the apostle who first receives comfort in affliction so that he can give it forth to others (1:3-7). In the first instance, the Corinthians are the receivers of comfort from the apostle. At this moment, however, the apostle has received comfort from them. They have been God's tools and agents in the life of the apostle. Among Christians (and indeed, in the world), there are no absolute givers and no absolute receivers. God alone in Christ remains the absolute Giver. We live in changing roles of receiving and giving, giving and receiving. Of course, the reciprocity may not take the form it does with Paul and the Corinthians; often we receive in order to give forth to others, and not to one who has given to us. In speaking in this way to the Corinthians, Paul elevates them remarkably. He does not leave them entrapped in a relationship of dominance and dependence, which they would have known quite well from Greco-Roman society, and which they experience from the other apostolic claimants. Paul allows them to be givers to him, just as God makes them givers. The dynamic that we find here obviously anticipates Paul's call to complete the Jerusalem collection in 2 Cor 8–9.

Paul underscores his need in his conclusion of his words of praise: "I abound beyond measure with joy in all our affliction." He has not left his earlier argument behind! The conjunction of joy and affliction corresponds to his preceding defense and description of the nature of the apostolic mission (4:7-15; 6:4-10). In praising the Corinthians, he implicitly draws them into acceptance of him as their suffering apostle. He likewise prepares for his narrative of Titus's report, which is filled with the apostolic theology of the cross.

(b) Titus's Arrival (7:5-7)

> [5]*For even when we came into Macedonia, our bodies had no rest, but we were afflicted at every turn — fighting without and fear within.* [6]*But God, who comforts the downcast, comforted us by the coming of Titus,* [7]*and not only by his coming but also by the comfort with which he was comforted by you, as he told us of your longing, your mourning, your zeal for me, so that I rejoiced still more.*

5 Paul now picks up the narrative of his concern for the Corinthians that he broke off in 2:12-13. In Troas, he had hoped to meet Titus, and to hear of the Corinthian response to his concerns for the church, concerns which had caused him to cancel his visit. But he did not find Titus there. In his anxiety over the Corinthians, he was unable to make use of the "open door" for the Gospel given to him, and departed for Macedonia.

Now he informs the Corinthians that the situation did not change when he arrived in Macedonia. He recalls his earlier description of his distress, but deepens the language theologically in view of his preceding argument. He still has "no rest,"[679] but now he speaks of having "no rest in our flesh" (ESV, wrongly, "bodies") rather than of having no rest "in my spirit" (2:13). The singular form "my" shifts to the plural "our," deflecting attention from Paul's person to his apostolic mission. Here he uses "flesh" in the theological sense of "the whole person," as he often does in Romans and Galatians, and as he has done already in 5:16, and probably 4:11. "Flesh" does not merely signify his body or outward life, as his concluding description makes clear: "but we were afflicted in every way: battles without, fears within."

Paul explains the hyperbolic "we were afflicted in every way" in the twofold statement that follows. His language recalls not only his description of apostolic existence (4:8), but also the benefit of his sufferings for the Corinthians: if he is afflicted, he is afflicted for their comfort (1:6). Apostolic existence is a *pro-existence,* an existence for others.

The expression "battles without" is clearly metaphorical. Paul is not concerned to describe what sort of strife or conflict he had to face in Macedonia. The situation of the church there was precarious and threatened, as is clear from his letter to the Philippians and the Thessalonian correspondence. He is now thrust into those dangers afresh, and describes them as expressions of the warfare that takes place through the Gospel in the fallen world. He describes his apostolic service in similar terms elsewhere in the letter.[680]

Paul likewise leaves "the fears within" undefined. He undoubtedly recalls his anxiety for the Corinthians, and wants them to hear it afresh. But now he has broadened his scope: he has many fears. The apostle is no hero of faith, but a mere weakling carried by the grace of God. He is just like the Corinthians — and the rest of us.

6 "But the One who comforts those brought low comforted us." The apostle's life does not run in a line that might be traced. It is interrupted not only by unexpected troubles but also by the wonder of God's grace.

God is the One, who comforts those brought low. Paul here emphatically characterizes God, recalling his naming of God as "the Father of mercies and God of all comfort" in the opening of the letter (1:3b-4a).[681] He thereby iden-

679. On the vividness of Paul's fresh use of the perfect form ἔσχηκεν, see the discussion of 2:13, p. 81.

680. See 6:7, "weapons of righteousness for the right hand and the left"; 10:3-5, "waging war, . . . destroying fortresses, . . . taking every mind captive." See Phil 1:30. Cf. 1 Tim 6:12; 2 Tim 4:7.

681. See also Paul's characterizations of God in 4:6 ("God, the One who said, 'Let light shine out of darkness'"), 9:10 ("The One who supplies seed to the sower and bread to the eater"), and 11:31 ("The One who is blessed forever").

tifies God, reminding the Corinthians who God is and how God acts in the world. He is not with the high and mighty as they imagine, but with the lowly.

The word Paul uses, *tapeinos,* may signify either humility or lowliness. In this context, the term clearly expresses the latter. Paul does not have in view a sort of self-humiliation by which one might gain or assure oneself of divine comfort and favor. He is not advocating a sort of medieval theology of humiliation. He speaks rather of "those brought low," who have "suffered" a humiliation that they have not sought, but which has come to them. It is those who have been brought low, by the action of their enemies or by circumstances beyond their control, whom God comforts.

Paul's characterization of God here draws on a rich biblical tradition that appears prominently in the book of Isaiah, and also in the Psalms: "'Comfort, comfort, my people,' says the Lord" (Isa 40:1).[682] The One enthroned above all things does not look up — there is no one above him — but down into the depths, where there is suffering and need (LXX Ps 112[113]:4-9).[683]

God uses earthly means to provide comfort: he comforted Paul with the arrival of Titus. This arrival was beyond Paul's control. The "when" and "how" of help lie with God, even for the apostle. He thus has the true God, and not an idol of his own imagination and planning.

7 Of course, it was not so much Titus's arrival, but the news he brought about the Corinthians that comforted Paul. His love for the Corinthians has been reciprocated: they, too, long for him. These close, personal relations were central to the life of Paul's churches.[684] He again mentions their desire for him in v. 11. Yet he does not seek to bind them simply to him in mutual love and longing, but to the other churches, especially the church in Jerusalem (9:14).

The "tears" of the Corinthians expressed not only their longing for Paul, but also their sorrow over their broken relationship. As the following context makes clear, the confrontation with a leading figure within the church stands in the background to the entire course of events, including the resolution that now has taken place. The tears of the Corinthians come in response not only to Titus, but also, even more, to the tears Paul shed as he wrote to them after that unhappy encounter (2:4).

At least for the moment, the Corinthians are zealous to defend Paul and affirm him as their apostle. Indeed, they have been overly zealous in their treatment of the one who provided the offense (2:5-11). Just as Paul affirms their tears, he likewise affirms their zeal or jealousy for him. He, too, is jealous in love for them, yet not for himself: he wants to wed them to Christ (11:2).

682. See LXX Isa 40:1-2, 11; 49:10, 13; 51:3, 12; 54:11; 61:2; 66:12-13.

683. See LXX Pss 9:39 (10:18); 17:28 (18:27); 33:19 (34:18); 81(82):3; 101:18 (102:17); 137(138):6. See Luther, *LW* 21:299 (The Magnificat).

684. See, e.g., Rom 1:11; Phil 1:18; 2:26; 4:1.

Paul therefore rejoiced. As we have observed, a rare reversal of roles has taken place. Normally, it is the apostle who is a channel of comfort to the Corinthians and others (1:3-7). They now have become God's means of comforting him in the midst of other unnamed troubles to which he refers in v. 5. The relationship between the apostle and his church is not one-way. He will not lord his authority over their faith (1:24). When and where God chooses, they must be the source of comfort to him.

(c) The Letter That Brought Grief (7:8-13a)

[8]For even if I made you grieve with my letter, I do not regret it — though
I did regret it, for I see that that letter grieved you, though only for a while.
[9]As it is, I rejoice, not because you were grieved, but because you were
grieved into repenting. For you felt a godly grief, so that you suffered no
loss through us. [10]For godly grief produces a repentance that leads to sal-
vation without regret, whereas worldly grief produces death. [11]For see what
earnestness this godly grief has produced in you, but also what eagerness
to clear yourselves, what indignation, what fear, what longing, what zeal,
what punishment! At every point you have proved yourselves innocent in
the matter. [12]So although I wrote to you, it was not for the sake of the one
who did the wrong, nor for the sake of the one who suffered the wrong, but
in order that your earnestness for us might be revealed to you in the sight
of God. [13a]Therefore we are comforted.

8 The grief and joy of the apostle and his church are intertwined. It was to avoid being grieved by them again that he decided not to visit them — and then wrote to them "with many tears" (1:23–2:4). The one who caused grief, did not grieve Paul (although, of course, as Paul's opening statement makes clear, he obviously did do so), but the entire church (2:5). Now Paul acknowledges that his tearful letter grieved the Corinthians. He continues to open his heart to them: for a time he regretted that letter, and the grief it brought them. But the grief was "only for an hour."[685] Paul now does not regret the grief the letter brought them.

9 He thus explains his joy at Titus's arrival, and his change of heart over the letter he had written: the grief he brought the Corinthians only worked them good, because it effected their repentance. The event follows the pattern of the word of the cross. The theology of the Corinthian correspondence is contained in a nutshell within it.[686] Through the apostle, God has wounded

685. Paul uses this concrete expression elsewhere for a short period of time that may seem very long (Gal 2:5; 1 Thess 2:17).

686. That is to say, the event reflects the "word of the cross" in relationship to human

the Corinthians in order to heal them. As Paul's prior regret makes clear, the story-line was by no means predictable. Matters might well have taken a turn for the worse. Indeed, Paul was anxious for the Corinthians to the point of paralysis in his apostolic mission (2:12-13). But the Corinthians were "grieved to repentance." They were "grieved according to God." That is to say, their grief was worked by God and rested in his hand. It had its time, but that time came to an end in their change of heart. Just as the Corinthians have been instruments of God in the life of the apostle, the apostle has proved to be the instrument of God in the life of the Corinthians. "Through us," he says, "you were grieved according to God." This took place so that the Corinthians might not suffer loss in any way. The healing that God works through wounding is complete and whole. God wills to restore us, not destroy us, even though he must perform the latter in order to accomplish the former. That is the essence of salvation: we must be stripped of our idols and given the true God.

10 Paul elaborates the nature of God-worked grief: it effects a "repentance unto salvation." It was the great temptation of liberal Christianity to forget or underplay the call to repentance that is inherent to the Gospel. Contemporary Christianity, especially its evangelical form, seems presently to face the same temptation.[687] Paul's Gospel contains no less a call for repentance than does Jesus' message of the kingdom. In neither case, however, is this "repentance" to be regarded as a condition that we must fulfill in order to come to salvation.[688] As Paul has already made clear, it is his letter to the Corinthians that God has used to effect repentance in them. Without in any way reducing human responsibility, God remains the author of repentance, working it through his word in its twofold form of demand and promise, law and gospel.[689]

As we have noted, not all grief brings this healing, saving repentance, to which no regret is attached: "the world's grief works death." In this context, one cannot help but think of the difference between Peter and Judas as they appear in the Gospel narratives. One came to repentance; one came to grief. Yet Paul most likely does not have something so immediate or drastic in mind: there is another form of grief that drains away life and joy, and brings death

---

fallenness, and not in connection to inexplicable suffering. The apostle speaks comfort to this suffering as well in this letter.

687. See above, p. 88, for H. Richard Niebuhr's analysis of liberalism.

688. Then we would be set before the two opinions that were current within medieval piety. Either one supposed that a simple sigh of grief was sufficient before God, or one again and again faced the tormenting question as to whether one's repentance was sufficient, whether one had truly grieved over sin and had truly turned away from it. See D. C. Steinmetz, *Luther in Context* (Grand Rapids: Baker, 1995), 1-11.

689. According to the report of Acts, the earliest church recognized that repentance was worked by God and thus spoke of God "*giving* to the Gentiles the repentance that is unto life" (Acts 11:18).

only very, very slowly. It is in this grief of hopelessness that the world without Christ lives and dies.

11 Paul reminds the Corinthians of their repentant grief: "Such eagerness! But what a defense, what indignation, what fear, what desire, what zeal, what vindication!" This response of the Corinthians has entirely to do with their relationship with Paul, as their apostle. Their eagerness is an eagerness to accept and support Paul (v. 12). Their defense *(apologia)* is a defense of the apostle, as Paul's following exclamations make clear.[690] Their indignation is on his behalf, most likely in view of the offender who stands at the center of the controversy. Their fear is not a fear of Paul, but of God who has given him apostolic authority (v. 15; cf. 10:9). Their "desire" and "zeal" are for the apostle, as we have seen already (v. 7). Likewise, their "vindication" or (one might even translate *ekdikēsis*) "vengeance" clearly has to do with Paul. He again recalls their rebuke of the offender, now placing it in a positive light, overlooking their excess.

Paul concludes his praise of them in a wonderful way that reflects the Gospel: "In everything you showed yourselves to be innocent in the matter." He has made clear that his comfort and joy have come from the repentance of the Corinthians. They turned away from the wrong they had done. This was the effect of Paul's letter. Yet he now speaks of them as having been entirely innocent, without guilt in the matter that has caused them both so much grief. He does something similar in the opening of the letter, when he speaks of his merely testing their obedience (2:9). But now his forgiving spirit becomes especially apparent. This forgiving spirit is an expression of the Gospel: the rebellion and failure of the Corinthians are completely overcome, done away with. They no longer exist. Love does not keep an account of evil (1 Cor 13:5).

12 The content and concern of the "tearful letter" that caused so much grief become clear here. The relationship between Paul and the Corinthians has been strained to the point of breaking as the result of the confrontation in Corinth to which Paul refers in 2:5-11. As we have noted, although the message of Second Corinthians is profoundly relevant beyond (or more precisely, in and through) its original occasion, that original occasion was remarkably concrete and specific.

Paul speaks of himself and the offender only in indirect terms here, as "the one acting unjustly" and "the one to whom an injustice was done." His language is distinctly forensic, and decided. Someone in the church has done him an injustice.

But Paul again sweeps that matter aside. His letter had obviously addressed this issue; otherwise it would not have caused so much grief, or worked such repentance. But he now places the letter in a larger context. It was not

690. Cf. 1 Cor 9:3.

written in order to right a wrong, although that was clearly its intent. In the hand of God it had a greater purpose. Through it, the Corinthians came to see for themselves, "in the presence of God" (and not in that of the absent apostle), that they in fact were eager "on (Paul's) behalf," i.e., eager to accept and defend him. It should go without saying that this eagerness has nothing to do with Paul, and everything to do with the apostolic calling and mission given to him.

Once more, Paul overlooks the guilt of the Corinthians, treating it under the Gospel, as non-existent. This is not a mere fiction on his part: he means and believes what he says when he speaks of Christ having become sin, that we might become the righteousness of God in him (5:21).

13a Again here we find an unhappy division of verses. The first word of v. 13 clearly belongs with what precedes, and rounds off Paul's narrative of his encounter with Titus that extends back to v. 5.[691] "On this account, we have been comforted." The comfort of the apostle does not come at the expense of the Corinthians. They are in his heart to live and die (v. 3). Whatever rebellion and guilt there may have been in Corinth, it is gone and forgotten. Paul's comfort and joy is that the Corinthians in their repentance are innocent of defection from the apostolic Gospel, and remain zealous for him as their apostle.

(d) Titus's Joy (7:13b-16)

> [13b]*And besides our own comfort, we rejoiced still more at the joy of Titus, because his spirit has been refreshed by you all.* [14]*For whatever boasts I made to him about you, I was not put to shame. But just as everything we said to you was true, so also our boasting before Titus has proved true.* [15]*And his affection for you is even greater, as he remembers the obedience of you all, how you received him with fear and trembling.* [16]*I rejoice, because I have complete confidence in you.*

13b Paul closes his appeal to the Corinthians by turning to Titus's joy over their reception of him. He seeks to draw the Corinthians into the community of the apostolic Gospel, not into a personal allegiance to him. For this reason, he seeks to bind them to others and not merely himself. Indeed, his comfort includes Titus's joy over the Corinthians. As we have noted, his rhetoric anticipates his appeal for the Jerusalem collection.

The dynamic remains personal, through and through. Titus had joy in the Corinthians' response. His spirit was refreshed. The apostle works first with persons, and not with plans and programs.

14 Paul already has told the Corinthians that he has great confidence in them, and boasts about them greatly (v. 4). He boasted to Titus about them,

691. The narrative is also anticipated by the closing words of his appeal to them in v. 4.

even before Titus's visit. This boast is noteworthy in more than one way. In the first place, human beings are not the proper object of boasting, according to Paul. All proper boasting is boasting in the Lord. Secondly, and even more remarkably, the conduct of the Corinthians up to the point of Titus's visit provided more grounds for the very anxiety concerning them that Paul recounts, than any confidence or boasting. The Corinthians had been far more a grief for the apostle than a joy. It is undoubtedly the case that Paul praises them here and throughout this section for a certain rhetorical and emotional effect: he seeks to win them with honey rather than with vinegar. Their relationship with him is far from being secured. By building on their positive response to Titus, he seeks to gain their allegiance fully. Yet his rhetoric remains shaped by the Gospel. At a deeper level, his boasting in them — which took place *before* their positive response — is nothing but a raw confidence in the Gospel that performs its work in them. Paul's boasting in the Lord does not exclude, but includes boasting in the Corinthians, *precisely in this otherwise unwarranted and unexpected form*. He boasts in them when they least deserve it, and hardly earn it.

It is for this reason that Paul's joy is so great. If in anything he boasted to Titus about them, the Corinthians did not put him to shame. He spoke "in truth" about the Corinthians, namely, out of the Gospel itself.[692] Just as he said all things about the Corinthians in this truth, so his boast to Titus came to be true. Paul's boast in the Gospel about the Corinthians came to reality. The word performed its work. The Yes of God in Jesus Christ came about afresh in the Corinthians (1:19).

15 Titus himself is concerned, with heart and life, about the fidelity of the Corinthians to the Gospel, and to the apostle who bears it. The warm personal relationships within Paul's circle again come to expression here: Titus's deepest feelings remained touched by the Corinthians, as he recalls their reception of him. Of course, Paul frames the matter for the greatest rhetorical effect. Titus recalls the obedience of the Corinthians. He was sent to them as an apostolic delegate: their reception of him was equivalent to the reception of the apostle himself.[693] Their obedience was an obedience to the apostle and his message. And that obedience, in turn, was nothing other than obedience to God. Paul will later insist on such obedience.[694] Paul thus characterizes the Corinthian reception of Titus as taking place "with fear and trembling," the same terms he uses with the Philippians for their obedience to God (Phil

692. This understanding of "truth" as the Gospel in its word about God and the fallen human being appears elsewhere in the letter. See 4:2; 6:7; 11:10; 13:8.

693. In this respect, the delegates of the apostle were like the apostle himself. See the brief discussion above, p. 4.

694. 10:5-6.

2:12).[695] This same understanding of apostolic authority appears elsewhere in Paul's letters, aside from the conflict situation in Corinth. This authority rests entirely in the Gospel that the apostle bears.[696]

16 "I rejoice that I have confidence in you in everything." Paul's last word in the body of the letter is to be taken as an expression of apostolic confidence in the Gospel: he does not gain assurance from their past obedience, he gains obedience from his past assurance of God's work in Christ. His affirmation is intended to have a definite rhetorical effect. Paul seeks to build up the success achieved in Titus's mission. He will continue to do so in the collection for Jerusalem. A battle has been won, but the war is far from over. This is clear from this happy narrative of Titus's mission itself: it begins with Paul's direct request to the Corinthians to "make room" for him (v. 2). The unit appears within the larger context of appeal, in which Paul openly asks the Corinthians to reciprocate his openness with them, and to break their ties with "unbelievers" (6:11-13; 6:14–7:1). If in recounting the Corinthian reception of Titus Paul makes it seem as if the Corinthians are nothing but saints, in the larger argument they appear to be nothing but sinners. His concluding rhetoric has to be seen for what it is, and taken with a few grains of salt. Paul's troubled relationship with the Corinthians has been the underlying theme of the letter from its opening onward. As we have noted, the apostle is realistic enough to recognize that a single swallow does not make a summer. There are more issues with which he must deal in Corinth. And there is more to come in his argument.

695. See also Eph 6:5.

696. See Rom 1:5; 6:16-17; 10:16; 15:18; 16:19, 26; Phil 2:12; 2 Thess 1:8; 3:14.

III. THE CLOSING OF THE LETTER: THE CALL TO SIMPLICITY (8:1–13:14)

The closings of Paul's letters are marked by a shift from the theme of the body to a reference to Paul's next contact with the church, either through representatives, or by a visit of his own.[1] In Second Corinthians, Paul's plan of sending of representatives, and his announcement of his visit appear in two distinct sections: an encouragement to the Corinthians to complete their collection for Jerusalem (2 Cor 8:1–9:15), and Paul's concluding assertion of apostolic authority (2 Cor 10:1–13:14).

These two sections of the letter-closing are sufficiently different in content and tone from the preceding argument that a number of interpreters have questioned their originality. In both instances, however, good reasons for the change in topic and tone are apparent.[2] Within the context of Paul's stormy relations with the Corinthians, his concluding, brief expressions of confidence in them in 7:5-16 are to be regarded as rhetorically motivated, intended to win

1. This marking of the turn from the body of the letter to its closing is admittedly early, much earlier than the usual marking of it as beginning at 12:14. Nevertheless, as long as 8:1–9:15 may be regarded as original to the letter, it marks the turn in Paul's attention to the collection, to his sending his delegates (8:16-24; 9:3-5), and to his own visit to Corinth (9:4). As Funk recognizes, the material bears the characteristics of the usual "apostolic parousia." See R. W. Funk, "The Apostolic *Parousia:* Form and Significance," in *Christian History and Interpretation: Studies Presented to John Knox* (ed. W. R. Farmer, C. F. D. Moule, and R. R. Niebuhr; Cambridge: Cambridge University Press, 1967), 250. That it has to do with the preparation of the collection does not diminish its function of announcing the visit of Paul's delegates and, in fact, his own visit. Furthermore, the argument of the body of the letter is obviously completed by Paul's rejoicing at the parousia of Titus with good news from Corinth (7:5-16, esp. vv. 6-7). As is obvious, 8:1–9:15, as well as 10:1–13:13, constitute distinct epistolary units, both of which, from beginning to end, are oriented to Paul's upcoming visit to Corinth. As is widely recognized, the demarcation of the closing of a letter is difficult (see Schnider and Stenger, *Studien,* 71-74). Paul's turn to speak of a visit or his sending of delegates in his stead is the clearest marker of that shift, as Funk has argued persuasively. The fact that it appears early here (and elsewhere, too) does not eliminate its significance. We must not imagine Paul's letters to be theological disquisitions that necessarily conclude with a few, brief words of exhortation and greeting. They are living communications, with living churches. In this lengthy closing of the letter, Paul continues to deal with matters that are not so much extensions of his preceding argument as they are extensions of the intended effect of that argument. Above all else, Paul is concerned to communicate not merely meaning but his presence. From this perspective, even 1 Cor 4:16-21, as early as it is in the letter, may be regarded as turning to "closing matters."

2. See the discussion of the function of 2 Cor 10–13 below, pp. 368-73.

the hearts of the Corinthians. His positive statements about them should not be read as a description of a fully restored relationship.[3] They rather serve as prelude to the appeal for the completion of the collection (8:1–9:15), and likewise to the strident argument of 10:1–13:14. They function nearly like a *captatio benevolentiae,* despite the fact that they appear late in the letter.

With regard to the collection chapters: as we have observed, Paul does not seek to bind the Corinthians to himself, but to Christ. He is concerned only that they recognize and embrace him as Christ's apostle. He thus underscores the comfort and joy that Titus received from them, and how Titus himself came to be bound to them with heart and soul, as the result of their warm reception of him.[4] Indeed, Titus acts not only as an agent of the apostle, but also at the prompting of God, and thus of his own accord.[5] Furthermore, Paul is not concerned merely with the Corinthians' relationship with his agent. Just as he seeks to bind them to Christ, he seeks to bind them to all other Christians and churches. This is fundamental to his purpose in the collection for Jerusalem.[6] The gift, by its very nature and intent, constitutes Paul's attempt to bring the Corinthians (along with all other participants) into *koinōnia* with all the other churches, and especially, of course, with the church in Jerusalem. He hopes for unity among *all* the churches and communication between them.[7] The Corinthians' gift is an expression of that unity.[8] Paul's announcement of the gift of the Macedonian churches serves this aim, even if he also thereby seeks to motivate the Corinthians to complete their promise.[9] Likewise, those who accompany Titus not only ensure the probity of Paul's dealings, but also serve as representatives of the churches to which the Corinthians are to be joined in this mission. Paul's concern to bind the Corinthians to the other churches is not new. As is evident in the present context, the Corinthian contribution for Jerusalem has long been his concern.[10] Paul's appeal to the Corinthians to complete their promised gift for Jerusalem is thus far from being a break in his argument or a digression from his main concern. Just the opposite: the Corinthian gift represents a concrete act of obedience to the Gospel that the

3. This remains so, even if Paul's confidence is grounded in Christ and spoken in earnest.

4. See 7:7, 13-16. The Corinthians received Titus as Paul's representative, of course, but Paul emphasizes the bond that came to exist between the Corinthians and Titus.

5. It was Titus who had begun the collection in Corinth (8:6). See further 8:16.

6. 8:13-15; 9:12-15.

7. This hope is esp. evident in the conclusion of the letter to Rome. See Rom 15:14-33.

8. 8:16-24; 9:12-15.

9. 8:1-6.

10. His aim of securing unity among the churches is also evident in his instructions concerning head coverings for women and is implicit in his admonitions concerning the celebration of the Lord's Supper (1 Cor 11:2-16, 17-34). His concluding greetings in First Corinthians, which include those of "the churches in Asia," bear the same significance (1 Cor 16:5-20).

apostle bears. Their participation in the collection will be an affirmation of Paul's apostolic authority and a fulfillment of his apostolic aims.

Furthermore, the collection chapters (8:1–9:15) and the stormy conclusion of the letter (10:1–13:14) are connected to one another fundamentally. Corinthian participation in the collection will be an act of the "simplicity" *(haplotēs)* of giving and receiving that Paul seeks to further in the church. As his own claim to "simplicity" makes clear, this communicative openness is the work of the Gospel, a fruit of its opening of communication between God and the fallen human being in Christ (1:12). It is no surprise, then, that Paul returns to this theme in the concluding chapters, as he expresses his fear that the Corinthians might be led away from "the simplicity which is directed toward Christ" (11:3). The simplicity of giving cannot be separated from the simplicity of receiving. Love finds its energy and source in faith; faith expresses its energy in love.

A. The Collection as the Confession of the Gospel (8:1–9:15)

Already when Paul wrote First Corinthians, the Corinthians were ready to participate in the collection. In that letter, Paul merely instructs the Corinthians on the completion of the collection in an orderly manner prior to his arrival (1 Cor 16:1-2).[11] He had planned to visit Corinth on his way to Macedonia. As we know, that plan was disrupted by the troubles in his relationship with the church. After an emergency trip to Corinth, and a disastrous confrontation between the apostle and a leading figure within the church, Paul cancelled the originally planned trip. Now Titus's mission has brought a temporary reconciliation with the apostle. Paul seeks to build on that success by taking up the matter of the collection again, binding the Corinthians not only to himself, but also to the other churches. He does not refer to his earlier instruction, but, in view of the passage of time, exhorts the Corinthians afresh to complete their promised gift. That is to say: Paul takes up the collection from Corinth right where he left off. Yet the circumstances have changed considerably. He is now coming to them from Macedonia, where the churches unexpectedly have made a sacrificial contribution to the collection. Paul now distances himself somewhat from his planned reception of the collection for delivery to Jerusalem. Titus, who already has facilitated healing in the relationship between Paul and the church, will precede him (8:16-17). Moreover, Titus will be accompanied by two others. In that way, the Corinth contribution will be received first by Titus and the representatives of the churches (8:18-24). Paul will arrive only later (9:1-5).

11. The arrangements concerning the delivery of the gift will be made when Paul is present (1 Cor 16:3-4).

As we have observed, the collection chapters are integral to Paul's larger purpose in the letter of binding the Corinthians to the other churches and to Christ. This concern is evident throughout the chapters, and finds expression in the twofold form of Paul's argument. In contrast to the usual pattern of Paul's theological argument, he introduces the topic of the collection with a lengthy exhortation (8:1-24). Instruction on the meaning of giving follows in second place (9:1-15, esp. vv. 6-15). This reversal of order is quite understandable, of course, since the Corinthians promised a gift for Jerusalem long before, but have not yet completed the collection of it.

In both his encouragement and his instruction, Paul makes appeal to the Corinthian relationship with other churches. In his encouragement, he points to the Macedonian churches as an example of the grace of giving (8:1-6), and likewise announces the representatives whom he is sending to facilitate the collection (8:16-24). The Corinthians are thus to demonstrate the genuineness of their love "in the presence of the churches" (8:24). In the instruction Paul gives to the Corinthians, the roles are reversed (9:1-15). The Corinthians now appear as the pattern for the Macedonians: the promised gift of the Corinthians provided the motivation for their generous gift (9:1-5). Likewise, Paul, in the instructional section of his argument (9:6-15), envisions the Corinthian gift as both effecting thanksgiving to God and creating a bond of love between Jerusalem and Corinth. This living and dynamic exchange between Corinth and the other churches is expressive of the rich theology of gift that guides Paul's argument.

1. *Encouragement to Complete the Collection (8:1-24)*

As we have noted, Paul regards the collection for Jerusalem not merely as serving to relieve need (although it does do precisely that) but, more fundamentally, as bringing about common thanksgiving to God and interchange among the churches. This concern is apparent from the very start of Paul's exhortation, in which he presents the Macedonians as an example for the Corinthians. They are an example, not of a moral virtue that is to be imitated, but of the grace of God that is to be sought. As is the case with Paul's exhortations elsewhere, he calls the Corinthians to a fresh experience of that which Christ has given to them and has done for them. Their "doing" flows out of what Christ has done and, indeed, is a reception of the grace of Christ. Christ stands between the Corinthians and the apostle, the Corinthians and the Macedonians, and all others. We may remind ourselves here of Bonhoeffer's rich insight into Christian fellowship: "I have community with others, and I shall continue to have it only through Jesus Christ."[12] Christ brings all of them into a relationship of

12. Bonhoeffer, *Life Together,* 25-26. See the lengthier citation above, p. 16.

giving and receiving, in which God remains the unqualified Giver, and therefore the recipient of all thanksgiving. Giving is spontaneous. It does not arise from compulsion; indeed, it cannot properly arise from compulsion, or it is no longer giving. The unfettered spontaneity of giving nevertheless does not exclude persuasion that is defined and shaped by what God in Christ has given and done. This form of persuasion is evident in the pressure that Paul brings to bear on the Corinthians. They are to "demonstrate" the reality of *their love* in the presence of the churches (8:24). Paul's wording here again makes clear that his argument does not rest on moral obligation, not even one that arises from gratitude. It rests instead on the reception of the gifts and grace of God in Christ, which themselves effect that reception, which itself issues in giving. As he does throughout the Corinthian correspondence, Paul here seeks to overcome the fatal separation of God's gifts from God the Giver, which brings the misrecognition and perversion of God's gifts.[13] He thus closes his instruction on the collection with a word of thanksgiving, to which he implicitly invites his readers: "Thanks be to God for his gift that is beyond all telling!"

a. The Grace of Giving in Macedonia (8:1-6)

8[1]*We want you to know, brothers, about the grace of God that has been*
given among the churches of Macedonia, [2]*for in a severe test of affliction,*
their abundance of joy and their extreme poverty have overflowed in a
wealth of generosity on their part. [3]*For they gave according to their means,*
as I can testify, and beyond their means, of their own accord, [4]*begging us*
earnestly for the favor of taking part in the relief of the saints — [5]*and this,*
not as we expected, but they gave themselves first to the Lord and then by
the will of God to us. [6]*Accordingly, we urged Titus that as he had started,*
so he should complete among you this act of grace.

As we have noted, Paul presents the Macedonians to the Corinthians as an example. Yet they are an example, not of generosity, but of the grace of God. Paul seeks to stir the Corinthians to a renewed experience of God's grace with their completion of their promised gift for Jerusalem. He later informs them that they have played an instrumental role in the Macedonian gift (9:2). In the willingness to give itself, then, there is to be an exchange, receiving and giving, between the Corinthians and the Macedonians. At this point, Paul remains silent about this role of the Corinthians. He first of all wants the spontaneity of the gift of the Macedonians to spur them to complete their contribution.

1 In this first movement of argument in the closing of the letter, Paul

13. He has asked the Corinthians earlier, "What do you have that you did not receive?" (1 Cor 4:7).

announces to the Corinthians "the grace of God" that had been given to the Macedonians. He thus turns immediately from his celebration of the Corinthian response to Titus, to the happy news of God's work elsewhere. This sudden shift is an implicit reminder to the Corinthians that they are not the only objects of God's love and care. Indeed, God's work in Macedonia is to spur the Corinthians to complete their own promised participation in the collection for Jerusalem. It is Titus who provides the continuity between the two units of the letter: Paul again is sending his emissary, whom the Corinthians recently have welcomed, to help in the completion of the gift for Jerusalem.[14] Paul thus builds on Titus's recent success in restoring the Corinthians, as he seeks to draw them more fully into the community of churches.

It is "the grace of God" given in Macedonia that Paul announces. In this context, "grace" signifies not merely God's favor but the concrete expression of that favor in the life of the Macedonian churches. Here the term *charis* (usually translated "grace") very nearly takes on the same meaning as *charisma, dōrea,* or *dōrēma* (all of which are usually rendered "gift"). Indeed, over against the last two terms, which focus more on the action of giving, *"charis-ma"* ("gift") may be regarded as a concrete expression of *charis* ("grace" or "favor") of a person. As we have noted, the concrete usage of the term *charis* is not unusual for Paul. It appears regularly in the prescripts and closings of his letters,[15] as well as in other contexts.[16] The significance of this overlap of "grace" and "gift" should not be overlooked. On the one hand, it makes clear that, even though Paul speaks of "grace" as the (undeserved) favor of God given once-for-all in Christ, he also presents it as a gift that arrives and is to be received again and again.[17] On the other hand, the same overlap in meaning shows that Paul presents "gifts" as acts of grace and giving. This is especially evident in the present context. His use of the term *charis* as "gift" implicitly includes the giver's favor and act of giving within the gift given: here he speaks of God as having "shed his grace" on the Macedonians. He goes on to speak of human gifts in much the same way. Paul understands true gifts as involving the self-giving of the giver. This idea comes to expression in various ways in the following context.

Paul also makes it clear that he understands the Macedonian act of giving as the reception of a gift from God. God is present and active in human giving in such a way that human givers are finally mere receivers. This profound theology of gift continues throughout Paul's argument in 2 Cor 8–9 and appears emphatically in his closing exclamation in 9:15: "Thanks be to God!"

14. Titus, most likely, is the bearer of the present letter.

15. E.g., Rom 1:5; 16:20, 24; 1 Cor 1:3; 16:23; 2 Cor 1:2; 13:13; Gal 1:3; 6:18.

16. See esp. Rom 1:5; 12:3; 15:15; 1 Cor 1:4; 3:10; Gal 2:9. He uses it in reference to human gifts in 1 Cor 16:3 and in the following context here, 2 Cor 8:4, 6.

17. The pronouncements of his letter prescripts make this understanding esp. apparent.

2 The grace of God that was given to the Macedonians was the grace of *giving.*[18] Paul uses the example of this gift to exhort the Corinthians, just as he will later inform them that their readiness to give prompted the Macedonian giving. As we have noted, Paul's encouragement takes place within a changing pattern of giving and receiving. It is not the Macedonians themselves or some virtue within them that serves as an example for the Corinthians, but the grace of God that has been given to the Macedonians. As Paul himself underscores, this grace arrived in an unexpected and extraordinary way — within the affliction of the Macedonians. Paul did not ask for or expect a contribution from them. The situation in Corinth is quite different. They are not facing persecution or trial. Paul has solicited their participation in the collection and already has instructed them concerning it (1 Cor 16:1-4). He does not ask the Corinthians to match the Macedonians' gift. This would not have been possible, even if the amount might have easily exceeded the Macedonian contribution. The magnitude of the Macedonian gift arises from their simultaneous joy and poverty. Paul, in fact, emphasizes to the Corinthians that their gift is *not* to be extraordinary. It is not to cause them affliction (8:12-13). They are not to compete with Macedonia. Gift-giving is not to become a competitive game, a sort of "Mediterranean potlatch," as was common in the Greco-Roman world.[19] Such competition would negate the giving, turning it into a mere means of self-assertion. Paul's following exhortation suggests that he is attempting to prevent, or perhaps even correct, this way of viewing the promised gift on the part of the Corinthians.

Paul underscores the extraordinary grace that was given to the Macedonians in two concise paradoxes. The first paradox is implicit, and yet obvious: in the midst of "much testing of affliction" the Macedonians had an abundance of joy. Like the apostle, who grieves yet always rejoices (6:10), they are recipients not only of the sufferings of Christ but also of the divine comfort given through him (cf. 1:3-7). Their experience is contrary to all human expectation, a mark of the presence of the unseen eschaton that they nevertheless see and possess in hope (cf. 5:16-18).[20]

In a second paradox, Paul speaks of this abounding joy cooperating with their "deep poverty" so as to abound in a wealth of generosity. God's

18. The opening ὅτι is to be understood as recitative, which is usual following a verb of knowing: "*that,* in much testing of affliction, . . ." (against the ESV, which makes it explanatory).

19. For a brief but useful survey of friendship and benefaction, see P. Marshall, *Enmity in Corinth: Social Conventions in Paul's Relations with the Corinthians* (WUNT 2/23; Tübingen: Mohr Siebeck, 1987), 1-34.

20. The pressure and persecution that the Macedonian churches faced are apparent in the Thessalonian correspondence and the letter to the Philippians. See also the account of Acts 17:1-15, concerning Paul's visit to Thessalonica.

grace works *sub contrario:* wealth is present within their poverty.[21] Before all else, this reality holds true in Christ, as Paul will remind the Corinthians shortly (v. 9). Of course, radically differing currencies are in play in this paradox, opposing conceptions of "poverty" and "wealth" that overturn human calculations. The poverty of the Macedonians is outward and visible, their wealth is inward and hidden. The former is temporal, the latter is eternal. Yet Paul is not content simply to await the arrival of the eschaton, in which all poverty shall be overcome. His very purpose here is to urge the Corinthians to participate here and now in the alleviation of need and poverty.[22] Contrary to our usual assumptions, the unbridgeable gap between the present and the eschaton does not lead to inaction, but to action in its highest form. The "simplicity" of the Macedonians is a witness to the already-present eschaton, the arrival of which — in judgment and salvation — will abolish all poverty. In their present wealth-within-poverty, the Macedonians participate in Christ, who out of his poverty makes all believers rich (8:9). They share in the pattern of God's work that is likewise found in the apostle, who, "being poor, makes many rich" (6:10).

The term *haplotēs,* which is rendered "generosity" in the major English translations (ESV, NIV, NRSV), should be interpreted instead in its usual sense as "simplicity," not only here, but also in 9:11, 13. There is no good reason to introduce an otherwise unattested meaning of the term in these contexts.[23] God's grace effects a "simplicity" in human beings that opens them to a receiving-and-giving in which hidden and self-seeking motives are overcome. As we have seen, Paul uses the same term to describe the transparency of his conduct toward the Corinthians ("the simplicity [*haplotēs*] and purity of God," 1:12), and he likewise worries that the Corinthians might be led astray "from simplicity [*haplotēs*] toward Christ" (11:3). The term thus brings to expression a fundamental theme of the letter, the communication between God and humanity that has been established in Christ. The "simplicity" of the Macedonians has expressed itself in their gift for Jerusalem. Paul characterizes their giving here as an act of communication, rather than one of generosity. As he goes on to recount, the Macedonians asked for "the grace" and "the participation" of the collection. They entered into a relationship of receiving from God and giving to others, which went beyond their own power (v. 3). In other words, Paul does not speak here of the Macedonians "having" riches, not even having them in

21. This is not at all to say that poverty is to be understood as wealth. To speak in this universalizing way would be naïve, to say the least.

22. 8:4; 9:1, 12. Aside from Paul's instruction in 1 Cor 16:1-4, one would not know that the contribution was intended for Jerusalem.

23. See BDAG, "ἁπλότης," 104; T. Schramm, "ἁπλότης," *EDNT* 1:123-24. The same is true of the adjective ἁπλοῦς in Matt 6:22 and Luke 11:34, and of the adverb ἁπλῶς in Jas 1:5.

magnanimity or generosity. He speaks instead of "the riches of their simplicity." "Riches" are not found in a possession — not even in a virtue that one might "possess" — but in free communication with God and with others, in free acts of receiving and giving. Paul will develop this thought in his theological instruction of the Corinthians (9:6-11).

3 Paul here repeats his report to the Corinthians in other words. Verses 3-5 present a theologically significant parallel to v. 2: the gift of God's grace has its expression in the willing and working of the Macedonians.[24]

The finite verb "they gave themselves" is postponed until v. 5. Here and in v. 4, Paul describes the manner in which this self-giving takes place. It takes the form of a wonder: the Macedonians gave according to their power, and also contrary to their power. The action of the Macedonians thus takes the form of God's action in Christ. It is the expression of power in weakness (cf. 12:9-10), which transcends all human possibilities (cf. 1:8). In this way it is manifest that it is the grace of God, not the power or goodness of the Macedonians, that is at work. Paul's asseveration "I bear witness" is no mere confirmation of the Macedonians' gift. It is a confirmation of the grace of God at work in them.

As Paul goes on to underscore, the Macedonian giving took place spontaneously. Its character as gift thereby remains intact. In the following context he likewise stresses that Titus himself is acting spontaneously in arranging the collection. Even though he received encouragement from Paul, it is God who has given him zeal for this endeavor (8:16-17). Paul similarly instructs the Corinthians that any gift they arrange must be given gladly, just as each one has determined. It must not arise from regret or compulsion (9:7). Paul will not compel the Corinthians to give. He seeks to preserve the spontaneity of their giving in the very nature and form of his exhortation. He does encourage them to complete their promised gift, and he makes considerable use of the social pressure of the witnesses to the Corinthian action, including, perhaps, some Macedonians.[25] Nevertheless, the apostolic exhortation remains bound to the grace of God. His encouragement is an encouragement to experience God's grace afresh, precisely by the "grace" of participation in the gift for "the saints." His thanksgiving to God at the conclusion of his argument makes the nature of his exhortation clear (9:15). The call to complete the collection takes the form that is present in all of Paul's parenesis: our doing and giving is already given and done within God's grace in Christ. All true giving, together with all true obedience, is a spontaneous participation in that grace, or it is not giving at all.

4 In the eagerness of the Macedonians, the roles of apostle and church were reversed. Paul did not need to appeal to them to participate in the col-

24. Again, the opening ὅτι is to be understood as recitative, against both the NIV and the ESV, which make it explanatory.

25. 8:16-24; 9:1-5.

lection, for "with much encouragement" they petitioned him to be included in this effort. More precisely, they asked for "the grace and fellowship of the mission to the saints." Paul again describes the collection as a "grace," locating the love and kindness of giving within the gift given. He also recalls his opening word concerning the "grace of God" given to the Macedonians. The grace of God given produces the grace of giving in its recipients, without in any way diminishing its unconditioned priority.

The second term, *koinōnia,* expresses the human experience of "fellowship" or "participation" with others that is present within the grace of God, and thus within all true giving and receiving. The Macedonian petition to share in "the *koinōnia* of the mission" was a request to share in the reality of community that is present in God's grace in Christ. Paul expands on this theme in his following argument.[26] As his continuing description of the nature and effect of the contribution makes clear, the *koinōnia* of which he speaks is not merely a joining together with the others who share in the contribution. It is a participation in a dynamic relation of giving and receiving.[27] Before all else, it is a participation in Christ, who stands between givers and recipients in order to join them in common thanksgiving (8:9; 9:15).[28]

The terms with which Paul describes the collection reinforce the preceding reflections. The *koinōnia* is that of "the *diakonia* to the saints." As we have noted, the term *diakonia,* which is usually translated "service" or "ministry," is here probably best rendered "mission." It expresses the idea of agency, task, or errand carried out at the behest of another.[29] Paul's characterization of the collection again underscores God's ultimacy as Giver. The Macedonians petitioned the apostle for participation in *God's* work.

Correspondingly, the recipients of this "mission" are merely "the saints." Were it not for 1 Cor 16:3, we would not know that Paul has the church in Jerusalem in mind as the recipient of the gift.[30] This underplaying of locality is of considerable theological significance. It reinforces Paul's following appeal to *equality* in difference and exchange.[31]

5 Only here does Paul complete the thought he begins in v. 3; the finite verbal form that governs the main clause finally appears. The overflow of joy and poverty, in which the Macedonians passively received God's grace, has its counterpart in their own action: "They gave themselves first to the Lord, and then to us by the will of God." As Paul will make clear shortly, it was the

26. See 8:13-16 and esp. 9:6-15.

27. See 8:13-15; 9:12-15.

28. Yet once more, see Bonhoeffer's comments in *Life Together,* p. 16 above.

29. See above, n. 4, p. 96.

30. In contrast, and quite naturally, Paul directly names Jerusalem as the recipient of the collection in Rom 15:25-29.

31. Cf. Gal 3:28.

Achaian promise to participate in the collection that prompted the Macedonian response (9:1-5).[32] Their "giving themselves to the Lord" does not refer to their conversion. Their generosity overflowed out of their affliction (v. 2). It is also the case, then, that their "giving themselves to the Lord" did not take place within the normal course of life as some special, self-prompted (and thus self-centered) decision to surrender themselves to "Christ's lordship." It was an act of faith and hope that was "pressed" out of the Macedonians by the trials that had come to them. Their giving was the work of God's grace in them. In giving themselves to the Lord, they were only affirming that which Christ had done for them: they had been possessed by God.[33]

The Macedonian gift took place contrary to Paul's expectations: ". . . and this not as we had hoped, but they gave themselves *first* to the Lord, and then to us by the will of God." As Paul has made clear, the Macedonian gift was spontaneous (v. 3). No request or encouragement to give came from the apostle. The apostle will not be lord over the faith of his churches. They are bound to him only through Christ (1:24). Apostolic authority rests entirely in the word of reconciliation.

In its "voluntary" nature *(authairetos),* its responsive spontaneity, the gift of the Macedonians was willed by God, apart from the apostle or his instruction. For Paul, the will of God does not restrain or prevent voluntary action. Quite the opposite: it creates the space in which true freedom is present. The Macedonians otherwise would have been compelled by circumstances, by hidden, personal motives, or by the arguments and persuasion of others. The limitation of apostolic (and therewith, of all pastoral) authority takes on added significance in this respect. Precisely *because of* the will of God (that operated beyond the apostle and his plans), not in spite of it, the Macedonians' giving was voluntary.

It was not merely a gift that the Macedonians gave, they gave *themselves,* first to the Lord, and then to the apostle, "by the will of God." Paul regards the whole person of the Macedonians as being present in their gift. This self-surrender of the Macedonians represents the very aim that Paul seeks to effect with the Corinthians. The apostolic purpose is not limited to the relationship between himself and his churches. As we have observed already, the gift is intended to bind the churches together in Christ. The Corinthian generosity is to be a generosity not merely toward Jerusalem but "toward all" (9:13). The recipients of their gift shall long for *them* (and not merely more gifts from them) "on account of the grace of God" that is "in" them (9:14). Giving, if it is truly giving, is a giving of oneself, just as true reception of a gift is the reception

32. In fact, the needy Macedonian churches had already supported Paul while he labored among the comfortable Corinthians (11:9). See further Phil 4:15. They had also sent the apostle a gift during an imprisonment, perhaps one that took place in Ephesus (Phil 4:10-20).

33. See 5:14-15.

of the giver. As we shall consider more fully below, Paul regards as fundmental to giving what postmodern philosophers have regarded as impossible to giving. This is so because he proceeds from the willing and working of God as unqualified Giver behind, before, and within all true giving. As is clear from the case of the Macedonians, the human participants — who have their own needs, and therefore cannot be absolute givers — give forth only from that which they have received from God.

6 The Macedonian gift has motivated Paul to send Titus — only just returned to Paul — immediately back to the Corinthians.[34] He has "encouraged" Titus to bring the collection to completion. In this context, as well as others, the verb *parakaleō* ("encourage") signifies a personal appeal: Paul has not asserted his apostolic authority by commanding Titus, but has made a request of him.[35] He thus leaves room for Titus's own decision — and God's work.[36] Titus's participation in this effort with the Corinthians is itself to be spontaneous (see v. 16). Just as Paul was moved by the appeal of the Macedonians, so Paul has sought to move Titus.

Paul urged Titus that, "just as he had made a beginning," he should also bring the Corinthian contribution "to completion." His appeal to Titus takes the same form as his appeal to the Corinthians (vv. 10-11), whom he seeks to persuade. Titus comes as Paul's representative, bearing his authority. Yet that authority is expressed in appeal that is based on the Gospel. The Corinthians are given the freedom of response that is given to all those within the sphere of the apostle's work.

Titus is to complete "this grace" with the Corinthians, namely, "the grace and participation of the mission to the saints." In the first instance, Paul wants the Corinthians to enter into an act of giving from the heart. His refraining from commanding them (or Titus) allows the "space" for this response. Naturally, the spontaneous contribution of the impoverished Macedonians is to encourage them as well. Indeed, the "grace" in which the Corinthians are to abound (v. 7) is the same "grace" that the Macedonians have displayed. Not only do we give only that which comes from God alone, our very act of giving is a work of God's grace.

34. Again, Titus was almost certainly carrying this letter.

35. The background of usage as "persuasion," not only in Greek rhetoric but also in Greek letters, in which the term παρακαλῶ expresses a polite appeal, is probably operative here. Perhaps, too, there are overtones of the Gospel as the basis of appeal (which is explicitly the case in Rom 12:1), given Paul's frequent use of παρακαλῶ in the biblical sense of "comfort" in the letter. It quickly becomes apparent in the present context that the Gospel here serves as the basis of Paul's appeal. See J. Thomas, "παρακαλέω," *EDNT* 3:23-27.

36. Paul's co-workers appear to have operated generally with the same freedom that we find here (1 Cor 16:10, 12). They were, then, in the fullest sense *co-workers,* who cooperated with the apostle willingly but did not always follow his requests.

b. The Appeal to the Corinthians (8:7-15)

7 But as you excel in everything — in faith, in speech, in knowledge, in
all earnestness, and in our love for you — see that you excel in this act of
grace also. 8 I say this not as a command, but to prove by the earnestness
of others that your love also is genuine. 9 For you know the grace of our
Lord Jesus Christ, that though he was rich, yet for your sake he became
poor, so that you by his poverty might become rich. 10 And in this matter I
give my judgment: this benefits you, who a year ago started not only to do
this work but also to desire to do it. 11 So now finish doing it as well, so that
your readiness in desiring it may be matched by your completing it out of
what you have. 12 For if the readiness is there, it is acceptable according to
what a person has, not according to what he does not have. 13 For I do not
mean that others should be eased and you burdened, but that as a matter
of fairness 14 your abundance at the present time should supply their need,
so that their abundance may supply your need, that there may be fairness.
15 As it is written, "Whoever gathered much had nothing left over, and
whoever gathered little had no lack."

Although he has delegated the task of completing the collection from the Corinthians to Titus, Paul provides his own encouragement to the Corinthians. Just as he encouraged Titus and has left room for an unencumbered response, so he encourages the Corinthians, explicitly indicating that he is not *ordering* them to complete their contribution (v. 8). The spontaneity of giving that arises from the Gospel does not exclude exhortation. It does, however, determine the form of exhortation. Paul's encouragement is twofold. In the first instance, Paul appeals to the Gospel as it is operative in the life of the Corinthians (vv. 7-9). He then renders his opinion that the completion of their gift will be beneficial for them (vv. 10-15). As is immediately apparent, this benefit is one that springs from the Gospel. Paul's encouragement of the Corinthians thus is based entirely on the Gospel, first in its work *in them,* and then in its work *for them.*

7 Much as he does in the opening thanksgiving of First Corinthians (1 Cor 1:4-9), Paul here names the gifts that have been bestowed on the church. The gifts, or more precisely in this context "the graces," that he lists match the ways in which he earlier has described the church as "having been made rich."[37] In the present context he adds "faith" to the gifts of "word" (i.e. speech, or rhetoric), and knowledge, in the same way that "faith" appears as the third element of his listing of gifts in 1 Cor 12:8-9a. Furthermore, while he earlier declares to the Corinthians that they are not lacking in any gift (1 Cor 1:7), he now urges

37. "In all speech" (or "word": λόγος) and in "all knowledge" (1 Cor 1:5).

them that, just as they abound in "all things," namely, in all "grace," so they are to abound in "this grace," namely, the grace that has been given in Macedonia.

Paul's appeal to the Corinthians also corresponds quite closely to his instruction concerning "gifts" (or, more precisely, "spiritual things," *pneumatika*) in 1 Cor 13:1-13. As the greatest and best gift, the Corinthians are to strive for love before all else (1 Cor 14:1). So, too, here Paul urges them to see that they abound in "this grace," namely, the collection for Jerusalem, just as they abound in the other gifts. He goes on to describe "this grace" as an expression of love (v. 8). The Corinthians' overestimation of the lesser gifts is a manifestation of their separation of the gifts from the Giver. They thereby have lost the gifts given to them. They have turned them into possessions.

The *abundant* grace given to the Corinthians stands in remarkable contrast to the experience of the churches of Macedonia, whose joy and poverty *abounded* within their affliction (v. 2). Paul by no means disparages the gifts that have been given to the Corinthians. Nor does he suggest that they are to feel ashamed of "the riches" that have been granted them (1 Cor 1:5; cf. 4:8).[38] He does remind them, however, that all they have has come to them as a gift (1 Cor 4:7). Furthermore, through the example of the Macedonians, he points them to the things that constitute the greater gifts. He has instructed them on this matter already in 1 Cor 13.

Paul includes two further elements in his list of the "graces" given to the Corinthians. They have been granted "all eagerness." Paul undoubtedly refers largely to the matters immediate to the collection. His attribution serves as a form of praise intended to motivate the Corinthians to complete their promised gift. The former eagerness of the Corinthians stirred the Macedonians to action (9:2). Now he is testing the love of the Corinthians by the eagerness of the Macedonians (v. 8). Paul goes on to speak of Titus's eagerness in regard to the collection, as well as that of the "other brother" whom Paul is sending with him to Corinth (8:16-17, 22). Paul very likely also recalls the recent eagerness that the Corinthians have shown for him in their reception of Titus (7:12). Their participation in the collection will bind them not only to the Jerusalem believers but also to the apostle.

Finally, Paul speaks of his own love toward the Corinthians as a "grace" in which they also abound. Correspondingly, their participation in the collection will be an expression of their acceptance of him as their apostle. Paul's fresh and direct affirmation of his love for them is likely intended to clear away suspicions, doubts, and reserve on the part of the Corinthians. His decision not to visit them, which has contributed to the tension in their relationship, was based, he affirms, on his love for them (2:1-4). He has likewise asserted that

38. The contrast with the Macedonian poverty (2 Cor 8:2), while entirely implicit, is nevertheless evident.

he has opened his heart fully to them (6:11). He will go on to protest to them that he loves them, despite all their suspicions about him (11:11; 12:15). That he names his love for them as a "grace" given by God not only affirms that love but calls them to participation in the apostolic mission and, at this moment, to participation in the mission of the collection.

8 Paul makes it clear that his encouragement is not a command. He is instead "proving" the genuineness of the love of the Corinthians by the eagerness of the Macedonians. He has indicated already that his request to Titus to complete the Corinthian collection was motivated by the unexpected request of the Macedonians to participate in the collection. Now he directly appeals to their example. Yet, as we have noted, he does not put forward the Macedonians as a moral example that the Corinthians are to follow. The Macedonians are an example of "the grace of God," the very grace that the Corinthians are to seek, in addition to all the other gifts that have been granted them.[39]

Paul is "proving" the genuineness of the love of the Corinthians. This proving is undoubtedly an expression of his apostolic authority, which the Corinthians have attempted to invert by proving the apostle (13:3). Paul already has indicated that his "tearful letter" was intended to test the Corinthians, to discover whether they were "obedient in all matters" (2:9).[40] The present proof is not for the apostle alone: the "proof" of this mission of the collection will take place "before the churches" (8:24) and will bind the Corinthians to Jerusalem in praise and thanksgiving to God (9:13; cf. Phil 2:22).[41] This proving of the Corinthians on Paul's part is not to be understood as a questioning of their love. It is just the opposite: an affirmation of that love. He expects that their love will be displayed.[42] This expectation is apparent, not only from his boasting about the Corinthians' eagerness to give (9:2), but also from his affirmation that they know (and thus have experienced) "the grace of our Lord, Jesus Christ" (v. 9). The proof for which Paul calls is not finally a proving of the Corinthians but a proving of God's work in them. This proof, in its sharing

39. As we have observed, Christ stands between them. See 9:12-15; 1 Cor 1:9.

40. Paul likewise has "proved" the "brother," namely the co-worker, that he is sending along with Titus and another (8:22).

41. This apostolic proving does not displace the call for Christians to "prove" themselves (11:28; 13:5). Nor does it substitute for God's final proving of human hearts, and of all things "with fire" at the final judgment (1 Thess 2:4; 1 Cor 3:13).

42. The connotations of δοκιμάζειν ("to prove") differ from those of πειράζειν ("to try" or "to tempt"), even if the usage overlaps. The former term implies a testing in order to form a judgment. The latter may do so as well but may also signal trial and temptation. Satan "tries" but never "proves." According to the letter of James, God finally does not "try" anyone (Jas 1:13-15). In this respect, God's testing of Abraham (LXX Gen 22:1: ὁ θεὸς ἐπείραζεν τὸν Αβρααμ) takes on profound significance: only in retrospect does it become apparent that the call to sacrifice Isaac was a proving of Abraham, not a destructive trial.

in the affliction of others, corresponds to the "proof" of affliction that came to the Macedonians (v. 2).

9 Paul follows his encouragement with an explanation *(gar)*. The proof of the love of the Corinthians is grounded in their knowledge of Christ's "grace," i.e., Christ's act of self-giving. Christ is much more than an example for them. Paul is reminding the Corinthians of the Gospel that they have received, and in which they participate.

It is "the grace of our Lord, Jesus Christ" that provides the pattern for the Corinthians. English translations generally interpret the act of Christ's grace as his entering into poverty by his divesting himself of his wealth. The participial expression *plousios ōn* is read concessively and located in past time: "*though* he *was* rich, he became poor" (ESV, NIV, NRSV). Wealth and poverty thereby are assumed to be sequential states. It is not at all clear, however, that Paul has in mind a sequence of poverty and wealth. Quite the contrary. Paul himself possesses riches that are communicated to others in (or through) his own poverty: "as poor, yet making many rich, as having nothing, yet possessing all things" (6:10).[43] The same is true of the Macedonians: the depth of their poverty abounded in the wealth of their simplicity (8:2). It is the pattern of Christ and "the word of the cross" that appears in both Paul and the Macedonians: he is "the Lord of *glory*" whom the rulers of this age *crucified* (1 Cor 2:8). In Christ, God's power is present in weakness, God's wisdom in foolishness.[44] The exchange of sin and righteousness that has taken place in Christ itself implies the simultaneity of these two realities, despite the movement from cross to resurrection that is apparent in Paul's statement: the resurrection is merely the manifestation of the righteousness that was hidden under sin in the cross (5:21). In all these instances, Paul speaks of a paradoxical coincidence of opposites, not a sequence of states. Likewise in the present context, Christ's wealth and poverty are simultaneous realities. The participial construction should not be interpreted as concessive but as modal: "for your sake he became poor, being rich."[45] Christ's wealth is present within his poverty.[46] Indeed,

43. Likewise, Paul's strength lies in his weakness (2 Cor 12:9-10).

44. 1 Cor 1:18–2:16.

45. The position of the participial construction after the verb suggests this sense as well: ἐπτώχευσεν πλούσιος ὤν. Paul's description of Christ's saving act overturns the usual conceptions of "poverty" and "riches," as is also the case with the grace of God given to the Macedonians (vv. 1-2) and with his own apostolic ministry (6:10). One might therefore read the participial construction in v. 9 as expressing Christ's true riches of self-giving and interpret the participle as causal, "For you know the grace of our Lord, Jesus Christ, who *because* he is rich, for your sakes became poor" (cf. Rom 2:4; 10:12).

46. Paul's description of Christ's saving work here parallels the "hymn" of Phil 2:6-11, in which Christ's "making himself nothing" (κενοῦν) and humbling himself (ταπεινοῦν) consist in his taking on humanity and suffering the death of the cross, not in his emptying himself of

Paul's description of the gift of salvation as an act of Christ's grace requires this sense: the riches of Christ, hidden in his poverty, are the riches that make the Corinthians rich. This simultaneity of wealth in poverty constitutes the life and existence that the Corinthians wish to deny.

Correspondingly, the poverty of Christ should not be understood as a former state that has now been left behind. It is the very means by which Christ here and now communicates his riches to the Corinthians. As Paul earlier has reminded the Corinthians, he wanted to know nothing while among them except "Jesus Christ, and this one crucified" (1 Cor 2:2). It is the crucified Christ who has become for them "righteousness, sanctification, and redemption" (1 Cor 1:30). The celebration of the Lord's Supper is a proclamation of the *death* of the one who is *Lord* (1 Cor 11:26). Paul shares in the sufferings of Christ and bears the deadness of Jesus in his body (1:5; 4:10). Christ was crucified in weakness, yet he lives by the power of God (13:4). He is the Crucified One, who lives. The nail prints remain in the hands of the risen Lord.

In what, then, does Christ's poverty consist? What are the riches that Christ communicates? In his metaphor of poverty, Paul makes no distinction between incarnation and cross.[47] He is speaking of the communication of salvation and thus surely has the cross in view. His language furthermore presupposes that an exchange has taken place between Christ and the Corinthians. It is *their* poverty into which Christ has entered, and *his* riches that have been given to them. Christ's poverty is thus to be understood as including the whole of human life under sin, death, and condemnation that he has taken on himself. Not merely the cross but also the incarnation lies within Paul's metaphor.

Correspondingly, the riches that Christ communicates consist in righteousness, life, glory, and comfort — in other words, the gift of salvation itself. Christ's riches include, yet transcend, his grace of giving. The Corinthians, who have been "made rich" in Christ (1 Cor 1:5), are yet "to be made rich" by the arrival of the eschaton (1 Cor 4:8). "Riches" here are nothing other than the final salvation that has broken into the present world.[48] These "riches" are not to be understood as a Corinthian possession but as a communicated good. The Corinthians have their riches in Christ's poverty, and they have them abidingly there. As we have seen, Paul is able to speak of the wealth of the Macedonians, as well as that of the Corinthians, as resting in "simplicity," the freedom of

---

deity. Paul's thought is distant from the *kenosis* theology of the nineteenth century, which attempted to account for the true humanity of Christ by supposing that the incarnation entailed setting aside divine attributes. See P. Althaus, "Kenosis," *RGG3*, 3:1243-46.

47. In this respect, Paul's statement here differs from Phil 2:6-11, where the incarnation and the suffering of the cross appear as two distinct, although obviously related, acts on the part of Christ.

48. See 2 Cor 1:6; 2:15-16; 3:6, 8, 9, 18; 4:6, 12; further, e.g., Rom 9:23; 10:12; 11:12, 33; Phil 4:17.

receiving and giving.[49] Salvation for Paul is properly understood as a gift, or as he says in this context, a grace that does not become a private possession, but a self-communication of the Giver.

In speaking of the poverty and riches of Christ, Paul again touches on the fundamental issue that has troubled the Corinthians' relationship with the apostle.[50] Their salvation has been effected by the weakness and sufferings of Christ, the Lord, in whom strength and salvation are present. On this point, Paul is thus emphatic: "*You* know the grace of our Lord, Jesus Christ . . . on account of *you* he became poor, in order that *you* by his poverty might be made rich." Correspondingly, Christ's act of grace took place for the sake of the Corinthians and their salvation. He became poor "in order that you *by his poverty* might be made rich."[51] *By means of his poverty,* Christ communicates his riches to the Corinthians. It is not by Christ's riches that the Corinthians are made rich, but by his poverty, in which those riches are hidden. Paul's language is shocking, especially for the Corinthians, who had a taste for finer things, especially when it came to apostles. Their upward striving has been countered by the condescension of Christ. Their twisted values are undone by his grace.

The final phrase in Paul's statement is critical: it is not true *in general* that poverty makes rich, but only *concretely,* in the grace of Christ, who acts out of *his* riches. The Corinthians have been made rich "by the poverty of *that one.*" Like the Baptist in the Isenheim altar, in his use of the demonstrative Paul *points* to the crucified (and yet risen!) Christ, whom the Corinthians are tempted to ignore and forget. Paul thus brings a reminder to the Corinthians that they are wealthy paupers: the crucified Christ is the mirror in which they see both their poverty and the One who communicates his riches to them.

According to Paul, then, through the poverty of his incarnation, suffering, and death, Christ confers the riches of salvation, life, and righteousness. The "grace of our Lord, Jesus Christ" — the expression commonly appears in the prescripts and closing of Paul's letters[52] — is unqualified here, as it is elsewhere. Paul does not introduce it with a prior reference to the grace of God. It is not a "grace" that had to be sought, as with the Macedonians (vv. 1, 4). He speaks instead absolutely of "the grace of *our Lord,* Jesus Christ" and presents that "grace" as the gift of salvation. The grace of Christ is an *absolute* gift. Paul thus attributes to Christ the role of giving that is otherwise reserved for God alone. Indeed, the saving exchange of sin and righteousness that appears in 5:21

49. 8:2; 9:11.

50. Paul's concise summary of Christ's work here corresponds remarkably to his argument in 1 Cor 1:18–2:16, esp. 1:26-31.

51. The NIV makes the poverty the vehicle, or intermediate means, by which we are made rich: "through his poverty." But the dative τῇ ἐκείνου πτωχείᾳ is better taken as expressing the direct means.

52. E.g., Rom 1:7; 16:20; 1 Cor 1:3; 16:23; 2 Cor 1:2; 13:13; Gal 1:3; 6:18.

as an act of God in Christ appears here as Christ's act of *self*-giving. Christ has taken our poverty upon himself and has given us his own riches. In so doing, Christ has acted as God.

These riches include all the earthly gifts of salvation, the *charismata*, which the Corinthians have misjudged and misappropriated. Paul began First Corinthians with thanksgiving to God for the way in which the church has been "made rich in [Christ Jesus]," so that they do not lack any gift as they await the revelation of Christ.[53] Among these gifts is the gift of love[54] and the grace of giving that Paul now urges upon the Corinthians.[55] As we have noted, Paul here reminds the Corinthians of Christ, who is not merely an example of giving but the source of their new life and existence, which is characterized by giving and receiving. The Corinthians know the grace of Christ. For this reason, and not because of any virtue in them, Paul is confident that their love is genuine.

10 Paul has just described what the Gospel does *in* the Corinthians. He now turns to what it is to do *for* them in the present moment. While his theological judgment is certain, he qualifies his practical judgment: "And I offer my opinion in this matter: [You ought to do this] for it is for your advantage. . . ."

He does not begin by naming this advantage to the Corinthians but seeks to motivate them by a reminder of their precedence in the collection. They not only were the ones who initiated the collection, but were the first to desire to do so more than a year before.[56] Among the churches of the apostle, both the "doing" and the "willing" to make a collection for Jerusalem began with the Corinthians. Paul will shortly inform them that it was their zeal that motivated the Macedonians (9:1-2). Here he simply wants to remind them of their priority and of the length of time that has passed since they initiated the project. His language suggests that the Corinthians have followed the instructions he gave them in 1 Cor 16:1-4: the "doing" of the project began with them. Funds have been collected. Yet the collection is not yet complete. Undoubtedly, the situation has been complicated by the strained relationship between the Corinthians and the apostle, especially by his decision not to visit them on the way to Macedonia.[57]

53. 1 Cor 1:5-7.

54. 1 Cor 13:1-13.

55. Cf. 2 Cor 9:10-11.

56. See the instructions to the church in 1 Cor 16:1-4.

57. Paul originally hoped to spend the winter in Corinth and then to receive help from the church when traveling further "through Macedonia" (1 Cor 16:5-6). His language suggests that he regarded the passage through Macedonia as an extension of his travel to Jerusalem. That would correspond to his original plan to visit the Corinthians twice (2 Cor 1:15-16). Perhaps the changes to the administration of the gift for Jerusalem that appear in 2 Cor 8:16-24 reflect the distance in his relationship to the Corinthians and his correspondingly altered travel.

11 "But now complete the doing as well." Since the Macedonians have made a contribution and the collection is being completed, the time has come for the Corinthians to finish the job. Their readiness "to will" the project is to have its complement in their "doing" of it, according to the means that are available to them at this moment.

The Corinthians' knowledge of the "grace of Christ" (v. 9) lies in the background of Paul's exhortation. Just as he follows the hymn of Phil 2:6-11 with the affirmation that God works both "willing" and "working" in believers, so here he calls for the "doing" of that which the Corinthians have "willed."[58] The work of Christ is to have its effect in the life of the Corinthians.[59] Paul's emphasis lies on the moment of opportunity: now is the time to complete the work with whatever resources are available. The readiness of the Corinthians to "will" the project must now be matched by its completion.

12 As Paul explains, "it is the thought that counts." It is the readiness of heart, the eagerness and spontaneity of giving, that matters, not the amount of the gift. No one need suppose that, because their means are limited, their gift lacks significance. We need not imagine that the Macedonian gift was financially large. In this respect, the gift that finally came from the Corinthians probably outstripped it. But the Macedonian contribution was by no means the smaller gift: here one cannot help but think of Jesus' word concerning the widow's mite.[60] Paul is not urging the Corinthians to give what they do not have. They are not to take upon themselves the role of "absolute givers" or benefactors.[61] This role belongs to God alone. Their gift will be acceptable in accord with what they have — which itself has been given to them! — and will not be measured by what they do not have. Later, in his instruction concerning giving, Paul emphasizes to the Corinthians God's ability to cause "grace" to abound to them, so that in all ways they would have an abundance for every good work (9:8). God remains the final Giver, who out of his own goodness creates givers who know and share in his goodness.

13 Paul explains further: "For it is not that there should be ease for others and affliction for you." He does not expect the Corinthians to match the giving of the Macedonians, which arose "in much affliction" (v. 2). This "grace" has not been given in Corinth. As we have noted, Paul does not hold up the Macedonians as a moral example, but as an example of the grace of

58. The language of "willing" (τὸ θέλειν) and "working" (τὸ ἐνεργεῖν) that follows the hymn of Phil 2:6-11 in vv. 12-13 likewise appears here in vv. 10-11 (τὸ θέλειν and τὸ ποιῆσαι). Just as in that context Jesus appears not merely as example but as saving Lord, so he does here: "willing" and "working" are worked by God through Jesus.

59. Cf. Rom 7:18, the picture of the human being confronted with demand, rather than grace.

60. Mark 12:41-44; Luke 21:1-4.

61. On this role in the Greco-Roman world, see again Marshall, *Enmity in Corinth*, 1-34.

God. The Corinthians are simply to seek a measure of that grace in their own situation.

The tenor of Paul's exhortation in this verse and the previous one suggests that the delay in the completion of the Corinthian gift is not merely due to the problems in the relationship between them and the apostle. Most likely some preparation of the gift had begun long before, according to Paul's former instructions concerning a weekly collection.[62] This would be the case, even if the strained relationship with Paul had disrupted the collection. He does not call the Corinthians to institute his instructions or to return to them. Perhaps he intentionally overlooks this matter, choosing instead to emphasize the former willingness of the Corinthians to share in the gift. They may now take care of the details of the collection themselves. His language in this verse, however, suggests that another factor is at work. The Corinthians are not to bring affliction upon themselves by their gift. As he has indicated, their gift is acceptable according to the means that are available to them at this time (v. 12). The delay in the Corinthian contribution seems to have arisen — at least in part — from their desire to deliver an impressive gift, one that would have placed them in the role of benefactors in relation to the church in Jerusalem. This role would have secured them a position of honor and prestige. The church has behaved in a similar manner toward Paul, who has refused to accept any compensation from them. The apostle will not allow any church, and especially not the church in Corinth, to place him under obligation.[63] This question has contributed substantially to the tension between Paul and Corinth.[64] In insisting on a modest gift that accords with the means available at this moment, Paul reserves the role of benefactor for God. Honor and thanksgiving belong to God alone, who is the source of all good. This theme comes to explicit expression in Paul's instruction in 9:6-15.

Paul's implicit curbing of the false aspirations of the Corinthians comes to expression in his final, positive word in this verse: giving is to take place out of *equality*. Christians are not to be divided into separate classes of benefactors and beneficiaries, or patrons and clients. Even in "the matter of giving and

62. 1 Cor 16:1-4.

63. Even with respect to the Macedonians, Paul insists on maintaining his independence and on securing the acknowledgment of God as the one benefactor (Phil 4:10-20). Admittedly he later names Phoebe, a member of the Corinthian church, as having become a patroness (προστάτις) of many, and of him as well (Rom 16:2). But one individual is not an entire church. It is likely, moreover, given Paul's vigorous protest (1 Cor 9:1-27; 2 Cor 11:7-11), that he accepted funds from her only after departing Corinth. This would fit not only the pattern of his dealings with Philippi but also his open claim in 2 Cor 11:9.

64. See 1 Cor 9:15-18: Paul must maintain his freedom from all in order to become the servant of all (1 Cor 9:19). See further 2 Cor 11:7-11; 12:14-18. Paul's practice obviously differs from that of the apostolic claimants in Corinth (2 Cor 11:12-15).

receiving" (cf. Phil 4:15), where there are obvious distinctions, they remain equals. Contrary to human judgments, the nature of this equality is based, not on sameness, but on *difference in dynamic exchange,* as becomes apparent in Paul's following description of giving and receiving.

14 This dynamic exchange is to take place in "the present moment of opportunity" *(en tō nyn kairō).* Paul's thought is concentrated on the Corinthian gift. Their abundance is to serve the want of the Jerusalem Christians, so that the abundance of the Jerusalem Christians might serve the want of the Corinthians. Paul does not envision a sequence of giving and receiving, or a return gift, which would be delayed. As with his own apostolic mission, with the Macedonians, and with Christ himself, two opposites are to meet in a single event. The material abundance of the Corinthians — Paul has just made appeal that the gift be given out of abundance and not bring them affliction — is to "be" for that which Jerusalem is lacking. This giving is to take place *in order that* the abundance of Jerusalem might "be" for the want of the Corinthians. Here Corinthian values and their apparent aspiration to the status of benefactors are overturned. The "abundance" of Jerusalem is to fill up what the Corinthians, who are "rich in things, but poor in soul," are lacking.[65] This abundance, like that of the Macedonians — who abounded in joy and "in the riches of their simplicity" (v. 2) — is obviously of a different order than that of material goods. As we have noted, the same form of giving takes place in Paul's apostolic mission (6:10) and in Christ himself (8:9). Paul elsewhere describes the gift of the Gentile churches for Jerusalem as the obligatory return of "fleshly" (i.e., physical and material) benefits in response to the "spiritual" benefits Jerusalem has shared with the Gentiles (Rom 15:27). The concentration on the single moment of exchange is lacking in that context, but the contrast in the nature of the gifts is the same. The Corinthian gift is a confession of the Gospel of Christ that binds them to Jerusalem and to all other believers (9:13). In giving, they, in their poverty, receive afresh the riches of the Gospel.

In this verse, as we have noted, Paul points to the present moment of opportunity. The exchange is concentrated. It is to take place in a single event. This understanding of the exchange as one of simultaneity is confirmed by Paul's closing statement and his following appeal to Scripture.

Paul summarizes his point by returning to his opening instruction (v. 13b). The exchange between Corinth and Jerusalem is to take place "in order that there might be equality." This appeal to equality reinforces the impression that Paul presupposes a simultaneity of exchange: it is not clear that a delay in a return gift would in itself allow equality. A subsequent, material gift from Jerusalem to Corinth no longer could take place in spontaneity but would be

65. H. E. Fosdick, "Shame our wanton, selfish gladness, / Rich in things and poor in soul" (from the third verse of "God of Grace and God of Glory").

encumbered by obligation.[66] There would no longer be equality but an initial benefactor and beneficiary. Their roles and relation already would have been fixed; the gratuity of any return gift would thereby be destroyed.

As we have noted, Paul understands "equality" in terms of difference, rather than in sameness. His conception of equality is thus vastly different from usual human conceptions, and especially those of the (post)modern world, which has largely lost the horizon of Scripture and therefore conceives of equality entirely in terms of sameness (no matter that it praises diversity).[67] The exchange that Paul describes is to take place in simultaneity. The abundance and poverty of the Corinthians and that of the Jerusalem Christians are of respectively different orders. They are *therefore* able to meet one another's need in a single, opportune moment. Paul by no means shoves aside material need in favor of spiritual values. He makes clear, however, that the Corinthians themselves are beneficiaries in the matter. As we have seen, he urges the Corinthians that their completion of the gift is for their *advantage* (v. 10). As Paul will shortly instruct the Corinthians, both parties are to recognize this mutual giving and receiving and the benefits that are conferred within it, both on themselves and on the other.[68]

It is evident that Paul understands the dynamic equality of giving and receiving as created and preserved by God, who within it all remains the ultimate Giver.[69] It is this vertical dimension of God's fundamental goodness that many

66. In Romans, Paul presents the return gift of the Gentiles to Jerusalem as one of a differing *kind,* and not merely one of delay (Rom 15:25).

67. It should be noted that an appeal to outward sameness as a basis for equity is not out of order in itself. Who would suggest, for example, that women should not receive equal compensation for equal work? It is the modern absolutizing of "sameness" that is problematic, the insistence that, in order for equality to exist, we must be the same in all possible ways. All human communities bear within themselves the tendency to compel conformity, rather than to delight in the created and gifted differences that exist among us. Only the Gospel can guard the church from this evil. For further reflections on this topic, see Bayer, *Freiheit als Antwort: Zur theologischen Ethik,* 55-59.

68. See 9:6-15.

69. Paul's understanding of equality has implications that extend well beyond the matter of material gifts. The theme of dynamic exchange appears, for example, in Paul's discussion of gender difference in 1 Cor 11:2-16, esp. vv. 11-12. As is clear from this text, he is by no means an advocate of the obliteration of a difference of role between husband and wife. Indeed, for Paul this difference is necessary to equality, which cannot be realized in sameness, but only in dynamic exchange. Nevertheless, it is rarely, if ever, recognized that the very bearing of the role of husband brings with it inherent weakness and lack, which can be met only by the strength and abundance of the wife. This reality of interdependence manifests itself in other ways. The wealthy, who have their own unseen poverty, need the poor. The strong likewise need the weak. The apostle of Christ received his "thorn for the flesh" (12:7). The Corinthians need the Macedonians, the Jerusalem Christians, and, above all else, the suffering apostle. Conversely,

if not most postmodern discussions have ignored.[70] The very possibility of a "gift" thereby comes into question, since a purely human exchange inevitably may be reduced to economics. Paul already has reminded the Corinthians of the unqualified grace of Christ, whose riches are the source of all giving, including that of the Corinthians (v. 9). He will return to this theme at the close of his exhortation (9:15). God's giving in Christ creates (thanks)givers, whose (thanks)giving does not constitute a return gift but remains an act of reception. The form of Paul's exhortation, which preserves the spontaneity of giving, is likewise dependent on the work of God to effect giving and receiving. It is God who has orchestrated the opportunity that stands before the Corinthians at the present moment; the need and abundance of both Corinth and Jerusalem finally come from him.

15 Paul understands the dynamic equality to which he calls the Corinthians to correspond with Scripture, "just as it is written." He appeals to the story of the Lord's provision of manna for Israel in the book of Exodus: "The one [who gathered] much did not have too much, and the one [who gathered] little did not lack" (Exod 16:18). The words describe the measuring of the manna in the wilderness that the Israelites had gathered, in which the differences in the amounts each one gathered for their family for that day wondrously disappeared. No one had too much: those who attempted to hoard it found that on the following morning it became full of worms and had begun to stink. One had to gather only that which was needed for the day (Exod 16:19-21). No one lacked enough to eat, either. At first reading, the passage to which Paul appeals seems odd. In the Exodus account, it is God who mysteriously effects equality in the collection of the manna. Paul, in contrast, is exhorting the Corinthians to participate in the collection for Jerusalem. It is their entrance into giving and receiving that is to facilitate equality. Upon reflection, however, Paul's appeal to this text is not at all strange. He began his

---

even the apostle needs the Corinthians in all their weakness, as the proof of his apostleship and his boast (1:12-14). Those who lead need those who follow, not merely as followers but, paradoxically, more often than not, as their leaders in faith, hope, and love. Otherwise, Acton's dictum would prevail. It is the weaker members of the body that are the more necessary (1 Cor 12:22). Not all have the gift of faith. God delights in speaking wisdom through the mouth of babes. This dynamic is nowhere more evident than in the Gospels, where it is not the Twelve but the most unexpected persons — the centurion, the Syro-Phoenician woman, and so on — who are given and display the greatest faith, even if the Twelve nevertheless remain apostles.

70. The more recent discussion was prompted esp. by the work of Jacques Derrida. See, among other works, J. Derrida, *Given Time I: Counterfeit Money* (Chicago: University of Chicago Press, 1992); J. Derrida, *The Gift of Death* (Religion and Postmodernism; Chicago: University of Chicago Press, 1995). In the latter, Derrida gives some attention to the Bible and Christian faith, without truly coming to grips with God's radical gift of himself (indeed, in death!) in Christ. Oswald Bayer has offered insightful reflections on the questions that Derrida and others have raised. See O. Bayer, "The Ethics of Gift," 447-68.

appeal to the Corinthians with the announcement of the grace of God given to the Macedonians that worked their participation in the collection (v. 1). He urges the Corinthians that they should "abound in this grace," namely, the grace of giving as well (v. 7). His confidence in their participation is based on their knowledge of Christ's self-giving grace that makes them rich in all things, including this grace (v. 9). Paul's appeal to the Exodus text drives home his message that God is the One who is the source of all human giving and receiving. In this exchange, no less than in the case of the measuring of the manna, God works the wonder of equality. This is the crowning point of Paul's closing appeal to the Corinthians, which he expresses — necessarily — in an exclamation of thanksgiving (9:15).

Other dimensions of this exodus context are relevant to Paul's thought here as well. By appealing to the gift and gathering of the manna, he reminds the Corinthians that all they have comes as a sheer gift from heaven. In his citation, he indirectly inquires of them, just as he has done earlier: "What do you have that you did not receive?" (1 Cor 4:7).[71] He will make the same point again, later in his instruction, by appealing to Isa 55:10-11, a text that compares the work of the word of God to rain and snow coming from heaven, which provides "seed for sowing and bread for eating" (9:10). In all giving, God remains the one, unqualified Giver. Indeed, only because of this absolute Giver can there be any true giving at all. Otherwise, all exchanges may be unmasked finally as "economic" transactions, even when they involve honor and recognition rather than money or material goods.

It is likely, too, that Paul intends the Exodus text to recall for the Corinthians their "location." They have not yet "arrived in the promised land." They have not yet become satiated and rich (1 Cor 4:8). They are still in the wilderness, along with all the wandering people of God.

In this respect, too, the Exodus text may serve as a reminder to the Corinthians that they are part of the one people of God, composed of both Jews and Gentiles. Prior to any action on their part, they have been made to share in Christ with the Jerusalem Christians, to whom they are therefore bound.

Finally, Paul's appeal to the equality wondrously effected in the collection of the manna reinforces our observations above concerning the simultaneity of giving and receiving in the exchange between Corinth and Jerusalem. Just as the leveling of the manna took place in the single event of measuring (Exod 16:18), so Paul understands that equality will be effected in this single exchange.

Perhaps his appeal to the event also hints at the spiritual benefit that the exchange with Jerusalem will bring the Corinthian church. The verb *pleonazō* that appears in Paul's appeal to Exod 16:18 (which closely follows the

71. William Walsham How, "We give Thee but Thine own, / Whate'er the gift may be; / All that we have is Thine alone, / A trust, O Lord, from Thee."

Septuagint) may signify not merely "to increase" or "to be more than enough," but in some contexts may take on the negative connotation of "having (*or* claiming) too much." The term borders on the idea of greed, through its association with violation of the natural order in Stoic thought.[72] Paul may thus be understood to say: "the one [who gathered] much did not claim too much [in greed]." Admittedly, Paul otherwise uses the verb *pleonazō* in a positive sense and employs another, related verb when speaking of greed or gaining unfair advantage. But he could hardly insert that other verb *(pleonekteō),* with its unmistakable sense of grasping and greed, into his allusion to the Exodus text without disrupting the parallel contrast of the absence of "abounding" and "lacking" that appears there. The very context of Paul's Exodus citation suggests that the wonder of equality in the manna served to thwart the problem of greed. It is followed by the story of those who attempted to reserve a portion of manna from one day to the next and thus to hoard it. The short account concludes with the note that the Israelites then collected each day as much as they needed for that day alone (Exod 16:19-21). In his citation Paul perhaps subtly hints at a fundamental benefit that will come to the Corinthians in their exchange with Jerusalem: they will be preserved from overreaching. In First Corinthians, he has more than once warned them of the danger of greed.[73]

c. The Gift-Delegation (8:16-24)

> [16]*But thanks be to God, who put into the heart of Titus the same earnest care I have for you.* [17]*For he not only accepted our appeal, but being himself very earnest he is going to you of his own accord.* [18]*With him we are sending the brother who is famous among all the churches for his preaching of the gospel.* [19]*And not only that, but he has been appointed by the churches to travel with us as we carry out this act of grace that is being ministered by us, for the glory of the Lord himself and to show our good will.* [20]*We take this course so that no one should blame us about this generous gift that is being administered by us,* [21]*for we aim at what is honorable not only in the Lord's sight but also in the sight of man.* [22]*And with them we are sending our brother whom we have often tested and found earnest in many matters, but who is now more earnest than ever because of his great*

72. See G. Delling, "πλεονάζω," *TDNT* 4:263-66. *Pss. Sol.* 5:16, although it employs a different vocabulary, expresses the same thought.

73. 1 Cor 5:10-11; 6:10. Now, however, Paul himself is under suspicion of acting in greed (2 Cor 7:2; 12:17-18). Perhaps the Corinthian suspicions are not accidental, but a projection of their own tendencies, and those of the apostles they admire, upon Paul (1 Cor 6:8; 2 Cor 11:7, 12-15, 20).

confidence in you. [23]*As for Titus, he is my partner and fellow worker for your benefit. And as for our brothers, they are messengers of the churches, the glory of Christ.* [24]*So give proof before the churches of your love and of our boasting about you to these men.*

Paul has already indicated to the Corinthians that he has encouraged Titus to bring to completion the "grace" that he began with them (v. 6). He now informs them that not only Titus but two others have departed to Corinth with him. It is probable that Titus was carrying this very letter and that the two other companions are present in Corinth as this letter is read to the church. Within the framework of the Gospel, Paul is quite prepared to apply social pressure to the Corinthians.[74]

One of Titus's companions had been chosen by the churches to accompany the collection. This is apparently not the case for the other companion. Paul apparently does not count him as one of his co-workers, either. Yet this one, too, serves as a representative of the churches. Paul has worked with him, knows him well, and vouches for his integrity. As Paul underscores at the close of this section, the Corinthian response will take place "in the presence of the churches."

Paul's announcement concerning the gift-delegation thus displays a subtle transition. His opening exclamation of thanksgiving for Titus's eagerness reflects his concern for the spiritual well-being of the Corinthians, who are to benefit from their participation in the collection (vv. 10, 13-15). His focus immediately shifts, however, to the readiness of the Corinthians (v. 19). He thus underscores their own spiritual vitality, to which he returns more than once (vv. 22, 24). Just as Jerusalem is not to become subservient to Corinth materially, Corinth is not to become subservient to Jerusalem spiritually. Paul makes it clear that the representatives have accompanied Titus to ensure the probity of Paul's dealings (vv. 20-21). Yet they serve at the same time as witnesses to the actions of Corinth. The Corinthians are to display "the proof of their love," not merely to Paul, but to the churches as well (vv. 7-8, 24). Again it is clear that Paul exhorts the Corinthians out of the Gospel itself and "the grace of our Lord, Jesus Christ." The "love" that they display will be only the love that they have received. As Paul makes clear shortly, their contribution will be a confession of the Gospel (9:13).

16 Paul gives thanks that God has given Titus the same zeal for the benefit of the Corinthians that Paul has just expressed in his own theologi-

74. The same dynamic appears dramatically in Paul's letter to Philemon. On the one hand, he obviously makes room for Philemon to fulfill his request for the manumission of Onesimus spontaneously, as an act of love worked by the Gospel. On the other hand, he brings remarkable pressure on Philemon to do so.

cal judgment (vv. 10-15), anticipating his closing thanksgiving concerning the collection (9:15). "Zeal" is no heat without light but is filled with knowledge.[75]

It is noteworthy that the Greek term for "thanks" *(charis)* is the same as that for "grace" and "giving." In this twofold usage the joy and pleasure of a relationship of receiving and giving implicitly come to expression. The return of thanks is finally no return gift to God. Even as the response and return of thanks, it is the reception of God's gifts. Paul again gives thanks, using this word dramatically and climactically in 9:15.

As we already have noted (v. 6), Paul leaves room for the spontaneous decision and response of his co-worker, just as he does with the Corinthians themselves. He thus gives thanks to God that God "has given" this zeal — as a gift — in Titus's heart. For the apostle, the work of the Gospel remains the free work of God.

Titus's zeal is "on behalf of" the Corinthians *(hyper hymōn)*, i.e., for their benefit. Their participation in the collection is for their advantage (v. 10). Their own lack is to be met by the abundance of those in Jerusalem with whom they are to share (v. 14). Paul here indicates to the Corinthians Titus's eagerness to assist them to sharing in this benefit. His words are obviously intended to strengthen Titus's hand in the completion of the project.

17 Titus's zeal for the Corinthians is expressed in his action:[76] he has gone forth to Corinth.[77] God's work of zeal in Titus's heart did not exclude, but included, encouragement from Paul. Yet that apostolic encouragement left room for the work of God and the spontaneity of response. Paul's emphasis again rests on that spontaneity: "being most zealous," Titus has departed for Corinth, "of his own accord." The language of the description, especially the reference to Titus's voluntary *(authairetos)* engagement in this mission, recalls Paul's account of the Macedonian contribution (vv. 1-4). The work of God proceeds on its own terms, not those of the apostle. In all of it, the remarkable independence of God's instruments is preserved. Paul's report of Titus's spontaneous action, together with that of the Macedonians, serves as an open invitation to the Corinthians to their own free and voluntary cooperation.

18 Paul's report concerning the delegation now shifts to the measures he has taken to ensure transparency and honesty in the collection of the gift for Jerusalem. While Titus has gone to Corinth voluntarily, Paul has sent with

75. Cf. Rom 10:2.

76. Usually the introductory ὅτι in this verse is taken to be causal, implicitly expressing the basis of Paul's *expression* of thanks. But it is just as natural to take the ὅτι as expressing the content of Paul's thanksgiving, and thus the basis of the thanksgiving itself.

77. Following contemporary epistolary convention, Paul writes from the perspective of the Corinthian recipients of the letter: by the time the Corinthians receive the letter, Titus not only has gone forth but has arrived. As we have noted, it is likely that Titus is the letter carrier.

him "the brother whose praise in the Gospel is throughout the churches."[78] Unlike Titus, Paul's co-worker, this brother, a delegate of the churches (vv. 19, 23), presently operates under Paul's direction: Paul sent him. In all likelihood, we should understand his renown in the Gospel as including not only fidelity to its truth but also an attractive presentation of its message. Paul's characterization of him probably constitutes an appeal to the Corinthians, who value effective rhetoric highly — too highly, as Paul well knows.[79] Paul's affirmation thus should be understood as relative. Normally, he speaks of praise of persons coming from God alone.[80] It nevertheless reflects Paul's remarkable generosity of spirit. Unlike many (supposed) leaders, including his opponents in Corinth, he feels no need to be center stage. He is quite happy to celebrate others, even when their gifts and reputation exceed his own, as they appear to do in this case. Here again it becomes clear that his defense of his apostolic calling is no defense of his person or privilege.

Paul's indication of the regard in which "the brother" is held throughout the churches represents again his attempt to bring Corinth into an abiding connection and fellowship with the other churches. This concern is evident already in First Corinthians,[81] and it remains fundamental to Paul's aim of securing Corinthian participation in the collection.[82]

19 The one whom Paul has sent, not only is known for his service in the Gospel, but also has been chosen by the churches to accompany Paul.[83] It is not impossible that this one is Apollos.[84] He might be one of the traveling companions that Luke names at this stage of Paul's mission in Acts, but this is far from certain.[85] Nor is there any reason to suppose that his list is complete, or that it pertains exactly to the time at which Paul wrote this letter to Corinth.[86]

78. It is not surprising that, in the ancient church, this brother was often identified as Luke. See Thrall, *The Second Epistle to the Corinthians*, 561-62. But it is highly unlikely that Paul has in view a written gospel.

79. See 1 Cor 1:12-17, 1:18–2:5; 2 Cor 11:6.

80. Rom 2:29; 1 Cor 4:5.

81. 1 Cor 11:2, 16; 15:1-11.

82. See also 9:13.

83. The situation obviously has changed since Paul wrote First Corinthians. At that time he indicated to the Corinthians that they should choose someone to bear their gift to Jerusalem. Paul will accompany that one only if it seems proper (1 Cor 16:3-4). Because of the Corinthian delay in completing their gift, the matter has moved beyond them.

84. See n. 6, p. xxi.

85. Acts 19:29 and also 20:4. Aside from an indirect statement in the mouth of Paul (Acts 24:17), Luke makes no mention at all of the collection for Jerusalem.

86. The lengthier list in Acts 20:4 corresponds to Paul's coming third visit to Corinth. It varies from the mention of Gaius and Aristarchus, who, according to Luke, were with Paul during the riot in Ephesus (Acts 19:29). The situation was fluid, as Paul's comments here also indicate.

Paul here continues to refer to the collection (1 Cor 16:1-2), or *"koinōnia"* (Rom 15:26), for Jerusalem as a "grace," i.e., a gift as an act of giving, as he generally does in his appeal to the Corinthians.[87] As we already have seen, it expresses the theology of giving that he develops at the conclusion of his appeal (9:15). As is evident here, this theology pervades his entire argument.

Paul is only secondary to the collection. His role is that of a mere administrator. Nevertheless, he shares in the eagerness of his associates and coworkers and, he hopes, of the Corinthians as well. He administers "the grace" of the churches, which is for the glory of the Lord — and for our eagerness.

As a "grace" itself, the collection is for the "glory of the Lord." Here again, Paul's theology of giving comes to expression, anticipating his final thanksgiving (9:15). God remains the final, unconditioned Giver, from whom not only all gifts but all giving flows. In giving, we receive. Only in this way can it be that the collection is for the Lord's glory, and not that of the human participants.

Paul's use of the divine name ("Lord") and not the generic designation ("God") recalls Israel's Lord, the God of Scripture, who there has revealed himself in self-giving love. As is often the case, Paul's reference to Christ in the near context (v. 9) associates him with the Lord who has revealed himself in Israel's Scripture. Paul's language here thus bears christological overtones, without clearly becoming a direct reference to Christ.

The collection serves not merely the glory of the Lord but also the "eagerness" or "readiness" of the Corinthians. Paul thus includes the Corinthians within the work of God, providing them encouragement to complete the collection. He has noted their early "willing" and "working" for the collection (v. 10), and immediately after this section he will indicate to them that their preparation stirred the Macedonians to their dramatic and sacrificial gift (9:2). The Corinthians themselves know the love of Christ, share in the Gospel, and are examples of its power. The completion of the collection serves the eagerness of the Corinthians that already has been manifest, securing their full participation in this work of God's grace.

20 Paul has made the arrangement for this delegate of the churches to travel to Corinth, lest someone there find fault with Paul in his administration of the collection. He is well aware of the suspicions that he somehow is attempting to defraud the Corinthians and has taken measures to show that they are baseless.[88] His actions are a concrete expression, in any case, of the aim he has expressed that no one should find fault with his apostolic mission (6:3).

Paul here describes the collection with an unusual term that is gener-

87. In 9:5 he names it a "blessing" (εὐλογία); in 9:13, a sharing or participation (κοινωνία). In 8:14, in reference to the gift, he speaks of the "abundance" (περίσσευμα) of the Corinthians.

88. See 12:14-18.

ally obscured by the translations: he speaks of it as a "fatness" *(hadrotēs).*[89] The usage may reflect the Septuagintal usage of the related adjective *hadros,* which appears in reference to the rich.[90] Whatever the semantic motivation of the Septuagintal usage might be,[91] it is likely that with Paul it has broader biblical overtones. In biblical idiom, "fatness" may signify the abundance that arises from the divine blessing of lands, fields, and vineyards.[92] Admittedly, the Septuagint uses another term *(piotēs)* to render the Hebrew in these instances. But the conceptual background of Scripture corresponds to Paul's thought in more than one way. He has just spoken of the gift that should come from the Corinthians as an expression of their "abundance" (*perisseuma,* v. 14). He also goes on, in reference to giving, to employ the agricultural metaphors of sowing and reaping, behind which stand the work and blessing of God, the Creator.[93] Paul's naming the collection a "fatness" fits both these themes. His shift away from the usual Septuagintal term *piotēs* may have to do with the more frequent association of *hadrotēs* with wealth.

Paul's reference to the collection of the churches as a "fatness" thus underscores its size. It is therefore entirely appropriate that Paul send representatives to ensure the transparency of his dealings. By virtue of its agricultural associations, the term also brings the reminder that this abundance is not a mere expression of wealth, but of the goodness and blessing of God, who has provided this abundance. Had Paul used the term "riches" or "wealth," he would have suggested that he deals with mere "possessions," or an illegitimate excess (cf. v. 15). He does not regard material goods as such: they are instead gifts of abundance that are to be communicated to others.[94] Indeed, he em-

89. ESV: "generous gift."

90. See LXX 3 Kgdms 1:9; 4 Kgdms 10:6, 11; Job 29:9; 34:19; Isa 34:7; Jer 5:5.

91. The term ἁδρός may signify "fullness" or "strength." The metaphorical usage in reference to the rich may have to do either with their corpulence or with their strength.

92. See, e.g., Gen 27:28, 39; Judg 9:9; Job 36:16; LXX Pss 35:9 (36:8); 62:6 (63:5).

93. 9:9-11.

94. Locke's theory of private property, based on rights derived from human labor, therefore has value only in relation to other human beings, and even then in only a limited way (see Locke's *Second Treatise of Government,* chap. 5, "Of Property"). Locke appeals to God's gift of the earth to humanity in common (Ps 115:16b), the fruits of which are distributed to each by their labor. He forgets, however, that the heavens remain the Lord's possession (Ps 115:16a). The distinction between heaven and earth is not a division: heaven still rules the earth. The thought of the psalmist is not that earth has been given over to human beings absolutely, but that the human being has been brought into God's rule over all things from heaven. As Paul reminds the Corinthians, the earth remains the Lord's (Ps 24:1; 1 Cor 10:26). The fruits of our labors, including those of Paul and Apollos, are not ours by any natural right but come to us from God (1 Cor 3:5-9). *Our very existence and all our labor come to us as sheer gifts.* Locke's theory of private property threatens to do what the Corinthians have done: to separate the gifts from the Giver. Paul thus counters Corinthian thought: the unconditioned gifts of God

ploys the language of "wealth" only metaphorically, in reference to spiritual and salvific blessings that by their very nature are present only in communication with God.

21 Paul explains the more basic motivation that underlies his decision: "For we take thought not only of that which is good before the Lord, but also before human beings." He thereby echoes LXX Prov 3:4 and anticipates the ethical instruction he gives in Rom 12:17.[95] As is clear from his wording, this expression of his aim and practice extends beyond the collection to the whole of his apostolic ministry. He is again implicitly defending himself against Corinthian suspicions, as he has repeatedly done in the asseverations of his sincerity and openness in the letter up to this point.[96] Yet Paul's commitment to doing that which is good in the sight of human beings has its limits, as is apparent from his decision not to visit Corinth as he had planned and promised. Pleasing God has priority over pleasing people, as Paul expressly indicates both in this letter and elsewhere.[97]

22 Paul has sent another representative alongside Titus and the delegate of the churches. Perhaps he is to serve as a second (or third) witness, confirming the integrity of the collection (cf. Deut 19:15). Paul has tested him "many times, in many ways." Yet Paul does not mention this purpose; rather, he emphasizes his role in the completion of the collection. Like Titus, he is quite zealous and now even more so "with much confidence" toward the Corinthians. It is Paul, of course, who has given him this confidence. Paul thus brings pressure on the Corinthians not to let this confidence fail, as he explicitly indicates in the following verses.

This second, unknown brother appears not to have been a co-worker, to whom Paul makes appeal, but a delegate, who accompanies Paul in order to assist him in the collection. Paul names him along with the other "brother" as an "apostle of the churches." Yet he is somehow more closely bound to Paul than the first and most likely has accompanied him for a longer period. His reputation is not as great, but his faithfulness is apparently unquestionable. Perhaps he was known only to one church, who sent him with the apostle. In any case, it is Paul who vouches for his integrity.

23 Paul now provides a summary description of the delegation to

---

free us for the spontaneous giving to others for which we have been created. In so giving, we finally receive God's gifts *as gifts*, and not finally as the fruit of our labors, even though our labors are not thereby obviated.

95. Paul's wording corresponds closely: καὶ προνοοῦ καλὰ ἐνώπιον κυρίου καὶ ἀνθρώπων. In contrast to English translations (ESV, NIV, NRSV), both the MT (מְצָא) and the LXX take the Hebrew verb as an imperative.

96. See 1:12-14; 2:17; 4:2; 5:11-12; 6:11-13; 7:2.

97. 5:11; see also Gal 1:10; 1 Thess 2:4.

Corinth. Titus is Paul's "partner" *(koinōnos)* and co-worker. To receive him is to receive Paul.

Paul then characterizes the two whom he has sent to Corinth as "apostles of the churches." As his following identification of them as "the glory of Christ" shows, the designation is honorific and theologically motivated. It is not to be regarded as a technical term but as an ad hoc metaphor. The churches are somehow present in those whom they have sent as apostles, as becomes apparent in the following verse.[98] It is likely, too, that, in using this description, Paul implies that these agents bear the Gospel to Corinth, just as apostles of Christ bear the Gospel. The Corinthian participation in the collection is, after all, a fresh confession of the Gospel (9:13). It is also a fresh reception of the Gospel, as Paul's repeated calls to the Corinthians to seek and share in "this grace" make clear.

As "apostles of the churches," Paul's agents are "the glory of Christ." The churches are not absolute or final. They themselves are the work of Christ, who is present and active in them and has priority over them.[99] Thus, just as the churches are present in their apostles, so Christ is present in them as well. Furthermore, Paul's language strikingly recalls his description of the "glory of Christ" as the content of the Gospel, which itself is radiant light (4:4). As a recipient and bearer of the Gospel, Paul has had his heart illumined by this light, which he bears in the earthen vessel of his body and life (4:6-7). In describing the representatives sent to Corinth as the "glory of Christ," Paul thus indicates that they bear Christ and his glory in their earthly lives. It is likely, too, that he has in view their Gentile identity; the Servant of the Lord is a light to the pagans.[100]

24 Paul's final appeal is that the Corinthians provide the proof and demonstration of their love — and his boasting — in the presence of the churches. He already has made clear to the Corinthians that he is not giving them an ultimatum, but testing the genuineness of their love (v. 8). He now asks for that proof in the presence of the churches.

His ethical appeal is thus entirely shaped by the Gospel. The "love" of the Corinthians is nothing other than the love of Christ that they have come to know and experience (v. 9). As we have noted, Paul goes on to describe their gift as a confession of the Gospel (9:13). The Corinthian "doing" is to arise entirely from what Christ has "done" for them, and this not as mere gratitude but as a fresh experience of the "grace" of Christ and of God. Paul's concluding, joyful thanksgiving drives home the confession of God as unqualified Giver.

98. The understanding of an apostle in the earliest church becomes apparent here as well: Christ is present in his apostles (cf. 13:3).

99. See 13:5; 1 Cor 12:12.

100. Isa 42:6; 49:6; cf. Col 1:27.

This appeal, based on and shaped by the Gospel, nevertheless does not exclude the pressure of the witness of others. The Corinthians are to show the love, which Paul is confident is theirs in Christ, before the churches.

They are also to verify Paul's boasting about them. Given their stormy relationship with the apostle, this boasting is perhaps the clearest evidence that Paul's ethic is based entirely on Christ and his work, and not on the fallen, human recipients of the Gospel. Paul has briefly mentioned the encouragement he has given to Titus (v. 17) and the confidence of one he has sent to Corinth (v. 22). He is about to bring further pressure to bear on the Corinthians by describing his boasting about them to the Macedonians.

2. *Instruction concerning the Collection (9:1-15)*

Paul inverts the usual order of his theology and ethics in dealing with the Corinthian collection. Normally, he first presents the Gospel, and then he calls his addressees to the new life that flows forth from it. In this case, his exhortation (chap. 8) precedes his instruction (chap. 9). This inversion is most likely due to his already having instructed the Corinthians concerning the collection. They need only a reminder of what they already know. Yet he brings a potent reminder of the meaning of giving in his concluding theological instruction (9:6-15). Had it not been for the disruption in his relationship with the Corinthians and the present situation in Corinth, we would not possess this dense and profound presentation of Paul's theology of giving.

The instruction falls into two distinct sections. In the first section, Paul directs the Corinthians to complete their collection prior to his own arrival: he has encouraged his delegation to help them in this regard as well (9:1-5). He thus takes up the threads of his prior instruction (1 Cor 16:1-4), which had been broken in the recent controversy between him and the church. Now, however, Macedonians, to whom Paul has boasted concerning the Corinthians, may well accompany him. He thus continues to apply the pressure of the witness of the churches that he already has brought to bear on the Corinthians.

a. The Promised Blessing and the Macedonians (9:1-5)

9 1*Now it is superfluous for me to write to you about the ministry for the*
saints, 2*for I know your readiness, of which I boast about you to the people*
of Macedonia, saying that Achaia has been ready since last year. And your
zeal has stirred up most of them. 3*But I am sending the brothers so that our*
boasting about you may not prove empty in this matter, so that you may
be ready, as I said you would be. 4*Otherwise, if some Macedonians come*
with me and find that you are not ready, we would be humiliated — to say

nothing of you — for being so confident. [5]*So I thought it necessary to urge the brothers to go on ahead to you and arrange in advance for the gift you have promised, so that it may be ready as a willing gift, not as an exaction.*

Paul stresses the superfluity of any further instruction on his part concerning the collection. Indeed, he has boasted to the Macedonians that "Achaia has been prepared for more than a year" (v. 2). This insistence that the Corinthians need no instruction, practical or theological, brings yet further pressure to bear on them. It binds them afresh to him as their apostle, since they must recall and implement the instruction that he has given them already. His indication of his boasting about them to the Macedonians likewise serves as an exhortation. At the opening of his encouragement to Corinth, he brought forward the Macedonians as an example of the grace of God at work. The Corinthians are to imitate them in that they seek God's grace for themselves (8:1-5). Now, however, in his instruction, he inverts the relationship of Macedonia and Achaia. As it turns out, it was the zeal of the Corinthians that stirred the Macedonians to action. Corinth was the instrument in God's hand in Macedonia, just as Macedonia is to be the instrument in God's hand in Achaia. The dynamic of equality worked by God extends to the grace of giving itself. In his report of the effect of their eagerness on the Macedonians, Paul elevates the Corinthians, making them the equals of the "rich" Macedonians, even as he encourages them to complete the collection of their gift. As he has hinted already, the delegation he has sent (and now, so to speak, is standing before the Corinthians) does not simply have the purpose of ensuring the integrity of his dealings. They also have come to Corinth in advance of the apostle in order to bring the Corinthian collection to its completion.

1 According to Paul, the long-standing readiness of the Corinthians renders any further word from him concerning "the mission to the saints" unnecessary. His affirmation largely serves as an exhortation, as becomes clear in this brief section. Paul does have another word for them, not only in the exhortation that he provides here, but also in his weighty theological elaboration of the nature of giving in vv. 6-15.[101]

2 Yet Paul's discussion of giving must be regarded as a reminder or development of his earlier instruction. He implicitly regards the Corinthian "eagerness" as having arisen from instruction. Again, there is no heat without light for the apostle.

As we have noted, in his report concerning his boasting "on behalf of" the Corinthians, Paul reverses the roles of the Macedonians and Corinthians.

101. He opens his instruction with the first part of a well-known "on the one hand . . . on the other hand" construction (μέν . . . δέ) that he closes off only in v. 6. He does have something to write to them, but does not want to overlook their earlier eagerness to share in the collection.

Behind the surprising grace given to the Macedonians stands the zeal of the Corinthians. The dynamic exchange of equality forms his entire encouragement and instruction of the Corinthians. He by no means belittles them for their delay in completing their gift. Just the opposite, he elevates them by underscoring the effect they have had on Macedonia.

This boasting on Paul's part again represents his faith in Christ rather than his confidence in the Corinthians. Of course, they had been ready to participate in the collection for some time. Paul had given instructions in First Corinthians as to how they were to prepare the collection.[102] But in the intervening period the relationship between the apostle and his church had become quite stormy. Much had transpired in Paul's relationship with Corinth in the year that had passed! He communicates his boasting about them from Macedonia in the wake of the crisis that has been resolved only recently by Titus's visit to Corinth. The conduct of the Corinthians could hardly have inspired confidence in the apostle. His boasting about them is a boasting in Christ.[103] At the same time, his report concerning his boasting signals to the Corinthians that his love for them and his confidence concerning them remained unbroken. Despite all that has transpired, they are in his heart "to die together, and to live together" (7:3).[104]

Paul has boasted that the Corinthians have been prepared for more than a year. They should have been, since they already had received sufficient instruction. He has sent his delegation to ensure that they are in fact prepared when he arrives (v. 5). Paul perhaps has stretched the truth a bit in his boasting about the Corinthians. The readiness of the collection has not yet matched the Corinthians' initial zeal. Paul's praise of the Corinthians obviously is intended to secure the former, even as it affirms the latter.

3 Until this point, it has appeared that Paul sent the delegation in order to help and encourage the Corinthians to complete their collection, and to prevent any doubts from arising concerning the integrity of his dealings. Now he indicates that he had another purpose in sending "the brothers." He does not want his boast that the Corinthian collection has long been prepared to be rendered void. He has been telling the Macedonians that the Corinthians are ready, and Paul wants to find them so when he comes. The delegation is an advance team that will ensure the success of the project. Paul thus strengthens the position of the delegation, who have arrived with this letter.

4 Paul's thought is completed in this verse, and the pressure on Corinth has intensified. It is possible, and indeed likely, that Macedonians will accompany Paul as he travels to Corinth. If they should do so, and if the Corinthians

102. 1 Cor 16:1-4.

103. See 1:14-15, as well as the rhetorically motivated words of 7:2-4, 14-16.

104. See likewise 8:7; 11:11; 12:14-15.

turn out not to be prepared to deliver the collection, Paul will be put to shame in the worst sort of way. This will be even more the case for the Corinthians, as Paul underscores. This is a serious threat for a first-century Mediterranean culture, which was oriented to honor and shame much more than the modern West. It must have been especially disturbing to the Corinthians, who show themselves to be quite conscious of their status in Paul's letters. As we have noted, it is likely that one reason for the delay in the completion of the collection was the Corinthian attempt to come up with an impressive sum, establishing themselves as benefactors. If some impoverished Macedonians should show up with Paul, who has boasted to them about Corinth, and found them unprepared, they would suffer a terrible loss of face. Paul knows how to persuade.

5 Paul repeats his third reason for sending the delegates, elaborating his point theologically and preparing for the instruction that follows in vv. 6-15. The apostle himself takes responsibility for the task he has assigned to the "brothers" he has sent: he has encouraged them to complete the collection in Corinth.

While he has spoken of "sending" the two delegates of the churches (8:18, 22) and of arranging their mission (v. 20), he now steps back a bit: he has *encouraged (parakaleō)* them to go in advance and to make preparations. They are to act with a measure of freedom and independence and are thus personally engaged in this work, as Paul has indicated already.[105]

All three delegates are to prepare in advance the "previously promised blessing."[106] Paul's description of the collection now takes on new theological overtones. In the first place, he now speaks of their "eagerness" and "readiness" as a concrete commitment, a promise that they have made. The question is whether they will fulfill their word. Second, he here describes the Corinthian gift as an act of verbal communication. This is true not only of the term "promise," but also "blessing" *(eulogia),* which connotes spoken words and, within biblical usage, often consists precisely in words that confer blessing. Third, his characterization of their gift as a "promised blessing" implicitly sets the Corinthians in the place of God, who has given the Yes to his promises in Christ (1:21). Generally with Paul, "promising" is *God's* action.[107] Similarly, in Scripture, human beings "bless" others, but their blessing of others is always a communication of God's blessing and not a gift of their own.[108] Paul by no means suggests that the Corinthians are thereby to replace God. Just the opposite: their entrance into giving brings a fresh knowledge of God the

105. 8:16-17, 22.

106. ESV: "the gift you have promised."

107. See, e.g., Rom 1:2; 4:13-21; 9:4, 8-9; 15:8; Gal 3:14-29; 2 Cor 1:21; 7:1.

108. See, e.g., Gen 27:27-29; 48:9-20; Num 6:24-25; 23:7-10.

Creator and Giver of all good, as Paul makes clear in his following instruction. Nevertheless, in giving, they act as God, the Giver, acts. In sharing in his goodness, they give forth this goodness to others. In using the word-combination "promised blessing," Paul implies that the Corinthians are to participate in the work of God, giving forth what they have received from him. Perhaps, too, he places their delay in completing the collection in a positive light: just as God's promises have their Yes in the crucified and risen Jesus, the Corinthian promise has taken a number of unexpected turns before it finally will issue in fulfillment.

Paul wants the "promised blessing" to be ready as a "blessing," not as "an instance of greed" *(pleonexia)*. The syntax strongly suggests that Paul does not speak of greed on his part (or on that of his delegates), but rather of greed on the part of the Corinthians: just as the "blessing" has reference to them, so does the potential of "greed."[109] If the Macedonians should appear with Paul and the "blessing" is not prepared, it will appear that the Corinthians are stingy, hoarding for themselves the earthly goods in which they abound. This reading of Paul's statement corresponds to the benefit to the Corinthians that he has named in citing Scripture: "The one [who had] much did not take too much [*pleonazō*]."[110] What the Corinthians have available to give is sufficient (8:12-13). They need only make good on their promise.

b. Giving and the Indescribable Gift (9:6-15)

[6]*The point is this: whoever sows sparingly will also reap sparingly, and*
whoever sows bountifully will also reap bountifully. [7]*Each one must give as*
he has decided in his heart, not reluctantly or under compulsion, for God
loves a cheerful giver. [8]*And God is able to make all grace abound to you,*
so that having all sufficiency in all things at all times, you may abound in
every good work. [9]*As it is written,*

> *He has distributed freely, he has given to the poor;*
> *his righteousness endures forever.*

[10]*He who supplies seed to the sower and bread for food will supply and*
multiply your seed for sowing and increase the harvest of your righteous-
ness. [11]*You will be enriched in every way to be generous in every way, which*
through us will produce thanksgiving to God. [12]*For the ministry of this*
service is not only supplying the needs of the saints but is also overflowing

109. Rightly NIV, "not as [a gift] grudgingly given"; wrongly ESV, "not as an exaction," and NRSV, "not as an extortion."

110. 8:15; Exod 16:18. See, too, Sir 14:8-10, which presents the vice of greed in terms of refusal to share.

> *in many thanksgivings to God.* [13]*By their approval of this service, they will glorify God because of your submission that comes from your confession of the gospel of Christ, and the generosity of your contribution for them and for all others,* [14]*while they long for you and pray for you, because of the surpassing grace of God upon you.* [15]*Thanks be to God for his inexpressible gift!*

Paul now instructs the Corinthians on the nature of giving, after having encouraged them to complete their gift for Jerusalem. Although he reverses the usual order of his argument, his ethics remain grounded in his Gospel. In a profound way, which exposes the reality of human existence itself, he makes it clear that all true giving is dependent upon the prior giving of God. His instruction on giving is a single unit, without any sharp breaks in the argument. This unity expresses a correspondence between the work of God as Creator and the work of God as Savior that is of fundamental theological significance.

A slight shift in Paul's thought is apparent at v. 12, even if it is not strongly marked. In the first movement of his instruction, Paul unfolds the nature of giving by appealing to the figure of agriculture, in which the labor (and "giving") of the human being is taken up within the unqualified gifts of the Creator (vv. 6-11). In the second movement of his thought, he unfolds the theological significance of this work of the Creator, which extends beyond the provision of our daily bread to the gift of righteousness and life in Christ (vv. 12-15). God not only supplies our need, but in Christ also creates the reception of his gifts in praise and thanksgiving. The entrance of the new creation brings light to the human heart, the recognition of the work of God, the Creator, in all its wonder.

6 Paul abruptly supplies the counterpart to his opening statement that the Corinthians do not need him to write anything to them concerning the "mission to the saints." Despite their long-standing eagerness, Paul does have something to say: "But this. . . ." Undoubtedly, their failure to complete the collection prompts his instruction. Yet there is likely another reason as well. Like the rest of Scripture, apostolic instruction has depths that can never be fully learned but bring forth ever-fresh experience.[111] This inexhaustible richness of the Gospel comes to expression in the exclamation of thanks with which Paul closes his instruction. His doxology is a confession that this theology cannot be grasped fully but invites ever again to growth in understanding. It is this invitation that Paul extends to the Corinthians as he urges them to complete the collection for Jerusalem.

In instructing the Corinthians concerning the nature of giving, Paul appeals to a fundamental biblical figure of human existence: sowing and reaping, and the temporal locations in which they are found, seedtime and harvest. In one way, this imagery differs from his prior appeal to the story of the gift of

111. See also Rom 15:14-15; cf. 1 John 2:26-27.

manna (8:15). As his citation of Exod 16:18 makes clear, in that event the Lord worked an equal distribution of the manna, no matter that some gathered more than others (8:15). In the figure of agriculture, Paul emphasizes difference. The one who sows sparingly shall also reap sparingly.[112] The one who sows "upon blessings" (or "bountifully") shall likewise reap bountifully. The manna came as a gift; it required no sowing, only the gathering up of the gift given from heaven. In agriculture, in contrast, the act of sowing is determinative. The amount one sows determines the amount one reaps. The measure in which one enters into the reality of giving determines the measure of the benefits that one receives from it.

At first sight, then, Paul seems to agree with the postmodern deconstruction of giving, according to which all gifts may be exposed as a hidden form of economic exchange. By its very nature, however, Paul's agricultural figure reveals that something quite different and wonderful takes place in giving. Despite the obvious difference between the gift of manna and the practice of farming, in another, more basic way, they are the same. Indeed, this correspondence is essential to the meaning of the gift of manna. The Lord fed Israel with manna in order that the people might know that "the human being does not live by bread alone, but by every word that goes forth from the mouth of the Lord" (Deut 8:3). Israel's lesson in the wilderness was intended to prepare it for the promised land, in which there would be seed to plant and crops to reap. Not only in the wilderness, but also in the land itself, Israel was to learn that the produce of the field comes as a sheer gift from God. This produce of the field is essential to human life and existence; without the fundamental goodness of God that is "richly and daily" granted to us, human life could not continue, no matter how much we labored, no matter how clever we might be. Paul pointedly borrows this lesson from the figure of agriculture in earlier instruction of the Corinthians concerning their leaders. He planted, Apollos watered, but

112. Paul here echoes LXX Prov 22:8a (ὁ σπείρων φαῦλα θερίσει κακά), a passage to which he will allude more directly in v. 7. As a whole, LXX Prov 22:8-9 varies from the MT, reinterpreting and extending the deed-recompense formulation that appears in MT Prov 22:8a (זוֹרֵעַ עַוְלָה יִקְצָר־אָוֶן), and adding further sayings, including the one Paul cites in v. 7. A similar affirmation of the connection between deed and recompense appears in LXX Prov 11:21 (χειρὶ χεῖρας ἐμβαλὼν ἀδίκως οὐκ ἀτιμώρητος ἔσται, ὁ δὲ σπείρων δικαιοσύνην λήμψεται μισθὸν πιστόν). According to Paul's Gospel, God's saving work in Christ transcends and interrupts this connection. Nevertheless, it also paradoxically confirms it: salvation does not come apart from judgment, but through it. As Paul puts it in this letter, God made the one who knew no sin to be sin, in order that we might become the righteousness of God in him (5:21). With respect to salvation itself, Paul himself insists — again in true paradox — that "what one sows, that shall one reap" (Gal 6:7b). The grace of Christ transcends this law of recompense, but it does not exclude it. We have seen the same pattern of thought in Paul's presentation of Christian hope and the final judgment in 5:1-10.

God was causing the growth in and among them (1 Cor 3:6). Human labor, while it is required and rewarded by God, is only secondary. It is God who gives all growth and who thus is not dependent on human instruments. The gift of the manna reveals the fundamental goodness of the Creator — not merely toward Israel, but toward all human beings — a goodness present and manifest in the whole creation, which was made for us and which, from its fields, nurtures us and provides for our daily needs.[113] Despite human sin and the enslavement of creation to vanity, the goodness of God remains in God's quiet (yet audible!) beneficence that sustains and supports all human life and existence.[114] It is celebrated in the Psalms,[115] and it appears in Luke's report of Paul's preaching in Lystra.[116] It is basic to the Lord's Prayer. Paul explicitly develops the theme in his following argument (vv. 9-10). It is clear, then, that he by no means reduces gift-giving to an economic transaction. Whether it is recognized or not, the practices of gardening, farming, and agriculture, no matter how small or how large they may be, are acts of participation in the goodness of the Creator, which stands behind and before all human labor. As Paul shortly reminds the Corinthians, not only does the harvest come from God, the very seed that is sown comes from him as well (v. 10). To farm is to enter into the work of God, without in any way displacing or qualifying the ultimacy of God's goodness and giving.[117] The same is true of giving. It differs from agriculture in that in true giving the human being must *knowingly* participate in God's unqualified goodness. This is Paul's point in this verse. To reap bountifully from what one gives is *not* to receive a wage for one's labor. God himself chooses the currency of the return. This is apparent, as we have seen, in the exchange between Corinth and Jerusalem. Insofar as material goods are concerned, the return of them is almost always delayed, and almost always comes not from the recipients of our gifts but from an unexpected source. In this sense, it is not a reward or economic return on investment that comes from one's cleverness. Nor does it arise out of mere luck. It is the reception of blessing, as Paul's wording ("upon blessings") implies. Sowing sparingly or bountifully in giving is not a matter of earning a wage by one's labor. It is the reality of faith, which has its works but which cannot be reduced to them. It a participation in the goodness of God, who supplies both seed and harvest.

Paul employs unusual language in the latter part of the verse that is generally obscured in modern translations: "And the one who sows *with* [or *upon*] *blessings* shall also reap *with* [or *upon*] *blessings*." The usage is rare. It appears

113. Gen 2:15-16.

114. Gen 8:22; 9:3. On this theme, see again Bayer, *Luther's Theology*, 95-119.

115. Pss 104:10-23, 27-28; 127:1-5; 145:13-16.

116. Acts 14:17.

117. Not even in genetically modified crops, we might add!

twice in LXX Gen 49:26 and likewise twice in Philo.[118] Neither offers a real parallel to Paul's thought. As in LXX Gen 49:26, the sense of the expression is probably that of bounty or abundance, which comes across in the English translations. Yet Paul's use of the term "blessing" *(eu-logia)* suggests that he understands bountiful giving as a "speech act," a response to the address of the good Creator, a "speaking forth" of the spoken blessing that has been received.[119] This reading correlates with Paul's following description of the Corinthian gift as a confession of the Gospel (v. 13). All our giving, or also our failure to do so, is a response to the prior goodness, grace, and blessing of God. Our response is that of faith — or of unbelief.

7 Paul follows his proverbial dictum with a concrete guideline for the collection: each one is to give "as they have determined in advance, not out of sadness or compulsion." All true giving must arise from spontaneous individual decisions, uncompelled by others. Faith cannot be forced, nor is it a mere communal phenomenon.

The yet-to-be-completed collection guides Paul's instruction here. According to his earlier directive, the individual members of the Corinthian church were to set aside a contribution each week, according to the way in which they might have prospered in that time. The collection would then have been prepared before Paul arrived.[120] Although this work had begun, it had not been completed. It had been broken off because of the recent controversy with Paul, if not also for other reasons. Now Paul has sent his delegation, who have arrived with the present letter. The collection must be completed rather quickly, according to the means that the Corinthians have available. There is a danger, then, that Christians in Corinth will be placed under pressure to contribute and will do so with regret or out of the feeling that they are compelled by circumstances or by the apostle and his representatives to present a gift. Paul therefore urges that each one is to give "just as they have determined in advance." They have been committed to the collection for some time and most likely have considered already what they would give. The need to complete the collection now should not necessarily change those prior decisions.

Paul elaborates and concludes his opening instruction with a proverb: "For God loves a joyful giver." The saying is almost certainly drawn from LXX Prov 22:8a, a text upon which Paul already has drawn in v. 6.[121] He nevertheless modifies the Septuagintal reading ("God blesses a joyful and giving person"), explicitly locating joy in giving ("a joyful giver") and announcing

118. See Philo, *Leg.* 3.210.2; *Mos.* 1.283.7.

119. On this theme and its significance for Christian ethics, see Bayer, *Freedom in Response,* 1-12.

120. 1 Cor 16:1-2.

121. See n. 112, p. 353.

that God loves such a person, rather than promising blessing that is yet to come. He thus removes any possible economic overtones from the saying. His announcement transcends the sphere of "works." God loves a *joyful giver,* and not merely gifts, which in themselves are ambiguous, no matter how large they are or what ends they ostensibly serve. Giving must come from the heart, apart from any recognition by others, or it is not giving at all. Entrance into this giving is participation in the unconditioned goodness of God.[122] As Paul will make clear in the latter part of this passage, it is a confession of the Gospel, where coveting has been overcome and love reigns.[123]

8 The relationship of communication and faith in God the Creator to which Paul here calls the Corinthians is not distant from the world, but it has its concrete earthly effects. Paul now elaborates his appeal to the figure of sowing and reaping and speaks to the Corinthians in a fivefold promissory assertion, which, through its repetition of the term "all" *(pas),* emphasizes the comprehensiveness and ultimacy of God's goodness. As we have seen, this giving of God does not exclude, but includes, the giving of the Corinthians: "And God is able to cause all grace to abound to *you,* that in everything, always having all self-sufficiency, *you* might abound unto every good work." The grace of the Creator encompasses the human being behind and before, in such a way that our giving is always a fresh entrance into the giving of God. The Corinthians are simultaneously to be both active and passive, both givers and receivers.[124] Precisely because of the grace of God given to them, they will be empowered and enriched to give to others.

The entire chain of promised blessings is contained within Paul's first word: "God is able to cause all grace to abound to you." Here again we meet Paul's usage of "grace" *(charis)* as a concrete expression of God's favor that comes close to the sense of "gift." Paul has urged the Corinthians to "abound" in the grace of giving, just as they abound in other "graces" (8:7). Now he asserts God's power to so act with them. The grace that God is able "to cause to abound" to the Corinthians is nothing other than the grace of giving. Even in the giving of the Corinthians, it remains *grace:* the favor and goodness of God, unearned and undeserved, which remains unconditioned by the "good works" of the Corinthians that flow forth from it.

As Paul makes clear, the grace of God has a purpose. The abounding of God's grace to the Corinthians is to cause *them* to abound "unto every good

122. 2 Cor 5:14; 13:11, 13; Rom 5:5, 8; 8:39.

123. 1 Cor 13:1-13; Rom 13:10; Gal 5:6, 13, 22; Phil 2:1. Paul speaks elsewhere of loving God as a reality for those who believe, e.g., 1 Cor 2:9; 8:3; Rom 8:28.

124. It should not be forgotten that Paul has defined the Corinthians by the figure of the field and its fruits in 1 Cor 3:5-9; 9:7, and he elsewhere uses such terms to describe his broader apostolic labors (Rom 1:13; 15:28; Phil 1:22). He likewise uses it in reference to the work of salvation (Gal 5:22-23; Phil 1:11) and its results in the lives of believers (Rom 6:21-22).

work." This does not mean that God's grace serves an end other than the display and giving forth of his goodness. The Corinthians are not obligated to offer a return gift. Their relationship with God cannot be reduced to an economic transaction. The grace of God is to bring the Corinthians into real participation in his grace; they are to receive and know that grace afresh, as they give it forth. Indeed, only in the giving forth of God's grace shall they know God's grace in its fullness.

Paul's description of the work of God's grace centers on the promise that the Corinthians will "in all things, at all times have all self-sufficiency [*autarkeia*].[125] Here he borrows a term from Stoic philosophy that expresses the attainment of mental happiness, accepting the good or ill that nature brings.[126] Paul's use of this language seems especially strange at first hearing, since throughout the letter, and especially in this context, he is instructing the Corinthians that life under the Gospel is not one of inwardness or self-contentment, but of communication with God and with others. Yet, just as he does with the Platonic concept of "the inner person" and other philosophical terms current in his day, Paul "baptizes" this Stoic language, reinterpreting it, and yet drawing an essential truth from it. Understood in the context of God's work as Creator (rather than that of a mute, impersonal "nature"), "self-sufficiency" is not an obstacle to giving and communication but its very prerequisite. The theme appears in Paul's exhortation to complete the collection: the Macedonians gave in self-determination (*authairetos,* 8:3); Titus has traveled to Corinth in the same way (8:17). True communication, receiving and giving, cannot take place apart from "self-sufficiency" and spontaneity. In this profound sense "individualism" is necessary to community.[127] Modern theology, in the priority it generally gives to "community," church, and kingdom, largely has lost sight of this truth. To the degree that we are not "self-sufficient" and therefore *need* others, we attempt to dominate or exploit them in one way or another. Bonhoeffer's words concerning Christian community, to which we have referred several times, apply again here, as does his warning about the "dark side" of any human community that is not centered in Christ.[128] The dramatic difference between Paul's understanding of "self-sufficiency" and that of the Stoics, a difference that also sets Paul apart from the postmodern deconstruction of "giving," is the obvious truth that for Paul "self-sufficiency" is an

125. Paul's thought stands in contrast to that of *Pss. Sol.* 5:16, in which the psalmist hopes for only a "measure of self-sufficiency" lest, because of abundance, he should transgress. The dynamic of exchange is missing with the latter.

126. The same borrowing appears significantly in Paul's "thanksgiving" for the gift of the Philippians (Phil 4:11).

127. That is not to say that the individual has priority over community, but that new persons and the new community of the people of God are created simultaneously in Jesus Christ.

128. See p. 16.

unqualified gift of God. "Self-sufficiency" is thus relative for the apostle. One does not have "sufficiency" in oneself, but only in relationship to the God who acts toward us in grace. We are therewith free with respect to our neighbors, not so that we might isolate ourselves from them, but so that we might serve them. Indeed, unless we are free from our neighbors, we cannot serve them, but in one way or another will seek to exploit them for the fulfillment of our needs. Paul's promissory assertion concerning "self-sufficiency" calls for nothing other than faith in the fundamental goodness of God. In this relationship of faith, and only in this relationship, in which we look to God in his promises to supply all our needs — material, emotional, and spiritual — we are granted the "self-sufficiency" that sets us free to love and serve our neighbor.

That this "self-sufficiency" does not issue in selfishness and self-contentment is due to the nature of God's grace and giving. As Paul makes clear in his following instruction, God does not merely provide our material needs. In his provision of these needs, God gives himself to us. The Corinthian temptation has been to separate the gift from the Giver. Paul's instruction here goes directly to this point. In giving himself to us, God elevates us, lifts us up to himself. We are made to be much more than mere dependents, beneficiaries, and clients. We are granted participation in God's very giving. We ourselves are made to be givers, just as God is the Giver. We are made to be Christ to our neighbor. This is Paul's message to the Corinthians concerning the collection. In a sense, then, in giving there is a "deification" of the human being that in no way displaces God; rather, it confirms God as the one Giver. Paul hints at this truth already in the present verse. Just as God is able to cause all grace to *abound* to the Corinthians, the Corinthians will *abound* in good works that flow out of their "self-sufficiency." By its participation in God's goodness, faith is active in love.[129]

The larger context makes it clear that this apostolic promise of "self-sufficiency in all things, at all times" should not be taken to mean that the Corinthians will never suffer want or need. Just as the sufferings of Christ belong to the apostle, they belong to the Corinthians as well. The Macedonians were granted the grace of giving in the depths of their poverty. The Jerusalem Christians, who shall fill the lack of the Corinthians, do so out of their need. The "self-sufficiency" of which Paul speaks furthermore does not exclude, but includes, the dynamic of exchange and equality among Christians. As Paul makes clear, it is the abounding of God's *grace* that works "self-sufficiency." Blessings lie in abundance with God, who grants them at the times and in the ways of his choosing. As both Paul's opening formulation and his following appeal to Psalm 112 make clear, God's power ("God is able to . . .") is experienced only within the reality of faith, into which we must enter again and

129. Cf. Gal 5:6.

again. The "self-sufficiency" which Paul promises will be complete only at the arrival of the eschaton when faith itself will be complete.[130] That is not to say, however, that "self-sufficiency" remains a mere ideal. Just as the new creation has entered into this world, so this promised "self-sufficiency" is to be tasted and known in the present, even if its fullness is yet to come.

9 Paul makes it clear that his rather Hellenistic assertion has its roots in the Scriptures: "just as it is written." He draws the promise of self-sufficiency from the image of the righteous person that appears in Psalm 112: "He scattered, he gave to the poor, his righteousness abides forever." The text employs the metaphor of giving as the image of sowing of seed that Paul himself uses in v. 6. In fact, the figure is heightened. Giving is pictured as a scattering, a broadcasting of seed. The language bears overtones of dissolution and dissipation. "Scattering" implies a free and indiscriminate giving to those in need, an apparent profligacy. The righteous seem to squander their resources.

Nevertheless, through a wonder, "their righteousness abides forever." There is a twofold sense, plus a measure of wordplay, in this usage of "righteousness" in the psalm. It first signifies the relationship of faith and fear of the Lord in which the righteous person lives (Ps 112:1, 7b). Their righteousness is the righteousness of faith that is lived in the face of need, threat, and danger.[131] "Righteousness" thus appears here as a reality that is fundamental to the human being as a creature, and not merely as a sinner. In context, it signifies the abundance of goods and the protection from enemies with which the righteous are blessed.[132] This second sense is essential to the wordplay in the psalm, which expresses the wonder of the abiding prosperity of those who scatter their goods. Despite apparent prodigality, the righteous unceasingly prosper.[133] Their "righteousness" is an abundance that comes ever again in blessing from the Lord. It thus abides forever. The psalm makes the point that the abundance of the righteous is not the result of their work or their hoarding of possessions. Just the opposite. It is blessing that is ever given and ever received afresh, in the relationship of trust and fear of the Lord, an abundance found in the relationship of receiving and giving. "Righteousness" signifies the relationship of fear and trust in the Lord in which all good, including material good, is to be found.

130. Paul's similar promise to the Philippians, that "my God shall fulfill every need of yours according to his riches in glory in Christ Jesus" (Phil 4:19), is likewise to be understood as bearing an eschatological horizon, yet including all present gifts that carry the Philippians to that end.

131. See Ps 112:4-8, 9c-10.

132. As is the case elsewhere in Scripture, "righteousness" has to do not merely with a declaration or status but with the concrete benefits that arise from a right relation with God, esp. vindication over against enemies.

133. See also Prov 11:24, where the same figure and a similarly worded promise of blessing appears.

Paul cites the psalm as a re-presentation of his assertion concerning God's power toward the Corinthians. The "self-sufficiency" that he promises in v. 8 reappears in the eternally abiding righteousness of v. 9. His recasting of "self-sufficiency" here becomes apparent. It is not found in an "introverted" state of contentment as in Stoic thought, but in the "extroverted" relationship of faith and fear of the Lord. In citing the psalm, Paul calls the attention of the Corinthians to this relationship with God. Just as the psalmist does not gain righteousness by his giving but gives out of the righteousness that already has been granted him, so, too, the Corinthians are to give out of the righteousness that already is theirs. As with the psalmist, this righteousness is the righteousness of faith. The entire purpose of the apostolic mission is to effect this righteousness of faith and communication with God that is given in and through the dramatic exchange that has taken place in Christ.[134] The righteousness of the Corinthians is not found in themselves, but in Christ.[135] The work of God the Creator and God the Redeemer is one.

As in the Septuagintal rendering of the verse (Ps 111[112]:9), Paul uses the term *penētes* to refer to the poor. It signifies impoverished day laborers (of which there are an increasing number in our world), in contrast with the term *ptōchoi,* which is often used in reference to beggars. Paul may simply have drawn on the Septuagint, but his usage may also serve to ennoble the Jerusalem Christians in relation to the Corinthians.

10 Paul extends his appeal to Scripture with an allusion to the book of Isaiah. He now refers again directly to the Corinthians ("you," pl.), as in v. 8. His assertion concerning God's power to provide becomes a direct promise here: the citation of the Psalm in the preceding verse presupposes the reality of faith into which Paul is inviting the Corinthians afresh.

The promise of provision and abundance is based in God the Creator, whom Paul characterizes as "the One who supplies seed to the sower and bread for eating."[136] What God does everywhere and always, God will also do for the Corinthians. Paul draws his characterization of God from Isa 55:10 by penetrating the simile that appears there. The Isaianic text speaks of "the rain and snow that come down from heaven" as watering the earth and causing it to bear fruit. It goes on to liken this unfailing work of the elements to the word of the Lord, which does not return to him without accomplishing his purpose. Yet the opening words of Isa 55:10 already hint at a second, interior

134. 2 Cor 3:9; 5:21.

135. 1 Cor 1:30.

136. Cf. Gal 3:5, where he characterizes God as "the One who supplies the Spirit to you," presenting the gift of the new creation (Gal 6:15) as the act of the Creator. See also 2 Macc 1:24-25, where the Creator is characterized as "the only One who supplies, the only One who is righteous, all-powerful, and eternal" (ὁ μόνος χορηγός, ὁ μόνος δίκαιος καὶ παντοκράτωρ καὶ αἰώνιος).

dimension to the utterance. The rain and snow come "from heaven." That is to say, they come from the Creator, whose thoughts and ways transcend human capacities.[137] Paul thus makes explicit what is implicit in the text, drawing attention to the work of the Creator that is described there.

Paul speaks, then, of "the One who supplies seed to the one who sows, and bread for eating." According to Paul and the text that he cites, the human being, in both need and abundance, in both receiving and giving, is encompassed by the goodness of God the Creator, who richly supplies all things. Behind and before any giving, there must be something to give. Paul has likened the abundance that may be given to seed that is sown, both in the opening of his instruction (v. 6) and in his citation of Ps 112:9 (v. 9). He now makes it clear that all that we have to give has come to us as a gift from God. He is the One (and the only One) who "supplies seed to the sower." Properly speaking the human being cannot "give." We can only give forth from that which we have received: "What do you have, that you did not receive?" (1 Cor 4:7). God is the One who supplies "bread for eating." The human tasks of sowing, tilling the land, collecting the harvest, winnowing the grain, grinding it at the mill, preparing dough, and baking bread are all presupposed and included in this bread. There remains, however, only One who supplies it. Apart from God all planning and effort are in vain. This truth is fundamental to all human life and labor.

The statement of promise appears, then, in the latter half of the verse: "[God] shall supply and increase your seed, and shall cause the fruits[138] of your righteousness to grow." Paul draws the Corinthians into the figure he has found in Scripture. Their gift now appears as "seed" that God supplies and increases. Out of this seed, God shall cause the produce of the Corinthian righteousness to grow. The Corinthians are to be taken up into the Creator's supply of all need, including their own. It is probably not accidental that Paul uses the plural noun *genēmata* ("fruits") to describe the produce of the Corinthian righteousness. It naturally appears frequently to describe the "fruits of the field." But it also suggests that the blessings received from God may be distributed so as to meet not only one's own needs but also those of many others.

Paul here speaks directly of the righteousness of the Corinthians, borrowing the language of Ps 112:9 that he has cited in v. 9. As in that citation, this righteousness bears a twofold sense. In the first place, it resignifies the *seed* for sowing as a blessing received from God. At the same time, it resignifies the *sowing* of the seed as the relationship of receiving from God and giving forth to others, the relationship of faith, in which the Corinthians are to live. In both

137. The text thus continues the thought of the immediately preceding verses, Isa 55:8-9. See also Isa 30:23; 44:14; 45:8, which in varying ways present the Lord's saving work as Creator in terms of his sending rain from heaven.

138. ESV: "harvest."

senses, although this righteousness is that of the Corinthians, it is extrinsic to them. The blessings that they have received are not properly their own but have come from God. Likewise, their giving is the work of God's grace, given to them in Christ (v. 8). Paul takes up this very theme in the completion of his thought in the following verse.

11 This verse should not be separated from Paul's preceding statement by a full stop, but by a comma: "[He] shall cause the fruits of your righteousness to grow, in everything [you] being enriched. . . ." Paul continues and completes his thought in this verse, rounding off the first movement of his instruction begun in v. 6 and drawing the elements of it together.

With his emphatic, twofold use of "all" ("being enriched *in all ways,* for *all* simplicity"), Paul echoes the promissory assertion of v. 8. Now, however, the "all" bears a new dimension. Paul no longer speaks of "reaping blessings" (v. 6) or "self-sufficiency" (v. 8), but of "being *enriched* in all ways." His wording especially recalls the "riches of simplicity" of the Macedonians (8:2), as well as the wealth of Christ that makes many rich (8:9). In both of these instances, Paul speaks of "riches" metaphorically: it does not consist in material goods, but in life and salvation. These "riches" are now included among "all" the ways in which Paul promises that the Corinthians will be enriched. Thus they will be "enriched unto all simplicity." Especially when one takes into account Paul's word concerning the Macedonians (8:2), it is clear that he here speaks of this "enrichment" effecting simplicity in the Corinthians. His summary statement is also a further description of the increase of the "fruits" of the Corinthians' righteousness (v. 10). The "enrichment" of the Corinthians "unto simplicity" is included within the "fruits" of their righteousness. Paul thus rounds off and completes the thought he began in v. 8: the Corinthian giving is the work of God's grace. For this reason, it results in thanksgiving — not to them, but to God.

We have noted that Paul's wording here recalls 8:2, where he speaks of the "riches of the simplicity" of the Macedonians. Here again, there is no sufficient reason to set aside the usual sense of the term *haplotēs* ("simplicity") in favor of the otherwise unattested sense of "generosity" (ESV, NIV, NRSV). Especially in this context, it is clear that Paul understands giving as a reality of receiving and giving forth, an openness to God and to one's neighbor, in which there are no hidden motives of personal gain. It is entirely to his point that he characterizes giving as "simplicity." This "simplicity" is life with an open hand to receive from God and to give forth to one's neighbor. The concept of giving thus is reserved for God alone, guarded from overtones of benefaction and patronage that were operative in the world of the Corinthians. Paul might be said to agree with Derrida that a gift is not possible — with respect to human beings.[139] But with God all things are possible, including absolute, unconditional giving.

139. See n. 70, p. 337.

The final phrase of this verse marks a shift in Paul's thought to the purpose of his mission, which, as he makes clear, goes beyond the supply of material needs to the effecting of thanksgiving to God and, as vv. 13-14 will show, the creation of the community that exists within this thanksgiving. His preceding characterization of the Corinthians as being "enriched unto all simplicity" — i.e., not merely granted material blessings, but also spiritually enriched — prepares for this transition in his instruction. As is clear from the following relative pronoun, it is the simplicity of the Corinthians that, through Paul, works thanksgiving to God. This work is possible only if simplicity is itself the work of God.

12 The thematic turn in the instruction is marked by causal *hoti* ("because").[140] Paul explains why he speaks of the Corinthian "simplicity" producing thanksgiving. It is first important to note that he does not speak of their *gift* as working thanksgiving, but their *simplicity.* It is their person and not their contribution that brings about thanksgiving.

Furthermore, while the relief of material need is essential to his mission, the purpose of that mission is larger. We do not live by bread alone, nor by mere material provision of our needs. This is true not only in the sense that we are dependent on God to provide our need. It is also true in the sense that every human being, consciously or unconsciously, has a "god," to whom they look for help.[141] The return of thanksgiving to God is the mark of the gift that has been received as a gift. It is not a return gift to God but the wondrous discovery of God in his love and care as the one, true Giver. The collection, or, more properly, the mission, thus "abounds" beyond the fulfilling of want "through many thanksgivings to God." It is not irrelevant that Paul speaks of "many thanksgivings." Thanksgiving cannot be reduced to a communal event. It must come from the heart, or it is not thanksgiving. "Many" thanksgivings come from many hearts.

It is likewise significant that Paul describes this mission as abounding "*through* many thanksgivings to God." This statement in particular makes clear that Paul by no means thinks of a return gift from those who receive the collection. It is highly significant that they offer thanks. In the end, however, it is God's gift itself that works thanksgiving *through* them.

Paul again describes the collection as a *diakonia,* a mission that has been entrusted to him and of which he is a mere agent of Another.[142] He thus implicitly associates it with his apostolic mission and, in his following description

140. An explanatory γάρ would have signaled a continuation of the preceding discussion.

141. We are here recalling again Luther's comments on the First Commandment in his Large Catechism, WA 30/1:400-401.

142. See 8:4, 19-20.

of its purpose, presents it in terms that anticipate his theological elaboration of God's ways with Jews and Gentiles in his letter to Rome.[143] In describing the collection as a "mission," he indicates that he himself bears an intermediate role, as will the Corinthians in their giving. The Corinthian simplicity works thanksgiving to God *through him.*

Paul describes the collection here as "the mission of this service." The genitive relation is epexegetic: the mission itself is an act of service in the worship of God. The term Paul uses for "service" *(leitourgia)* was used in secular Greek for public service. The collection might well be conceived as serving a public good. But Paul's point in this context is that the purpose of the collection transcends this need. It works thanksgiving to God. His concluding instruction is centered on praise, thanksgiving, and petition. The "service" that he ascribes to his mission, then, should be understood within the context of worship, the priestly service that was associated with the term *leitourgia.*[144] His language here resonates with his later description of his apostolic ministry as a priestly offering of the Gentiles (Rom 15:16), and with his description of the Corinthian gift as an act of priestly service (Rom 15:27).

13 An unmarked shift in subject takes place here. While in v. 12 Paul speaks of the *diakonia,* he now speaks of the Jerusalem Christians, picking up the logical subject of the thanksgivings in v. 12b. Nevertheless, he continues to express the action in participial form, continuing the thought of v. 12 and describing the nature of the thanksgiving worked by the mission. The mission is a proving of God's work in the Corinthians, as Paul already has indicated to them (8:8). Thus the recipients of the collection (the Jerusalem Christians remain unnamed throughout Paul's instruction) shall glorify God. The Corinthians themselves are mere vehicles of God's work. Paul furthermore now characterizes the thanksgiving of v. 12 as praise *(doxazō).* The gift is not forgotten, but the Giver, and the Giver's work, stands at the center of this thanksgiving. Above all else, the recipients of the collection shall find the Giver in the gift.

They shall glorify God for two inseparable wonders. First, they shall do so in response to "the subjection that is your confession [with respect] to the Gospel of Christ." Paul's roundabout manner of expression has its point. It is not the Corinthians who appear as subjects, but it is purely and entirely God's work in them: "their confession *to* the Gospel of the Christ" is worked by God and the Gospel itself.[145] Paul describes this confession of the Gospel

143. See esp. Rom 11:33-36; 15:16, 25-33.

144. For a brief discussion, see H. Balz, "λειτουργία, κτλ," *EDNT* 2:347-49.

145. See Rom 6:17 and esp. 15:9, where Paul describes Christ as an agent (διάκονος) of God for the Gentiles, to *glorify* God, citing LXX Ps 17:50 (18:49) in reference to Christ *confessing* God's name among the Gentiles. See further Phil 2:11, which, borrowing the language of Isa 45:23, speaks of God working the confession of Jesus as Lord by "every tongue."

as a subjection to it, just as he does in Rom 10:3.[146] He will shortly inform the Corinthians that he is awaiting the completion not only of the collection but of their obedience to Christ (10:5-6). He thus anticipates his description of faith as obedience in his letter to Rome;[147] he thematically comes close to his depiction there of the rule of Christ as one that both subjugates and saves the Gentiles.[148] Likewise, his presentation of the common praise of God ("by one mouth") of Jews and Gentiles as a sign of hope in Romans is not far from his thought here.[149] Paul subtly brings to expression the priority of the faith of Jerusalem over the Corinthians: they rejoice that the Corinthians have joined them in the confession of the Gospel of Christ.

The genitive "of Christ," with which Paul here defines the Gospel, recalls the crucified and risen One, who by his poverty made the Corinthians rich.[150] Here, just as he does regularly in this letter, Paul gives priority to Christology and brings constant reminders of the cross.

The second reason why the recipients of the collection shall glorify God is the "simplicity of [your] sharing [*koinōnia*] toward them and toward all." Again, the Corinthians do not come directly into view. It is the work of God through them that is of significance.

Paul again describes their contribution as a "simplicity," underscoring the receiving and giving forth that is inherent to the confession of the Gospel and the life of faith. Especially in this context it is clear that he regards this "simplicity" as a work of God in the Corinthians.

It is the "simplicity of [their] *koinōnia*" that calls forth praise to God. By referring to this "sharing" or "participation," Paul recalls the dynamic of equality, the simultaneous meeting of one another's need, that he has described in his appeal to the story of the manna (8:14-15). The praise that the Jerusalem Christians offer for the Corinthian confession of the Gospel suggests that the exchange that appears in Rom 15:26-27 also appears here: Jerusalem has shared its spiritual benefits, and the Gentiles are indebted to help them materially. The exchange in Romans is spread out in time. Here it is again compressed into the moment of sharing. The collection is simultaneously a confession of Christ and a meeting of needs. In one and the same act there is receiving and giving.

Yet Paul suggests that the Jerusalem Christians are not merely interested in the gift that shall come to them. They glorify God also for the simplicity of the Corinthians' sharing "toward all." Paul already has indicated that the

146. The genitive relation in the expression ἡ ὑποταγὴ τῆς ὁμολογίας ὑμῶν is again to be understood as epexegetic.

147. Rom 1:5; 6:17; 10:16; 15:18, 16:19, 26; esp. 6:17 and 10:16.

148. Rom 15:7-13.

149. Rom 15:5-6.

150. 8:9; see also 2:12; 4:14. This designation is not uncommon with Paul in any case: Rom 1:9; 15:19; Gal 1:7; Phil 1:27; 1 Thess 3:2; 2 Thess 1:8.

collection is not to be a one-time event, but simply one opportunity in the life of faith. This is clear from his promissory assertion, his appeal to Scripture, and his following elaboration (9:8-10). The occasion of the collection is to encourage the Corinthians in this life of receiving and giving, and thus to bind them to all other churches. Their withdrawal from God, the Giver, is also a separation from others, a retreat into themselves.

14 Using a genitive absolute, Paul marks his continuing description of thanksgiving as contained within the twofold description of the praise of God that precedes it.[151] The Gospel itself creates community. We need not manufacture it by our plans or programs. We need only receive the community of dynamic exchange that the Gospel creates: "and they shall long for you." This "longing" for the other — in the eyes of the Jerusalem Christians, the Gentile Corinthians were radically "other" — is not a mere emotion. It includes action, the only action that the impoverished believers in Jerusalem could take: "they shall long for you, in petition on behalf of you." The distance between Corinth and Jerusalem does not hinder their fellowship. It merely reduces it to its essential nature: they are bound together by God in Christ. Paul knows this fellowship with his churches.[152] Paul has invited the Corinthians to labor with God in petition for him (1:12). Others shall now labor for them.

Jerusalem and Corinth are to be bound together, yet not because "boundary markers" that distinguish Jew and Gentile are set aside. They do not come together in a "sameness" born of the ideal of a united humanity. Pentecost notwithstanding, Babel is not yet behind us. They remain what they are: Jerusalemites and Corinthians, Jews and Gentiles. Furthermore, as Paul makes clear, it is not any quality or virtue in the Corinthians that binds Jerusalem to them. Christ stands between them in order to bring them together. Only in Christ do they come together. Otherwise they would seek to force the other to conform to their respective ideals. Because of "the surpassing grace of God" that is upon the Corinthians, these Jewish believers long for them. Paul here characterizes the grace of God as "surpassing," "exceeding," "extreme." It transcends all human thought and expectation. This has been his theme. His instruction concerning giving is nothing other than a description of the wondrous working of God's grace (v. 8). His encouragement to complete the collection is a call to grasp and know that grace of God afresh (8:7). His last word concerning God's grace especially recalls his first word concerning the remarkable grace of God given in Macedonia (8:1). His description of it here as "surpassing grace" deflects all attention away from the Corinthians, or any comparison they might be tempted to make between themselves and the Macedonians. It is not the persons or the churches that are outstanding, but the grace of God "upon them."

151. καὶ αὐτῶν . . . ἐπιποθούντων ὑμᾶς.

152. See Phil 1:4, 19.

15 Paul's theology ends in doxology, a doxology that he himself speaks on behalf of the Corinthians, the Jerusalem Christians, and all who are involved in the collection. All of them fade into the background. Thanksgiving belongs to the one true Giver alone. Again he uses the term *charis;* his thanksgiving is implicitly nothing other than the reception of the *charis,* the grace and giving of God.

Paul now shifts attention from God's grace to the concrete gift that God has given. For this indescribable gift, this gift beyond all telling, Paul gives thanks. The term that he uses, *anekdiēgētos,* signifies that this gift cannot be recounted, narrated, or told. It implies a story that is beyond all telling, a story that again and again calls forth amazement, wonder, and praise. He subtly recalls the Isaianic word to which he has alluded in v. 10: as the heavens are higher than the earth, so the Lord's thoughts are higher than our thoughts, and the Lord's ways higher than our ways (Isa 55:10-11). Paul's thought also comes close to that of Rom 11:33-36, where, taking up biblical tradition, he praises God's "unsearchable judgments" and "untraceable footsteps."[153] This later text is not unrelated to the thanksgiving here: Paul writes it in response to God's dealings with Israel and the pagans.[154] The passages are complementary. There his attention is directed to the wonder of God's untraceable ways; here he focuses on the unspeakably wonderful gift of God.

But what is the gift that Paul has in mind? We know its contours. It involves God's self-giving in Christ, the wonder of his taking upon himself our poverty, sin, and guilt; the wonder in which he has made us rich.[155] It entails Christ's grace, which not only meets our every need but also elevates us to share in the divine giving. It includes God's creation of true community, in which the reality of giving is present. We cannot go further than a mere outline of the dimensions of this gift. To attempt to define the gift that Paul names, to pin it down and describe it without reserve, would be to violate his intentional silence. He himself names it merely as a "gift," leaving any further definition aside. The story of God's gift of himself for our salvation cannot finally be told in full. It is unspeakably wonderful. Yet precisely because it is unspeakably wonderful, it must be spoken and retold again and again. If we could narrate it and tell it in full, we would cease speaking it. But it can never be exhausted, never fully explored, never fully explained or defined. It is to issue ever afresh in thanksgiving, praise, song — and giving, not only with the Corinthians, but also with us.

153. In biblical tradition, see esp. LXX Hab 1:5 (Acts 13:41), also LXX Job 5:9; LXX Ps 76:20 (77:19); Wis 17:1.

154. See Rom 11:25-32.

155. See Rom 5:15-17.

B. The Legitimation of Paul as Apostle (10:1–13:14)

While the tone of Paul's argument in these chapters changes dramatically over against 1:1–7:16, the theological content remains remarkably constant. As with all letters, the letter represents Paul's attempt to overcome the distance between him and the Corinthians. In this instance, his physical distance from them is the result of their spiritual distance from him. He already has sent a letter sufficiently severe in its tone to grieve them (7:8), a letter that he affirms was written with tears (2:4). Second Corinthians thus serves as a substitute for Paul's personal presence, performing a pastoral function in an epistolary manner. This is especially true of the body of the letter, which Paul dramatically frames with his burning concern for the Corinthians.[156] The positive tone of the body, especially 7:5-16, is part of this expression of Paul's love. The closing of the letter, in contrast, prepares for the visit that Paul has not canceled and will not cancel (1:15-16). In view of this coming visit, he asserts his apostolic authority, even to the point of threatening severity and punishment.[157] He prefers, when necessary, to be stern in his letters, so that he may be gentle when he is present.[158] This is his *modus operandi*. The operations of the apostle thus follow the pattern of God's saving operations. God first addresses us at a distance (and in wrath) in the written "letter" in order to then come close and give himself to us in the meekness and gentleness of Christ: the still, small voice of the Lord's presence comes only after the wind, earthquake, and fire (1 Kgs 19:12). Paul holds back from even greater severity toward the Corinthians in the letter only in order to avoid "terrifying" them (10:9). This latter statement bears considerable irony: Paul is known for weighty and powerful letters, but also for a weak and pitiful presence (10:10).[159] His implicit threat serves to decrease the probability that he will need to engage in confrontation in Corinth. The letter itself, especially the closing, is to perform that work in advance.

In all probability, then, the final chapters, 10–13, do not constitute a separate composition or letter fragment, but are integral to the letter. The details of Paul's contact with the Corinthians fit the earlier part of the letter so remarkably well that one must assume either that 2 Cor 10–13 was added shortly after the composition of the first part of the letter or, as seems more likely, that they belong to the letter as it was originally composed.[160] Not only

156. 2:1-13; 7:5-16.

157. 10:6; 13:2.

158. See 1 Cor 4:16; 2 Cor 13:10. Paul thus operates like God, whose severity is apparent in the written Law but who is present in the "meek and gentle" Christ (cf. 10:1).

159. He challenges this characterization of him with the assertion that he is the same person when present in deed as he is in word in his letters (10:11).

160. On this question, see I. Vegge, *2 Corinthians, a Letter about Reconciliation: A Psychagogical, Epistolographical, and Rhetorical Analysis* (WUNT 2/239; Tübingen: Mohr Siebeck, 2008).

does Paul repeatedly call his upcoming visit his "third visit,"[161] he refers to a difficult preceding visit that likely corresponds to the one mentioned in 1:23–2:4,[162] and he inquires specifically about Titus's conduct while Titus was with the Corinthians.[163] The frequent, direct, and even emphatic references to himself in the first-person singular, including the hints and announcements of his visit,[164] mark the material as a letter closing, just as letter closings elsewhere with Paul are marked by such characteristics. As we have noted, the encouraging and positive appeal for the Jerusalem collection (chaps. 8–9) is not out of place, either, in relation to Paul's sharp tone in 10–13. It, too, prepares for Paul's following assertive tone. In calling for the Corinthians to complete their contribution to the collection, Paul seeks to bind the Corinthians to his apostolic labors before he admonishes them.[165]

It is hard to see how 2 Cor 10–13 could serve Paul's purposes apart from the setting within the letter in which they appear.[166] Correspondingly, 2 Cor 1–7 lose something of their concreteness when separated from the closing chapters. While in the earlier chapters Paul speaks of his adversaries in Corinth only indirectly and merely hints at the issue at stake in Corinth, in 2 Cor 10–13, we finally learn what the controversy is all about. The whole matter between the Corinthians and Paul turns on the question of the legitimation of an apostle. The problem has been forced upon Paul because the church has been attracted to other claimants to the role of apostle in Corinth. If in 2 Cor 1–7 Paul's adversaries are silent and hardly appear, in 10–13 they become audible and visible.

Likewise, while in 2 Cor 1–7 Paul first and primarily describes the apostolic *mission* given to him, in 10–13 he describes *himself* as an apostle in mission. This difference may appear at first to be overly subtle. But it bears profound theological significance. Paul, who is an "eccentric" and has his life in Christ, speaks of his person only after he has described his *diakonia,* his mission (cf. 4:1–7:16). Admittedly, that mission involves his whole body and life. But Paul's apostolic calling is not dependent upon his own gifts and powers, which become the centerpiece of his argument — admittedly in irony — in 2 Cor 10–13. If in the body of the letter Paul is buried, in 2 Cor 10–13 he has been raised.

The prominence Paul gives to himself and to his opponents in the argument of 2 Cor 10–13 is bound up with two theological developments that strongly

161. 12:14; 13:1.

162. 12:19-21; 13:2.

163. 12:17-18; cf. 7:5-16.

164. 10:2, 11; 13:1, 10.

165. Conversely, had Paul presented the request for the collection after 2 Cor 10–13, he might as well have not asked at all.

166. These chapters have sometimes been associated with the earlier "severe letter" that Paul avers was written with tears (2:3-4; 7:8).

suggest that these chapters were part of the original letter. First, Paul's message in these chapters remains grounded in the "word of the cross" that he develops in the body of the letter. His assertions of authority in 2 Cor 10–13 are framed by his ironic request for permission to speak with boldness, and then, later, with his request to boast as a fool.[167] On the one hand, through their assumed servility, these petitions expose the false pretension of the Corinthians, who imagined that they were competent to judge the apostle. On the other hand, Paul's assumption of this subordinate role expresses the theology of apostolic calling that he presents in 1–7: the power of Christ, and therefore apostolic authority, is exercised in weakness. It is noteworthy that the theme of "weakness" does not appear *expressis verbis* in chaps. 1–7. Of course, it is present within the concrete paradoxes that Paul offers there: comfort is given in affliction, life in death, light in darkness, and so on.[168] Contrastingly, the theme of weakness appears only in 10–13, and there prominently, in reference to Paul himself.[169] Christ's power is perfected in Paul's weakness (12:9). Paul uses the language of weakness in 2 Cor 10–13 as a summary of the theology of 1–7, and as the defining term of his own apostolic claim. The shift to the language of "weakness" corresponds to Paul's shift to speaking, or more precisely, to "boasting," about his own person. This theological correlation does not establish the unity of the letter, of course. But it shows how the closing of the letter further develops the theology of the body. At the very least, it *suggests* that the letter was composed as a single piece.

A second theological development of 2 Cor 10–13 also argues for the unity of the letter, perhaps even more strongly. The bare assertion of authority with which Paul begins these chapters, ironically presented in terms of weakness though it is, would hardly have won over the Corinthians.[170] By itself, it would have at best placed Paul on the same ground as his opponents. It more likely would have further damaged his relationship with the Corinthians, since the opponents could point to their possession of gifts and powers that the Corinthians prized. Paul himself seemed to have nothing to offer. But then he goes on to boast — as a "fool" — in his weaknesses. We have noted how the theme of weakness first appears in 2 Cor 10–13 as a summary of the theology of 1–7 in reference to Paul's person. Paul's weaknesses fill out nearly the whole of the fool's speech in 11:22–12:10. But why should an argument for apostolic authority based on weakness have been persuasive with the Corinthians? Why should they not have rejected him as a sorry loser or strange masochist? According to all the evidence we have, the Corinthians entertained no naive optimism. They cherished no hope in a power present in weakness.

167. 10:1; 11:1, 16.

168. E.g., 1:3-7; 4:6, 7-11.

169. 10:10; 11:21, 29, 30; 12:5, 9-10; 13:3, 4, 9.

170. See esp. 10:1-11.

Otherwise, Paul would long have been their hero. The Corinthians cherished a hope of power present as power. As they recognized, the meek do not normally inherit the earth but are plowed under it. Paul's boasting in his weakness in 2 Cor 10–13 is built upon his prior announcements of comfort in affliction, life in death, and deliverance out of hopeless situations.[171] That is to say, it is based on the resurrection of the crucified Jesus from the dead, in whom the apostle and all believers share. The christologically specific nature of Paul's argument from weakness is fully apparent only against the backdrop of 2 Cor 1–7. Not even the word of Christ to the apostle is clear apart from this setting (12:9). What does it mean for Christ's power to be perfected in weakness? Unless this saying is grounded in the resurrection of Christ, it is subject to becoming a mere utopian ideal. Only once, in 13:4, does the theme of participation in the crucified and risen Jesus come to expression in these chapters. This delayed reference links Paul's present argument with the argument of 2 Cor 1–7, which supplies the necessary background to Paul's thought here. The "foolishness" of Paul's boasting loses its force if it is detached from his description of the apostolic calling as the bearing of the deadness and life of Jesus (4:10-12). Likewise, Paul's description of his labor as a "tearing down," even while his proper work is "building up," makes sense only in the context of Christ's death and resurrection.[172] The argument of 10:1–13:14 is largely dependent on that of 1:1–7:16.

As we have noted, it is only in this second unit of the closing that Paul *directly* addresses the issue in his contention with the Corinthians, namely, his legitimacy as the apostle of Christ to Corinth. From its very beginning, this section is marked by the use of first-person-singular self-references. This increase in usage is not unanticipated: in Paul's defensive statements in the opening of the letter, and again in his appeal to the Corinthians at the end of the letter's body, Paul speaks self-referentially in the first-person singular. He also does so in the collection chapters, as is characteristic of any letter closing. But the concentration of the usage here stands out.[173] In these chapters, Paul places himself at the center of the battle. This is so, even though Paul's argument throughout the letter is fundamentally a defense of the apostolic mission, and not a self-defense.[174] He is the test case with the Corinthians as to the nature of the apostolic ministry and its legitimation. The focus on Paul in the closing is not unanticipated in the letter. As we have noted, a similar concentration of first-person-singular references appear in Paul's opening defense (1:12–2:17) and at the end of the body of the letter (6:11–7:16). In the body, Paul

171. 1:3-7; 4:7-12.

172. 10:4; 12:19; 13:10.

173. Out of the 239 relevant first-person singular forms in the letter, 163 of them appear in the last four chapters.

174. 12:19.

makes it clear that the apostolic mission itself is at stake in his contention with the Corinthians. The first-person-singular self-references in 2:13 thus shift to the first-person plural forms of 2:14, which, aside from one exception (5:11), continue until Paul's appeal to the Corinthians at the end of the body. He defends *his* calling as apostle to the Corinthians only after he has explained and defended the nature of the apostolic mission itself.

This observation corresponds to the way in which 2 Cor 10–13 are dependent on Paul's earlier argument.[175] It is worth recalling Paul's insistence that the treasure of the Gospel is carried within an earthen vessel (4:7). Salvation and life are hidden behind hardship, suffering, and death. This is true, not only for the crucified Christ, but also for his apostle. The argument of the letter's body thus stands behind and fills out the content of the closing, providing its focus upon Christ and the power of the closing. Conversely, as we have noted, the theme that God's power is present in weakness comes to expression explicitly only here in the closing, even though it implicitly pervades the argument of the body. Paul now pointedly interprets for the Corinthians what he has said to them in other terms.

Paul's confrontational statements, as well as the irony and even sarcasm that he employs, function within a rhetoric that is shaped by God's dealings with human beings in the Gospel. Paul must (first) "tear down" before he can engage in his proper work of "building up."[176] He prepares for his third visit in the closing of the letter by addressing the Corinthians with the severity that is necessary to this end. He prefers to do so in this letter, from a distance, so that, if it is at all possible, he may perform his proper work while he is with them (13:10). There are thus good reasons for regarding these chapters as original to the letter as Paul composed it.

This final section of the closing falls into three distinct units. In the first of these, Paul *asserts* his apostolic authority, albeit in an ironic manner (10:1-18, see vv. 1-2). Yet he does not offer bare assertions. He appeals to the obvious fact that it was he who first came to Corinth with the Gospel. The Corinthians are thus included within the field of labor that the Lord has allotted him (10:12-18). His argument and the assertions that arise from it are "eccentric," based not on himself, but on the Lord. This first argument of the closing is Paul's "proper" argument.

His argument shifts from "proper" to "improper" form in a second, lengthy movement (11:1–12:13) that is largely filled out by his "fool's speech" (11:22–12:10). His opening request to be bold (10:1-2) now becomes more specific. Paul expresses the wish to be foolish (11:1) and then takes the part of a fool, ironically playing to the tastes of the Corinthians and adopting the stan-

175. See the discussion above, pp. 369-71.

176. 10:4, 8; 12:19; 13:10.

dards of his opponents (11:16-21). The material does not lack straightforward statements of purpose. But much of Paul's discourse is ironic. He plays the fool in order to unmask the foolishness of both the apostolic claimants and the Corinthians who are attracted to them. He intends to subvert the perverted structure of their false judgments through "the word of the cross," which he bears in his body and life. In this concluding movement of his argument, he finally makes his personal qualifications as apostle the central issue. But he does so in a manner that the Corinthians never imagined.

He finally brings this argument to bear upon the Corinthians as he prepares to visit them the third time. They are going to have to face this Paul, whether they like it or not. As is always the case at the very close of his letters, he summarizes his argument in terms of the problems that he is addressing. He thus becomes quite concrete in reference to himself, to his co-workers, and to the Corinthians. The fundamental themes of the letter appear in concentrated form within this particularity. The presence of Christ legitimates the apostle — and the church. On this issue Paul and the Corinthians are agreed. They disagree as to what the marks of that presence might be.

1. Paul's Lowly Appeal and Bold Assertion of Authority (10:1-18)

a. The Lowly Appeal to Be Bold (10:1-6)

10 1 *I, Paul, myself entreat you, by the meekness and gentleness of Christ*
— I who am humble when face-to-face with you, but bold toward you
when I am away! — 2 *I beg of you that when I am present I may not have*
to show boldness with such confidence as I count on showing against some
who suspect us of walking according to the flesh. 3 *For though we walk in the*
flesh, we are not waging war according to the flesh. 4 *For the weapons of our*
warfare are not of the flesh but have divine power to destroy strongholds.
5 *We destroy arguments and every lofty opinion raised against the knowl-*
edge of God, and take every thought captive to obey Christ, 6 *being ready*
to punish every disobedience, when your obedience is complete.

Paul's opening address in this closing unit sets both the terms and the tone for all that follows. It serves simultaneously as an introduction to his first argument within this section and as an anticipation of the remainder of the letter.

Although Paul does not take up again the military imagery that he introduces here, he nevertheless plays upon it until the very end of the letter. Furthermore, his closing threat and exhortation to the Corinthians in 13:1-4 and 13:5-10 take up the themes of 10:1-6 and 10:7-11, in the wake of his intervening argument:

- the threat of warfare (vv. 4-6) has its counterpart in the threat of severity (13:2);
- the meekness of Christ (v. 1) has its counterpart in the weakness of the Crucified (13:4);
- Paul's assertion that he is "of Christ" has its counterpart in his call to the Corinthians to test if Jesus Christ is in them (13:5);
- the charge that Paul's presence is weak has its counterpart in Paul's rejoicing in his weakness (13:9);
- Paul's definition of his authority as one of edification rather than destruction appears both at the opening and in the ending of this unit of the letter (v. 8; 13:10).

Paul provides brackets around his argument, forming an inclusio and clarifying his message.[177] Before all else, Paul makes clear that his "warfare" does not constitute his proper work as an apostle, even if it is necessary to his work. Just as "the letter" must kill in order for the Gospel to give life, so the apostle must first destroy in order to build.[178]

Likewise, as Paul makes clear shortly (vv. 9-11), his assumption of a humble, almost servile, stance (vv. 1-2) serves to disarm and unmask the Corinthians in their supposed superiority, and thus to reassert the Gospel, in which the power of God is hidden in the weakness of Christ and Christ's apostle.

1 Despite the sharp turn in the argument, the beginning of this new section is marked grammatically as a continuation of that which precedes: "*And* I myself, Paul. . . ."[179] The Corinthian participation in the collection is itself a submission to Paul's apostolic authority and thus directly related to the argument that now appears.

Paul's self-reference here is the most emphatic in all his letters: "I myself, Paul. . . ." Only his forceful appeal to his authority in Gal 5:2 ("Behold, I, Paul, say . . .") comes close to it.[180] His delay in calling attention to his person is understandable. At an earlier stage of the problems that had developed in Corinth, there was a group that attached itself to Paul, his gifts, and his authority.[181] Paul wanted none of that adulation, and will not have any of it now.[182] As we have observed, it is only because he has defended the nature of true apostolic authority in the body of the letter that he is now able to communicate his claim to that authority to the Corinthians. Even now that claim is fraught with difficulty.

177. Cf. Heckel, *Kraft in Schwachheit,* 49-51, who offers a similar analysis of this unit.

178. 10:8; 12:19; 13:10.

179. One might have expected asyndeton. Instead we have δέ, a marker of continuity.

180. See also Eph 3:1; Col 1:23; Phlm 9; and solely with the emphatic "I, myself," Rom 7:25; 9:3; 15:14; 2 Cor 12:13.

181. 1 Cor 1:12.

182. 1 Cor 1:13; 3:5.

With the sort of ironic twist that is common in these chapters, in the very next breath, Paul deflates his implicit appeal to his authority: "I appeal to you by the meekness and gentleness of Christ." As we have seen already, Paul's term for "appeal" *(parakaleō)* signifies a polite request. It is the kind of language used in diplomatic letters.[183] Paul will not and cannot force the recognition of his authority as apostle. He only can call for it to be recognized: he makes this clear from the very start in this letter (1:12-14).

It is "through the meekness and gentleness of Christ" that he appeals to the Corinthians. The second term, *epieikeia,* which signifies clemency or mildness in judgment, may function epexegetically, explaining what Paul means here by speaking of Christ's meekness.[184] Paul will not be severe in his contention with the Corinthians, his following threats notwithstanding.[185] It is "through" the meekness and mildness of Christ that Paul makes his appeal. As in Rom 12:1, he thereby signals both the basis of the appeal and the means by which he makes the appeal. As his following address shows, the latter is the dominant thought here. He is reminding the Corinthians of Christ and calling them back to Christ, not to himself.

Paul's reference to the "meekness of Christ" recalls Gospel tradition, and specifically that of Matthew.[186] It is altogether likely that Paul appeals here to "the earthly Jesus," who is obviously significant to his instruction of the Corinthians, as is apparent from the Lord's Supper tradition.[187] But it is hardly likely that he is pointing merely to a past example. He speaks at the same time of the risen Lord. Indeed, as quickly becomes clear, the question of the presence of Christ is at the center of the debate over the apostle.[188]

Paul here recalls the "word of the cross" and the Christ who suffered there, rather than the Christ of the Corinthian imagination. He speaks ironically, exposing the Corinthian pretensions. This tone becomes apparent in the latter part of the verse: "[I] who, on the one hand, according to [my] personal presence am lowly among you, and, on the other hand, while absent, am bold toward you." The first part of Paul's statement, "according to personal presence, lowly among you," is not to be understood *simply* as Paul's description of his demeanor. This thought is obviously present, since the self-description follows the appeal to the meekness of Christ and is juxtaposed to Paul's "boldness." But

183. See n. 92, p. 18. On this topic, see C. J. Bjerkelund, *Parakalô: Form, Funktion und Sinn der parakalô-Sätze in den paulinischen Briefen* (Bibliotheca Theologica Norvegica 1; Oslo: Universitets Forlaget, 1967), 108.

184. The ESV, NIV, and NRSV render the term "gentleness."

185. See 10:6; 13:2.

186. Matt 5:5; 11:29; 21:5 (Zech 9:9-10); cf. 1 Pet 2:21-25. Even if neither of Paul's terms appears in the Petrine text, the thought is obviously proximate to his appeal.

187. 1 Cor 11:17-34.

188. 10:7; 11:4; 13:3-6.

this juxtaposition itself already bears an note of irony. Paul is not expressing his own judgment. He begins already to take up the taunting characterization of vv. 10-11, that while his letters are weighty, his personal presence is pathetic. He is not merely pointing to a humility that he exercises while present in Corinth;[189] he is admitting that his personal presence is "lowly," as his opponents like to point out.[190]

2 The reading of Paul's self-description as bearing an ironic tone is confirmed in his following request of the Corinthians. Admittedly, the irony of Paul's request goes missing in almost all translations, including the ESV, NIV, and NRSV, which understand Paul to ask that he might not (need to be) bold when he comes to Corinth.[191] The negation is taken in relation to Paul's boldness ("I beg not to be bold, when I am present"), rather than in relation to his presence ("Not being present, I request to be bold"). This general misreading is rather surprising, since in the end it is clear syntactically that the negation is to be related to Paul's presence.[192] The usual translation of v. 2 misses the obvious

189. This is the impression one gains from the ESV and NRSV, which translate Paul as speaking of himself as "humble when face-to-face" with the Corinthians. The NIV represents Paul as confessing that he is "timid" when face-to-face. This rendering, which appears to be based entirely on the juxtaposition with Paul's boldness, takes ταπεινός outside its normal range. Furthermore, the translation "face-to-face" that appears in all three of these English versions focuses too narrowly on personal presence. Only a dozen lines later Paul uses the same phrase (κατὰ πρόσωπον) in an adverbial sense: the Corinthians are "looking at things according to appearance" (v. 7). This idea is already in play here in v. 1.

190. The adjective that he uses (ταπεινός) is more often associated with a lowly state than with a lowly mind. See, e.g., 2 Cor 7:6; 11:7; 12:21; Rom 12:16. The verb ταπεινόω and the substantive ταπείνωσις are likewise primarily associated with being humiliated outwardly and a state of humilation or lowliness. To signify humility or lowliness of mind, the compound ταπεινοφροσύνη is often used.

191. It must be admitted that the same is true of the commentaries: if there is one that takes the reading offered here, I have not yet found it. Nevertheless, both the syntax and the context of Paul's thought are compelling. The Vulgate, moreover, takes the reading offered here ("rogo autem ne praesens audeam . . ."), which suggests that at least some ancient interpreters did so as well.

192. The text reads: "δέομαι δὲ τὸ μὴ παρὼν θαρρῆσαι. . . ." The confusion arises because the particle μή, which negates an articular infinitive, normally falls between the article and the infinitive. This usage is frequent. In 2 Corinthians alone, see 2:13; 3:13; 4:4. Nevertheless, one can hardly overlook the presence of the participle παρών between the particle and the infinitive, which itself may well be negated, rather than the infinitive. The placement of the negation *after* the participle is usual in such constructions and results in clarity (2 Macc 14:32; 3 Macc 1:11; Bel [OG] 1:8; Matt 22:23; Acts 21:21; 25:24). At this point, commentators seem to have been confused by the grammars, which ignore the participle, and take the construction as a negated articular infinitive (thus, wrongly, BDF §399.3). Within biblical literature, the closest parallel to the syntax found here appears in Heb 11:3 (εἰς τὸ μὴ ἐκ φαινομένων τὸ βλεπόμενον γεγονέναι), which must be rendered according to the pattern suggested above if it is to make any sense at

parallel (and, indeed chiasm, or x-pattern) that is formed with the latter part of v. 1 (ABBA): Paul, who is lowly among the Corinthians but bold when absent *(apōn),* requests to be bold although he is not present *(mē parōn),* with the boldness with which he reckons to be bold toward some (when he is present). Paul is not speaking straightforwardly, asking to be spared a confrontation. This is especially clear from the end of v. 1. He is speaking ironically, not at all sparing the necessary confrontation with the Corinthians.

Paul's language is ironic: "And I *request,* while not present, to be *bold.*" Boldness does not normally wait for permission. The connection with the preceding appeal *(de)* suggests that the "I request" (v. 2) provides the object and content of the "I appeal" (v. 1). The two verbs are related semantically in any case. Just as *parakaleō* presents a polite request, *deomai* ("I request, ask, petition") often appears in a request made of someone regarded as a superior.[193] Paul continues the ironic tone that he has struck in v. 1.[194] By *requesting* to be bold, Paul disarms the complaint that appears in the mouths of his opponents in v. 10: his *parousia* (presence) does not match his *parrēsia* (boldness).[195] If he, in all meekness and mildness, requests of the Corinthians to be bold in the present letter, the charge of the adversaries can no longer stand.

Indeed, he makes his point even more sharply by implying that the situation in Corinth is not going to be pleasant when he arrives there. He asks to be bold with the confidence with which he calculates that he will act with boldness toward "certain ones" who miscalculate him as "walking according to the flesh." One should not overinterpret the *modus operandi* that he articulates in 13:10, where he speaks of his present confrontation of the Corinthians as a means of avoiding severity when he arrives. His confrontation of the Corinthians from a distance does not mean that he will not act decisively when he

---

all: "so that which is seen has come about not from that which is visible." The biblical usage of anarthrous infinitives preceded by μή with a participle confirms the reading offered here. These constructions are a bit more frequent than those with an articular infinitive (16x), probably because most of them involve a participle (esp. δύναμαι, 9x) that takes an object infinitive. While a few instances might be debatable, breaking with the pattern offered here generally results in absurdity: e.g., "Fear the one . . . who is able not to kill the soul" (Matt 10:28). Sus 1:23 in both the OG and Theodotion becomes outright scandalous if it should be read in the way the translations and interpreters read Paul's statement: αἱρετόν μοί ἐστιν μὴ πράξασαν ἐμπεσεῖν εἰς τὰς χεῖρας ὑμῶν ("it is preferable for me doing so [i.e., committing fornication] not to fall into your hands"). Of the biblical usage of the anarthrous infinitive with a preceding negation followed by a participle, this example most closely approximates Paul's statement here, since the participle πράξασαν requires no object as complement.

193. This is true, for example, of virtually all of the Lukan usage.

194. The rendering "I beg" (ESV, NIV) is too strong and deflects attention from the issue at hand. It is obviously precipitated by the interpretation of the verse as an expression of desire to avoid confrontation on Paul's part.

195. See pp. 70-71 above.

is in Corinth. Everything depends on the Corinthian response. Indeed, Paul's present argument depends in considerable measure on his threat to exercise severity when he comes to Corinth. His argument has force only if the Corinthians take this threat seriously.[196]

Paul's petition to act with boldness anticipates further contention over the legitimation of the apostle in Corinth. His request here is the first in a series of ironic expressions of the desire to speak as a fool, which finally issues in the "fool's speech."[197] It is likely that the "certain ones" against whom Paul intends to act boldly are the "super-apostles" whom Paul names later.[198] Of course, the church as a whole has tolerated these apostolic claimants. But at this point, Paul seeks to drive a wedge between the church and the false apostles by singling out the latter as the objects of his attack.

Paul uses more than one term for "boldness" in this verse. He begins with a term *(tharreō)* that connotes daring or courage, i.e., a bold spirit. He concludes with a term *(tolmaō)* that is associated with action. Between the two, he again uses the term "confidence" *(pepoithēsis)*, which, as we have noted, conveys the passive idea of trust in something.[199] It has an object. The term again recalls the Gospel, with which the apostle has been entrusted.

One reckoning is set against another reckoning, one judgment against another judgment. "Certain ones" judge Paul to be "walking according to the flesh."[200] That is to say, they regard him as living according to mere human powers: he is weak in appearance and constantly subject to difficulties, trials, and suffering.[201] Where, they asked, are the charisma and power that belong to a legitimate apostle? Where is Christ and his power? Probably, too, they judged that Paul operated with deception and self-serving motives, especially after his failure to visit Corinth as he had promised.[202] Yet even if his integrity is included in the judgment against him, his weakness constitutes the primary charge. It is this issue that determines Paul's response in vv. 7-10. In any case,

196. For this reason as well, the usual reading of v. 2 as Paul's appeal not to be bold when he arrives is quite misleading.

197. 11:1, 16-21.

198. 11:5; 12:11.

199. See above, p. 56.

200. As we have noted, "walking" is a rich biblical idiom that pictures human life and existence as a road to be traveled to an end. See the discussion at 5:7, p. 232. It was taken up in earliest Christianity, and esp. by Paul.

201. To do something "according to the flesh" connotes both the weakness and the waywardness of the fallen human being. Within the Corinthian correspondence, see, e.g., 1 Cor 1:26; 10:18; 2 Cor 1:17; 5:16; 11:18.

202. This overtone is present both in Paul's earlier protest concerning his "walking" with integrity (4:2) and elsewhere in his use of the expression "to walk in the flesh" (Rom 8:4; Gal 5:16).

it is Paul who frames the issue here: the phrase "according to the flesh" is his own.[203] If this language is also that of his opponents, it is so only derivatively. To this human reckoning, Paul opposes the *confidence* that has been given to him. He reckons to act in boldness when he arrives.[204] This conflict of judgments — or more precisely, the conflict between the practical reasoning of the fallen human being and the Gospel — is the fundamental battle that we encounter repeatedly in the letter. Paul brings it to explicit expression for the first time in the following verses.

3 Paul follows his humble threat with two explanatory statements (v. 3, vv. 4-6). The first of these is both a concession and a correction. Paul immediately concedes that he "walks in the flesh." In other words, he is subject to weakness, distress, and suffering. This has been his theme in this letter, and also in his self-description in First Corinthians.[205] Yet he does not concede that he "walks according to the flesh." It is clear from Paul's threat in v. 2 that he regards this judgment as a serious error, a challenge to the Gospel itself. As is clear from his earlier response to the Corinthians in 1 Cor 3:1-3, "being fleshly," or in this case, "walking according to the flesh," cannot be reduced to the question of morality (or, more properly, immorality). It has to do with the operation of God's power in the apostle and in the world. This is evident from the contours of the contention between Paul and the Corinthians that appear in the following chapters. Not only "certain ones" but the entire church has been looking at the apostle according to appearance (v. 7), and not according to faith (cf. 5:7). They have not perceived that God's saving power runs its course contrary to all human judgments and reasoning. It does so necessarily, so that we might be delivered from the idolatry of the worship of created gifts. The Corinthians have not heard "the word of the cross," even though the apostle has proclaimed it to them.

Paul thus abruptly switches metaphors, in a sharp response to the false opinions in Corinth. He rejects the judgment that he "walks according to the flesh" with the assertion that he does not "war according to the flesh." He is not merely following the course that God has set for him in his "walking." He must also wage war, and must do so against the judgment of the Corinthians. The figures of warfare and weaponry appear elsewhere in reference to the life of a Christian.[206] But here Paul employs it specifically in reference to his calling as apostle.[207] God's defeated captive, led in a *triumphus,* wages war even within that procession to death.[208] Precisely *within* the weakness of the apostle, who

203. See Rom 8:4; Gal 5:16.

204. See 1:17; 3:4.

205. 1 Cor 4:6-13.

206. Rom 6:10-13; 7:23; 13:12; Eph 6:10-20.

207. See also 1 Cor 9:7; cf. 1 Tim 1:18; 2 Tim 2:4.

208. Cf. 2:14-17.

lives "in the flesh" and bears the deadness of Jesus (4:10), the power of God is at work.

4 The second, lengthier explanation now follows, filling out vv. 4-6. Paul's rejection of Corinthian judgments has prepared for his description of the state of war that exists between him and the Corinthians. Having clarified the first term, Paul now turns to the second. As is already clear from the repetition of the phrase, the fundamental question is whether Paul, according to his pointed correction of Corinthian opinion, wages war "according to the flesh." Paul now provides an explanation as to why this is not so.

The reason lies in the weapons that have been placed in his hands. The weapons are not Paul's own. The imagery again drives home the point that the powers that operate in the apostle are extrinsic to him. They are not "fleshly" but "powerful for God."[209] But what, precisely, are these weapons? Paul leaves them unnamed. It is necessary for the Corinthians themselves to recognize them. In the "hardship list" of 6:3-10, he has provided an indication of what those weapons are. The "weapons of the right hand and the left" that serve as the apostolic panoply include "glory *and* dishonor, slander *and* praise, being regarded as deceivers *and yet* true." The "earthen vessel" of his earthly body and life is a weapon of the Gospel and knowledge of Christ that Paul bears. It is necessary for the power of Christ to be perfected in the weakness of the apostle, just as it was perfected in the cross.[210] The apostle thus necessarily battles with two hands: Christ's power is present only within weakness. Jesus triumphed in his death on the cross. This understanding of the apostle's weapons explains the irony that he employs in his boasting in these concluding chapters, including his meek request to be bold in the present context.

Note that Paul has turned a defense into an offense. Or more accurately stated, he has never regarded it as necessary to defend himself. He recognizes that he is at the center of the controversy, as is evident in his opening words in this chapter. At various points in the present letter, he has indicated that he regards his argument as something other than a defense.[211] He will soon make clear to the Corinthians that his purpose all along has been their edification (12:19). The real debate does not have to do with his own person. It has to do with the Gospel, which Paul already has presented to the Corinthians as "the word of the cross" (1 Cor 1:18).

His first task, however, is that of destruction. The weapons that have

209. The expression δυνατὰ τῷ θεῷ probably should be interpreted in terms of a *dativus commodi* (cf. 2 Cor 2:15). It remains possible that the dative expresses association (cf. Rom 6:10-11; Gal 2:19) and thereby cause: "powerful with God," i.e., empowered by God, as in the Septuagintal δυνατὸς ἰσχύι (which renders גִּבּוֹר חַיִל), e.g., LXX Ruth 2:1; 1 Chr 5:2; 4 Kgdms 5:1.

210. 12:9-10; cf. 1 Cor 1:23-24.

211. 3:1-3; 5:12; 6:11-13; 7:2-16.

been placed in his hands are for the destruction of fortresses. As is already clear, this violent conquest is achieved by means of weakness. It is not to be generalized, as if it might be achieved by all the powerless throughout the world, but is contained within the paradox of the cross, where God's weakness is manifest as more powerful than human beings (1 Cor 1:25). Paul immediately discloses the nature of the metaphor: "we are destroying [human] reckonings." He has declared war on the very "reckoning" that regards him as "walking according to the flesh." As is clear from the term that he employs, the objects of his assault are the practical judgments of human reasoning. This battle is Paul's fundamental purpose in the letter as a whole.[212] The Corinthians, like the apostle, are called to "walk by faith, not by appearance" (5:7; cf. 5:12). Like the apostle, they are no longer to "know anyone according to the flesh" (5:16).[213] But this is precisely what "certain ones" are doing in their "reckoning" concerning the apostle. Paul is called to destroy such false judgments.

5 The concluding participial clause of v. 4 belongs properly with v. 5a. Paul here continues the description of his warfare, continuing his metaphor of siege: "[we are destroying] every exalted thing raised up in rebellion against the knowledge of God." By his lowliness (v. 1), the apostle destroys the things that are exalted, just as God in Christ puts to shame the wise, the powerful, and the noble (1 Cor 1:26-28). As he has indicated to the Corinthians more than once, he is not defending himself. He is on the offensive. Yet the glory that accompanies the apostolic mission is apparent only to faith (3:8-11). The minds of the sons of Israel were hardened and unable to see it (3:13-14), just as the "god of this age" blinds the minds and thoughts of unbelievers (4:4). The nature of that hardening and blindness now becomes apparent. Paul is called to destroy the "exalted things" constructed by the minds and hearts of fallen human beings, the "Babels" we erect in opposition to the knowledge of God. We, together with all our thoughts, must be taken captive by the word of God, just as the apostle himself is led in God's triumphal procession (2:14-17).

Paul's language here is somewhat difficult, and obscured by the translations. He speaks of the destruction of every "exalted thing" *(hypsōma).* Both the ESV and NIV eliminate Paul's metaphor by rendering the term in reference to Paul's preceding work concerning "reckonings." Thus the ESV has "every lofty opinion," and the NIV "every lofty pretension." It remains a question whether this elimination of Paul's metaphor is warranted.[214] The term *hypsōma* and the expression in which it appears ("every exalted thing") anticipate Paul's following reference to his taking captive "every mind" (or, "every concept,

212. See esp. the reflections on the letter's purpose, pp. 104-7.

213. See the discussion on p. 247.

214. The NRSV partially retains the metaphor by the rendering "every proud obstacle."

plan"; *noēma*, also with a *-ma* ending).[215] It is better to allow Paul's metaphor to stand and to let it be interpreted by his following statement: "We are destroying reckonings and every exalted thing, and we take every mind captive to the obedience of Christ."[216] This decision admittedly mixes the metaphors of destruction and the taking of captives. But Paul mixes the metaphors in any case. No matter how one reads v. 5a, it is transitional.

The basic interpretive question is where the shift in metaphor begins. The difficulty with supposing that it takes place in v. 5a is that one must then understand that, when Paul speaks of "[destroying] every exalted thing," he refers to the "minds" that he takes captive.[217] Rather than destroying "opinions" and "pretensions," Paul destroys "minds" (admittedly, "minds at work," *noēmata*) and thus persons. But would Paul destroy persons? How can one destroy those whom one takes captive — unless perhaps one leads them in a Roman triumph? As this latter reflection makes clear, the difficulties are only apparent. The "minds" that Paul takes captive are nothing other than the Corinthians themselves. This understanding becomes apparent in v. 6: Paul uses *noēma* in metonymy for the "mind" and whole person, as he has done elsewhere. Indeed, in his unusual usage of *noēma* ("conception, plan") for "mind" in this letter, he effectively identifies persons with their purposes and thoughts.[218] The transition in Paul's metaphor in v. 5a fits into the figure that he employs in the closing of the letter: his authority as an apostle is for the edification of the Corinthians, not for their destruction.[219] He must, however, first destroy the Corinthians in their false imaginations ("every exalted thing") in order to take captive every mind (including the Corinthians) in obedience to Christ. The Spirit gives life only to that which has been put to death (3:6). Paul's calling as apostle is not to effect merely a change of minds, but a change of persons. The cross of Christ does not merely do away with the world's wisdom, strength, and boasting. It does away with the wise, the things that are strong, and the exalted (1 Cor 1:26-31).

215. Here the ESV, NIV, and the NRSV render νόημα as "thought," even though they translate it as "mind" in 3:14 and 4:4. The ESV and NIV are obviously influenced by their decision to render ὕψωμα as a cognitive act. But consistency with Paul's earlier usage and conformity to his material metaphor here suggest that "mind" is to be preferred, even though νόημα signifies "thought" and refers to "mind" only in Paul's extended use. See the brief discussion of νόημα above, pp. 165-66. The rendering "taking every thought captive" conflicts (again) with the metaphor Paul employs here. How does one take a "thought" captive? One might better do so with a "mind," and thus with the whole person.

216. Apparently that is what Stephanus did in marking the versification as it stands.

217. It should be noted that neither the ESV nor the NIV escapes this problem, since they both translate v. 5b as Paul's taking every *thought* captive. Every lofty thought is destroyed. Every thought is taken captive. Unless one imposes a sequence on the text, the problem of mixed metaphors remains.

218. 3:14; 4:4; 11:3.

219. 10:8; 13:10.

The "knowledge of God" is on the offensive, pressing its attack against "everything raised up in rebellion" against it.[220] The expression is a pointed reference to the Gospel and its effect. The suffering apostle is an aroma of the knowledge of Christ (2:14), just as the Gospel is "the light of the knowledge of the glory of God in the person of Jesus Christ" (4:6).[221] Paul warned earlier that there are some among the Corinthians who have "no knowledge of God" (1 Cor 15:34). Now the entire church appears to be in jeopardy. Correspondingly, in the present context, Paul immediately goes on to refer to the establishing of "obedience of Christ" as the object of his warfare. He conquers by the "meekness and mildness of Christ" (v. 1). What his opponents among the Corinthians regard as his weakness is in reality his very weapon in his battle.

As we have noted, Paul shifts his metaphor of conquest from the destruction of fortresses to the taking of captives: "we take every mind captive to the obedience of Christ." Unfortunately, the English versions obscure a significant dimension of Paul's thought in this verse, not only by translating *noēma* as "thought" ("every thought captive"),[222] but even more by limiting the genitive expression "obedience of Christ" to the idea of obedience to Christ.[223] Genitive usage is inherently rich semantically. One therefore must take care not to eliminate the range of connotations it engenders, particularly when a verbal noun such as "obedience" appears. The idea of obedience to Christ is present here, as Paul's following reference to obedience by the Corinthians in v. 6 makes clear. Nevertheless, as Paul's language of destruction and edification (i.e., death and life) also makes clear, he speaks more fundamentally of the obedience that *comes from Christ* and his saving work.[224] The apostle understands — with the Corinthians, he understands all too well! — that the new obedience of Christians is nothing other than the palimpsest of Christ, his rewriting their hearts with his life and righteousness (3:1-3). Christ captures the rebellious by giving himself over to death for their sake. Only because of his death for them can they live for him. Their new life of obedience is nothing other than his resurrected life that has taken possession of them (5:14-15). As the apostle of Christ, Paul takes captives, not by the mere wisdom of moral instruction or ethical appeal, but by the Gospel. The conquest of the Corinthians takes place through the utter weakness of the cross. "The obedience of Christ," which has

220. On the translation of the term ἐπαίρομαι, see the brief discussion on p. 423.

221. One cannot help but recall Isa 53:3-4, which speaks of God's Servant as "despised and rejected, . . . as one from whom people hide their face, . . . he was despised, and we did not reckon him [of any worth]."

222. This rendering is entirely possible, but as is clear from the discussion above, it does not fit this context. See pp. 165-66.

223. I.e., an objective genitive.

224. The thought contained in the expression thus comes close to that of "the obedience of faith" (i.e., the obedience that is faith). See Rom 1:5; 6:17; 10:16; 16:26.

its source in the risen Lord, takes its form from Christ. It does not look at the things that are seen, but at the things that are unseen (4:18).[225] It sees the glory of God in the crucified Lord.

6 Paul continues and completes the metaphor of warfare and conquest. The destruction of fortresses and the taking of captives are followed by the requital of any subsequent act of rebellion: "And we have in readiness the avenging of all disobedience, whenever your obedience is full." The language of obedience both participates in Paul's military metaphor and extends beyond it into his apostolic aim with the Corinthians. The intent of a military campaign is the subjugation of those in resistance, the obtaining of their "obedience." The punishment of rebellion is regarded as "vengeance" *(ekdikeō, ekdikēsis)* exercised against the violation of the "justice" that already has been established in conquest. Obedience is also the object of the apostolic service of the Gospel. Paul thus speaks of the "fulfillment of [the Corinthian] obedience," expressing the eschatological triumph of God in Christ. Once the Corinthians have submitted themselves to Christ, instead of wavering as they now do, Paul, like a commanding general, is prepared to avenge all disobedience.

But what does he have in mind in this figure? Within the metaphor, the threat makes sense, because resistance might still arise within a conquered city. But the very object of Paul's campaign is the obedience of Christ. If the obedience of the Corinthians is complete and "fulfilled" within "the obedience of Christ," how could disobedience possibly arise? Paul almost certainly has in view the false apostles, whom he regards as outside the community of faith and, in fact, agents of Satan (11:13-15). His following address to "anyone who trusts that they are of Christ" (v. 7) suggests the same. Something similar may be said of his later threat "not to spare," since in this connection he refers explicitly to his previous visit, during which someone challenged his authority (13:2; 2:5-11). In other words, in this last word within his military imagery, Paul is serving notice that he intends to effect the separation from the false apostles for which he already has called (6:14–7:1).

b. The Bold Assertion of Authority (10:7-11)

[7]Look at what is before your eyes. If anyone is confident that he is Christ's, let him remind himself that just as he is Christ's, so also are we. [8]For even if I boast a little too much of our authority, which the Lord gave for building you up and not for destroying you, I will not be ashamed. [9]I do not want to appear to be frightening you with my letters. [10]For they say, "His letters are weighty and strong, but his bodily presence is weak, and his

225. In other words, the genitive, while it certainly bears an objective sense, is fundamentally a genitive of source that bears overtones of possession and quality.

speech of no account." [11]Let such a person understand that what we say by letter when absent, we do when present.

Now Paul not only addresses the Corinthians directly, he names the issue that stands between him and the church, which has guided his argument throughout the letter. The legitimation of the apostle is at stake. The question at hand is the mark of apostolic legitimacy. Opposing apostolic claimants now appear in Paul's address. He speaks to the Corinthians as if they are under their sway. He does not present an argument but asserts his authority and hints at its dimensions. He likewise hints at his coming visit to Corinth and at the confrontation for which he is prepared.

7 Paul's first word is to the church as a whole: "You are looking at [mere] appearance."[226] His earlier explanation for his lengthy defense of apostolic ministry was that he wanted to provide the Corinthians a response to those who "boast in appearance, and not in heart" (5:12). This explanation was overly generous. In reality, the Corinthians themselves are the problem. Only because they are attracted to outward displays of power and rhetoric do the opponents hold influence in the church.

Nevertheless, Paul turns directly to the opponents in vv. 7-11. His second word is directed to the apostolic claimants, that is, to "anyone" who imagined oneself to be the apostle of the church in Corinth. A confidence of this kind had to be individual in nature, of course. It is likely that Paul reckons with another confrontation with someone who had managed — at least temporarily — to assert his claim to apostolic status above all others in Corinth. Other contenders were present. This contest was not yet finally decided. That is to say, it is likely that there was contention, not only between the apostolic claimants and Paul, but also competition among them. Paul shortly refuses to enter into any comparison of himself with the others, as he indicates that they themselves do (10:12). This in-fighting among the apostolic claimants meant that it was possible for one or another of them to hold sway over the church, or at least a large segment of it, at a given time. It is not surprising, then, that Paul's "painful visit" to Corinth involved a confrontation with some individual who held sway in the church. Nor is it unexpected that the opinion of the church shifted so rapidly in favor of Paul after that confrontation. In his mention of the event, Paul makes nearly nothing of their changed allegiance (2:5-11). It may have meant very little. Furthermore, as we have noted, his words in 7:2-16 must be taken as supporting a fragile reconciliation with him on the part of the Corinthians, rather than a description of a permanent change in the church. Paul's address to "anyone" who trusts that one is of Christ corresponds, then, to the

226. Both the theme of false judgment according to appearance (cf. 5:12) and the placement of the verb (τὰ κατὰ πρόσωπον βλέπετε) argue against the rendering of the ESV.

situation as it appears in the letter. The contention over the legitimation of an apostle had to end with the triumph of a single figure, even if that outcome is not apparent in the church at this moment.

The language that Paul uses to describe this apparent apostolic claim is itself of significance: "if anyone trusts that they are *of Christ.*"[227] The overtones of an apostolic claim in this expression are especially clear in light of Paul's later description of the Corinthian contention with him: "you are seeking proof of the Christ who speaks in me" (13:3). Already in First Corinthians Paul had to deal with factions within the church, divided by their allegiance to various figures, including a group who regarded themselves — in contrast to all the others, probably on the basis of an apparition — as being immediately "of Christ" (1 Cor 1:12). The reappearance of that language here suggests that, even at the outset of the problems in Corinth, to be "of Christ" implied an apostolic claim — indeed, a claim that was meant to trump claims of allegiance to earthly leaders.[228] In any case, the problem of the proper legitimation of an apostle was present incipiently when Paul wrote First Corinthians, as his defense of his apostolic calling and his role as "father" of the Corinthian church confirm (4:1-21; 9:1-27). Whether being "of Christ" was conceived as deriving from supposed contact with the earthly Jesus, or, more likely, as access to a heavenly Christ (12:2), is finally irrelevant. Paul here reflects the mutually exclusive claims of multiple apostolic contenders within the church. It is a claim that he himself makes: he is an apostle of Christ (1:1).

The apostolic claim to be "of Christ" does not exclude, but includes, the understanding that Christ is imparted to the church through an apostle. All sides agree on this point. The question is, Which Christ? And this question is settled by the decision as to who is the legitimate apostle.

Paul's response to the claim of the opponent is a simple assertion and attack: "If anyone trusts that they are of Christ, let him reckon again, against himself, that just as he is, so also are we." Paul makes a probing charge against the claim of the one who makes the claim to be "of Christ." As he signals by his first word, he by no means accepts this claim, which appears based on self-confidence: "if anyone trusts *in himself,* that he is of Christ. . . ." Paul calls this one to a fresh inward reckoning. Paul, too, is an apostle: "so, too, are we."

227. Note the significant, interesting, and yet not finally decisive variant represented by $\mathfrak{p}^{46}$: ὅτι καθὼς αὐτὸς ὁ Χριστός, οὕτως καὶ ἡμεῖς.

228. In First Corinthians, Paul immediately asserts that Christ remains undivided, that he alone was crucified for our salvation, and that all the Corinthians have been baptized into his name (1 Cor 1:13). Every Christian is "of Christ." As Paul's language concerning Christ "being divided" makes clear, all the factions imagined that they participated in Christ through their favored leader. That an apostle is "of Christ" implies that he imparts Christ to those who adhere to his message. The question at stake in Corinth is which "Christ" is being imparted, the crucified Christ or another one.

Indeed, such a one is to reckon again, "to himself," that Paul, too, is "of Christ."[229] The implicit charge corresponds to the situation of competing apostolic claims in Corinth that we have suggested above, with the assertion that one is "of Christ," serving to trump the claims of others. Paul now joins the battle. He already has rejected any self-confident claim to apostleship. He will present his own standard in his following argument: "Not the one who commends himself is approved, but the one whom the Lord commends" (10:18). The terms of the battle are set.

In the remaining argument in this section, Paul again takes up the first-person-plural form, tacitly, but clearly, acknowledging that he is not the only apostle in the world. He thus stands apart from the competition in Corinth, as he also has done in a similar way in his characterization of himself alongside Apollos as a mere co-worker of God (1 Cor 3:1-9).

8 Paul is quite prepared for the contention as to who should be recognized as apostle in Corinth. As the series of introductory particles in this verse indicates, his statement here is to be regarded as an extension of his claim to be "of Christ."[230] By preemptively indicating that he has something "most exceedingly" to boast about his authority, he anticipates his response to the "boasting" of his opponents in the "fool's speech."[231] If he should boast, he will "not be ashamed." As is the case elsewhere with Paul, the language of shame implies a contention, as it often does in the Psalms.[232] This contention is taking place with the Corinthians. But Paul's warning is also directed at all potential opponents.

Paul boasts that his authority is not his own; it has been given to him by the Lord.[233] His conception of authority is thus decisively extrinsic. The weakness of his own person and his lack of rhetorical gifts therefore do not detract from this authority in the least. As he goes on to make clear to the Corinthians, his authority is not dependent upon his powers, but upon Christ, who is present in his weakness (12:9-10).

229. The usage of the verb λογίζομαι with the preposition ἐπί governing the genitive is quite rare. Probably the preposition with the genitive here expresses perspective or relation. See BDAG, "ἐπί," 365.

230. The infrequent combination ἐάν τε γάρ is found with Paul elsewhere only in Rom 14:8. While the presence of the τε is text-critically questionable, it is probably to be included as the *lectio difficilior.* It is the τε that binds v. 8 to v. 7; this construction is difficult to interpret unless one recognizes that the claim to be "of Christ" is a claim to apostolic authority.

231. The comparative adjective is best taken as superlative in this context.

232. See, e.g., LXX Pss 34(35):4, 26; 68:7 (69:6); 70(71):24; 85(86):17; Isa 50:7; Rom 1:16; Phil 1:20.

233. It is difficult to determine whether the case of the relative pronoun ἧς has been assimilated to its antecedent (ἐξουσίας) or whether the genitive suggests a partitive idea: "the authority of which the Lord gave to us." Probably assimilation has taken place here. Cf. John 4:14; 1 John 3:24, where the same question arises.

In speaking directly of his authority, Paul speaks of it in its proper sense: it is an authority for edification, and not for the destruction of the Corinthians. The biblical image of the people of God as a temple, which Paul has employed already, likely lies in the background.[234] Given the preceding metaphor of siege, it is even more likely that Paul's language implies the image of a city. The two belong together in antiquity, in any case. The twofold imagery "destroying" and "building" is reminiscent of the calling of Israel's prophets to announce judgment and salvation, especially as it is found in the book of Jeremiah. Judgment and destruction must come, but out of sheer grace, the Lord promises to rebuild Jerusalem and plant his people again in their land.[235] Like God himself, the apostle must perform his alien work of destroying the false judgments of the Corinthians before he can perform his proper work of building them up.[236] Even in this beginning of his contention with them in the closing of the letter, he signals to them unequivocally that his authority is finally an authority for their benefit and growth. He will do so again in 12:19, and yet a third time as the last word in his argument, in 13:10.

9 Yet Paul will not boast to the Corinthians concerning his authority: "Lest I should appear as if I wanted to frighten you through letters." His tone clearly remains ironic. If his apostolic authority is for the edification of the Corinthians, they have nothing to fear from his boast. But the Corinthians have accepted the charge of his opponents. Paul therefore feigns cautious self-restraint here.

10 He seeks to drive a wedge between the Corinthians and the apostolic claimants. The singular figure whom Paul addresses in v. 7 is replaced now by a plurality: "*they* say, his letters are weighty and strong." Paul knows that the apostolic claimants present a united front against him, even if they also contend with one another.

The charge of the opponents holds Paul back from his boast: "(his) letters . . . are weighty and strong, but the presence of his body is weak, and his (spoken) word is worthless." The opponents concede the power of Paul's letters, but argue that the weakness of his person demonstrates his inadequacy, and disqualifies his apostolic claim.[237] They thus call attention to the stark difference between Paul's *parrēsia* and his *parousia*.[238] In his opening ironic request for

234. 1 Cor 3:10-17 (cf. 6:19); 2 Cor 6:14–7:1.

235. See Jer 1:10 and esp. 24:6; LXX 38:28 (MT 31:28); LXX 49:10 (MT 42:10); LXX 51:34 (MT 45:5[4]).

236. See the discussion of "edification" in connection with 12:19, p. 468.

237. See Shi, *Paul's Message of the Cross as Body Language*, 172-86, who argues that Hellenistic conventions concerning the marks of manhood and (conversely) the physiognomy of slaves may have been operative in the background.

238. Mitchell, *The Birth of Christian Hermeneutics*, 81. See also the brief comment on p. 52.

permission to be bold "while not present," Paul has touched on this issue (vv. 1-2). To the extent that the Corinthians accept the judgment of the opponents, his letters may be discarded. Paul's adversaries have the advantage. Not only are they present in Corinth, where they may display their powers, they are able to make use of Paul's weak appearance and lack of rhetorical skill. His "word" is worthless. Paul concedes as much: he is unskilled, unversed in (the spoken) "word" (11:5). Paul can't preach. Or at least he cannot preach according to the standards and tastes of the Corinthians.

Here the fundamental issue with which Paul deals throughout the letter again emerges explicitly. The power of God begins where the power of the apostle ends. The difference between the power of Paul's letters and the weakness of his person is nothing other than the difference between the treasure of the Gospel and the earthen vessel in which it is placed (4:7). Christ's power is perfected only in weakness (12:9-10). The mercy and comfort of God that constitute salvation are granted only to those who suffer (1:3-7). The powerful Corinthians, who imagine that the kingdom has arrived for them in its fullness (1 Cor 4:8), desperately need the weak apostle, who bears the "deadness of Jesus" in his body and yet lives by faith in things yet unseen (4:10; 5:7). Like the crucified Christ, whom he follows, the apostle is the mirror of the Corinthians, in which they may see themselves as they truly are. At the moment, the Corinthians are blind to this truth, preferring heroes who match their own imagination.

11 The plurality of opponents again shifts to the singular: Paul again focuses upon the likelihood of an individual confrontation in Corinth, as he does in v. 7. Again he calls for a fresh "reckoning," as he does there. He is "destroying" the false judgments of practical reason (v. 4).

Now he presents an implicit threat: he is going to appear in Corinth. What he is "by word" through letters, he is also "by deed" when present. His appeal to his epistolary "word" counters the judgment that his (spoken) "word" is worthless and implicitly points to his unquestionable knowledge (11:6). The "weight and strength" of his letters shall soon be apparent in his "deed." This is again his point, as it was in vv. 3-6. He sets the threat of his action over against the appearance of his weakness. The apostolic work of destruction is about to take place. Paul has made use of a similar threat in First Corinthians, contrasting the mere spoken word of "some" among the Corinthians with decisive action on his part: "the kingdom of God does not consist in word, but in power. What do you want? Shall I come to you with a rod, or with love and a spirit of gentleness?" (1 Cor 4:20-21; see 4:18-19). The confrontation that arose in that second visit was disastrous.[239] Paul now hopes for something better. His threat is an expression of apostolic audacity, not the power of his

239. See 2 Cor 1:23–2:11.

person.[240] The confrontation and "retribution" of any disobedience will take place without force, by the power of the word. But it will require decisive action on Paul's part, which he is prepared to take, as he signals here and elsewhere in the closing. He hopes that the present threat will remove the need for action when he finally arrives (13:10).

c. The Corinthians as the Boast of the Apostle (10:12-18)

> 12*Not that we dare to classify or compare ourselves with some of those who are commending themselves. But when they measure themselves by one another and compare themselves with one another, they are without understanding.* 13*But we will not boast beyond limits, but will boast only with regard to the area of influence God assigned to us, to reach even to you.* 14*For we are not overextending ourselves, as though we did not reach you. For we were the first to come all the way to you with the gospel of Christ.* 15*We do not boast beyond limit in the labors of others. But our hope is that as your faith increases, our area of influence among you may be greatly enlarged,* 16*so that we may preach the gospel in lands beyond you, without boasting of work already done in another's area of influence.* 17*"Let the one who boasts, boast in the Lord."* 18*For it is not the one who commends himself who is approved, but the one whom the Lord commends.*

In the first instance, Paul explains his assertion of apostolic authority by rejecting the standards by which his opponents in Corinth commend themselves. They are without understanding when they measure themselves by and compare themselves with one another.

Paul instead grounds his claim to authority in his "proper" commendation, namely, the Corinthians themselves. Their faith in the Gospel of Christ is the demonstration of Paul's apostolic calling. The mark of Paul's authority is that God has allowed him to reach the Corinthians with the Gospel. His aim, therefore, is to reach beyond the Corinthians with the Gospel, to those who have not yet been reached.

His last word clarifies the standard of boasting and the nature of commendation: "Let the one who boasts, boast in the Lord." This appeal to the text of Jeremiah that Paul has cited already in 1 Cor 1:30 stands at the theological center of his legitimation as apostle, defining both "foolishness" and "boasting," the terms that predominate in his argument and that appear in this material in remarkable concentration.[241] In a larger sense, it stands at the center of all of Paul's dealings with the Corinthians; his correction of the

240. See 3:1-18.

241. Rightly, Heckel, *Kraft in Schwachheit,* 303.

false standards of the apostolic claimants is nothing other than a pointed interpretation of his earlier correction of the Corinthians' adoration of human wisdom, power, and honor.

12 Paul explains *(gar)* the assertion of his authority, an authority that sets him apart from his opponents. He neither includes himself among them nor enters into comparison with them, as they commend themselves. Even if he has been compelled to commend himself by the Corinthians (5:12) — as he does immediately in this letter (11:1–12:13) — Paul will not commend himself in the terms that the Corinthians require.[242] The Corinthians are his commendation (3:1-3). They themselves ought to commend him (12:11).

Paul's opponents, who draw comparisons with one another and not merely with Paul, do so without understanding what they are doing. The term Paul uses to describe the failure of his opponents is deliciously ironic. This verb for understanding is a compound form *(syn-iēmi)* that appears at the end of a list of similar compounds with the prefix *syn-* ("together"). Paul will not compare himself *(syn-krinō)* with those who commend themselves *(syn-istanō);* when they compare themselves *(syn-krinō)* they do not understand *(syn-iēmi).* The opponents make comparisons in which they put things together, but they cannot put it together.

The irony is deeper yet. Paul speaks within the context of biblical tradition, in which the lack of "understanding" is not merely an intellectual deficiency but godlessness and unbelief. In Rom 3:11, for example, Paul cites the biblical Psalms that announce that "no one understands, no one seeks for God."[243] Correspondingly, he appeals to the Isaianic announcement of the effective proclamation of "Good News" so that "those who have not heard shall understand" (Rom 15:21; LXX Isa 52:13[15]). In both instances, lack of understanding is godlessness. By their self-comparisons and judgments, the apostolic claimants in Corinth thus show themselves to be unbelievers and godless. Paul later designates them with even worse names (11:12-15). His charge that they "do not understand" also anticipates his closing appeal in this unit to Jer 9:23-24 (LXX 9:22-23): the one who boasts is to boast that they have *understanding,* and know the Lord.[244] Although Paul rewords the text with language from the Psalms, the original form likely resonates in the background: the opponents boast in themselves, not in the Lord.[245] Their godlessness is manifest in their misunderstanding of the work of God.

13 The lack of understanding of the opponents displays itself in their comparisons: they boast with respect to "immeasurable things." Paul will not

242. Cf. 4:2; 6:3-10.

243. See LXX Pss 13(14):2; 52:3 (53:2).

244. See n. 260, p. 397, on the Septuagintal reading of this passage.

245. Rightly, Heckel, *Kraft in Schwachheit,* 193.

do so. He has a measure by which he boasts, which, limited though it may be, reaches as far as the Corinthians: he will boast only "according to the measure of the standard of which God has measured us a measure." This standard *(kanōn)* is the Gospel, as Paul makes clear in v. 14. The Gospel is the measure. God has measured to Paul a measure of the Gospel. This measure includes the Corinthians. Paul has expressed himself in similar terms in First Corinthians: through the Gospel, he has become their one and only "father" (1 Cor 4:14-15).

The English translations, as well as the commentaries generally,[246] misunderstand Paul's reference to "immeasurable things" *(ta ametra)*, reading Paul as rejecting a boasting "beyond [proper] limits."[247] This interpretation is achieved only by an extremely free translation of the text. The rendering of *ta ametra* as "immeasurable things" remains the most likely reading, given the usage of this language in biblical tradition,[248] as well as Paul's contrast between measurement according to a standard *(metron tou kanonos)* and the *a-metra* (alpha privitive). Paul's thought here corresponds to his admonition to the Roman Christians "not to think more highly of oneself than one ought to think, but to think with sound judgment, because God has measured to each a measure of faith" (Rom 12:3). The standard *(kanōn)* of the Gospel has its counterpart in the faith that grasps the Gospel. There is, to be sure, a warning against hubris both in Romans and in the present context, which is the thought that guides most translations and commentators. But as Paul's charge that his adversaries are "without understanding" makes clear, his attack upon the apostolic claimants is much more than a moralistic warning against hubris, which was common in Hellenistic culture, and of which the opponents most likely would have been conscious. Paul does not merely challenge a boasting that exceeds its proper limits. He is concerned to destroy *the human judgment* and understanding that sets the standards of boasting. He holds to the *standard* "of the measure measured to him," namely, the Gospel, and refuses to adopt an "alien *standard*" (v. 16). The same thought appears in Rom 12:3: God distributes faith according to his own "measure." It is not given to us to penetrate the mystery of why and how God distributes faith as he does. These matters remain immeasurable.[249]

246. E.g., Harris, *The Second Epistle to the Corinthians,* 709-10; Thrall, *The Second Epistle to the Corinthians,* 2:644; Furnish, *II Corinthians,* 481. The Greco-Roman awareness of the danger of hubris, which is surely relevant in this context (e.g., the oft-cited Delphic oracle μηδὲν ἄγαν, "nothing too much"), is here allowed to overrun Paul's thought in context, as it has done in H. D. Betz's important work *Der Apostel Paulus und die sokratische Tradition: Eine exegetische Untersuchung zu seiner Apologie 2 Korinther 10–13* (BHT 45; Tübingen: Mohr Siebeck, 1972), 70-89.

247. Thus ESV, NIV, NRSV.

248. LXX Isa 22:18; 3 Macc 2:4, 9; 4:17; Sir 16:17; 30:15.

249. This understanding lies behind Paul's earlier reminder to the Corinthians "not to go beyond the things that are written," lest one "become puffed up" over against another

The limited measure that God has given to Paul and, by implication, to each apostle allows place for the work of God, which transcends all limits and boundaries. Paul's language in this context is again paradoxical. He has been "measured a measure" by God, and yet he "has attained" as far as the Corinthians (vv. 13b-14). Indeed, he hopes "to be made great," i.e., elevated in esteem and "magnified" — at least according to his standard — by the increase of the Corinthians' faith (v. 15). He hopes therefore "to abound" (cf. 9:8) and to evangelize the regions beyond the Corinthians (v. 16a). The limited measure that has been measured to the apostle is nothing other than a measure of "the Gospel of Christ," which has no limit to its working (v. 14). This work of the Gospel is not merely geographic. Its power is manifest in the creation of faith in the human heart, and here, especially, in the hearts of the Corinthians (vv. 14-15). In the apostle, the boundaries of human weakness meet with boundless power, just as they do in the crucified and risen Christ.

Paul's opponents understand Christ and his power to be present within their powers. This human judgment makes the legitimation of an apostle also a matter of human judgment. According to Paul, in doing so, these apostolic claimants are "without understanding," and godless (v. 12). They are blind to the judgment of God on the human being in the crucified and risen Christ, and therefore also blind to the work of God. It is not merely that they have measured wrongly. They lack the proper standard *(kanōn),* the Gospel of Christ, which, as the work of God, judges all human works, powers, and reasoning, and cannot be judged by them. It is not merely that their judgments are false, but their entire reasoning is false because it remains merely human, and does not rest in God's work and judgment in Christ.

It is not the case, then, that a certain measure of boasting is proper, but must not be exceeded. Paul is not criticizing excessive boasting, he is insisting on eccentric boasting. All proper boasting is "eccentric," a boasting in the Lord, who performs his own work, as he chooses, in and through his apostles. Paul makes this point emphatically in v. 17: "Let the one who boasts, boast in the Lord."

Here Paul emphasizes that it is God who has "measured of a measure" to him. The extent of his ministry lies in God's hands. He has a stewardship for which he will be held accountable — woe to him, if he does not preach the Gospel! (1 Cor 9:16) — but the credit or blame for the success or failure of his ministry does not belong to him, but to God. Paul's thought here corresponds to his earlier description of himself as a co-worker with God alongside Apollos. He is a *diakonos,* an agent of another (1 Cor 3:5-9). He has used the same term to describe himself in this letter (3:6). His labors in the Gospel are the partic-

(1 Cor 4:6). The differing callings given to Paul and Apollos, onto whom Paul has transposed the figures of agricultural laborers and builders, rest finally in the purposes of God, and more fundamentally, in the work of God that takes place through each of them.

ular form of "receiving and giving" that have been granted to him as apostle: "I delivered to you as of first importance what I also received" (1 Cor 15:3; cf. 11:23).[250] He has been entrusted with the Gospel, as a steward (1 Cor 4:1; cf. 1 Thess 2:4). As we have noted, the Corinthians are looking for a genius, but God has sent them an apostle.[251]

The work of God does not exclude the ambitions and labors of the apostle, but includes them. It sets Paul free by providing him with the boundary that prevents his goals and aspirations from becoming unlimited demands and utopian dreams. The apostle is aware that a limited measure has been measured to him. It is only by the grace of God that he is who he is. Yet he labors more than all others, especially with the Corinthians (1 Cor 15:10; cf. 2 Cor 6:5; 11:26-29). Just as he does in the letter to Rome, Paul here expresses the hope that the sphere of his mission will be expanded beyond the Corinthians to those who are yet unreached (vv. 15-16).

14 Paul elaborates by stating the obvious: in his claim that the Corinthians lie within the sphere of his apostolic authority, he is by no means overreaching. He has come as far as the Corinthians with the Gospel of Christ.[252]

As he often does in this letter, Paul brings the Corinthians a necessary reminder by describing the Gospel as the Gospel *of Christ*.[253] He already has spoken of the "Gospel of the glory of Christ, who is the image of God" (4:4). The Good News remains the Good News of the crucified Jesus, now risen. Paul does not proclaim himself, but Jesus Christ as Lord (4:5).

As we have noted, the work of God does not exclude the work of the apostle, but provides it with the "space" in which it takes place. This thought comes to expression again here: Paul has "attained" or "arrived" as far as the Corinthians. The course of his life is determined by the course of the Gospel and by "the measure" that God "has measured" to him. But this recognition by no means does away with his ambition for the Gospel. He goes on to speak of his ambitious aims beyond the Corinthians.

15 Verses 15-17 are a single, lengthy statement that clarifies Paul's apostolic aims for the Corinthians. The thought is a continuation of v. 14, which serves to "de-center" the Corinthians, in much the same way as his word about the grace of God given in Macedonia does with respect to the collection.[254]

250. These confessions, which involve human instruments, do not contradict, but rather complement, his insistence that he received his Gospel from heaven itself (Gal 1:12).

251. See once more Kierkegaard, "Of the Difference between a Genius and an Apostle."

252. As becomes clear in Romans, Paul regards his apostolic authority as extending to the entire Gentile world. Yet where he has not been the first to bring the Gospel, he speaks of his authority only very carefully. See, e.g., Rom 15:14-16.

253. 2:12; 4:4; 9:13; cf. 1 Cor 9:12.

254. Paul operates similarly with the church in Rome, which was also tempted to regard itself as the center of God's purposes. See Rom 1:13-15; 15:17-29.

Paul's statements here are self-descriptive. They appear in participial form, although this cannot be represented in translation. First of all, he does not boast in "alien labors with respect to immeasurable things." These "alien labors" are clearly the labors of others. Paul again sets himself apart from his opponents in Corinth and implicitly charges them with this improper boasting: it is he, not they, who reached Corinth with the Gospel. Yet the term "alien" also signifies that Paul does not boast in labors that are alien to the Gospel, those that do not properly belong to his apostolic calling. This interpretation of the term is reinforced by Paul's opening repetition of his insistence that he does not boast "with respect to immeasurable things," but maintains the measure God has granted him (v. 13).

Paul then states his purposes positively. He has the hope of "being made great," being "magnified" by the Corinthians. He is by no means shy in stating his aims. Yet these aims have to do with the Gospel, and not with Paul's person. The greatness that he seeks is "according to [his] standard," for an "abundance" that extends beyond both him and the Corinthians. It is not accidental that the language of receiving and giving reappears here.[255] The giving forth of the Gospel that he has received is the mission given to the apostle. The greater things for which he hopes from the Corinthians are conditioned by their faith. He is not concerned with counting heads, but with the work of God in human hearts. By the growth of the Corinthians' faith, Paul will be set free for a larger sphere of mission. This hope undoubtedly includes the hope of financial support. Despite his unswerving refusal to accept compensation from the Corinthians, he appears prepared to accept assistance for projects beyond them. He had expected that the Corinthians would help him directly in his travel from them to Judea (1:16).[256] More fundamentally, however, the growth in the Corinthians' faith is their edification. As he tells them earlier in the letter, his entire purpose as an apostle is the furtherance of their faith (1:12). This faith, which is to bring joy to the Corinthians (1:24), is not merely an outward confession of their lips but the living confession of their lives.

16 The "abundance" that Paul seeks is the evangelizing of the yet-unreached regions beyond Corinth. The language of reach and extension continues throughout Paul's description of his mission. For the apostle, the Gospel is no mere doctrinal statement but a power that performs its work in the world. It has a course to run. In his ambition as an apostle, Paul merely seeks to keep up with the word that has been given to him. His self-description here obviously stands very close to his declaration of his apostolic aims in

255. See 8:2, 7; 9:8, 12.

256. In a similar manner, he indicates to the Roman Christians that he hopes to be aided by them in a mission to Spain (Rom 15:24).

Romans. There, too, it becomes clear that Paul understands his mission as a fulfillment of the words of Scripture that empower and guide his work.[257]

Paul rounds off his description of his apostolic purpose by repeating his opening denial that he will not "boast by an alien standard with respect to the things prepared." His formulation changes in the wake of his argument. Paul now indicates that he will not boast by some "alien standard," i.e., a false measure, a standard other than the Gospel itself. For Paul, boasting can take place only in reference to "things" that already have been "prepared."[258] The human being is no initiator or creator and cannot be properly a "worker," but only a "co-worker" who enters into the work of God that already is complete in itself. Even our individual tasks have been prepared. Out of the Gospel, God "measures" each one "a measure" of work (v. 13).

17 Paul completes his description of his apostolic aims with an appeal to the book of Jeremiah that he has cited in his earlier instruction of the Corinthians (1 Cor 1:31; Jer 9:23): "Let the one who boasts, boast in the Lord." This word, which appears without an introductory formula, is more a strong allusion than a direct citation. It undoubtedly recalls not only the book of Jeremiah but also Paul's citation of the text in 1 Cor 1:31.

This word completes the thought of vv. 15-16, standing in contrast to Paul's preceding statement, to which it belongs syntactically: the hope that Paul has (v. 15) means that he does not boast "by an alien standard" with respect to the things prepared by God (v. 16), *but* (citing the Jeremianic exhortation) "Let the one who boasts, boast in the Lord" (v. 17). Paul addresses something more profound than the mere refusal to boast in someone else's work. He is not concerned with false *judgments* in Corinth, he is concerned with the false *reasoning* behind those judgments, the lack of understanding — the godless "foolishness" — that is characteristic of the fallen human being.[259]

In its Jeremianic context, the admonition appears in the wake of an or-

257. See Rom 15:17-21, esp. v. 21.

258. The expression εἰς τὰ ἕτοιμα stands in parallel contrast to εἰς τὰ ἄμετρα (v. 15). The rejected comparison with "alien labors" (ἐν ἀλλοτρίοις κόποις), i.e., the labors of others (yet with overtones of misplaced labors), is now replaced by a rejected comparison with an "alien standard" (ἐν ἀλλοτρίῳ κανόνι). Paul shifts attention from the objects of judgment to the standard of judgment. He thus speaks here of the "things prepared by God," not "things worked by other persons." This point becomes esp. clear in v. 17 — against, e.g., Harris, *The Second Epistle to the Corinthians,* 723-24, who combines the two thoughts, understanding "things prepared" as prepared by others as God has allotted their work to them. But this reading misses the thrust of Paul's argument against the false criterion of judgment employed by Paul's opponents.

259. Similarly, Heckel, *Kraft in Schwachheit,* 177. Not merely the values but the practical reasoning of the Corinthians is the problem. At this point Pickett's conclusions must be deepened. See R. Pickett, *The Cross in Corinth: The Social Significance of the Death of Jesus* (JSNTSupp 143; Sheffield: Sheffield Academic Press, 1997), 183-92.

acle of the devastating judgment that is coming upon Jerusalem. The disaster that is coming is not predictable or comprehensible, even to the wise (Jer 9:12). It is a judgment that must be declared and made known by the Lord (Jer 9:12-16). In the face of this judgment, the Lord thus warns:

> Let not the wise person boast in their wisdom, and let not the strong boast in their strength, let not the wealthy one boast in their wealth, but let the one who boasts, boast that they have understanding, and know me, that I am the Lord who does kindness, judgment, and righteousness in the earth (Jer 9:23-24).[260]

The word to the wise, which stands at the head of the warnings, recalls the failure of the wise, concerning which the Lord rhetorically asks in Jer 9:12. The word of the Lord here clarifies the nature of that failure. As is clear in the second rhetorical question in 9:12, the Lord must first announce his purpose before anyone can declare it to others. It cannot be known otherwise. Consequently, for wise persons to boast in their wisdom is to cut themselves off from the true understanding that comes from hearing the Lord's word. In the face of the coming disaster, the same applies to the boast in strength or in wealth. Both are worthless. These false judgments proceed from the false imagination that life and abundance may be measured by these goods (which, after all, are mere gifts from the Lord). As is the case with Paul, the Jeremianic text is directed against the false reasoning of human beings who imagine that they have life and good in themselves and their powers. True "boasting" rests in the knowledge of the Lord, and specifically in the knowledge of the Lord in his works of mercy, true judgment, and righteousness. Human beings were not made to live within themselves, but to live in a relationship of communication with the Lord, in hearing and receiving, and then responding in "boasting" and praise.

Paul's wording of the text, which corresponds directly to his citation of it in First Corinthians, is a modification of the text of Jeremiah, with a borrowing of language from the Psalms. Using the language of the Psalms,[261] Paul interprets the admonition that one is to "boast that they know the Lord" as

260. The Septuagintal rendering omits the personal pronoun from the Hebrew "and knows me" (וְיָדֹעַ אוֹתִי), so that the following clause becomes the object of the verb: "and knows that I am the Lord, who performs mercy and judgment and righteousness upon the earth" (καὶ γινώσκειν ὅτι ἐγώ εἰμι κύριος ποιῶν ἔλεος καὶ κρίμα καὶ δικαιοσύνην ἐπὶ τῆς γῆς). The text of 1 Sam 2:10, which is expanded to include a parallel to Jer 9:23-24 (LXX 9:22-23), remains closer to the MT Jer 9:23: one is to boast that one "has understanding and knows the Lord" (1 Kgdms 2:10). It varies from LXX Jer 9:22 by substituting φρόνιμος/φρόνησις for σοφός/σοφία, and δυνατός/δύναμις for ἰσχυρός/ἰσχύς. Apparently this reading of 1 Sam 2:10 has a long history, since it seems to appear in 4QSam.

261. See esp. LXX Ps 5:12(11), but also MT Pss 20:8(7); 34:3(2); 44:9(8).

boasting "in the Lord." He locates the object of boasting entirely outside the human being. Paul radicalizes the extrinsic nature of this boasting, which is present implicitly in the text.

In First Corinthians, Paul employs the text to summarize and explain his apostolic proclamation, which he there describes as "the word of the cross" (1 Cor 1:17-18). The whole of his argument, and especially 1 Cor 1:26-31, receives its structure and content from Paul's opening citation of Isa 29:14 and from the text of Jeremiah that Paul cites at the close (1 Cor 1:31). Here, too, Paul's topic is God's undoing of the false wisdom of the human being that imagines that God may be judged according to human standards. Before all else, God's saving work entails delivering human beings from the idols of wisdom, power, wealth, and social standing. This work of God has taken place in Christ, crucified in weakness and foolishness, who is God's wisdom and power (1 Cor 1:23-24). Paul underscores to the Corinthians that God's work includes their very deliverance: by God's doing, they are in Christ Jesus, who (thereby) became to them "wisdom from God."

In the present context, Paul addresses the other side of God's work, namely, the apostolic mission. Paul will not boast "by an alien standard," but he will fulfill the Lord's exhortation in Jeremiah, "Let the one who boasts, boast in the Lord." It is God who creates and increases faith. The apostle is a mere instrument, a co-laborer, through whom God performs his own work. The boast of an apostle, no less than that of the objects of his mission, must be radically extrinsic, or it is no true boasting at all. Paul's bodily weakness and rhetorical inability are not an obstacle for the work of God. They are its vehicle. The life and mission of an apostle is nothing other than the life of a Christian written large; it consists in a relationship of communication, in which God's power is present and performs its work *within human weakness.* God's saving work necessarily operates in the paradox of the cross. Otherwise we would not be saved — from ourselves.

18 In a final explanation of this word of Scripture, Paul returns to his opening refusal to enter into any comparison of himself with others, rounding off his argument (v. 12). As we have seen for Paul "boasting in the Lord" by no means excludes self-reference. Indeed, it requires telling what the Lord has done "for me." "Boasting in the Lord" thus provides self-reference its proper form. It is the Lord who has commended Paul to the Corinthians. They are his commendation (3:2). It is Paul who reached them with the Gospel, just as he hopes to reach others. Behind and before Paul is the work of God, in which alone he boasts. The thought is the same as Paul's word in First Corinthians: "His grace toward me was not empty, but I labored more than all of them. Yet not I, but the grace of God with me" (1 Cor 15:10). Paul therefore need not and will not commend himself. Nor does he need the approval of the Corinthians. The evidence of his calling as apostle comes from God alone, who works savingly in and through the crucified Christ. Paul's approval therefore appears in a form contrary to all human judgments. It is present in the faith of the Corinthians, even though they are in danger of ignoring it.

2. *Paul's Foolish Boasting (11:1–12:13)*

Having rejected any boasting that is not properly a boasting in the Lord, Paul proceeds to boast quite improperly concerning his apostolic qualifications. From the very start, his argument in this section is laced with the irony that appears in his opening address in chapter 10. Now the request to speak boldly becomes more specific: Paul requests permission to be foolish, or more precisely, he asks the Corinthians to bear with him and accept him as a fool. It is only fitting that they should do so. The wise Corinthians should be happy to have a fool as their apostle. As Paul points out, this is precisely what they have been happy to do in their embrace of the apostolic claimants. In asking the Corinthians to allow him to be foolish, Paul lets them in on the game he is playing. The entire controversy concerning Paul and his opponents should be clear to them by now. His request to speak foolishly is intended to force the Corinthians to acknowledge their role in Paul's contention with his opponents. They themselves are the problem. He tells them so at both the outset and the close of his argument.[262]

Correspondingly, Paul twice asks the Corinthians to accept him as a fool, and he closes the argument by confessing that he has become foolish.[263] These requests and Paul's confession make clear that he regards what he is doing as improper. Indeed, it is not only improper but ungodly. As has become clear from Paul's charge that his opponents are "without understanding" and his appeal to Jer 9:23-24, his understanding of "foolishness" is finally drawn from the Scriptures and from Jewish Wisdom literature.[264] To be "foolish" is to live in unbelief and godlessness. As he states explicitly, it has been forced upon him by the Corinthians.[265] They are the ones who are thinking and behaving in an ungodly manner. Paul's twofold request that they bear with and accept him as a fool further serves to punctuate his argument, marking its stages. Despite Paul's opening wish that the Corinthians might bear with a bit of foolishness from him (11:1), he does not fully take up the part of the fool until after his second, more pointed request (11:16).

In the first part of his argument, Paul provides the basis and grounds for

262. 11:3-4; 12:11-13.

263. 11:1, 16; 12:11.

264. See Heckel, *Kraft in Schwachheit,* 304.

265. 11:17.

what he is about to do (11:1-15). He again boasts about his apostolic mission to the Corinthians (11:7-11), and does so now much more concretely than he has done in 10:12-18. Nevertheless, Paul's boasting in this opening unit remains entirely proper, based on the Gospel. Indeed, Paul appeals to the "truth of Christ" in asserting it (11:10).

Only in the second part of his argument, after he has made clear why he must play the part of the fool, does Paul fully enter the game and offer his "fool's speech" (11:22–12:10). His foolishness consists in his doing precisely what he has rejected: he ranks himself alongside the apostolic contenders, comparing himself with them in the superficial matters that cannot be measured. Once more, before he begins his "speech," he emphatically rejects what he is about to do (11:16-21). Yet here Paul brings a further ironic twist to his argument, in that he only briefly names the standards by which the opponents measure themselves and then quickly turns to boast in his labors, sufferings, and weakness. These elements, once introduced, become the stay of Paul's argument. Ironically, in the end, even as a fool, Paul does not speak as a fool, but as the apostle of Christ. Yet, to speak as a true apostle is nothing but foolishness in the eyes of the Corinthians.

In his closing word, Paul makes it clear to the Corinthians that it is they who have forced him to speak and to act as he has done (12:11-13). Just as Christ was "made sin" in order that we might become "the righteousness of God," Paul, as Christ's apostle, has become the fool for the sake of the Corinthians in order that they might know "the wisdom of God that is hidden in a mystery" — that is to say, that they might know the crucified Christ as their wisdom (1 Cor 1:18–2:16).

a. The Reasons for Paul's Foolishness (11:1-15)

Before he enters into his foolish boasting, Paul provides a lengthy word of introduction that explains the reason and basis for his comparing himself with the "super-apostles." In the first place, he has betrothed the Corinthians to Christ, and he worries that they are all too easily led astray from Christ by those who have arrived in Corinth with another Gospel (11:1-4). In the second place, Paul regards himself as in no way inferior to these apostolic claimants, whom he now names "super-apostles." Paul mentions the two points at which he has been under attack: his lack of rhetorical skill (11:6) and his refusal to accept compensation for his labors among the Corinthians in the Gospel (11:7-15). The latter issue has long contributed to the unsettled relationship between Paul and the Corinthians (1 Cor 9:1-18). They obviously have regarded it as a mark of his inadequacy. Paul — rhetorically uneducated though he may be! — reframes their doubts concerning him on this matter by raising the question as to whether he sinned in so acting. Set in the context of God's work, rather than that of the cultural expectations of the day, the Corinthian judgment is exposed as deficient. Paul's refusal to accept support from Corinth is no sin at all. It is Paul's boast, as the Corinthians have heard from him already (11:10; cf. 1 Cor 9:15). This practice, by which Paul participates in the Gospel he proclaims (1 Cor 9:23), marks Paul out as apostle in distinction from the pretenders, whom Paul now charges as false apostles and agents of Satan (11:12-15). Paul thus expresses the basis of his concern that the church is being seduced and corrupted.

(1) Paul's First Request to Be Foolish: Parental Concern (11:1-4)

> **11**[1]*I wish you would bear with me in a little foolishness. Do bear with me!* [2]*For I feel a divine jealousy for you, since I betrothed you to one husband, to present you as a pure virgin to Christ.* [3]*But I am afraid that as the serpent deceived Eve by his cunning, your thoughts will be led astray from a sincere and pure devotion to Christ.* [4]*For if someone comes and proclaims another Jesus than the one we proclaimed, or if you receive a different spirit from the one you received, or if you accept a different gospel from the one you accepted, you put up with it readily enough.*

1 There is asyndeton here, a break of connection with the preceding argument. Paul's expression of unattainable wish, "O, that you would endure from me a little bit of foolishness!", may be taken in two senses.[266] In the first instance, despite its unreal form, it constitutes a request of the Corinthians to allow him to speak foolishly. It echoes his opening request to be bold (10:1-2), making the permission he seeks more precise and heightening the form and content of his petition. It also has its parallel in his second, explicit request to play the fool in 11:16. As an unattainable wish, Paul's wish likely also bears a second sense. The "foolishness" that Paul requests the Corinthians to endure may be understood as that which *they* regard as foolish, namely, the weakness of the apostle. The "word of the cross" that the apostle bears is foolishness to the perishing wisdom of this world, which the Corinthians have embraced (1 Cor 1:18-27). He only wishes that they might endure this bit of foolishness from him!

Paul follows with an immediate retraction: "But, indeed, you do endure me." The statement is again ironic. Paul plays off the second sense of his preceding wish. The Corinthians endure the apostle whom they regard as substandard, incompetent, weak, and suspicious. They are long-suffering with him, bearing with him, despite the deficiencies they find in him. Yet, as he indicates by his expression of an unattainable wish, they do not truly bear with *him,* as the apostle of the crucified Christ.

266. On the usage, see BDF §359.1.

2 Paul presents the first explanation for the foolishness in which he is about to engage. He has betrothed the Corinthians to one husband, Christ, and seeks to guard their purity until he finally presents them to him. The pathos that drives him to this extreme thereby becomes understandable. As he has already done and will do again in this letter, Paul assumes the role of father to the Corinthian church.[267] The thought flows out of his preceding reminder that it was he who first reached the Corinthians with the Gospel. He has expressly claimed the role of father on this basis already.[268] The figure of paternity that Paul employs asserts the authority for which he has argued in 10:12-18. In arguing from the Gospel in this way, Paul again sets himself above any sort of judgment that the Corinthians might render, and likewise above any need to enter into comparison with the apostolic claimants in Corinth.[269] As is especially apparent in their unhappiness over Paul's refusal to receive support from them, the Corinthians have regarded themselves as benefactors and sponsors of (true) apostles. This self-understanding is shaped by the culture and values of the world. Paul wages war against it with the Gospel.

Paul's assumption of the role of father also sets limits to his apostolic authority. The betrothal of a daughter means that the father's role is drawing to a close. It is the marriage of the woman and the man that is of fundamental importance. The father steps aside and disappears from the scene once his responsibility has been fulfilled. Paul again underscores that the role of the apostle, as significant as it is, remains of a temporary and secondary nature. The image of the wedding indicates that Paul's thought is eschatologically oriented: the presentation to Christ (v. 2) takes place on the last day. Nevertheless, the eschaton has entered the present in the reality of faith; Paul will not be lord over the faith of the Corinthians. By their faith — insofar as they have faith — they stand (1:24). Paul's self-characterization thus again calls to mind the words of John the Baptist, who likewise uses the figure of marriage to describe his secondary role in relation to Jesus. As the friend of the groom, he confesses: "He must increase, but I must decrease." Grünewald's Isenheim altar again presents the image that Paul is conveying. Paul is putting all apostles, including himself, in their proper place.

Paul is compelled to speak in foolishness, not because of his own person, but for the sake of the Corinthians, whom he seeks, as any father would, to present as a pure bride to her husband. He is zealous for them with "a zeal of God." The expression bears rich overtones. In the first instance, it remains within Paul's metaphor, as a description of a father's godly zeal for his daughter.

267. 6:13; 12:14-15.

268. See 1 Cor 4:14-15, where Paul asserts his role as father to the Corinthians, using this very argument.

269. See 1 Cor 4:1-5.

At the same time, it also reflects the biblical figure of God as the caring and zealous father of his people.[270] Paul shares God's own zeal for the Corinthians. His zeal therefore, thirdly, may recall the zeal of Phinehas for the Lord's cause with Israel: Paul's zeal is likewise radical and, in a sense, expresses the same concern for the purity of God's people.[271] Probably, too, the expression suggests that Paul's zeal "of God" is a zeal that is given to him by God as the apostle to the Corinthians.

As the father of the Corinthian church, Paul has betrothed the church to Christ "as a pure virgin." The Isaianic image of Jerusalem as the bride of the Lord lies in the background.[272] The identification of Christ with God, which is inherent to the figure, is rooted deeply in early Christian tradition and may be traced back to Jesus himself.[273] The span between betrothal and marriage is to be understood as that between Paul's arrival with the Gospel and the last day, in which the apostle will present the Corinthians to Christ. By its very nature, the figure points to Paul's role as father of Christ's bride and the consummation of that role at the *parousia.* As Paul has indicated more than once to the Corinthians, he and the church are bound together in Christ's saving work.[274] This bond appears once again here.

Correspondingly, the "purity" of the church as a virgin betrothed to Christ consists in the faith that has been brought to it in the apostolic Gospel. This aspect of the metaphor is clear, not only from the way in which it is correlated to Paul's role as father to the Corinthians, but also from the fear that he expresses. He is worried that their "minds might be seduced," and he is concerned all the more in that they happily bear with the proclamation of another Jesus and with the reception of another Spirit and Gospel (vv. 3-4). The purity that he seeks is the purity of faith. This faith is the presence of the new creation, which changes the entire course of earthly life. The biblical figure of Israel's idolatry as infidelity to the Lord, its faithful and loving husband, lies in the background as well.[275]

270. See esp. Isa 63:15-19, and also Jer 3:1-5, 19-20, where the figure of husband shifts to that of father.

271. Num 25:1-13.

272. See Isa 49:18; 61:10; 62:5.

273. A similar figure appears in Ephesians, although here the apostle does not come into view: the focus rests on the redeeming work of Christ, even in the midst of an exhortation to husbands (Eph 5:25-33). According to the testimony of the Synoptic Gospels, Jesus took up this image in reference to himself, in a remarkable claim to authority (Mark 2:19-20; Matt 9:15; Luke 5:34-35). It appears indirectly in the Johannine witness of the Baptist to which we have referred above (John 3:28-30), and likewise in the book of Revelation (19:5-10).

274. See, e.g., 1:12-14, 20-22.

275. See esp. the book of Hosea, but also elsewhere in the prophets, e.g., Jer 2:23-37; Ezek 16:15-63.

3 Paul adds a new figure to that of betrothal and marriage, or, more precisely, he expands the figure with a brief, yet significant recollection of the biblical narrative of Eve's transgression. Within the Scriptures, primal events do not remain in the past as mere memories but remain present in the world even now. The recounting of them reveals the battles that are taking place here and now within the world.[276] This is true of Paul's recollection of the encounter between Eve and the serpent. He already has warned of the wiles of Satan and will do so shortly again in completion of the thought he introduces in this verse (2:11; 11:14). Here, however — for the only time in his letters — he speaks of "the serpent." The narrative of Eve's temptation and fall is revelatory for the present. Nothing is more up-to-date than the foundational events, to which Paul has already alluded more than once in 3:18–4:6. The Corinthians and the world in which they live are "figured out" within the text, in a way that they could not otherwise conceive or imagine.[277]

As we have noted, the figures of vv. 2-3 are joined. Not only does Paul's appeal to the primal sin explain the cause for his concern for the Corinthians, the figure of betrothal and marriage places the narrative of Eve and the serpent in a new context. The disruption of the communion between the human being and God that took place in the primal transgression is not final but — through the wonder of God's grace — has become a mere delay, a betrothal that awaits its consummation in marriage. Paul's thought corresponds remarkably to Johannine theology, in which the same figure appears, and likewise to the brief word of Jesus in the Synoptic tradition in which he identifies himself as the bridegroom.[278]

Paul fears that somehow the minds of the Corinthians might be seduced, just as the serpent deceived Eve by his guile *(panourgia)*. Paul leaves those who might seduce the Corinthians unnamed for the moment. His focus rests entirely on the biblical narrative that exposes the forces in conflict in Corinth.[279] He will name them soon enough (vv. 12-15).

In Paul's fear concerning the Corinthians, we encounter again his reckoning that they are in real danger of being turned away from Christ. This entirely legitimate concern is juxtaposed to his unshaken confidence that God's work in them in Christ remains intact and unthreatened; the thought is im-

276. Cf. Ps 78:1-4.

277. Yet again I am recalling Christopher Seitz's title *Figured Out: Typology and Providence in Christian Scripture.* That Scripture is revelatory of the world is apparent in Paul's use of the narrative of the giving of the Law in 2 Cor 3: he appeals to the text not because he is confronting advocates of Judaizing but because it reveals truths about the Law, the Gospel, the apostolic mission, and the Corinthians that otherwise would remain hidden.

278. John 3:29; Mark 2:19-20; Matt 9:15; 25:1-10; Luke 5:34-35.

279. Not surprisingly, Paul's language here is quite close to that of the Septuagintal rendering of the narrative, esp. LXX Gen 3:1, 13.

plicit to the apostolic claim he presents in 10:12-18. These two dimensions of his thought should not be played off against one another, or qualified or limited. Their relation cannot be resolved — at least not this side of glory.

Paul thus implicitly acknowledges the cleverness of evil, which transcends not only the Corinthians' capacities but also his own. "Satan" is no mere metaphor for Paul, no mere personification of an impersonal power of evil, but precisely the power of evil, fully personal in nature. Paul fears that "somehow" — he knows not how — the Corinthians might be seduced. Satan operates with a guile and craftiness that goes beyond Paul. This is so, even if "we are not ignorant of [Satan's] plans" (2:11). If he could penetrate this mystery, he would be able to prevent it. He cannot, and must therefore seek to protect the Corinthians by the power of the Gospel. Yet he does know the pattern of Satan's work, its telltale marks, the form that it takes within the world. As he shortly makes clear to the Corinthians, he can recognize Satan's agents (vv. 12-15).

Paul likens the serpent's deception of Eve to "the corruption" of the minds[280] of the Corinthians.[281] He interprets this "corruption" as a seduction, but the metaphor is not that of "thoughts" being "led astray" (ESV, NIV, NRSV). The "seduction" is a "corruption," the ruin of the mind and heart.[282] The fundamental concern of the letter thus again comes to expression here, in much the same way as it does in 4:3-6: the thinking and acting minds of the

280. Paul again uses νοήματα ("plans, conceptions") in metonymy for "the minds" or faculties of the person. See above, pp. 165-66.

281. It is fairly clear that the verb φθείρω should here be translated "seduce," so long as we understand seduction (i.e., a leading astray) as a person's moral corruption or ruin. See, e.g., BDAG, "φθείρω," 1054. Paul is building upon Satan's deception of Eve. Consequently, the Corinthians appear in the role of the woman. The verb φθείρειν normally signifies "to corrupt, to ruin," but it also appears in Hellenistic literature in the context of moral corruption, including the moral corruption of a woman (or man) in illicit sexual relations. In the general sense of moral corruption, see 1 Cor 15:33, where Paul cites the Greek dramatist Menander in a way highly relevant to the present context: μὴ πλανᾶσθε· Φθείρουσιν ἤθη χρηστὰ ὁμιλίαι κακαί. In the context of seduction, see, e.g., Philo, *Jos.* 445.3; *Decal.* 124.2; *Spec.* 4.203.5; Epictetus, *Discourses,* 3.7.16. It is surely this sense that is present for Paul and his readers, given the preceding metaphor in v. 2. The ESV, NIV, NRSV take a half-step in this direction, probably under the influence of the prepositional phrase ("from the simplicity . . ."), rendering the verb as "lead astray." As a result, however, they ignore the sense of the verb ("to corrupt, to ruin"), and also lose the powerful metaphor of seduction that Paul so obviously employs. All three versions render φθείρειν in 1 Cor 15:33 as "ruin" or "corruption." See further their renderings of φθείρω in 1 Cor 3:17 and 2 Cor 7:2. It would have been better if they had remained consistent in their rendering.

282. Paul interprets the seduction of the minds of the Corinthians as corresponding to the deception of Eve. The seduction is entirely noetic. Sexuality is metaphorical. Paul thus stands at a distance from any thought of the serpent having seduced Eve into sexual relations, even if one might say that Paul interprets the temptation and fall of Eve as a seduction by the serpent.

Corinthians are the field of battle that the Gospel has brought into the world, as Paul makes clear in his opening boldness in 10:4-6. The practical judgments of the Corinthians seem entirely rational and legitimate to them. They do not realize that the heart beats faster than the head can think: their reasoning and judgments are predetermined by the images and idols of their imagination and affections. They cannot by their own reason or understanding remove themselves from the battle that is taking place in them. It is being fought above and beyond them by higher powers. They are the battleground between Christ and Satan, between the true God and "the god of this age" (4:4). The significance of Paul's lengthy discourse concerning the glory of the new covenant becomes apparent here. The story of Moses' veil does not have to do with the threat of Judaizing. It reveals the effect of the Gospel on the human mind and heart under condemnation and death.

Paul fears that the minds of the Corinthians might be "seduced from the simplicity that is directed toward Christ."[283] The "simplicity" for which Paul hopes again represents a significant aspect of his fundamental concern in the letter. Just as he has conducted himself in "simplicity and purity" toward the Corinthians (1:12) and has called them to the simplicity of giving and receiving (8:2; 9:11, 13), he now expresses his fear that the minds of the Corinthians might be "corrupted [i.e., seduced] *away from* the simplicity directed toward Christ." The preposition "from" *(apo)* functions within the metaphor of betrothal. "Seduction" implies the violation of union with Christ in an illicit union with another (cf. 1 Cor 6:15). Correspondingly, "simplicity" expresses the openness and freedom of communication, the communion with Christ to which the Corinthians have been called. Paul's discourse on the new

283. Although it is a difficult call, it is likely that the longer reading, "seduced from the simplicity *and purity* that is directed toward Christ," is secondary. Admittedly, the external evidence (including $\mathfrak{p}^{46}$ ℵ* B 33) is strongly in its favor. If this longer reading is original, however, one must assume that copyists accidentally omitted καὶ τῆς ἁγνότητος and thus produced the shorter reading. The omission most likely would have been occasioned by the matching endings of the nouns and the similarity of the words: ἁπλότητος καὶ τῆς ἁγνότητος. This omission is possible. But it seems more than a bit odd, since scribes would have anticipated the term ἁγνότης rather than ἁπλότης: Paul has just spoken of his betrothal of the Corinthians to Christ as a "pure virgin" (παρθένος ἁγνή). Is it likely that the scribes would overlook this term and retain the rather infrequent term ἁπλότης? It is entirely conceivable that scribes added the reference to purity in order to maintain the metaphor that Paul introduces in v. 2 and to supplement or correct Paul's rather infrequent and unexpected reference to "simplicity." The transposed order ἁγνότητος καὶ τῆς ἁπλότητος (D*) then becomes understandable, since the tendency would have been widespread, and the locus of the insertion arbitrary. The fathers of the fourth and fifth centuries who refer only to "purity" and not "simplicity" would seem to be indicative of this tendency. For the opposite judgment, see Metzger, *Textual Commentary*, 514-15. In the end, whether one retains the longer reading or not, there is very little difference in Paul's meaning.

covenant in 2 Cor 3 and his elaboration of it in 4:1-6 lie in the background of his thought. Paul continues to identify Christ with God, drawing not only on the biblical image of the Lord as the husband of Israel, but now also on the communion of God with humanity in paradise that was ruined by the guile of the serpent. This communion is fulfilled in Christ, the man (*anēr*, v. 2) who is God. As we have noted above, within the witness of Scripture, the ruin of the human relationship with the Lord described in Gen 3 is transformed by the unfathomable love of God into a mere period of waiting for the consummation of the marriage between God and his people. The entrance of the eschaton into the world in Christ facilitates Paul's characterization of the present waiting as a betrothal to Christ, who shall yet come to bring in the eschaton in its fullness.

Paul's use of the term "simplicity" should be understood in contrast to the guile *(panourgia)* of the serpent and the cleverness ascribed to him in the biblical text on which Paul draws (Gen 3:1). While "simplicity" could be regarded as a virtue in moral contexts (esp. in early Jewish writings), in the intellectual realm it was regarded as a defect. "Simplemindedness" was disdained, just as it is now.[284] Yet Paul is calling the Corinthians to "simplemindedness," one that rejects the wisdom that God has shown to be foolishness in the crucified Christ (1 Cor 1:18-19). The Corinthians must become fools if they wish to become wise (cf. 1 Cor 3:18).

4 In a second step of his explanation of his zeal, Paul sets aside his metaphor and speaks directly of the danger in which the Corinthians stand, as it presents itself outwardly. The ironic tone with which he opens this passage reappears. Paul again challenges the judgment of the Corinthians. They imagine themselves to be generous in enduring him, despite his deficiencies. He now wryly charges that they "endure it well" when someone brings them another Jesus, another Spirit, and another Gospel.

Paul here expands his preceding reference to "Christ" into a threefold form that is of fundamental theological significance. The risen Christ, to whom the Corinthians have been betrothed and with whom they have been called into communion, is none other than the crucified Jesus. As Paul has made clear within his discourse in 2 Cor 3, the apostolic mission establishes this relationship of communication with God by the outward proclamation of the Gospel and the inward gift of the Spirit, who re-creates the darkened human heart. The human relationship with Christ, and thus with God, is dependent upon the proclamation of the Good News of the crucified Jesus,

284. See LSJM, "ἁπλοῦς," 190-91; O. Bauernfeind, "ἁπλοῦς, ἁπλότης," *TDNT* 1:386-87. E.g., Isocrates, *Ad Nicoclem* (Oration 2), 46: ἁπλοῦς δ' ἡγοῦνται τοὺς νοῦν οὐκ ἔχοντας ("And they regard the simple as having no sense").

through whom the Spirit is given.[285] As is clear from the metaphor of betrothal, Paul's focus here rests on the relationship of personal communication established by the Gospel. He thus first speaks of Jesus. References to the Spirit and the Gospel then follow. Yet the three realities are obviously bound together in his thought. Where there is "another Jesus" there are "another Spirit" and "another Gospel."

Paul describes the situation of the arrival of an individual in Corinth who proclaims "another Jesus," by whom the Corinthians receive "another spirit" and accept "another Gospel." In each of these expressions, Paul draws a contrast between his apostolic mission and that of the intruder. This is apparent even in his use of the first-person-plural form, by which he indicates that he speaks of his apostolic mission and not of himself. The "one who comes" proclaims a Jesus "whom we did not proclaim." The Corinthians thereby receive a spirit that they "did not receive," and they accept a "gospel" they "did not accept." Paul's wording makes clear that he recalls his initial arrival in Corinth with the Gospel, and he contrasts it to the danger to which the Corinthians are now exposed. Apostolic claim is set over against apostolic claim. It is clear from Paul's concluding irony, "You endure it well!", that the "reception" *(lambanō)* of "another spirit" and the "acceptance" *(dexomai)* of "another gospel" are implicit in the *proclamation* of "another Jesus."[286] The Corinthians tolerate it happily when they hear something different. Their sophisticated tastes are eclectic.

Paul speaks of a single, yet indefinite intruder arriving with a "different Jesus." His wording supports the scene in Corinth that we have described already. The reference to an individual is generic, not definite. There is, furthermore, no reason to suppose that "the one who arrives" comes from Jerusalem or that he claims the support of the Jerusalem apostles.[287] As an important center of commerce and trade, Corinth had quickly become a destination for Christian preachers. This is already apparent from the divided loyalties that appear in First Corinthians, as well as the Corinthian awareness of the activi-

285. See 1 Cor 12:1-3, where the confession of the crucified Jesus as Lord is, for Paul, the distinguishing mark of the presence of God's Holy Spirit in a world filled with many spirits, "gods," and "lords." The same dynamic, in a different context and configuration, appears in Galatians. See esp. Gal 3:1-5, in which Paul's thought approximates that found here.

286. Paul speaks similarly in his appeal to the Corinthians in 6:1, when he urges them "not to receive the grace of God in vain." Here the "reception" of "grace" is its arrival in Corinth with the apostolic Gospel, not the response of the Corinthians to that grace as it was proclaimed.

287. See the discussion of Paul's opponents in Corinth, pp. 100-110. We have already noted there Käsemann's entirely correct judgment against Schlatter's thesis that the church awaited an arbitrator of their dispute with Paul from Jerusalem. See Käsemann, *Die Legitimität des Apostels,* 14-16; Schlatter, *Paulus, der Bote Jesu,* 631-32.

ties of other apostles and itinerant preachers.[288] The Corinthians have "countless teachers" (1 Cor 4:19). This situation corresponds to Paul's word about the many who "peddle the word of God" (2:17). Multiple apostolic claimants have arrived in Corinth, as is apparent from Paul's frequent use of the plural in reference to them.[289] Each has come with a claim to apostolic status that had to be defended against the others (10:12); "many boast according to the flesh" (11:18). These battles are of no interest to Paul. He is concerned about the Corinthian willingness to endure each new overture.

Paul charges that, when someone arrives, they proclaim "another Jesus" and "another Gospel." His warning is just as serious as that which appears in Gal 1:6-9. It presupposes that the proclamation differs not merely in style but in content from that which Paul himself delivered. Yet he does not spell out what that distorted Gospel might be. This silence has led to various conjectures concerning the message of Paul's opponents in Corinth, and the purpose of the letter itself.[290] But Paul does not remain entirely silent about his adversaries in Corinth. Far from it! He labels them in terms that are just as harsh as those he uses in Galatians, and does so here much more directly: they are false apostles and agents of Satan, who disguise themselves as apostles of Christ (11:13-15). Paul is by no means shy about expressing his judgment concerning his adversaries in Corinth. We should expect that he expresses the views that he regards as heretical within the letter. He can hardly imagine that the Corinthians see the issue clearly, given his characterization of them. As we have observed, this rules out the problem of Judaizing, which appears nowhere in this letter or, for that matter, in First Corinthians either. We should also be cautious about theories concerning the Hellenistic background of the opponents, even if it is clear that they are basically Hellenistic in their orientation, despite their Jewish heritage. Furthermore, the apparent competition among the apostolic claimants in Corinth strongly suggests that their messages varied. This variety might well have entailed variations on a theme, but it strengthens the suspicion that they did not have a single, coherent proclamation to offer in opposition to Paul. It might well have been useless for him to attempt to delineate their message(s), which may well have been subject to change in time. If "some" in Corinth had once offered a reinterpretation of the resurrection, they seem to have been silenced, at least temporarily, by Paul's response in First Corinthians (1 Cor 15:12). Paul does not mention this issue now. What he does address explicitly is their "peddling the word of God,"[291] their judgments based on ap-

288. 1 Cor 1:10-17; 9:3-12.

289. 10:10, 12-13; 11:5, 12-15, 22-23.

290. See again the discussion of Paul's opponents and the purpose of the letter, pp. 100-110.

291. 2:17; 11:12-15.

pearance,[292] and their boasting and self-comparisons.[293] There is every reason to take these explicit judgments as describing the fatal flaws in Paul's adversaries in Corinth. As we have noted, Paul deals with practical judgments, not with explicit theological formulations of his opponents. As *judgments,* these practical judgments themselves bear an implicit theology, indeed, a theology in close connection with life. It is already apparent that, whatever their particular theological distinctives might have been, Paul's adversaries in Corinth shared a common *praxis* that stood in the sharpest contradiction to the proclamation of the crucified Jesus and "the word of the cross." They regarded the power of Christ as being revealed in power — particularly their own gifts and powers — and not in weakness and suffering. This practical human reasoning, according to Paul, is a violation of the Gospel. It is this human reasoning, together with all the judgments that flow from it, that the Gospel overturns.

In this respect, Paul's concentration upon "Jesus" in this verse is significant. As we have noted, Paul implicitly identifies the risen Christ (v. 3) with the crucified Jesus (v. 4). He furthermore places the name of Jesus at the head of his threefold description of the mission of his adversaries.[294] Normally, one would expect him to begin with the Gospel. In placing his reference to Jesus first, he emphasizes that the Gospel has to do with the earthly Jesus, who suffered and died. But he also thereby orients his charges to the apostolic claims of his opponents. It is likely that we know a fundamental element of their theology from Paul's word to the Corinthians: "since you are seeking proof of Christ speaking in me" (13:3). On this matter Paul, the Corinthians, and the opponents are in agreement. Christ speaks in his apostles. The only question was, Which Christ? According to the apostle, Christ is known only as the crucified Jesus now risen. This knowledge of Christ requires that our judgments as fallen, veiled, and blinded human beings must be overturned; "even if we have known Christ according to the flesh, we know him thus no longer" (5:16). Only through the crucified and risen Jesus is the Spirit given. Only the proclamation of this Jesus in word and life is the apostolic Gospel.

Paul gives his statement an anticipatory form that reinforces his opening wish that the Corinthians bear with him. The "on the one hand" *(men)* does not find its counterpart, leaving it to readers to fill in the blank from what Paul has said.[295] The Corinthians gladly endure "another Jesus," but will they endure the real Jesus borne by the suffering apostle?

292. 5:12; 10:10-11.

293. 5:11; 10:12-18; 11:16, 21b; 12:1.

294. The move anticipates the closing benediction in 13:13.

295. The "hanging" μέν appears elsewhere, with a similar effect (Rom 1:8; 2:25; 7:12; 10:1; 11:13; 1 Cor 6:4, 7; 11:18; 12:28; 2 Cor 9:1; 12:12).

(2) Paul's Equality with the Super-apostles — and More (11:5-15)

[5]Indeed, I consider that I am not in the least inferior to these super-apostles. [6]Even if I am unskilled in speaking, I am not so in knowledge; indeed, in every way we have made this plain to you in all things. [7]Or did I commit a sin in humbling myself so that you might be exalted, because I preached God's gospel to you free of charge? [8]I robbed other churches by accepting support from them in order to serve you. [9]And when I was with you and was in need, I did not burden anyone, for the brothers who came from Macedonia supplied my need. So I refrained and will refrain from burdening you in any way. [10]As the truth of Christ is in me, this boasting of mine will not be silenced in the regions of Achaia. [11]And why? Because I do not love you? God knows I do! [12]And what I am doing I will continue to do, in order to undermine the claim of those who would like to claim that in their boasted mission they work on the same terms as we do. [13]For such men are false apostles, deceitful workmen, disguising themselves as apostles of Christ. [14]And no wonder, for even Satan disguises himself as an angel of light. [15]So it is no surprise if his servants, also, disguise themselves as servants of righteousness. Their end will correspond to their deeds.

Paul provides a second reason for his desire to act foolishly (cf. v. 1) and now begins to hint at the boasting in which he is about to engage; he regards himself as in no way inferior to his opponents (v. 5). He immediately turns his attention to the point at which the Corinthians undoubtedly harbor suspicions concerning him.[296] He has not accepted any compensation from them for his apostolic labors among them. This practice has been, on the one hand, an affront to them, and on the other hand, incomprehensible. It has led them to suspect that Paul does not measure up to the standards of an apostle. The other apostolic claimants have been more than happy to accept remuneration from their followers, as would have been a common practice for philosophers of the day. In response, Paul reasserts his commitment to his practice, intentionally wounding the pride of the Corinthians (vv. 7-11), and distinguishing himself from his opponents, whom he now attacks in the sharpest terms (vv. 12-15). What he has done among the Corinthians is equal to the powers they profess, but his mission is entirely different from theirs. He came to give freely. They came to take freely. The difference between Paul and the pretenders is the difference between Christ and Satan.

5 This further word of explanation *(gar)* should be understood in relation to Paul's opening expression of his desire to be foolish, as a parallel to the

296. 1 Cor 9:1-27; 2 Cor 12:14-18.

parental zeal he first offers as the ground for his foolishness (vv. 2-4). In his judgment, he has been in no respect inferior or lacking in comparison with the others who claim the role of apostle in Corinth. He has not yet boasted and become the fool, but he now indicates that if he enters into self-comparison with his opponents, he won't come out behind.

He now, for the first time, gives his adversaries a name, to which he is about to add a whole series of names. He calls them apostles "beyond measure" *(hyperlian),* "super-apostles." The expression is surely Paul's own creation. It appears nowhere other than here and in 12:11, and in both instances, in the context of Paul's comparison of himself with the other apostolic claimants. Even the adverbial adjective "beyond measure" *(hyperlian)* appears to be a neologism. The name is a dry witticism that is obviously not to be taken seriously. Paul plays upon the inappropriate comparisons that his opponents draw between him and themselves (10:12-18).[297] They are paragons of power who are beyond comparison in their own mind, and also — more fundamentally — beyond comparison according to the misguided standards by which they judge themselves. They have no understanding that Christ's power is manifest in weakness, and that apostles appear to the world as those condemned to death (1 Cor 4:9). Nevertheless, if comparisons are to be made — and Paul now feels himself compelled to make them — Paul in no way will come up short.

6 Paul immediately makes a concession. In so doing, he refocuses attention on the essential matter of the contention. He is "unversed in word," that is, untrained in rhetoric. As Paul is aware, his opponents have made much of this obvious lack, which is a manifestation of the apostle's weakness in the eyes of the Corinthians (10:10). The issue between them is long-standing and arises not merely from a gap in Paul's education but from the Gospel itself. Already in First Corinthians, Paul warns the Corinthians that "the word of the cross" is not compatible with any "wisdom of word." The Gospel cannot be shaped into a proclamation that is designed to match the tastes of its hearers. It is necessarily offensive, or it cannot save (1 Cor 1:17-18). Precisely as the friendliness of God, the Gospel remains "seeker unfriendly." The "wisdom of word" is a manifestation of the wisdom of the world that God has made foolish in the cross of Christ (1:18-25). Rhetoric and substance, form and content cannot be separated finally, even if they may be distinguished. Paul therefore did not aim at offering the Corinthians any superiority in speech *(logos)* or wisdom when he first proclaimed to them the Gospel, "the mystery of God." Indeed, he was

297. Paul does not refer to the Jerusalem apostles or the Twelve with this expression, as a number of interpreters assume. We must not forget that the Corinthian church retains the right to approve its own apostles (3:1-2), also that it has been remarkably dilatory in its collection of funds for Jerusalem, which is hardly a mark of respect. See Sumney, *Identifying Paul's Opponents,* 159.

present with them "in weakness, and in fear, and in trembling," so that their faith might not rest on human wisdom, but on God's power (1 Cor 2:1-5). In the present context, he points to the deficiency in his training: he is unskilled and unversed in rhetoric *(idiōtēs tō logō)*.

He admits the deficiency only to set it aside. He is not unversed in knowledge. Indeed, he has made this knowledge manifest to the Corinthians, "in every way, in all things." The claim — already essentially a boast — is not small.[298] Yet it is not strictly personal; Paul shifts the participle in this verse to a plural form, subtly indicating that the knowledge of which he speaks does not belong to him alone, but belongs to him as Christ's apostle. He may not have mastered the rhetoric that the Corinthians expected and required, but he certainly was capable of communicating the Gospel to them. If they had not recognized that gift up to this point, they certainly should recognize it in the present letter! Paul here recalls what he says in other terms in 1 Cor 2:6-16. The rejection of the wisdom of the world does not mean the rejection of wisdom. Just the opposite! It means the embrace of true wisdom. The Gospel has its own wisdom, just as every dimension of human knowledge has its own vocabulary and its own rules of thought.[299] This wisdom of the Gospel, moreover, remains different from all human knowledge and overturns its practical judgments. Wisdom bears its own "grammar" and form. The Gospel therefore also has its own rhetoric, which is different from the rhetoric of the world, just as its subject matter is different The apostle speaks "the wisdom of God hidden in a mystery" (1 Cor 2:7). As a "mystery," it is not accessible to the present world or its rulers. This wisdom of God does not exclude the human labor of learning, study, and practice, as is clear in Paul's own claim in this context. Yet it clearly transcends it. As Paul makes clear to the Corinthians in his earlier argument in First Corinthians, as well as in 2 Cor 3, the wisdom of God must be given by God. It must be revealed — not apart from human capacities and effort, but from beyond them (1 Cor 2:9-16).[300] No simple formula may be offered by which to separate a "wisdom of word" from "the wisdom of God." Nevertheless, it is absolutely necessary to do so. This separation is no mere mental act but an art taught by the Spirit — and therefore does not take place apart from labor in the Scriptures. It takes place by the operation of the Word in the heart and life of the one who proclaims the Word. Proclamation is a whole body-and-life event that neither we nor the apostle can control but must suffer as God's work in us.

7 Paul has requested to be bold, and he does not shrink back from it here. He turns to the other long-standing issue that has troubled his re-

298. Cf. 1 Cor 8:1-3.

299. On this theme, see Bayer, *Theology*, 74-82.

300. See the reflections on this theme offered in Bayer, *Theology*, 15-82.

lationship with the Corinthians, and maintains his ironic tone in doing so: "Or did I commit a sin, humbling myself in order that you might be exalted, [in] that we proclaimed the good news of the Gospel to you without charge?" As we learn shortly from Paul, his refusal to accept compensation from the Corinthians has led, strangely, to suspicions not only that he is incompetent but also that he is unscrupulous (12:14-18). Here he forces the question on the Corinthians as to whether his practice constitutes a sin. It certainly has contributed to the tension between them. Just as the Corinthians had hoped to establish themselves as benefactors in their contribution for Jerusalem, so they likely expected that they should have become benefactors and, most likely, patrons of their apostle. This would have entailed obligations that Paul refuses to accept, not only in the case of Corinth, but in the case of other churches as well.[301] The vehemence with which Paul defends his practice in the following verses, and the same vehemence with which he does so in First Corinthians,[302] strongly suggests that the Corinthians harbored this expectation and that it was fundamental to their dispute with Paul. Indeed, Paul's refusal to accept funds could not have become the basis of suspicions that he was seeking to defraud them financially unless they also expected that "their apostle" would welcome the common social relation of benefactor and beneficiary, probably in the form of patron and client. Paul's following reference to the gift of the Macedonians to him while he was in Corinth and the hyperbolic language he uses to describe it point in the same direction (v. 8).

Paul "humbled" himself in order that the Corinthians might be "exalted." Paul thus sharpens the question as to whether he committed a sin in delivering the Gospel without charge. Once again, he indicates that he bore the Gospel not merely in his mouth but also in his life.[303] The medium of the message must share in the message. The pattern of Paul's service recalls "the grace of our Lord, Jesus Christ," as well as Paul's earlier description of himself as "having nothing, yet making many rich" (8:9; 6:10). His language comes especially close to that of the Philippians "hymn" concerning Christ's humility (Phil 2:6-

301. Paul thanks the Philippians for the support he accepted when absent from them, serving elsewhere — including Corinth (2 Cor 11:9). The same is likely true of the help that he received from Phoebe, who was part of the Corinthian church, and whom he names explicitly as having become a patroness to him (Rom 16:1-2). It is apparent that Paul, in his letter of thanks to Philippi, seeks to prevent them from imagining that he had become their beneficiary, or that any return gift might be due from him (Phil 4:10-20). His comparison of Corinth with other churches in 12:13 makes it clear that, in other churches, Paul has been willing to accept financial support. He obviously has special concerns with regard to Corinth, almost certainly related to their relative affluence and apparent tendency to assume the role of benefactor.

302. 1 Cor 9:27.

303. See once more Schlatter, *Paulus, der Bote Jesu*, 533: "As the herald of Jesus, he recounted the history of Jesus' passion, but he not only recounted it, he experienced it as well."

11). Apostolic service takes the form of the crucified and risen Lord, whom it serves. Not only is the gift of salvation free, there is no charge for the costly delivery, either. Paul has made this point earlier to the Corinthians (1 Cor 9:15-27). He does not want his mission of proclaiming the Gospel to be merely a matter of fulfilling the obligation that has been laid upon him. He wants to be a participant in the Gospel he proclaims. This participation is his "reward." He therefore refuses to accept the compensation that rightfully is due him. As we have noted, this decision sharpens the question of Paul's having sinned. In the eyes of the Corinthians, he has sinned and is a sinner, since he has broken a social norm. Indeed, he has broken not only a social norm, but also the instruction of the Lord that those who proclaim the Gospel should get their living from the Gospel (1 Cor 9:8-14; Deut 25:4). Just as Christ was made sin and yet was the righteousness of God, so Paul has "sinned" and yet has acted in righteousness. The Corinthians will have to decide whether they will judge Paul by their standards, or by the standard of the crucified and risen Lord.

8 Paul now confesses his "sin" hyperbolically: "I robbed other churches, taking [my] wages from them for the mission to you." Not only his practice, but his exaggerated description of it depreciates the Corinthian church. They well imagined that they should be benefactors and patrons. Paul has made them into mere beneficiaries of the lowest kind. He has made them precisely what they are! In his *praxis* he has preached the Gospel to them. They are seeking God up high, where they imagine that they belong. But God is not to be found there. If they are to find God, they must seek him in that which is lowly. And at this moment, they must meet Christ in the suffering apostle.

9 Paul now becomes quite concrete about his practice while in Corinth and, in so doing, further humiliates the Corinthians. His description of his "sin" is probably to be understood as a restatement of his preceding hyperbole, the opening connective "and" notwithstanding. Even when he came to be in need while in Corinth, he did not "benumb anyone,"[304] i.e., he did not overburden them with his needs (ESV "burden").[305] The Macedonians provided

304. Although the verb καταναρκᾶν was very early interpreted as meaning "to burden" (Jerome, Vulgate, Peshitta) and is generally given this sense in English translations, it expresses the idea of "numbing" or, more precisely, as a transitive verb, "benumbing." See BDAG, "καταναρκάω," 522; H. Balz, "καταναρκάω," *EDNT* 2:265. But what sort of figure is it? Danker sees satire in Paul's usage and suggests both "knocking out" or "shaking down" (i.e., defrauding). The former is more likely, esp. since the verb bears the intensifying prefix κατα-. Paul exaggerates the suspicions of the Corinthians in order to show how absurd they are.

305. According to the Lukan report, Paul first worked as a tentmaker with Aquila and Priscilla when he arrived in Corinth. Once Silas and Timothy arrived from Macedonia, he devoted himself to "the Word" (Acts 18:1-5). It is probable that they brought funds from the Macedonians, and Paul perhaps refers indirectly to their arrival in the present verse. It is not out of the question, either, that Paul recalls gifts from the Macedonians to him while he was in

for him. Again, the lowly Macedonians! Paul has already pointed to them as an example of the grace of God in their gift for Jerusalem (8:1-5). Now he reminds (or perhaps informs) the Corinthians that it was the Macedonians who paid for his ministry to them, above and beyond any proper expectations. The churches that he "robbed" were the churches of Macedonia.[306] Now the insult is complete. The Corinthians, who imagined themselves benefactors, are in fact beneficiaries of the poor Macedonians. Paul truly shames them; or more properly stated, he helps them to find their true place in the order of things. In the end, he is merely preaching the Gospel to them through the grace given in Macedonia: "We are beggars! This is most certainly true."[307] This is what it means to be a human being. Only those who know and confess that they are unworthy beggars, who have been granted the unmerited bread of grace, are in the position of giving forth this bread to others. Otherwise their gifts, no matter how great they might be, are merely gifts to themselves and to their own reputation. The Corinthians are bound to be beneficiaries of the apostle, and not his patrons.

Paul kept himself from becoming a burden to the Corinthians and insists that he will continue this practice. Paul does so in order that he might share in the Gospel, and as he indicates in 1 Cor 9:12, does so in order to avoid providing any hindrance to it. The wisdom of that practice is now manifest: Paul is able to show that the Corinthian suspicions about him are groundless, and at the same time to point out the manifest difference between him and the other apostolic claimants.

10 Paul's humiliation of the Corinthians serves his cause in his contention with them. His reminder to them of his refusal to "benumb" or "burden" them is no mere passing comment. It constitutes a permanent marker in their relationship that Paul not only refuses to forget but promises to make known "in the regions of Achaia." Paul tends to speak of his churches in terms of their political designations as Roman provinces, and does so again here in reference to Corinth, just as he does at the outset of the letter and in the collection chapters.[308] He thereby accentuates the extent of his boasting. He is carrying out his contention with the Corinthians, and the entire province is going to hear about this matter. Paul will not be silenced.

Paul therefore boasts, and he introduces the boast with an asseveration:

Corinth in Phil 4:16: it is not entirely clear that he speaks of gifts sent to him in Thessalonica alone.

306. The plural form "I robbed *other churches*" indicates that Macedonia included a circle of house churches, as did Corinth and Rome.

307. These are Luther's "last words," written just two days before his death (WA TR 5:168.35).

308. 1:1; 9:2; see also Rom 15:26; 1 Cor 16:15.

"As the truth of Christ is in me!"[309] In contention with the Corinthians, he provides his response to their unexpressed opinion of him with the formal tone of an oath.[310] The oath itself implicitly expresses the essential matter of the dispute, the question of the presence of Christ in the apostle (13:3). As Paul earlier made clear to the Corinthians, his refusal to accept wages for the proclamation of the Gospel is nothing other than his own participation in the Gospel (1 Cor 9:23). He would rather die than surrender this boast (1 Cor 9:15). Driven as it is by the saving reality of the Gospel, Paul's boast is contrary to the social expectations of the Corinthians. He, in fact, has experienced the reality of deliverance from want by the arrival of "the brothers from Macedonia."[311] In a twofold way, then, the "truth of *Christ*" is in the apostle, in his eccentric desire to provide the Gospel without charge, and in his experience of deliverance within that practice.

It is "the *truth* of Christ" that is in the apostle. The Gospel is embodied in his life and practice, which are an expression of this truth. Paul has described the apostolic mission in these very terms, as "the manifestation of the truth" (4:2). The one who bears "the word of truth" (6:7) is regarded within the world as a deceiver (6:8). Nevertheless, he can do nothing against the truth, but only act for it (13:8), even if the Corinthians regard it as a lie. Again, the question is whether they perceive Christ in the apostle, or whether they have been blinded and deceived.

11 Paul has given clear indication that he regards himself to have a contention with the Corinthians. His attack on their self-esteem is aimed at their defeat. He wages war against all their "reckonings" (10:3-6). As he repeatedly tells them, however, the authority that has been given him as apostle is not for their destruction but for their edification (10:8; 12:19; 13:10). According to his own presentation of his mission, righteousness is given only where condemnation first arrives. Life is given only to the dead. Paul must wound the Corinthians in order for them to be healed. He acts out of love and quite understandably finds it necessary to affirm his love for them here. He does not aim at "winning" at the cost of the Corinthians "losing." The apostle and his church must "win" together in Christ.

Paul's final word in this verse is usually overtranslated. One might do better to leave off the last words in translation, which are only implicit in any case. Paul does not quite say "God knows that I love you." He says, "God knows." This statement is undoubtedly to be taken as an affirmation of his love.

309. He later argues that his boasting is not foolishness, because in it he is only telling the truth (12:6).

310. See the parallel form in Rom 14:11, and also Gal 1:20.

311. The gift may well have been unsolicited, as was the case with the later gift from Macedonia for which he gives thanks in Phil 4:10-20.

Yet the original expression bears a measure of reserve that is lost in translation.[312] Paul's love for the Corinthians is a matter finally known by God. God is the audience to both the apostle and the church.[313]

12 Paul's argument has reached a turning point. Vv. 12-15 are transitional. Now he directs his attention to the other apostolic claimants in Corinth, whom he already has named derisively.

He echoes his preceding expression of determination to keep himself from burdening the Corinthians, using a doubled verb: "and what I do, I shall do [further]." He is not going to change his practice. In this way, he hopes to cut off any opportunity for his opponents to boast that they bear apostolic authority. Paul is no pragmatic. He operates contrary to the tastes and judgments of the Corinthians. His adversaries are "seeker friendly." Paul instead confronts the Corinthians with the "word of the cross," which has brought judgment on all that the world values. He trusts that the Gospel finally will perform its work in them.

13 Paul now calls things by their proper names. The intruders, who have come with "another Jesus," "another Spirit," and "another Gospel," are nothing other than "false apostles, deceitful workers." The latter designation of itinerant preachers, who received their wages from their proclamation, almost certainly reflects Synoptic tradition.[314] Paul's refusal to accept remuneration sets him apart from his adversaries. These apostolic claimants are "crafty, wily [*dolios*] workers"; the adjective *dolios* is related to the noun that signifies "fish bait" and bore connotations of trickery.

Paul expands the two names he applies to the opponents in a verbal description: "they transform themselves into apostles of Christ." The transformation is a mere guise, of course. Only Christ works saving, eschatological transformation.[315] Paul charges his opponents with merely pretending to be apostles in order to take advantage of the Corinthians. As "deceitful workers" they work deceit.

14 The sharpness of Paul's accusation against the apostolic claimants in Corinth is unsurpassed in his letters. Not even the warning in Galatians

312. Cf. 12:2, 3.

313. We may again recall the picture of the "devotional address" that Kierkegaard describes. See above, p. 95.

314. More specifically, it reflects Q-material, however one might want to define it: Matt 9:37-38 par. Luke 10:2; Matt 10:10 par. Luke 10:7; cf. Luke 13:27, "workers of unrighteousness." See also Phil 3:2, "evil workers."

315. See Phil 2:6-11; 3:21. Paul's "transformation" of the pictures of workers, builders, and stewards in reference to himself and Apollos is an act of interpretation of Scripture, a transposition of its forms to his person. This "trans-forming," however, is not an act of the imagination for Paul but revelation of that which is real and true: the Corinthians are to learn from it "not to go beyond that which is written" in their own thinking (1 Cor 4:6).

matches the charge that he makes here in its directness: the opponents are agents of Satan.[316]

It is no wonder, says Paul, that the "false apostles" transform themselves into apostles of Christ. Satan transforms himself into an angel of light. His thought is obviously related to the Genesis narrative of the temptation, in which the serpent is described as being "craftier than all the beasts of the field" (Gen 3:1), and in which Eve attempts to exculpate herself by claiming that the serpent deceived her (Gen 3:13). It is difficult to discern whether there are early Jewish traditions that may have influenced Paul as he makes the claim that Satan disguised himself in this way. An early Jewish (or Christian) apocalypse describes the devil as coming to Eve in order to tempt her, adorned with "the form and brightness of an angel" (*Apoc. Mos.* [*Vita Adami et Evae*] 9:1). But it may well be that the apocalypse is influenced by Paul, and not the other way around. Paul's words might bring to mind the narrative of the fall of the king of Babylon in the book of Isaiah in this connection, especially Isa 14:12: "How you have fallen from heaven, you shining one, son of the dawn!"[317] But the Isaianic figure does not engage in deception. He is instead guilty of pride and overweening ambition.[318] The only possible connection between Paul's thought and the Isaianic text lies in the reference to the implicit promise of "light." The "shining one, bringer of dawn" is an ambiguous figure. He appears to bring light, but he does not have the authority or power to do so.[319] In that sense he is a deceit. In this limited way, the thought of Isa 14:12 parallels that of Paul and could be regarded as a source of his thought. In the pattern of the pretense of the king of Babylon, Paul may find a figure of Satan. This is essentially what the later church fathers did in identifying "Lucifer" with Satan.[320]

Paul, in any case, again describes Satan as presenting the danger of deception. He obviously recalls his opening expression of concern that the Corinthians might be taken in, just as Eve was seduced by the guile of the serpent (11:3). The nature of the deception now becomes clear: it lies in false appearances. The Corinthians, who look at things according to appearance, are highly susceptible to being led astray (10:7). The light that is the knowledge of God's glory is hidden in the person of the crucified Jesus, who is the

316. "If we or an angel from heaven should proclaim a Gospel different from what we proclaimed . . . may they be accursed!" (Gal 1:8).

317. Cf. Luke 10:18.

318. Not until the third century did Christian interpreters connect the figure in Isaiah 14 with Satan. See, e.g., Origen, *Commentarii in evangelium Joannis* 12.78.

319. The Septuagint has "bearer of the dawn, early-riser" (ὁ ἑωσφόρος ὁ πρωὶ ἀνατέλλων). The first term appears in several other passages in reference to the dawn of creation (Job 11:17; 38:12; LXX Ps 109[110]:3). The term is positive, even if the figure is a failure and thus a fraud.

320. See H. A. Kelly, "Teufel V: Kirchengeschichtlich," *TRE* 33:124-34.

Christ (4:6).[321] The Corinthians, who are light in him, must have nothing to do with darkness (6:14), especially with the darkness that disguises itself as light.[322]

15 Paul now makes explicit the connection with his preceding expression of concern. If Satan transforms himself into an angel of light, it is no great surprise that his agents *(diakonoi)* disguise themselves as agents of righteousness. In his description of apostolic service, Paul reaches back to take up his foundational description of the apostolic mission in 2 Cor 3. Once more, now in negation, he echoes the Isaianic association of "light" with "righteousness."[323] Apostles are mere *diakonoi,* agents of Another,[324] who have been entrusted with a mission.[325] The apostles of Christ bring the gift of Spirit and righteousness. Paul's adversaries in Corinth are likewise agents, who also carry out a mission. They offer a glory that appears to accredit them as agents of righteousness. But this glory and righteousness are merely outward and visible. Their work is pretense and deceit, just as Satan, who has commissioned them, is the master of deceit. The gift of righteousness is the surprising end *(telos)* of the Law (3:13). In contrast, Paul asserts concerning his adversaries, "their end [*telos*] will be according to their deeds." This is the state of the game that is being played out in Corinth. The warning to the Corinthians could not be sharper.

b. Paul's Rejection of Boasting — and Paul's Boasting (11:16–12:10)

After considerable delay, Paul finally enters into boasting, comparing himself to his opponents in Corinth. Even here, he asks not to be taken as a fool, before he finally expresses his willingness to be regarded as such. It would not have crossed the minds of the Corinthians that Paul's boasting should be regarded as foolish, had Paul not repeatedly made it clear that it was so. His reserve concerning "boasting" communicates unmistakably to the Corinthians the utter impropriety of judging apostles by human standards. When Paul presents his boast, he quickly changes the terms by which he is to be measured — from the boast of his opponents to the standard of service to Christ. In the end, Paul is no fool of the Corinthians. He is the fool of Christ.

321. It is quite understandable that we find in the New Testament a reference to Christ as the "morning star" (φωσφόρος, 2 Pet 1:19), a counterpart to the failed "dawn bringer" (ἑωσφόρος, Isa 14:12). Cf. Rev 2:28; 22:16.

322. See Luther, *LW* 14:31: "The lies of this world cannot become lies without first having become truth. The godless do not go to hell without first having gone to heaven. They do not become the devil's children until they have first been the children of God."

323. See above, n. 227, p. 158.

324. 3:6; cf. 1 Cor 3:5.

325. 3:3, 7, 8, 9; 4:1.

(1) Paul's Second Request to Be Foolish (11:16-21)

> [16]*I repeat, let no one think me foolish. But even if you do, accept me as a fool, so that I too may boast a little.* [17]*What I am saying with this boastful confidence, I say not as the Lord would but as a fool.* [18]*Since many boast according to the flesh, I too will boast.* [19]*For you gladly bear with fools, being wise yourselves!* [20]*For you bear it if someone makes slaves of you, or devours you, or takes advantage of you, or puts on airs, or strikes you in the face.* [21]*To my shame, I must say, we were too weak for that! But whatever anyone else dares to boast of — I am speaking as a fool — I also dare to boast of that.*

Paul intensifies the irony in this second request to be foolish, or more precisely, in the request to be a fool. He now qualifies what he is going to do and likewise aims his ironic statements directly at the Corinthians. In their self-supposed wisdom, they are the fools.

16 "Again I say: no one should suppose me to be a fool." Paul resumes the wish that he has expressed in v. 1, turning it into a request. He is going to speak foolishly, but he wants the Corinthians to recognize that he is speaking eccentrically, outside himself. As he has indicated to them, when he was once "beside himself" (in the earlier confrontation in Corinth), it was for the sake of God and of God's purposes among the Corinthians (5:13). Yet he is prepared for them to receive him as a fool, if they will only do so. He, *too,* wishes to boast just a little bit, just as his adversaries do.

17 Paul now begins to define the nature of the foolishness in which he is about to engage. He is not going to speak "according to the Lord." He is going to boast, just as many boast "according to the flesh" (v. 18). This is the only instance in which this opposition between "the Lord" and "the flesh" appears in Paul's letters. Otherwise Paul contrasts acting "according to the flesh" with that which is "according to the Spirit." The change in language is almost certainly due to Paul's christological concentration in the letter.[326] The crucified and risen Lord is the standard.[327]

He is going to speak "in foolishness, in this state of boasting." The term that Paul uses here for "foolishness" *(aphrosynē)* may connote insanity, in contrast with the alternative term for "foolishness," *mōria,* which suggests stupidity. The former connotation is surely present in this context. Paul speaks "in" foolishness, "in a state of" boasting. His earlier description of his having been "beside himself" (most likely in the ugly confrontation in Corinth) finds its

326. See, e.g., 11:4; 13:13.

327. Had Paul spoken instead of "the Spirit," his point would have been unclear, perhaps even misunderstood.

counterpart here. "Boasting" for Paul is nothing other than the wild speech of those who are insane or mentally disturbed, a "tale told by an idiot." Paul is going to enter into a spell of insanity.

18 Paul now joins the crowd: "Since many boast according to the flesh, I also shall boast." As in 2:17, his reference to "many" again suggests that he is not battling against a united front, but against a number, perhaps even a considerable number, of opponents, each of whom has staked out his own claims to apostolic authority. The Corinthians have many teachers (1 Cor 4:19).

"Boasting according to the flesh" refers to the comparisons the apostolic contenders make among themselves (10:12-18). Despite their irrelevant and superficial standards, Paul heads straight into the fray.[328]

19 Paul, who sets aside propriety for the sake of the Corinthians, addresses them ironically in explaining *(gar)* his boasting: "For you, being [wise and] reasonable, gladly endure fools." Paul characterizes the Corinthians as *phronimoi,* as those with good sense and practical wisdom.[329] They therefore can afford to bear with those without sense, the *a-phronoi.* They therefore are able to bear with Paul just now. The apostle has long been stupid *(mōros),* while the Corinthians are wise and understanding (1 Cor 4:10).

20 Now Paul shifts attention from himself to the apostolic claimants in Corinth. His irony becomes sarcasm, as Paul attacks the Corinthians in their fleshly judgments. The wise Corinthians endure it well, "if someone enslaves you, if someone devours you, if someone takes you in, if someone exalts themselves, if someone strikes you in the face." Each of the five figures of speech that Paul employs describes in a drastic manner how the Corinthians allow themselves to be taken advantage of. Their wisdom is truly marvelous! The first figure, "if someone enslaves you," likely plays upon the military imagery with which Paul begins his address to the Corinthians (10:3-6). Not only does Paul wage war, the other apostolic contenders do so as well, even if they do so "according to the flesh." The Corinthians, in their wisdom, are all too happy to surrender themselves as slaves. The second figure, "to devour someone," probably also signifies the unjustified surrender of the Corinthians in the contention with which they should have engaged. Paul employs similar language and imagery in Gal 5:15. Perhaps there is also a suggestion that the adversaries exhaust the Corinthians of their goods, since the term "devour" could be used figuratively in this way.[330]

328. See esp. 5:16; 10:2-3.

329. The adjective φρόνιμος, which overlaps in its field of meaning with σοφός, tends to connote good sense and practical judgment, while the latter has overtones of cleverness. In the present context Paul speaks of himself as "foolish" in the sense of "senseless, insane" (ἄφρων), so that it is clear that he ironically contrasts the Corinthians with himself as having sound judgment. The practical judgments of the Corinthians remain the fundamental issue with which he deals throughout the letter.

330. LSJM, "κατεσθίω," 925.

The third figure probably builds upon the image of a military defeat, but with the added twist of the idea of deception: the Corinthians endure it when someone "takes them," not by force, but by cunning.[331] Paul uses the same language to describe the Corinthians' suspicions concerning him (12:16). The fourth figure most likely also makes use of military imagery: "if someone rises up in rebellion [*epairetai*]." Admittedly, this verb often is understood to signify mere haughtiness.[332] But the use of the term elsewhere (esp. in the middle form) to signify an armed uprising,[333] the military resonance of the other terms, and the rather obvious recollection of Paul's preceding use of the same term in a military context (10:5) all strongly suggest military imagery here as well. Paul pictures the Corinthians as ruling — although not very well! — and unnecessarily succumbing to an attack upon their rule. The final figure, "if someone should smite you in the face," is obviously a violent expression of disrespect. As such, it is certainly not at odds with the preceding military language, especially the immediately preceding image of rebellion. It very likely also held a particular connotation for the Corinthians, who apparently were quite familiar with the traditions concerning Jesus, including his betrayal (1 Cor 11:23-26). Jesus was beaten by Roman soldiers and also, according to Johannine tradition, given a blow to the face by one of the underlings of the high priest.[334] The language of "striking someone in the face [*or* cheek]" is difficult to find in Greek literature. It has obvious biblical connections, in which, again, there are overtones not only of shame but also of defeat.[335] The Corinthians are illegitimately subjecting themselves to shame by their behavior.

Indeed, the entire series of images, with their overtones of battle and contention, picture the Corinthians in the place of the apostle, who is on the offensive in the battle he wages against "every lofty thing that has risen up in rebellion against the knowledge of God" (10:5). In contrast to the apostle, the Corinthians have signed their own "Munich Accord," having settled for a false peace with the false apostles. Paul thus employs a twofold irony. On the one hand, he presents to the Corinthians a scathing critique of their conduct. On the other, he shows them that he holds them in the highest esteem.

Paul again represents the contention in Corinth as that of the claims of particular individuals who each want to be recognized as the apostle of the Corinthians. Despite the number of Paul's adversaries in Corinth, they do not seem to be united, even if they jointly reject Paul as apostle. Before all else, Paul continues his campaign to win the hearts and minds of the Corinthians.

331. LSJM, "λαμβάνω," 1026.

332. Thus the ESV, NIV, and NRSV: "to put on airs."

333. E.g., Josephus, *J.W.* 2.365; 4 Kgdms 18:29; 19:10; 2 Esd 4:19; 1 Macc 8:5.

334. Matt 26:67-68; Mark 14:65; John 18:22-23; 19:3.

335. E.g., 1 Kgs 22:24; Ps 3:7; Lam 3:30. See also Matt 5:39.

21 Paul continues ironically. To his disgrace and dishonor, he has been weak with respect to the Corinthians. He has not taken advantage of them, as the others have. He has not boasted "according to the flesh," as the rest have done. The irony is again double. It is not truly shameful that Paul has not abused the Corinthians; it is merely strange that they so readily tolerate abuse from others. Furthermore, as Paul shortly makes clear, his true boasting lies in his weakness, in which Christ's power is perfected (12:9-10).[336]

Nevertheless, Paul plunges ahead in feigned recklessness in order to remedy his failure: "And in whatever someone might be bold — I speak in foolishness — I also shall be bold." As the connective particle *(de)* indicates, this last word before the "fool's speech" rounds off his second apology for boasting (11:16). Paul is now ready to play the fool.

(2) Paul's "Super-qualifications": The Fool's Speech (11:22–12:10)

As Paul explicitly indicates, he now speaks in boldness in the same matters in which "anyone else" might be bold. He follows the pattern of boasting of the apostolic claimants in Corinth. It is at this juncture in the letter that "mirror-reading" of the claims of Paul's opponents finds its best warrant.

The lengthy boast falls into four unequal and differing sections. Paul briefly presents the credentials of his Jewish heritage (11:22). He then compares himself with the others as a messenger and servant of Christ. He does so in a lengthy list that begins and ends with his labors, but which consists basically in the hardships of his apostolic service (11:23-29). His narrative of his ignominious escape from Damascus, an extension of his list of hardships, rounds off this element of his boasting (11:30-33). Just as Paul's opening assertion of his Jewish credentials and his closing reference to "appearances and revelations of the Lord" clearly counter the boasts of his adversaries, so the list of hardships and the story of the escape from Damascus are almost certainly a counterclaim to their claims of wonder-working (11:30-33; cf. 12:12). Almost from the start, then, Paul overturns the boasting of his adversaries, happily boasting in his weaknesses. He correspondingly provides only an indirect report of his "revelation," describing it as if it were that of another person, and couples it with the narrative of the "thorn in the flesh" that was "given" to him (12:1-10). The "fool's speech" is completely ironic. Paul subverts the standards by which the Corinthians presume to judge an apostle.

336. See also 11:30; 13:3-4, 9.

(a) Paul the Jew (11:22)

[22]*Are they Hebrews? So am I. Are they Israelites? So am I. Are they offspring of Abraham? So am I.*

22 Paul presents his Jewish credentials, which may be supposed to match substantially those of the other apostolic claimants. It is again apparent that there are multiple contenders for recognition as apostle: the singular form of v. 21 ("someone") shifts to the plural. Their open claim to Jewish identity does not in itself indicate that they appeared in Corinth as advocates of Judaizing. As we have noted, where Jews are inclined to Hellenize, to the point of reversing their circumcision, there can hardly be much pressure upon Gentiles to Judaize (1 Cor 7:18). As we have seen, 2 Cor 3 is not directed against Judaizing either.[337] The typical themes of the Law, works, and circumcision are lacking. Nor does Paul charge the false apostle with Judaizing or warn the Corinthians against it. For Paul, the story of the giving of the Law serves to expose fundamental realities about God's dealings with fallen humanity. The Corinthians were attracted to the claims to authority in any case. It is no surprise that they had a taste for the exotic.

The elements of Paul's boast correspond in part to his boast "in the flesh" in Phil 3:5, and likewise to his affirmation of his heritage in Rom 11:1. The claim to be a "Hebrew" most likely emphasizes ethnolinguistic identity: the distinctness of race, culture, and language.[338] In contrast to the two other passages, Paul here places the ethnic claim in the first position. Obviously a claim to apostolic authority, which implied direct contact with Jesus, would not have been convincing had it come from a Gentile who could not speak Aramaic.

The second claim, to be an "Israelite," obviously recalls the history of the people as the people of God and their special relationship to God and God's promises. It obviously bears an ethnic dimension. The Israelites are the members of the twelve tribes. Yet if "Hebrew" has linguistic overtones, "Israelite" connotes the hope and privileges of Israel. It is the first element in Paul's affirmation of his Jewish identity in Rom 11:1 and likewise appears at the head of the list of the benefits he ascribes to his kinspeople in Rom 9:4.[339] In the New Testament, it most frequently appears in honorific addresses to Jews in Acts.[340]

The claim to be "of the seed of Abraham" is obviously ethnic and thus

337. See the excursus on Paul's opponents and the purpose of the letter, pp. 100-110.

338. See Acts 6:1. In Phil 3:5 the linguistic dimension is likely primary, since Paul has already identified himself ethnically ("of the race of Israel"); unlike many Diaspora Jews, Paul spoke Aramaic, as did his parents. See also, e.g., Gen 39:14; Exod 1:15; Deut 15:12; Jdt 10:12; 2 Macc 7:31.

339. See also Rom 9:6, where "Israel" obviously signifies "the people of God."

340. Acts 2:22; 3:12; 5:35; 13:16; 21:28. See also John 1:47.

stands in contrast with the preceding designation. Proselytes could and did join the nation of Israel and thus shared in its hope. But the "seed of Abraham" remained intact. This claim likewise appears in Paul's self-identification in Rom 11:1. Whether one associated it fully with promise (as Paul did) or understood it in terms of obedience to God, the term designated Jews as the recipients of blessing and the channels of blessing for the world.[341] This connotation would not have been irrelevant to the Corinthians or to the apostolic claimants. In all these claims, Paul matches his opponents and simply reminds the Corinthians of what they in all likelihood already knew.

(b) Paul the Messenger of Christ (11:23-29)

> [23]*Are they servants of Christ? I am a better one — I am talking like a madman — with far greater labors, far more imprisonments, with countless beatings, and often near death.* [24]*Five times I received at the hands of the Jews the forty lashes less one.* [25]*Three times I was beaten with rods. Once I was stoned. Three times I was shipwrecked; a night and a day I was adrift at sea;* [26]*on frequent journeys, in danger from rivers, danger from robbers, danger from my own people, danger from Gentiles, danger in the city, danger in the wilderness, danger at sea, danger from false brothers;* [27]*in toil and hardship, through many a sleepless night, in hunger and thirst, often without food, in cold and exposure.* [28]*And, apart from other things, there is the daily pressure on me of my anxiety for all the churches.* [29]*Who is weak, and I am not weak? Who is made to fall, and I am not indignant?*

Paul shifts from merely insisting that his Jewish heritage is equal to that of his opponents to asserting that he is superior to them as a messenger *(diakonos)* of Christ. In making this new claim, Paul acknowledges afresh that he is speaking as one who is insane. He is beside himself.

The terms of the question Paul raises are clearly his own, not those of his adversaries: "Are they ministers [*or* messengers] of Christ?"[342] He again emphasizes that an apostle carries out the mission of another; an apostle is an agent and ambassador of Christ. The list of experiences that follows serves as a counterclaim to those presented by his opponents. Both the terms of the question Paul presents here and the content of his larger argument strongly suggest that his opponents never imagined presenting claims to apostolic authority in terms of service and suffering as Paul does. As his description of his escape from Damascus further suggests, the opponents' self-commendation as

341. See Gen 12:1-3; 15:1-6; 17:1-27, and esp. Gen 22:15-18; further, with Paul: Rom 4:13-18; 9:7-8; Gal 3:16-29.

342. See 1 Cor 3:5; 4:1.

apostles was based on "signs, wonders, and mighty deeds" (11:30-33; cf. 12:12). Paul's commendation is based on his weakness. The list of qualifications he presents is similar in some measure to Stoic catalogs of hardships.[343] Yet the Corinthians are no Stoics! Paul does not presuppose agreement on their part that the hardships he has suffered legitimate him as an apostle. Nor is he seeking their sympathy. He is seeking to turn their world upside down. He must do so as one who bears "the word of the cross." The list begins and ends with reference to Paul's labor (11:23, 27-29). But the manner in which he describes that labor and the terms by which he does so convey the idea of hardship, as is explicitly the case in v. 27. Paul's credentials lie not in what he has accomplished but in what he has suffered.

23 Paul now asserts, not merely that he is equal to his adversaries, but that he is superior to them. In all probability, he is echoing their claims against him. Yet the question, "Are they ministers [*diakonoi*] of Christ?" reflects Paul's understanding of the apostolic calling, not theirs. As we have noted, the term *diakonos* primarily signifies agency, or action on behalf of another. The idea of service is included within this meaning, but it is not the sole or primary sense of the term. In the present context, which Paul frames in terms of labor, the idea of service is clearly present: an apostle, according to Paul, is a "minister of Christ."

While he introduced the list of 6:3-10 with the characterization of himself (and other apostles) as emissaries (or ministers) of God (6:4), he now speaks of apostles as ministers of Christ. Christ is the one who sends them. They perform the service to which he commissions them. As those sent by Christ — Christ's ambassadors (5:20) — they re-present Christ to the world. Their mission takes the form of his mission. They are subject to suffering, just as he was.

Paul is a minister of Christ "above and beyond" the others: the adverb he employs *(hyper)* also appears within his ironic characterization of his adversaries as "super-apostles" (*hyperlian apostoloi,* 11:5). Paul is super, even beyond these super ones. Of course, he describes himself as perfectly crazy for speaking in this manner.

Now comes the list, which begins in a sort of staccato: "in toils exceedingly so, in imprisonments exceedingly so, in beatings surpassingly, in deaths many times."

As we have noted, Paul begins the list with a reference to his labor, but even here uses a term *(kopos)* that signifies the labor as "toil" and "suffering."[344]

343. This present list stands closer to the Stoic hardship catalogs than does 6:3-10, in which the hardships are interwoven with a listing of God's works in and upon the apostle.

344. See also 6:5, where, in a different order, a number of the hardships that Paul lists here also appear: ἐν πληγαῖς, ἐν φυλακαῖς, ἐν ἀκαταστασίαις, ἐν κόποις, ἐν ἀγρυπνίαις, ἐν νηστείαις.

He describes his "toil" more concretely at the conclusion of the list (vv. 27-29). The Corinthians have heard this boast from Paul already, even if they have not heard it quite so sharply: "[God's] grace did not become empty with respect to me, but I labored more than all of them [i.e., all the other apostles]. Yet not I, but the grace of God that is with me" (1 Cor 15:10). In this earlier boast as well, Paul makes it clear that his boast is not in himself but in the grace of God. He has long been "eccentric."

Paul's reference to his excelling toils naturally follows his claim to be superior as a "minister of Christ." But he immediately sets aside that theme and turns to the hardships that he has endured. His credentials lie fundamentally in his *passiones* not in his *actiones*. We know of only two imprisonments from the Lukan report in Acts.[345] Yet even prior to an extended imprisonment in Jerusalem, Caesarea, and Rome, Paul speaks of numerous imprisonments, and not merely the one that he endured in Philippi.[346]

In his earlier description of his commendation as apostle, Paul also speaks of "beatings" that he had endured (6:5). Now he indicates that he is "surpassingly" beyond the other apostolic claimants in beatings. Many of these likely came from mobs, as did his stoning. He received official Roman beatings with rods as well, as he recounts in v. 25.

Paul concludes the staccato with the dramatic: "in deaths many times." His language — as also in 1 Cor 15:31 — is hyperbolic. Yet it cannot be reduced to mere hyperbole.[347] The beatings that he endured could well bring death. The same is certainly true of the stoning he received (v. 25).[348] The threat of death was hardly new for Paul, even if an official Roman "sentence of death" brought him that threat in new measure (1:9). As one who bears the treasure of the Gospel, he also bears in his body "the deadness of Jesus" (4:10-12). He has been as good as dead more than once — indeed, many times. He lives, not because he was not truly given over to death, but because he was delivered.

24 Paul now becomes more specific and begins to enumerate the afflictions he has endured. The "forty minus one" that he received five times from "the Jews" should be counted among his Jewish credentials. It indicates that Paul remained in contact with synagogues even during his mission to the Gentiles, and that they, conversely, regarded him as one of their own, one who was subject to the punitive measures available to the Jewish community. The punishment follows the Deuteronomic instruction for the administration of justice to a guilty party in a contention (Deut 25:1-3). Since the community ad-

345. Acts 16:16-40; 21:27–28:31.

346. It is therefore possible that Paul was imprisoned in Ephesus, as we have suggested in reference to Paul's report in 1:8-11 of the "sentence of death" that rests upon him.

347. See above, p. 36.

348. See also the brief Lukan report in Acts 14:19-20.

ministered the punishment, it was easily extended to communal judgments. As we know from rabbinic materials, it was administered by Jews under Roman rule long after Paul's time.[349] We have no Lukan report that Paul underwent such punishments, even though Luke presents Paul as regularly seeking out the synagogue or at least a Jewish place of meeting on the Sabbath as the starting point for his proclamation of the Gospel. According to Luke, this was true in Corinth as well and likewise brought trouble, although apparently not for Paul himself.[350]

25 The enumeration continues. Paul follows the reference to punishments he received from the Jewish community to those he received from Roman officials: "Three times I have been beaten with rods." The rods, bundled with an axe *(fasces)*, borne by the attendants of Roman magistrates, were symbols of Roman authority. They could be used not only for beatings but also for executions.[351] According to the Lukan report, Paul experienced such a beating in Philippi.[352] His other experiences would have been similar.

We likewise know of the stoning that Paul reports from Luke: "Once I received a stoning." It took place in Lystra, after the crowds turned against Paul and Barnabas (Acts 14:19-20). If Paul had been in "deaths many times," this event was surely one of them. Luke presents a rather reserved report that leaves open whether Paul merely recovered consciousness or if a "resurrection" took place.

In contrast to Paul's two previous claims, there is nothing in the Lukan account that corresponds to Paul's next report: "Three times I have been shipwrecked. I have spent a night and a day in the deep." These shipwrecks must have taken place before the one that Luke reports as taking place during Paul's voyage to Rome as a prisoner (Acts 27:1-44). The Lukan report of Paul's rather bold scolding of the ship's crew ("You should have listened to me, and not sailed from Crete!"; Acts 27:21) seems quite natural when one considers that he had traveled more than most (v. 26) and already knew the dangers of autumn weather on the Mediterranean. He had been through it all before, more than once.

Just as he does in the list of the trials of all believers in Rom 8:35-37, Paul here makes no distinction between afflictions that come from human beings and the sufferings that arise from natural events. His apostolic mission, with its travels and dangers, brought both of them upon him.

26 Paul's reference to his three shipwrecks marks a turning point in his list of afflictions. The earlier part of the list is devoted to general descriptions

349. E.g., *m. Kil.* 8.3; *m. Ter.* 11.3; *b. Ber.* 58a.

350. Acts 18:12-17.

351. See Furnish, *II Corinthians*, 516; Harris, *The Second Epistle to the Corinthians*, 803-4; Thrall, *The Second Epistle to the Corinthians*, 2:803-4.

352. Acts 16:22-24.

of the suffering he has endured at the hands of human beings (v. 23). The enumeration of specific hardships stands in the middle of the list (vv. 24-25). The shipwrecks add the dimension of the hardships of travel. He continues that theme here, again speaking more generally of his trials, just as he did of his experiences of persecution in v. 23.

Paul's opening word, "in travels many times," extends the preceding reference to the three shipwrecks and serves as the head term for the series of eight "dangers" that Paul presents. Travel in the ancient Mediterranean world was not uncommon. But it was by no means safe. Paul presents an entire array of threats: "in danger from rivers" (bridges were rare), in danger of robbers (Roman authority extended only so far), in danger from kinspeople (as the lashings show, Paul could not count on Jews being his friends), in danger from Gentiles (but he was not safe among the pagans, either), in dangers in the city (not only Rome but also other large cities in antiquity, not least Corinth, could be characterized as moral cesspools),[353] in danger in desolate places (from the elements, as well as from bandits), in danger in the sea (as the shipwrecks attest), in danger from false brothers (see Phil 1:17!).

27 Paul now rounds off the list that he began in v. 23, returning to his opening claim that he outstripped his adversaries in "toils." By postponing any reference to his labors, he subtly communicates that the legitimation of an apostle lies in suffering rather than in labor, even though labor is obviously required of him. He underscores this point by expanding his reference to "toils." It now becomes "toil and hardship," incorporating the list of hardships that precede. Correspondingly, he does not describe his "toil" in terms of accomplishments in the continuing list, but as "hardship." He has been "in sleeplessness many times, in hunger and thirst, in fasting many times, in cold and nakedness." He speaks of the physical hardships of his service to Christ. The "fastings," which obviously duplicate the previous reference to "hunger and thirst," probably reflect the claims of his adversaries, who maintained the Jewish practice.[354] By placing the reference to "hunger and thirst" first, Paul makes clear that his many instances of "fasting" are not self-chosen exercises but periods in which he lacked sufficient food and drink.[355]

28 Paul supplements the list with a further burden: "Apart from these things, there is, besides, my daily anxiety, my concern for all the churches." His "superiority" as apostle consists in his lowliness. He does not speak of his accomplishments in planting or building churches, or in any of the remarkable deeds he might have performed. The other apostolic claimants undoubtedly offered letters of commendation from other churches that described their work

353. Tacitus, *Annals* 15.44.

354. On fasting in earliest Christianity, see Mark 2:18-20; Matt 6:16-18; Acts 13:2-3.

355. Cf. Phil 4:12.

in precisely such glowing terms.[356] Paul's commendation remains eccentric. It rests not in what he has done but in his existence and service for others. He has made his love and concern for the Corinthians clear in this letter, not only in his repeated, explicit statements,[357] but also in his framing of the body of the letter around his distress concerning them and their relationship with him.[358]

29 Paul's closing rhetorical questions clearly belong to his preceding indication of his concern for the churches. This pastoral concern extends to each person: "Who is weak and I am not weak? Who stumbles and I do not burn?" Like Christ, of whom he is a minister, Paul does not remain cold and aloof, full of power and indifferent to the state of others. He is bound to others, just as he has indicated to the Corinthians, and shares in their condition. If they are weak, he too is weak. He is speaking of something more here than the accommodation that he makes for the sake of others.[359] He is bound to his churches and each of their members, so that he participates, heart and soul, in all that they experience. That he is weak when someone in his churches is weak means that he is often thrust into weakness. He likewise shares in their failures: "Who stumbles and I do not burn?" In biblical idiom, which pictures life as a path to be traveled, to stumble is to transgress.[360] When this happens to another, Paul "burns." The metaphor conveys the burning of emotion, the precise nature of which may vary from context to context.[361] Paul is not concerned to express the particular emotion(s) with which he "burns," although sorrow and love are surely involved, and perhaps, too, anger at the cause of the failure. What he expresses, again, is his unreserved participation in the failure of another: "if one member suffers, all the members suffer together with it" (1 Cor 12:26), especially the apostle. In this concern, together with all his hardships, Paul more than surpasses the others who claim to be apostles in Corinth.

(c) Paul the Wonder-Worker and the Escape from Damascus (11:30-33)

30*If I must boast, I will boast of the things that show my weakness.*
31*The God and Father of the Lord Jesus, he who is blessed forever, knows*
that I am not lying. 32*At Damascus, the governor under King Aretas was*
guarding the city of Damascus in order to seize me, 33*but I was let down*
in a basket through a window in the wall and escaped his hands.

356. See 3:1.
357. 1:14, 23-24; 6:11-13; 7:2-16; 11:11; 12:14-18; 13:7-10.
358. 2:12-13; 7:2-16.
359. See 1 Cor 9:19-23.
360. E.g., Pss 73:2; 119:165; Prov 3:23; Isa 3:8; Sir 9:5; 23:8; Matt 5:29-30; Rom 9:33; 1 Cor 8:13.
361. See, e.g., LXX Gen 45:27; LXX Lam 2:4; 2 Macc 4:38; 10:35; 3 Macc 4:2.

Paul's brief narrative of his escape from Damascus does not mark a break in his presentation of his claims but serves as a continuation of Paul's preceding assertion of his superiority as a "minister of Christ." This narrative, together with the preceding list of hardships, offers to the Corinthians the "signs of an apostle" that they required, which Paul's adversaries offered in a very different form: "signs, wonders, and mighty deeds" (12:12). Paul's ironic, almost mocking asseveration in v. 31 lends strong support to this reading, which is likely in any case, given Paul's opening presentation of his Jewish credentials, the tone of his boasting throughout the speech, and his reference to visions and revelations as a distinct and separate corroboration of his claims. He is parodying the pattern of boasting set by his opponents, a pattern that included the "signs of an apostle." Indeed, in the present narrative, as well as in the following account of his vision, he may well be offering a substitute to the claims of a commissioning vision offered by his opponents.[362] The commissioning appearance of the risen Christ to Paul on the road to Damascus was very well known. He himself has reminded the Corinthians of it in 1 Cor 9:1. In the present context, however, he omits any reference to this christophany. In the place of his dramatic Damascus vision, he gives an account of his ignoble Damascus escape, which he will supplement with a vision narrative in the following section. Seen in this light, Paul's story is wonderfully ironic.

30 Paul's programmatic comment "If boasting is necessary, I will boast of the things concerning my weakness" serves both as a conclusion to the list of hardships, which he has ended with reference to his weakness (v. 29), and as the introduction to his brief account of his escape from Damascus. It likewise anticipates the concession he makes in 12:1.

The comment is no mere aside. It expresses the "eccentric" boasting that belongs not only to the apostle but to all Christians.[363] Paul concludes his fool's speech by returning to this theme. It stands as the theological signature of all his boasting (12:9-10).

31 Paul prefaces his story with a formal Jewish oath, swearing by the divine name itself, in Christianized form. His formal appeal to the divine name ("Blessed One") sets this asseveration apart from the somewhat less formal and less distinctively Jewish appeal to "God as my witness"[364] or simply to "God"[365] that he uses elsewhere.[366] The oath approximates Paul's lengthier solemn affirmation of the divine benefits that have been accorded Israel (Rom 9:1-5, esp. vv. 1, 5). The oath most likely reflects those used by Paul's adversaries

362. So also Heckel, *Kraft in Schwachheit*, 307.

363. See, e.g., Rom 5:1-5.

364. 2 Cor 1:23; 1 Thess 2:10; Rom 1:9-10.

365. Gal 1:20.

366. See *b. Ber.* 23a.

in Corinth in asserting their claims to apostolic status. One can only imagine that such an oath was then followed by the report of a wonder or mighty deed that they had performed (12:12). It is perhaps not irrelevant that an oath based on the divine name, which is otherwise infrequent in the Babylonian Talmud, is attributed to Honi the Circle-Maker in his petition for rain that received a miraculous answer.[367]

32 Paul somehow got himself into trouble in Damascus. The "ethnarch" (tribal ruler), who was the governor *(stratēgos)* of the city, was guarding the city in order to seize him.[368] Paul's report that immediately after his conversion he "departed to [Nabatean] Arabia, and returned again to Damascus" (Gal 1:17) by no means suggests that he spent time in contemplation and reflection after his conversion. It appears that he did just the opposite: he immediately began preaching Christ among the pagans (Gal 1:16).[369] Otherwise it is hard to imagine that he could have gotten himself into so much trouble with the Nabatean authorities so quickly.[370]

33 Paul's story ends not with a wonder but with a whimper: "and through a little door, I was let down in a wicker basket through the wall and escaped his hands." No angel appears from heaven, no mighty deed of God accomplishes his deliverance. His escape from the city is mundane. He is let down through the wall in a wicker basket, the sort of thing that was used for

367. See *b. Taʿan.* 19a, 23a.

368. On epigraphic evidence for the association of the titles στρατηγός and ἐθνάρχης, see J. Taylor, "The Ethnarch of King Aretas at Damascus: A Note on 2 Cor 11,32-33," *Revue Biblique* 99 (1992): 719-28. Paul's statement here is the only indication we have that Nabatean rule extended to Damascus itself; nevertheless, as Taylor observes, appealing to the work of Theodor Mommsen, precisely in this period the Nabatean kingdom had extended greatly. Cf., however, E. A. Knauf, "Zum Ethnarchen des Aretas 2 Kor 11:32," *ZNW* 74 (1983): 145-47, who argues that there is no evidence that Aretas IV held Damascus and that the dating of Paul's flight is difficult. Taylor seems to have the better case. The narrative has relevance for Pauline chronology and might provide a second (if somewhat weaker) link to external history, alongside the Gallio inscription (by which Paul may be located in Corinth in A.D. 51 or 52). The terminus ad quem for Paul's escape is the death of Aretas in A.D. 40. This would place Paul in Damascus somewhere between 37 and 39. See R. Jewett, *A Chronology of Paul's Life* (Philadelphia: Fortress; London: SCM, 1979), 30-33.

369. See M. Hengel and A. M. Schwemer, *Paul between Damascus and Antioch: The Unknown Years* (Louisville, Ky.: Westminster John Knox Press, 1997), 106-26.

370. Luke reports that Paul was preaching in the synagogues of Damascus, which is not unlikely either. In Luke's account of the incident, it was the Jews of Damascus that held a council and decided to kill Paul. Luke has them watching the gates of the city (Acts 9:19b-25). Unless they planned a secret action, which seems unlikely, given the Lukan report, they could not have carried out their decision without the agreement of the authorities who ruled Damascus. Paul, who had received both lashes from the Jews, and rods from the Romans, obviously was quite capable of making everybody angry. It is possible that both the Jewish authorities and the Nabatean ruler had a common cause in this instance.

carrying salted fish.[371] Paul appears silly, humiliated, and weak.[372] He appears precisely as he is.

(d) The Heavenly Revelations and the Thorn in the Flesh (12:1-10)

12[1]*I must go on boasting. Though there is nothing to be gained by it, I*
will go on to visions and revelations of the Lord. [2]I know a man in Christ
who fourteen years ago was caught up to the third heaven — whether in
the body or out of the body I do not know, God knows. [3]And I know that
this man was caught up into paradise — whether in the body or out of
the body I do not know, God knows — [4]and he heard things that cannot
be told, which man may not utter. [5]On behalf of this man I will boast, but
on my own behalf I will not boast, except of my weaknesses — [6]though if
I should wish to boast, I would not be a fool, for I would be speaking the
truth; but I refrain from it, so that no one may think more of me than he
sees in me or hears from me. [7]So to keep me from becoming conceited be-
cause of the surpassing greatness of the revelations, a thorn was given me
in the flesh, a messenger of Satan to harass me, to keep me from becoming
conceited. [8]Three times I pleaded with the Lord about this, that it should
leave me. [9]But he said to me, "My grace is sufficient for you, for my power
is made perfect in weakness." Therefore I will boast all the more gladly of
my weaknesses, so that the power of Christ may rest upon me. [10]For the
sake of Christ, then, I am content with weaknesses, insults, hardships,
persecutions, and calamities. For when I am weak, then I am strong.

In his final boast, Paul turns to "appearances and revelations of the Lord," obviously echoing the claims of his opponents. A commissioning appearance of Christ, or here, a plurality of them, served to substantiate the claim to be an apostle sent by Christ.[373] In the previous section, Paul avoided mention of the Damascus road appearance of Christ to him, substituting for it his lowly escape in a basket from Damascus. This report, too, serves as a substitute for the Damascus christophany and likely would have been recognized as such by the Corinthians.[374] Here he describes the remarkable experience of the rapture to heaven as if it came to another person: "I know [a certain] person in Christ."[375]

371. E.g., Athenaeus, *The Deipnosophists* 3.89.3.

372. On a possible counterimage in a heroic "wall-climbing" in a military conquest, see Furnish, *II Corinthians*, 542. Against such a backdrop, Paul appears as an antihero.

373. In the Lukan account in Acts, Paul himself receives multiple visions from the Lord, even after the Damascus road encounter (Acts 16:9; 18:9-10; 23:11; 27:24, and esp., 22:17-21).

374. See 1 Cor 9:1.

375. Even in Galatians, where he describes his calling, he speaks of the event, not in terms of his experience, but in terms of the work that God performed upon him (Gal 1:15-16).

In place of the commissioning of an apostle, we hear only of the experience of "one in Christ." This transposition of the apparition to another person is not merely a rhetorical ploy. It bears an implicit theological statement: the reality of the new creation is present with Paul, just as it is with all believers. Just as Paul lives, and yet it is no longer Paul, so the vision came to him, but in a fundamental theological sense, it was no longer Paul who experienced it.[376]

Second, while Paul distances himself from the revelation, he nevertheless describes the "thorn for the flesh" that was given to him in order that he "might not exalt" himself. His report of his petition and the response of Christ supplant a report of the content of the revelation. As the apostle of Christ, Paul has been granted weakness and trouble in order that Christ's power might be present with him. The legitimation of an apostle lies not in strength but in weakness.

1 Having twice requested permission to speak foolishly before he entered into boasting, he twice expresses reserve about boasting in the midst of doing so. As with his requests to speak as a fool, a mild statement is followed by a stronger one. Paul now sets aside the reserve he has expressed in 11:30 ("*if* boasting is necessary") and states the matter directly: "Boasting is necessary." It is necessary, of course, only because of the Corinthians, who have been attracted to the boasting of Paul's opponents. As Paul immediately indicates, "Boasting is not useful." It violates the meaning and purpose for which the gifts of the Spirit are given within the churches (1 Cor 12:7).

Paul nevertheless will go on to "appearances and revelations of the Lord." The noun *optasia,* which generally is translated in English as "vision" (ESV, NIV, NRSV),[377] should be rendered instead "appearance" or "apparition."[378]

376. Cf. Gal 2:20.

377. But see the Lutherbibel 1984 and the Einheitsübersetzung 1979, both of which rightly have *Erscheinungen,* i.e., "appearances."

378. The terms ὅρασις and ὅραμα are used much more frequently in the LXX and the NT in reference to visions. While the usage of the term ὀπτασία overlaps with these terms, it bears a distinct sense of its own. While ὅρασις and ὅραμα express the *reception* of a visual revelation, ὀπτασία signifies *the object or person perceived.* An ὀπτασία might well be a ὅρασις or ὅραμα, but not all "visions" have to do with an apparition of a person (or a thing). Even if they involve seeing things or persons, they have to do primarily with words, events, or actions (e.g., Gen 15:1; 1 Sam 3:10-14; Ps 89:19; Jer 24:1-10; Acts 12:7-10). Consequently, the first two terms appear to be nearly exclusively related to an inward vision, a revelation to the eye of the mind. In this respect, ὀπτασία bears a broader range of meaning: an apparition may well take place outside the mind, as an external experience. The relatively limited usage of ὀπτασία in the LXX and New Testament clearly involves external appearances. In some instances, no visionary experience is involved (Add Esth 4:17; Mic 3:2; Sir 43:2, 16). Twice in Lukan usage the noun ὀπτασία appears with the verb ὁράω: one "sees an appearance." While one might well speak of "seeing a vision" as a mental revelation (e.g., Acts 2:17: ὁράσεις ὄψονται), in both these Lukan contexts it is clear that the noun refers to an extra-mental "apparition." Those

The term signifies the appearance of an object or person. In contrast, a "vision" (expressed in Greek by *horasis* or *horama*) implies a mental image or perception. It is oriented to the subject who receives the revelation, rather than the object revealed.

The pairing that Paul employs, "appearances and revelations of the Lord," probably should be taken as a hendiadys, expressing one thought. The single preposition that governs both terms and the following genitive modifier, which likely does the same, both suggest this reading. Furthermore, when Paul summarizes his experience, which intimates an encounter with the Lord, he speaks only of "revelations," most likely summarizing both aspects of the experience in the latter term (v. 7). The pairing may well reflect the language of his adversaries, who might have claimed to have had apparitions of Christ. The pairing with "revelations" implies that what was seen bore a meaning and significance that could be communicated to others. Paul himself focuses on the aural and verbal dimension of the experiences given to him. At the same time, the pairing of "revelations of the Lord" with "appearances" suggests that these "revelations" are not merely those that might be given to any believer but specifically those given to apostles. It is likely that the genitive modifier, "revelations *of the Lord*," signifies the Lord as the object of the revelations, even if the genitive relation includes the idea of source.

The context and scope of Paul's argument, which is directed to the legit-

---

gathered at the hour of prayer at the temple recognize that Zechariah has "seen an appearance" (namely, of Gabriel, who is explicitly said to have appeared to him, Luke 1:22; cf. v. 11). Likewise, the disciples on the Emmaus road report to the risen Jesus that certain women came to them saying that "they had seen an appearance of angels," who said that Jesus was alive. These were the "two men in luminous clothing" who suddenly "stood next to them" (Luke 24:4). Paul's words to Agrippa "I was not disobedient to the heavenly apparition" (Acts 26:19) should almost certainly be taken to refer to the appearance of Christ (Acts 26:16), which his traveling companions saw as well. It was not a "vision" that was experienced inwardly but an appearance from without. The usage of ὀπτασία in Theodotion's Daniel (Dan 9:23; 10:1, 7, 8, 16), which must be explained over against the much more common choices of ὅρασις and ὅραμα, appears to conform to the meaning suggested above, since in all the contexts in which it appears Daniel sees an apparition, first of Gabriel (9:23), and then of the one in human form (10:1, 7, 8, 16). Theodotion takes these apparitions to be extra-mental events. The apparition of Gabriel is specifically set apart from the prior vision (ὅρασις) of Gabriel that Daniel had received (Dan 9:21). The concentrated usage of ὀπτασία in the Pseudo-Clementine *Homily* 17 (17.5, 13, 14, 15, 16, 17, 18, 19, 20), which appears in a debate between Peter and Simon Magus concerning the validity of dreams and visions, also gives evidence of the sense of ὀπτασία as "apparition," even if all the apparitions here are mental. The two uses of ὀπτασία in *Mart. Pol.* (5:2; 12:3) might be thought to deviate from the meaning suggested above, since they have to do with the event of his martyrdom. Yet it is his pillow, set ablaze, that appears to Polycarp. His vision might well be characterized as an apparition. On the usage and meaning of ὀπτασία, see Michaelis, *TDNT* 5:372-73.

imation of an apostle, suggest this focus as well. Paul must boast of "appearances and revelations of the Lord" because the Corinthians apparently expect reports of apparitions of Christ from an apostle. These apparitions were likely regarded as evidence for the presence of Christ in the apostle (13:3). The same interest on the part of the Corinthians may well be reflected in the faction that claimed to be "of Christ" (1 Cor 1:12). Some of the Corinthians found in their "apostle," whoever it might have been, a direct link to the risen Christ. The criterion of the reception of "revelations" also corresponds to the Corinthian interest in "spiritual" powers: together with tongues-speaking, revelations were a regular element within the worship of the church (1 Cor 14:6, 26).[379] It is only natural that the Corinthians would require them of their apostles.[380] It may well be that the Corinthian overestimation of speaking in tongues is connected to their interest in apparitions of Christ. Paul's own report of the revelation he received involves a transport to the heavenly realm and entailed unutterable words.[381] Quite likely his Jewish adversaries claimed something similar. In the heavenly realms, one might indeed receive the power to speak "with the tongues of angels" (1 Cor 13:1). Paul's brief, opening defense of his apostolic calling in 1 Cor 9:1-2 also makes very good sense when placed in the context of demands for "appearances and revelations" of Christ. Paul appeals to his having seen "Jesus, our Lord" (1 Cor 9:1).[382] This is sufficient. But as the very form of his rhetoric shows, the Corinthians were well aware of this claim: "Have I not seen Jesus, our Lord?" Neither that commissioning vision nor the fact that they themselves are evidence of his apostolic calling is sufficient for them. This reserve on their part suggests that they sought more evidence from Paul, which apparently included ongoing *heavenly* apparitions of Christ.[383]

379. As the book of Acts and Paul's letters make clear, visions and revelatory experiences were widespread. Luke in particular attests that they represent a fulfillment of divine promise (Acts 2:17-21; Joel 2:28-32). In normal instances, "revelations," the laying bare of heavenly realities, served the instruction and edification of others (1 Cor 14:6, 26; Gal 2:2; Rev 1:1). Such "revelation" did not stand in contrast to Scripture but included the unfolding of its meaning (Rom 16:25). Yet "revelation" was clearly more than the interpretation of the biblical text (e.g., Gal 2:2; Acts 11:28-30).

380. In this regard, see Rev 1:1 (cf. 22:6), which by its supra-local and, indeed, universal claim, suggests a claim to apostolic authority. Likewise, Eph 3:5, which, however, extends the revelation of the mystery of God's purpose to the prophets as well.

381. Cf. *T. Job* 48:2-3.

382. In Gal 1:12 Paul describes his own reception of the Gospel as coming about "through a revelation of Jesus Christ." As becomes clear in context, the genitive is to be understood as an objective genitive: God revealed his Son in Paul (Gal 1:16; cf. v. 24). This revelation cannot be described as simply a revelation to Paul, whether inward or outward. It involves Paul's entire life and person, in whom Christ and the Gospel were manifest in all their power. Paul's thought in Galatians corresponds to his larger message to the Corinthians in this letter.

383. On this point, see rightly Georgi, *The Opponents of Paul,* 281-82.

The Lukan account in Acts suggests that revelations were given to the apostles, and especially to Paul. Luke reports that Paul received a number of revelations beyond his original encounter with Christ on the way to Damascus.[384] One of them, in fact, came to Paul during his initial mission in Corinth.[385] Paul does not report that revelation, but another that is far more dramatic.

2 Paul first distances himself from his revelatory experience. He continues to do so through v. 5. It is not Paul who was given this revelation but a certain "person in Christ," whom he knows. It quickly becomes clear that it was Paul himself who received this vision (v. 7). At this point, Paul is "beside himself" (cf. 11:23), not in foolishness, but in the sober realism of the Gospel. His distancing himself from his own experience is not to be understood as a mere act of humility. It is a theological judgment that corresponds to the "eccentricity" that he has expressed repeatedly in this letter: his sufficiency is not of himself but God (3:5-6); he bears the deadness of Jesus in his body in order that the life of Jesus might be manifest in him (4:10). This theology is summarized in his well-known statement in Galatians, "I live, yet no longer I, but Christ lives in me" (Gal 2:20).[386] Consequently, he speaks of "a person in Christ" to whom this remarkable revelation was given. He thereby implicitly broadens the range of recipients of such a revelation. It might be given to any person "in Christ," i.e., to any believer, and not merely to an apostle. Indeed, the person remains anonymous. Paul only indirectly concedes that he is the recipient of the revelation.

Paul locates the revelation at a specific time. It took place "fourteen years ago."[387] If Second Corinthians was written in A.D. 54 or 55, the experience took place around A.D. 40. This places it relatively close to the escape from Damascus, which must have occurred between 37 and 39. In both cases, Paul reports events from the early, relatively unknown years of his apostolic mission, while he was in Tarsus.[388] The revelation was given to him when he was a nobody.

His reasons for dating the experience are probably manifold. Within the prophetic literature, visions appear at distinct and significant moments in the

384. Acts 16:6-10; 18:9; 22:17-21; 23:11; 27:23-26. See also the vision given to Stephen, who is also counted among the select group of "witnesses" to Christ — by Paul himself (22:20) — witnesses, who, in Luke's usage, are none other than apostles. Likewise Peter is granted a significant vision (10:9-16).

385. Acts 18:9.

386. See also Rom 6:5-11; 7:24-25; 1 Cor 15:10.

387. This period obviously does not correspond to Paul's second trip to Jerusalem fourteen years after his encounter with Christ (Gal 2:1).

388. See Gal 1:21; Acts 9:30. If the "first missionary journey" took place in A.D. 47 or 48, Barnabas would have sought out Paul in Tarsus around 44 or 45 (Acts 11:25-26). See further Hengel and Schwemer, *Paul between Damascus and Antioch*, 151-77.

life of Israel.[389] By reporting only an indistinct and relative time of his vision, Paul, for the moment, preserves his anonymity. He also relativizes the temporal significance of his apostolic mission; in the light of the new creation, the dates and times of earthly events are of secondary importance.[390] Nevertheless, the temporal reference indicates that the event itself was singular and that Paul possesses definite information about it.

The revelation was given in a dramatic transport to the heavenly realms. Paul's description of that transport, "whether in the body . . . , or outside of the body," which he emphatically repeats in v. 3, expresses the extraordinary nature of this revelation. In the matter of "appearances and revelations of the Lord," as well as in everything else that counts, Paul is superior to his opponents (v. 7; cf. 11:23).

His description of his revelatory transport challenges any monistic anthropology, i.e., any attempt to reduce human existence to a bodily existence that either defines or is defined by self-consciousness.[391] The same is true, as we have seen, of his earlier description of apostolic hope, which includes an intermediate state in which one is "absent from the body and present with the Lord" (5:6-8). Nothing that Paul says here calls into question the hope of the resurrection that he so vigorously defends in 1 Cor 15:1-58. Nevertheless, his dramatic reserve about the nature of the revelation given to him calls into question any attempt to limit personal existence to bodily existence. Indeed, within the experience of that revelation, bodily existence became an entirely secondary matter.[392] In this heavenly transport, the weakness of the body was transcended (4:10; 10:10). The one so transported did not know whether they were in the body any longer or not: "God knows!" Paul understands personal identity to continue outside the body. Indeed, the experience outside the body (if, indeed, it was that) transcended normal bodily experience. Paul prefers to be absent from the body and present with the Lord (5:8). Conversely, Paul's ignorance as to whether he was in the body or outside of the body leaves open the possibility that he was caught up into heaven bodily, as in the reports of the seers in the Jewish apocalypses.[393] No hidden Platonism, which seeks escape from bodily life, lurks in his thought.

The one whom Paul knows was snatched up "as far as the third heaven." He was, in other words, caught up into the highest heaven, where God himself

389. E.g., Isa 6:1; Jer 1:1-3; Ezek 1:1-3.

390. Cf. Rom 13:11.

391. See again the helpful reflections in Gestrich, "Luther mit Leib und Seele," 289-314.

392. This point is perhaps reflected in *1 En.* 70:1–71:17 but otherwise differs from Jewish traditions of tours of heaven, which take their start from the stories of Enoch (Gen 5:24) and Elijah (2 Kgs 2:9-11). See Furnish, *II Corinthians*, 525; Thrall, *The Second Epistle to the Corinthians*, 785-86.

393. Early rabbinic tradition also knew of journeys to heaven: *b. Ḥag.* 14b.

is present.[394] To enter into this heaven is to enter into the presence of God. The revelation is, after all, an "apparition." Paul's circumlocution implies this extraordinary experience without stating it directly. The same experience is reported in varying ways in Jewish apocalyptic literature.[395] Paul stands within this Jewish tradition and speaks in Jewish terms, as undoubtedly his adversaries did as well. Indeed, he nowhere else speaks of a visionary ascent to heaven, only of the revelation of Christ to him here on earth. In all probability, the "apparition and revelation" he describes follows the pattern provided by the opponents, who themselves seem to have offered reports that were similar to the apocalyptic journeys that we find in early Jewish writings.[396] At the same time, Paul's brief report differs considerably from these accounts of ascents through the heavens to the divine throne. While these apocalyptic revelations are given pseudonymously to figures that appear in Scripture (such as Adam, Abraham, or Moses), Paul makes the recipient of the revelation anonymous.[397] If Paul's opponents in Corinth made use of this form in their claims to "appearances and revelations," as is likely, they presumably did so in their own name. Furthermore, Paul offers no detailed narrative of travel through the heavens, nor does he provide an account of his entrance into the divine presence, even though the visual wonders that the seer encounters play a large role in the reports of ascent in Jewish apocalypses. Paul says nothing of these wonders. He speaks only of the aural experience of "unutterable utterances" (v. 4). In stark contrast to the apocalypses, the very point of which was to convey some sort of message, he offers no report of the revelation that the "one whom he knows" received.

As we have noted, the experience of being "snatched up into heaven" appears in the Jewish apocalyptic literature, where it also may be characterized

394. The tradition that there are three heavens appears to be older than the seven-heaven tradition. The tradition of three heavens (as opposed to two) seems to have been drawn from 1 Kgs 8:27 ("the heaven, and the heaven of the heavens"; cf. 2 Chr 6:18; Deut 10:14; Neh 9:6). See *Midr. Ps.* 2.114 (236a); Str-B 3:531; *T. Levi* 2:1–3:10; *Apoc. Mos.* 37-40; *2 En.* 42:3. On the tradition of seven heavens, see *b. Ḥag.* 12b; *b. Menaḥ.* 39a; *Exod Rab.* 196; *Apoc. Mos.* 35:2; *2 En.* 1-20; *Ascen. Isa.* 6:1–9:42; *3 Bar.* (five heavens, but corrupted?); *Apoc. Abr.* 9:1–32:6. There is also rabbinic tradition that denies that an ascent to the highest heaven is possible: see *b. Sukkah* 5a.

395. E.g., *1 En.* 14:8; *T. Levi* 2:1-12; *T. Ab.* 10:1-2 (see both recensions).

396. For a survey of early Jewish journeys to heaven, see, inter alia, M. Himmelfarb, *Ascent to Heaven in Jewish and Christian Apocalypses* (New York: Oxford University Press, 1993); A. Segal, "Heavenly Ascents in Hellenistic Judaism, Early Christianity, and Their Environments," *ANRW* 2.23.2 (1980), 1352-68; G. Strecker, "Entrückung," *RAC* 5:461-76; J. D. Tabor, *Things Unutterable: Paul's Ascent to Paradise in Its Greco-Roman, Judaic, and Early Christian Contexts* (Studies in Judaism; Lanham, Md.: University Press of America, 1986), 57-111.

397. Did the apostolic claimants offer revelations that they had received directly in their own name? Or did they use a transparent pseudonymy, in which they placed themselves in the role of an Abraham, an Enoch or a Moses? If so, Paul mimics their style without following them.

as an anticipation of what is to come.[398] Paul's language suggests that he understands this experience in the same way, since he uses the same description of being "snatched up" to describe the experience of all believers at the *parousia* (1 Thess 4:17). What Paul experienced anticipates what is given finally to all Christians, and is already possessed by them proleptically in the presence of the Spirit (3:18).

3 Paul repeats his exceedingly brief report in this verse and the next, expanding and explaining it. He now emphasizes the exalted status of the one who had the vision, which he already has introduced at the end of v. 2: "I know such a one!" He prepares for his boast in v. 5 and, most likely, somewhat mockingly offers a parallel to the claims of his opponents, who suppose that they possess an exalted status on account of the revelations they claim to have received. While Paul is speaking of his own experience, he locates it outside himself, in the "one in Christ." The one with this exalted status is nothing other than a simple Christian to whom a revelation was given.

Again Paul expresses his ignorance as to whether this experience was "in the body" or, as he now puts it, "without" the body.[399] Perhaps the slight change in wording is insignificant. Or can it be that Paul indirectly speaks of one of the many "deaths" in which he has found himself (11:23)?[400] In any case, by repeating this description of the one who was given the revelation, Paul underscores the extraordinary nature of the event. God alone knows whether "such a one" was transported in the body or without the body.

4 Paul now completes his repeated report. He knows that "such a one" was "snatched up into paradise." The term "paradise" appears as a loan word from Old Persian in both Greek and Hebrew. In the Hebrew Bible it retains its original sense of an enclosed park or garden.[401] In Jewish usage it came to refer to the Garden of Eden, as is incipiently the case in the Septuagintal rendering of Gen 2:8.[402] In the Jewish pseudepigrapha, Qumran literature, and rabbinic

398. See *1 En.* 71:16-17; also *1 En.* 14:8; 39:3-4.

399. It is not surprising that scribes tended, consciously or unconsciously, to repeat the ἐκτός of v. 2. The reading χωρίς is unexpected, has good external attestation (𝔓[46] B D*), and is therefore likely original.

400. Cf. *Apoc. Mos.* 37:1-6, where Adam is transported posthumously, without the body, into paradise.

401. Song 4:13; Eccl 2:5; Neh 2:8.

402. We find: "Καὶ ἐφύτευσεν κύριος ὁ θεὸς παράδεισον ἐν Εδεμ κατὰ ἀνατολάς." While the Septuagint retains the understanding of "Eden" as a location, it translates גַּן as παράδεισος ("an enclosed garden"), which in the Achaemenid period had come to be associated with royal parks and gardens. This rendering appears not only in the continuing Genesis narrative but also elsewhere in the Septuagint as a reference to the Garden of Eden (e.g., LXX Isa 51:3; LXX Ezek 28:13; LXX Joel 2:3). It marks the beginning of the association of the term "paradise" with the Garden of Eden.

writings, it comes to refer to the place of God's dwelling, as well as that of the deceased righteous.[403] In some contexts it refers to the age to come, which already exists, even if it is hidden.[404] The eschaton is thus given a "locality." The original reference to the Garden of Eden is not lost in this usage, which comes to expression in a number of contexts.[405] The age to come is a renewal of the conditions of the original Garden, and yet it transcends that Garden. The way to the Garden, which was once closed — a "paradise" according to the original usage is an *enclosed* garden — shall be opened. The seers of the Jewish apocalypses journey not merely to the highest heaven, but they often are said to be given a revelation of paradise, a foretaste of the eschaton.

It is again likely that Paul echoes the claims of his adversaries in Corinth, who may very well have claimed to have been transported to paradise. The claim to speak with "the tongues of angels" (1 Cor 13:1), might well be coupled with this claim, since a visit to paradise not infrequently entails an encounter with angelic beings who guide the seer, or who surround the divine throne.[406] That Paul recounts hearing "unutterable utterances" strengthens this suspicion. His inclusion of a reference to "paradise" makes clear that his thought remains apocalyptic. That is to say, his transport to heaven was not a quasi-Platonic exploration of an immaterial world. Heaven for him holds already the saving realities of the age to come. His experience, which he presents as that of a mere Christian, was a foretaste of the salvation that is yet to come to the world.

Unlike the seers of the Jewish apocalypses, and almost certainly unlike his opponents, Paul is not able to give any report of the revelation given to him. Unlike the apocalypses, he says nothing of the visual dimension of his transport. His attention here, as elsewhere, is directed entirely to words. The revelation he received in paradise was essentially an audition, not a vision. As his immediate elaboration of his report makes clear, the "utterances" that he heard were not "inexpressible" but "unutterable." The words *(rhēmata)* that he heard must remain secret. They were matters "which are not permitted for a person to speak." The visit to paradise and encounter with God was not a pre- or supra-linguistic experience but a speech event. Verbal communication took place.[407] Yet that which was said may not — or at least, may not *yet* — be

403. E.g., *b. Ber.* 12b; *b. Ḥag.* 14b; *1 En.* 32:3; 60:8; *Apoc. Mos.* 37:1-6. On "paradise," see Charlesworth, *ABD* 5:154-55; BDAG, "παράδεισος," 761; Str-B 4:1118-65. See, too, Luke 23:43.

404. On the eternal state, e.g., *b. Ber.* 28b; *b. B. Bat.* 16a; *Exod. Rab.* 307; on the preexistence of paradise, esp. *4 Ezra* 3:6; 6:2; 7:123; 8:52; *2 Bar.* 4:3; 59:8; furthermore, within the New Testament, Rev 2:7.

405. E.g., *1 En.* 32:1-6; *2 En.* 8:1-8; *4 Ezra* 8:52.

406. E.g., *1 En.* 20:7; 60:1-6; *2 En.* 30:8; *Apoc. Mos.* 25:1-3.

407. Against Bultmann, *Der Zweite Brief an die Korinther,* 224, who rightly affirms that ἄρρητος here signifies "unutterable" but interprets the experience as "ecstatic-mystical." For Bultmann, the meaning of the experience (and thus its verbal dimension) is the fruit of

communicated to others. This reserve sets apart the revelation given to Paul as far superior to anything that his adversaries might report. In this respect, he is also set apart from the prophets. He is more like those who speak in tongues, who in their spirit utter mysteries (1 Cor 14:2). But he is beyond them as well. He was granted the knowledge of exalted divine secrets. At the same time, the prohibition against telling what he has heard places him beneath his opponents. He has nothing about which he might boast. Furthermore, his presentation of the revelations as the experience of an anonymous Christian conveys the understanding that this "apostolic" experience, which outstrips the claims of the adversaries, is in reality an experience that could be — and finally shall be — given to every Christian. Indeed, it already has been given to every Christian, according to Paul, even if not in the same form: "we *all,* with unveiled face," behold "in a mirror the glory of the Lord" (3:18). What has been given to Paul in a special way is nothing other than the experience of all Christians written large and shall come to fulfillment for them as well.[408]

5 Paul is prepared to boast of "such a one" who was given these revelations. Yet he will not boast in himself, except for his weaknesses. Of course, Paul is the one who was carried into paradise. As we have noted, he distances himself from himself, not simply as a rhetorical move, but as a theological statement. He has made clear that the experience he was granted effectively belongs to any and every Christian. It belongs to them, not as a natural possession, but as the reality of the new creation, in which they share in Christ. Paul is prepared, then, to boast in Christ. Yet Christ dwells in weakness, including the weakness of the apostle. Paul therefore is not prepared to boast in himself in any other way than in his weaknesses. He has already said so (11:30), and he will make the point again profoundly in the conclusion of his report (12:7-10).

6-7a Now comes the turn in Paul's report. Given the nature of his account of the revelations, it is fairly clear that he is speaking of himself, even if he is "beside himself." Here and in the following verse he makes it obvious that he is describing an experience given to him.

---

the originally prelinguistic experience. The interpretation reflects the essence of Bultmann's program, but not of Paul's message. Indeed, Paul is not at all sure that the experience was "ecstatic." Whether he was outside himself — i.e., his body — only God knows.

408. Paul's earlier word to the Corinthians — that God, by the Spirit, has revealed "what eye has not seen, and ear has not heard, and which has not arisen in the human heart" (1 Cor 2:9-16) — corresponds to what he says here. There he speaks of that which he can communicate as an apostle, by "spiritual words" (v. 13). But the matters he communicates are finally given to human understanding and placed within the human heart by the Spirit of God (vv. 10-12). The Spirit operates not apart from the apostolic word but through it. By the work of the Spirit, then, "God's wisdom in a mystery" (v. 7) and "the mind of Christ" (v. 16) belong to every believer. They both have them and do not have them yet, but they must await the eschaton — into which Paul reports that he was carried in the present text.

The explanation he provides *(gar)* relates to the latter part of his statement in v. 5. He will not boast on his own behalf, except in his weaknesses. This implies that he might, in fact, boast on behalf of himself, which, in turn, implies that Paul might redirect his boasting on behalf of the anonymous Christian into a boast on his own behalf. If he should decide to do so, he will not be a fool, because he will be telling the truth. In other words, Paul is making clear in no uncertain terms that he could well boast about himself and his experience, if he wished to do so.

He refrains from this boasting because he does not want anyone to "reckon" or ascribe something to him beyond what they *see* with respect to him, or *hear* from him, "even with the surpassing thing of the revelations."[409] He is not permitted, after all, to speak the utterances that he heard. He is permitted only to speak the Gospel as a word of faith (4:5, 13). This is what the Corinthians are to hear from him. But what are they to see? In the first instance, they see the weakness of his bodily presence. They also see and hear his contemptible skill as a speaker (10:10). They see one who must face insults, needs, persecutions, and straitened circumstances, as Paul again reminds them shortly (v. 10). But precisely in this weakness, they see the power of Christ (v. 9). Paul bears the deadness of Jesus so that the life of Jesus might be manifest in him (4:10). This is his message to them: in this way he is their servant on account of Jesus (4:5). The Corinthians are thus to see the love of Christ in the apostle who loves them (5:14-15; 11:11; 12:15).

7b Along with the surpassing revelations of the Lord, Paul was also sent affliction from Satan. The visit to heaven is accompanied by visits from hell. Paul's report of these attacks, together with his petition and Christ's response, stand in the place of a report of a heavenly revelation that is characteristic of the Jewish apocalypses, and almost certainly was likewise characteristic of the claims of the opponents. The transport to the third heaven and to paradise is not properly Paul's own experience, but it is that of "one in Christ." Nor are there any revelations to report. What was heard in heaven must remain in heaven. Paul thus makes good on his pledge that he will boast only in his weaknesses (v. 5), and he counters his adversaries' claims of ethereal revelations with his account of earthly suffering in which he received a revelation from Christ.

Twice, at both the beginning and the end of the account, Paul states that affliction was given to him "in order that I might not exalt myself."[410] As the

409. As the editors of NA^{27} and UBS^{4} recognize, together with the ESV, NIV, and NRSV, v. 7a belongs with v. 6. The decision is largely determined by the recognition of the originality of the connective διό, which marks the beginning of a new period; on which, see Metzger, *Textual Commentary*, 516.

410. It is no surprise that the repetition resulted in textual variants that omit the final clause. The twofold form is well attested, however (including $\mathfrak{p}^{46}$ B). The emphatic repetition, furthermore, makes good sense in context. So also, Metzger, *Textual Commentary*, 517.

connective "therefore" *(dio)* itself makes clear, Paul's account of his affliction is an extension of his determination not to boast. The "superiority *(hyperbolē)* of the revelations" might lead Paul to "present himself as superior" *(hyperairō)*. Paul is not different from others. He himself might do what he accuses the Corinthians of tolerating and his adversaries of doing.[411] Although they are the "super-apostles" (at least in their own mind), he is superior to them.[412] Yet he will not boast.

His decision to refrain from boasting does not stand alone. The action of God that he suffers prevents him from exalting himself. What others see in Paul (v. 6) includes the affliction brought to him by Satan's angel (v. 7). Paul speaks quite directly of a "thorn for the flesh" as having been *given* to him, or, more likely, *for* him. The purpose of the "thorn" in preventing self-exaltation, as well as Paul's wider usage of "flesh" in reference to the fallen human being, indicate that the dative relation, "for the flesh," is to be taken as a benefit for Paul.[413] But how can God be at work and, indeed, "give" to Paul through Satan and Satan's angel? How does God work good through suffering and evil? Paul does not answer the endless questions that might be raised at this point. Yet, here, at the very start of his account, he implicitly provides an answer that is more than sufficient for the final questions of the human heart. God uses evil, even Satan himself, for Paul's good. Who can explain this wonder?[414] Is there any story line that we might draw that can explore its depths? It is the story of Christ's cross being replayed in Christ's apostle. Paul himself is giving an account of it. Yet he cannot see to the bottom of it; he cannot figure it out. Indeed, he *resists* the evil that has come to him by the only means available — prayer. If God's dealings with Paul took place in a recognizable story line, resistance to "the will of God" would have been disobedience. The "thorn" was given to Paul to prevent him from exalting himself. If that were its sole purpose and sufficient explanation, Paul should have accepted it as God's will. Protest would have been blasphemy. But Paul does resist. He petitions the Lord three times that "the thorn" might be removed from him, just as Jesus resisted the cross three times in the garden. Paul's action, like that of Jesus, sets a pattern: Christians are protesters against death[415] — except at the point at which they, like Jesus, must accept it. [416]

411. See 11:20; cf. 10:5.

412. 11:5, 23; 12:11.

413. Whether one then should categorize the dative as a *dativus commodi* or a *dativus incommodi* remains open. What is a disadvantage to the flesh, and Paul's fallen person, is an advantage to Paul, as his account makes clear. In this matter, the Holy Spirit has his own grammar.

414. Cf. Luther, *LW* 33:175-78, 289-92 ("The Bondage of the Will").

415. Christoph Blumhardt, "Wir sind Protestleute gegen den Tod." The citation is well known but generally without specific reference. I have drawn it from a sermon preached by Oswald Bayer in the Stiftskirche, Tübingen, July 1, 2012.

416. One thinks here of the original German title of Bonhoeffer's *Letters and Papers*

Nevertheless, Paul's petition, like that of his Lord, was rejected. The answer that he received could not answer his questions. Nevertheless, Christ's answer was sufficient for Paul. His petitions ceased. He came to accept the work of God that he was called to "suffer," without being able to fully understand or explain it. It was simply enough to know that Christ's grace was sufficient for him and that Christ's power finds its purpose and place in his weakness. What Paul recounts here is an instance of the comfort that abounds within the sufferings and afflictions that are his in Christ.[417] This apostolic existence is nothing other than Christian existence written large.

The term *skolops,* which is generally translated "thorn," signifies a pointed object. In the three instances it appears in the Septuagint, it refers to thorns.[418] Elsewhere it is used often for larger objects, especially the pickets or stakes used in constructing palisades.[419] It also appears in Plutarch (A.D. 45-120) in connection with impalement as an alternative to crucifixion.[420] Yet Paul here can hardly be thinking of impalement or crucifixion.[421] He has received the *skolops* and petitions the Lord to remove it three times, characterizes it as continuing beatings, and does not at all suggest that death impends for him. The usage of the Septuagint is not determinative for Paul, but Paul's usage basically corresponds to it, without necessarily being dependent on it. The traditional rendering as "thorn," which is drawn from the Septuagint, is perfectly acceptable, although "spike" is also possible.

Paul immediately interprets the "thorn for the flesh" by the apposition: "an angel of Satan." The term *angelos* might be rendered "messenger" (ESV, NIV, NRSV). But Paul most likely offers his report as a counterclaim to the claims of his adversaries to have been transported to heaven, as Paul himself does indirectly in vv. 2-4. Angels are a regular feature of these journeys, both as guides and as they are gathered in array surrounding the heavenly throne. The angel sent from Satan to Paul in his earthly weakness replaces the angel of a transport and the vision of angels at the throne of God. The one transported to heaven remains bound to the weakness of flesh and subject to the attacks

---

from Prison (ed. E. Bethge; New York: Macmillan, 1972), namely, *Widerstand und Ergebung* ("Resistance and Submission"), which characterizes Bonhoeffer's thought as it appears in his letters, and esp. his opening account, "After Ten Years," in 1942-43.

417. 1:3-7.

418. LXX Num 33:55; LXX Hos 2:8(6); Sir 43:19.

419. E.g., Appian, *Bellum Civile* 5.4.36.16. See LSJM, "σκόλοψ," 1613; BDAG, "σκόλοψ," 930-31; G. Delling, "σκόλοψ," *TDNT* 7:409-13.

420. Plutarch, *Moralia* 499d: "ἀλλ' εἰς σταυρὸν καθηλώσεις ἢ σκόλοπι πήξεις;" See also Philo, *Flacc.* 84.1, "ὁ δ' οὐ τετελευτηκότας ἐπὶ σταυρῶν καθαιρεῖν, ζῶντας δ' ἀνασκολοπίζεσθαι προσέταττεν." See Hengel, *The Cross of the Son of God*, 124. Later, Origen connects a "stake" with the "cross," *Contra Celsum* 2.55.

421. Against Schlatter, *Paulus, der Bote Jesu*, 666.

of hell. Even if one should translate *angelos* as signifying a "messenger" here, one nevertheless should take it as referring to an angel. Paul is hardly speaking of his adversaries, even if he has described them in similar terms (11:12-15). There are a number of them, but only one who has come from Satan. They take advantage of Paul's weakness, but the angel from Satan is a cause of weakness. It is not at all strange that Paul should speak of an "angel of Satan." Like the afflictions of Job (Job 1:6–2:13), Paul's afflictions came to him as a blow from Satan. In Matthew's gospel, Jesus speaks of "the devil and his angels" (Matt 25:41). The same understanding appears in the New Testament apocalypse (Rev 12:7, 9) and elsewhere in early Jewish writings.[422]

This angel of Satan cuffs and buffets Paul, just as Satan or other angels appear delivering blows in Scripture; one thinks again of the experience of Job.[423] He delivers Paul beatings, regularly or, perhaps, continuously; the present tense of the verb suggests an ongoing trial. But what sort of affliction does Paul have in mind? He speaks only metaphorically, and intentionally so. Interpreters long have speculated on precisely what Paul had in mind, but this is largely beside Paul's point. There are three primary possibilities.[424] It is unlikely, as we have noted, that Paul is speaking of his adversaries, a view common in the early fathers. Nor is it likely that he is speaking of sexual temptation, a view common in the medieval period, which arose from the misleading Latin rendering "*stimulus carnis.*" Perhaps we should be hesitant to conclude that Paul refers to some physical affliction or malady, even if this conclusion seems the most likely.[425] The periodization of the interpretations suggests that each time reads its own concerns into the text. The idea that Paul suffered from a malady of the eyes is unlikely, as it derives from a misreading of a metaphor in Gal 4:15.[426] Epilepsy has been a popular alternative, but it is not compelling. It might be that Paul suffered from migraine headaches,

422. E.g., *T. Dan* 6:1; *T. Ash.*6:4; *Exod. Rab.* 250. See U. Heckel, "Der Dorn im Fleisch: Die Krankheit des Paulus in 2Kor 12,7 und Gal 4,13f," *ZNW* 84 (1993): 70; Str-B 1:139 (h); 1:984 (a).

423. See Job 2:7; 2 Sam 24:17.

424. On this question, see Heckel, "Der Dorn im Fleisch"; Thrall, *The Second Epistle to the Corinthians,* 809-18.

425. See Heckel, "Der Dorn im Fleisch," 78-80, 83-85, who rightly points out how sicknesses or physical disabilities are frequently attributed to Satan in Scripture and early Jewish literature, and that these maladies are associated often with blows. See, e.g., Luke 13:10-17; Job 2:7; Acts 10:38. He makes a very good case that the weakness that Paul describes in Gal 4:13-14 is also associated with Satan: you Galatians, Paul says, "did not spit me out." Spitting was an apotropaic act, intended to ward off demons or evil (e.g., *T. Sol.* 7:3).

426. The Galatians' willingness to "tear out their eyes" and give them to Paul metaphorically expresses a love that is ready to make tremendous sacrifices, much like the modern being willing to "give one's right arm."

which would fit the metaphor of beatings.[427] But in the end, only God knows the affliction that was given to Paul. Indeed, it may well have been a variety of afflictions: Paul identifies the "thorn" with a messenger of Satan. The numerous beatings that this one delivers may encompass all of the sufferings that the apostle names and more (11:23-33).

8 Paul did not simply accept the thorn in his flesh, even if it was given by God: "Three times I appealed to the Lord, that he might remove it from me." He was a poor Stoic: he did not seek mere self-contentment or the power to persevere. But he was a good Christian, who was not afraid to bring his petition to Christ in prayer, and most likely his lament as well.[428] That he petitioned the Lord "three times" corresponds to the implicit understanding that appears in the Scriptures (and beyond) that an action is brought to completion by its third occurrence.[429] This understanding of a thrice-repeated act as bringing its completion applies to prayer, as is apparent from Jesus' prayer in Gethsemane, which Paul's report naturally recalls.[430] The concreteness of Paul's account implies deliberate, specific prayer and, as with Jesus, bold resistance. With the third petition, Paul ceased further to ask for the removal of the thorn. The answer he received was not the one for which he asked, but it was one that was more than sufficient for him.[431] His appeal to the Lord is nothing other than an appeal to the crucified and risen Christ, who speaks to him in response to his prayer.

9 Just as the angel of Satan appears on earth in place of the interpreting angel of apocalyptic visions in heaven, so the usual report of the heavenly revelations, which the adversaries offered, is replaced here by the word of Christ to Paul in the midst of earthly weakness and suffering. Paul here presents a report of apostolic revelation in the form in which it must be communicated. In the place of "unutterable utterances," he is given, for his comfort, a definite word from Christ, which he passes on to the Corinthians. This word did not match their heavenly tastes, but it spoke to their earthly needs.

Christ did not remove the thorn from Paul. Yet Christ did not remain silent or give him a dismissive No! He gave Paul an answer that arrived, not simply from the heights of the divine throne, but from the depths of human

427. See Heckel, "Der Dorn im Fleisch," who includes a thorough survey and critique of the alternatives.

428. Rightly noted by Heckel, *Kraft in Schwachheit*, 317.

429. E.g., Exod 23:14; Num 22:28; 24:10; 1 Sam 3:8; 20:41; 1 Kgs 18:34; Mark 14:30 (and par.); John 21:14; Acts 10:16; and in this very letter, 12:14; 13:1.

430. Mark 14:41 and par. See also 1 Kgs 17:21; Dan 6:10.

431. Paul describes his experience as apostle in a related way in 4:16-18: although his outer person is being destroyed, his inner person is made anew day by day. As Luther notes, Christ's method is not to remove the evil from the person but to remove the person from the evil. See above, n. 409, p. 216.

suffering and need. Christ spoke to Paul as the one who himself was "crucified in weakness" but "lives by the power of God" (13:4). His answer contains within itself the wonder of his own suffering and deliverance. His word to Paul is inseparable from his person: "My grace is sufficient for you, for power is perfected in weakness."

Christ's grace is sufficient for Paul. Like the self-sufficiency *(autarkeia)* that Paul promises the Corinthians (9:8), the sufficiency of Christ's grace is a sufficiency in communication. Paul's relief comes not in the removal of the thorn but in an abiding relation with Christ. As he has repeatedly made clear in this letter, salvation is granted not through the possession of gifts and powers but in participation in Christ, one that takes the form of verbal communication. Here and elsewhere with Paul, grace is before all else personal favor. It would be a mistake, therefore, to equate "grace" with "power," despite the close connection between them. The power of Christ never becomes Paul's possession, but it remains a constant gift of Christ's grace. Weakness and power paradoxically coincide in Christ's apostle, just as they do in Christ himself.

Nevertheless, Christ's grace for Paul is not an abstract or general experience of Christ's favor. It is found in the work of Christ that remains present in his person. Paul has already reminded the Corinthians that they know the "grace of our Lord, Jesus Christ" quite concretely: "Being rich, he for your sake became poor, in order that you, through his poverty, might become rich" (8:9). Christ's self-giving love in the incarnation and cross is present afresh in the suffering of the apostle.

Christ gives Paul a word of explanation as to why his grace is sufficient for him: "For power is perfected in weakness." This word of Christ to Paul appears in a surprisingly general form. It is not surprising that there was a scribal tendency to make Christ's word definite: "for *my* power is perfected in weakness." Yet the statement without the qualifier is more likely original.[432] Nevertheless, Christ's word to Paul should not be interpreted as a general statement, but as a christologically grounded absolute. It is not a statement about what happens at all times and all places in the world. If that were so, the Corinthians would have recognized it long before. The rulers of this age would not have crucified the Lord of glory (1 Cor 2:8). Christ's word is specifically bound to Christ's cross and resurrection. The form in which it appears constitutes an *absolute* claim that is yet to be established in the world. This will only come at the resurrection of the dead. Then, and only then, all other rulers,

432. A number of important witnesses read, "For *my* power is perfected in weakness" ($\aleph^2$ A D^1). Yet the witnesses that lack "my" are even stronger (e.g., $\mathfrak{p}^{46vid}$ $\aleph^*$ B D^*), and there is inducement from the end of the verse, where Paul speaks of "the power of Christ," to read it into the opening words. The general statement is decidedly the more difficult and thus is to be preferred.

powers, and authorities will be done away with (1 Cor 15:24). God's power then will remain alone, as power absolute.

As Christ's word makes clear, "power" (i.e., the absolute power of God) has a goal or end. It is to be "perfected in weakness." It is contrary to all human expectations, especially as they are voiced in the thought of Thomas Hobbes. For him, human power, in its striving at good and well-being, always seeks to increase itself in the domination of other human beings.[433] God's power moves in precisely the opposite direction: the One who dwells "in a high and holy place" dwells with the lowly (Isa 57:15). The One who is seated on high does not look up but looks down, far, far below, to the poor and needy in order to lift them out of dust and ashes (Ps 113:4-9). Christ's word to Paul stands within this biblical tradition. The goal of God's power is not to increase itself (which could not be done) but to lower itself so that it is present and dwells within human weakness and need. This is precisely what has taken place in the resurrection of Christ, the Crucified One. As Paul repeatedly has made clear, and will do once again, the risen Christ is none other than the crucified Jesus (13:4). Weakness remains in the Risen One, even though it has been decisively overcome; one need only think of the Gospel reports of the nail prints in Christ's hands to recognize this truth. What is true for the risen Christ is also true for the apostle and for all Christians. God wills, through Christ, to dwell in human weakness. The christological specificity of this word is not to be forgotten, or else one will land in a liberation theology of one form or another, or in an abuse of the earthly powers and roles of authority that have been temporarily granted to us.

Paul follows the word of Christ to him with a word to the Corinthians: "I shall therefore most gladly boast much in my weaknesses in order that the power of Christ might encamp upon me." He immediately broadens the sphere of reference of Christ's word beyond the thorn for his flesh to include all his weaknesses and thus addresses the issue at stake in Corinth. This boasting in weaknesses should not be regarded as means by which Paul gains Christ's power. It is the response of faith to the word of Christ. Otherwise, he would only repeat the Corinthian error in passive-aggressive form. He does not intend to launch a new competition for recognition in masochism. Paul boasts in his weaknesses, he does not glorify them. They are neither self-imagined failures or self-attained deprivations. His opening word, which is of fundamental importance, takes on fresh significance here: the thorn was *given* to Paul (v. 7). He did not seek it or ask for it. Just the opposite. Nor does he seek or ask for new problems. The Corinthians make enough trouble for him already. Weaknesses and afflictions are received passively. They arrive unexpected, unannounced, and undesired. To boast in one's weaknesses, as Paul does, is to

433. T. Hobbes, *Leviathan* (ed. E. Curley; Indianapolis, Ind.: Hackett, 1994), xix-xxi, 58.

speak in faith.[434] It is to await the fulfillment of the Yes of God, given already in Jesus, in one's own body and life (cf. 1:20). It is to be operated upon by "the grace of Christ," which is sufficient in itself, and requires no assistance to its end by those to whom it is given.

Nevertheless, within Christ's grace (and not as a condition to it) there is a place for response. Paul boasts in his weaknesses "in order that the power of Christ may encamp upon me." The grace given must be received, even if that reception is worked by grace itself. The grace of Christ, which appears within Christ's word to Paul as a presupposed, unconditioned reality, grants Paul the freedom of boasting in his weaknesses. In the definite word by which it arrives, grace establishes the relationship and response of faith.

Paul describes this relationship here in imagery drawn from Israel's sojourn in the wilderness. He wants "the power of Christ" to "encamp" upon him, that is, to "dwell as in a tent upon him [*episkēnoō*]."[435] Earlier in the letter, he uses the image of a tent, drawn again, no doubt, from Israel's story, to characterize earthly life as temporary, a mere anticipation of the building in heaven we await (5:1-4). It is likely that Paul has the transitory nature of earthly life in view in his use here of tabernacle language. He thereby underscores the dramatic condescension of Christ, who, although he is risen Lord, wills to cause his power to rest upon Paul's frail, earthly frame. As he already has indicated to the Corinthians, he bears the "deadness of Jesus" in his mortal body in order that the life of Jesus might be manifest in him (4:10-12). His language here is unique in that he stresses his desire that the "power of Christ" might "dwell *upon*" him.[436] He thereby emphasizes that the distinction between Christ's power and his weakness abides. Power is "perfected" in weakness. Power overcomes it without doing away with it. As Paul makes clear in 5:1-10, this relation shall take a different form at the eschaton, when "the mortal will be swallowed up by life" (5:4; cf. 1 Cor 15:53). Nevertheless, as Paul's reference to the crucified and risen Jesus shows (13:4), even when Christ's power has its final triumph over our weakness, the relationship between our inherent weakness and Christ's power will remain. Paul does not describe here a reality of the present life only, but a reality that endures into all eternity.

Paul speaks not of "Christ" but of "the power of Christ" encamping upon him. This shift is slight, but significant. It obviously arises from the word of Christ given to him, in which the transition from person to power takes place: Christ's grace implies the presence of power. It is a power that is sufficient for Paul in all his human weaknesses, not least in the attacks from Satan's angel.

434. Cf. 4:13; Rom 5:1-3.

435. Cf. the similar language in John 1:14; Rev. 7:15; 21:3.

436. As is fairly common in Greek, the emphasis appears in the preposition ἐπί reappearing in the prefix of the verb ἐπι-σκηνόω.

This transition in thought implies ultimate, absolute power, as becomes especially apparent when one considers the qualification ("my power") introduced by the secondary reading. Absolute power can belong only to God. In speaking of "power" as the benefit that he brings, Christ identifies himself with God. The same identification is implicit in his word concerning his "grace." In the proper sense, as unconditioned favor and giving, "grace" and "power" belong to God alone.

10 A second explanatory statement follows. If the first is oriented to Paul's life as a whole, the second is immediate to Paul's circumstances: "therefore I am well content with weaknesses." In his preceding explanatory word, Paul, in his response to Christ's word to him, has broadened it to encompass the whole of his life. He continues that broadened scope of his response here: he will boast in weaknesses and is well content with weaknesses. Now he becomes specific, listing four elements of apostolic experience: "[I am well content] . . . with assaults, with distresses, with persecutions, and with straitened circumstances." The terms recall the list of hardships with which Paul opens his "fool's speech" in 11:23-27. In bringing this speech to a close, he rounds it off by returning in summary to the opening, forming an inclusio. The second and fourth terms, "distresses" and "straitened circumstances" ("hardships"), have appeared already in the list of "Paul's hardships and God's works" (6:3-10, esp. v. 4). The first and third terms, "assaults" and "persecutions," are new. While the former term *(hybris)* may well refer to the forces of nature (e.g., Acts 27:10, 21), it may also refer to attacks by persons (e.g., Sir 10:6, 8) and likely does so here. In this list, Paul thus alternates between references to violence done to him by other persons and the hardships he has endured in his travels. The four terms provide a complete summary of his apostolic credentials.

Weaknesses, assaults, distresses, persecutions, and hard times come to Paul "on behalf of Christ." The phrase, which falls at the end of the list, modifies the list. Paul does not say that he is *content* on behalf of Christ (ESV, NIV). He says that *weaknesses and hardships* come to him on behalf of Christ (NRSV). This thought is present in Christ's word to Paul: "power is perfected in weakness" (v. 9).[437] It likewise appears in Paul's unusual opening word, that he does not want the Corinthians to be uninformed "on behalf of our affliction," an affliction that is an instance of the sufferings of Christ in which he shares (1:8). Paul's description of the purpose of Christ's death, "that those who live . . . might live *on behalf of* him who died and was raised" (5:15), finds its expression in the life of the apostle. Out of this experience, Paul makes appeal "on behalf of Christ" (5:20). The apostle serves the risen Lord, not fundamentally in his *doing* (although he is highly active), but in his *suffering*

437. See also the Lukan report of the word of the Lord to Ananias concerning Paul: "I will show him how much he must suffer on behalf of my name" (Acts 9:16).

and being *delivered*. Christ's power comes to perfection *not* in his gifts and abilities but in his weakness.

Paul is "well content" in these weaknesses and hardships on behalf of Christ. The term "well content" was used as a summary of Epicurean thought by Philodemus of Gadara.[438] If the Corinthians made the connection, Paul would here appear as the anti-Epicurean, who does not seek pleasure. He seeks Christ.

Paul concludes his "fool's speech" with a final explanation of his contentment with his troubles: "For when I am weak, then I am powerful." This last word makes clear that the life of the apostle, as difficult as it was, was not a constant disaster. That there were times of trial implies also that there were times of deliverance and times of peace. Paul is content to meet the hardships because when he is weak, then he is powerful. The statement is obviously paradoxical. It is not that weakness attempts to subvert power, as Nietzsche supposed.[439] Nor is it the case that the weakness is outward but the strength is inward, as with the Stoics. Paul's statements in 4:16-18 are not to be taken in that sense.[440] The paradox is based in Christ and his saving work. When Paul is weak, then he is powerful. The power is not his, nor does it become his, as the temporal limitation of his statement makes clear: "*when* I am weak, *then* I am powerful." The power that comes to Paul remains the power of Christ. Nevertheless, Paul here openly says, "Then *I* am powerful." His statement implies a real and effective *koinōnia* with Christ, in which the apostle shares in Christ's power, even if that power remains the possession of Christ alone.

This relationship of communication, in which weakness and power abidingly remain in exchange between persons, does not belong to the apostle alone. Paul consciously presents himself as a model of the Gospel at work for the Corinthians, as an answer to the model of self-possessed power of his opponents. His confession "when I am weak, then I am strong" is not to be understood as a conditional statement.[441] It is not that he must first make himself weak in order to experience Christ's power. It is rather that, "just as

438. The aim was for a "well-content life" (ἡ εὐδοκουμένη ζωή). See G. Schrenk, "εὐδοκέω, εὐδοκία," *TDNT* 2:739.

439. E.g., Friedrich Nietzsche, *Beyond Good and Evil* (trans. R. J. Hollingdale; New York: Penguin, 1973), 118.

440. Nor does Paul speak in the same way as Philo, who interprets the burning bush as an encouragement to those in affliction, "your weakness is your strength" (*Mos.* 1.69). For Philo, the strength is an inherent quality, just as the briar bush, although weak, has thorns and (in this case) burns with fire. For Paul, the power present in weakness remains extrinsic, although present.

441. Thus, wrongly, T. B. Savage, *Power through Weakness: Paul's Understanding of the Christian Ministry in 2 Corinthians* (SNTSMS 86; New York: Cambridge University Press, 1996), 176, 177-90, who interprets the presence of Christ's power in Paul's weakness as taking

the sufferings of Christ abound to [him]," so, too, "through Christ, comfort abound[s] to [him] as well" (1:5). Paul did not seek the thorn for his flesh. It was given to him. Human weakness is not a condition to be fulfilled. It is a reality that is already present, into which Christ himself has entered and participated to the utmost extent in the cross. In Christ and in the Gospel, therefore, weakness performs a hermeneutical function.[442] It exposes the truth about us as human beings: we are weak, not only in being subject to suffering and death, but also in being under the power of sin.[443] Within the sphere of the Gospel, weakness opens saving communication with God in Christ, in confession, lament, thanksgiving, and praise. The weakness of the apostle has performed this function already with the Corinthians: through his weakness, God has worked their faith. The question is whether they will continue to grasp the power of Christ, which is present only in weakness, or substitute other powers for it.

c. Paul's Confession of Foolishness (12:11-13)

> 11*I have been a fool! You forced me to it, for I ought to have been commended by you. For I was not at all inferior to these super-apostles, even though I am nothing.* 12*The signs of a true apostle were performed among you with utmost patience, with signs and wonders*[444] *and mighty works.* 13*For in what were you less favored than the rest of the churches, except that I myself did not burden you? Forgive me this wrong!*

Paul brings his "speech" to a close by confessing that he has now become a fool. Before he entered into his boasting, he twice requested permission of the Corinthians to act foolishly (11:1-4, 16-21). Now that he has boasted, he confesses that he has done so quite improperly. The threefold "apology" suggests

---

place in Paul's humbling himself. In the end, one runs the danger of making humility a mere tool to gain power.

442. Rightly Heckel, *Kraft in Schwachheit*, 321.

443. Rom 5:6; 8:3; 2 Cor 11:29.

444. The pairing "signs and wonders," which appears esp. in connection with the Exodus in Scripture (e.g., Exod 7:3; 11:9-10; Deut 6:22; 7:19; 11:3; 29:2; Pss 78:43; 135:9; Isa 20:3; Jer 32:20), had clearly become a stock expression for the phenomena associated with divine deliverance. It thereby recalled the Exodus and implicitly announced the fresh experience of the pattern of the Lord's work in a new context. See, e.g., LXX Esth 10:8; Wis 8:8; Mark 13:22; John 4:48; Acts 5:12; Rom 15:19. Although this pairing is clearly marked with a τε in the present verse (σημείοις τε καὶ τέρασιν καὶ δυνάμεσιν), it is ignored by the ESV, NIV, and NRSV. The additional reference to "power" or "deeds of power" serves either as a summary of the other two terms (e.g., Bar 2:11; Rom 15:19; 2 Thess 2:9) or as a reference to a demonstration of God's power that is less tightly bound to the theme of deliverance (e.g., Acts 2:22; Heb 2:4).

the attestation of a witness (cf. 12:14; 13:1). Paul is making a formal confession to the Corinthians that he has become and acted like a fool.

Yet, the ironic tone of all three of his appeals concerning his foolishness makes clear that he is not confessing a sin. Indeed, his concluding appeal for forgiveness in this context is a sharp correction of the Corinthians: "Forgive me for the injustice I did you by not burdening you financially!" The same sort of irony appears in the other apologies. The Corinthians already bear with the foolish Paul (11:1). Indeed, he is ashamed that he has not been more foolish already, since the Corinthians gladly suffer fools — namely, the apostolic claimants who abuse them (11:19-21). Now, having confessed that he has become a fool, he lays all the blame for it on the Corinthians: "You compelled me!" Paul is in a contention with the Corinthians. His battle for their hearts and minds is a battle as to who is in the right, whose judgment will prevail. The question, again, is the legitimation of an apostle. What it means to be a Christian is therewith decided as well. As Paul has made clear throughout the letter, in this question the Gospel itself is at stake.

11 Paul's conclusion to his boasting ends with the brief confession we have noted: "I have become foolish." He follows it with an immediate reversal, in which he addresses the Corinthians: "You have compelled me, for I ought to have been commended by you." He already has indicated to the Corinthians that they themselves are his letter of commendation (3:1-3). They are the demonstration of the Christ who speaks in him, whose power is present in his weakness (13:3; 12:9). They themselves are Paul's commendation, should have spoken up already, and boasted (in the proper sense, "in heart") on his behalf (5:12). Because the Corinthians have not fulfilled their responsibility, Paul has had to do so.

Paul grounds his case in the same manner that he introduced the cause of his boasting: he lacks nothing with respect to the "super-apostles" (11:5). Here is a second mark of the inclusio, with which he rounds off his argument in this section. The name by which he describes his opponents is, again, in all probability one of his own making. It is a derisive hyperbole, one intended to expose their pretensions. Paul is lacking in nothing with respect to them, especially now that he has become a fool.

Here Paul continues the paradox of the working of Christ's power in his weakness. He does so in another hyperbole: "I am lacking in nothing, even if I am nothing." This is not a false, self-serving humility. Nor is it an expression of an inferiority complex. Paul is quite aware of his gifts and has pointed already to his knowledge as the most prominent of them (11:6). Paul's overstatement is a confession that spiritual gifts remain gifts that flow forth from the Giver, through him, to others. They do not become qualities or possessions of his own: "What do you have, that you did not receive?" (1 Cor 4:7). Remarkable gifts are present with Paul, just as the power of Christ rests upon him in his weaknesses; in no way is he lacking over against the "super-apostles." Boast as they might, they remain little nothings, too.

12 Paul supplements his claim that he is in no respect lacking over against the "super-apostles" with the assertion that "the signs of an apostle" had "been worked" among the Corinthians themselves. It is unlikely that Paul at this juncture is introducing a new element into the contention. The expression summarizes the boasting of the "fool's speech," particularly Paul's account of his ignoble escape from Damascus, which stands as a counternarrative to the claims of his adversaries. In all probability, the expression "signs and wonders, and powers [*sēmeiois te kai terasin kai dynamesin*]" represents Paul's own language, borrowed from biblical tradition and early Christian usage. Paul's use of it here shows that it was shared by the Corinthians and, no doubt, by the apostolic claimants as well. It comes remarkably close to Paul's description of his apostolic mission in Rom 15:18-20, written only shortly after this letter.[445] As the form of the expression, with the connective combination *te kai,* suggests, and as is confirmed by Paul's usage in Romans and further by the pairing of "signs and wonders" in biblical tradition (including the book of Acts), the third descriptive, "powers," appears as an elaboration of the other two elements. Paul does not speak of "signs, wonders, and powers" but of "both signs and wonders, and deeds of power."[446] The third element, "deeds of power," serves as a restatement of the pairing: "signs and wonders, i.e., deeds of power." In context, it recalls the word of the risen Lord to Paul's petition: "my power is perfected in weakness" (12:9), linking the "signs and wonders" to Christ's work in Paul's weakness. It thus supplies an implicit corrective to the Corinthian misunderstanding of "signs and wonders" that had been exploited by Paul's opponents.

The pairing "signs and wonders" reflects biblical language, especially the prophetic signs associated with the exodus, but also with the Lord's further acts of judgment and deliverance.[447] As attestations of the apostolic

445. See esp. v. 19a, "in the power of signs and wonders, by the power of the Spirit."

446. Strangely, despite the usage of combination τε καί to mark pairings (e.g., LXX Gen 37:10; Acts 2:10-11; Rom 1:14; 3:9; 10:12), the biblical tradition of the pairing "signs and wonders," and Paul's parallel language in Rom 15:19, the major English versions misrepresent Paul's expression here, presenting the three elements in a simple series. Admittedly there are textual variants here, but the τε καί has solid attestation (𝔭[46] א* B), and the alternate readings may be explained by the same motivation that appears in the English versions: the triplet of terms seems to require the dissolution of the pairing of "signs and wonders." It is worth noting that, in other contexts, "power" or "powerful deeds" appears along with the pairing yet is distinguished from it (Bar 2:11; Rom 15:19; 2 Thess 2:9; Heb 2:4). See, however, Acts 2:22, where the order is inverted (ἀποδεδειγμένον ἀπὸ τοῦ θεοῦ εἰς ὑμᾶς δυνάμεσι καὶ τέρασι καὶ σημείοις). The inverted pairing "wonders and signs" also appears in some instances elsewhere (e.g., Wis 10:16; Acts 2:43; 6:8; 7:36).

447. See, e.g., Deut 6:22; LXX Ps 134(135):9; Isa 8:18; LXX Jer 39(32):20. In Isaiah 20:3 the prophet, naked and barefoot for three years, himself appears as a "sign and wonder."

message[448] and as portents of coming judgment and salvation, "signs and wonders" were part of the life of the earliest church.[449] Yet apart from the crucified and risen Lord, "signs and wonders" no longer serve the Gospel, but other powers.[450] True "signs and wonders" are given only together with hardships and persecution.[451] Paul's stance is thus reflected in early Christian tradition. Here he reminds the Corinthians that the Christ who is present in an apostle is the crucified Christ now risen.[452] The apostle through whom "signs and wonders" have been worked suffers the same rejection as the crucified Jesus of Nazareth, whom God marked out with "powers, wonders, and signs" (Acts 2:22).

It is therefore no surprise that Paul's claim concerning the "signs of an apostle" is marked by features that signal a correction of his opponents, and a decisive one at that. First, Paul presents his claim in the passive voice. It is not that *he* had worked "signs and wonders" and "deeds of power" among the Corinthians, but they "had been worked" among them.[453] The passive form corresponds to Paul's language in Rom 15:18-20, where he speaks of "what Christ has worked through me." It also recalls again Paul's account of Christ's word to him: "power is perfected in weakness" (12:9). Correspondingly, according to Paul, these "signs" have taken place among the Corinthians "in all perseverance" (or "endurance") — the first commendation of an apostle (6:4). The "signs of an apostle" appear only in affliction. Yet Paul is no hero; he was with the Corinthians "in weakness, in fear, and in much trembling" (1 Cor 2:3). He neither glorifies suffering nor makes himself out to be a model of virtue. Paul does not work the "signs of an apostle," not even in his perseverance. As he makes clear to the Corinthians from the start of the present letter, affliction is filled with comfort, a comfort that itself produces perseverance (1:6). Indeed, the fundamental sign of the apostle is that he does not fail (4:2, 16), despite hardship, affliction, and death itself. This perseverance, without question, is *not*

448. This is esp. clear from the story of Simon Magus (Acts 8:9-24).

449. E.g., Acts 2:19, 43; 4:16; 5:12; 6:8; 14:3; 15:12. The precedent and background lay in the signs of attestation given to Moses and in the exodus (e.g., Exod 4:1-9; 11:9-10; Deut 4:34), which had been repeated in Jesus and now in his saving work (Acts 2:22; cf. 10:38). See also Heb 2:4.

450. E.g., Acts 8:10; 2 Thess 2:9; Rev 13:13-14; 16:14; 19:20.

451. Acts 4:29-31; 6:8; 9:15-16; 14:22. Here one cannot help but think of the Matthean witness to Jesus' response to the demand for signs: "no sign shall be given [to this adulterous generation] except the sign of Jonah, the prophet" (Matt 12:39; cf. 16:4). Here, too, the sign of the cross stands above any other sign.

452. 4:10-12.

453. Paul's language is similar to his boast in Romans concerning what Christ "had worked through [him], with the power of signs and wonders" (15:18). Here, too, he is merely passive (even in all his labors); Christ alone was at work through him.

Paul's own but comes from the power of the risen Christ. The "signs and wonders, and deeds of power" that took place in Corinth came about in the context of perseverance.[454] In locating the "signs" within the endurance of suffering, Paul makes it clear that the "signs of an apostle" are found only under the sign of the cross of the risen Lord. As apostle, he "suffers" the work of God, namely, the affliction and comfort given in Christ, in order that others might receive comfort through him.[455] The Corinthians regard the "signs of an apostle" as deeds of power, worked by the apostle, in whom the risen Christ is present. Paul corrects this misunderstanding. In the first place, it is not an apostle who works signs. He is only the vehicle for them. Furthermore, it is Christ *crucified* and risen who works the signs of an apostle. Just as this Christ lives by the power of God, his deeds of power take place only in the apostle's weakness (13:4). For this reason, Paul lacks nothing over against the "super-apostles," despite his being nothing (v. 11). The radical extrinsicism that is characteristic of Paul's understanding of salvation as a relationship of communication again comes to expression here.

13 Paul now turns the argument around. It is not that he is in any way inferior as an apostle. Nor is it the case that "the signs of an apostle" had been absent in Corinth. It is the question as to whether Paul has made the Corinthians inferior to any of the other churches. Paul's apostolic authority has been recognized elsewhere. Is there any way in which the Corinthian church received less than the others? Only in that Paul has not burdened them financially! Again he expresses the matter hyperbolically: "I did not benumb you!"[456] He was far from overburdening them and wearing them out, as the Corinthians apparently suppose (v. 16). The issue of his refusal to accept compensation is long-standing.[457] Within the church it has raised suspicions about him that he already has addressed once[458] and is about to do so again.[459] At this point

454. Unfortunately, both the NIV and the NRSV basically ignore the datives (σημείοις τε καὶ τέρασιν καὶ δυνάμεσιν), equating them with the "signs of an apostle." The ESV, however, rightly connects them to Paul's perseverance.

455. *Pace* Heckel, *Kraft in Schwachheit,* 299-300, it is not clear that the expression "signs of an apostle" belongs to Paul's adversaries, nor that these signs appear here simply as deeds of power, apart from the decisive work of faith in the hearts of the Corinthians. Even in this context, where the faith of the Corinthians remains unexpressed, the "signs and wonders" worked in *perseverance* implicitly belong to the comfort and salvation given to the apostle to communicate to the world out of the sufferings of Christ that are likewise given to him (1:3-7). As Paul makes clear, his very speech as apostle arises from the affliction and deliverance that come to him (4:13). In this distinctive manner, the "signs and wonders" worked in Corinth belong essentially to the apostolic proclamation. It does not take place without them.

456. On the meaning of the verb καταναρκάω, see n. 304, p. 415.

457. 1 Cor 9:15-18.

458. 11:7-11.

459. 12:16-18.

he dismisses the matter with obvious irony: Forgive me this injustice! In his contention with Corinth, Paul knows himself to be in the right.

3. *Paul's Preparation for the Third Visit (12:14–13:14)*

In concluding the letter, Paul now speaks directly of his pending, third visit to Corinth. As we have seen, the letter as a whole takes its orientation from Paul's decision to cancel his previously announced visit to Corinth (1:15–2:4). This change in plans was prompted by his distress over the situation in the church, a distress that paralyzed him at a crucial point in his mission and altered the course of his actions. Paul frames the entire body of the letter around his profound concern for the Corinthians, signaling to them his love (2:12-17; 7:5-16). The visit that he is now prepared to make is intended to further the healing of their wounded relationship. Titus's mission brought a reconciliation of the Corinthians to Paul. Fragile though that reconciliation may be, Paul seeks to build on it, first in his encouragement to them to complete their promised contribution for Jerusalem (8:1–9:15), and then in his direct, sharp, and yet ironically humble address to the Corinthians concerning the apostolic claims of his opponents (10:1–12:13). Already in his "confession" of having become a fool, he turns his attention away from the adversaries to the Corinthians themselves. It is they who have compelled him to become a fool, since they have not supported and commended him as they ought to have done. In this final section of the letter, the opponents disappear entirely. Paul is focused upon his ultimate concern throughout the letter: the Corinthians themselves. Their recognition of him as their apostle is the fundamental issue in the letter, and it comes to the fore as he prepares to visit them. In these closing words, Paul openly speaks to the Corinthians, both about the suspicions that they have harbored concerning him and about the problems that he must address in Corinth. As in the "fool's speech" (11:22–12:10), in this final section of the letter the "mirror-reading" that is necessary to discerning the context of Paul's argument finds a sound warrant. No reconstruction of the theology of the opponents can find such firm grounding as the concerns Paul expresses and addresses here.[460]

The material falls into three distinct sections. The first two of these are marked by Paul's notice to the Corinthians that his third visit to Corinth now stands before them (12:14-21; 13:1-10). In the first of these sections, Paul reaffirms his love and overwhelming concern for the Corinthians, even in the face of their suspicions about him (12:14-21). Here it is apparent, however, that apostolic love is tough love: Paul is not afraid to name the problems as they stand in Corinth. Correspondingly, in the second section (13:1-10), his tone

460. See the excursus on Paul's opponents, pp. 100-110 above.

shifts: apostolic love is not divorced from apostolic authority. It is this authority that has been the matter of contention between Paul and the Corinthians. Paul now threatens, as he already has done,[461] to bring the contention to a decisive conclusion by virtue of the power of Christ, who is present in him.

Both of these sections are bipartite. Paul first addresses concerns of the Corinthians (12:14-18; 13:1-4), albeit in strikingly different tones, and goes on to express his apostolic concerns (12:19-21; 13:5-10). In both instances, his address to the Corinthians is determined by his repeated announcements that his third visit is now pending (12:14; 13:1).

The final section of the letter (13:11-14) contains the closing exhortations, greetings, and apostolic grace-pronouncement that are typical of Paul. The content of these last words is determined, of course, by the needs of the Corinthians at this moment.

a. Paul's Love and His Purpose of Edification (12:14-21)

The sharp rebuke that follows the "fool's speech" is now replaced by expressions of love and concern for the Corinthians. These expressions of love have an edge. Paul now directly confronts and corrects the Corinthians' misperceptions of him.

(1) Paul's Parental Love and the Corinthian Suspicions (12:14-18)

14Here for the third time I am ready to come to you. And I will not be a burden, for I seek not what is yours but you. For children are not obligated to save up for their parents, but parents for their children. 15I will most gladly spend and be spent for your souls. If I love you more, am I to be loved less? 16But granting that I myself did not burden you, I was crafty, you say, and got the better of you by deceit. 17Did I take advantage of you through any of those whom I sent to you? 18I urged Titus to go, and sent the brother with him. Did Titus take advantage of you? Did we not act in the same spirit? Did we not take the same steps?

As we have noted, in this first subsection Paul addresses the concerns of the Corinthians. He will take up his own concerns in the following one.

14 Paul announces to the Corinthians and reminds them, "Behold! This is the third time that I am ready to come to you!" The church was founded on Paul's first visit, which can be dated fairly precisely because of the Gallio inscription found at Delphi (A.D. 50-51).[462] After two intervening letters (the

461. 10:2, 11.

462. Acts 18:12-17; for the inscription, see École Française d'Athènes, *Fouille de Delphes,*

second of which is our First Corinthians, written, most likely, from Ephesus, circa 53), Paul visited Corinth again (again, most likely, from Ephesus) with the unhappy result that he reports in the present letter (circa 54). The visit was followed by the "tearful letter" (2:1-4). He is now prepared to visit them again.

Paul's tone here shifts noticeably in comparison with his preceding irony. The sharp rebuke turns to expressions of love. The prior announcements of his upcoming visit, which include threats of severe action,[463] turn into assurances that Paul will not financially burden the Corinthians. He knows of their suspicions and shall address them shortly (vv. 16-18). He again (for the third time!) uses an infrequent figure of speech, by which he describes his possible "misuse" of the Corinthians: "I shall not benumb [with my needs]."[464] He thus picks up his preceding hyperbolic insistence that he has not "worn" the Corinthians "numb," in contrast with his practice in other churches. Just as he has not worn out the Corinthians financially in the past, he shall not do so in his present visit, despite their fears and suspicions.

The Corinthian suspicions presuppose a fraudulent or opportunistic beneficiary who exploits the generosity of a benefactor.[465] Paul reframes the matter, simultaneously affirming his love for the Corinthians and asserting his authority. He is their parent, who wants to give to them. He does not intend to take anything from them; he wants them, their hearts, and their affections. Just as salvation does not consist in possessions but in a relation with God through Christ, so the apostle is bound to the church, not by an economic exchange, but by a relationship of love and, indeed, the relationship of salvation itself. He is bound to them, to die with them, and to live with them (7:3). The salvation of the apostle cannot be separated from the salvation of the church, and vice versa (1:12-14). The metaphor of parenthood already has appeared in the body of this letter: "I speak as to children, open [your heart] to us as well!" (6:13). His emphasis rests on the relationship of open communication and affection that is to exist between them. It appears again implicitly as Paul begins to make excuses for his boasting as a fool: his betrothal of the Corinthians to Christ presupposes his role as their father (11:2). For Paul, this metaphor of the relationship between apostle and church is not arbitrary or changeable. In his earlier use of it in First Corinthians, he elaborates it theologically: "For

---

vol. 3: *Épigraphie*, fasc. 4: *Inscriptions de la Terrasse du Temple et de la Region Nord du Sanctuaire* (ed. André Plassart; Paris: Éditions de Boccard, 1970), 26-32 (no. 286), plate VII.

463. See 10:2, 11, and esp. 10:6, which likely has reference to the coming visit: "καὶ ἐν ἑτοίμῳ ἔχοντες ἐκδικῆσαι πᾶσαν παρακοήν" ("We have in readiness the avenging of all disobedience"). Correspondingly, Paul here uses the infrequent expression "Ἰδοὺ τρίτον τοῦτο ἑτοίμως ἔχω ἐλθεῖν πρὸς ὑμᾶς" ("Behold, this third time I am ready to come to you").

464. For the meaning of the verb καταναρκάω, see again n. 304, p. 415.

465. The situation is not unknown in the Pauline churches. See 1 Thess 4:11-12; 2 Thess 3:7-13.

even if you should have ten thousand tutors [*paidagōgoi*] in Christ, you do not have many fathers. For in Christ Jesus, through the Gospel, I begot you" (1 Cor 4:15).[466] Apostle and church are bound together by the Gospel. For the Corinthians to recognize Paul as "father" is to recognize him as the apostle through whom they were given life by the Gospel. In the figure of parenthood, Paul addresses the matter of contention between him and the Corinthians in the most fundamental way. They themselves in their faith are the evidence of his apostolic calling, which derives from the Gospel alone. As we have seen, it is not an absolute authority but has its end in the faith of the Corinthians, which, in turn, will have its consummation in their being wedded to Christ (11:1-4).

Paul follows his avowal not to wear out the Corinthians with his needs (as if he could!) with two explanatory statements. The two complement one another, along the lines that we have described already. In the first instance, he indicates that he is much more concerned about them than he is about any sort of help or remuneration he might receive from them: "For I do not seek your possessions, but you." He returns yet again to the theme that runs through the letter, that his life and salvation have been bound to that of the Corinthians, and theirs to his, in Jesus Christ.[467]

The second explanation reasserts the role in which Paul stands to the church. As his children, they have no obligation to store up a treasure for him. This obligation lies with him as their parent. Here again, Paul's long-standing refusal to accept compensation from the Corinthian church comes to expression. The Gospel establishes his parental role toward them. For the sake of its work in the Corinthians, he will accept no remuneration from them.[468] His decision is an open expression of his parental relationship toward the Corinthians. It undoubtedly serves to hinder their tendency to think of themselves as his benefactors, or perhaps even his patrons, and thus to regard their apostle as subject both to their generosity and to their judgments.

Paul presents his monetary relations with the Corinthians in a specific form. He does not speak of the daily needs that parents are obligated to supply for their children, but of parents "storing up treasure" for them. The ideal obviously comes from wealthy families, who seek to make provision for children to establish themselves once they reach maturity.[469] It may be associated with

466. See Phlm 10. In a related way in Gal 4:19, Paul describes himself in a maternal role, indeed, in pregnancy, as he awaits the "formation of Christ" in the Galatians — namely, the arrival of the eschaton. See further 1 Thess 2:7-11, where Paul employs the images of both father and mother, in the nuture and care of the church.

467. E.g., 1:12-14; 2:1-4; 6:11-13; 7:4.

468. See again 1 Cor 9:1-18; 2 Cor 11:5-11; 12:13.

469. See, e.g., Plutarch, *Moralia* 526a-c, cited in G. Strecker and U. Schnelle, *Neuer Wettstein: Texte zum Neuen Testament aus Griechentum und Hellenismus* (Berlin: Walter de Gruyter, 1996), 2/1:513.

an inheritance, a figure to which Paul appeals in other contexts.[470] As Paul's following statement makes clear, it is not impossible that Paul has his death in view. In employing this language and the imagery it calls forth, Paul gives an eschatological orientation to his figure and circumscribes his role, much as he does earlier in 11:1-4, where he appears as the father of the bride. Just as in that context, the father is present only in order to transfer the bride to her husband, so Paul, the parent of the Corinthians, has the duty of "storing up a treasure" for them so that, at the last Day, they themselves may stand. This limitation of his role by no means suggests that their relation ends in the eschaton. It merely takes a new form: they remain one another's boast (1:14).

15 Already in the figure of "storing up treasure," Paul has shifted the terms of his relationship with the Corinthians, from the financial matters with which they were concerned, to the relationship and life with which he is concerned. This metaphor continues: "And I shall most gladly spend, and be spent up, for the sake of your lives." The proverbial statement now becomes personal. Paul owns it for himself emphatically in his use of the duplicative pronoun "I" *(egō)*. His spending and self-giving refer most naturally to his service to them in the Gospel, which he offers to them without expense on their part.[471] His service to them costs him anxiety and concern, trouble and distress, dishonor and shame, and perhaps even life itself. We need only recall the lists in 4:7-15 and 6:3-10. Paul is thrust into affliction, and there granted comfort, so that he might bring comfort to the Corinthians (1:3-7). As he tells them, "All things are for your sake" (4:15). He is prepared "to be spent up" for the Corinthians. This expression of the heightened cost that he is ready to pay for them makes sense only in the context of the apostolic afflictions.

More precisely, he is glad to be spent for the sake of their "lives" *(psychai)*. Paul is ready to be spent for the personal life and existence of the Corinthians, their true vitality. Here, as well as elsewhere with Paul, *psychē* does not signify a part of a person, but the whole person viewed in terms of one's animating inward life.[472]

Paul then poses the rhetorical question: "If I so exceedingly love you, shall I be loved the less?" Although he gladly spends himself for his children, the Corinthians, they remain aloof from him and attached instead to his opponents. Paul's question is intended to show the Corinthians that their dislike for him is without explanation or excuse. It is an invitation to embrace him afresh as he comes to visit them.

16 Paul is prepared to let the matter stand: "Be that as it may be!" The

470. E.g., Rom 4:13-14; 8:17; 1 Cor 6:9-10; Gal 3:18, 29; 4:1, 7, 30; 5:21.

471. See 1 Cor 9:18: ἵνα εὐαγγελιζόμενος ἀδάπανον θήσω τὸ εὐαγγέλιον.

472. See, e.g., the contrast between Adam and Christ in 1 Cor 15:45; also, e.g., Rom 11:3; 16:4; Phil 2:30. See A. Sand, "ψυχή," *EDNT* 3:500-503; BDAG, "ψυχή," 1098-1100.

Corinthians will have to decide this matter by the time he arrives. He shall have to deal with things as they stand then. He turns his attention to their suspicions about him. He has not burdened them, as they well know. Yet they imagine he is an unscrupulous character who took them in with guile. The Corinthians have reached this conclusion by some absurd calculus. This is Paul's point. Perhaps his refusal to accept funds has contributed to their suspicions. Perhaps his failure to visit them has done so as well. But it is perfectly clear that the Corinthians' distrust of Paul is groundless. The wisdom of his determination not to accept remuneration from them proves itself, even if it contributed to their suspicions about him.

17-18 Paul now points to the conduct of his representatives as indicative of his own. In all probability, he refers to the recently dispatched representatives of the collection, who were present with the Corinthians as this letter was first read. After the general question, "There was no one whom I sent to you, through whom I defrauded you, was there?", Paul makes his query specific. If, as seems likely, he refers to the very persons who carried the present letter and who then stood before the Corinthians, his question to the Corinthians would have been quite pressing. They had to respond immediately to his probing.

The wording Paul employs, "I encouraged Titus and sent the brother," corresponds to that in 8:16-18, where Paul speaks of the collection delegation. In that context, however, he speaks of sending two "brothers" to Corinth, along with Titus (8:16-24). Did Paul send two or three representatives? Or is this discrepancy evidence that 2 Cor 10–13 represents a different letter that has been joined to 2 Cor 1–9? The resolution to this question lies most likely in the present context. At this juncture Paul is dealing with suspicions against himself. He refers to those that he has sent to Corinth as representatives of his conduct and character. One of the brothers whom Paul has sent to Corinth is not, properly speaking, his representative but has been "hand-picked" by the churches (8:18-19). Paul quite understandably does not mention him here. Even though he also speaks of the other brother as an "apostle of the churches" (8:23), this other brother is relatively unknown. He is, however, known by Paul and has been proven in many times, in many ways (8:22). He is obviously a representative of the apostle, even if he is not a co-worker of Paul.

Throughout these verses Paul employs aorist indicative forms of the verbs. This usage need by no means signal that he refers to a past event (thus suggesting that chaps. 10–13 were composed later than 1–9). Letter writers in antiquity not infrequently take the perspective of the recipients of their missives, describing their writing as a *fait accompli:* i.e., they employed the so-called epistolary aorist.[473] Paul uses it elsewhere, not only in reference to

473. See BDF §334; BDR §334.

writing,[474] but also in reference to sending persons.[475] The same phenomenon appears in Paul's initial reference to Titus and the brother, whom he "encouraged" and "sent," even though they did not depart until he gave them the letter. The question as to whether Titus had defrauded the Corinthians would have been relevant already by the time the letter was first read. Paul, furthermore, undoubtedly intended the letter to be read more than once, and thus even after Titus's departure.

Just as Christ's life extends into that of Paul, Paul's life and witness extend into that of his co-workers and representatives. In First Corinthians, Paul indicates to the Corinthians that he sent Timothy to them in order for him to be a model of his conduct and a pattern for them.[476] His final question to the Corinthians here presupposes the same modeling by Paul's representatives. Just as Titus has not taken advantage of the Corinthians, neither has Paul. His pattern of conduct, which stands before the eyes of the Corinthians at the time they have the letter, is a reminder of Paul's own conduct. Thus Paul's question: "Did we not walk by the same Spirit — and with the same footsteps?"

In all probability Paul's language of "walking by the same *pneuma*" is to be taken as a reference to the Holy Spirit, even if it includes Paul's own spirit. For Paul, "walking," or the conduct of the life of faith, *always* takes place by the power of God in the saving work of Christ.[477] In Gal 5:17 he expressly describes Christian living as a "walking by the Spirit." In the same way, for Paul the imitation of conduct does not take place through the emulation of a moral example. It takes place by the power of the Gospel, which imparts new life. Paul thus characterizes Timothy in the first place as his "child," in whom his "ways" appear (1 Cor 4:17). The Corinthians likewise are to imitate Paul because they already are his children (1 Cor 4:15-16). For this reason, too, the Thessalonians could become imitators of the churches of Judea, persons whom they had never seen (1 Thess 2:14; cf. also 1:6). The bond between them is not the power of virtue but the power of the Spirit.

(2) The Contention Reframed (12:19-21)

19 Have you been thinking all along that we have been defending ourselves to you? It is in the sight of God that we have been speaking in Christ, and all for your upbuilding, beloved. 20 For I fear that perhaps when I come I may find you not as I wish, and that you may find me not as you wish

474. Rom 15:15; Gal 6:11. In both instances, the letter is basically complete. Paul speaks retrospectively.

475. Phil 2:25, 28; Phlm 12.

476. See 1 Cor 4:16-17.

477. Rom 6:4; 8:4; 13:13; 1 Cor 3:3; 2 Cor 4:1-2; 5:7; 10:2.

> — *that perhaps there may be quarreling, jealousy, anger, hostility, slander, gossip, conceit, and disorder.* [21]*I fear that when I come again my God may humble me before you, and I may have to mourn over many of those who sinned earlier and have not repented of the impurity, sexual immorality, and sensuality that they have practiced.*

Paul has reframed his relationship to the Corinthians in his assertion of his parental love, overturning their assumptions. Now he overturns their perception of his arguments to them concerning his apostolic calling by once again reframing the contention between him and the church.

19 Earlier in the letter, more than once, Paul challenged the Corinthian assumption that he is commending himself to them.[478] They suppose that the legitimation of the apostle rests with them, namely, with their judgment. Paul wants them to understand that his legitimation rests *in them,* namely, in their faith (1:24). Here, at the end of the letter, his tone sharpens as he addresses the Corinthian misunderstanding directly: "You have long supposed that we are presenting a defense to you." That the Corinthians imagine that Paul is defending himself to them implies not merely that he must legitimate himself to them but that he has failed or has been found wanting.[479] He is an impostor. The Corinthians suppose, as Paul has ironically observed, that they have been wronged (v. 16). A contention exists between them as to who is in the right. Paul himself has taken a combative tone from the opening of chapter 10 onward. The "boldness" with which he has addressed the Corinthians has included not only unsparing judgments of them but also irony and sarcasm.[480] The apostle to the Corinthians contends with the Corinthians. As the representative and advocate of the crucified and risen Christ, he must do so (5:20). Normally a contention ends with a winner and a loser. Either the Corinthians are going to be shown to be in the right, or it is Paul who will finally triumph. Paul seeks that triumph, a triumph which is not his own. But his love and his aim of "edifying" the Corinthians remain unswerving. He seeks to win the hearts of the Corinthians, their fresh reconciliation to God. In the end, as we have noted, there can be no winners and losers. Either both Paul and the Corinthians shall win, or they both shall be defeated together. It is not without significance that Paul indicates that he speaks on behalf of the *edification* of the Corinthians, and not on behalf of the Corinthians themselves. As they are in themselves, they must be done away with in order for their "edification" to take place.

Paul thus reframes the matter. He seeks their edification. Of course, the

478. 3:1; 5:12.

479. Cf. 4:1, 16.

480. 10:7; 11:1, 19-21; 12:11-13; also 11:5-11.

contention is necessary. He must destroy fortresses and bring down every lofty thing raised up against the knowledge of God (10:4-6). Nevertheless, just as the "letter" that brings death is followed in Christ by the Spirit who brings life, so Paul's work of demolition is only a prelude to his real work, that of edification. In the end, he is not presenting a defense to the Corinthians. This conclusion is wrong on two counts. In the first place, they are not in a position to judge him. Second, his purpose is not to judge and destroy them but to build them up. He thus addresses them here as "beloved," just as earlier in his contention with them he has insisted on his love for them.[481] Paul leaves the subject of the love unexpressed.[482] In all likelihood, he speaks not only of his own love but also of the love of God in Christ, in whose presence he speaks. Their contention, after all, is not only with him, but with God, who already in Christ has reconciled them to himself (5:19).

According to Paul, the Corinthians have supposed "for a long time" that he has been presenting a defense. This "long time" extends back into the past, long before the writing of this letter, as Paul's repeated references to his supposed commending himself "again" make clear.[483] The Corinthians had taken a negative view of their relationship with Paul, already, at the very least, at the unhappy confrontation during his second visit (2:5-11). The same attitude was present even earlier in the church, as is clear from Paul's protest in First Corinthians, where he in fact offers a "defense" (*apologia*, 1 Cor 9:3).[484] There, too, he shrugs off any judgment that the Corinthians might render concerning him and warns them not to judge matters "before the time" but to wait "until the Lord comes, who will bring to light the things hidden in darkness, and manifest the purposes of hearts" (1 Cor 4:1-5).

Paul's reframing of the situation once again recalls Kierkegaard's "devotional address."[485] Paul speaks not in the presence of the Corinthians who are to judge his words but in the presence of God, who judges both speaker and hearers. What Paul says to the Corinthians is for their edification.

There is something further in Paul's statement. He returns to the language he has used to describe his apostolic mission in 2:17: he speaks "in the presence of God, *in Christ*." His words to the Corinthians are not arbitrary. They are not his own but are given to him by Another. As the apostle of Christ, he echoes God's Yes in Jesus (1:19-20). His speech comes from beyond the final judgment into the present time. It is not subject to the judgment of the

481. As he does in 7:1, Paul also frequently addresses his audience as "beloved" in his exhortations: Rom 12:19; 1 Cor 10:14; 15:58; Phil 2:12; 4:1.

482. He addresses acquaintances elsewhere as "my beloved": Rom 16:5, 8, 9, 12.

483. 3:1; 5:12.

484. Even here Paul understands himself as defending his apostolic calling, not himself.

485. See the description above, p. 95.

Corinthians; quite the contrary, it judges them. The boldness and freedom of this apostolic speech is not indeterminate. It bears the concrete form of the crucified and risen Christ, in whom the veil that lies upon human hearts has been removed (3:14).[486]

The metaphor of "edification," which is especially frequent with Paul, is based on the more fundamental metaphor of the church as the temple of God. The language of "edification" occasionally appears in both Jewish and Hellenistic contexts, and even with Paul, as a metaphor for human life or moral development apart from any clear connection to the image of a building.[487] But Paul's appeal to temple imagery is quite prominent, especially in the Corinthian correspondence, so that in all likelihood it is operative here as well.[488] The metaphor obviously communicates growth and development in Christian living, not merely that of the individual, but that of the entire community. It presupposes a fundamental, defining form. As Paul's statements show, the work of deconstruction and demolition must necessarily precede the constructive work of God. As is often the case literally in Europe, churches were built upon the sites of former pagan shrines and altars, which had to be torn down in order for the new building to stand. This is true for the work of the apostle, not only corporately, but also individually. Idols must be torn away from human hearts in order for Christ to dwell there. Furthermore, as Paul's instruction in 1 Cor 3:10-17 makes clear, Jesus Christ alone serves as the foundation of the new building (esp. 1 Cor 3:11). Any and all construction upon that foundation must conform to the crucified and risen Lord if it is to stand the test of final judgment. It must consist of that which has come to reality in Christ, namely, "faith, hope, and love" (1 Cor 13:13). The "building" that is the work of those who claim to be apostles or teachers is no mere human project but, if it is valid, proceeds from the reality that has been laid already in the foundation. Paul's prior image of planting, watering, and the growth of a crop to fruition confirms this reading of his "architecture" (1 Cor 3:6-9). "Edification" is something much more than mere moral development. It is a growth in Christ and in faith. This is Paul's aim for the Corinthians as he writes this letter.

20 Paul follows his reframing of his contention with the Corinthians with two explanatory statements, in this verse and the following one. Both explanations build on the sharpness of his preceding attack, which remains the unstated premise of Paul's conciliatory statements here. Both explanations

486. See also 1 Cor 2:6-16, where Paul makes clear the nature of his speech as the "speaking of the wisdom of God that is hidden in a mystery," namely, the mystery of the cross, the understanding of which is given by the Spirit of God alone.

487. See LXX Pss 27(28):5; 126(127):1; Epictetus, *Dissertationes* 2.15.8 (cited by O. Michel, "οἰκοδομέω, κτλ.," *TDNT* 5:137). See also BDAG, "οἰκοδομέω," 696; J. Pfammatter, "οἰκοδομή, οἰκοδομέω," *EDNT* 2:495-98.

488. See 1 Cor 3:10-17; 6:19; 2 Cor 6:14-18.

contain vice lists, which Paul, for the sake of his argument, separates into two distinct types.

Just as Paul earlier apologized for the "foolishness" he was about to practice by appealing to his fear for the Corinthians (11:1-4), so here he appeals to his fear for the Corinthians in explaining the tone of his argument. He attributes his sharp tone to a weakness that he bears for them. Everything he has spoken, he has spoken for their edification, even if it has been the destructive work that must precede construction. As is generally the case in the letter, Paul describes his action as a *speaking*, rather than writing.[489] Effectively, he is present with the Corinthians, addressing them directly.

In expressing his fear, he makes it clear that he does not aim at defeating the Corinthians and triumphing in his own right. He hopes that he will find a certain sort of persons in Corinth when he comes — genuine Christians. He fears, however, that when he comes, he will find them not as he wants. And they will find him to be not as they want. He will be something other than the apostle they desire: God will again humble him and display in him the weakness that the Corinthians despise. Rather than edification of the Corinthians that Paul seeks, there will be a continued contention with the Corinthians that Paul seeks to bring to an end for their good.

The list of vices that Paul fears he might find among the Corinthians displays distinct similarities to the list of the "works of the flesh" that appears in Gal 5:19-21.[490] In contrast to that list, Paul here presents the vices of selfishness and factious behavior separately from those of immorality.[491] This concentration of the vices of division stands in contrast to Paul's tone toward the Corinthians. While they suppose that Paul is defending himself against their legitimate complaints, he communicates his love toward them and his purpose of edification. Although he walks in the flesh, he does not wage war according to the flesh but seeks to triumph by the meekness and gentleness of Christ (10:1, 3).

His characterization of the situation he fears further corresponds to the report he received from Chloe's slaves that he addresses in the opening of First Corinthians: "I hear that there are matters of strife among you."[492] Paul fears that matters have not gotten better, but have gotten worse. The term that he

489. The exceptions appear in 1:13; 9:1; 13:10, i.e., the opening, the collection instructions, and the closing of the letter.

490. The central section of the list (elements seven through ten) corresponds precisely to the list that we find here: ἔρις, ζῆλος, θυμοί, ἐριθεῖαι (strife, jealousy, outbursts of anger, factions). The two following elements are likewise related conceptually to the present list: διχοστασίαι, αἱρέσεις (dissensions, divisions).

491. In that case, too, however, Paul concludes his exhortation by addressing sins of strife and jealousy (Gal 5:26).

492. 1 Cor 1:11; see vv. 10-17.

uses there (*eris*, "strife") appears at the head of the list here. As we have noted, the other apostolic claimants sought to establish their cause not only over against Paul but also over against one another (10:12-18). Already when Paul wrote First Corinthians, varying allegiances to leading figures had brought about divisions within the church (1 Cor 1:12). This problem undoubtedly has continued until the present moment and forms the background of Paul's well-founded fear.

No two vice lists in Paul's letters contain precisely the same elements. He does not present them according to a defined pattern of a moral ideal. In some measure, the variety of the lists is due to Paul's forthright and vivid descriptions of the problems in his churches. Yet the lists are likely also reflective of Paul's perception of the issues in each instance. In the present list, the reference to strife, jealousy, and the like might be a somewhat standard way of describing a fractious situation. As we have noted, several elements of the list appear in the same order in Gal 5:20.[493] Some elements of the list correspond to Paul's description of the ungodly in Rom 1:29-32; after all, the Corinthians are behaving as unbelievers.[494] Paul has warned the Corinthians more than once against becoming "puffed up."[495] It is not accidental that Paul includes "instances of pride" or "being puffed up" in his list. It is difficult to interpret the final element of the list: "matters of disorder" or instances of disorderly conduct *(akatastasia)*. But what sort of "disorderly conduct" does Paul have in mind here? Earlier in this letter he uses it to refer to the instances of public disorder, the riots that he has endured as an apostle (6:5). In First Corinthians it appears in relation to order in Christian worship: "God is not a God of disorder, but of peace" (1 Cor 14:33). Perhaps Paul has in mind here disruptions that involved physical violence or the threat of it. This situation is certainly imaginable in Corinth, where at the founding of the church violence had broken out.[496]

21 Paul divides the expression of his fear into two distinct units. He

493. "Strife" (ἔρις) appears in the list in Rom 1:29-32; "strife and jealousy" (ἔρις, ζῆλος) in Rom 13:13; likewise "jealousy and strife" (i.e., reverse order) in 1 Cor 3:3. A warning against factiousness appears in Phil 2:3 (cf. 1:17).

494. Rom 1:29-30: πεπληρωμένους . . . ἔριδος . . . ψιθυριστάς, καταλάλους ("filled with . . . strife . . . [they are] whisperers, slanderers"). The last two elements presented here appear in reverse order of the related nouns in the present verse.

495. 1 Cor 4:6, 18-19; 5:2. As the last instance shows, "being puffed up" may entail, not merely a false sense of superiority over against other human beings, but the imagination that one stands above divine judgment. The Corinthians have become proud of their toleration of the one who "had his father's wife." This vice may thus be linked to the following list that describes immoral conduct.

496. See the Lukan report of the earlier situation in Corinth during Paul's mission there (Acts 18:12-17).

does not repeat the verb, implicitly connecting this second articulation of his fear with the initial unit. Now Paul's response to the Corinthians, or, more precisely, God's work in Paul, becomes the focus of his fear. He fears that God might humble him in relation to the Corinthians, that he might "mourn many who previously have sinned and have not repented." At the opening of his argument for his apostolic authority, Paul characterizes himself as "lowly [humble] among you, according to personal presence, and while absent, bold toward you" (10:1). He thereby ironically concedes what the Corinthians have judged concerning him already. His letters are powerful, but his presence is weak (10:10). Paul's previous visit could only have confirmed that impression. He now expresses the fear that he might *again* come to them and have God humble him. The last time he came to the Corinthians, he came "in grief" (2:1). Not only did he grieve them, but they grieved him (2:2-3). The letter that followed that disastrous encounter was written "through many tears" (2:4). He hopes that he will not have to face the same situation again.

Paul does not fear that *he* will have to humble himself and thus embarrass himself before the Corinthians.[497] Rather, he fears that *God* will humble him, or more precisely, in his words, that "my God" will do so. His language again reveals a profound understanding of his apostolic labors, particularly in his role in admonishing and correcting the church. It is not that Paul will humble himself before the Corinthians. This would make him a mere moral example for them. In that case, he only would sink into their strife, becoming one more self-justifying voice among many.[498] He fears instead that God will humble him in relation to the Corinthians. If he must mourn over them, it will be a mourning worked in him by God. Without in any way removing or obviating his own work, Paul understands his labor with the Corinthians as something "suffered" rather than accomplished. As we have noted more than once, Paul does not live a purpose-driven life, but a God-driven life. His own goals remain secondary to the larger work of God that is being worked in him.

Paul expresses the fear that "*my God* will humble me toward you." He characterizes God as his God only infrequently. In doing so, he obviously emphasizes God's particular dealings with him and the relationship with God in which he himself lives.[499] The language is biblical, reflecting especially the language of the psalmists.[500] The apostle does not speak abstractly or in mere dogmatic statements about God. He speaks because he believes, even in the

497. According to both his judgment and, in a certain respect, that of the Corinthians, he has humbled himself already by preaching the Gospel to them free of charge (11:7).

498. Self-humiliation is no humiliation at all. See Col 2:18, 23.

499. See Rom 1:8; Phil 1:3; 4:19; Phlm 4.

500. E.g., Pss 3:7; 7:1; 18:2; 22:1; 31:14; 86:2; 91:2; 118:28; 140:6. It also appears in the words of dereliction (Mark 15:34; Matt 27:46).

face of circumstances that speak the opposite (4:13; LXX Ps 115:1 [116:10]). His dogma is dogma in life, set against all appearance. Personal though it is, however, Paul's language is not privatistic. It contains the implicit invitation to the Corinthians to know the God who is the God of the apostle. Paul's mission is that of reconciliation of the world to God (5:20). Like the God of "Abraham, Isaac, and Jacob," the God of the apostle — who is the same God, according to Paul himself — is not merely for them or him alone, but for all the world.

Paul hopes to avoid a visit in which God again humbles him in relation to the Corinthians. This desire is not the hope of escaping problems or of avoiding personal embarrassment. As Paul affirms to the Corinthians shortly, he is quite happy to be weak while they are strong (13:9).[501] In shifting the description of his fear to his own humiliation, Paul shifts the burden of the problems in Corinth. As we have noted, he is reframing the contention with the Corinthians. As the apostle of Christ, Paul anticipates his taking the sins of the Corinthians unto himself, mourning them in the place of the Corinthians. He signals to them unmistakably that, even in his severity, he is not working against them, but for their good. This humiliation and mourning that Paul fears refer to the same visit and same confrontation in which Paul threatens to act with boldness and unsparing severity toward the Corinthians (10:11; 13:2). Meekness and severity, gentleness and a rod meet in Paul's apostolic authority.[502] Unbending insistence on truth and discipline coincides with the tenderness of a parent. They meet in the form of the "word of the cross." The power of Christ is present within the weakness of the apostle, whom God *again* may humble and cause to mourn those who have previously sinned. In this very weakness of his bodily presence and speech, which the Corinthians together with his opponents despise, the destruction of fortresses takes place (10:4-6).

Paul fears that he will mourn over those who previously have sinned but have not repented of the "impurity, immorality, and licentiousness that they practiced." He singles out the sexual transgressions that have taken place within the church, listing them separately from the sins of conflict.[503] As we have noted, this division of the vice lists allows Paul to express the depth of his pastoral concern. He *mourns* the *many* who have engaged in immorality and have not repented. The three vices of "impurity, immorality, and licentiousness" appear in Gal 5:19, with "immorality" placed as the first member.[504] "Impurity," which naturally has cultic overtones, not only in Scripture, but

501. See 1 Cor 4:9-14; 2 Cor 2:14-17; 4:7-15.

502. Cf. 1 Cor 4:21.

503. In the vice list of Gal 5:19-21, in contrast, Paul sandwiches the more-or-less overlooked vices of strife, conflict, and arrogance between the "open" sins of immorality and intoxication and carousing. Likewise in Rom 13:13 the two types of vices are listed together.

504. See also Rom 13:13-14; 1 Thess 4:3-8; Eph 5:3-14, esp. 3-5; cf. Eph 4:19 and Col 3:5.

also in the Greco-Roman world, signifies defilement and pollution, and thus the shame or dishonor that is attached not merely to deeds but to the persons who perform them.[505] "Immorality" *(porneia)* generally signifies an act of fornication or prostitution. The term for "wantonness" *(aselgeia)* denotes an act as lawless and reckless, perhaps with overtones of the violence that is done to another in any illicit sexual relation. As is the case with Paul's vice lists generally, this brief piling up of related terms describes evil from a number of perspectives, underscoring its dimensions and depth.

Paul fears that *again* God will humble him toward the Corinthians when he comes to them. In so speaking, he obviously refers to his second, difficult visit to Corinth. As we have observed, while it is unlikely that the figure with whom Paul had a confrontation in Corinth was the immoral man of 1 Cor 5:1-13, it is entirely probable that this confrontation had to do with instances of immorality that the Corinthians happily tolerated, and even celebrated. Paul here speaks of "many" who previously sinned and who had not repented. The egregious instance of immorality that Paul addresses in 1 Cor 5 was only one case among many: "a little leaven, leavens the entire lump of dough" (1 Cor 5:6). The Corinthians' tolerance of this flagrant transgression only encouraged other less shocking, but no less serious, evils.

The immorality that Paul combats among the Corinthians was not merely a matter of occasional moral failures that the Corinthians had failed to address. It had theological underpinnings. Some clues to the thinking of the Corinthians appear in Paul's instruction in 1 Cor 6:12-20. His opening words there, "all things are permitted for me," appear to be a Corinthian slogan, which they obviously applied to the question of sexual conduct. Paul tacitly accepts the slogan — which appears to be a distortion of his Gospel — but immediately corrects it in two fundamental ways. In the first instance, he briefly indicates that, while all things are permitted, not all things are beneficial (1 Cor 6:12). The human being is not autonomous but lives under one power or another. Already in these first words there is an implicit correction to the Corinthians' false estimation of "knowledge" as an absolute and liberating good (1 Cor 8:1). Second, and correspondingly, Paul reasserts the end of God's saving work in the crucified and risen Lord (1 Cor 6:12-17). God's purposes are not fulfilled in the enjoyment of present earthly life but in the transformed life of the resurrection, which is nothing other than the life of the risen Lord, in whom we have been made to share by the power of the Spirit (1 Cor 6:13-17). Salvation means that we do not belong to ourselves, but to God (1 Cor 6:18-20). The denial of the resurrection, which some in Corinth had embraced, was not divorced from the problem of immorality, but bound up with it.[506] Undoubt-

505. See, e.g., Rom 1:24; Dio Cassius, *Roman History,* 46.18.6.

506. See 1 Cor 15:33-34.

edly, those who sought to exercise authority in Corinth, especially the apostolic claimants, contributed to the Corinthian error. On this score, however, Paul does not lay the blame on his opponents. We find at most a hint that the Corinthians' association with the apostolic claimants was an inducement to immorality in Paul's appeal to them to break with the opponents. Like Israel in Babylon, they are not to touch what is unclean (6:17), and they are to cleanse themselves of all defilement of *flesh* and spirit (7:1). The former charge should certainly not be limited to moral concerns, but it may well include them; there is no participation between "righteousness and lawlessness" (6:14). In any case, Paul places the blame for failure, or here, the cause for his mourning, not with the opponents but with the Corinthians themselves. It is these "many" whom he seeks to bring to repentance. The Corinthians regard themselves as the judges of the apostles. They collect and select their own teachers. Had the apostolic claimants clashed with the Corinthian view of the world, they likely would have been rejected, just as the Corinthians are tempted to do with Paul.

b. Paul's Threat of Severity and His Call to Self-Examination (13:1-10)

With his second reminder to the Corinthians that he is prepared to visit them a third time, Paul's tone shifts. Having expressed his parental love and concern for them, he now indicates his readiness to bring his contention with them to a decisive end. In the contrast between 12:14-21 and 13:1-14, the radical shift between 1:1–9:15 and 10:1–13:14 that constitutes the macrostructure of the letter is found *in nuce.* Paul's love for the Corinthians penetrates his severity toward them here, just as it does throughout 10:1–13:14. He follows his threat of severity (13:1-4) with an appeal to them to judge themselves, so that he might avoid a confrontation with them (13:5-10). He is not concerned with his own triumph, but with their healing and wholeness in Christ (13:9). He thus preaches the Gospel, not merely with his mouth, but also with his conduct toward the Corinthians. He bears the message of Jesus in his body and life.

(1) Paul's Threat of Severity (13:1-4)

13[1]*This is the third time I am coming to you. Every charge must be established by the evidence of two or three witnesses.* [2]*I warned those who sinned before and all the others, and I warn them now while absent, as I did when present on my second visit, that if I come again I will not spare them —* [3]*since you seek proof that Christ is speaking in me. He is not weak in dealing with you, but is powerful among you.* [4]*For he was crucified in weakness, but lives by the power of God. For we also are weak in him, but in dealing with you we will live with him by the power of God.*

By use of a figure drawn from Scripture, Paul communicates to the Corinthians that he understands himself to be in a contention with them, and he asserts his apostolic authority over them in no uncertain terms. At the same time, he makes clear to them that this authority is nothing other than the authority of the crucified and risen Christ, nothing other than the power of God, which appears paradoxically in Paul's weakness. The Corinthians are not to be misled by outward appearance but must gain the eyes of faith.

1 In this second reminder that he is about to visit them a third time, Paul presents his relationship with the Corinthians as one of a legal contest, a contention. He cites Deut 19:15b without comment. His interpretation of the text follows implicitly, in his words to the Corinthians. The Deuteronomic injunction regulates the disposition of accusations of wrongdoing within Israel. It presupposes a contention between two parties, who are to bring their case before the "priests and judges," that is, they are to bring their case "before the Lord" (Deut 19:17). Violations of the rights of a neighbor are sins that bring guilt before the Lord. This understanding comes to expression in the first part of the verse, which Paul does not cite. He picks up the second part of the verse, focusing on the contention between two parties. It is this matter that the injunction regulates: "Upon the mouth of two witnesses and three, every matter shall be established."[507]

Paul interprets the text rather creatively. At least in the first instance, the "two witnesses, or three" are no longer two or three persons, but Paul's three visits to Corinth: the founding visit, the visit from Ephesus that led to confrontation, and the third visit that Paul now has planned. Paul's appeal to his visits makes clear what "matter" has to be resolved: the question in dispute is Paul's authority as an apostle, just as it has been throughout the letter. Paul's first visit to Corinth already provides a witness to this authority: "Are you not my work in the Lord?" (1 Cor 9:1c). Whether they are willing to acknowledge it or not, the Corinthians are "a letter of Christ" administered by the apostle (2 Cor 3:3). The difficult and sorrowful second visit notwithstanding, Paul's third visit to Corinth will bring the final witness that establishes his apostolic authority before the church.

The concrete language of the biblical text that Paul retains is lost in most English translations: it is "by the mouth" of two or three witnesses that a matter is established. The wording of the text implies the agreement of the multiple witnesses, who are presented in a vivid, physical figure as speaking with a single mouth. The emphasis, furthermore, lies on their verbal testimony: "the mouth" is obviously a metonym for speech. The means by which a case is established corresponds to the form of Paul's following warning, in

507. Aside from the abbreviation of the reference to the (mouth of) "three" (witnesses), Paul's citation corresponds to both the MT and the LXX.

which he underscores what he has *said,* and now *says* in advance of his visit. He threatens severity in the face of the Corinthian insistence on proof of the Christ who *speaks* in him (vv. 2-3). The legitimation of the apostle rests on the "word" of the Gospel spoken out of weakness in faith. This theme runs like a scarlet thread through the letter: contrary appearances notwithstanding, Paul's word to the Corinthians is not Yes and No but the unqualified Yes of God given in the crucified and risen Christ (1:18-20). Having the same Spirit of faith as the psalmist, Paul "believes, therefore [he] speaks" (4:13). His "mouth is open" to the Corinthians, his heart is opened wide to them (6:11). Before all else, the apostle bears and brings to them "the word of the cross" (1 Cor 1:18). It is by this means, and not by any power or charm of his own, that his case shall stand. Yet the establishing of Paul's case as apostle cannot lead to the defeat of the Corinthians. As an apostle of Christ, who brings the "word of reconciliation" (5:19), he must also win the restoration of the Corinthians. As Paul makes clear early in the letter, the salvation of the apostle and that of the church cannot be separated.[508] This understanding comes to the fore in his call to self-examination on the part of the Corinthians (vv. 5-10).

In a quite subtle way, therefore, Paul's appeal to Deut 19:15 — which he leaves uninterpreted and thus open — may bear a second sense. The "two witnesses and three" may be understood to refer not only to Paul's three visits but also to three persons. The first of these is Paul himself. The second is Christ, who speaks in the apostle. Then there is the third witness, who is added to the other two witnesses in the form of the Deuteronomic injunction. This third witness will be the Corinthians themselves, in whom Jesus Christ dwells — or perhaps is yet to dwell (v. 5). This is the truth that Paul is called to serve as apostle (v. 8).

2 Paul's primary use of Deut 19:15 remains, however, the underscoring of the significance of his visits to Corinth, and the upcoming third visit in particular. Here he reminds them of a warning that he issued during his second visit to Corinth: "I have said beforehand, and I [now] say beforehand, as present a second time, and now absent . . . that should I come a third time, I shall not spare [you]." If Paul's second visit to Corinth brought a confrontation, to which Paul responded with grief and sorrow over those unrepentant of flagrant sins, the third visit will bring unmitigated severity.[509] His language here is reminiscent of his warning in 1 Cor 4:18-21, where he threatens to come to his "children" with a rod. The matter has now come this far.

Paul issues his warning not only to "those who have previously sinned" but also "to all the rest." At this point, the entire church is responsible for its

508. 1:14, 21-22. See also 4:14-15; 7:3.

509. Cf. 2:1, as well as Paul's preceding expression of his fear for the Corinthians (12:19-21).

failure to deal with the problems in its midst. In much the same way that Paul earlier has reproached the Corinthians for their failure to deal with the grievous instance of immorality in the church (1 Cor 5:1-13), he now threatens the entire church that he will be unsparing in his severity with them. Of course, he has no other power or authority than the word given to him as apostle. But that "word" is much more than a mere human word. As he has informed them already, "the kingdom of God does not consist in words, but in power" (1 Cor 4:20).

3 Paul's sentence is not yet complete. He has threatened the Corinthians with severity, "since" they "seek proof of the Christ who speaks" in him. In all probability, the criterion of "Christ speaking" in the apostle is shared by both Paul and the Corinthians. But they understand the criterion in radically different ways. We have a solid clue to the Corinthian understanding of "Christ speaking" in Paul (or rather, the absence of it) in his earlier report of the way in which his opponents characterize him: "His presence is weak, and his rhetoric is contemptible" (10:10). Paul counters that assessment here, asserting that the Christ who speaks in him "is not weak toward you but is powerful among you." Paul's understanding of what it means that Christ speaks in him becomes fully clear only in the following verse. But it is apparent that Christ's power is manifest in the weakness of the apostle, just as Christ himself has communicated to Paul (12:9). The Corinthians understand weakness to be excluded or removed by power. This is rational. Paul understands power to be present and effective only within weakness. This is the word of Christ. Correspondingly, and as Paul's following statement makes clear, he understands Christ's speaking "in" him in an all-encompassing manner. As we have noted often, Paul, as the apostle of Christ, bears the message of Christ not merely in his words but in his entire body and life. In and through Paul's weakness, Christ speaks to the Corinthians. It is there that Christ displays his power.

4 Paul follows his assertion concerning the operation of Christ's power in and through him with two explanatory statements. The first statement concerns Christ: "For also he was crucified out of weakness, but he lives out of the power of God." The "also" (i.e., the adverbial *kai*) has reference to Paul's immediately preceding statement that Christ is powerful among the Corinthians; this same Christ, who exercises his power among the Corinthians, is the One who was crucified.[510] The Corinthians regard Christ quite differently.

510. Despite the witnesses that present a concessive form of Paul's statement — καὶ γὰρ εἰ ἐσταυρώθη ἐξ ἀσθενείας . . . (including ℵ[2] A D[1]) — it is likely that the εἰ is secondary. The reading is more difficult as it stands. In the first place, one must then account for the adverbial καί as we have done. Second, if the opening clause of v. 4 is concessive, then the paradoxical presence of power in weakness (and weakness in power) may be removed: "*although* he was crucified in weakness, he lives by God's power." Weakness and power are then set in a simple

Paul here corrects them. Indeed, according to Paul, Christ was crucified "out of weakness [*ex astheneias*]," not, as the main English versions (ESV, NIV, NRSV) have it, "in" weakness. The difference between the two readings is of fundamental importance. For Christ to be crucified "out of" weakness means that weakness was, or had become, inherent to him. Weakness *belongs* to Christ. Paul here plays the Philippians hymn that tells the story of the Incarnate One, in a slightly different key (Phil 2:6-11). Weakness is inherent to the humanity into which Christ has entered (cf. 8:9). It was finally out of this weakness (and not by external forces) that Christ was crucified. Here, for the only time in the letter, Paul speaks directly of the crucifixion, implicitly taking up the theme of "the word of the cross," which he introduces in First Corinthians.[511]

The crucifixion is not the end of the story, of course: "but he lives out of the power of God." This latter declaration may be taken in more than one sense. In the first place, Christ lives out of the power of God that has operated, and continues to operate, upon him; Christ is the Crucified One, who lives, the human being in whom God exercises his saving power. Yet the parallel with the opening statement suggests something more. Despite the clear distinction between Christ and God that Paul expresses here (he does not speak of Christ living out of his own power), the thought that Christ lives "out of the power of God" conveys the understanding that, just as weakness is inherent to Christ, God's power is inherent or essential to him as well. In his previous statement, which has prompted this explanation, Paul speaks not of God's power but of Christ, who acts in power among the Corinthians (v. 3).[512] He thus simultaneously identifies Christ with God while distinguishing him from God.

The Corinthians suppose that, where there is power, no weakness may be present. This, after all, is how the world works. One should therefore wish to gain power and rid oneself of weakness. This should be the way to salvation. Paul is instructing the Corinthians, as he has done throughout the letter and now does in a summary manner, that the opposite applies. God's power is present and operative *only* within weakness. It overcomes it without removing it. This is true in the crucified Christ, now risen. It is also true of Paul, as Christ's weak apostle, in whom Christ's power is perfected. Paul's opening benediction of God makes sense in this light: the comfort and mercy that spring from God come to the apostle, to the Corinthians, and to all of us, *only in affliction;* the sufferings of Christ are given to believers in order that they might know the decisive, final, saving comfort of God (1:3-7). God operates in this manner in

---

opposition, and Christ's crucifixion becomes merely a stage on his way to life. This reading is at first sight easier to understand and therefore less likely to be original.

511. See 1 Cor 1:18–2:16, esp. 1:18.

512. He likewise identifies the crucified (and risen) Christ with the power of God in 1 Cor 1:24, just as he does the Gospel (1 Cor 1:18; 2:5; Rom 1:16).

order to save us from our addiction to power and our worship of it. This is Paul's message in the opening chapters of First Corinthians. By locating his saving power nowhere else but in the crucified Christ and the message of the cross, God brings to nothing all human wisdom, power, and honor.[513] God saves us from ourselves. This is the Gospel upon which the Corinthians seem to have only a feeble grasp, if they have grasped it all.

Paul's second word of explanation necessarily follows: the Corinthian question is about the Christ who speaks *in him.* Paul's word about himself takes the same form as his word about Christ. The formal parallel expresses the material reality of Christ speaking in the apostle: "For also we are weak in him, but we shall live with him out of the power of God [directed] toward you." Like the crucified Christ now risen, Paul's weakness remains. He participates in Christ. He is weak because he shares in Christ's weakness. But he also shall live with Christ, "out of the power of God directed toward you." Here Paul breaks from the wording that he used to describe the operation of God's power in Christ. Paul shall live *with Christ.* The power of God that is inherent to Christ is not inherent to Paul. Only by virtue of sharing in Christ is the power of God operative in Paul.

This operation of God's power in Christ is not for the apostle alone. It has its goal outside him: the saving power of God is directed to the Corinthians. As Paul already has made clear to the Corinthians, his salvation and their salvation are bound together. The apostle cannot be saved without his church, nor the church without its apostle (1:21-22). They are one another's boast (1:14). Paul is thus prepared to "die together, and live together" with the Corinthians (7:3).

Paul's description of the working of God's saving power in Christ confirms what we have suggested already. When Paul speaks of "the Christ who speaks" in him, he does not refer simply to his own speech, although this is certainly included.[514] His entire life, in which he bears the "deadness of Jesus," is the vehicle through which God makes known the life of the risen Jesus to the world. Paul is a visible sermon, preached before the eyes of the Corinthians. They require only the word of the Gospel in their ears — and in their hearts — to open their eyes to the truth that is being announced to them.

(2) The Call to Self-Examination (13:5-10)

5Examine yourselves, to see whether you are in the faith. Test yourselves. Or do you not realize this about yourselves, that Jesus Christ is in you? — unless indeed you fail to meet the test! 6I hope you will find out that we

513. Again, see 1 Cor 1:18-25 and also 1:26-30; 2:1-5.

514. See 4:15.

have not failed the test. [7]But we pray to God that you may not do wrong — not that we may appear to have met the test, but that you may do what is right, though we may seem to have failed. [8]For we cannot do anything against the truth, but only for the truth. [9]For we are glad when we are weak and you are strong. Your restoration is what we pray for. [10]For this reason I write these things while I am away from you, that when I come I may not have to be severe in my use of the authority that the Lord has given me for building up and not for tearing down.

The Corinthians seek proof of Paul's apostolic credentials, namely, the proof of Christ speaking in the apostle (v. 3). Paul has threatened to provide that proof in unsparing judgment of the church upon his third visit (vv. 1-3). Yet that proof is already present in the power of Christ that is at work in and among the Corinthians (vv. 3-4). Paul thus calls the church to test itself. His certainty of the work of Christ among the Corinthians does not exclude his call for them to examine themselves. Paul's turning of the tables on the Corinthians is again an obvious assertion of his apostolic authority; he is not unapproved, and he hopes they recognize it. Yet, as we have seen already, both in the letter at large and in the present context, apostolic authority does not aim at the condemnation of the Corinthians, but rather at their vindication — even in their contention with him. Here, too, Paul makes it clear that, in his contention with the Corinthians, he does not seek their defeat. He is well content to appear to be unapproved, so long as the Corinthians do what is right. For the apostle, there can be no winner and loser in this contention; his validation as apostle to the Corinthians necessarily includes their validation and strengthening as true Christians. Paul's last word in preparation for his visit is thus a repeated description of the nature of his apostolic authority: it is for edification, not for destruction. For that reason he has written to them boldly so that he need not be severe on his arrival there.

5 The evidence of Paul's apostolic calling lies in the Corinthians themselves. If they question his apostolic authority, they must question themselves: "Try yourselves, as to whether you are in the faith. Test yourselves." As the articular usage and the metaphor of locality make clear, "faith" for Paul is not merely a human disposition or response. This is particularly apparent when Paul is dealing with the question of the resurrection. When he speaks of faith in this context, he stresses the content of faith (*fides quae creditur,* i.e., objective faith, "the faith that is believed"), even if the act of believing (*fides qua creditur,* i.e., subjective faith, "the faith by which [it] is believed") is not lost from sight.[515] For Paul, faith not only takes its orientation from the content of the Gospel, it is born of it. Indeed, faith's origin in the proclaimed word is of fundamental

515. See 1 Cor 15:14, 17.

importance for Paul; because faith involves the act of believing, faith (which re-creates the whole human being) must know that it has arisen, "not by the wisdom of human beings, but by the power of God" (1 Cor 2:5). Correspondingly, in the present context, Paul speaks of faith as a "place."[516] The Gospel creates a "space," so to speak, and transfers us to that location. Paul's language is obviously similar to that which he uses elsewhere of being "in Christ."[517] If the latter expression emphasizes the crucified and risen Christ as the locus of God's saving work, the parallel expression of being "in the faith" emphasizes the communication of that saving work to the human being. In speaking of being "in the faith," Paul demarcates the Gospel as the place within which God's work takes place.

Despite the doubts of the Corinthians, which ironically jeopardize their own standing, Paul expresses the expectation that they will pass the test they are to perform upon themselves: "Or do you not [approvingly] recognize yourselves, that Jesus Christ is in [and among] you?"[518] The self-examination that Paul urges is no exercise in introspection or navel-gazing. In the first place, the plural form of the second-person pronoun includes both individual and corporate examination. There is no reason to exclude either from the scope of Paul's statement. Second, Paul makes clear that the question of the legitimacy of faith is decided not by any quality inherent to the Corinthians or by any progress they might have made in Christian living. It is decided by whether or not they recognize that "Jesus Christ is in [and among] them." In shifting the terms of the self-examination from faith to Christ, Paul clarifies and defines the nature of the test. For the Corinthians to be "in the faith" is to have Jesus Christ in and among them. The shift in terms corresponds to the observation we have offered above: in speaking of being "in the faith" (rather than being "in Christ"), Paul emphasizes the effect of God's saving work on the human being. Paul describes that saving effect as the dwelling of Christ within the individual believer and within the believing community.

The question then arises as to how the presence of Jesus Christ is to be recognized, if the Corinthians are to test themselves by it.[519] In the face of

516. See also 1 Cor 16:13, where he calls them to "stand in the faith."

517. In this letter see, e.g., 2:17; 3:14; 5:17, 19; 12:2, 19.

518. In this context, the verb ἐπιγινώσκω clearly signifies "approving recognition" (and not mere knowledge), just as it does in 1:13, 14; 6:9, and also in 1 Cor 14:37; 16:18, and, most likely, 1 Cor 13:12.

519. Paul's use of "Jesus Christ," in which the name of Jesus qualifies the title "Christ," is also indicative of Paul's understanding that the One who indwells the Corinthians is the crucified and risen Jesus. The same emphasis appears elsewhere in the letter (1:2, 3, 19; 4:5, 14; 8:9), esp. where Paul simply uses the name "Jesus" (4:5, 10, 11, 14; 11:4, 31). Admittedly, the variant reading "Christ Jesus" (represented by א A 326 1175) is somewhat more strongly attested than

Corinthian misunderstanding, Paul already has clarified who "the Christ" is who speaks in him: it is the Christ who was crucified out of weakness and who lives out of the power of God (vv. 3-4). The mark of the presence of Jesus Christ is power within weakness, righteousness within sin, life within death, comfort within suffering.[520] This is true for both the apostle and the Corinthians. Conformity to Christ is "suffered" rather than achieved by discipline or devotion. To be indwelt by Christ is to be thrust into the conflict between God and the fallen world. For the Corinthians to recognize this truth about themselves will mean that they must surrender their dreams of earthly power and glory. They will have to come to themselves, to mourn the unrepented transgressions in their midst, to recognize their frailty and mortality. They will have to recognize the presence of Christ in the suffering apostle who also shall soon be in their midst. They will have to receive the comfort of God that is given through him in order that they themselves may be comforted. Following the pattern of the apostle, they will have to share that comfort "with those who are in any and every affliction" (1:4). Within its passivity, faith is exceedingly active. As is apparent from Paul's definition of the self-examination the Corinthians are to perform, the confirmation of faith lies within the reality of faith itself. This confirmation does not involve a circular logic, but a call to believe *(fides qua creditur)* the Gospel *(fides quae creditur)* already proclaimed. Paul's call to the Corinthians to test themselves is a call to a fresh act of faith, a fresh "grasping" of the truth that had been given to them already. They are to recognize that Jesus Christ is in and among them, and not just any "Jesus," as Paul has made clear, but the Crucified and Risen One. To fail this test is not merely to do evil (although it certainly entails that) but to commit the ultimate evil, to disbelieve the message of the apostle. We must not overlook the form of Paul's question to the Corinthians: he regards Christ as present in and among the Corinthians and expresses that judgment.

There is no overlooking that, in his next breath, Paul raises the question as to whether the Corinthians are "in the faith" after all: "unless, perhaps, you are unapproved." But this is the pattern of assurance and warning that we have seen repeatedly in this letter. From the perspective of God's work in Christ and the message of the Gospel, Paul speaks with unconditioned certainty of the faith and salvation of the Corinthians. From the perspective of the Corinthians themselves, especially in view of their recent behavior, it is an entirely different story. Within the space of a few short verses, he can address them both as

---

"Jesus Christ" (B, D, a Vulgate manuscript, and the Majority Text). However, while the thought that "Christ" is "in" someone appears in the Pauline letters, Paul does not speak elsewhere of "Jesus Christ" or "Jesus" being "in" someone, even if the idea appears in other forms (4:10, 11; Gal 6:17). It is likely that scribes reversed the unexpected order of the terms.

520. See 12:9-10; 5:21; 4:10; 1:5.

unbelievers and as believers.[521] His certainty concerning the Corinthians does not lie in the Corinthians, but in Christ.

6 Paul returns to his contention with the Corinthians over his apostolic calling: "And I hope you know that we are not unapproved." He has acknowledged their perspective on the issue indirectly in his warning in v. 3: the Corinthians are seeking proof of the Christ who speaks in him. He now has reframed the issue by reminding them precisely who the Christ is who speaks in him. In view of this corrective and his turning of the tables on the question of proof, he freshly asserts his apostolic authority. It should be fully apparent to the Corinthians that the crucified and risen Jesus is present in him, whose regular experience is that of suffering and deliverance. As he does elsewhere in this letter when speaking of his apostolic authority, Paul employs the first-person plural; the issue is not that of Paul's person, but the legitimation of an apostle.[522]

7 Paul follows his exhortation with a long-delayed description of his petition for the Corinthians. What usually appears in the opening of his letters comes to expression here only after Paul's lengthy love letter and battle with the Corinthians. His concluding words bring a reminder that, as the apostle to the Corinthians, he is a mere agent of God. Verses 7-9 take the form of an inclusio, beginning and ending with Paul's expression of his prayer for the Corinthians, and in the middle describing his aim and motivation as God's agent.

"We pray to God that you not do any evil." Paul intercedes for the Corinthians. His intercession for them is again a reminder that there is Another present, to whom both apostle and church must render account. The contention between them is taking place before God. Paul is not the opponent of the Corinthians, even if he must contend with them. He believes the best about them, hopes the best for them, and endures all the things that they do to him.

Even if Paul's prayer refers in the first place to the contention between him and the Corinthians, and their recognition of him as apostle, his statement here encompasses the whole of his apostolic mission. This is apparent in the contrast Paul draws between the Corinthians doing "evil" (or "that which is bad," *kakos*) or doing "good" *(kalos).* He is not concerned with their allegiance to him as a person, but with the conduct of their lives. His earlier expression of his fear of the moral disorder he might find in the church upon his visit displays a solicitude over the same matters (12:20-21). The very wording of Paul's contrast, *kakos* ("bad") versus *kalos* ("pleasingly good"), expresses his

521. Cf. 5:20–6:2; 6:11–7:1.

522. See, e.g., the first-person singular usage, in the context of plural usage in 1:13, 17, 23, and then the shift to the first-person plural in 2:14-17, after the extensive use of the singular in 2:1-13. Paul's use of the first-person singular signals that he is speaking of himself, even in the larger context in which the plural appears. The plural, again, signifies that he is not strictly speaking of his own person, but of matters pertaining to his calling as apostle.

desire that the church know and experience that which is beneficial and that it will not have to suffer the effects of evil.

Paul's aim, moreover, is nothing less than the complete obedience of the Corinthians, that they do no evil whatsoever. He has stated that purpose in other terms already (10:6). This goal may seem strange for one who insists that the reality of evil remains in the human heart throughout this body and life.[523] But the aim that he pursues for the Corinthians has already come to reality for them in the crucified and risen Christ. He makes this point repeatedly in his letters.[524] He seeks for them to grasp what belongs to them already. That the attainment of his aim lies beyond the present life does not diminish in the least his hope for it or his striving after it.[525] He understands that the eschaton has entered into the present: "if anyone is in Christ, there is a new creation" (5:17). The presence of this saving reality shapes his entire purpose.

In the following pair of clauses, Paul states his motive in his intercession for the Corinthians, and by implication for his entire mission: "not that we might appear approved, but instead that you should do what is good, and we should be as ones who are unapproved." Paul recognizes that selfish motives might well lie behind any mission or pretense of mission. He has made the point repeatedly to the Corinthians that they themselves are his commendation as apostle. If only they would behave properly, he himself would have his approval. But that is not his purpose! He does not seek, of course, that they reject him, but rather that they recognize him as their apostle and thus receive afresh and abidingly the Christ and the Gospel that he bears.

Paul is fully prepared to make an exchange with the Corinthians. He has just asserted (in inverted form) that he is approved as apostle, and he has called into question whether they can stand the test as to whether they are Christians (v. 5). But he is more than happy to trade places with them! He prays that they might do no evil, but rather do "the good," so that he might be as one who is unapproved. He is ready to lose in his contention with the Corinthians if only he wins them for Christ. He is ready to be the "sinner" in order for them to be righteous. Indeed, he prays that it might be so. The apostle thus takes on the form of Christ in relation to the Corinthians. He will take up this theme again in v. 9.

8 Paul attaches two explanatory statements to his petition, in this and in the following verse. The first is a restatement of the nature of apostolic mission: "For we are not able to do anything against the truth, but [only] on behalf of the truth." Paul is a servant of the Gospel, which he has described

523. See Rom 7:7-25, esp. v. 24; for a discussion of this text, see Seifrid, "The Voice of the Law."

524. E.g., Rom 6:1-11; 7:4-6; 1 Cor 5:7-8; 6:9-11; Gal 5:24-26.

525. Cf. Phil 3:12-16.

elsewhere in this letter as "the truth," which he makes manifest to "every human conscience" (4:2). The "word of truth" is essential to his commendation as an apostle and agent of God (6:7). The "truth of Christ" is in him (11:10). Paul's understanding of truth is thus vastly different from that of Albert Schweitzer, who appealed to this verse frequently as a justification of his modern and post-Christian views. Paul's understanding goes beyond a "scientific worldview," with its vain hope for (or pretense of) a final objectivity that can explain all things. He understands that truth is found in the Gospel, which is God's saving response to human blindness, and to the lies and deception — a deception simultaneously human and demonic — that lie behind that blindness.[526]

Paul cannot act in his own interest, contrary to the Gospel, but only on behalf of it. By naming the Gospel as truth, Paul again asserts his apostolic authority. In resisting that authority, the Corinthians are deceived and under the influence of the false apostles, who, as the agents of Satan, practice deception (11:12-15). Nevertheless, it is once again apparent that Paul's apostolic authority includes the good and the salvation of the Corinthians. The truth that he must serve is furthered and manifest in the good conduct of the Corinthians; his confession that he must serve the truth explains his prayer for the spotless conduct of the Corinthians. Despite having questioned whether the Corinthians are "approved" and are Christians at all, Paul here speaks from the certainty that he has expressed concerning them, that "Jesus Christ" is in and among them (v. 5). This is the truth of the Gospel, on behalf of which Paul acts and must act.

9 Paul's second explanation of his readiness to be "unapproved" while the Corinthians are "approved" in the faith is an expansion of that faith, an expression of the form of his entire mission as an apostle. Just as the first explanation is grounded in the truth of the Gospel, the second explanation is grounded in the apostolic calling: "For we rejoice when we are weak, and you are strong." Paul here openly embraces the form of the apostolic mission, which has proven to be the cause of offense to the Corinthians. He likewise rounds off the theme that he introduces in his benediction of God at the very beginning of the letter: when he suffers affliction, it is for the comfort and salvation of the Corinthians (1:6). Death is at work in him in order that life might be at work in them (4:12). The indwelling of Christ's power in Paul's weakness does not result in a turning inward on Paul's part. Just the opposite, it brings a turning outward. The power of Christ that is operative in Paul in his weakness is not for Paul alone but for the Corinthians and all the world (12:9-10). This is the form of the life of an apostle.

In conclusion, Paul restates his petition for the Corinthians, forming

526. 4:3-4; 11:3, 12-15.

an inclusio with v. 7: "And this we pray: your restoration." His summary of his prayer for them strikingly takes up the opening exhortation of First Corinthians, where he urges "that you all say the same thing, and that there not be any divisions among you, and that you be made whole [*or* restored] in the same mind, and the same opinion" (1 Cor 1:10). Nothing has changed since the initial problems that broke out in the Corinthian church, other than matters becoming worse.

The term Paul employs, *katartisis,* may signify "wholeness," "a completion," or "furnishing," but also "restoration" or "a bringing-back to order."[527] In this context, it is clear that the latter set of meanings is operative. As in his opening expression of his petition in v. 7, he focuses on the strife and immorality that he fears continue to be present within the church (12:20-21). It is clear at the same time that this restoration, or coming to wholeness, entails a fresh reconciliation with God through Christ, and thus with Paul as well (5:20–6:2, 11-13). But Paul allows this reconciliation to remain in the background of his petition and intercedes for the wholeness and well-being of the Corinthians.

10 In voicing his petition for the Corinthians and explaining its basis, Paul changes the tone of his confrontation with them to one of mildness. He concludes his message to them by stating his purpose in writing: he wants to avoid exercising the severity he has threatened (v. 2). The authority that the Lord has given him as apostle is to edify, not destroy the Corinthians. Paul thus returns to the opening theme of his legitimation as apostle (10:1-11). He began there with the ironic request for permission to speak boldly, even though he is not present with the Corinthians (10:2). His pattern of dealing with them forcefully in his letters, but mildly in their presence, has become familiar to them, and it has been used against him within the church. Paul himself confirms that opinion, just as he has done earlier in the letter, when he explains his reason for failing to visit Corinth as he had promised. He wanted to spare them (1:23; cf. 1 Cor 4:21) and determined not to come to them "again" in grief (2:1). Instead, he wrote to them "through many tears," and very likely with a measure of the severity he now has warned that he will use (2:3). As Paul makes clear in his appeal to Deut 19:15 (v. 1), the game is now up. Nevertheless, he still wants to avoid a confrontation, and he repeats his earlier description of his apostolic authority (10:8): its aim is to build up, not to tear down, even if the latter becomes necessary. As we have noted, the apostolic mission follows the pattern of God's dealings: God, in remaining distant, first puts to death by "the letter," in order that, in coming near to us in Christ, he might make alive by the Spirit.

527. See BDAG, "καταρτίζω," 526.

c. Closing Exhortations, Greetings, and Grace-Pronouncement (13:11-14)

Although no two letters of Paul are alike, the final three elements of the letter correspond to the variable pattern that appears elsewhere. As is especially apparent in this letter, Paul does express himself arbitrarily in these last words but continues to speak to the needs of the church.

> [11]*Finally, brothers, rejoice. Aim for restoration, comfort one another, agree with one another, live in peace; and the God of love and peace will be with you.* [12]*Greet one another with a holy kiss.* [13]*All the saints greet you.* [14]*The grace of the Lord Jesus Christ and the love of God and the fellowship of the Holy Spirit be with you all.*

11 Paul regularly inserts exhortations into the conclusion of his letters, almost always discernibly directed to the particular circumstances within the church he addresses, as, for example, when he urges the Corinthians to submit to "the household of Stephanas" (1 Cor 16:15), or when he urges Euodia and Syntyche to be of one mind (Phil 4:2). Just as the openings of Paul's letters are "words on target," so the concluding exhortations are directed to the needs of Paul's hearers.[528] It is especially apparent that Paul's concluding exhortations here are directed to the immediate needs of the Corinthians. He picks up his preceding description of his prayer for the Corinthians and his aim for them as apostle (v. 9), and likewise recalls the message of comfort from his opening benediction (1:3-7). The call to be of one mind and to be at peace has obvious relevance for the strife within the church, which must have been in considerable measure bound up with the contention over apostolic leadership (12:20).[529]

The term *loipon*, by which Paul signals that he is concluding the letter, is often rendered "finally." The term connotes this sense here, and similar contexts as well. But it would be more properly rendered "beyond these matters" or "otherwise."[530] This turn to "other matters" is not a setting aside of the concerns over which Paul has labored in the letter. It is a placing of those immediate concerns within the larger context of God's saving dealings with the church.[531]

528. On this topic, see J. A. D. Weima, *Neglected Endings: The Significance of the Pauline Letter Closings* (JSNTSupp 101; Sheffield: Sheffield Academic Press, 1994), 77-155, 208-15.

529. See 10:12-18; cf. 1 Cor 1:10-12.

530. See BDAG, "λοιπός, ή, όν," 602.

531. This turn is apparent in Phil 3:1 and 4:8, where Paul addresses the temptation to Judaize and the apparent strife within the church, after having dealt with the Philippians' concern over his imprisonment and with their own exposure to persecution. Likewise, 1 Thess 4:1 marks a shift to instruction of the fledgling church, after Paul has expressed his love for

The simple call to the Corinthians to "rejoice" is a reflection of Paul's preceding expression of his own joy at his being weak while the Corinthians are made strong (v. 9). Just as his salvation is bound to theirs and theirs to his, so their joy is bound to his joy. Paul makes this connection explicit earlier in the letter: "[I am] persuaded concerning all of you, that my joy is the joy of all of you" (2:3). Paul's exhortation to the Corinthians to rejoice is a call to rejoice in the exchange that is made on their behalf in the apostle, through whom they are made strong and granted comfort and salvation. It is simultaneously a call to embrace afresh the Gospel in which the fundamental exchange of sin and righteousness has been made for them in Christ.[532] Paul's call to rejoice is thus intended to lift the eyes of the Corinthians above their present contention with the apostle to see the unconditioned good that God has given to them in Christ. In this respect, Paul's call to the Corinthians to rejoice parallels his repeated calls to the church in Philippi to do the same. In that context, he seeks to turn their attention from the immediate circumstances of his imprisonment to the greater work of God that is taking place in and through that imprisonment: "You, too, rejoice, and rejoice together with me!" (Phil 2:18). The Philippians are to rejoice in the face of the challenges that confront the church from without and within. They are to "rejoice in the Lord, always" (Phil 3:1; 4:4).[533] In the present context, Paul omits the defining phrase "in the Lord," perhaps because it could deflect attention from the apostolic mission by which God delivers comfort to Corinth.

The connection of Paul's call to rejoice to his earlier expression of joy in v. 9 is confirmed by his second exhortation to the Corinthians, "Be restored!" or, as one might render it, "Be made whole!"[534] What Paul prays for the Co-

---

them and offered them comfort in the face of the persecutions that have separated them. In 2 Thess 3:1 Paul moves from dealing with the question of the coming of the day of the Lord and forged letters purportedly from him to deal with broader concerns concerning the church.

532. The call to rejoice (χαίρετε) is clear enough (although the NRSV takes it, wrongly, as closing, "farewell"). See the parallels in Phil 3:1; 4:4; 1 Thess 5:16.

533. See also 1 Thess 5:16, written to a church under similar pressure.

534. The English versions have done a rather poor job in representing Paul's exhortations here. The ESV, NIV, and NRSV translate the middle/passive form "καταρτίζεσθε" in an active sense: "Strive for full restoration!" (NIV); "Aim for restoration" (ESV); "Put things in order!" (NRSV). But in the relatively infrequent cases in which the context indicates the usage of the middle form of the verb καταρτίζω, it takes an object, which is lacking here. Furthermore, the interpretation of the verb that the English versions offer runs counter to Paul's prayer for the Corinthians in v. 9: restoration is God's work, not theirs. It is much more likely that καταρτίζεσθε here should be taken as passive. All three versions likewise gloss over the form in 1 Cor 1:10 — ἦτε . . . κατηρτισμένοι — a perfect middle/passive form that in all probability should be taken as passive ("that you might be restored"). They translate the verb instead in the active voice as "agree." In both instances, the English translations overlook the fact that Paul elsewhere employs passive imperatives of this kind: they are a necessary expression of his Gospel (e.g., Rom 12:2; 2 Cor 5:20). God's work in us has priority over any work of our own.

rinthians, he now calls them to receive (v. 9). Indeed, the exhortation takes a passive form. It might be better characterized as an apostolic pronouncement that imparts the Gospel to the Corinthians, rather than an exhortation. Of course, the Corinthians are to respond to this word. But their response must be a response of reception, an act of faith that grasps what is given by God, through the apostle.

As we noted in reference to v. 9, Paul's desire that the Corinthians "be made whole" reflects a long-standing concern that extends back at least as far as the writing of First Corinthians (1 Cor 1:10). Paul there appeals to the Corinthians to be "restored" in "the same mind [*nous*]" and in "the same judgment [*gnōmē*]." He seeks the restoration of the community to wholeness in view of the factions that have divided the church (1 Cor 1:11-12). Such a healing of the believing community is surely the primary sense of his pronouncement here as well. Just as Paul calls the Corinthians to the same mind and judgment there, he here urges them to be "intent on the same thing." Strife and jealousy within the church top the list of his concerns as he anticipates his third visit (12:20).

At the same time, there is probably also an individual appeal in this apostolic appeal: the community cannot be made whole unless its individual members are themselves made whole. The other elements of his exhortation entail an individual dimension, including the preceding call to rejoice. In other contexts, moreover, Paul urges and hopes for the "restoration" and "bringing to wholeness" of individual persons.[535] This understanding is included in his pronouncement.

The third element of his exhortation is also passive in nature and thus also appears as an effective apostolic pronouncement: "be comforted."[536] The thought is obviously bound up with the two preceding elements: to rejoice and be made whole as a church (or also as individuals) involves sharing in the comfort of the Gospel. But Paul's pronouncement recalls even more powerfully his opening benediction, in which he blesses God for the comfort that he receives in Christ and gives forth to others, to the Corinthians in particular. This comfort, we should remember, is nothing less than sharing in salvation itself (1:6). The call to receive the comfort of the Gospel afresh is likewise an implicit reminder to the Corinthians that they have not been and cannot be removed from suffering within this body and life. Paul's word calls the Corinthians to a realistic understanding of themselves and the world.

535. Gal 6:1; 1 Thess 3:10.

536. Once again the English versions (ESV, NIV, NRSV) fail to represent properly Paul's exhortation "παρακαλεῖσθε." In this case, it is virtually certain that we find here a passive usage of the verb, since the middle form with the meaning "to comfort" is nearly unattested in biblical Greek (LXX 1 Kgdms 15:11 bears a different sense; 2 Macc 7:6 similarly is better rendered "have mercy" or "show comfort"). The broader biblical usage overwhelmingly points to the passive, as does Paul's own usage throughout this letter, esp. that in 1:3-7, which this word recalls.

The fourth exhortation deals directly with the unity of the church: "be intent on [*or* give attention to, *phroneō*] the same thing." The wording is slightly different from the twofold exhortation in 1 Cor 1:10, but the thought is nearly the same. Here Paul speaks of the intent and aims of the Corinthians, calling them to focus on the same matter. It is a call for them to transcend their differences, to find a unity above and beyond the matters that divide them. This call will involve their setting aside their upward strivings, in whatever form they may take, whether in the tongues of angels or in the rhetoric of "apostles." It will especially mean a change in their taste in leaders. It will mean a learning to live with that which is lowly and weak (cf. Rom 12:16). It will mean setting aside factiousness, vanity, and selfish ambition. It will involve learning to see others as bearing greater importance than oneself. It will mean learning to seek the things that concern others (Phil 2:2-4). Above all else, it will mean seeking the profound humility that has been given to us "in Christ Jesus," not merely as an example, but as a gift (Phil 2:5). The Corinthian church can come together only by coming to Jesus and by embracing Jesus' apostle.

The last element of the exhortation, "be at peace," rounds off not only the exhortation but the entire letter.[537] As we noted at the outset, in reference to Paul's opening apostolic pronouncement of "grace and peace," Paul almost always closes off his letters with an inverted echo of that announcement, forming an x-pattern, or chiasm: grace-peace / peace-grace.[538] Here Paul follows the call to peace almost immediately with his usual pronouncement of Christ's grace (v. 13). He thus envelops the letter within the Gospel, signaling that all that he has said to the church in addressing its particular needs is nothing other than an expression of the Gospel.

As is apparent in corresponding contexts, the "peace" that Paul pronounces upon the Corinthians and to which he calls them is the reality of the age to come into the present, which they are to know and experience.[539] This *shalom* in the first instance has to do with the experience of the heart that is made in faith: joy and peace come by the power of the Spirit in believing (Rom 15:13).[540] Yet it is by no means limited to the inner life. As the presence of the age to come, it anticipates the final divine triumph over evil that will usher in peace throughout the creation.[541] Paul's call to peace thus surely also includes a call to cease the warring within the church; earlier, in admonishing the Corinthians for their disorderly assemblies, he reminds them that God is

537. It is not at all clear that one should render εἰρηνεύετε as "live in peace" (ESV, NIV, NRSV), rather than the passive understanding, "be at peace," even if in this instance the former is possible.

538. E.g., Rom 15:33; 16:20; Gal 6:16, 18; Phil 4:9, 23; 1 Thess 5:23, 28.

539. See the brief discussion above of Paul's opening "grace-pronouncement," pp. 9-10.

540. See also, e.g., Rom 5:1; 8:6; 14:17; Gal 5:22; Phil 4:7.

541. See, e.g., Rom 2:10; 16:20; Eph 2:17.

a God of peace, and not of disorder (1 Cor 14:33).[542] In calling them to peace, he seeks to overcome the disorder that has manifest itself in the warring of the community. His call is thus both a pronouncement and an exhortation, both individual and corporate. It is a call to faith that has its works.

Paul's concluding statement gives his exhortations the form of a conditional promise: "[do this and] the God of love and of peace shall be with you." The form and content of the declaration come remarkably close to the one that appears in the conclusion of the letter to the Philippians, where Paul promises the presence of "the God of peace" (Phil 4:8-9). Similar statements appear in the conclusions of First Corinthians and Galatians.[543] In all these instances, the condition to be fulfilled is not a mere act of the human being (which might then be thought to secure divine favor). It is rather an entrance into the reality and gift of salvation already given. In the present verse this is apparent from the form and content of the exhortations themselves. As we noted, two of them take a passive form: "to be restored" and "to be comforted" is not to act but to be acted upon. Likewise, "to rejoice" is no self-induced action for Paul but an act of faith and hope that sees and embraces the Gospel. Similarly, "to be intent on the same thing" means in the end to give attention to all that God has given to us in Christ, and finally to be intent upon Christ himself. "To be at peace" is thus to participate both individually and corporately in the decisive, eschatological *shalom* that God has worked in Christ. Here, in particular, it becomes apparent that the conditional promise that Paul sets before the church is a gift that has been given to them already. The condition is fulfilled not by what the Corinthians do but by what God has done for them. The exhortations that Paul sets before the Corinthians represent a call to the Gospel in the concrete form it must take within the church at this time.

The promise that Paul sets before the church is the saving presence of God: "the God of love and of peace shall be *with you*." As we have seen throughout the letter, Paul understands salvation as consisting finally not in an endowment with power or benefits but as a relationship of communication with God that has been established in Christ.[544] This thought comes to expression here, as it will again in v. 13. The gifts of salvation are not given to us apart from the Giver. To attempt to separate the two, as the Corinthians have done, is fatal. The Christian life is one of the experience of God's power in our weakness, God's righteousness in our sin, Christ's riches in our poverty.

542. In light of the same promise of peace, he likewise urges the Roman church "to pursue the things of peace" (Rom 14:17, 19).

543. 1 Cor 16:22 ("If anyone does not love the Lord, let them be accursed. Marana tha"); Gal 6:16 ("And as many as keep order according to this standard, peace [be] upon them and mercy, and upon the Israel of God").

544. See 1:3-7; 3:18; 4:7-15; 12:9-10, and many other contexts.

The Corinthians would like to thrust all this away and have power in and for themselves. They therefore are tempted to thrust away Paul and, with him, Christ as well.

Paul's understanding of salvation as a communicative relation is not limited to this letter or to the Corinthian correspondence. It comes to expression elsewhere in the conclusions of his letters as a summation of the Gospel. In Romans (in unconditioned form), he pronounces the apostolic blessing, "[May] the God of peace be with all of you" (Rom 15:33). He presents the same promise, as here, in a condition, in Philippians (Phil 4:9). While the promise Paul pronounces here in Second Corinthians bears particular relevance for the church, it is by no means a mere occasional expression. It represents an encompassing summary of his Gospel.

It is striking that these two promises of God's saving presence in Romans and Philippians identify God in the same way as Paul does here in Second Corinthians: "the God of peace." This characterization of God appears elsewhere with Paul. In Romans, his pronouncement of blessing finds a counterpart in his subsequent promise that "the God of peace shall tread Satan under your feet, very soon" (Rom 16:20). In a similar way in First Thessalonians, he pronounces the blessing "May the God of peace himself sanctify you entirely, and keep the whole of you . . . blamelessly at the coming of our Lord, Jesus" (1 Thess 5:23). A pronouncement of peace appears in Gal 6:16 as well. The presence of God is the presence of God in saving power. Just as the gifts cannot be separated from the Giver, the Giver cannot be separated from the gifts. Here and elsewhere, Paul summarizes those gifts, and salvation itself, as the decisive and final arrival of *shalom,* eschatological peace that is both inward and outward, vertical and horizontal. It brings both a new relationship to God and a new relationship to all creation.[545] The repeated appearance of this term in the conclusion of Paul's letters, in his pronouncements of blessing in the letter openings, and as a regular characterization of God marks its fundamental significance in his conception of salvation as an all-encompassing gift that makes right the world, even as it makes right with God.

Finally, we should not overlook that here, as well as in the other instances we have cited, Paul *identifies* God. The genitive forms "of love" and "of peace" not only signal that God is the one source of love and peace, they also name God. As he has done before,[546] Paul reminds the Corinthians that God is the source of all good that is present in the world, and that this goodness is an expression of who God finally is. Before and beyond all else, God is a God who wills to work peace, to bring salvation to the world. This truth obviously does

545. Elsewhere, too, Paul describes salvation as "peace." The significance of Paul's summary statement in Rom 5:1 should not be underestimated. See also Rom 8:6; 14:17.

546. Cf. 1 Cor 14:33.

not set aside the cross, the work of the "letter" in bringing condemnation and death, or the work of the apostle, who must bring destruction before he can work the edification of the Corinthians. Nevertheless, Paul's identification of God bears the promise of the Gospel, that God's purpose for the Corinthians and for the world is that of blessing and salvation.

It is likewise significant that Paul here identifies God uniquely for the Corinthians. It is "the God of love and of peace" who shall be with them. Nowhere else in his letters does he characterize God in this way. The expansion of his usual reference to "peace" should most likely be understood as a further definition of this reality provided for the sake of the Corinthians. Paul again underscores the person of the Giver, who is present within the gifts; to speak of "the God of love" conveys the understanding that salvation is not merely the possession of benefits but a living relationship with a loving God. This particular reminder that God is a God of love obviously recalls "the love chapter," 1 Cor 13, in which Paul describes the abiding eschatological reality of love that has now entered into the world. It is of profound significance that Paul there personifies "love" in action: it is patient and kind, it is not jealous, it does not brag, it is not arrogant (1 Cor 13:4). The description implies that love is embodied in a person, and thereby points to Jesus, and likewise to God. In that context, Paul urges the Corinthians to pursue love as the highest of all gifts (1 Cor 14:1): in that gift the Giver is most fully recognized. They must be warned against focusing on the trivial gifts, including that of knowledge (1 Cor 8:1-3; 13:8-10). Paul's word here brings a reminder of that earlier instruction. It is also obviously related to his preceding call to be restored, to give attention to the same matter, and to be at peace. For the Corinthians to do so means that they are to share in the reality of love that God has granted in Jesus Christ. Paul significantly returns to this theme in a final word in v. 13.

12 Paul's call for the Corinthians to "greet one another with a holy kiss" provides a transition to his communication of greetings from others to the Corinthians. He thereby reminds them that "the saints" (or "holy ones") are bound to one another, not only in their local assembly, but in all places.

The exhortation to greet one another "with a holy kiss" also appears in 1 Cor 16:20, Rom 16:16, and 1 Thess 5:26 ("all the brothers [and sisters]").[547] Perhaps it is implicit in the call in Phil 4:21 to "greet every holy one in Christ Jesus." Greeting another or departing from another with a kiss was obviously an expression of honor;[548] it communicated a bond of love and affection.[549] Paul's

547. See also 1 Pet 5:14: ἀσπάσασθε ἀλλήλους ἐν φιλήματι ἀγάπης.

548. This is evident, for example, in the "Judas kiss," since it is only Jesus, and not the rest of the disciples, who receives a kiss. The kiss of betrayal marks out the leader, to whom special honor is due (Mark 14:44-45; Matt 26:48-49; Luke 22:47).

549. See, e.g., Luke 7:45; 15:20, and also the kiss of Judas, Mark 14:44-45 (and par.); in

designation of the kiss as "holy" indicates that it is a marker of the community of faith; it is the kiss shared among "holy ones," and among them alone.[550] They have been made into a family of brothers and sisters in Christ, and thus they know a bond of love, affection, and honor in relation to one another.

The question arises as to whether it bore a liturgical significance. Was it a regular element of the gathering of earliest Christians for worship? The primary occasion for the practice of Paul's exhortation would surely have been in assembling for worship. Paul, moreover, names this kiss "holy," thus setting it apart from usual social practice. To some scholars, the connection between Paul's call to a "holy kiss" and his pronouncement of a curse on anyone who does not love the Lord and his appeal "Marana tha!" ("Come, Lord!") in 1 Cor 16:20-22 suggests a connection to the celebration of the Lord's Supper, which Paul understands as anticipation of the Lord's coming.[551]

Several considerations call for a qualified judgment on this question. In the first place, even though Paul designates this kiss as holy, the greeting with a kiss was already an established social practice. While the "holy kiss" certainly marked out the Christian community, it is hard to think that the practice would have been reserved only for gatherings of the church for worship, even if that was the primary occasion of its expression.[552] The Roman house churches, where Paul enjoins the practice (Rom 16:16), were, after all, *house* churches, where Christians most likely had social contact beyond the meetings for worship.[553] Surely the greeting with a kiss would have been practiced in social settings beyond the gathering for worship. Second, Paul's exhortations to practice this greeting appear only at the conclusion of his letters, including First Corinthians, where he provides instruction concerning the celebration of the Lord's Supper. The placement of the instruction within the closing greetings of the letter suggests something less than a fixed liturgical instruction related to the opening of worship. Furthermore, when Paul corrects the abuse of the Lord's Supper on the part of the wealthy (who had neglected the needy), he makes no mention of this greeting or its significance. Naturally, it would not (and indeed, could not) have been practiced during

---

departure, Acts 20:37. On the practice, see G. Stählin, "φίλημα," *TDNT* 9:138-41; H.-J. Klauck, *Herrenmahl und hellenistischer Kult: Eine religionsgeschichtliche Untersuchung zum ersten Korintherbrief* (Neutestamentliche Abhandlungen 15; Münster: Aschendorff, 1982), 352-56.

550. Cf. the refusal of Joseph, "a God-fearing man," to kiss the pagan Aseneth (*Jos. Asen.* 8:4-7).

551. Klauck, *Herrenmahl und hellenistischer Kult,* 355-56.

552. Even if K. Thraede's argument against the liturgical significance of the practice is overstated, this point stands (see his "Ursprünge und Formen des 'Heiligen Kusses' im frühen Christentum," *JAC* [1968/69]: 124-80).

553. W. Klassen, "The Sacred Kiss in the New Testament: A Example of Social Boundary Lines," *NTS* 39 (1993): 131.

the worship of the church, but only at the opening of the worship, as the congregants gathered. The absence of the "kiss" from Paul's corrective instruction on the Lord's Supper suggests that he does not regard the greeting as closely connected to the celebration. Even in 1 Cor 16:20-22 his greeting to the church appears between his exhortation and his concluding words on the coming of the Lord. The practice of the holy kiss surely marked not only a boundary between the church and the world, but also between daily life and the entrance into worship. In that sense, Paul instituted it as an element of worship. Third, the call to a greeting with a "holy kiss" appears in only four of Paul's letters, two of them written to the Corinthians. The practice might be presupposed in Phil 4:21, and perhaps even elsewhere, where no mention of it appears. A greeting with a kiss may well have been customary in Paul's churches and beyond. But it could hardly have been regarded as a *previously* fixed element of worship if Paul on occasion had to call churches (some of which he himself had founded) to the practice. There is no indication in these contexts that he is calling them back to something from which they had lapsed. He is giving new meaning to a greeting that was already customary[554] or, perhaps, calling them to a new practice that will do them good. Paul's exhortation, which designates the kiss of greeting as "holy," establishes the practice within the churches he addresses, i.e., it elevates and universalizes a practice that might have been a matter of personal, selective judgment. He might be said to create an element of the liturgy, or perhaps, to establish a marker of entrance into corporate worship. His creation or furtherance of this practice in these churches had significance for other churches (and had a lengthy history in the ancient church),[555] but we should not overlook the particularity of Paul's exhortations. In Rome, not only was there a large circle of house churches but there also was tension between conservative Jewish Christians and the rest of the largely Gentile group. The call to the holy kiss would have been an expression of mutual love, acceptance, and respect between all believers. In Thessalonica, where there was both separation of house churches under the threat of persecution and a considerable amount of confusion, the call to greet "all the brothers [and sisters] with a holy kiss" would have marked the unity of the church under pressure. It is not accidental that in the same context Paul must instruct the church to have this letter read to all the believers (1 Thess 5:27). In Corinth, where Paul twice must call the church to greet one another with a "holy kiss," his exhortation reinforces the unity of the church in the face of factions and strife. Karl Barth

554. That the designation is Paul's is clear from 1 Pet 5:14, which speaks instead of a "kiss of love."

555. On which, see G. Stählin, "φίλημα," *TDNT* 9:138-41; K.-M. Hofmann, *Philema Hagion* (Beiträge zur Förderung christlicher Theologie, 2nd ser., vol. 38; Gütersloh: C. Bertelsmann, 1938), 90-144.

is reported to have responded to the question as to whether we shall see our loved ones again in the life to come with the wonderful line, "Yes — and the other ones, too!"[556] What Barth anticipates in heaven, Paul institutes here on earth. This point is clear in the present context.

Paul follows his exhortation to the greeting with a holy kiss with greetings from "all the churches." None of Paul's other concluding greetings has so wide a scope. Even in First Corinthians, a greeting comes from (only) "all the churches of Asia" (1 Cor 16:19) and all the "brothers" who are with Paul (1 Cor 16:20a).[557] The greeting here stands especially in contrast with Paul's communication of greetings from particular persons.[558] It likely arises from Paul's engagement in the collection for Jerusalem at that time, which brought him into contact with representatives from the wide circle of his churches, and Jerusalem as well. Yet the greeting very likely is also intended to serve as a reminder to the Corinthians that they are not the only Christians in the world, but live in a far-reaching "communion of the saints." Paul brings a similar reminder in the opening of First Corinthians: the Corinthians have been called as "holy ones, together with all those who call upon the name of the Lord, their Lord and ours" (1 Cor 1:2). Likewise, in 1 Cor 11:16 and 1 Cor 14:33, 36, Paul's exhortations are based on the communion and connection between the church in Corinth and all other churches. As brief as this greeting may be, it bears a potent message for the Corinthians. Just as they are to practice a greeting with a holy kiss internally and thus recognize and accept one another, they are also to recognize the larger community of churches, of which they are only a part.

13-14 Paul's opening pronouncement of grace (1:2) has its counterpart in this closing pronouncement of grace (13:14). Both of them are to be regarded as blessings, given as an effective word from the apostle. As we have noted, they complete a bracket around the letter (grace-peace / peace-grace), communicating to the church that all Paul has said to them springs from the Gospel. The letter was intended to be read in the worship of the church and therefore itself bore liturgical significance. As in a number of other instances, this pronouncement of grace is Paul's last word.[559] Just as he has called for the Corinthians to greet one another and has reminded them of their fellowship with all the churches, so here he emphasizes that this blessing is intended for all of

556. E. Busch, *Glaubensheiterkeit: Karl Barth, Erfahrungen und Begegnungen* (Neukirchen: Neukirchener Verlag, 1987), 91.

557. The greeting of Phil 4:22, "all the holy ones greet you," is likely to be understood as a reference to the Christians where Paul is imprisoned.

558. E.g., Rom 16:21-23; 1 Cor 16:19b; Phlm 23.

559. Gal 6:18; Phil 4:23; 1 Thess 5:28; 2 Thess 3:18; Phlm 25. There are minor variations in wording among these: "may the grace . . . be with your [pl.] spirit, brothers [and sisters]" (Gal 6:18); ". . . be with your spirit [pl.]" (Phil 4:23); ". . . with all of you" 2 Thess 3:18; ". . . with your [pl.] spirit" (Phlm 25).

the believers in Corinth.[560] As is the case with the opening pronouncement of grace, this pronouncement is for the whole church and each member of it.

Paul here significantly expands his usual pronouncement of the grace of Christ; it now becomes "the grace of our Lord, Jesus Christ, and the love of God, and the fellowship of the Holy Spirit [be] with all of you." He underscores that the pronouncement is a blessing directed to every believer within the church.

In this context grace, love, and fellowship (or "communion," *koinōnia*) refer to "things," realities that Paul wants the church to know and experience, and not actions (even though the first two nouns are verbal nouns). Paul wants grace, love, and this communion or fellowship "to be with" all the Corinthian believers. With the first two expressions, therefore, the genitive modifiers express the source (and therefore also the possessor) of the benefit: "the grace of our Lord, Jesus Christ" is the grace that comes from Jesus and belongs to him; "the love of God" is the love that comes from God, and likewise belongs to God. The third substantive, *koinōnia* ("fellowship" or "communion") is an abstract: the genitive modifier "of the Holy Spirit" in this case expresses the "content" of this *koinōnia,* in this instance, a participation in a person. At the same time, because communion with a person is presented here in the metaphor of "content," the genitive again may suggest the idea of source, as in the first two instances. This is clearly the case in Paul's parallel usage in Phil 2:1, where his appeal on the basis of the *koinōnia* of the Spirit appears sandwiched between "comfort in Christ," "consolation of love," and "feelings and mercies." In that case, the "fellowship of the Spirit" includes participation in that which the Spirit works. The same idea is likely present here: Paul's expression "fellowship of the Spirit" conveys not only a relationship in which the Spirit is communicated to us but also one in which communication and sharing is created between persons, a sharing within the community of believers.

Paul wants the Corinthians to know and experience afresh the presence of "the grace of Jesus," "the love of God," and "the fellowship of the Spirit." By its very nature, this presence must be understood as a living communication of Christ, God, and the Spirit. This blessing naturally applies to each and every believer in the Corinthian church; Paul explicitly speaks this blessing upon "all" of the Corinthians. Yet for the same reason, the pronouncement of blessing is corporate as well.

As we have noted, this closing word of Paul is an expansion of his usual closing pronouncement of grace. What is noteworthy here, therefore, is not that the reference to Christ appears as the first word. This is to be expected. What is remarkable is that Paul expands his usual reference to Christ's grace to include God's love and the fellowship of the Spirit. That he expands his

560. See also 2 Thess 3:18.

normal usage in this way suggests that the blessing he pronounces, even with its distinctions, is to be regarded as a unity; in some sense the grace of Christ, the love of God, and the fellowship of the Holy Spirit signify a single reality in which the Corinthians are to participate. This suggestion is confirmed by the setting of each of the expressions within the Corinthian correspondence.

The first of these, "the grace of Christ," recalls the opening pronouncement of grace of which it serves as a counterpart. There Paul pronounces upon the church "grace and peace from God, our Father, and our Lord, Jesus Christ" (1:2). As we noted in that context, for "grace and peace" to proceed from God and Christ means that Paul effectively identifies Christ with God. Paul's instruction to the Corinthians concerning giving confirms that judgment: God, in the end, is the only true Giver and therefore the final and only source of "grace" (9:15). The grace of God can only be *given* to the churches of Macedonia (8:1). But the grace of "our Lord, Jesus Christ" is a spontaneous act of giving (8:9). Indeed, this reference to the grace of Christ, who "being rich . . . became poor" for the sake of the Corinthians, stands in nearest proximity to this closing pronouncement of grace. The blessing of "the grace of Christ" implies the fresh experience of the wonder of Christ's saving gift of himself in the incarnation and the cross and, at the same time, the recognition that Christ's favor is nothing other than the favor of God.

The second expression, "the love of God," surely reflects Paul's preceding characterization of God as "the God of love and peace" (v. 11). In that case, too, Paul has expanded his usual closing identification of God as "the God of peace."[561] It is significant that these two references to "the God of love" and "the love of God" appear only here at the end of the letter. Paul does not speak directly of *God's* love elsewhere in the Corinthian correspondence. Implicitly, the love of God is found within the grace (and love) of Christ. As is the case with his reference to the "grace of Christ," his reference to God's love serves as a counterpart to the opening of the letter. Paul there blesses God as "the Father of mercies, and God of all comfort," taking up his preceding description of God as "the God and Father of our Lord, Jesus Christ" (1:2-3). As both this interweaving of expressions and the substance of Paul's following benediction make clear, the mercies and comfort of God are known only through the sufferings of the human Christ (1:5). Insofar, then, as Paul's final pronouncement of "the love of God" upon the church reflects this opening benediction, it reflects the understanding that the love of God is known through Christ alone. This is also implicit in the way Paul has expanded his final "grace-pronouncement" to include the love of God. Furthermore, although Paul has not spoken of the love of God up to this point in the letter, he earlier has spoken of the love of Christ in a highly significant manner, as a

561. Rom 15:33; 16:20; Phil 4:9; 1 Thess 5:23.

saving reality that possesses the human being (5:14). Paul presents the "love of Christ" as a power that "constrains," and thus that masters and rules him. Christ's love appears there as a spontaneous act that redeems human beings and makes them Christ's own. In other words, Paul presents Christ as acting as God, thereby implicitly identifying Christ with God. Furthermore, Paul elsewhere, especially in First Corinthians, speaks of "love" as an eschatological gift and reality that has entered the world in Christ (1 Cor 13:1-13).[562] The description of this reality corresponds to the humility and self-giving that appear in Paul's descriptions of Christ.[563] Paul thus implicitly associates the "love of God" with Jesus in a twofold way in the Corinthian correspondence, both as (1) a love received in the mercy and comfort given to the crucified Jesus and as (2) a love given by the risen Lord. By virtue of Paul's more proximate, verbal reference to "Christ's love" in 5:14, it is the latter of these ideas that is surely more prominent here; without in any way blurring the distinction between God and Christ (whom Paul has just named separately in the preceding blessing), it would have been hard for the Corinthians to think of "the love of God" without thinking of the "love of Christ."

Paul's final reference — to the "fellowship" or "communion" of the Holy Spirit — brings a decisive reminder of his message to the Corinthians; namely, salvation consists not of the possession of gifts but of communion with the Giver. This communion, according to Paul, is effected by the Spirit, who is given through the apostolic mission and the Gospel, with which Paul has been entrusted. The whole of 2 Cor 3 appears here in highly concentrated form: the Corinthians are a letter written by "the Spirit of the living God" (3:3); Paul has been made an agent of the new covenant, which brings the gift of the Spirit (3:6); and the Corinthians have thereby been brought into a saving, face-to-face relationship with God (3:17-18).[564] The Spirit is nothing other than God in his saving presence in communion with and indwelling the human being. Yet, as is apparent in the present context, this identification does not overrun the distinction that Paul obviously allows to stand.

It is of fundamental significance, too, that Paul identifies the Spirit not only with Israel's God but also, implicitly, with Christ. This is apparent already in 4:4-6, where Paul, having identified the Spirit with Israel's Lord, goes on to name Christ the "image of God," the person in whom God's glory is displayed, and the Lord whom Paul proclaims. Elsewhere in the Corinthian correspondence, Paul does not speak of the *koinōnia* of the Spirit, but of the *koinōnia* "of God's Son, Jesus Christ," into which the Corinthians have been called (1 Cor

562. See also 1 Cor 8:1; 16:14; 2 Cor 8:8, 24.

563. See, e.g., in this letter, 8:9; 10:1.

564. In that context, we may recall, Paul identifies the Spirit with the God of Israel and of Scripture (3:17a; cf. 3:3).

1:9), and the *koinōnia* of Christ's "blood and body" in the Lord's Supper (1 Cor 10:16). In a similar way, in Second Corinthians, Paul instructs the Corinthians that there can be no *koinōnia* of "light with darkness," just as there can be no agreement between Christ and Beliar (2 Cor 6:14-15). For the Corinthians to bear happily the proclamation of a "different Jesus" is for them to receive "a different spirit" (2 Cor 11:4). Likewise, in Phil 2:1 Paul locates the *koinōnia* of the Spirit "in Christ Jesus." The blessing of the "fellowship of the Spirit" that Paul invokes upon the Corinthians is not a different fellowship from that of the "fellowship of Christ," of which he otherwise speaks in varying ways. In this indirect manner, Paul identifies the Spirit not only with God but also with Christ. Yet even in this identification, the distinction between the two remains, as is obvious from both the present context and others.

Paul's language here is thus incipiently Trinitarian, even though he obviously does not use the categories of "person" and "substance" that played large roles in later debates. With him we find merely the juxtaposition of identification and distinction. This grace-pronouncement is not an isolated phenomenon within Paul's letters, even if it is remarkable here in its threefold form. Something similar appears in the summary description of the apostolic mission in 1:21-22. We likewise have noted the progression of identification that takes place in 3:17–4:6. A form similar to the one we find in this closing of Second Corinthians appears in Paul's discussion of spiritual gifts in 1 Cor 12:4-6: the same Spirit, the same Lord, and the same God work varieties of gifts, bring varieties of tasks, and work varieties of effects. Paul's point here fails if there does not exist a fundamental identity of the Spirit, Lord, and God whom he names. As is well known, Romans 6–8 develops chapter-by-chapter with a progression of references to God, Christ, and the Spirit. Similar forms appear in other passages.[565] It must not escape our notice that, in all these contexts, Paul's "Trinitarian expressions" serve as clarifications of the Gospel. The earliest Christian confession is the confession of Jesus as risen Lord.[566] It is out of this confession that Paul's incipiently Trinitarian formulations emerge. At the risk of anachronism, we may say that Paul's Trinitarian theology is nothing other than an explication of his Christology. This is especially apparent in the present verse, where Paul offers his last word to the Corinthians. As we have observed more than once, Paul above all else seeks to make clear to them that the salvation brought to them through the Gospel is one of a relationship of communication with God, the Giver, not one of the private possession of gifts. The beginnings of a doctrine of the Trinity, as they appear with Paul, present this understanding of God in an unfolding of the Gospel. The apostle speaks only of the "economic Trinity" and invites no speculation concerning

565. E.g., Rom 1:1-4; 2 Thess 2:13; perhaps, too, 1 Cor 6:9-11.

566. E.g., Acts 2:36-38; 1 Cor 12:3; Phil 2:6-11.

the "immanent Trinity."[567] The God who saves is found solely and entirely in the crucified and risen Jesus. It is this God of all comfort, who is present as the Spirit in the Gospel of Christ, whom Paul has proclaimed afresh to the Corinthians in this letter.

567. On this question, see Bayer, *Luther's Theology*, 334-36.

Authors Index

Hebrew Old Testament Index

Proverbs

Ecclesiastes

Song of Songs

Isaiah

Greek Old Testament (Septuagint) Index, with Apocrypha

New Testament Index

1 Corinthians

2 Corinthians

Ephesians

Philippians

Extrabiblical Literature Index